CW00860194

RECOLLECTIONS FROM MY JOURNEY THROUGH LIFE

RECOLLECTIONS FROM MY JOURNEY THROUGH LIFE

SHAUKAT HASSAN

To order additional copies of this book, contact:
Xlibris
844-714-8691
www.Xlibris.com
Orders@Xlibris.com
819060

DEDICATION

To my wife, Nipa Hassan, for her love and support
To my wonderful children, Fareen Hassan and Nayeem Hassan
and
To my loving parents and siblings

CONTENTS

PART THREE

INTERFACE WITH REALITY

ACKOWLEDGEMENTS

One day shortly after my immigration to Canada some thirty years ago, I was having a post-dinner chat with my friend Sharfuddin Syed about politics in Bangladesh. He had heard that I worked for a strategic studies institute in Bangladesh and that I was a member of a small team that regularly provided briefing to Bangladesh President Ziaur Rahman on contentious international issues. He was very curious to know about those briefings and about the president himself. He had heard mixed messages about the president from other people, both positive and critical. Since I frequently met the president over a two year period, he wanted to know what I thought of him. Toward the end of our talk, assessing the richness of my experience, he told me that at some point in my life I should write all this down.

As years passed, more and more people came to know me and my past work. After coming to Canada, my work expanded in terms of thematic areas and issues, as well as embraced many countries and continents. I was constantly travelling in line with my work, and I was often asked at lunch or dinner parties within our community about my latest trip. And, on occasion, someone would urge me to write a book about my 'adventures.'

My brothers and sisters, who knew about my work and travels, also never failed to remind me that as soon as I retired I should sit down to pen my life's story. They saw this as an important part of our family's history.

I retired from the Canadian federal public service in the summer of 2014. For the next five years I was engaged in consultancies all over the world. With the advent of COVID-19, my travels stopped and I decided that now was the time to do some introspective writing. But my first inclination was to expand my PhD thesis that I had written in 1986 into a book. I had collected a huge amount of information during my doctoral research, which I could not incorporate into my thesis. But due to a number of reasons I had to decide against it.

Instead, I decided to listen to my well-wishers and write a memoir of sorts, which recalled some salient moments from my journey through life. I had to contact many people in many countries to help me remember certain incidents, to provide me with greater details, or to verify or confirm facts. I thank them for their indulgence.

There were many events or incidents that were noteworthy that deserved mention in my memoir, but I avoided including them to protect individuals or prevent embarrassment. However, I have occasionally named names in the book but always with good intention; I apologise for any failing on my part on that score. I have tried to be factually as accurate as possible, although I readily concede that I may have failed here and there, and if so, I beg forgiveness.

A manuscript always benefits from input from others. I wish to thank two persons for reading my manuscript and for providing me valuable feedback and suggestions: Chowdhury Ishraq Uz Zaman (Sanin) and Abdur Rahim. They are authors in their own right and were kind enough to invest their time and effort to comment on my manuscript. This work benefited considerably from their thoughtful critique.

And finally, I wish to thank my wife, Nipa Hassan, for her patience and understanding and for the freedom she afforded me to undertake and complete this endeavor. I also wish to thank my children, Fareen and Nayeem, for their encouragement along the way.

PROLOGUE

My thirst for travel to see the world and its many wonders started in my pre-teen years. Illustrated Comic Books like the *Prisoner of Zenda*, *The Count of Monte Cristo*, *Robin Hood*, *The Three Musketeers*, *Robinson Crusoe*, *Gulliver's Travels*, *The Adventures of Marco Polo*, *The Black Arrow*, *The Odyssey*, *The Knights of the Round Table*, *William Tell*, and *The Mutiny on the Bounty* were just a few among the tens of others that triggered my fertile imagination and unending day dreaming. I imagined myself to be there as I pored through the pages of the Classics Illustrated; I became a part of the stories I read.

Next were the Greek, Roman, Norse, and Persian mythologies that fed into my imagination. The tales of King Agamemnon amassing a massive fleet to rescue Helen from Troy, of Odysseus' wanderings, of Jason and the Argonauts, of Ali Baba and the Forty Thieves, of the Norse hero Beowulf, and of the twelve Labors of Hercules enchanted me. The English tales of Camelot and King Arthur and of Robin Hood and his band of merry men delighted me. The condensed anthologies of great warriors in my father's library introduced me to Charlemagne of the Carolingian Empire; Macedonia's Alexander the Great; Sparta's Leonidas; Persia's Cyrus the Great; China's Sun Tzu; Mongols Kublai Khan, Genghis Khan, and Tamerlane; Roman general Julius Caesar; Carthaginian general Hannibal, Moorish general Tariq ibn Ziyad and American general George Patton.

I was only around ten years old when I started correspondence with pen pals in far-off lands. I recall one particular day when I received the first letter from my new Japanese pen pal, Keiko Ito. My heart fluttered as I carefully opened the pink envelope. A light scent spread in the air as I unfolded the translucent page that contained dried, pressed flower petals and a couple of exotic Japanese postage stamps. A wave of warmth and excitement enveloped me. As I examined the colorful postage stamps, I looked at my mother and remarked that I would like nothing better than to travel the whole world and see other peoples and their cultures and customs. My mother replied, "The Almighty usually grants the wishes of the innocent and pure of heart. You might want to make your wish known to Allah." And that was what I did from that day on every time I joined my parents at prayer time. I prayed for the opportunity to travel.

I started my travels when I was a teenager. Five decades later, I had been to six continents and experienced the traditions, the novelties and the quaintness of many cultures. My journey was full of events that both delighted me and saddened me.

It opened many windows to a world of wonderment that I was eager to experience; it was enriching. But it also gave me glimpses of pain and suffering, of inequality and injustice, of man's inhumanity towards fellow men, and of his cavalier if not arrogant attitude toward our planet. Along the way, there were cultural shocks and clash of values that I had to negotiate.

I was baffled when the stewardess on JAL 004 flight from Tokyo to San Francisco served us an appetizer of dumplings of bat meat dipped in a light sauce. Until then, I never knew that some people actually ate bat meat! Or that people ate snakes that I saw skinned and hung from strings in mobile kiosks in the streets of Hong Kong. I was also in a quandary when a special dish of roasted ham garnished with pineapple slices and cloves was served at my host's table in my honor. My dietary restriction against eating pork rebelled against what was a sumptuous dish prepared by my hostess. I was torn between making my host happy by eating the slices of ham served on my plate and my religious injunction against it.

I was nonplussed by the political upheavals of the early 1970s in America's campuses, and by the air of vehemence that pervaded my own campus. While I wholeheartedly embraced the antiwar demonstrations in the early seventies in the United States, I found it very disrespectful when antiwar students spat on the white uniforms of fellow students training for the Reserve Officers' Training Corps (ROTC). I was shocked to witness streaking in the University of Colorado campus. More broadly, I was amazed by the lack of knowledge of other cultures and peoples and of the naiveté of the average American, and yet they had the knowledge to maneuver robotic vehicles on the surface of Mars from planet Earth.

My development work often put me in the midst of crisis situations that often led me to question my faith in man's capacity to govern justly. I was numbed by the death and destruction I witnessed during the Tamil-Sinhalese conflict. I found myself sympathizing with the citizens and activists of Ukraine's Euromaidan revolution. And I spent five years in fear of whether I would be among the next victims of Taliban bombing in Afghanistan as I sought to improve the governance of that country.

I learned valuable lessons from my interactions with different governments, militaries, academics, international organizations, non-governmental organizations, media and citizens' groups. I met countless men and women from all walks of life who enriched my life in small or large measures. These experiences, I would like to think, made me a better person, even perhaps a citizen of the world.

This book is about that journey. Its pages narrate some of the poignant moments of my life, and I am happy to share them with my readers.

PART ONE

IN THE BEGINNING

Recollections from My Journey through Life

Kabul. August 30, 2011. The terrorists had positioned themselves both inside and outside the Blue Mosque that was a stone's throw from my residence. I had just gone into my first ruku, a bending at the knees in preparation for sajdah, when a terribly loud explosion shattered the serenity of my surroundings. This was followed by the sound of crashing glasses as all the windows of my bedroom splintered into pieces. Anurag came running to my room to see whether I was still okay, and to escort me to the highly secure Safety Room.

Within a short time we learned that a Taliban suicide squad, mainly Sunni extremists, had carried out the attack against the Shia worshippers and nearly a hundred of them had died instantly and many more were severely wounded. As I collected my thoughts inside the Safety Room, I couldn't help thinking that had it not been for Gareth who had prevented me from going to the mosque that morning I could have been one of those hundred dead within one week of my arrival in Kabul!

It was one phone call that had brought me here. It was early spring of 2011. I was representing Canada in an inter-governmental meeting with European colleagues at the UNODC headquarters in Vienna. My cellphone began vibrating in my trouser pocket. I pulled it out discreetly and noticed the 202 area code; it was a call from Washington DC.

Thinking that it must be important, I quietly stepped outside the conference room to take the call. It was Bert Spector, an American anti-corruption expert and a colleague who had accompanied us as an observer in the joint European Union/Canadian mission to Yaoundé, Cameroon the previous year to hold a series of meetings with the Vice President and other high government officials on issues pertaining to much needed governance reform in Cameroon.

After mutual greetings, he cut to the chase; would I be willing to go to Afghanistan on an assignment? He explained to me that in October 2010, his Washington DC-based international development firm, Management Systems International (MSI), had launched a USAID-funded $26.5 million anticorruption project in Kabul after winning the competitive bid. After five months, the project was on the rocks because two chiefs of party

3

(COP), one replacing another, had failed to manage the project (in USAID parlance, a COP is akin to a director of a project). MSI had to send a senior official from Washington DC to salvage the project and hold it together until they found an acceptable COP who could pull it together and keep the multimillion-dollar project afloat. Bert thought I was that person. I hesitated, knowing how dangerous Taliban-controlled Afghanistan was at the time, and my immediate instinct was to say no. He told me that I didn't have to give him an answer right away and proposed to send all the relevant documents to me to read up on the project; he proposed to call me after I return to Ottawa so that we could discuss it further.

Several days later, I returned home to Ottawa and pored over the documents Bert had e-mailed to me. The project was essentially to work with and train Afghan government officials to detect and combat corruption in its various manifestations to usher in good governance throughout the Afghan civil service. It required reaching out to various Afghan provinces to work with the provincial governments under the watchful eyes of the provinces' warlords, and to liaise with the relevant senior cabinet minister and his officials, as well as to regularly report to the Afghan president. The project's primary target was to strengthen the High Office of Oversight and Anticorruption (commonly called HOO) that the Afghan government was obliged to establish to monitor corruption in the government and the public service; it was a precondition for receiving international financial assistance.

I had been working as the governance and anticorruption policy lead in the Canadian International Development Agency (CIDA) for nine years. I had developed CIDA's anticorruption policy and had been advising and assisting my colleagues in the geographic branch of CIDA to mainstream anticorruption policy into CIDA's governance projects in over eighty countries. But being in the policy branch, I was removed from doing actual programming; so here was a chance for me to directly implement what I had been preaching for years at CIDA. On the other hand, the political and security situation in Afghanistan was nightmarish with most of the country under the control of the Taliban and the warlords with competing interests, and so how successful would I be if I took up this challenge? This gave me a long pause.

That evening after dinner, my wife Nipa and I sat down with our usual mug of tea and After Eight chocolate mint sticks. Every evening, that was a special time for us when we shared our day's work with each other and talked about family, relatives, and friends and of what lay ahead. I told her about the job opportunity in Afghanistan and explained what the job entailed. She had concerns but well grounded: What would happen to my public service job? How long would I be gone for? How safe was it in Kabul? Would it cause any disruptions to our son's studies at the University of Westminster in London? And so on. I answered her questions as best as I could. She remained calm throughout. She knew that she had wanted me to explore job opportunities outside Canada. In fact, noting that I had always worked in the capitals of other countries—Canberra, London, Ottawa—her preference was Washington DC. And Kabul wasn't Washington DC! But, ultimately, she left the decision to me. Next day, I called my mother in Dhaka, Bangladesh, who was very alarmed and asked me, "Why of all the places in *Khoda Ta'alah*'s green earth do you want to go to such a hellhole?" Later in the day, Bert called. I gathered courage and told him that I was willing to take up the challenge. It was a momentous decision for me not quite knowing what I was signing up for.

I shall return to my experiences in Afghanistan in a later chapter; let me instead divert your attention to my earlier life.

The Story Unfolds

I was born on a cold day in December in my mother's village of Lostimanika in the district of Comilla in East Pakistan (now Bangladesh).

Lostimanika was an average-sized village some two miles west of River Meghna, one of the three mighty rivers flowing through Bangladesh into the Bay of Bengal. It was also an important village because it had the only domed *masjid* (place of worship) in an area comprising multiple villages, and the *masjid* was located within my grandparents' homestead. Like any other village in East Pakistan, Lostimanika was bearing the full brunt of the cold, merciless winter.

Doors and windows of homes were kept shut to keep out the biting cold wind, and charcoal fires in cow-dung-lined earthenware were lit inside the homes to keep them warm. In my maternal step-grandma's (*nani's*) home, I lay wrapped up in warm clothes with pillows all around me. I also had a round black kohl dot placed on the side of my forehead to ward off evil spirit from doing newborn me harm. Extra fires were also lit; one was located at the foot of the outdoor steps leading to mother's room, and another was placed inside the door of the room. These additional precautions were also to ward off evil spirits.

Neither my father nor my maternal grandpa (*nana*) was present at my birth, but they arrived within a day or two upon hearing the news. Nana being a *pir* (a holy man or spiritual guide) had thousands of disciples, many of whom came to see him to convey their best wishes for me; they also brought material gifts, and some brought token cash. According to Mother, when Nana visited Mother and me in our room for the first time, he whispered the Shahadah—"La ilaha illallah Muhammadur rasulullah" (There is no deity but God and Muhammad is his messenger)—into my ear, recited some verses from the Holy Quran, kissed my forehead, and then folded the cash he received from his disciples and put it inside one of my clenched fists.

So I started my life with the knowledge that there was only one God to worship and Muhammad (peace be upon him) was his messenger and with fifteen rupees in cash in my hand; not a bad haul for barely a week old boy! Father, however, came to see me empty-handed, which raised eyebrows among the village women, only to be silenced by nani's piercing stares. But gossip among the village women did not stop; how could a *sahib* and an army officer to boot visit his wife and his first newborn without gifts? they wondered loudly!

I was one of ten children born to my mother Jamila, who herself was only sixteen years old when I was conceived. My delivery was not only normal as village births go but also not so normal in the sense that there were several women fussing around Mother after she delivered me. Although my actual *dai ma* (midwife) was Saifan's mom, each of the women present thought of herself as the midwife, liberally dispensing do's and don'ts to Mother.

As *pir sahib's naatee* (holy man's grandson), I was the darling of the village, and extra care was taken to see to my creature comforts. It wasn't until later years that I realized how weak my immune system was and how physically weak that made me compared to my siblings, who grew up unfettered by the soft touches reserved for any firstborn. My siblings would often play out in the rain while I sniffled and caught a cold indoors, not to mention the frequent bouts of tonsillitis.

Two years later, twins followed, both of whom died within a few hours of their birth. According to Mother, there was not a soul around to tend to them. She recalled that tears were flowing from her eyes as she lay in bed helplessly watching her young ones die. She was young, uninformed, and quite confused in matters of motherhood. She was also frail from lack of proper medical care while carrying the twins, without any emotional or physical support from her stepmother, and with a husband away at his first new job most of the time. She felt traumatized and blamed herself and Father for the death of my twin brothers.

A year after the twins died, my sister Lily was born on September 11, 1954, which became a day of infamy for a different reason many decades later. Two months later, Nana arranged a twelve-year-old boy named Anwar to come to our home as our servant, who gave our family lifelong selfless service. Father called him Anu for short, which Anwar resented because even at that young age, he felt that it belittled him and reduced his importance. When Anu retired, Mother tried to make it up to him by giving him ownership of land and property, while my sister Lily attended to his medical needs. He is very old now and remembers us fondly as he bides his time in his own village.

Two years later, my brother Mahboob was born, and shortly thereafter, Mother contracted smallpox, a highly infectious airborne disease. She was bedridden for a month, with lesions and blisters all over her body. She was quarantined in a room, and no one was allowed to go near her. Anu was the only person who tended to her, and with each change of clothes, her outfits, bedspread, and pillow cases were burned to prevent the spread of the disease. The Hindu doctor who looked after Mother had Anu rub butter over her blister marks after she recovered. It took many years for the blister marks to disappear completely; most other smallpox patients who recovered were not as lucky. During this time, another servant, Ismail, from my father's village, Gourshar, took care of the household work.

My brother Mahboob, who was only a few months old then, had to forego breast milk and subsist on bottled cow milk and warm water. But he suffered from a serious ear infection that lasted for a painfully long time. Mahboob was followed by another brother, Selim, who was the only one to be born in a hospital. Since Selim grew up to have a mind of his own and preferred a solitary lifestyle away from the family, we used to tease Mother that they had switched babies in the hospital and that Selim was really not our brother; Mother never liked that! The rest of my four siblings came in two-to-three-year intervals.

The Teen Bride

My mother still gets teary-eyed when she recalls her sad childhood. She was born in the village of Lostimanika in the district of Comilla, which was then a part of undivided India. She was the youngest of three siblings. The eldest was a brother, Bazlur Rahman, who died when he was only a few years old. Her sister Qamarunnessa passed away in September 2019.

Her mother, Khadija Khatun, died young, and her father, Maulana Shamsuddin Ahmed, remarried soon after. Mother recalls that her stepmother Ambia Khatun's first priority was to rid herself of the three stepchildren by marrying them off as soon as possible. Nani was eager to build her own nest unsullied by the presence of stepchildren. So my mother's elder sister, my *khala,* was married off to my nani's uncle, Abdul Mannan, an elderly man whose wife had died leaving behind several children most of whom were older than my khala. My khala, only twelve at the time and a child herself, had to cater to the demands of this large family, her in-laws and her own children.

Getting rid of my mother was even more dramatic. Mother recalls being woken up from her nap one afternoon and being hurriedly readied for a "ceremony." Suddenly decked in a clean sari and some *alta* (lac dye used by village women to paint the borders of their feet) on her feet, she was led to the formal sitting room and made to sit down in the center of a *chowkee* (a four-legged bedstead). Some female family members sat behind her.

The *maulvi* (Muslim priest) who would conduct the wedding and the man who would marry her entered the room and sat next to her. Mother was told to follow the instructions of the maulvi, which she did. Within minutes, marriage vows were exchanged, and my thirteen-year-old mother became a married woman. Mother recalls that she had hardly seen my father before and that he left immediately after the wedding that very afternoon. He returned to Dhaka where he had recently joined work in a private company on Simpson Road, Sadarghat, by the Buriganga River in Old Dhaka. It wasn't until many weeks later that he visited Mother in Lostimanika.

Confusion Regarding My Birth Year and Name

My birth year is unclear to me. As a young boy who just began to read, I remember seeing in my dad's private desk drawer a tiny three-by-five-inch notebook with torn pages and the front and back covers missing. This was very unlike Father, for he was very meticulous and disciplined. All the scribbles in the notebook were in blue or red fountain pen ink. On one page, there were a couple of names; one name read "Showkat Ali 1951." My nani called me Hassan, which became the name everyone called me by, and so at some point in my life, "Hassan" replaced "Ali" as my last name. My uncle Fazlul Hossain added "Shah Mohammad" to my name, the thinking being that a longer name enhanced a person's status. So Shah Mohammad Shawkat Hassan was the name in my first passport issued by the Pakistan government, for I was a Pakistani citizen then.

However, I was not happy with my name. I wished my name was Tariq after the Muslim general Tariq ibn Ziyad of the Umayyad Caliphate who had captured the Iberian Peninsula from the Spanish king Roderick in AD 711. Father occasionally narrated to us histories of Muslim conquests, and I had been quite impressed that the name Gibraltar was the anglicized derivation of Jabal Tariq (rock of Tariq), honoring General Tariq.

In any case, I was stuck with "Showkat," which was then a very common name in Pakistan. I resolved to change the spelling of my name to make me feel slightly uncommon and started spelling my name as "Shaukat." Also, early on at some point in my life, the year of my birth was changed to 1952, although I don't know why, and so all subsequent documents show this changed birth year. Later on, I learned that it was a common practice to reduce a child's age by a year or two to meet age limits imposed by school admission requirements or for entry into government service. This was due to frequent political disturbances in the country that led to school closures, delayed graduation, and hence the fear of exceeding the maximum entrance level age limit.

The Empire Gets a New Recruit

My father was an army captain in the Fourth Baluch Regiment of the British Indian Army under the overall command of Lord Archibald Wavell, who was the viceroy of India at the time; Father had seen action in as far away as Tripoli and close at home in southern and eastern Afghanistan. After the Second World War ended, he resigned from the army but served as an advisor in the Pakistan Army during the 1965 India-Pakistan war, and as Mukti Bahini (liberation force/ freedom fighters) instructor who set up the Palatana Training Camp in Agartala, eastern India, during the Bangladesh Liberation War in 1971. He trained thousands of militia who fought alongside the regular Bengali armed forces who defected from the Pakistan Army to fight for independence. He regularly commanded forays to disrupt enemy supply lines and occasionally attacked enemy strongholds.

Over the years, many genuine Mukti Bahini members used to visit Father to pay homage and regale each other with their exploits about fighting the Pakistan Army. One story we heard many times over was how a platoon of enemy soldiers retreated into a mosque in Mainamati,

Comilla, in the face of Mukti Bahini attack and barricaded themselves inside waiting for reinforcement to arrive. The Bengali freedom fighters climbed to the top of the dome of the mosque, blew a hole there, and dumped burning red chilies. The acrid smell and smoke forced the enemy soldiers to open the door to the mosque and surrender. In another military operation in Kasba, Comilla, Father and Brigadier Khaled Musharraf took heavy incoming artillery fire; one shell exploded nearby, and shrapnel went through Musharraf's kneecap and pierced Father's abdomen, spilling his intestines. We have a photo of that incident taken by an Indian war correspondent showing Father in a stretcher with a soldier holding parts of his intestines in his hands as he was being taken to the makeshift field hospital.

In the course of his military career, Father was wounded many times, and there were many visible scars on his body even until his death in 2008. Two years after Bangladesh's independence, a small delegation from the prestigious Bangla Academy—an autonomous institution set up in 1955 to promote and foster the Bengali language, literature, and culture—visited Father in our house in Hafizabad Colony, Eskaton, to interview him, explaining that the academy had embarked on a project to capture the history of Bangladesh's liberation effort. Father advised them to wait a few more years until the dust settled to write the true and complete history of the liberation war.

In hindsight, I think that was a bad advice because what has been subsequently written by various governments and other writers contains many untruths, lies, and exaggerations; genuine freedom fighters who gave their blood or their lives were shunned aside, while those who did not contribute or even fought against the Bengali nation were promoted as liberation heroes by vested interests. Today, these unscrupulous opportunists enjoy the full benefits of the freedom fighters' welfare trust, while the genuine warriors of our independence war languish in poverty and pain. This is undoubtedly one of the greatest tragedies of the war of 1970–71.

As a young boy, I was very proud of my father's many military and civilian medals, and I would often hold them in my hand and admire them; Mother even bought me brass and silver polish so that I could polish them. One military medal was for being able to shoot a bullet through seven rings placed in a straight line over a distance and hit the bull's-eye at the end; he was indeed a sharpshooter. He also had several medals for poetry recitation, and I remember that, at least on one occasion, he recited a long poem for us to our great delight. All his medals were seized by the marauding pro-Pakistan Bihari paramilitary force, the Razakars, from our house in Dhanmondi, Dhaka, during the Bangladesh War.

However, after he left the British Indian Army, he appeared to have been disillusioned by the death and destruction he witnessed around him. Wanting a normal peaceful life, he married a woman from a respectable family from the town of Comilla; but he was not happy with his in-laws. He felt unappreciated by his mother-in-law in particular.

One anecdote that I heard from my paternal grandma (*dadi*) was that Father had been trying hard to please his mother-in-law. So during one of his visits to his in-laws, he purchased the biggest fish he could find in the market and presented that to his mother-in-law. She looked at it, and far from appreciating the gesture, her only remark was that somebody else had bought her an even bigger fish! There was no thank-you, no appreciation of any kind. Mercifully, however, the relationship with that family ended because his wife eloped with another army man from the Mainamati Cantonment to Karachi, West Pakistan.

Father was at an all-time emotional low and sought an alternate path and spiritual guidance. According to my dadi, he used to love to go duck hunting in the marshes with his dog but gave up hunting soon after leaving the army. He would go away from home wandering for days, which caused great concern to dadi. She doted on him, affectionately calling him *amar shuju* ("my shuju," his full name being Mohammad Shujat Ali).

His resignation from the military caused financial burden on Grandma's household. My grandpa had died when Father was very young, leaving Grandma with the burden of raising their large family with modest income from farming. There were days when there wasn't enough food for the household, and according to Mother, dadi would wrap her sari around her stomach very tightly so that her hungry tummy wouldn't make any grumbling noise and let everyone know that she hadn't eaten.

Three of her six sons died in that struggle. Through grit and hard work, dadi raised the remainder of her family and also earned the respect of her village. When Father received his commission in the British Indian army, fortune smiled on the household. His salary provided them an income that was huge by the standards of the village, and it catapulted my grandma's household into nonpareil economic prominence and earned it the sobriquet *bepari bari* (merchant house).

All that, however, changed when Father left the military; with the sudden loss of substantial income, Grandma had to tighten her purse considerably. When she died silently in bed after her *Isha'a* (nighttime) prayer after eighty plus years, she died with the respect of her family and the admiration of the entire village.

In Search of a Meaning

After leaving the army, Father spent many months wandering aimlessly. One day, Father heard of this pir, Maulana Shamsuddin Ahmed, and went to visit him in the village of Lostimanika. The pir was known throughout *Homna thana* (an administrative unit comprising scores of villages) and had thousands of followers. Soon after, my father decided to become a disciple of the pir. Ever the opportunist, it was not long before the presence of this young, fair, and handsome military officer caught my nani's eye, and she at once resolved to marry off my mother. The pir became my maternal grandpa (nana), whom I vaguely remember since he died when I was only four and a half years old; he was known to be a soft-spoken, spiritual man removed from earthly matters and happy to leave everything that concerned the here and now in my nani's hands.

He did, however, have a soft spot for my mother and my khala, who he recognized had to live under the dark shadow of their stepmother; he allegedly expressed his concern about marrying off my mother at the tender age of thirteen, but my nani would brook no objections from

Nana, whom she felt knew nothing of worldly matters, and should confine himself to providing spiritual guidance to his disciples. My nana's inability to protect my mother and khala from nani's shenanigans continues to be a bitter reminder and a cause for considerable ire in my sister Lily; my mother had confided in Lily many details of her life, most of which were sad and painful, and so more than anyone else among us brothers and sisters, Lily continues to feel the pain and disregard that Mom endured, for which to this day she cannot forgive nani for her stepmotherly conduct.

My nana had a calming influence over Father and gave him solace and a reason to be hopeful. Several years after my parents' wedding, Father got a job in the Jamal Soap Factory in the inland port town of Narayanganj, some fifteen miles southeast of Dhaka, the capital city of then East Pakistan. He rented a two-room building with the kitchen to be shared with the landlord in the suburb of Dharmatola, Narayanganj. The rent was thirty-five rupees, one-tenth of Father's monthly salary.

Hazrat Ali, the owner, was a kind man, and his wife was very supportive of my mother, perhaps because she was a child bride. My parents started enjoying conjugal life for the first time since their marriage three years earlier, and I was conceived soon after in Narayanganj. My nana came to visit my parents for the first time and, upon learning that my mother was pregnant with me, resolved to take her with him to his village home for better care. As mentioned above, I was born in Nana's house in Lostimanika.

A New Abode for the Young Couple

When my nana had come to visit Mom for the first time in Dharmatola, he felt that my parents should move to a house of their own. During that short visit, he would get into a rickshaw and scour the town looking for a suitable house for my parents; sometimes Father would accompany him. He finally found an independent house in the mixed Hindu-Muslim neighborhood of Amlapara whose address was 17 Harakanta Banerjee Road. It was a spacious house with two bedrooms, another bedroom-cum-sitting room, a detached kitchen, and dining room with a garden forming the central courtyard. The enclosed garden was a particular delight because of all the fragrant flowering trees and plants such as *beli, rajanigandha, hasnahena, bokul,* etc., which scented the whole house at night.

The strong fragrance of hasnahena (a type of night-blooming jasmine) supposedly attracted a type of snake at night, so we always shut the window that overlooked the flower plant before going to bed. The wide walkway from the garden to the external courtyard gate had an overhead wood lattice covered in red grape vines, but the grapes were not sweet; our cook would use them to cook one of our favorite dishes called *tok*. From the outside courtyard gate to about twenty feet into the garden and parallel to the side boundary wall was a row of palm and coconut trees. My parents liked the house and bought it for 13,000 rupees with Nana's help.

Three months after my birth, Father brought Mom and me to our own house in Amlapara, Narayanganj. Accompanying her was a maid servant named Jainab. Jainab had a checkered background. Her husband had deserted her and she had no kids, which left her slightly deranged. She would talk to herself incessantly and occasionally vanish, only to be found on treetops by villagers looking for her. Everybody thought she was under the influence of some *bhooth* (evil spirit/ghost), and they would dunk her head in tubful of water to ward off the evil influence, but nothing worked. I don't know why such a person would be sent to help my mother with a young baby, except that she was from Mother's village, everybody knew her to be a kind soul, and she supposedly loved me very much.

In addition to several relatives staying with us, we had frequent visitors in our new home including my two step-khala, Jotsna and Najma. I remember visits by my great-grandmother (*boroma*) as well, who loved me very much. I remember visiting her in her village of Mahmudpur, Comilla, in the summertime and whiling away the long days playing with village kids in the pumpkin and melon fields on the sandy shoals (*balu char*). At the day's end, she would always bathe me in the river. On one such occasion, she told me how, when she was young, huge screeching birds used to fly low over her village nearly popping people's eardrums; she was referring to fighter planes and bombers heading east to fight the Japanese during the Second World War.

She was also extremely protective of me. I remember that, at least on one occasion, she shielded me from getting caned by Father for not being in bed for my afternoon nap as was the imposed custom. Since Father was usually at work in the afternoon, I would often skip the afternoon nap to play with the neighborhood kids. Occasionally, Father would come home in the afternoon and find me missing and, being short-tempered, would fly into a rage. When I finally came home, he would be waiting for me with a cane in hand, which was usually a thin branch from our guava tree. I got badly caned on several occasions. My brother Mahboob who would also get caught did not fare any better. But what I remember most was my mother crying helplessly every time Father took to the cane.

One day, we received the sad news that boroma had died during a severe storm when the tin roof of her home collapsed on her as she slept. At the time of her death, she was a very old woman who was bent forward from her hips and relied on a walking stick, and though no one knew exactly how old she was, elderly villagers would point to grand old banyan trees and the last great flood in the region as reference points and opine that she was well over hundred.

I grew up under the eyes of a very strict father who insisted on us living a disciplined life. He had transferred his military discipline, order, and a no-nonsense approach into our home. That meant there was set time for everything: time to take the afternoon nap, time to play outside, time for the *hujur* (religious tutor), and time for evening study to do our homework and prepare for next day's classes.

When my sister Lily and I were little, I recall Father lecturing us that we must learn how to wash our own clothes, cut our nails, shine our shoes, mend clothes, sew buttons, and do other things so that we became self-reliant, because in a few years' time, there weren't going to be any servants to hire, and so I learned to do all that and more including learning to braid my mother's hair.

Even our hujur was strict, instructing my sister and me to always drink water sitting down, never to exhale into the glass while drinking, never to pee standing up and always wash after, never to swear or utter bad words, never to miss our prayers, and always to roll up my pants above my ankles when at prayer. But, most importantly, we were instructed to always remember the order of things: Allah, the creator of heaven and earth and of all things living and nonliving, reigned supreme; immediately below him were one's parents, and below them were he and maulvis like him; to question this order or to deviate from these beliefs and practices was to let *shaitan* (Satan) get a foothold into our lives, which was a big no-no!

Early School Years

I was admitted to kindergarten I in Narayanganj Preparatory English School in 1957 at the age of five. For the first two years—KG I and KG II—a teenaged servant girl named Rezia held my hand and walked me to and from school. The school had a dress code: white shirt, navy blue tie and shorts, white socks, and black shoes, with white handkerchief in pocket. I liked our school uniform because I thought that it made us look quite smart.

I remember the beginning of each school year was a time of great joy; it was like spring in the calendar year. The most exciting part were the brand-new books with the smell of fresh print in each page, the new writing pads waiting to bear witness to calligraphy that we were learning in our handwriting class, the replenished stationery, and the brown paper wrapping we diligently did to preserve the new book covers from getting soiled from daily use.

Our headmistress was a Scottish lady whom we called Mrs. Hubbard. She was also our piano teacher, and in the piano class, she played the piano while we sang nursery rhymes. I remember that we always followed our teacher's instructions meticulously, especially copying her face and hand gestures while she acted out the nursery rhymes, so much so that once she sneezed during a recitation and the whole class sneezed after her, thinking that it was a part of the recital; the teacher paused and simply smiled.

Most of our teachers were English or Anglo-Indian. We followed an English curriculum and celebrated English events, among which the most memorable one was the Guy Fawkes Day on November 5, the day when Guy Fawkes attempted to blow up the British Parliament. Our school was a three-story square building with classrooms on three sides and an open central space where we gathered for the morning assembly and sang the national anthem. On every November 5, we burned the effigy of Guy Fawkes at the place of assembly, with accompanying fireworks; then the teachers distributed sweets presumably to celebrate our success in burning the would-be arsonist!

I also joined the Boy Scouts, and my classmates and I eagerly digested the stories about its founder, Lt. Gen. Lord Robert Baden-Powell, and of the worldwide scout movement. I happily embraced the Scouts movement and its goals; camaraderie; discipline; skills such as leadership, teamwork, adapting to hardship, learning self-reliance, cooking, applying first aid, and tying various types of knots. In our senior year, we went to the Scout Jamboree in Madhupur Jungle, now the Madhupur National Park, about 3.5-hour drive north from the capital, Dhaka.

The teachers were very strict and always seemed to be competing with each other to gain favor with the headmistress. It was not surprising, therefore, that our favorite period was the game period. We usually played carom, ping-pong, ludu, or bagatelle, while the girls preferred to focus on drawing, painting, needlework, and other artistic pursuits. Sometimes we stayed behind even after school ended to continue playing with each other.

On one such occasion, we were playing hide-and-seek when a class friend named Sanjay discovered me in my hiding place and playfully threw at me a handful of sawdust from the chalk box that went right into my eyes. I was in pain and couldn't open my eyes. Another class friend called a rickshaw and took me home. My mother was shocked. She immediately took me to Tanbazar, a bustling section of the town, where the only eye doctor, realizing how dangerous it was for my eyes, sat me down and delicately flipped my eyelids as he gently washed my bloody red eyes with water. He then administered some eye drops and bandaged both my eyes, telling us that the bandage must remain until the next day, when I must visit him again for further checkup and eye drops. He also said that there was a good chance that my eyes would be permanently affected and that I would need eyeglasses soon. A month later, he prescribed corrective lenses for me, and Father took me to the Opticsman in Gulistan, Dhaka, where I got a pair of Rodenstock frames.

Over the years, my eyes deteriorated further. I wore contact lenses for a while but had to abandon them and return to wearing prescription glasses permanently. I was too young to hold any grudge against Sanjay, but I learned later that he was killed by the Razakars during the Bangladesh War.

Since class 5 was the final year in that school, students of classes 4 and 5 jointly put up a play every year in honor of the graduating class; the parents were invited to attend. The play was usually held in the green-roofed auditorium of the Narayanganj Tennis Club, which had an attached dining hall that was the favorite meeting and drinking and dining place of all the Englishmen and the few non-Englishmen in the town. During my graduation, I remember the play staged that year was *The Merchant of Venice,* and I dressed up in a frilly outfit to play the part of Portia; what I remember even more is my stage fright and wondering when the play will end so that I could go home.

A Typical Day

In our house, each day started with my parents getting up before the sound of *ajan* (call to prayer by the muezzin) before sunrise. Following their *fajr* prayer, Father would recite Sura Yaseen, considered to be the most important verse in the Holy Quran because of its focus on monotheism, prophethood, and resurrection. Well into my preteen years, I remember waking up to Father's recitation of Sura Yaseen.

Every morning at dawn, we would hear knocks on the outside gate that opened into our courtyard garden. Usually, it would be a pair of young Hindu girls with bamboo baskets in hand out to gather fresh flowers for their *puja* (worship). Their nimble fingers would meticulously pick up every *shiuli* flower (night jasmine) that had fallen on the ground overnight. The shiuli was used by Hindus and Buddhists for worship.

According to one Hindu mythology, Princess Parijataka had fallen in love with the sun, but when the sun deserted her, she committed suicide. A tree sprung from her ashes, which could not stand the sight of the lover who had abandoned her, and so it flowered only at night and shed them like teardrops before the sun rose. Apparently, these were the only flowers that Hindus offered to their gods that were picked from the ground and not plucked directly from the tree.

The shiuli had other uses as well. In those days, the orange-red tubes at the center of the flowers were dried and used as dye for clothing. We were lucky to have a beautiful flowering shiuli tree in our courtyard garden, which endeared us to our Hindu neighbors; no one else in our neighborhood had a shiuli tree.

During weekends, my sister Lily and I were joyfully immersed in our own little universe that included playing hide-and-seek, jump rope, hopscotch, and reciting nursery rhymes among other pursuits; one of our favorite pastimes was to play what we called *jola bhat,* where we cooked rice and *dahl* in miniature *hari-patil* (earthenware pots) over a chulha under the shade of a mango tree in our inner courtyard. Those were blissful days indeed!

Continuing with the daily routine, our breakfast usually depended on the season; during the winter months, it was usually a variety of *peetha* (cake made from rice flour) with fresh *khejoor rosh* (date juice) or *goor* (molasses); during the summer months, it was inevitably squeezed *aam* or *kathal* (mango or jackfruit) mixed with milk and *moori/cheera/khoi* (puffed/flattened rice); while at other times, it was *parata* or roti with *bhaji* (curried vegetables) or dahl (curried lentils). When our English *baburchi* (chef) arrived a few years later, porridge, eggs, toast, butter, and marmalade were added to our breakfast menu.

After breakfast, Lily and I went off to school, Father went off to work, and Mother went off to the kitchen for the day's cooking. Our school ended at 1:30 p.m., when we came home, showered, had lunch, and then took a nap; I, of course, was on the lookout to escape from the afternoon siesta to play with my neighborhood friends. After the nap, it was hujur, homework, and study time. When Father returned from work in the evening, we gathered for evening snack when Mom and Dad had tea or coffee and we kids drank either Ovaltine or Horlicks milk. We then did our ablution and lined up behind Father for our Maghreb prayer. At the end of each *salat* when we raised our hands in supplication, I remember always asking God to grant me my wish to travel and see the whole world.

From the stories I heard from Father and the books I read, I was fascinated by other cultures, traditions, and peoples. I joined the Pen Pal Club promoted by the country's English language daily *Morning News* and soon had pen pals from Japan, Poland, Rumania and Brazil with whom I regularly exchanged letters, postcards, and postage stamps. We exchanged stories and information about each other, about our lifestyles and about our countries; this opened up a whole new and exciting world to me and increased my hunger to travel and meet other peoples around the world.

I am convinced now that God indeed heard my prayers, for I have traveled all over the world and in every continent except the Arctic and the Antarctic. I wished that my children would also have this opportunity, and I am happy to say that our daughter, who lives in London, and our son, who lives in Oslo, also travel widely and frequently both as a part of their work and also on their own as they broaden their appreciation for humanity with all its wonders and diverse beauty.

Over the years, we have frequently traveled as a family to exotic destinations that have enriched our lives greatly; we continue to do so to this day. Now that I am retired, traveling and vacationing have become very relaxing for me especially because all the vacation planning from start to finish is done by our daughter Mumu with the help of her brother Mishu.

Like other kids, my childhood had its ups and downs. I was not interested in studies and therefore had average grades as a student. But I was an avid reader of Greek, Roman, Norse, Persian, and Hindu mythologies. I found the stories of gods, goddesses, warriors, and their exploits absolutely fascinating.

Since my father was a military man, at home we had plenty of books on military histories, biographies of ancient and modern warriors, and military expeditions. I also loved to read books on famous people, such as Alexander the Great, Julius Caesar, Genghis Khan, Charlemagne, Richard the Lionheart, Winston Churchill, General George Patton, Mahatma Gandhi, and the Mughal emperors, to name a few.

I also remember getting hooked to the *Hardy Boys* series and read all the forty-one titles available then. As an avid reader of comics, I learned about the Trojan War from the Classics Illustrated titled *Iliad* a long time before I read Homer's *Iliad* and *Odyssey*. Of course, I loved to read *Archie, Jughead, Veronica and Betty* comics as well, even at school, sometimes placing the comics on my lap below my desk at school so that teachers won't notice, only to desist for a few days when someone else got caught and punished.

When I was not immersed in reading, I always looked for a way to get out of the house to play with the neighborhood boys, and there were plenty of them. I did get into quarrels with them off and on whether it was over marbles or kites or something really stupid. I remember having a heated argument over how many seconds there were in a minute. My friend said five seconds, while I argued sixty seconds, because my mother had said so. This led to us to not talking with each other for a few days.

Among my other childhood activities were flying kites from our flat rooftop, playing marbles in the street with the objective of winning the other guy's prettiest marbles, and playing ping-pong in the Narayanganj Rifle Club. I remember the disappointment in the faces of table tennis players whenever we ran out of Helix ping-pong balls made in England and had to substitute Olympia balls made in China, which were considered to be decidedly inferior in quality. I had built up quite a reputation in my preteen and early teen years as the table tennis champion of the club.

I loved to play carom and often went to the Narayanganj Bar Academy near our house to play carom with carom champions in the evening. I also played a great deal of soccer and cricket. Playing soccer in the rain when I visited my nani in her village during the summer was especially fun, but quite stressful for nani because she was torn between letting her grandchild enjoy his summer visit and the high chance of me catching a cold, which happened often; indeed, tonsillitis was my middle name in those early years, until one day I received homoeopathic treatment that permanently cured me and spared me any surgery. I have been partial to homoeopathy ever since. My homoeopathy doctor was a Hindu, and sadly, he lost his life during the Bangladesh War.

I also had an air gun, though I don't remember how I came to possess it. I would shoot the small pellets at the birds in our trees in our courtyard, until one day I actually shot a sparrow in its wings, and it fell from the tree on to the ground. As I tried to pick it up, it tried to hop away chirping wildly. I finally caught it and felt its warm heart beating wildly; I also noticed blood on its wing. The excitement of successfully shooting a bird gave way to remorse, and I promised myself I would never use the gun again, and I never did. Mother cleaned the blood with diluted Dettol and put the bird in a cage to let its wing heal and, after a few days, opened the cage door, and we watched the sparrow fly away to freedom. I was very relieved.

However, the fun of catching sparrows didn't die yet. Several years later, when we moved to Dhanmondi, Dhaka, I would often visit my nephew Fayez, who was of my age, and we would shut the door and windows of the room when a sparrow came in and chase it nonstop until it collapsed with fright, when we would grab it and hold it in a cage for a few days before releasing it later. I enjoyed visiting Fayez. His father, Ahmed Fazlur Rahman, who was my cousin, was a man of few words but always smiled and inquired how I was when I visited them. Fayez's mom was our favorite *bhabi* who loved me and my brothers and sisters dearly, and was always happy faced, smiling and serving us tasty snacks. She loved gardening and always had bouquets of rajanigandha in her house.

Occasionally, there would be kite fighting competition held between neighborhoods in a place by the Narayanganj railway station called Chashara. It was an elaborate affair. All participants would diligently make their multicolored paper kites and lace their kite flying strings with a mixture of powdered glass and rice glue in a process called *manja*.

The idea was to fly your kite from under or dive down from the top of an opponent's kite so that the glass-laced string would act like a knife against the opponent's string and sever it. Every time one side managed to cut the string of the opponent's kite, the victor's drums and trumpets would go full blast announcing to everyone near and far that the other side had lost a kite. The objective was to eliminate opponent's kites from the sky. Those who were really skilled could use their own kite to snag the adversary's kite that was cut and haul it over to his side. The side whose kites were the only ones flying in the sky would be declared the winner and would get the championship cup.

My summer holidays at my nani's place in Lostimanika, away from my parents, were blissful indeed. No one there told me that I had to maintain any routine, take afternoon naps, or study. I played all day with village kids, running after brightly colored butterflies with long sticks tipped with sticky sap from the gum tree, or chasing flying cotton fluffs as the wind blew them off the prickly cotton trees, or jumping off of blackberry tree branches (*jam gach*) into a pond, or watching cockfights.

Summer was usually the rainy season when the water level would rise significantly everywhere. One memorable incident was when, one day, I was standing at the water's edge when I saw a snake slithering toward me. I panicked and jumped into the river to escape the snake, and soon I saw the snake swimming away below me. I fainted and started sinking. Villagers on nearby boats harvesting jute from stems that were shoulder deep in water dived and hauled me out of the water. By then, there was considerable commotion, and as I came to, I learned that someone had placed me on his head and spun me around to expel the water I had swallowed, and my nani had administered salt into my mouth from the tip of a *dao* (a curved knife with wooden handle). Such were the superstitions I grew up with!

I remember watching friendly mud wrestling with competitors wearing only lungi, which is a cloth wrapped around the waist below the belly, but pulled up like loincloth. They wrestled each other down in clay courtyards that were drenched with water to make them muddy and slippery. I watched intervillage *kabadi* (contact team sport) competition with intense cheering on both sides. I also saw historical dramas such as *Sirajuddaula* (the depiction of bringing down a favorite king of Bengal by British colonialists) on mobile stages that went from village to village.

Occasionally, there would also be *mela* (fair) where all sorts of goodies like trinkets, cosmetics, clothing, and household items were sold, including different types of sweets. It would be an occasion for everyone, especially for young boys and girls, to dress up in bright colors and mingle with each other and with people from neighboring villages.

I witnessed how crops were harvested; jute fibers and spices were dried under the sun in the courtyard; cattle tied side by side and tethered to a central pole made to go round and round to crush grains under their hooves; how rice and wheat were made into flour in *dhekis* (tool village women used to thresh or separate grains from their husks), and how fish were caught with huge nets (*jaal*). I was always fascinated by the rainbow colors of kingfishers perched on tree branches on the banks of ponds waiting patiently for a fish meal. I also witnessed cows being corralled into tight enclosures to allow bulls to mount them. Girls around me seemed to know what was going on and usually giggled, but I had no clue until much later.

Every year, February 2 was a special day because it was *urs*, or the anniversary of *pir sahib*'s (my nana's) death. It was held in Nana's home in Lostimanika, and thousands of his disciples gathered to commemorate this occasion. It was a grand religio-social coming together. The usual food served were spicy beef curry, lentils, and rice, and a dozen or so cows and goats were slaughtered for the occasion.

Temporary fires were built by digging out holes in the ground that were long strips where chopped tree trunks and branches were dumped as firewood. Huge copper/bronze cooking utensils separately laden with meat, lentils, and rice were placed over these dugouts with fire burning below as the food got cooked. Oars of boats were used as spatula to ensure the food didn't get burned at the bottom of these utensils, and once cooked, the food was served on earthenware plates to all the guests seated on bamboo mats across the entire courtyard.

Once, I sat down with them as well, and I can still vividly remember how tasty the food was. According to Nana's disciples, the food was so delicious because it was *niyamat,* which in English means divine blessing. Until my departure for the States, attending the urs was our annual ritual. For Mother, it was a time for sadness and joy; sadness because it was Nana's death anniversary, and it reminded her of her loving father; joy because all her relatives from far and wide came, and she got to meet and spend precious time with them.

The trips themselves to the villages whether to visit my nani, dadi, or boroma during my summer school holidays that usually lasted two to three months were very memorable also because of the excitement and trepidation of traveling over mighty and sometimes unpredictable rivers. Summers were also the season of frequent thunder, lightning, and heavy downpours.

Until the late '60s, the principal mode of travel was on riverboats and launches (coal-powered boats on riverine routes). Bangladesh, which was formed over the last ten thousand years by silt from the Himalayan mountain range brought down by rivers, lies in the world's largest river delta—the Ganges delta system. The country is basically a flat alluvial plain through which flow fifty-four rivers from India and three from Myanmar; while the exact number of rivers in the country is difficult to count because some rivers dry up during the winter months while others change their names in different regions, estimates vary between 250 to 800 rivers, tributaries, distributaries, and rivulets crisscrossing its territory.

During the rainy season, the mighty Brahmaputra, Jamuna, Padma, and Meghna Rivers, as well as lesser rivers, swell several times their normal sizes, not only facilitating riverine travel but also instilling fear in the hearts of the travelers. The common mode of travel was by boat, where the boatman would stand in the rear of the boat, drop his pole to touch the riverbed, and push against it to move the boat forward through water.

In deeper water where the pole could not reach the riverbed, one or two people would be on the riverbank pulling the boat forward with ropes tied to its mast. When one had to cross from one side of a huge river to its other side, the sails would be hoisted to catch the wind as the boatman steered the boat with his wooden rudder.

I recall many of these moments when we had to cross the mighty Meghna river with its other side nowhere in sight, and the boatman asking us to pray for safe crossing. Mother and other adults would suddenly go quiet, hold on to each other tightly, palpable fear in their faces, as they silently prayed for God's mercy. In moments like these, I recalled nighttime fireside chats in our village of how another village had lost its boatman and its passengers when mighty waves swallowed up the boat with none of the passengers to be seen ever again; the speculation was that if the waves didn't kill them, the crocodiles surely dragged them down and finished them off.

Before modern bridges were built over the mighty rivers, European-built ferries plied between Narayanganj and Daudkandi, and Narayanganj and Aricha Ghat. We used to drive our cars onto these ferries, disembark from our cars, and sit in the cabin, and then drive off once we reached the other side.

But before the ferries came, launches were our primary mode of transport over long distances. The cabin at the center on the top of the launch adjacent to the captain's space was reserved for sahibs (gentlemen) where we would usually sit, while the rest of the passengers would be below deck and on deck. Unless the weather was being difficult, the river journeys were pleasant. The summer breeze, the panoramic view of the pristine verdant countryside, and the seagulls feasting on the fish that were churned up by the launch in its wake are images that still remain vivid in my mind.

One could also order snacks from the kitchen below deck that somehow appeared enticing. The stops along the river route constantly changed because riverbanks frequently collapsed in the face of the never-ending onslaught by the rising, turbulent waters. When the launch arrived at a makeshift stop, it would try to get as close to the bank as possible. Then a ladder was lowered to form a bridge between the launch and the riverbank with two people at either end holding on to a bamboo pole shoulder high to serve as a rail so that passengers could hold on to it while disembarking. So traveling to and from our villages was an adventure by itself.

Summer visits to my father's village in Gourshar wasn't as much fun primarily because there were no children of my age to play with. There were also no young people in the village to relate to. My dadi, while loving and caring, didn't have much time for me because she was always busy with farm-related chores.

There were many stories about her that went around. One story related by one of my cousins was about dadi sitting down to pray. Occasionally, she would throw down her *jai namaz* (prayer mat) in the center of the inner courtyard so that she could keep an eye on her surroundings. One day, she was in the middle of her prayer when out of the corner of her eye, she spied a cow had somehow slipped out of its tether and was leaving the cow shed and heading toward the field. She immediately shouted, "Someone! A cow is loose and heading towards the field!" A farmhand nearby heard her warning and ran after the cow to catch it. Ever since then, her grandchildren teased her, "Dadi, what kind of namaz was that! When Allah asks you why the cow was more precious to you than your namaz, what will you say?" Her reply was "Tora boojbina, choop kor!" (You won't understand, hush!)

She never missed her namaz. She would start her day with namaz way before sunrise and work continuously through the day and into the night. She was always very mindful of the needs of the day laborers who worked in the fields, especially with regard to meals. There was a hujur who resided in dadi's household rent-free in exchange for giving religious lessons to everyone.

When the laborers returned from the fields after a day's backbreaking work, they would wash up and start eating dinner often forgetting to utter *Bismillah-ir Rahman-ir Rahim* (Arabic for "In the name of God, the merciful and compassionate"), which all Muslims are enjoined to utter before placing food in their mouth. The hujur never failed to castigate them for not remembering to say grace.

One day, dadi got really tired of hujur's failure to appreciate the hard work the laborers did and that they would be so hungry that it was natural that they would occasionally forget to say bismillah. She suggested that the hujur should accompany the laborers to the field the next day because hands-on work in the field would be good for the soul. The hujur agreed. When they returned from the field that day, while everyone was busy washing themselves before sitting down to dinner, the hujur forgot about washing up and sat down for his meal. Everyone was served their meal except the hujur, who was told to wash up and then say bismillah before he could touch his food. He got the message and felt quite humbled.

Our main annual celebrations included the two Eid holidays: Eid ul Fitr, after a month of fasting; and Eid ul Adha, usually two months and ten days later, when during both occasions, we dressed up in new clothes, went to the morning prayer in the *idgah* (large open-air gathering place where Eid prayers were conducted by the imam), and then visited each other, exchanged gifts, and feasted all day. The best part was when we received *iddies* (money) from our elders, a tradition that we still practice in our home.

The other big occasion was our national day, August 14, when Pakistan got its independence from Britain. On that day, the rooftop of every Muslim house was festooned with small triangular multicolored paper cuttings and tiny Pakistani paper flags glued to long strings that stretched from a mast hoisted in the center of the roof to all corners of the rooftop, with the normal-sized Pakistan flag flying high at the top of the mast. And those who had radios could listen to special programs all day long.

My childhood was full of other forms of entertainment as well. Vendors would holler down our street announcing all sorts of wares and entertainment. Our favorites were the snake charmer and monkey dancer, who would be called into the house to put on their show for a small price. It was exciting and sometimes scary to watch snakes come out of the charmer's basket and sway side to side along with the charmer's pipe music, or watch a hat-wearing monkey perform tricks.

In the 1950s and '60s, Narayanganj was full of monkeys freely roaming across town from tree to tree. We had a huge mango tree over our *gosholkhana* (bathroom) that was detached from the house but had no roof covering, and monkeys would occasionally throw fruits at us when we were bathing or steal stuff that was put out in the sun to dry. One of our servants was always on the lookout to prevent theft. Another common denizen at that time were innumerable crows. Occasionally, one would mistakenly sit down on a live electric wire running along the streets and get electrocuted; hundreds of other crows would then mill around and caw incessantly until shooed away by throwing stones at them.

Often we would see a mongoose enter our house through the open sewerage drain in the rear, and we would all tense up thinking that there must be a snake in the vicinity, for nothing attracts a mongoose like a snake. Mongoose also came to kill chickens that Mom kept in a netted enclosure on one side of the courtyard; luckily, the chickens were always the first ones to cackle and panic, and our servants' job was to block the mongoose's retreat and kill it, which rarely succeeded.

The barber would be called frequently into our house to cut our hair as we sat out in the sun on a *mora* (knee-high round bamboo seat) in the courtyard. On rare occasions when we were deemed to have been good and well-behaved, Father would hire a black-and-yellow Chevy taxi, most of which were of the '30s and '40s vintage to take us to the capital city of Dhaka to a posh hair salon; after which we would go to Rex restaurant, which was famous for its beef samosas and chicken cutlet, or to Sweet Haven for *muglai parata,* or to Baby Ice Cream for some tutti-frutti, all located in bustling Gulistan.

Sometimes Father took us to the Narayanganj Tennis Club for a wonderful lunch. These rare occasions were sublime. A regular treat at home was getting freshly churned butter in clay pots from the *Rocket,* a paddle steamer that plied between Dhaka and Khulna since colonial times. The texture and taste of the butter was unlike any one finds in the market; it's like I can still taste it.

It was also a time of social change, not all of which was welcomed by parents. I was in class 5, the final year at the Narayanganj Preparatory English School. Wearing pants with flared legs called "teddy pants" and pointed shoes with shoelace on the side was the new rage, but as much as I wanted to dress like other youngsters my age, I was scared of Father's disapproval. It required Mother's direct supplication for Father to grudgingly tolerate my teddy look.

For adults living in towns, the principal form of entertainment outside the home was going to the movies. Father hardly ever went to the movies, but I did, with Mother and a maid servant. There were two movie theaters, Asha and Hongsho, initially in Narayanganj, and in the absence of television, the only way of knowing what was playing where was the periodic musical band that traversed the streets carrying huge posters of actors and actresses. They loudly played their trumpets and drums to attract the people out of their homes into the street to distribute their leaflets announcing the latest movie in the cinema halls.

There were other processions as well. In the months of September to October every year, Bengali Hindus carried the effigy of their god Durga accompanied with band music through the streets and dumped them in the Amlapara pond as a part of their puja ritual. The effigy being made of clay easily dissolved in the water and was an efficient way of disposing the god once the puja ended.

The Hindus paid homage to goddess Durga, who, according to Hindu legend, vanquished the evil shape-shifting buffalo Mahishasura over a ten-day period, symbolizing the victory of good over evil. This puja that is celebrated only by Bengali Hindus was started in the late 1500s in the province of Bengal by the landowners and merchants during the harvest festivities to promote commerce and trade.

It was an essential part of our cultural and religious festivities and quite exciting to us kids. We often joined these processions never bothering about which religion it was part of. Another annual ritual we witnessed was on the Tenth of Muharram (the first month in the Islamic calendar), which was the remembrance of Ashura (religious commemoration of martyrdom) when shias marched through the streets flagellating their chests and shoulders with chains and knives as a symbolic show of repentance.

We watched from inside our house through our windows as the shia followers marched past us screaming, "Hassan Hussein, Hassan Hussein," which were the names of the prophet's two grandsons who were slaughtered by the second Umayyad Caliph Yezid I in the Battle of Karbala in October AD 680. Blood would drip from their shoulder and chest; it was gruesome and scary. I did not understand the depth of their passion over an event that took place over 1,300 years ago, but I wondered how painful it must be to deliberately flagellate themselves,

31

and that how merciless they could be with anyone who crossed their path.

I am also reminded of another scary time when there was Hindu-Muslim riots in early 1964 when Muslims were incensed by an event in distant Kashmir where Hindus supposedly showed disrespect to Prophet Mohammad (PBUH); this triggered mass attacks on Hindus in East Pakistan. I remember my father secretly turning our home into a sanctuary for the Hindus of our neighborhood to protect them from marauding Muslim fanatics; many Hindus were welcomed to our home in the dead of night and hidden under our beds and in other hiding places.

The other painful experience that was very personal to me and to my immediately younger brother Mahboob was our circumcision, commonly known as *mussalmani*. Both of us were circumcised at the same time. I remember changing from shorts to lungi. I was made to sit on a *piri* (a low wooden stool), with my two hands going around the outside of my legs and coming up from the inside to grab on to my ears, which lifted my legs wide open with my genitals exposed, and the *hajam* (person who does the excision) then did his work. I was blindfolded so that the large-sized scissors would not scare me and was asked to bite on a stick so as not to bite my tongue. There was no anesthesia. I was tightly held in place by someone behind me.

I recall giving out a deafening scream when the prepuce was severed. As my blindfold shifted, I could see the scissors on the floor and the hajam holding a thin strip of white muslin over a candle, and after it had caught fire and the whole strip turned black, he blew out the fire and then wrapped the burnt black fabric around just below the glans penis. I was released with the strict instruction that I must keep on wearing lungi until told otherwise and to keep my hands away from my genital area.

While all this was happening to me, Mahboob was kept in another room with his ears stuffed so that he wouldn't hear my scream. Then it was Mahboob's turn. Our younger brother Selim heard my scream from another room, and thinking that the hajam had cut off my penis, he grabbed the longest knife he could find in the kitchen and, brandishing the knife, started in the direction of the hajam, screaming that he will kill him. It was with great difficulty that Selim was restrained, while the hajam was already on his back foot ready to flee the house, delayed only by the time it took to count his cash payment.

Our house was home to many cousins, uncles, and other relatives, and was generally lively. Our family pastime was playing carom and ludu (snakes and ladders), and sometimes *bagaduli* (bagatelle), family games that are still very popular in the countries of South Asia. Everyone in our household was an excellent carom player, and every carom game was an excitement. Mother's stepbrother, my Anis mama, and my cousin Yunus bhai, same aged, were very ticklish, so much so that the mere suggestion of tickling them would make them feel tickled and they would fall apart laughing. So when they played carom, the opponents would frequently say, "Tickle, tickle," and their game would fall apart, causing them to lose.

The family tradition of playing carom has rubbed off on my siblings and me; each of my brothers including mother is an excellent carom player, and to this day, we play competitive carom every time we get together. On that note, the summer of 2018 is particularly memorable. Mother and I were visiting my brother Shahalam and his wife Luann in their beautiful spacious home in Irving, Dallas. Two of the youngest brothers, Sohel and Tawfiq, had also relocated to Dallas from New York and Dhaka.

One late afternoon, we sat down for a doubles game, Mother and I, who were always a formidable team, versus Shahalam and Sohel. We got clobbered, the score was 0-28, which is called a nil game in carom. It was one of those rare happenings destined to be family lore, to be told and retold a hundred times in family gatherings with consternation to the listener. I believe Mother took it hard, for no one had ever inflicted a nil game on us; she and I will never live it down! Our aura of invincibility was gone forever.

But what was priceless was the shock in my brothers' faces that they could actually pull it off and the tremendous joy and exhilaration they felt. If I recall correctly, they immediately called every member of our family to tell them about this unbelievable moment. Whenever we got together after that summer, the victorious brothers would assure Mom and me that they will not talk about that day, which was their way of reminding us that we were no longer the carom hotshots we once were! I am, of course, very proud that my brothers are such good carom players.

In any case, returning to my childhood days, Father also loved to play carom, but he always insisted on having his childhood friend Asgar as his partner, because whenever he lost, he took aim at his friend Asgar and exclaimed, "Pura game-ta harlam tomar jonno!" (We lost the entire game because of you!) But at the next game when Asgar would refuse to be his double's partner, Father would never take no for an answer. Aside from playing carom, Father also occasionally invited his business partners to our house to play contract bridge all night, as they smoked capstan cigarettes from tin cans and nonchalantly farted away one after another as if in competition.

Many of the relatives in our house were boarders who attended colleges and universities in the city. Money was tight, but Mom always managed. My cousins used pencils rather than pen so that they could reuse their notebooks by erasing previous notes. My mom sold her gold bangles she got at her wedding to pay for my youngest uncle Nawab's university tuition and fees; Mom was happy that Uncle completed his master's degree successfully. Years later, after father died, leaving behind unresolved land issues among his brothers, Mom had proposed a fair solution to a land dispute to Uncle Nawab, but he flatly refused her; that day, Mom recalled with sadness the sacrifice she had made for him and the recompense she got from the ingrate.

To New Jobs and New Homes

After a few years in the soap manufacturing company, Father landed a job with a much better salary in a Greek, subsequently British-owned jute exporting company called Ralli Brothers Limited that was located in Godenail on the other side of the Sitalakhya River that bordered Narayanganj. We moved to the second floor of a big house that the company called bungalow. We had a white-bearded chef by the name of

Shona Miah whom we lovingly called *dadu* (big brother) who introduced us to English food—namely, roast beef, roast chicken, mashed potato, potato chop, roasted vegetables, caramel pudding, and whatnot. We loved his cooking. Dadu used to call my baby brother Mahboob, Johny. He stayed with us for many years accompanying our family whenever we moved to a new location.

An English family—Michael, his wife Margaret, and their three children, Peter, Elsie, and Helen—lived on the ground floor. They were much older than my sister Lily, my brother Mahboob, and I. They were a happy and boisterous family whose laughter and joy would reverberate across the garden as they played hide-and-seek or badminton or tennis in courts adjacent to but a part of our bungalow compound.

Since the town of Narayanganj was on one side and Godenail on the other side of the river, we had to take diesel-powered launches from Godenail to go across the river to Narayanganj. The company had three such launches named *Alexander, Swift,* and *Anne,* which regularly transported me back and forth during school days. The launches docked in Bondor, right across from the offices of James Finlay Company on the other side of the road.

One vivid recollection from that time is when all the students from my junior high school, Narayanganj Preparatory English School, which was right next to the Pak Bay Building on the main road, lined up on the street and waved Pakistani and British paper flags as young Queen Elizabeth II and Prince Philip drove by in their motorcade. The year was 1961, and it was the royals' first South Asian trip to greet their former subjects.

The other memorable event was in 1962 when I was in grade four and I was awarded the first prize—a cricket bat—in an arithmetic competition; I had answered correctly all fifty questions within the allotted time. While I was happy and proud to own a new cricket bat, a notable outcome was that Mrs. Bennett, an extremely large black woman who taught us English and who was known to show no mercy to errant students and beat their outstretched hands with a wooden scale, was quite impressed by my achievement and became friendly toward me, which was a great relief indeed.

It was when my father was at Ralli Brothers Ltd. that, one day, a big fire destroyed several godowns that were stacked with jute bales ready for export to Dundee, Scotland, which was the world center for jute manufacturing at that time. His colleague Mr. Khair, who was in contention with him to be the next manager of the company, pinned the blame on him. An inquiry board was constituted, which interrogated the staff and workers and established that Mr. Khair was behind the fire; he was sentenced to jail for several months. My father was absolved of any wrongdoing.

After this incident, and a year into the job, Father decided to quit Ralli Brothers Ltd. He moved the family back to Amlapara and then took up the job of general manager of Daulatpur Jute Mills in the district of Khulna in southern Bangladesh.

Shortly thereafter, he took the family to Daulatpur but admitted me to the newly established Residential Model School in Mirpur, Dhaka. Modeled after British Eton, the school's mandate was to train elite military and civil service officers under British supervision. Our principal was a British military colonel. If memory serves me right, I was in the Humayun House (all dorms were named after Mughal emperors at that time).

Every morning before sunrise, we would hear the shrill whistle summoning us to the parade ground for an hour-long intense physical exercise and a couple of laps around the field; after which we would be given a glass of buffalo milk. It was all fat, smelly, gross, and undrinkable, and inevitably we would take the milk to our dorms and flush it down the toilet. We would then shower and gather en masse for our fajr prayer. Among my good memories in those short eighteen months that I was there was that I learned to play field hockey.

During my first visit with my family in Daulatpur, I saw how proud my family was to own the latest electrical gadget, a Philips reel-to-reel tape recorder that Father had purchased recently. I learned that many weekends were spent recording songs by several young girls from the neighborhood who were known for their melodious voices.

Father quit his management job in the jute mill and returned to our home in Amlapara, Narayanganj, to establish his own partnership company, SAS Jute Exporters; the acronym SAS stood for Shujat (his name), Afajuddin Faqir, and Sabur Khan (names of his two partners). He bought a two-storied building in Sitalakhya in the southern part of Narayanganj where he set up his office.

Sitalakhya, with its excellent riverine connection with the port city of Chittagong on the Bay of Bengal, was Pakistan's Dundee, for most of the jute processing and exporting companies were located there. Sitalakhya's riverfront was laced with jute godowns and jetties lined with huge wooden boats laden with raw jute. The jute would be off-loaded from the boats into big rectangular metal buckets that ran on very narrow gauge rails set on top of the jetty, and laborers would push these loaded buckets into the godowns where the jute was sorted into various grades according to quality, weighed, and then compressed into one-ton bales for shipment in huge container ships down the Sitalakhya River to the port of Chittagong for export to European destinations, usually Dundee, Rotterdam, and Antwerp, and sometimes to Brazil.

Occasionally, the jute carried by boats from the hinterland would be damp from river spray or wet from the rain despite the tarpaulin cover, and these had to be spread out to dry in the sun in front of the godowns by the riverbank before they could be weighed and processed.

What was also amazing to me as a kid was how the price of jute was negotiated by the jute grower and the purchaser. The latter, usually our office purchase manager, and the jute grower himself or the jute merchant would hold out their hands as if they were shaking hands. A handkerchief, a piece of head wrap, a waist wrap, or anything of a similar nature would be thrown on top of the hands so that no one could see what was happening as they negotiated their price. Under the cloth, they touched each other's fingers to indicate their offers and counteroffers until an agreement was reached. If the negotiation between the jute merchants and the office buyer ended in disagreement, then the merchants would go to Dad hoping to get a better purchase offer. Often, Dad would then go to the godown to check the quality of the jute himself, and if the quality was good, he would make a better offer to make the seller happy and for future business.

It was interesting to see the jute growers from Father's and Mother's villages who were our relatives and friends always depart happy faced because they would get from Father the price of jute they expected. When we visited the villages during our summer holidays, we would be invited to their homes and treated like royalty.

Father's most reliable jute purchaser was his childhood friend Asgar, who stayed with us and whom we called *taloi*. He would often travel to North Bengal, where the jute was of a superior quality, and would fetch a better international selling price. He would carry thousands of taka in his six-by-fifteen-inch multilayer cloth money bag tied around his tummy and covered by his jacket with which he purchased boatloads of jute for our jute exporting company. A bonus purchase was the highest-quality and the tastiest flattened rice called cheera, which was a better substitute for Quaker oats on the breakfast table. We loved to eat it with mango or jackfruit juice, thickened milk, and clotted cream.

As his jute exporting firm prospered, Father became increasingly philanthropic. He built a *madrasa* (school for Islamic instruction), orphanage, and a mosque in his rural town, Debidwar, and established scholarships for children from poor families. In 1968, he founded the Debidwar College in Comilla, which sentimental villagers later renamed as Debidwar Shujat Ali College during Father's absence from Bangladesh. Since none of us would return to Bangladesh to take care of these properties, Father decided to hand over our private college to the government, and it is now the Debidwar Shujat Ali Government College.

The college has produced many graduates holding elite positions in the Bangladesh society and government, as well as overseas. Many years later, I was attending a conference at the East West Center in Honolulu, Hawaii, during which time I also attended a presentation by a Bangladeshi professor from the University of Hawaii on a new type of energy-efficient low-fuel chulha, a U-shaped clay cooking stove used in South Asian villages. It was an impressive presentation. After the presentation, I walked up to the professor to congratulate him, and in the course of our conversation, he told me that he was in fact a graduate of my father's college; it was heartwarming to me to hear that.

A Stepsister Arrives

Before we moved to Sitalakhya from Amlapara, we had a surprise addition to our family—a stepsister from my father's previous marriage named Nilufar, nicknamed Khushi, three years older than I. She had opted to leave her mother and stepfather in Karachi, West Pakistan, and come to live with us.

She was fair skinned, very manipulative, and on the naughty side. Having recently become a teenager, she loved to wear tight-fitting *salwar kameez*. One day, she put on a kameez that was so tight that she couldn't breathe. She tried to pull it off over her head but couldn't and called out to me for help. I remember her sitting on her haunches and me standing up in front of her and both of us using all our combined might to pull the kameez over her head. That was the first time I saw how a teenage girl in a bra looked like.

She loved to flaunt herself in front of the neighborhood boys, and I, the younger brother, suddenly became every neighborhood teenage boy's best friend. They would offer me their shiniest marble or a chocolate bar or let me win in games just so that they could get close to her. She was, however, attracted to a boy named Jalal, whose father was a kerosene dealer, a profession that was looked down upon by Amlapara's business class, even more so after Jalal's father built what was considered to be an ugly, gaudy house that had several different-colored columns of pebbles glued on its front wall from the roof level to the ground.

Since Khushi was the eldest child and a daughter, she was given her own room that had a back door that opened into the roadside balcony. What my parents did not know was that she would frequently let Jalal visit her at night by secretly unlocking the balcony door for him, until she got caught one night. Father put a huge padlock on the outside of that door. He also took off his belt and whipped her back, leaving bloodstained lashes on her fair skin. Mother cried and yelled at him and told him he could never do that again. That was the first time she had ever yelled at him and also the first time Father had backed off. But that didn't stop Khushi. One evening, she eloped with a much older cousin of ours we called Bahar bhai. In desperation, Father sent his childhood village friend Asgar Ali to scour every seedy hotel in Narayanganj and Dhaka until they were found in a hotel in Jatrabari on the outskirts of Dhaka.

That was it. Father wasn't going to put up with any more nonsense. He immediately decided to marry her off swiftly before there was further family scandal. Our tall, handsome office manager named Badruzzaman Chowdhury, nicknamed Notu, was Father's immediate choice. He secretly sent his friend Asgar to Rajbari in the district of Faridpur to check out Notu's family's social and economic status. Asgar returned with happy news; Notu was the eldest son of a *jamindar,* a landed aristocratic family from the Rajbari Jamindar Bari. My parents were very excited, and without further ado, messages and visits were exchanged between them and us until the couple was married.

My new *dulabhai* (brother-in-law) was charming, fun-loving, and outgoing. He easily won the hearts of everyone, especially Mom's. Once he bought Mom the most expensive sari, Mom could never stop talking about it. He would bring baskets of fruits and sweets whenever he visited us. He was particularly nice and attentive to me, once taking me in a speedboat on the Sitalakhya River to go duck hunting in the marshes. When 7-Up was introduced in Pakistan, he took Lily and me to the old Dhaka Tejgaon Airport restaurant and treated us to the drink; I remember my whole body shuddered because of the strong fizz. He loved to take us to English movies playing at Naz Cinema in Gulistan, Dhaka, where we watched *The Guns of Navarone*, which was a real treat. He was also a talented banjo player.

Khushi's arrival caused many disruptions in our family. From day one, she tried to revive her mom's relationship with Father and to replace my mother with her mother. She secretly wrote letters to her mom, which, thankfully, were not reciprocated. She even convinced me to write a letter to her mom inviting her to come visit us; I had no idea what she was really up to. When Father found out, he was furious, but Mother was forgiving, explaining to Father that it was natural that a young girl would miss her mom and want her. Father tried to explain to Mother that she was being very naïve and didn't understand her stepdaughter's manipulation and deception.

My sister Lily and brother Mahboob were being coached by an Anglo-Indian teacher we called Mrs. Ahmed in preparation for admission to an English medium school. However, with Khushi's arrival, Lily was sent off to a Bengali school to keep our stepsister company, which totally changed the trajectory of Lily's future. While serving in the military and frequently traveling to Europe on business had opened up Father's eyes to progressive ideas, and he was progressive in many ways, there were certain old-fashioned ideas that he still held on to, such as the notion that boys were more valuable to a family than were girls.

His attitude toward and treatment of Mom and Lily were anything but progressive. Mom did not object because she was quite naïve and did not dare to challenge Father's whims and decisions. Lily is the only one among us siblings who attended the vernacular school. The whole family blames Father to this day for his discriminatory disposition and for this egregious folly. By the time our youngest sister Tina arrived, Mother and we brothers had a stronger voice, and Tina was admitted to an English medium school together with the youngest in the family, Tawfiq. Father was somewhat "reformed" and did not or could not object.

Father had saved up enough money to buy a used gun-metal-colored jeep open at the top and on all sides except for the windshield. The jeep's frame and inside seats were all metal, and every ride was cold and windy. The road from the town center to Father's office in Sitalakhya was a narrow single lane in disrepair. At night, truckloads of pebbles and sand were dumped at various spots on the road for repair work the next day. This stopped office traffic in the morning because cars, rickshaws, baby taxis, and pushcarts could not climb over the pebbles. They all waited for my father's arrival during morning office time because his jeep was able to climb over the pebbles and flatten the road surface for the rest of the traffic to follow behind him. In no time Father become the savior and the darling of Sitalakhya.

Sometime later, he bought a brand-new blue Ford Prefect. We were all excited to take a ride in it, but there was no driver. We had to hold our horses until Father was able to hire a driver a few days later. A year on, Father made substantial profit from his jute export business and bought two Volkswagens simultaneously, a green and a white one, but the white one was totaled shortly thereafter by one of his partners' brother who went off the road into the roadside ditch as he tried to pick up his cigarette that slipped from his fingers onto the car floor.

The High School Years

Two years after opening his Sitalakhya office, Father moved the family into the top floor of the office building. Being a military man himself, Father wanted me to attend the prestigious Faujdarhat Cadet College established in April 1958, located outside the port city of Chittagong. I passed the admission test but unfortunately failed the medical examination because I was assessed to be flat-footed. Father was disappointed, but I was even more disappointed because my somewhat romantic idea of attending the nation's first cadet college was dashed!

The alternative was to write the test for St. Gregory's High School and St. Joseph's High School, both located in Narinda, Dhaka. I passed both the admission tests but chose to attend St. Joseph's High School in grade six. Between the two, St. Joseph's had the reputation of being more elitist; I couldn't resist that.

For a whole year, we lived in Sitalakhya, and every weekday, I was driven to school in Dhaka, fifteen miles away. Today that doesn't sound very far, but back then, only taxis and buses plied that route that was so narrow that two vehicles coming from opposite directions had to partially go off the paved surface to avoid head-on collision. Besides, noncommercial traffic was limited to a few private cars owned by a handful of rich people, and so it was quite unusual for me and stressful for my parents for me to be on that highway five days a week.

The weekday routine included returning home from school at around 3:00 p.m., and then Mahboob and I heading toward the Sitalakhya River, walking over the silky jute fibers laid out to dry, and then jumping from the jetty into the river with a staffer named Sher Ali to play and swim for about half an hour. Contrary to his name, *sher*, which meant lion, Sher Ali was anything but that. He was a tall, skinny skeleton of a guy, slightly bent, obsequious, but quite jovial in nature. His job was to make sure we didn't drown, as we dog-paddled rather than swam, because of which we are very poor swimmers to this day having never received proper swimming lessons.

While in Narayanganj, aside from going to Dhaka to attend school, I also took bus trips to Dhaka by myself on various occasions. One occasion was to watch a wrestling match where I was impressed to see Pakistan's Olympic wrestling team comprising Aslam, Akram, Goga, and the Bholu brothers. It was shocking to me to hear their trainer tell the audience that each ate two roast chickens and six eggs for breakfast. I wondered what they had for lunch and dinner. I also went to see the wondrous *Circarama* at the Dhaka Outer Stadium. It was a huge white circular tent, and the audience inside experienced the feeling of moving forward with the people or objects in the film as they watched the documentary.

When I finished grade six, St. Joseph's High School relocated from Narinda in old Dhaka to what was then called Ayub Gate in Mohammadpur (renamed Asad Gate after independence) at the opposite end of an expanding city. It was too far from home now, and Father decided to rent a house close to my school. He rented a newly constructed two-storied independent house at 10/1 Iqbal Road, Mohammadpur. It was a brand-new suburb under construction, and only a handful of houses had been completed. Our nearest neighbor, three minutes' walking distance from us, was the famous musician Bedaruddin Ahmad, who was also the founder principal of the famous Bulbul Lalitakala Academy.

My immediate siblings Lily and Mahboob and I together with our chef dadu started living in Mohammadpur, while Dad split his time between us and Mother in Sitalakhya. Mahboob and I went to St. Joseph's High School, while Lily went to Bengali Medium Lalmatia Girls High School and then to Azimpur Girls High School, both in Dhaka.

Six months later, Father rented a house at 617 Dhanmondi, Road No. 18, and the whole family was once again together. We had very influential neighbors; on one side was the Speaker of the National

Assembly of Pakistan, Abdul Jabbar Khan, and on the other side was Ruhul Quddus, who later became the principal secretary to Prime Minister Sheikh Mujibur Rahman.

Dhanmondi was also a fairly new neighborhood with only a handful of houses, and on a clear day, we were able to see from our rooftop Rayerbazar adjacent to Satmasjid Road, with Buriganga River on the opposite side, a good mile from our home. A few streets away from our house was the house of Ahmed Fazlur Rahman, a CSP (Civil Service of Pakistan) officer of the Agartala fame. He had been named as a coconspirator with Sheikh Mujibur Rahman trying to secede from Pakistan, and both were jailed by the Pakistan government for a number of years. While in jail, he had translated the works of the famous Persian poets from Farsi to Bengali. When he was released from jail after serving his sentence, he employed his tremendous business acumen to build a veritable business empire that his family now enjoys. He was Fayez's father mentioned earlier and also my distant cousin.

I was now in grade seven and had passed my driving test at the Arambagh Police Station, Motijheel, in our Volkswagen. Father now bought several cars in rapid succession: first, a Morris Minor, and then a Ford Cortina, and we had two very reliable Hindu drivers, Kala Chand and Rashik. Having learned how to drive, I frequently drove then, and my usual destinations besides going to school were the United States Information Service (USIS) on Topkhana Road, which later relocated to Road 8A, Dhanmondi; the Alliance Française de Dhaka on Mirpur Road, where I registered to learn French; and the Goethe Institute on Road No. 2, where I registered to learn German.

There was a very cute American girl, the daughter of an American diplomat, who was in my French class. I was very much attracted to her and wanted to be friends with her, but I didn't have the guts to approach her. One day, I resolved to find out where she lived, so after class, I waited in my car to follow her. I was happy to see her driver going in the direction of my home. Then he turned into the driveway of the first corner house on Road 8B, the same road I took to go home; I was happy to see that she lived only a few streets away from where I lived. Since then, whenever I took that road, I always looked toward her upstairs verandah hoping that I would catch a glimpse of her. I never did. Her name was Tina. When my youngest sister was born, she was so pretty, notwithstanding her big eyes, I proposed that we call her Tina.

Being a new driver and loving to drive very much, I decided to go to the beach town of Cox's Bazar, which was about 165 miles driving distance from Dhaka. A couple of my siblings, our driver, and I took off for the Cox's Bazar Beach, which was nearly one hundred miles long and considered the "longest natural unbroken sea beach" in the world.

Since Cox's Bazar was totally undeveloped at the time, there were no hotels or motels, only a handful of what they called cottages. These cottages were single story, spacious, with provision for several beds according to one's need, with cold, red-colored cement floors, and windows with green shutters. Nevertheless, we were happy to be at the beach all by ourselves, far from the gaze of parents.

During the ebb, the receding waters of the Bay of Bengal left a huge stretch of pristine white wet sand that immediately turned bright red without fail as the tiny red crabs emerged from their holes onto the surface. I decided that it might be fun to try to squash them under my wheels. So with the driver beside me, I started driving up and down a stretch of the beach to run over those crabs, but to no avail because the crabs dashed into their holes before I could reach any of them. Neither the driver nor I realized how close to the water's edge we were, and at one point, the back wheels of my Volkswagen lost traction and started spinning in the wet sand; the more I tried to dislodge the car, the deeper I went into the hole.

It was a precarious situation because soon the tide would come in, and the Volkswagen would be partially submerged and might even get dragged to the ocean as the waters receded. The driver ran to the cottage manager's office and explained what had happened. The next thing I saw were several people approaching the car with wooden planks on their shoulders; they placed the planks behind the spinning wheels and then asked me to try to move in reverse gently as they pushed the car from the front. It worked; the rear wheels were on the planks, and with traction regained, I steered sideways and drove off the beach to firmer ground.

It was a scary experience but a lesson well learned. That evening at dinner, as we recalled the events of the day, we realized that we had too much at stake for our parents to hear about this; I would lose my driving privilege and the driver would be fired. So my siblings, the driver, and I swore to each other that our parents were not going to hear about this ever! And they never did.

We also went on school trips. One memorable trip was organized by our elderly geography teacher with horn-rimmed glasses, Brother Lorenzo, who had lived in East Pakistan for decades. He was an avid cyclist and had crisscrossed the country in his bike. He decided to take the entire class of seventeen students to see the new power station in Demra, about ten miles from our school on the Buriganga River as it swung around the city.

The day before our trip, we were instructed to bring several broadsheet newspapers, which we folded and shoved between our shirt and T-shirt to protect our chest and throat from the wind in order not to catch a cold as we biked to and from our destination. Another bike trip was to the famous Balda Garden, a three-acre botanical garden with over 650 rare species of plants at Wari, an old district of Dhaka. It was once the private garden of a wealthy jamindar (landlord) Narendra Narayan Roy, whose grandson donated it to the government in 1962. Both the trips were fun and informative.

My high school and college days were extremely happy and fun days. In high school, Brother Lorenzo was one of our favorite teachers, and he could read teenage minds very well. One day in class, he was teaching us about the origins of plant seeds in various continents, and as he proceeded to write their names on the blackboard, he said, "I don't want to hear you boys back there giggling like girls," and then wrote "rapeseed." Of course, one smart-ass student couldn't resist and asked, "Brother, does this mean we should not eat that seed to stay out of trouble?" That got him an hour's detention after school to write one hundred lines of "I shall observe decorum in my classes at all times."

Brother William Sheehan, our biology teacher, was a young man from Chicago and the strictest of them all; anyone coming to class late netted an automatic detention after school. After our graduation, he had gone to Chicago to visit with his family but met a girl with whom he fell in love and never returned to Dhaka; he had abandoned his calling and opted to have a married life.

Brother Nicholas, who taught us English, was soft spoken and the kindest of them all; he authored a booklet containing similar-sounding English words but with different meanings, which was very helpful to students. Our Bangla teacher was a no-nonsense fellow, and we being weak in Bangla, since we were from the English medium, dreaded his class. We also had a few VSOs (Volunteer Service Overseas) from UK schools.

While most of the brothers were of serious demeanor, Brother James sporting orange beard was loud and boisterous and a joker of sorts. He loved to spin tall tales. One such tale was that America was so advanced that if a tire in a multiwheeled trailer truck had a puncture, the driver did not need to stop to replace it; all he had to do was push a button on his dashboard, and the punctured tire would automatically recede to the top as a replacement tire fell in its place while the truck kept on moving nonstop. Not knowing better, and not daring to disbelieve a brother, we were impressed indeed.

He loved to bet students, saying, "I'll bet you a quarter that . . ." and if he lost the bet, which he sometimes did, he would pull out a dollar from his pocket and say, "Give me the change." Of course, none of us had any American coins, and so we could never collect the quarter! Our headmaster, Brother Gerald Kraeger, was hawk eyed and kept tabs on every student; hardly anything passed without him knowing about it. I must have been in his good book because he gave me a very good recommendation letter when I applied for admission to U.S. universities. He did not forget to mention that I "did not take part in any political disturbances or in any anti-state activities," which was the standard refrain every referee included in his reference letter as was customary at the time!

Our school had lots of sports teams, and I was the captain of our cricket and field hockey teams. I really sucked at basketball and couldn't dribble the ball at all, so I stayed away from basketball. We named our class hockey team the Phagocytes, having recently learned the word in our biology class. We had a very strong debating team, and twice we went to the national finals only to lose to Viqarunessa Girls High School; losing to the girls was hard for the boys to swallow.

There were two outdoor concrete table tennis tables in our school that were always in use. We played lots of soccer, and our favorite moments were when we could kick the soccer ball over the school boundary wall into the grounds of St. Francis High School, the girls' school next door, so that we could go get the ball and eye the girls. I dare say that the girls loved to see us as well. The only ones who would have none of that nonsense were our Catholic brothers and their Catholic sisters. We always got stern looks from the game teacher, and sometimes he would stop our soccer game as punishment. We also had a canteen outdoors next to the ping-pong tables that always had warm samosas, shingaras, cookies, and cold beverages; prominently displayed in the center of the back wall was the sign "Baakir naam faki" (Deferred payment means no payment).

At home, my siblings and I looked forward to watching our favorite television programs at night; *The Adventures of Robin Hood, Danger Man, Man from UNCLE, Danger Is My Business,* and later *Mission Impossible* were among our favorite shows. But it was also study time, and we were not supposed to be watching TV then, so we turned off the lights in the TV room and posted a servant by the gate, and as soon as he saw the headlights of Father's car turning onto our street, he would signal us, and we would immediately turn off the TV and rush upstairs to our study desks.

When Father dropped by our study areas to check up on us, we would be stressed out from the fear that he might hear our racing heart beats. On weekends, we played badminton and cricket in our garden. My sister Lily was quite creative while playing cricket with me; as she faced the ball, she would always keep her inside leg ready to stop the ball in case her bat didn't; her inside leg was always ready to be deployed as a second bat! She was lucky that we played cricket with tennis ball and not the real hard cricket ball.

When I reached grade ten, the final year of high school, some of us got to be designated as school prefects, which was one thing we eagerly looked forward to because we could pull rank, show off, and, most importantly, issue detention slips to misbehaving students or those who violated school rules. Of course, we were frequently reminded by the senior prefect not to get carried away in dishing out detention slips and definitely not to victimize anyone to get even. The latter did happen but only once, and the senior student was denied the privilege of continuing to be a prefect, which was a very loud signal to the rest of us prefects.

In November 1968, we wrote our O Level Examinations administered by Cambridge University, England, and fourteen out of seventeen of us passed in first division, the second best record in the school's history. Our best boy scored 8 (highest achievable was a score of 6 in six subjects); only one boy from St. Joseph's had scored 6 out of 6 until then. Our graduation ceremony was held in the ornate conference hall of Hotel Shahbag, which was converted to a Post Graduate Hospital (commonly known as the PG Hospital) after Bangladesh's independence. We all felt that we had broadened our intellectual horizons considerably and felt grateful to the brothers for the kind of education we received. When I went to the United States after finishing college, I felt that the material I studied in my freshman year was a rehash of what I had learned in final year of high school.

At the time of my high school graduation, Father was with the Pakistan Jute Delegation in Europe. He was so pleased to hear of my academic achievement that he bought me a Leicaflex camera from Holland as graduation gift. I took many rolls of pictures with that camera, especially during our family trip to the beach in Cox's Bazar. There being no photofinishing shop in East Pakistan at that time, I gave the rolls to Father during his next trip to Europe to wash and develop them, hoping to see color prints. When Father returned, he told me that to get color prints, the photo shop told him to use color film, not black-and-white film; I cannot believe how uninformed I was then!

However, it did incentivize me to read up on photography, and within a short period, I purchased a photo enlarger from the Kodak representative in Dhaka and started developing my own black-and-white prints in a makeshift darkroom. I should mention that many years later, during one of his trips to the UK, Father had given the Leicaflex camera to his British friend Lord R. E. B. Wilcox to have it cleaned in London, but the camera was never retrieved from Lord Wilcox. During one of my stopovers in London, I actually contacted Lord Wilcox to convey my father's greetings and to inquire about my camera. He invited me to lunch with him at the famous India Club on the Strand in London and promised to get the camera from the shop and hand it over to Father during Father's next visit to London. Unfortunately, Lord Wilcox died shortly thereafter, and his office could not give us the address of the camera shop; my camera was permanently lost. It had been sent to be cleaned because of the salt residue on the lens when a wave accidentally hit it as I was taking photos from waist-deep water off Cox's Bazar Beach.

The Taste of College Life

After our O Level exams, Urdu-speaking students went back to West Pakistan, as the western wing of Pakistan was known, before East Pakistan broke away to become the independent nation of Bangladesh. Some Bengali students went either to Karachi Grammar School or to Aitchison College in Lahore, West Pakistan, to continue their grades eleven and twelve schooling before sitting for their Advanced Level Certification (A Levels) prior to going overseas for higher studies. The rest of us went to colleges in Dhaka, primarily the Notre Dame College.

Going to Notre Dame College was a natural choice for us, because for most students from the English medium schools, it was the normal segue within the Catholic schooling system in then Pakistan. We understood and were at home with its norms and culture. Notre Dame College aspired to imparting the finest level of education and to the highest level of civic responsibility and citizenship for its graduates under the watchful eyes of its principal, Father Vanden Bossche, and the other Fathers of the Holy Cross, as did the schools we came from. Also, the college was rated to be at par with, if not better than, the prestigious Dhaka College, and the two were considered to be the best in the country.

Notre Dame College was established by the Roman Catholic priests from the Congregation of Holy Cross. Originally known as St. Gregory College, it was established in Laxmibazar, Old Dhaka, in November 1949, but was moved to Motijheel, Dhaka, and renamed Notre Dame College as a tribute to the University of Notre Dame, Indiana, the alma mater of many of the college's faculty members. We were admitted in January 1969, joining the first-year batch that entered five months earlier in August of the previous year. We graduated in June 1970 with HSC (Higher Secondary Certificate) degree, which was equivalent to the Cambridge A Level. All of us who came from St. Joseph's High School secured first-division results.

Life in college was barrels of fun as well. My small group of friends included Shamsuddin Ahmed, who subsequently joined the American Express Bank to build a career in banking and then went to the World Bank and then to the University of Hawaii to study business and finance that led to a PhD in economics; he is currently the chairman of Prime Bank Securities Ltd., Dhaka, and plays golf in his spare time.

Another boyhood friend was Gulam Faruq; we were friends from grade six at St. Joseph's. He followed me to the United States a year after I did and married beautiful Laura, a Sophia Loren look-alike. After graduating from the University of Oregon with a BA in physics and math, he worked for the UO Computer Center for a few years and then joined tech giant Intel in 1979, where he worked for thirty years until he resigned to lead a quiet life and pursue his passion of making furniture and machining. Sulaiman Tanvir was the third friend, the only one among us who studied Latin and went to England to study chartered accountancy. We lost track of him as he seems to have vanished into the ether.

We made our mark among the college kids in our batch at Notre Dame within the first few weeks. Father Joseph Peixotto, who taught us physics, gave the new year's first class quiz to his first-year students. The next morning, there was a buzz around the bulletin board besides the stairs that led to the first floor. As I walked up to the board, the students stared at me and parted to let me reach the board. Father Peixotto had posted the quiz scores; Faruq got 93/100, Shams got 95/100, and I got

97/100. Apparently, nobody had ever gotten scores in the 90s from Father Peixotto before; that day, we earned a special admiration and respect from our batch mates.

Our teachers also admired us, except for Sir Shaha, who taught us Bangla. He didn't have a high opinion of students who had come from the English medium schools because we were relatively very weak in Bangla, our native tongue. Indeed, our scores in Bangla language and literature tests were always lower than those of Bangla medium students.

To make matters worse, Sir Shaha had noticed that a bunch of boys in our class were always gawking at something outside through the side windows every day he came to class. One day, he walked silently into the classroom and looked out the window and saw a girl in the distant high-rise changing her clothes. Apparently, she changed her clothes every day during that hour in preparation for her departure to her classes, and she knew full well that boys were watching her. From that day onward, Sir Shaha kept those side windows closed during his class time. After class, he had also gone to that building, tracked the girl's floor and apartment, and informed her parents about her voyeuristic behavior. Her window remained permanently sealed thereafter.

Since Bangla was quite hard for those of us from the English medium instruction and it was a mandatory subject through school and college, it was a great relief when my friends and I completed our first-year final exam in Bangla and walked out of the exam hall. But the elation was short-lived. The minute we came out of the exam hall, we heard the terrible news that Prof. Mohammad Abdul Hai, the author of *Biletey Shaarey Shaatsho Deen (750 Days in England)*, which was one of our Bangla textbooks and the source of some of the questions in the HSC first year exam, had committed suicide by throwing himself in front of a moving train that morning. We were stunned by the news and kept speculating what could have caused him to take his own life. There were all sorts of theories: marital discord, financial trouble, it wasn't a suicide someone pushed him, etc. Whatever the reason for this tragedy, it was a real blow to the university's Bengali department.

We had mixed feelings about the courses we had to take in college. We dreaded the organic chemistry class because we had to memorize the periodic table, the organic formulas, structures of compounds, how chemical bonds were formed, and how structures and characteristics of compounds changed accordingly. In every class, the teacher would call out someone's name to come to the blackboard and draw the organic structure of a particular compound and explain its particular characteristics; without fail, our stress level would spike knowing that someone would goof up and the whole class would get an earful.

My favorite teacher was Father Ambrose Joseph Wheeler, who taught us botany and zoology. His lab assistant was a medical college student, Aslam Sultan Hassan, who later joined me at the University of Oregon and then graduated from the Oregon Medical School in Portland, and retired as an associate professor of physiology from the University of Illinois at Urbana-Champagne. Father Wheeler's lectures on genetics were particular interesting and inspired me enough to toy with the idea of studying genetics.

In those days, perhaps because of Pakistan's limited foreign currency reserves, students needing foreign currency to study abroad had to choose a subject that was approved by the government. The State Bank of Pakistan had a list of approved subjects to study overseas. Since biology or genetics was not on the list but biochemistry was, I declared the latter as my subject of choice for higher studies overseas and got the bank's foreign exchange release approval.

We sat for our final Higher Secondary School Certificate (HSC) examination in June 1970. These were national examinations administered countrywide. It was customary for students of one college to be placed in another college to write their exam scripts. The examination center that year for the students of Notre Dame College was Jagannath College, which was predominantly for Hindu students.

It was a politically tense year because the people of East Pakistan had been agitating against the central government for political equality and economic justice for a number of years. They had launched frequent civil disobedience movements to force the government of Pakistan to address the existing anomalies in society, but the government of Gen. Ayub Khan showed no concern and was callous, which infuriated the ethnic Bengali people of East Pakistan. Unable to contain the mass

53

uprising in January 1969, Gen. Ayub Khan handed over power to army commander Gen. Agha Mohammad Yahya Khan in March 1969, who suspended the Constitution and declared martial law.

Soon after, in November 1970, East Pakistan was hit by the Bhola cyclone, which was the deadliest tropical cyclone in recorded history and had killed half a million people; the lukewarm response of the Yahya government to this tragedy further convinced the people of East Pakistan that the government with its seat in West Pakistan did not give a hoot about the eastern wing of the country and the sufferings of the Bengali people.

It was in this tense environment that the students of East Pakistan sat to write their exam scripts. Three invigilators walked up and down the exam hall to ensure no one was cheating on their exams. Most of us went to the Jagannath campus at least an hour before the exam started because of the fear of political demonstrations and road closures. We checked out our assigned seat per our roll numbers.

My seat was on the very first bench in the first row near the entrance door. No one knew who would be sitting next to them. After waiting nervously for the bell to ring, when it finally did ring, we rushed to take our seats. The student sitting to my left at the other end of my bench introduced himself as Dobir. As we arranged our pens, pencils, erasers, slide rules, and instrument boxes on top of our bench, the exam questions and writing scripts with official seals on them were handed out to us facedown by the invigilators. The invigilators kept looking at their watches, and when it was time, we were told to turn over the question paper and start our exam. What I saw next shocked me. Dobir pulled up his right pant leg and pulled out a knife with a sheathed six-inch blade that was hidden inside his sock. He then placed the blade right in front of him on the bench in full view of the invigilators. The invigilator nearest to us saw that instantly but after a brief uncertainty decided not to confront him.

Except for a few policemen with their .303 Lee Enfield rifles guarding the entrance to the college building, there was no security on campus. The times were such that violence could erupt any moment anywhere. Dobir pulled out handwritten notes from his pocket and started copying them into his answer sheet. He completed the three-hour exam in just over two hours, submitted the answer script to the invigilator, and left. I didn't see him in the afternoon exam. I never saw him again, and I do not know what his results were; I only imagined that surely the invigilator must have written a note on the answer script stating that the student cheated during the entire exam.

During the chemistry viva voce examination that was held within my college, I was asked what numismatist and philatelist meant. Since I was an avid stamp and coin collector, it was easy for me to point at myself as I answered the question. This was the only question I was asked, and while it had nothing to do with chemistry, I learned later from the chemistry lab assistant that I had gotten such high marks in my chemistry written exams that the teachers conducting the viva felt asking me questions on chemistry would be a waste of their time. I got 25/25. My fellow students were surprised to see me walk in and walk out of the exam room in a few minutes. In any case, my friends and I secured first-division honors nationally.

Here, I should add that I had an impressive stamp collection with my album containing fantastic stamps from all over the world, including the most sought-after, first-day cover of the moon landing; when I left for the United States, I left my stamp album in my younger brother Sohel's care.

During our college days, Shams, Faruq, Tanvir, and I would occasionally take Faruq's red Toyota Corona for a spin in the vicinity of our campus. One favorite hangout was a new restaurant called Flamingo on North-South Road, which started serving hamburgers for the first time in the city. This sounds bizarre today, but that's how it was back then. We also went to picnic in the outskirts of Dhaka.

After college graduation, Father Wheeler proposed that we take a day off and visit Dhaka's famous historical sites. He asked us to list the places we should visit and draw up an itinerary. We were stumped because none of us knew what these historic places were, much less saw them. Seeing us struggle with this, Father Wheeler said, "OK, boys, I'll show you these sites myself." It was because of Father Wheeler's initiative that we became familiar with our history and archeology; we visited the seventeenth-century Lalbagh Fort; Ahsan Manzil, which was the palace of the Nawab of Dhaka; the Star Mosque; Balda Garden; etc. This outing encouraged us to take a longer trip to southeastern Bangladesh, which was mostly mountainous being the southern tip of the Himalayan range. Shams, Faruq, Tanvir, and I once again packed into the red Corona and headed south to the Chittagong Hill Tracts (CHT), Kaptai, and Cox's Bazar.

CHT, with its mountainous terrain, was home to many indigenous tribes of the Tibeto-Burman, Dravidian, and Austric stock, who have remarkable cultures, traditions, and languages of their own, quite unlike those of the Bengali people living in the plains of Bangladesh. There were over two million indigenous peoples in the country, with the majority concentrated in the CHT. They belonged to roughly twelve tribes, of which the Chakmas and the Marmas predominated. Among the other ethnic groups were the Tripura, Lushai, Mro, Khyang, Pankho, and Tanchangya. We visited the Chakma people to get a glimpse of their livelihood. Years later, I met the same-aged Debashish Roy, the titular Chakma king, during my work on indigenous issues in Southeast Asia. Debashish was a member of the United Nations Permanent Forum on Indigenous Issues, and we met during meetings in Dhaka and Bangkok.

During that trip to the CHT, we visited Kaptai Lake, which was artificially created by the construction of Kaptai Dam on the Karnaphuli River as a part of the Karnaphuli Hydroelectric Project. It was Bangladesh's largest lake. Its average depth was 30 meters, with a maximum depth of 150 meters. The dam itself was 671 meters long and 55 meters high. Funded and built by the United States from 1956 to 1962, its objective was to increase the country's electricity output, but the environmental disaster it caused had huge political and security ramification for the country.

It triggered tribal unrest leading to open insurgency for several decades, and not without reason. The lake flooded 220 square kilometers of farmland, which was 40 percent of the total arable land in the area; 680 square kilometers of forest land went under water; and nearly 18,000 families comprising 18 percent of the local population were displaced and their lives uprooted forever. It alienated a significant chunk of the tribal population, and although chaotic and often half-hearted resettlement plans and rehabilitation measures were undertaken, the grievances of the tribal people were neither seriously nor satisfactorily addressed.

The permanent encampment and occasional deployment of military forces in the region to maintain law and order and security against insurgent forces that found sanctuary across the border continue to be costly in terms of resources and lives. Things were sufficiently calm then for us to stay overnight at a hotel in Kaptai and next day rent a speedboat to see the lake and its scenic splendor. From there, we went to Cox's Bazar to enjoy the world's longest continuous pristine beach. On the way back, we stopped at Ramu to see the pagodas, Buddhist monasteries, and the four-meter-high bronze Buddha statue. All in all, it was an eye-opening and fun trip for the four of us.

From the time I started visiting the USIS during my high school years, I had been poring through various American university brochures, eagerly reading every page and dreaming about going to the States for higher studies. During my final year at Notre Dame College, I applied to three universities in the United States: University of Michigan, Notre Dame University, and University of Oregon for the 1970 fall semester. Luckily, I got accepted by all three universities, but unluckily, I was offered scholarship only by the University of Oregon. Getting a scholarship was extremely important to me because I was supremely aware that I had by then six younger siblings whose educational expenses would be a heavy burden on Father.

I showed the acceptance letter to Mother, who showed it to Father, who, I was told, broke into a smile. He was happy because all his friends' children were going to mother England to study chartered accountancy, while I was blazing the trail as it was across the ocean to America, and with a scholarship to boot. Father happily helped me with all the government approval and foreign exchange-related paperwork, for the scholarship covered only my academic expenses and not my living expenses.

While Father was happy, Mother was far from happy. She was happy for me but very sad that I had opted to go to a faraway land. She kept imagining horrific scenarios: who would cook for me, feed me, wash my clothes, and look after me, what if I fell sick, and myriad other concerns flooded her mind. As the day of departure neared, her sadness and bouts of crying increased. One day, she told me that she had heard from her friends that boys who went to America lost their ways; they started smoking, married American girls, and never returned home. I promised her that I would do none of that, and I kept my promise.

PART TWO

THE QUEST FOR KNOWLEDGE

Journey to the Unknown

I left the comfort of my home and my siblings, particularly my two-year-old sister Tina and one-and-a-half-month-old brother Tawfiq on September 16, 1970, to go to a land unknown to me except for the stories I heard about it. I also felt different from my other classmates because I was the only one among them who had opted to go to America; the rest who went overseas chose the United Kingdom to further their higher studies, most of them to study chartered accountancy, the sexy subject at that time.

But at the airport I had the jitters because I was about to break a law. Tucked under the sole of my foot inside my sock was a five-pound note, even though it was illegal to carry foreign currency unofficially out of the country. To meet educational expenses, the procedure then in place was for the State Bank of Pakistan to send a check every semester to the education counsellor in the Pakistan embassy in Washington DC, who was then to forward it to my bank account on campus. At the time, the counsellor was AMA Muhith, who was later the finance minister of Bangladesh from 2009 to 2018, and who knew Father well.

As I passed through airport security, I was stopped by a fierce-looking bearded official who asked me to step aside to undergo full body check. I thought my goose was cooked and imagined that I would be in jail in no time; I worried less about myself and more about family honor, Father's anger, and Mother's emotional and mental breakdown. He took me to a tiny adjacent room with a faded blue curtain that was pulled across the door and asked me whether I was carrying any foreign currency, assuring me that he was going to definitely find out if I did.

Unwilling to part with the only foreign cash I had, I decided to lie and told him that I had no foreign money on me. With a smirk on his face that said, "Yah, that's what they all say, but I know better," he asked me to undress down to my underwear. As I started to take off my clothes one by one, my heart grew fainter, my mind got clouded, and my hands started sweating and shaking a bit; at which point he said that that was a typical reaction of people who lied to him, thus making me more nervous. My mind went blank not quite knowing what will happen to me. He checked my coat, shirt, and pant pockets, and the insides of my shoes.

I was waiting for him to ask me to take off my socks, thinking that my end was near and that there was no going to America for me. Just then, his superior officer pushed aside the door curtain and stepped into the room and, seeing me almost naked, called out to him, "That's enough. Come with me," and turned to me and said, "Get dressed and go." I was so numb by then that it took me a while to get dressed and move on. I don't know what a near-death experience is like, but I must have come pretty close to it! I was also ashamed that I had lied and broken a law but took solace in the thought that it was all worth it to go to America.

I boarded a Japanese Airlines (JAL) flight to Bangkok and then to Tokyo landing past midnight. The connecting flight to San Francisco wasn't until late next day, but there were no hotel rooms available in Tokyo, so JAL put me on a taxi to a hotel in Yokohama some twenty miles away. About forty minutes later, I was in a beautifully appointed room with wood paneling all around me; too tired to appreciate further, I dressed down, put on the kimono that was neatly laid out on the bed, and just went to sleep.

When I woke up in the morning and pulled open the drapes to look outside, I was struck by the rustic beauty; the hotel was nestled in a wooded area, and everything appeared to be very peaceful and quiet. I decided to take a walk; every direction I looked at it was neat and tidy, and everything smelled so fresh. The air was rather warm, precursor to the typhoons that were on their way. I wondered how nice it must be to live in such bucolic surroundings all year round.

That afternoon on September 17, 1970, I took the taxi to Tokyo Haneda Airport and left for Frisco. A few hours into the flight, the pilot announced that we were crossing the international dateline, and then the stewardess started distributing Certificate of Crossing of the International Date Line with the JAL logo, date and time of crossing, and our name on it; we were all pleasantly surprised and happy to receive this gift.

A second surprise was when food was served that contained a ball of something in light syrup; I asked the stewardess what it was, and she smiled and said that it was bat meatball! I could not bring myself to eat it. I began to sense then that I would come across many such delicacies that would be new to me and that I would have to decide whether I want to be brave or stick to what I was familiar with. I landed in Frisco the same day, having gained a day, from where I flew to Portland, Oregon, where I was picked up at the airport by Richard Tacke, a close friend of Father Wheeler, my biology teacher at Notre Dame College. I was lucky to be in the right Portland because I learned from my friend Wahabi Taha, whom I would meet later, that he had ended up in Portland, Maine, and all my foreign friends teased him, saying, "What can you expect from an Arab!"

Richard drove me to his home in his big station wagon where I met his wife Eileen and their children. They were both very welcoming and nice to me. He asked me about Father Wheeler, whom they hadn't seen in years, and about my educational plan. She, on the other hand, was focused more on the immediate and said that she was cooking a special meal in my honor.

When dinner was served and we were all seated around the table, she lifted the cover off a large tray containing a ham roast garnished with cloves and slices of pineapple around it. She asked her preteen son to say grace and then handed the slicing knife to her husband as she explained with delight that she usually served ham either during Thanksgiving or during Christmas, but since a friend of Father Wheeler was visiting the family from across the ocean, this was a special occasion.

I did not have the heart to tell her that ham is forbidden to a Muslim. Perhaps she did not know that I was a Muslim or that Muslims do not eat ham, bacon, or pork, or if I had told her that I cannot eat ham, she might have offered me a precooked substitute from the fridge, but that would have taken the joy out of her. She was so happy and delighted with the special meal she had prepared, which brought smiles in the faces of her husband and children, that I kept quiet, said bismillah (a Muslim invocation that means "in the name of Allah"), and ate the slice given to me. I declined seconds with the excuse that I was still full from all the food that was served in the plane. It was the first time that

I had eaten something forbidden to me by my religion. Before retiring, I kneeled by my bed and sought forgiveness from Allah for knowingly violating the injunction. I hoped that making my hostess happy and appreciated would count for something to Allah the All Merciful!

The next morning, as I took leave, I thanked my host and hostess profusely for their hospitality. When Richard went to the garage to take his car out, Eileen took the opportunity to pull me aside and share her distress with me: she said that she very much wanted her young son to join the seminary to become a priest and do God's work, but her husband was opposed to it. She implored me to ask Father Wheeler when I corresponded with him next to help change her husband's mind. I assured her that I would convey her message, which I subsequently did, and Father Wheeler did intercede. Her son subsequently did join the priesthood, making her extremely happy that he was going to do God's work. Richard drove me to the bus depot and put me on the bus to Eugene. I learned recently from my friend Aslam that Richard had died in a car crash in 1979.

I was impressed by the bus ride and by everything I saw around me as I eagerly took in the view outside during the 110-mile ride south from Portland to Eugene. Everything looked, felt, and smelled differently from where I came from. I asked the bus driver the name of the tree that had all its leafy branches growing downward and touching the ground; he told me that they were called weeping willows. Two and a half hours later, I took a taxicab from the Eugene bus station to the Office of International Student Services (ISS) at the University of Oregon campus. I stepped out of the taxi and saw a beautiful tree-covered picturesque campus. I was very happy to be in America and felt a warm glow wash over my body. I was not even seventeen then.

Stepping into a New and Exciting Academic Life

At the ISS Office, I reported to Liz Litchman, a tall, bony lady with a happy face. She greeted me warmly and with a huge smile. She was the international student coordinator. We chatted for a short while, and then she walked me to the office of Dr. Kenneth Ghent, who was the foreign student advisor and who also taught mathematics part time. Dr. Ghent welcomed me warmly as well, sat me down, inquired about my journey, and then briefed me on most of the stuff that I needed to know. Mrs. Litchman then introduced me to the rest of the office staff, gave me a package containing a brochure and other information sheets about the university, and walked me to my dorm, the four-storied Watson dorm in the Watson-Hamilton Complex, a short distance away.

The boys' and girls' dorms were alternate buildings of the Hamilton Complex. The resident assistant, a short elderly lady, welcomed me with a smile and informed me that I had been assigned a single room on the third floor as requested, gave me the key to the room, apprised me of the dorm hours for visitors, and handed me a set of printed material about dorm rules and procedures to read. She told me that I should strictly observe dorm rules and also cautioned me that although Watson was an all-boys dorm, girls frequently visited Watson because there were three varsity football players from the University of Oregon football team living on my floor. So I shall be seeing lots of girls during visiting hours, and I should try to get used to it.

She also mentioned that sometimes the girls used the floor bathroom although they were not supposed to, so I should knock before I entered just in case, and, of course, I should report to her if there was any untoward incident. Luckily for all of us, there was never any untoward incident when our floor had female company. But what really got me was coming face-to-face with naked men walking in and out of the showers. What was even more embarrassing was when I did not have the time to return to my dorm for a quick shower after a sports activity or PE class and had to enter the communal shower at McArthur Court with naked men milling around in the huge shower area. I couldn't very well wrap a towel around me because I would be the only one doing that and everyone would stare at the prude! I did not want to be the butt of jokes in the locker room.

I settled down into my room whose layout I really liked; it was well designed for the needs of an undergrad. The entire back wall comprised two sliding windows; looking out, I saw another four-storied dorm, which was a girls' dorm. I bought a few nature posters and the poster of the Desiderata to break the monotony of the bare walls of my room. When I lay down in my bed, I would frequently read the Desiderata, which I found inspirational. One other writing that I recall from my childhood was the *Bangla Adorsho Lipi,* which was a book of wisdom, with every Bengali vowel and consonant in the fifty-letter Bengali alphabet giving rise to a wise and inspirational statement.

My floor had only single-occupancy rooms and one multiple-occupancy room, which was more like a big suite, which the three football players shared. The other three floors had double-occupancy rooms. The basic amenities were all there; however, there was only one telephone per dorm located in the entrance area on the ground floor. There were ample community spaces for multiple activities on the first floor. All the dorms of Hamilton Complex shared a central kitchen and dining area. Since I had a full meal plan, one big and immediate adjustment I had to make was to come to dinner between 6:00 p.m. and 8:00 p.m. This was initially hard for me to do, for I was used to having dinner at home at around 9:00 p.m., as was customary among city people in my country. I tried to have dinner just before closing time but found that often the main items or items of my choice were no longer available. There were many times when I skipped dinner because I was not hungry that I had to walk to McDonald's with fellow sufferers to grab a bite. I recall a tall pillar by the McDonald's arch that advertised, "6 million burgers sold"; that was in the fall of 1970. These days, McDonald's no longer posts their hamburger sales figure by their red and yellow arch; it is probably in the trillions by now.

Over the next few weeks, I eagerly crisscrossed the 295-acre campus along the Willamette River to get a better feel for it, familiarizing myself with places of interest such as the magnificent mixed Lombardy-and-Greco-Roman-styled Fenton Library (renamed as Knight Library in 1994); the campus bookstore, where I subsequently worked for several years selling electronic stuff; the McArthur Court, where most of our physical education courses took place, including being the home to our basketball team (we used to camp outside its doors the previous night to be the first ones through the door to appropriate the floor-level bleachers before every NCAA home game). Also included in my tour were the newly constructed lighted indoor tennis courts with five courts and the outdoor tennis courts with eight courts; and the historic Hayward Field, which was the home of the university's top-ranked track-and-field teams and also the on-campus home of the varsity football team until 1966.

Our most favorite hangout was the Millrace Restaurant with a slowly spinning waterwheel behind it; it was located across a fast-moving stream, and we had to cross an arched bridge to get to the restaurant that remained open until midnight on weekends.

Although we had six seasons in South Asia, the fall season on campus was a whole new experience; the leaves in the trees would start to change colors from green to yellow to orange to pink to red, which I had never seen before, and as they accumulated on the ground, the entire campus seemed to be immersed in a blanket of colorful leaves. It was a delight to behold and fun to walk over them between classes. And there were squirrels and chipmunks everywhere, running all over the place, busily stashing away acorns and other nuts for the coming winter. Many of my classes were held in buildings that were nineteenth-century, four-storied wooden structures with wooden staircases that creaked. Deady Hall, which was built in 1873 and home to the Mathematics Department, was the oldest, and I had to climb its creaky stairs to the fourth floor to get to my math classes several semesters.

I resolved to get the most out of my undergraduate experience. I found the American students very friendly and inquisitive about foreign students generally, and pretty soon I made quite a few friends. They invited me to their dorm rooms, which I found generally cluttered. Guys' rooms had typical boy stuff with stolen road signs, license plates, psychedelic posters, posters of seminude or nude girls, *Playboy* or sometimes *Penthouse* magazines by their bedside, empty beer bottles, sometimes a baseball bat and ball or the odd-shaped American football—in short, totally messy.

Girls' rooms were filled with girlie stuff including stuffed animals, pictures of their dogs or cats, sometimes pictures of their parents or siblings, potted plants on the windowsill, and not infrequently strips of warning taped to the mirror inside their cupboard that read, "Pill a day keeps the stork away," or caution note on the inside of the door that read, "Did you remember to take your pill?" Dorms would organize lots of activities, including intramural activities, in which I eagerly participated; it was a great way of meeting people and making friends.

I also immersed myself fully in academia. Over the three quarters that comprised the first academic year, I focused on biology and related courses, until one day it dawned on me that I was spending a better part of each week in the basement biology lab. On certain days of the week, I hardly saw what the weather outside was like because I was cooped up in the lab with petri dishes doing cell cultures. I seriously asked myself whether I was willing to spend the rest of my life working in laboratories and concluded that I wasn't cut out for that. Since, among the elective subjects, political science fascinated me most, I decided to switch my major to political science, although I was concerned about my father's reaction; it was one of the best decisions I made in my life.

My Life Changes its Trajectory

I officially changed my major in the sophomore year and started taking multiple political science courses from very engaging professors. I loved Thomas Hovet Jr.'s lectures on the United Nations, international law, and comparative foreign policy; George Zaninovich's lectures on Balkan politics and on Yugoslavia; Arthur Hanhardt III's lectures on German politics, especially on Ostpolitik; and Joseph Fiszman's lectures on Marxism, Socialism, and Eastern Europe. There were other professors whose names I cannot now recall who taught us armistice and Korean politics, the rise of Japan, China and Formosa, Soviet politics, American foreign policy, the arms race and détente, third-world government and politics, Arab politics and OPEC, European coal and steel community, and the politics of apartheid, to name a few.

I was resolved to exhaust the undergrad courses offered by my department. The course offerings by other departments across the disciplines were equally varied and rich. I particularly remember the courses offered by the History Department where I studied the Cuban

Revolution; the Bolshevik Revolution; the struggles of revolutionaries Fidel Castro, Che Guevara, and Simon Bolivar; African colonial history; and Latin America's colonial history. The anthropology courses were a window to the cultures and societies in the African continent. They also inspired me to study African literature in my English classes, which I found fascinating.

The sociology courses were particularly interesting. On the first day of my SOC 101 class, the opening statement of the sociology professor was "Does anyone know what a sociologist is? I'll tell you. A sociologist is a person who is continuously amazed at the obvious." I was hooked. Other head-turning courses I took were the Deschooling of Society, the Unlearning Process, the Politics of Waste Mismanagement, and the Throwaway Society, the latter in line with the beliefs of the "tree-hugging generation."

The course that aimed to teach us planetary consciousness and the need to preserve and conserve by applying the strategy reduce, reuse, and recycle was something of a chuckle for me because while it was a new discovery for the throwaway societies of the West, third-world societies from where I came regularly practiced the three Rs. It was also interesting to watch how the United States reacted to the OPEC oil embargo of 1973. Whereas before the oil crisis, every lightbulb on campus was lit up from dusk to dawn; when the embargo started, the campus went partially dark since only strategically located lightbulbs inside buildings or outside on campus were lit. Dorm hours, library hours, and restaurant hours were reduced. We were all told to conserve energy and water. Suddenly, there were bumper stickers that read, "When yellow, let it mellow; when brown, flush it down," or, "Don't californicate Oregon."

I was intent on getting a broad liberal arts education, and over the four year undergraduate program, I registered in courses on philosophy, history, psychology, anthropology, sociology, languages, English, you name it. I studied French and German for two years and Mandarin for six months. I was truly thrilled by this whole new universe that unfolded before me, and I was going to make the most of it.

But there were unforeseen or embarrassing moments here and there as well. On the first day of my philosophy class PHI 101, the professor walked in wearing run-down jeans, a shirt that looked like it had been worn for weeks, and disheveled hair; I was shocked that the class teacher would appear so unkempt. As if that wasn't enough of a shock, he told the class that we were going to leave the classroom and walk over to a pub a couple of blocks away to discuss philosophy over beer and pretzel. I didn't drink beer, nor did I like the salty taste of pretzels, which I had seen for the first time. However, the real problem was that he adopted the Socratic method of teaching, but the students were not sufficiently versed in philosophical discourse to meaningfully engage in the Socratic exchange.

Another shock was when I walked into a psychology class, human sexual behavior, to see if I would like to register in that course. At the U of O, during the first two weeks of registration, one could sit in different classes to check them out before actually registering for the course. When we took our seats in the classroom, we saw what looked like two round cellophane rings, one small and the other slightly larger, on each student desk. The teacher came in, allowed a few minutes for the nearly hundred students to settle down, picked up the two items, and said, "This is a question for the guys. Do you know what these are?" No one answered. He continued. "These are diaphragms, one for big girls and one for little girls." Then one after another, he asked several male students which one would be used by which girl, to which every male student he asked replied that obviously the big one was for the big girls and the small one for the little girls. None of the other guys in the classroom raised our hands in disagreement. Of course, we guys were all wrong. Then what followed in the next half hour was labelled as a desensitizing session that involved reseating with boys and girls facing each other and uttering the names of intimate body parts of the opposite gender. Coming from a conservative Muslim society, the whole experience was quite embarrassing to say the least.

In another incident, in my first anthropology class, when the shorts-and-T-shirt-clad thirty-something teacher was handing back our marked test scripts, he noticed an empty seat. He asked whether anyone knew who sat there. A female student raised her hand and said that she knew him. The teacher smiled and asked her, "How many times?" I was shocked at the insinuation. Among other shocks, I could not believe that students could put up their feet on the seat in front or smoke in the presence of the teachers; this was so disrespectful from where I came. I continued to experience cultural shocks throughout the first year, and they were notable indeed. Of course I did not share any of this with my parents because I knew that my mother would ask me to come home instantly!

It was symptomatic of the times. The late '60s and early '70s were a crazy time both in the United States and around the world. In the States, there was the Ku Klux Klan, or the KKK movement, which was a white supremacist hate group born in the American South, occupying the extreme right fringe of the political spectrum. They believed in the superiority of the white race and sought to eliminate the blacks, Jews, and immigrants from the homeland. At the opposite end was the Weather Underground Movement, which was a radical left militant movement born in the Ann Arbor campus of the University of Michigan and grew out of the anti-Vietnam War movement. It carried out bombings, riots, and jail breaks. There were frequent massive protests against the Vietnam War led by peace activists and leftist intellectuals on college campuses. One iconic figure was Hollywood actress Jane Fonda whose antiwar protests were marked by her visits to North Korea and to North Vietnam in 1972 in defiance of her government. Joan Baez's protest songs also moved us; she too visited North Vietnam in 1972 at the invitation of the Hanoi government.

Students across the country were so agitated that there were numerous violent altercations with the police, the most violent being the Kent State University campus riots in May where four students died and nine were wounded by the Ohio National Guard. At one point, even the students of vaunted Harvard University locked up their establishment-leaning professors inside their classrooms for a few hours. Students who enrolled at the Reserved Officers' Training Corps (ROTC) to become commissioned officers of the United States Armed Forces were taunted, heckled, and sometimes spat on by the antiwar demonstrators. I had friends both among the ROTC and the demonstrators. In fact, there was an ROTC officer in our dorm, and his life was made miserable. Nobody would sit with him at the meal table. When I took my tray and sat down with him in the corner of the cafeteria one day, he advised me to move away if I didn't wish to fall prey to the antiwar hecklers.

Up north across the border, the Vive le Quebec, which was a rallying cry for Quebec separatism and became a movement that demanded Quebec's sovereignty from the rest of Canada, was in full swing. It was greatly fuelled by Gen. Charles de Gaulle's "Vive le Quebec libre" controversial speech delivered during his 1967 official visit to Canada. The Biafra Movement in Nigeria, which pitted Nigeria's Christian and animist southeastern states against the mostly Muslim northern states, was triggered by the persecution of the Ibo people living in the north and the control of the lucrative oil production in the Niger Delta. Although the Biafran rebels surrendered in January 1970, coups and countercoups continued to destabilize the state.

The anti-Shah movement in Iran also triggered many demonstrations especially on campuses that had Iranian students. At the University of Oregon, where we had many Iranian students, I witnessed demonstrations and clashes between them and the police. I witnessed blindfolded students with their hands tied up standing on flatbed trucks being driven around campus mimicking what America's friend, the Shahinshah of Iran, and his secret service SAVAK were doing to Iranian student demonstrators in Iran. And, of course, there was the Bangladesh War in full swing as well.

Truth be told, it was thrilling for me and my friends to be in the midst of all this, and the courses offered by many American universities reflected this aggressive, antiestablishment, protest-driven mood. Notwithstanding this challenging environment, my overall academic experience was healthy, meaningful, and rewarding; I found the teachers to be very knowledgeable, helpful, and considerate, and the subjects offered by various departments very exciting and thought provoking.

Off to Hollywood

After the first quarter ended in mid-December 1970, students started leaving campus to return home to spend Christmas with their families. David Barnett, a philosophy student whose dorm room was next to mine, asked me whether I was going home for Christmas. I told him that home was too far away for me, that Muslims did not usually celebrate Christmas, and that I would be staying on campus over the holidays since I had nowhere to go. He immediately invited me to his home in Encino, a short distance from Beverly Hills in California, to join his family to celebrate Hanukkah.

Since I had never heard of Hanukkah before, he explained to me that it was an eight-day celebration in the Hebrew calendar, which fell anywhere between late November and late December in the Christian calendar. It celebrated the successful revolt by the Jewish people against their Greek-Syrian oppressors and commemorated the rededication of the Second Temple in Jerusalem in the second century BC.

I was excited that I would have the chance to learn about a different faith and culture and happily agreed to go with him. We got into his Ford Mustang convertible with its roof folded back, which was a very hot car for the peppy generation of that time, and began our drive south toward California. On the way, we stopped at a small town called Roseburg for gas. David was pumping gas, and I was sitting in the front passenger seat when suddenly a car came to a screeching halt. It was a police car, and it reversed and stopped parallel to our car. A burly police officer walked up to our car, plunked his hands down on the passenger side door, stared at me, shaking his head in disbelief, and then looked up at David and asked, "Where did you pick this up, boy?" He referred to me as "this" and not "him," immediately dehumanizing me because in his mind, I was an illegal Mexican who must have entered the United States unlawfully. David quickly replied, "He is my friend from Pakistan. Is something wrong, officer?" The officer barked, "From where?" Realizing the ignorance of the police officer, David replied, "Umm, India." "Where? I don't care, boy. Get him out of here" growled the officer.

David rushed into the gas station to pay for the partially filled tank of gas, got into the car, and immediately started to drive, making sure to stay within the speed limit so that he is not given a speeding ticket or we are not hauled into jail. Throughout this ordeal, the police car remained behind us all the way and stopped only after we left Douglas County and crossed over into the next county where the police officer had no jurisdiction.

That was my first brush with American cops, and it was unpleasant to say the least. David apologized to me, explaining that these were hick-town cops who probably never left Roseburg in their entire lifetime and therefore did not know better. But in my mind, I began to doubt the assertion that in America, a person is innocent until proven guilty. To me, it appeared that American cops had a different modus operandi—namely, a person, especially a nonwhite, was guilty until proven innocent. This sense was reinforced in me by other altercations with the American police in later years.

We finally arrived at David's home in Encino, and I was immediately impressed by the Maserati in their driveway. His father, Philip Barnett, was a very rich lawyer, and the opulence of his home and office reflected that. His parents graciously received me. The menorah, which symbolized the Israeli nation and its mission to be the light for other nations, was already lit, which to me mimicked the Hindu celebration Diwali, or the Festival of Lights.

Philip, was a friendly and humorous man. When he learned that I was from Pakistan, he insisted on taking me to his office to show me his prized possession. Sometime later, he drove David and me to a high-rise building in downtown Los Angeles, took the elevator many stories up, and then he opened the French doors to his office and with a flourish ushered me inside. Once inside, he threw his arms forward and uttered, "Ta-da!" Since he was so excited to show me something, I was desperately looking for it. I saw the expensive paintings on his office wall, the very well-appointed office, the superb view of Los Angeles through his office windows, but nothing else. Then I inched closer to one of the wall paintings; at which point, unable to contain his disappointment, he said, "No! No! Look there," as he pointed to a carpet on the floor. "It's a jute carpet!" East Pakistan had just started to manufacture jute carpets, and we had plenty of them at home, and so it was hardly an object to marvel at for me. But, apparently, he was the first one among his circle of very rich friends to possess one, and no one else had one, and therefore it trumped even the expensive paintings on his walls, and he was one-up on his friends. Hiding my surprise, I congratulated him on his prized possession!

He was also a generous man. One weekend, he drove all of us some fifty miles to a newly opened Mexican restaurant for breakfast only to find it closed!

During the course of my stay as their guest, I was struck, however, by Philip's liberal use of promiscuous language. When I had arrived at his home, David had introduced me to his family, but his young sister was not present then. When she came home later, Philip introduced her to me and then remarked, "Can you believe it—she is twelve and she is still a virgin. Which twelve-year-old California girl is still a virgin, you tell me?" One evening, as his wife was setting the table for dinner, he asked me rhetorically, "Do you know who my favorite woman is? It's Barbara Streisand. I would give anything to have her." I looked up at his wife, who just shrugged her shoulders and smiled, letting me understand that she had learned over the years not to let her husband's banter bother her.

To note, Barbara Streisand was only twenty-eight years old at that time and already famous as a singer and a Hollywood actress. She went on to become a famous Hollywood icon and the recipient of many awards including the Grammy, Oscar, and Tony awards.

Philip instructed his son David to show me a really good time, not to miss Universal Studios, Disneyland, Beverly Hills, Hollywood Boulevard, and certainly not Sunset Strip. So almost every day when I was there, David and I went out. We went to the Universal Studios at Universal City and Disneyland in Anaheim, both of which were a real treat.

At the Universal Studios, we had a tour guide. We were about twenty people in our group. The tour guide gathered us at one place and, seeing the diversity of faces, asked us to raise our hands if we were from outside the United States. More than half the people raised their hands. The tour guide asked a gentleman with raised hands in front of her where he was from. He replied, "Pakistan." David and I were at the back of the group, and I called out that I, too, was from Pakistan. "Which part of Pakistan are you from?" I asked. "From East Pakistan," he said. "Me too," I said, adding, "Which city?" "Dhaka, I live in Dhanmondi," he said. "Me too!" I said. "Which street?" "Road No. 18," he said. It turned out that both of us lived on the same street at opposite ends, but we never met, only to meet at the Universal Studios in Los Angeles. There was a loud round of applause from our group as the tour guide nodded her head at the remarkable coincidence.

The Disneyland visit was like a fantasy trip with visitors subjected to surprises and scares besides the regular rides and entertainments. David took me to Sunset Strip on Sunset Boulevard one evening and explained to me that it was famous for all the sexy prostitutes plying their trade. He drove down the boulevard slowly so that I could see the hookers in skimpy outfits. They all looked very young and were smiling and eyeing us, although I was wondering whether it was us they were looking at or David's spiffy, shiny red Mustang convertible!

But what was truly mind blowing was the play called *O. F. Ostrogoths* for which David bought tickets for us to see. It was a satirical play mocking the Catholic Church and its priests who acted out their homosexuality on stage. The theater was oblong in shape with seats at two levels on all four sides and the stage in the center. Actors dressed only in stiff cone-shaped hats and robes with cords hanging by the sides and no clothes underneath feigned homosexual acts on each other alongside mocking references to the Holy Bible. They pushed aside their robes during the fake act, and one could see they were stark naked. David's introduction to Los Angeles and its offerings were totally beyond my expectations and far removed from the Hanukkah celebrations I came to Encino for.

The Bangladesh Liberation War, 1970–71

By the end of my first year at U of Oregon, war was brewing in the South Asian subcontinent, which officially lasted from March 26 to December 16, 1971. Nearly twenty-four years of sustained socioeconomic exploitation and political discrimination by the government of Pakistan against the people of East Pakistan had come to a head, and the ensuing Bengali national and self-determination movement pitted the Bengali population against the armed might of Pakistan.

On March 26, Pakistan launched an all-out indiscriminate attack against Bengali civilians, especially targeting East Pakistan's military and police personnel, the political parties, and the students who were spearheading this revolution. My father being an ex-military man was a primary target, and our house in Dhanmondi was bombed, resulting in a roadside corner of the house getting totally demolished.

Having received a secret message that he was going to be picked up any moment, Father fled the city disguised as a peasant wearing a lungi and T-shirt. To get through military checkpoints, he held a sack of belongings on his head with one hand and someone's child on his hip with the other hand, pretending to be a peasant returning to his village. To make it look convincing to the Pakistani soldiers manning the check post, he walked barefoot some ninety miles from Dhaka toward the eastern border to Agartala, India, with a few stops on the way. It was a very long and difficult walk for him, with swollen legs and blisters on his feet when he arrived in Agartala. There, he opened the Palatona Training Camp to train Bengali freedom fighters, the Mukti Bahini, to fight the Pakistani military.

During that time, communication with home was very difficult and time consuming. The only means of fast communication was landlines, but for that too, one had to go through the telephone operators. I had to call the operator in the States and request her to connect me with the number at my home. She would then call the operator in Pakistan and request the connection. The operator in Pakistan would then call my home number and ask the call receiving person to hold on as she reconnected with the U.S. operator, who then called me and put me through. This took multiple tries and much patience, and often the line would get disconnected in the middle of the conversation requiring a repeat of the whole tedious process. One barely got to talk to his parents besides saying, "Hi, how are you? I'm fine." It was also very expensive, three dollars per minute.

But this was an abnormal time as war raged at home, and telephone, telegram, and telex services were down. I was glued to radio news and to newspaper reports, not knowing what had happened to my family, and with Father being a military man, I feared the worst. I learned later that Father Wheeler had visited Mother after Father fled to India and, seeing her predicament and mindful of the fact that my father was a benefactor of the college as well as a member of its governing board, offered her sanctuary at the Notre Dame College premises. Mother thanked him but declined to accept the generous offer.

She then decided to flee herself. She buried all her jewelries under the ashes of the chulha (cooking stove that uses firewood) and left Anu in charge of the house. She fled Dhaka with my seven brothers and sisters and two cousins, Rafiqur Rasul and Ezazur Rasul, who had been hiding in the university lavatory for several days to escape from being picked up by the military. Her obvious place of refuge was her village in Lostimanika, but response from there was tepid because my youngest step-aunt, Najma, strongly opposed her presence, arguing that since she was the wife of a military person, their home would be a primary target of the Pakistan military. Not wishing to put her stepfamily in jeopardy, Mother fled with her young children to her grandma's place in Mahmudpur and then to the village of Gobindapur, the home of a disciple of my nana.

Two of my teenaged brothers—Mahboob and Selim—left her to join Father in Agartala in eastern India and train as Mukti Fauj. Newspaper reports that the Pakistan military was particularly targeting young girls and had picked up university and college girls from their hostels for use by their soldiers in their camps struck fear in me because my sister Lily was a teenager then. The military came looking for Father, ransacked the house, and subjected Anu to extensive beating to extract information about the family's whereabouts. Mother's jewelries, however, remained safe.

I was very disappointed at the pro-Pakistan stance by the United States government. Pres. Richard Nixon wanted to show the American people a major foreign policy achievement by his Republican administration by establishing for the first time diplomatic relations with Communist China and had secretly sent Secretary of State Henry Kissinger to Beijing to lay the groundwork for a presidential visit to China. The go-between in this delicate development was Pakistan, who facilitated Kissinger's trip as well as kept it totally secret from the rest of the world and from the American public. This obligated the United States to support Pakistan in the military conflict in East Pakistan.

I felt that the American people were being kept in the dark about the ongoing massacre in East Pakistan and felt the importance of going public. First, I wrote a full-length article with the sensational title "Bengal Blood on US Hands" in our campus newspaper the *Daily Emerald* to attract attention. It did just that, for I was invited by a local radio station to speak to its listeners on what was happening in East Pakistan.

I also founded the Bangladesh Student Association and became its first president. During that time, in the entire West Coast, there were only three Bengalis from East Pakistan in Oregon—Jamal Rahman, Shahryar Ahmed, and myself—only one East Pakistani student in the state of Washington, and about fifty families in the state of California concentrated mostly in the greater Los Angeles area.

I took every opportunity to speak publicly about the war to inform the American people of their government's policy. It took me all the way to the Los Angeles Town Hall, where we gave a public presentation on the East Pakistan situation, which angered a West Pakistani so much that he picked up his chair to hit me over the head.This incident was captured by a photographer present at the town hall meeting and printed in the *Los Angeles Times* the next day. I also drafted a letter on behalf of the Bangladesh Student Association that was signed by my friend Jamal Rahman, which was printed either in the *Times* or *Newsweek* magazine, and which appeared in the Internet a few years ago. We successfully raised US$100K for Bangladesh and sent the money to Indira Gandhi's Relief Fund in Washington DC. We also undertook to create a telephone directory of East Pakistani students in the West Coast at the time.

As we pressed on with our pro-Bangladesh movement, there was a huge backlash against us from the West Pakistani students on campus. They became positively hostile toward us, constantly threatened us, and reported us to the Pakistan embassy in Washington DC as destructive anti-state elements working actively against the interests of the state of Pakistan. The Pakistan government immediately retaliated against me by suspending the foreign currency remittances to cripple my overseas studies.

By then, I was under considerable emotional and financial stress. Then one day, a letter arrived from the office of Sen. Edward Kennedy, who had just returned after touring the refugee camps outside Bangladesh's eastern and western borders with India. His letter stated that he had met my father in Agartala, who had asked him to convey to me that he was all right and that I shouldn't worry. That letter brought me tremendous emotional relief.

Also, my radio interviews in Eugene brought sympathetic responses from two sources. Dr. Ghent, the director of the Office of International Student Services, supplemented my university scholarship with a Ford Foundation Grant for the years 1971 and 1972, which replaced the money I was getting from home that was cut off by the Pakistan government. He also talked with the Oregon state government officials to arrange food stamps for us. Food stamps could be used in lieu of hard cash to buy food stuff at the grocery stores. While we were very grateful to get the food stamps, which we used for several months, I cannot forget the disapproving looks some people gave us at the grocery checkout stand when we started using them to pay for our groceries. They seemed to be thinking that we foreigners were ripping off the system big time!

In the summer of 1971, Aslam Sultan Hassan, Father Wheeler's lab assistant at Notre Dame College, arrived from Bangladesh, followed by Gulam Faruq in the fall. Together with another friend, Shahryar

Ahmed, the four of us moved into the attic of a house that was for rent; the house belonged to one of the chefs of our dormitory complex. It took the whole morning for us to shift our stuff, and then we went downstairs to her kitchen to cook our afternoon meal. The landlady sat in the kitchen the whole time knitting and stewing over how long it was taking for us to cook our Bengali food. After we were done cooking, eating, and washing up, which took a couple of hours and beyond the landlady's expectation, she got up stone-faced and told us that she refuses to "put up with this" and ordered us to move out of her house by the end of next day. We were shocked that we were ordered to leave when we had just moved in that morning. We immediately spread out looking for an alternative place and were lucky to find a two-bedroom apartment on the edge of campus. It was a tremendous relief to find a place with a kitchen of our own and not have the landlord looking over our shoulders.

One day, a very elderly couple, George and Mae Kobilkin, knocked on our apartment door. They told us that they had heard my radio interview and were deeply touched by our financial predicament. They handed us a forty-dollar check to buy the month's groceries and promised to provide us with a check every month as long as the need existed. This was a tremendously kind gesture from a couple we did not know. We learned subsequently from Mae Kobilkin that George Kobilkin was a White Russian who had fought the Bolsheviks and the Mensheviks, and immediately after the October Revolution in 1917, he had jumped onto a ship in Vladivostok and fled to Seattle, from where he worked his way to Eugene, where he met Mae and married her. They owned an apple orchard in the outskirts of Eugene and had no children. They were heaven sent indeed!

The war was finally over, and former East Pakistan became an independent, sovereign Bangladesh. Father recuperated from his wounds and returned home with a few Indian rupees in his pocket. Our family wealth was gone. The Pakistan Army had looted all the banks, including the vaults of the State Bank branch in Dhaka, which contained some gold bullion. With no cash in the banks of the new country of Bangladesh, Father decided to withdraw some money from his London bank account, which was a joint account with his partner Afajuddin Faqir but found the account empty. Faqir, who had remained in Dhaka during the war and hobnobbed with the Pakistan military, had withdrawn all the money and deposited it into his own personal account. When Father confronted Faqir after the war, Faqir replied that he withdrew the money for safekeeping thinking that the Pakistan military was going to find him and kill him anyway; however, Faqir refused to return the money. Father had to build up his life anew. A few years later, I learned that Faqir had resettled his family in London, but his wife had transferred all the money from their joint account to her personal account and had divorced him after that. I felt a sense of divine justice at this comeuppance!

After returning to Dhaka, my parents found our Dhanmondi home unlivable because of the bomb damage. They found refuge for several months in a house at 10 Circuit House Road; after which time they bought a flat in Hafizabad Colony, New Eskaton, Dhaka. The new government was losing its grip over the people whose expectations exceeded the government's ability to meet them.

In the face of new nationalism, all English medium schools were converted to Bengali medium schools, but the quality of education deteriorated fast because of lack of proper policy, lack of funding, lack of teachers, many of whom had lost their lives in the war, and general countrywide indiscipline and chaos.

Father was seriously worried about the education of my two younger brothers, Mahboob and Selim, who had been in the Palatona Training Camp with him. He wrote to me stating his concerns that he could compromise on many things but not on education. As the eldest son, I had to do something. I went to the principal of South Eugene High School, Eugene, and explained to him our predicament and asked him whether my two brothers could get admitted in his school. I also told him that we had no money to pay the out-of-state tuition. The principal was sympathetic and promised to give the issue his serious consideration. A few days later, the school called and informed me that both my brothers would get the high school admission letters and that their educational expenses would be waived. An official letter with I-20 forms for both would be issued shortly. I was ecstatic and informed Father of the good news. Mahboob and Selim arrived in Eugene and started high school in the fall of 1972. My sister Lily, who remained in Dhaka, completed her matriculation in 1972, her intermediate education at Eden Girl's College in 1974, and then went to Dhaka University to study sociology. I was sad that I could not attend her wedding in Dhaka in April 1975.

The Four Musketeers

With my family picking up the straws and gradually restoring their normal lives, normalcy was also returning to my life in Oregon. I used to write long handwritten letters to Mother, which she kept in a pile. I heard later that Father noticed those long letters and one day asked Mother, "When does your son find the time to study when he is writing such long letters?" The four of us—Shahryar, Aslam, Faruq, and I—settled down in our two-bedroom apartment comfortably. We took turns cooking.

One day, I had the craving to eat *khichuri,* a rice-lentil mixed dish, but none of us knew how to cook it. So I wrote to Mother for the recipe and cooking instructions. I learned later that Mother cried as she dictated the recipe because how unfortunate I was that there was no one there to cook for me! I was happy to get the recipe and put the letter inside my pants pocket. When I put my pants to wash, I had forgotten to take out the letter, and so when it came out of the clothes washer, the ink writing on the letter was no longer there; the recipe was gone.

Resolved to eat khichuri nonetheless, I cooked rice and dahl separately and then mixed the two together and pretended that we were eating *latka khichuri.* It tasted deliciously, perhaps because *nai mamar cheye kana mama bhalo* (a Bengali saying, "Better to have a blind uncle than no uncle").

Sometime later, a Bengali youth contacted us. He explained that he had come from West Germany via some Caribbean country and had no place to stay, and could we allow him to crash at our place for a few nights until he figured out what to do next. We took pity on him and let him sleep in the couch and gave him a sleeping bag. Since he had no money, he proposed to do the cooking for us as long as he stayed with us. We thought that was a good deal. So one day, we returned from our classes and were eager to sit down for dinner. We asked him what he had cooked, and he replied that he had cooked dahl, chicken, and beef. We positively salivated, but then we watched him dish out chicken and beef from the same utensil. We all stared at him in shock. He then calmly explained that cooking chicken and beef in separate utensils was too much trouble and time consuming, so he just cooked them together! "After all, both will be going into the same tummy, no?" he asked. Luckily for us, he took off for California shortly thereafter.

Our roommate Aslam was a jolly, happy-go-lucky fellow, very friendly and always smiling, who could not start his day without a cup of tea. Every morning, he would get out of bed rubbing his eyes with his knuckles, and the first thing he did was fill up the kettle with water and set it on the stove. He was also incurably romantic. As a medical student at the Dhaka Medical College, he had fallen in love with a girl named Putul. To win her affection, Aslam even learned to sing Rabindra Sangeet (songs written by Nobel laureate Rabindranath Tagore), which were her favorite. One day, when he was practicing Rabindra Sangeet in our apartment, someone knocked at our door. It was one of our neighbors who asked, "Is someone dying here? I am hearing mourning sound." To foreigners not familiar with Rabindra Sangeet, it could sound like someone is mourning, but, nevertheless, our neighbor's comment, while funny, was also very insulting to us and particularly to Aslam.

When Aslam had left Dhaka for Oregon, he and Putul had promised each other that they would regularly write to each other and that there was a future together for them. But shortly thereafter, Putul stopped replying to Aslam's letters. When I went to Dhaka to visit my parents in December 1973, Aslam wrote a long letter to Putul, handed it to me, and asked me to hand deliver it to Putul and bring back her written response. I did as demanded, but Putul did not give me a reply, so I came back empty-handed. Putul had fallen in love with another fellow; it was very hard on Aslam. He coped with his frustrations by facilitating the romantic liaisons of the rest of us. When another roommate, Gulam Faruq, was smitten with a lovely girl named Laura during a talk to high school students and resolved to walk her to her home after class, Aslam pushed Faruq's bike all the way to her home, staying an appropriate distance behind to allow Faruq to hold Laura's hand and exchange sweet nothings undisturbed.

Aslam and I used to watch lots of movies at the theaters. Our special target was the weekend matinee movie for a dollar, and on occasions, after the matinee, we would switch to another hall to see another movie without paying. My most memorable recollection is when we went to watch the much-talked-about triple X-rated movie, *Deep Throat,* which had taken the public by storm when it was released. Aslam and I decided that we had to see it but were also scared in equal measure. Having resolved to see it, we waited till the last moment when the lights in the movie theater went off before entering it so that no one would see us. But it didn't help when the lights came on after the movie ended, and we could see that we were the only eighteen-year-olds in the theater full of adults and seniors who did not hide their stares.

Aslam was also quite easy to tease because he often did quirky things. He used to follow grocery flyers meticulously and could never resist a good sale. One weekend, we woke up and found Aslam missing. After a while, we heard some hard kicks on the front door. When we opened it, we found Aslam standing at the door with multiple cartons of eggs held between his chin and his two hands below his navel. He had noticed in the weekend flyer that eggs were on sale for twelve cents a dozen instead of the normal eighteen cents a dozen, and had gotten up early and walked several miles to catch the sale before the eggs were sold out. While his valiant effort saved four of us undergraduates a few cents, we were eating eggs for breakfast, lunch, dinner, and between-meal snacks for the next few months!

He was also very particular about money matters. Every purchase we made, every bill we paid had to be split four ways equally. We would joke with him, what if the amount was an odd number, do we chop up the cent four ways? But the bottom line was that Aslam brought us much joy and entertainment, often bursting into laughter, making our undergraduate life more wholesome and fun. I thoroughly enjoyed his company, and I still miss him very much. He was, and I am sure continues to be, a great human being.

His roommate, Faruq, who was his parents' only child, was a quiet sort of a guy, studious and serious in demeanor, constantly pulling at his one beard on his chin, desiring a simple, uncomplicated life, and satisfied with the minimum. In contrast to me, he preferred to write short letters. So, one day, he bought a pad printed with pro forma letters on each page. All he had to do was tick off the appropriate words or phrases, tear the sheet, and mail it. For example, the first line would read, "Dear Father/Mother/Brother/Sister/Grandpa/Grandma . . .," and he would simply tick off "Father" if that's whom he was writing to. The next line read, "I am doing very well/OK/so-so/not good/in terrible shape," and he would choose the appropriate description he wanted, and so on. He couldn't be bothered to take the time to write a real longhand letter in some detail to his parents.

His minimalist approach extended to eating as well. He bought a special biscuit for breakfast, explaining to us that each biscuit contained one egg, two toasts, bread, and butter, which he could eat in minutes while we prepared our egg, toasted and buttered our bread, and took longer time to eat and then wash up; according to him, he had to do none of that and was saving so much time! We argued with him that he was missing out the real taste of the genuine stuff, but he wouldn't be budged. He was given to the world of computers. He graduated with a baccalaureate in physics and math and, after graduation, joined Intel from where he retired thirty years later. He still lives in Oregon. He had found his soul mate in Laura, and they continue to enjoy a blissful wedded life.

Our third roommate, Shahryar, with whom I shared my room, graduated with a journalism degree and has built a successful career in newspapers, but we have all lost contact with him. In those days, 45 rpm records were in vogue, and I had brought a whole bunch with me from Dhaka. I used to play them whenever I felt homesick. One day, Shahryar listened to a record, and then with a puzzled look, he asked me, "What does *Ei dotala raatey* mean?" The actual words were *Ei utola raatey,* meaning "In this bewildering night" and not "In this two-storied night!" Having attended the American International School in Dhaka, his Bengali was a lot to be desired.

Another dear friend, Jamal Rahman, was a happy and friendly face, confident, and quite articulate in his speech and actions. He is now settled in Seattle and is an active member of a Christian-Jewish-Muslim triumvirate promoting interfaith dialogue, tolerance, and peace. His elder brother Kamal relocated from Chicago to Eugene, and the three of us became great friends over the years. His father, Ataur Rahman, was Bangladesh's high commissioner to Canada at the time. After his term was over, he returned to Dhaka, where I met him briefly in our house. He had come to see my father to intercede on his behalf with President Zia on some foreign ministry-related matter.

By the beginning of 1972, we no longer needed assistance from the Kobilkins or the food stamps. My enhanced scholarship and my new part-time job in the university bookstore provided me the financial stability I needed. I became politically very active on campus. I ran for election as the undergraduate representative in the University Admissions Committee and also for the post of student senator and got elected to both positions.

At the Admissions Committee, our principal job was to scrutinize admission applications and select students for undergraduate admission per university policy and set criteria. One day, it was raining cats and dogs, and the committee chairman, who liked to bike to campus, came to the meeting totally soaked. He was in a god-awful mood. In that meeting, where he was the dominant voice, we ended up rejecting most of the applicants. I could not help thinking how he getting soaked in that morning's inclement downpour had affected his mood, attitude, and disposition, and undermined some innocents' future! As student senator, we mostly dealt with policies regarding student conduct, relations, and needs, as well as drafting rules and regulations to guide student life on campus, including disciplining errant students. I found both these responsibilities quite demanding but highly rewarding.

I also signed up for the International Student Speakers Club. Foreign students were regularly encouraged to reach out to the community and share their cultures, traditions, knowledge, and experience with the American public. I went out to speak before many church groups, junior high and high schools, at fairs and various other community events. These exchanges were mutually beneficial, and both sides learned a lot from each other because of natural curiosity.

However, sometimes these got out of hand, and there were moments of hilarity and discombobulation. In one church group presentation, after I talked about how different my society was from the American society, one very elderly lady asked me with great seriousness whether dogs in my country barked in Bengali! My Egyptian friend Wahabi Taha was asked during one of his presentations how far the pyramids were from the Cairo airport. He jokingly replied, "Little less than one hundred camel lengths," explaining to her that in Egypt, distance was measured not in miles but by the length of a camel, which was the primary mode of transportation. The audience was surprised but believed him nonetheless.

It was incredible to notice how naïve and uninformed the average American was! Wahabi took full advantage of their naiveté, but sometimes it was not funny. Once, a few friends and I drove up to Portland, Oregon's largest cosmopolitan city, to spend the day sightseeing. As we were walking down the pavement, Wahabi noticed that an elderly lady was trying to squeeze her car into the only remaining parking spot. So Wahabi gestured to her that she should follow his hand signal to back into the spot. She gratefully accepted his help. Before one knew it, she banged her car into the parked car behind her, damaging its front fender. Wahabi had deliberately not signaled her to stop. The woman was in shock as Wahabi gave her the thumbs-up and walked away. We were equally shocked at his meanness and told him that he would never be invited to join us in future road trips ever.

Notwithstanding this incident, our road trips were always fun, exciting, and sometimes unpredictable. On another occasion, five of us were traveling in the freeway when we saw a Dairy Queen (DQ) sign at a distance. Our Lebanese friend Izziddin Tabbara was driving, while our Iranian friend whose name I cannot now recall was sitting with me in the backseat. We stopped at the DQ to snack. The Iranian wanted a milkshake, but their milkshake machine was out of order, so he had a tall glass of milk instead. But he was upset that he could not have his milkshake and kept expressing his disappointment repeatedly when we were back on the road. Fed up with his whining, Izziddin abruptly stopped the car by the roadside, came around, and opened the back door of the car, pulled out the short Iranian, and grabbing him by his midsection shook him up and down several times, and then set him down and said, "There! Now you have your milkshake. Just shut up!" While the Iranian was as much shocked as he was pissed, the rest of us broke out into laughter and savored the moment at the expense of our Iranian friend.

There was hilarity in our classrooms as well. One Monday in a class, the teacher asked me how my weekend was, to which I replied, "I had a gay time." The class went silent. The teacher grinned, walked over to me, and explained to me what I had said, and suggested that perhaps I would like to rephrase it. Quite embarrassed, I quickly pointed out that I am a product of the British school system where "gay" did not mean what it meant in America and that what I meant was that my weekend was full of carefree, lighthearted fun. The times were different.

In another instance, a Chinese girl who had gone to the beach with her friends one weekend was asked how her weekend was. She replied that her friends were a wild lot; they swam, played beach ball, ate roasted marshmallows, and camped in the beach overnight, and, in general, they "fucked a lot." What she meant to say was that they "fucked around a lot," but not being familiar with the American idiom, she used the phrase incorrectly, conveying a meaning that couldn't be further from the truth. Such misuse of idiomatic expressions was quite common among foreign students, often resulting in embarrassing moments.

Interactions with American black friends were challenging as well, not only because of their accent but also because of their language and mannerism. During my four undergraduate years, I noted the evolution of their greetings from "What's happening, brother?" to "What's happenin', bro?" to "What's hap?" accompanied by contorted hand gestures. Many of the foreign students did not know that one cannot use the N-word. Also, on more than one occasion, I witnessed American students, both black and white, greeting female foreign students with a peck in the cheek at weekend parties, to which some of them recoiled not knowing what to make of it.

But what was most striking to some of us was the general ignorance of American students and people at large of the world outside America. They hardly knew what was happening around the world, appeared to have a shallow knowledge of other countries and peoples, had very limited knowledge of other religions besides their brand of Christianity, and hardly had any knowledge of world history or world geography. It seemed that the average American's life revolved only around beer, barbecue, baseball, basketball, and football (not soccer). But perhaps it is not a fair comparison, since we, who were mostly a part of our countries' elite, were comparing ourselves with everyday Americans, who we're not.

Campus life for me and my friends was indeed exciting. The academic resources at our disposal were rich, which made academic life exciting and rather easy. Our social life was equally rich. We threw weekend parties in our apartments by rotation. We would usually order a keg of beer, play the latest disco songs, munch and drink, and talk and dance until the wee hours of the morning, always mindful of the need not to be too loud.

To avoid someone complaining to the cops about noise, we usually invited all our neighbors to the party. Since our friends who came to our parties were students from all over the world, thus giving our parties an international face, our parties soon became the most sought after. Even students from our rival, Oregon State University, and other universities were frequent visitors, which helped us to build useful liaisons and networks. These friendships sometimes led to invitations to visit other countries. Sometimes our parties created friction as well.

Many pretty sorority girls came to our parties because they were fascinated by men from other cultures and countries speaking with different accents. This usually did not go down very well with the fraternity boys, who saw international students as unwelcome competition. There were numerous occasions when a sorority girl came to me after the party to inquire about a particular foreign student and get his campus coordinates. On a few occasions, friendships became long-lasting or a girl would visit her new boyfriend's country.

Besides studies and library hours, my friends and I were engaged in a variety of sports. We played a lot of indoor tennis during the winter or when it rained, and outdoors during the summer. Aslam and I regularly hit the courts to play singles, or mixed doubles when we had female companions, which was often the case. We frequented the courts usually after dinner and played until midnight when the lights went off. I remember thinking that we would never get tired of playing tennis even at old age; for me, it was sheer joy when Aslam and I were in the courts, and I believe Aslam felt the same way. I also played badminton indoors whenever I could. I sometimes wondered what fun it would be to be a badminton coach and teach junior high and high school kids. What I missed playing, though, was cricket and soccer, games I regularly played at home and was very good at, but games that had no roots then in North America.

The University of Oregon was ideally located between the Pacific Ocean in the west, the desert in the east, and mountains and forests in the north and south. One had the blessings of three completely different terrain, flora, and fauna to enjoy. The beach in the coastal city of Florence was only sixty miles, or an hour's drive west, and we frequently went to the coast during the summer months. On one summer day at the beach, a Pakistani friend had his picture taken with his dog. Intending to send it to his mother in Lahore, he wrote on the back of the picture, "The one on the left is me!" Some of his friends called him a moron from that day on.

We would drive up the coast on Interstate 101 through the coastal cities of Florence, Coos Bay, Cannon Beach, Newport, and Tillamook, which was famous for its cheese. I remember driving through Interstate 101 all the way south through the redwood forests just south of the Oregon-California border to Tijuana, Mexico, and northward all the way through the state of Washington to the border with Canada. The view of the Pacific coast was spectacular, and the trip was simply enchanting.

During one of these summer drives, I stopped at Mo's Seafood and

Chowder, which was famous for New England-style clam chowder. At the time, the restaurant was on a floating boat. The owner, Mohava Niemi, known to everyone as Mo, was an elderly lady who sat down at our table as I was downing a bowl of clam chowder. As we chatted, she learned that I was from Pakistan. At once, her eyes lit up with a smile, and she said that she had something to show me before I left. When I was done, she took me to her dinky little office on top of the boat and pointed to a picture hanging behind her desk. It was a picture of her with a smiling Bengali, Huseyn Shaheed Suhrawardy, the fifth prime minister of Pakistan from September 1956 to October 1957. He had come on a state visit to the United States in July 1957 at the invitation of Pres. General Dwight Eisenhower. During the talks, he agreed to lease out an air force base to the U.S. Air Force for signals intelligence purposes against the Soviet Union at the height of the Cold War. Eisenhower was pleased at this concession and arranged for Suhrawardy to tour the United States before he left. During his West Coast visit, one stop was Mo's restaurant, where he had clam chowder and a photo op with Mo herself! She recalled the prime minister's visit with nostalgic delight and asked me to sign her visitor's book, which I did.

I also went east to the Oregon desert twice; once just before graduation with a friend from Arizona whose passion was collecting rattles from rattlesnake tails. We went at night. His friend drove a heavy truck whose wheels caused enough vibration on the desert floor to get the rattlesnakes to shake their rattles to ward off enemies. We stood on the back of his truck, which had powerful search lights mounted in front and the sides, loaded gun on hand, and we shot off the rattles from the snake's tail. My friend was a sharpshooter and was able to collect eight rattles that night before we headed back home; me, zero! My second visit to the desert region was to Pendleton after graduation when my friend and roommate Shahryar Ahmed got a job as the copy editor of the Pendleton daily, the *East Oregonian*.

Eugene and the other major cities like Corvallis, Salem, and Portland were located in the Willamette Valley, which was very rich in beautiful streams, lakes, and falls, among which the Multnomah Falls is the most famous. Located 116 miles from Eugene on Multnomah Creek in the

Columbia River Gorge, it is fed by underground springs, snowmelt, and rainfall, and the spectacular waterfall is 620 feet tall. I went there several times with friends and jumped off the cliffs into the pristine waterhole and stood under the waterfall as the cold mountain water fell on my head and shoulders; in the hot summer day, it was simply exhilarating!

I also went rapid white water rafting, not in an inflatable raft but in a kayak, from Finn Rock, just east of Eugene. I did not need to paddle because the fast-moving water seized my kayak and speeded me forward. I had to use my paddle to steer my kayak away from the jutting underwater rocks that were clearly visible in the crystal-clear water. But the speed of the water was such that I could not keep up and ultimately hit a rock, which tipped my kayak and me overboard. I could not hold on to the kayak, and in the struggle, I lost my glasses, without which I was blind as a bat.

I was panicky trying to find something to grab on to, as well as use my hands to protect my head from the jutting rocks below. As I struggled to keep my head above water in order not to drown in the rapids, I heard someone shouting over the sound of the rapids that I should not fight the rapids but just allow myself to be carried forward, or else I will tire myself out and drown. I managed to catch a sideways glimpse and noticed a man running on the shore alongside me.

I tried to do exactly as he instructed me when he yelled again asking me to try to stretch out my arms and grab the tree branch some distance from me that was sticking out across the gushing river just above the water surface. As I came close to it, I lunged sideways and managed to grab and hold on to it even as my body was being swept away by the force of the water. He urged me not to lose my grip and to try to inch my way toward the bank, while he himself got onto the branch and started crawling toward me. After a while, he reached me, and we grabbed each other's hand as he slowly pulled me ashore. It was a harrowing experience for me, for I had thoroughly underestimated the power and force of the rapids and the merciless currents under the surface. Many years later, I narrated this incident to my young son and daughter. My son, who was only a few years old, was so concerned that he asked me, "*Abbu*, did you die?" I assured him that I did not!

Among other places my friends and I visited were the foothills of the active volcanic Mount Saint Helens and the Olympic National Forest, both in the state of Washington. Eight years later, in May 1980, Mount Saint Helens erupted, making it the most disastrous eruption in U.S. history; its ash rose eighty thousand feet (fifteen miles) into the atmosphere, spreading over eleven U.S. states and two Canadian provinces.

Another memorable event was a visit to Crater Lake about 130 miles southeast of Eugene. The lake was formed when Mount Mazama blew its top some 7,700 years ago, and snowmelt and rainwater filled its crater. The Crater Lake is over 1,940 feet deep, making it the deepest lake in the United States and the ninth deepest in the world. It is over five miles across. It took us an hour to hike down from the roadside to the icy blue water's edge and more than two hours to get back up.

The redwood forests further south as one enters the state of California are primarily covered by grand old sequoia trees and Douglas firs. According to the U.S. National Park Service, the sequoias can grow to a height exceeding 350 feet (equivalent to a thirty-five-story skyscraper) and are easily the oldest living things on planet Earth. Fossil records show that the relatives of the coastal redwoods thrived in the Jurassic era 160 million years ago. Besides the height of the sequoias whose tips blend into the sky, it was fascinating to see a two-lane highway run through a tree trunk! Among the interesting signs we saw during our redwoods trip was one that said that bears were able to detect women in menstruation and that it is inadvisable for women to visit the redwoods during that time.

Summer Jobs: Fun and Perilous

My first summer in America, the summer of 1971, was rough. Since the Pakistan government had cut off my money from home, I had to find a job to support myself. Summer was the time when the university did its entire campus-wide cleaning and repairing jobs because there was hardly anyone on campus at that time. Those taking summer courses usually moved to off-campus housing. I signed up with the dormitory housing office and joined the cleaning crews to air out the mattresses, wash the windows, clean and polish the floors and the staircases, assist in the repair or replacement of broken furniture, mirrors and lampstands, and sometimes help the garden crews. The pay was $1.20 per hour.

But that summer was not a total loss. Since by that time I had become friends with many freshman guys and girls, there were about ten of us who used to do things as a group. Two of our American friends owned cars, one a Chevy Impala, which we used to go to the beach several times. Once on our way back from the coast, Barbara Guardino, who owned the Impala, asked me whether I would like to drive on the way back. Both of us completely forgot that I did not have a driving permit. I took the wheels and drove us back to campus totally oblivious to the fact that if the cops had stopped me, I would probably have been in jail. That was a terrible oversight.

Talking about the law, there was another incident that transpired in a public park when I was not so lucky. Inside the park, I was taking in the beautiful view sitting on one side of a small lake. A young boy probably around ten was fishing on the other side of the lake. I could see that he had hooked a fish but did not know how to reel it in. So I went over to him, and standing behind him, I put my hands over his hands holding the fishing rod and started showing him how to release and pull the line to slowly draw the fish closer to him. Suddenly, I heard a voice behind me saying, "May I see your angling license, sir?" Rather startled, I said that I was actually not fishing and that I was simply showing the kid how to use his fishing rod. He maintained his poker face and said that that constituted fishing and again asked to see my license. I told him that I did not have one. He then asked for my ID and then wrote out a ticket for forty-four dollars. I told him that I was a student and that I did not have that kind of money to pay the penalty. He pointed to the flip side of the ticket and told me that I had the right to go to court and appeal before a judge.

Grudgingly, I accepted the ticket, and with great trepidation, I went before a judge to plead my case. The judge heard me out and said that he sympathized with me and noted that I was a foreign student and unfamiliar with U.S. laws. Then he said, "Son, ignorance of the law is never a good defense. Henceforth, make sure you know the law. I'm reducing your penalty to twenty-two dollars, and you can pay it in installments over the next three months, OK?" I thanked him for halving the penalty and for spreading the payment period over three months and left the court somewhat relieved, but I had learned an important lesson regarding the law.

Subsequent summers, however, were fun and adventurous, although not without peril. In the summer of 1972, my two brothers, Mahboob and Selim, and some friends and I went to an island on the Pacific Ocean off the coast of Oregon near the Oregon-Washington border to do summer jobs. All of us found jobs in two canning factories on the island. We rented an old home all to ourselves; it was well preserved, although its ocean-facing wooden front side was totally weather beaten from the slamming ocean breeze. The island, with only a handful of homesteaders, was very pretty with quaint houses and flower gardens everywhere and quite green for a rocky outcrop. It was still sunny after work when we usually barbecued and enjoyed our dinner outdoors. Summer life in the peaceful island was idyllic indeed.

But before summer ended, we faced two tragedies. In the bean canning factory where I worked, we were thoroughly briefed on the hows and whys of our work, with special emphasis on workplace safety. We were required to wear the factory outfit, special shoes, goggles, and those who had long hair were told to make sure to wrap up their hair in a tight bun and keep it under a mesh net.

One day in early summer, a teenage guy with longish hair was apparently negligent. He was perched up high on a steel walkway parallel to a conveyor belt. When he reached out over the conveyor belt to straighten a fallen can, his hair popped out of his loosely tied hair mesh and got caught in the moving machinery. As his hair got wrapped in the machine, it pulled him over the belt and then spit him down three floors; he died instantly. The emergency siren blared, and the factory stopped work immediately, called the medics and the police to the scene, and also declared the next day as intensive safety training day. As they wrapped up his body, I caught a glimpse of his bloody head and saw that his face was smashed beyond recognition.

I was so shaken that I quit my job in that factory the next day and went over to my brother Selim's fish canning factory where they smoked and canned oysters and sturgeons. I liked my new job much better than the previous one because there were no machines in the section of the factory I worked. My job was in fact quite simple—to slit six-to-ten-foot-long sturgeons from head to tail down the belly and then to shove them onto the conveyor belt that took them to a machine that sliced them into precisely measured pieces.

But tragedy struck that factory too, and this time, it was closer to home. One day in the middle of summer, the factory manager came running to me and asked me to come with him immediately. As he ushered me into his jeep, he told me that my brother Selim had an unfortunate accident and was in the emergency unit of the hospital. My heart sank, and my whole body went numb.

Selim had opted to go out to sea on fishing boats. When the fishing nets were hauled on board, the crew on top of the boat would shovel the fish into the boat's covered hold that was lined with a foot of ice to keep the catch fresh until the boat reached shore. Selim's job was to be down in the hold to distribute the fish evenly and then shovel ice over them to cover and refrigerate them. He was required to wear specially designed boots with steel toes and heavy woolen padding inside, plus special overalls and jacket to protect him from the intense cold inside the covered hold.

He had been doing that job well until one day he did not respond to calls from the top. The captain got worried and sent a crew member down, who found Selim unconscious and lying flat on the bed of ice. He was immediately hauled up from the boat's hold, and a rescue helicopter took him off the ship and flew him to the island hospital. At the emergency unit, no one would tell me anything, so I had to wait for the doctor. When he came out, he told me that Selim had collapsed from hypothermia; apparently, he had been standing on the ice for extended periods, and his padded boots could not prevent the cold from seeping upward to his lower body, which lost body heat precipitously until he suddenly collapsed. The doctor was worried whether they would have to amputate his legs.

I panicked, not knowing whether I should call my parents in Bangladesh immediately or wait since whatever happened would be beyond their control. I opted to wait, more out of fear of facing my parents' questions than anything else. I do not remember how long Selim remained in the emergency, but I was certainly relieved to hear the doctor telling me that the worst was over and that he will recuperate fully as well as retain his legs.

After that frightful incident, which scared the daylights out of all of us, Selim became the butt of jokes and tease from my friends who treated him and Mahboob like their own little brothers. A Chinese friend from Hong Kong named Dexter Ngai, who subsisted only on two-minute noodles, insisted that Selim cannot be allowed back onto the fishing boat until both his legs were fully insured by the Lloyd's of London! Then Dexter added, "And while we are at it, let's insure his family jewels too." All Selim could do was grin and bear it. My other brother with me in Oregon, Mahboob, spent his spare time reading cowboy books in which cowboys, the law, the bad guys, and the native Indians constantly shot at each other. My friends would tease him, "Mahboob, are you still reading those cowboy and Indian stories where A shoots B, B shoots C, and C shoots D, but nobody dies?"

****

There were lots of things that were happening on campus aside from political demonstrations. Every summer, people from *Encyclopedia Britannica* descended on campus to recruit and train students to be sales people to go door to door to sell the encyclopedia. Often these student-turned-salesmen were sent to cities across the country. A good salesman could earn up to $2,500 toward next year's academic costs, but most of them had disappointing stories to tell.

Hollywood Studios would also come to campus to recruit extras for the films that were being shot in the summer in Oregon or neighboring states. Once, a *Playboy* crew came to campus to select girls for the

Playboy spread because they were running a special states series, and this one was on "Girls from the Beaver State." One got to see the prettiest girls on campus that day; they were primarily sorority girls. Conventional wisdom was that most of these girls joined sororities to catch rich upper-class husbands from among the fraternity boys, and vice versa. Toward the end of the '70s decade, the university gained the notoriety of being one of the best party schools in the West Coast, a reputation sealed by the 1978 filming of National Lampoon's raunchy *Animal House,* starring John Belushi and Kevin Bacon in the Phi Kappa Psi sorority on the U of Oregon campus. All the extras in the film were University of Oregon students.

I think it was in my second year that I could save up enough money from my part-time job at the university bookstore to buy a secondhand Volkswagen, but, regrettably, I could enjoy it only for a few months. One weekend afternoon, I had driven to my friend Ginny Wood's house for lunch. When I left her place to return to my apartment, I couldn't find my car. Ginny and I scoured the area surrounding her place, but to no avail. She drove me to the police station, where I reported that my Volkswagen was stolen; they took down as much information as I could give them.

Two weeks later, the police came by my apartment to inform me that my Volkswagen was found in the town of Walla Walla in the eastern part of the state of Washington near the border with Oregon, some 350 miles northeast of Eugene. Ginny, who had been feeling guilty that my car was stolen from near her house, proposed to drive me to Walla Walla in her Ford Pinto to recover the Volkswagen. Seeing no alternative, I accepted her kind offer. We drove for nearly six hours to the Walla Walla police impound only to find the car stripped of all its essentials including the eight-track tape recorder that I had recently installed in the car. It was a total write-off because I could not afford to buy car insurance. I was very sad that not only had I lost my car but also I could not afford to buy a replacement car.

Ginny also felt my sadness, which brought both of us closer together. Toward the end of that summer, Ginny invited Aslam, Faruq, Shahryar, and me to her parents' house 140 miles south of Eugene. It was a beautiful house with a lovely swimming pool on top of a hill in the sparsely populated lumber town of Grants Pass. There we met her family, including her younger sister who was deliberately named Holly by her parents. The poor girl was constantly teased by everyone because her name was Holly Wood! She never forgave her parents for naming her Holly. The town itself was historic, having been named after civil war general Ulysses S. Grant's victory at Vicksburg. Among the town's big attractions included the picturesque Rogue River, famous for its rafting, and the Oregon Caves National Monument, thirty miles further south.

Father came to visit us next summer after finishing his tour of Europe as a member of the Bangladesh Government Delegation. Since *jolpai achar* (pickled olives) was my favorite, especially the way my mother prepared it, Father had to carry a big bottle of achar for me. In those days, South Asian food was not readily available in the grocery stores, unless one went to a specialized store that carried some.

When he landed in New York, the customs people examined it and said that he could not carry food into the country. Father told us that he explained to the officials that it was essential medicine for his diabetes. They let him keep the achar, and I was very happy that customs officials hadn't confiscated it, which would have devastated Mom.

Father had contracted diabetes after he lost a part of his pancreas and a good length of intestine when machine gun bullets ripped through his midsection during the Bangladesh Liberation War in 1971. While the field doctors in Agartala, India, and then his British doctor in London removed most of the shrapnel fragments lodged in his body, those fragments too close to his heart were left untouched. He was assured that the body itself will slowly get rid of them without the complications of risky surgery. However, his British doctor cautioned him that during security check at airports, the buzzer would go off because of the metal in his body. He was advised to always carry with him his barium X-ray and the doctor's letter when he traveled abroad to show to airport security officials that there were metal fragments lodged inside his body. I shudder to think how miserable airport security check would have made him during his international travels in this post-9/11 world.

Mother also told Father that he must not forget to go to a photo studio and have portrait pictures taken with his sons during his visit. So I made an appointment at a photo studio to have our pictures taken. The photographer for the session was young and pretty. She positioned us the way she wanted and asked us to smile for the camera. But Father was old generation and felt that he must look serious in order to look dignified and simply refused to smile. After several failed attempts to make him smile for the camera, the pretty photographer then simply said, "Dad, think of me!" The next thing she saw was the biggest ear-to-ear smile ever from Father, and she just clicked away. She knew exactly how to draw a man's attention. When we related this story to Mother some years later, she just nodded her head side to side, while Father sat there with a sheepish smile. I am glad that we had taken those pictures because they definitively prove that I did have a headful of shoulder-length hair, unlike my shiny, bald head now!

Just before Christmas 1973, my family sent me money to buy a return ticket to visit them during the Christmas break. It was a brief fifteen-day visit only. They were living in Hafizabad Colony, Eskaton, at the time. My itinerary took me through the Calcutta Airport in India, which was the last stop before reaching Dhaka, Bangladesh. As I was going through customs check, the Indian customs officer reached across the table and grabbed the pen from my pocket, saying, "My son will be sitting for his matriculation exams. He needs a pen."

I was shocked. But keeping my cool, I explained to him that I had purchased the Sheaffer pen as a gift for my father. I had also had his named inscribed on it, and I asked him to see it for himself. The officer verified that I was indeed speaking the truth. Seeing that other customs officers were staring at him, he hesitatingly returned the pen to me. I swore then that I would never travel through Calcutta Airport again, and I never did.

When I finally reached home, we were all happy to see each other. I also went to our village home in Gourshar to see my dadi. In the course of our chat, I showed her the photo of my blonde American girlfriend that I had in my wallet. She looked at the photo and said, "She is so pretty, but why did she dye her hair?" I explained to her that that was her natural color. She looked at me feeling offended. "Are you going to teach me the ways of the world? God gave girls black hair. She shouldn't have tampered with God's plan." I realized that there was no point in trying to convince her otherwise.

This reminds me of another similar incident that I learned of after my marriage. My wife Nipa was a few years old when my father-in-law returned to East Pakistan from Ireland after completing his medical studies. One day, she returned from kindergarten with teary eyes, and when asked what happened, she showed her drawing of a tree with a score of zero on it. The next day, my father-in-law took her to her teacher to sort it out. When he showed the drawing, the teacher immediately said that this girl had no sense of reality: "Dekhen-na, meye-ta patagulo lal ar komola rong diyechhe. Bolen-to dekhi, patar rong-ki orokom hoy kokhono?" (Look! She painted the leaves red and orange. Tell me, are leaves ever that color?) My father-in-law smiled and then explained to him that indeed in the northern climes when fall approaches, leaves do turn bright yellow, orange, pink, and red. And Nipa had seen this because they lived in Ireland for a few years and had drawn her tree accordingly. It was amazing how a sheltered life could lead to perceptions of different realities. In any case, my Bangladesh visit flashed by, and I had to return to Oregon without delay in order not to miss late registration for winter 1974. I graduated in December of that year.

My four years at Oregon U was academically and socially quite rewarding, and I had lots of memories to fall back on. Almost every day seemed like a fun day. The evenings were fun as well, as I watched my favorite late-night talk show, *The Johnny Carson Show*, which brought comedy into American bedrooms for thirty years from 1962 to 1992. Johnny Carson was viewed nearly by all as a puckish, effortless, wholesome comedian and, together with his sidekick Ed McMahon, brightened up the night with interviews and jokes with guests from across the entertainment world. One of my favorite jokes was about how thin the walls of American homes were. Johnny asked one of his guests, "How thin are the walls of your home?" "They are so thin I can hear my neighbor next door walking in her room," replied his guest. "How about you?" Johnny asked his second guest. "Oh! I can hear my neighbor flushing her toilet," replied the second guest. "How about your home, Johnny?" asked his third guest. "Oh! The walls of my home are so thin that I can hear my neighbor change her mind," replied Johnny as the entire audience reeled in laughter.

The other world-class comedian was Bob Hope, and I never missed the chance to watch him emcee the Oscar Awards night. He was the perfect comedian, and there was hardly an occasion when he didn't floor the entire audience. He was most loved, though, for bringing Christmas cheers to thousands of American troops serving overseas, particularly in Vietnam.

I also seriously watched the Republican and Democratic national conventions without fail every four years; I found the American electoral process mind boggling but fascinating. No other country in the world had presidential elections that ran for several years, and what was even more bizarre to the outside observer was that American presidents were not elected by the people but by an electoral college, an archaic instrument in the modern age! It skewed the popular mandate, and so many a president who had lost the popular vote to his opponent got elected nonetheless. At the time when this book is going to the printers, the Democratic nominee Joe Biden has been elected by a huge popular vote and electoral vote as the next president of the United States but Donald Trump is refusing to acknowledge that.

To the Centennial State: Surprises and Shocks

My four-year undergraduate program at Oregon had zoomed by. My roommates and I graduated in our respective fields with distinction. I graduated with a BS in political science and was inducted into Pi Sigma Alpha, the National Political Science Honor Society. Aslam graduated with a biology degree, Faruq with a math and physics degree, and Shahryar with a journalism degree. Jamal had already left for Berkeley in the summer of 1972.

I had been exploring my options to pursue my masters since the summer of 1974. I ruled out the hustle and bustle of the East Coast, preferring a state similar to Oregon's magnificent mountains, waterfalls, lakes, rivers, and plains. I also wanted to go to a university that had a reputable graduate program in international relations. Cost was also a major concern. I applied to the graduate programs at the University of Colorado, Boulder, and the University of Washington, Seattle. First, I got a letter of admission for the winter quarter 1975 from the latter, but with no offer of scholarship. Then I received a letter of admission to the graduate program in international relations at the University of Colorado. It came with a graduate scholarship, and to make it more enticing, I would get a bursary for my accommodation as well. I bade good-bye to my roommates and friends and flew to Boulder to start my master's program in January 1975.

At that time, the University of Colorado at Boulder had two high-rise student residence towers named Darley and Stearns Towers, in addition to normal student residence halls. Since I was now a graduate student, I applied for the position of resident advisor in the Darley Tower, and was lucky to get it; my high academic achievement, my very active extracurricular life in Oregon, my outgoing and friendly nature, my public relations capability, and the strong recommendations that highlighted all these and more all helped me to net this plum position. I was very happy to have the penthouse suite on the fifteenth floor, which was the highest floor of the tower. It came with lots of perks, privileges, and authority. I settled down quite comfortably, hardly anticipating all the interesting experiences I would have in the next eighteen months while staying there.

I was in overall charge of the tower but reported to the director of housing. I was responsible for the welfare of the mostly upper-class students residing in the tower. We had multiple committees and designed our own social activities calendar, although some activities were clearly not a part of the calendar and were spearheaded by rambunctious, fun-loving individuals without my knowledge.

It was Saturday, the second day of spring 1975. I heard some commotion in midmorning. Looking down from my window, I could see scores of excited students milling around each other, indicating that clearly something out of the ordinary was happening at the ground level. Thinking the worst, that it could be some kind of a protest against the university or specifically against the housing administration, I quickly got dressed and went down. The minute I walked outside the tower building, I was stunned to see about two dozen students, male and female, stark naked, urging others to take off their clothes and join them; everyone was excited and in high spirit. Every few minutes, a big cheer went up with lots of clapping all around as more and more naked residents came out of the Darley and Stearns Towers and joined the assembled nude bunch.

Seeing my shocked look, a few students came up to me and explained that among the wild things that happened on the Colorado campus, one was streaking, where both male and female students, sometimes joined by young faculty, ran completely naked across campus to herald the advent of spring! The usual number of streakers varied anywhere from one hundred to one thousand, although spectators lining up the route to encourage them numbered ten to fifteen times as much.

Surprisingly, this year, it was happening on my watch because this spring's streaking was being initiated by a handful of residents of the Darley Tower, who already had their route that meandered through residence halls, fraternities, and sororities marked out. The whole event, running completely naked from one end of campus to the opposite end, which I was told started in this campus in 1974, was gleefully covered by the local newspapers, especially the *Daily Camera*.

However, I could not believe that the senior administration or the senior faculty of the university would allow streaking on campus, and I particularly worried whether I would be held responsible since it originated at Darley Tower and whether I would lose my resident advisor's position for failing to stop it. In any case, I needed to brace myself for what might be coming next. But after a tense weekend because of wide newspaper coverage, I was relieved to see little reaction from the university authorities, and my position as resident advisor was still intact.

But I was not to be spared from embarrassment so easily. Spring was also the time for some kind of a lottery held jointly each year by the two towers, the details of which my memory fails me now. In any case, unluckily I was one of the winners. I had won six months' supply of tampons! Everyone thought that that was incredibly funny, and, henceforth, girls living in the two towers would regularly knock on my door when they needed them. It was becoming so embarrassing for me that I asked the girls in my friends circle whether there was a way out for me. One girl suggested that I should write to the supplier and advise them of an address change, giving the address of a senior female resident. Thankfully that worked, and the tampons henceforth were delivered to the new address. But many a girl in the two towers thanked me for the free six-month supply and occasionally invited me to join in the pizza fest paid for by what would have been tampon money!

As spring rolled in and the weather warmed up a bit, I hit the covered tennis courts. No one had told me that Boulder had an elevation of over 1,600 meters, while Eugene was only 130 meters above sea level, placing Boulder twelve times higher in elevation. This had a significant effect on my tennis game, as I discovered that tennis balls bounced differently at different elevations. The balls I used were bought in Eugene, which bounced much higher in Boulder than they did in Eugene. To play a decent game, I had to purchase new tennis balls in Boulder, which were heavier and furrier, causing the balls to bounce normally in the higher altitude. I had to adjust my game to this new reality.

There were other phenomena too that I was unfamiliar with. One day, I was seated in a chair in my room and tying my shoelaces to go out to play tennis. I had placed my racket and a tennis ball on the top of the table. As I was tying my shoe laces, I noticed from the corner of my eye that the ball slowly rolled to the edge of the table, stopped without falling, and then rolled back to the other end and then to the opposite direction again and so on just like a pendulum. It was freaky, but I knew that there had to be a scientific explanation for this.

As I narrated this incident to the international student advisor, he explained to me that the two student towers were situated at the base of the mountains and were right in the path of the wind that blew as if through a tunnel toward the valley where the campus was located. To prevent the towers from buckling in the face of this continuous onslaught from the wind, the towers were built with a flexible structure to arrest rigidity and allow them a degree of sway. The side-to-side rolling tennis ball was the manifestation of the tower swaying ever so lightly, which we couldn't normally detect.

On another day, I suddenly heard a swooshing sound that came from the bathroom. I got up to check and was surprised to see that there was no residual water on the commode. I learned later that the swirling wind above the exhaust vent of the bathroom on the fifteenth floor often created a suction effect and sucked the water out. These were among some of the never-seen-before moments to which I had to adjust while living in the penthouse. But with glass windows on two sides of my penthouse suite facing the mountains, the view was magnificent, especially at night in the winter months when I could see hundreds of skiers with torches in one hand skiing down the mountain slopes. It was like a freeway at night with miles of moving headlights coming toward you, but much prettier.

My extracurricular activities were much more limited in Colorado than was the case in Oregon. The people I got to interact with regularly were graduate students whose number was fewer than the undergraduates I interacted with in Oregon. We also had less time to spare, since graduate students had to focus more intensively on their courses, research, or labs.

Despite that, six of us found ourselves naturally gravitating toward each other, and pretty soon, we bonded as a close knit group. We regularly met between classes and in the weekends. Abdallah from Palestine was the weakest link in our group. He was always a happy face but weak in English and generally appeared to be lost all the time. Elizabeth, whom we called Babette for short, was from France and decidedly a quick thinker and always on the go. Gunter was German, and Hans was Austrian, both with a philosophical bent and measured in approach; for them, the universe was ordered and there was a place and time for everything. Gisela, also German, was the chain smoker and resigned to almost anything. Outings with this group were mostly cultural that included trips to Denver, some thirty miles southeast from Boulder campus, to go to the ballet or to the opera or to painting exhibits. We also went to solo concerto, orchestra, and sometimes to the symphony organized by the U of Colorado Music School in the campus auditorium.

We did take one long-distance trip in the winter of 1975 to go west to the Pacific coast when we had to drive through the mountain passes. It was one of the most hazardous trips I had ever undertaken. As we crossed the Rocky Mountain in Utah, we had to drive through miles of dense fog so much so that we could barely see the windshield wipers of the car; although we had fog lights, these were of limited use only.

Since we were taking turns to drive, Abdallah was driving when we hit the fog. His driving was very shaky, as he kept on pushing on the accelerator and the brakes intermittently, as the rest of us were panicking. I offered to drive, but he wouldn't let anyone drive, thinking that he must prove to us that he is man enough to drive through that hazardous patch. Even if he had agreed to let someone else drive, there was no way we could have stopped to switch driving under those dangerous conditions. So until we reached the clearing and left the fog behind us, Abdallah had hung on to the steering wheel but had to put up with our screams and shouts.

Babette was upset at how we had lost faith in Abdullah's driving and gave us an earful. A year after we had graduated with our master's degree, I learned that Babette had married Abdallah. Whether it was out of pity for the way we used to tease him or it was to give him sanctuary in France because his homeland in Ramallah, Palestine, was constantly under attack by the Israelis, I do not know. In any case, after we crossed Utah, it was fairly easy driving all the way to the Pacific coast, and all of us thoroughly enjoyed the few days of beach living.

I also had a separate group of friends, mostly girls and two Jewish guys, with whom I spent time eating, partying, going to varsity games, and visiting Colorado's scenic sites. One of the girls was a close friend of a Saudi prince studying at the university whose name I cannot recall now. He was known for his dazzling lifestyle, sports cars, and female companions. He hardly ever went to classes and was decidedly un-studious. He was also into recreational drugs and drinks.

One day, he drove his brand-new Lamborghini Countach that he had imported from Europe into a lamppost in the freeway to Denver.

Although he was lucky to come out of it unscathed, the sports car was totaled. We were surprised to see him driving a Porsche Carrera the following week. When asked about it, he explained that he just called the Saudi embassy in Washington DC and had them arrange the Porsche for him. I was very curious and asked him about his profligate lifestyle. He merely shrugged his shoulders and said that the "understanding" with his government was that he could have anything he desired while studying in the United States on the condition that he must return to Saudi Arabia after finishing his studies.

On March 1975, Faisal bin Musaid, who had gotten his bachelor's degree in political science from the U of Colorado a few years earlier and who was into heavy drugs, had returned to Saudi Arabia and assassinated his uncle, King Faisal. A week after the incident, my supervisor, Prof. George Codding, and I went fishing. As we discussed what had happened in Saudi Arabia, he gave me a worried look, saying that he hoped that the Saudi prince currently on campus was sane enough not to pull a stunt like that when he returned to his homeland.

This prince was quite friendly, quite easy with his money, and often invited us to his parties, which we diligently declined because of the free flow of drugs. To break the ice with us, one day, he insisted on taking us to Denver, Colorado's mile-high capital, to show us a good time. While I was not too keen to go, one of his girlfriends who was in our group was eager to go and persuaded us to accompany her.

None of us was prepared for what followed next. He took us to a place that was three stories high and quite plain looking from outside. The heavyset bouncers at the door smiled and welcomed him, which told us that the prince was a frequent visitor. Since we were accompanying him, we were allowed inside with no questions asked. As we absorbed the loud ambiance inside, with drinks flowing, music blaring, and people dancing, he casually informed us that the ground floor was for heterosexuals, whereas the two upper floors were for kinky people: the next floor up was for homosexual people only, both lesbians and gays, while the topmost floor was for threesomes and multiple partners. Both the top floors had only psychedelic lights and drinks and drugs galore.

Essentially, it was a place for free drink and drug-infused, uninhibited sex with many choices and partners.

My friends and I looked at each other with disbelief, and we all had the same thought. When the prince went to order cocktail drinks for us, we turned around and walked out of that place, got into our cars, and without looking back just drove away, relieved to be heading back to the dorm. Although I didn't know where the prince was taking us to in Denver, in my mind, I castigated myself for not directly conferring with the prince to find out about our destination ahead of time, and that as the resident advisor, I had failed to display good judgment. Thank God we did not have cell phones then and could escape easily without the prince stopping or following us. In any case, it was quite an experience, if only for the knowledge that such places indeed existed in the '70s in the United States. The prince got the message that we really didn't care for his company and his idea of fun.

Chaos back Home

Meanwhile, there were developments at home in Dhaka of which I was unaware. First, there was the good news. In the spring of 1975, I received a letter from Father informing me that my sister Lily was getting married in April. They had been receiving marriage proposals for her hand in marriage, and Father had decided on an engineer from the Engineers Corps of the Bangladesh Army, and Lily had acquiesced. Unfortunately, I was not able to attend because of my studies. Immediately after the wedding, I received a handwritten letter from Lily's husband, Shafiqul Karim, telling me that he was looking forward to meeting me in the not-too-distant future. It was not until several years later that we actually met.

Then there was bad news. The economic situation in Bangladesh during the administration of Awami League had been significantly deteriorating because the government had failed to manage public expectations that were high following independence after twenty-four years of negligence by the Pakistan government. By 1975, there was also widespread famine. Political agitation had ensued, and the government's ability to administer the country had been slipping away fast. On August 15, 1975, Prime Minister Sheikh Mujibur Rahman was assassinated in a military coup, and the country plunged into chaos and uncertainty.

My father, who was then the chairman of the Bangladesh Jute Association, was in Belgrade, Yugoslavia, as a member of the jute delegation to East Europe during the time of the coup d'état. On the day of the assassination, he and Jute Secretary Chisti went to a restaurant for breakfast, not aware of what had happened in Bangladesh. As the waiter brought their order of croissant, marmalade, orange juice, and coffee to them, he asked where they were from. Father replied that they were from Bangladesh. The waiter stood there shocked, and then with a hand gesture signifying the slicing of the throat, he said that he will not serve food to people who killed their prime minister and immediately started walking back with the food tray. Mr. Chisti and Father were shocked to hear the news that the prime minister was dead and watched in dismay as the waiter walked away with the food they had ordered. The delegation cancelled the rest of their trip and immediately returned home.

The reaction of the waiter was understandable. Prime Minister Sheikh Mujibur Rahman had vowed to pursue a socialist policy and had joined the Nonaligned Movement, endearing him to the nonaligned leaders. To demonstrate Yugoslavia's political and ideological support and goodwill, Marshal Tito of Yugoslavia became the first world leader to come to Bangladesh on a state visit in January 1974. My father and mother were invited to Bangabhaban (presidential palace) by the prime minister to welcome Marshal Tito.

It was also at the time when I had gone home from the United States for the first time for a short visit. My siblings and I were waiting eagerly to hear from our parents about the reception at Bangabhaban. When they returned home, Father was smiling and Mother was ebullient. The first thing Mother said was that she couldn't believe that a man could have such a soft hand. The prime minister had introduced her to Marshal Tito, and the president had shaken Mom's hand.

My mom was to be outdone by my wife Nipa a couple of decades later when Prince Charles and Lady Diana came on a royal visit to Canada in October 1991. Nipa excitedly waited in line in front of our parliament building in downtown Ottawa, hoping to shake Princess Diana's hand. But she ended up shaking Prince Charles's hand because Diana was on the opposite side. Nipa refused to wash her hand for a couple of days because it would wash away the royal touch!

In any case, back to the United States. Toward the end of summer of 1975, my group of friends and I drove up to Wyoming for about a month, some of us for a summer job and some to unwind from the compressed summer semester's course work. There, we rented a lumber cottage in Laramie, which served as a base from which we traveled to historic towns and sights. Our guide was Kerry Forbes, an adventurous, fun-loving Wyoming girl who knew her state like the back of her hand. We traveled from Cheyenne, Wyoming's capital situated in the south, through Laramie, Casper, all the way north to Sheridan and Jackson Hole to see the Grand Teton Mountains, a truly magnificent sight to behold. The Grand Teton, which literally means "the big tit," is the tallest of the three peaks, which were named by French trappers as "Les Trois Tetons" or "the Three Tits." It was no surprise that the female companion-hungry French trappers would look up at those mountain peaks and name them thusly.

Driving through Wyoming felt like driving on top of the world, for one drives on high-elevation flatland for hundreds of miles with nothing between him and the sky touching land in the distance. Wyoming was and still is a sparsely populated state. We passed through many dinky towns with population less than fifty. One town had a population of only one according to its welcome sign. It had only one two-storied ramshackle building divided into a ground floor comprising a general store and a side storeroom in the front and a room with iron bars that served as a jail in the back, with living quarters upstairs.

There was a gas station in front of the building. When the only person went to the washroom or to bed, the town was at a standstill or asleep. I asked that person how he survived since it seemed like it would be weeks before someone would pass through his town. He explained to me that the town had been designated as a postal depot by the U.S.

Postal Service, and people came from far and wide to buy postage stamps and first day covers.

About the only recreational activities in this sparsely populated state as far as we could deduce were rodeo, open-air concerts, and musical dramas for younger folks and fishing for older folks. I recall Vice President Dick Cheney, who had grown up in Casper, Wyoming, making frequent trips there to go fishing. In the evenings, we drove from our rented place to the top of the mountains to watch the sunset, where we saw young kids on fancy motorcycles smoking pot and drinking beer. Wyoming appeared to be a place where one could be as carefree as one desired.

Crossing the Rockies

I returned to Eugene during the 1975 Christmas break to spend the holidays with my two brothers, Mahboob and Selim. As I mentioned above, it was a group drive with my Colorado friends who wanted to see the beautiful Pacific coast. Once that was done, they drove back to Colorado, while I stayed back in Eugene.

I bought another Volkswagen with the intention of driving back to Boulder. Since it was winter, I decided to post an advertisement in the Oregon bookstore bulletin board offering a ride to anyone who would like to go to Boulder. I got a call from a girl who said that she was also attending school there and would be happy to get a ride. We agreed that she would share driving and gas with me. We started off in the afternoon, and she agreed to drive the first leg eastward up to the foothills of the Rockies, where I would take over. Halfway between Pendleton and the mountain, I took over. It was already nighttime. She decided to move to the backseat and sleep while I drove. The weather was beginning to turn nasty with a blizzard heading our way; I had to decide whether to continue driving or stop until the blizzard passed. I decided not to stop for fear of getting bogged down in the heavy snow that the blizzard was sure to dump on the top of the mountain.

The uphill drive was tremendously difficult because the Volkswagen's climbing power was really poor as the speed fell from 50 mph to 40 mph to 30 mph to 25 mph, and it occasionally lost traction. With much difficulty, I managed to cross the mountain pass as the blizzard shifted its direction away from me. I was now going slightly downhill, but I could see that the road ahead swerved left around the mountain. I tried to steer the car leftward to remain on the road, but my wheels lost traction, and I kept going forward until I went off the cliff. I remember rolling down six times and landing upright on soft snow at least a hundred meters down in the ravine. I then looked behind me to see whether my passenger was all right, but she was nowhere to be seen; instead, there was snow in the backseat.

What had happened was that during the roll, the rear windshield had popped out and fell off, and since there were no seat belts in the back, she was thrown out. I panicked thinking that I must have killed my passenger. I couldn't open either of the front doors but managed to kick and break the glass on the passenger's side and crawl out with great difficulty. The roof of my Volkswagen had dented inward, and the front and back ends had no fenders anymore.

I desperately looked around for the girl and finally spotted her red scarf halfway between the ravine where I was and the mountain cliff that I was blown off of. The blizzard had dumped so much snow that it covered the rocky sides of the mountain, and both she and my car landed on soft snow. Even though it was past midnight, I could see clearly because of the reflected light from the white snow all around me. I called out to her to see if she was OK, but there was no reply. I was desperate, not knowing what to do.

Then I heard the rumble of a semitrailer truck up on the mountain road. The driver of the truck had noticed the track mark of my Volkswagen going straight off the cliff and slowed down to check. As he craned out of his window and noticed my green bug, I waved at him and called out for help. He hollered back, asking whether I was OK. I told him that I was but perhaps not my passenger as I pointed my finger in the direction of the red scarf. He hollered back that he will get help. He immediately got onto his citizens band radio to alert other truck drivers of the accident until the message got relayed to the nearest police station.

After sometime, a police helicopter arrived followed by an air ambulance. The ambulance extracted my passenger, while I was pulled into the police helicopter, and both of us were flown to the hospital. After I was put on a stretcher, they piled several blankets on top of me and tightened the restraints over me. Within minutes, I started shaking violently while a couple of male nurses held me down tightly. I passed out.

When I came to, the attending physician told me that the violent shaking of my body was a danger point and that they were relieved to see me pull through. He also assured me that the female rider, who had lacerations on her head, forehead, shoulders, arms, and feet, was also doing OK and that she had not suffered any internal injuries, thanks to the fresh snow that had cushioned her when she was ejected from the car. I couldn't help thinking that it had to be a miracle that both of us survived the fall. We received good medical treatment and were discharged by the end of the day. The police drove us to the bus station where we took the bus to Boulder. My second Volkswagen again was a write-off. It seemed like Volkswagens and I were having difficult relationships!

My MA was an eighteen-month program, but I wanted to finish it as early as possible, so I took the maximum allowable courses at the graduate level and also opted to go to summer school. Since I had also received a graduate teaching assistantship, I was assisting two professors with their courses and grading: Problems and Politics in the Third World, and International Law. I enjoyed lecturing on some of the topics in both the courses immensely.

I also needed to choose a master's thesis topic. My graduate supervisor, Prof. George Codding, told me that choosing the right topic was extremely important because he had seen students abandoning their thesis topic after working on it for months and then struggling to find a new topic after wasting precious time. I, however, did not have that problem because I knew exactly what I wanted to explore.

I had been fascinated by Professor Hovet's lectures in Oregon on the

United Nations and on Secretary-General U Thant's work. U Thant was the first non-European secretary-general and had held the post for a record ten years. He was a soft-spoken Burmese diplomat thrown into the chaos of a bipolar world and into a United Nations in turmoil after the assassination of his predecessor, Dag Hammarskjold.

Since he was not as aggressive as the West wanted him to be, his docile demeanor came under much criticism. He was regularly pilloried in the western press and by western leaders, principally by the Americans. I floated the idea of critically examining how successful this Asian Buddhist diplomat was in comparison to the two previous European Christian diplomats and whether the United Nations was able to recoup its prestige as well as the dignity of the office of the secretary-general under his leadership.

After some exploratory discussion, Professor Codding approved the idea, and I followed it up with a formal thesis proposal to the thesis approval committee. After the thesis topic was approved, Professor Codding and I sat down to identify my research needs and the chapter-by-chapter submission schedule. After completing all my departmental course requirements, I plunged into my thesis work with gusto.

I finished my master's thesis on "U Thant, the United Nations and the Office of the Secretary General" without a hitch. My supervisor was pleased with the commendations the thesis received from fellow faculty members who had read it. I graduated in the summer of 1976 with a master's degree in international affairs. In the process, George and I became great friends and kept in touch until his death in December 2001.

The West Coast Calls Back

Since my brothers were in Eugene, I had the natural tendency to return to the U of Oregon. I also wanted to do my doctoral studies under Prof. Thomas Hovet, who had once been an advisor to Secretary-General U Thant and still retained lots of important contacts there. I applied for doctoral studies at the University of Washington, Seattle, and the University of Oregon and got accepted at both places but was offered a teaching assistantship in the latter. As a graduate teaching fellow, I assisted in the teaching and grading of two undergraduate courses: International Relations and Law of the Seas, which I greatly enjoyed doing.

But one year into my doctoral program, the department informed me that it had to curtail my assistantship because of a new federal government directive with regard to federal funding. I was told that the then Ronald Reagan administration felt that money spent on foreign students was money wasted; therefore, the federal grant that the university was receiving could no longer be used to finance my doctoral studies.

Faced with this volte-face, I was in a dilemma on what to do. Without an alternative source of funding, I had no choice but to abandon my doctoral studies. Professor Hovet, who had a high opinion of my academic abilities and had mentored me through my undergraduate studies, was quite sympathetic to my plight and asked me whether I would like to work at the United Nations. Since he still had good contacts there, he said he could arrange something for me. I was happy to hear that but thought I should first inform Father about my financial predicament and seek his opinion as well.

When I wrote to Father describing my situation and about the offer of help from Professor Hovet, he replied that while it was my decision ultimately, I should also think about my young country, Bangladesh, the investment that my country had made on me by releasing precious foreign exchange for my education, and the contributions I can make if I came home instead of staying behind in the West. He genuinely believed that I had tremendous opportunities to personally flourish in Bangladesh and might seriously consider returning home. I pondered over his response for several days and also discussed it with Professor Hovet. In the end, I decided to honor Father's advice and returned home, abandoning my doctoral studies.

PART THREE

INTERFACE WITH REALITY

At Home, but What to Do?

My return coincided with a wonderful thing happening to our family. My sister Lily gave birth to a lovely baby girl on January 28, 1978; they named her Tanya. She was the first child to be born among us brothers and sisters. There was a lot of joy, happiness, and mirth in our family. We were also happily engaged in our respective activities.

After a day's hard work, we played volleyball or badminton in the evening on grass courts in our spacious lawn. We had a distant cousin named Babul living with us at the time. He was a comic character. Whenever the volleyball or the shuttlecock went to his side, he lunged forward to hit it even if it came to his partner. So his partner would often yell, "Leave it," and he would yell back, "*You* libit," in his village accent, and we would all crack up. It was absolutely hilarious to play with him, and we thoroughly enjoyed it.

Father was happy when I returned from the States. My brother Mahboob also returned home from Oregon. Father, being a businessman, encouraged both of us to explore opportunities to establish a business. He informed us that he would help us whenever we needed his help and advice. We were excited to receive this assurance.

Father was an influential man in Bangladesh and was highly respected by the military, the government, and all the political parties. He was one of country's senior-most military officers with a British military pedigree, a respected parliamentarian, a popular politician in his district of Comilla, a successful businessman, and a well-known philanthropist having founded a college, an orphanage, and built a mosque.

He had been elected as a member of the National Assembly of Pakistan in 1970, and then as a member of the Constituent Assembly in 1972, and then as a member of the Bangladesh Parliament in 1973 from the Awami League. With the assassination of Prime Minister Sheikh Mujibur Rahman in August 1975, after a period of political turmoil, Gen. Ziaur Rahman became the president of Bangladesh in April 1977. He then started actively pursuing Father to join his party and his cabinet. He frequently sent Brig. Nurul Islam Shishu to our house to try to convince Father to join Zia's cabinet and also to consult with Father regarding cabinet selection.

Father declined to join General Zia's cabinet because General Zia was planning to bring into his cabinet anti-Bangladesh elements, prominent among whom was Shah Azizur Rahman, who had denounced the Bengali nationalist struggle, collaborated with the Pakistan Army, and also led the Pakistan delegation to the United Nations in November 1971, where he emphatically denied that the Pakistan Army's Operation Searchlight was a cover for genocide. After Bangladesh's independence, Shah Azizur Rahman was arrested as a collaborator but subsequently pardoned by Sheikh Mujibur Rahman in 1973 under a general amnesty. But Father, who had given blood like many other Mukti Joddha and had personally trained the Mukti Bahini in Agartala for the liberation of his country, could not stomach the thought that avowed anti-Bangladesh people would be his colleagues in Zia's cabinet.

However, in deference to General Zia's request, Father agreed to run for parliament from Ziaur Rahman's Bangladesh Nationalist Party (BNP) during the General Elections of February 1979. He ran against a formidable opponent, Muzaffar Ahmed, the leader of the pro-Moscow leftist National Awami Party (NAP-M), whom he had roundly defeated twice before.

One day during the campaign, Father received an invitation from the Russian ambassador to have dinner with him. Since Father had just returned to Dhaka after a few weeks of hectic campaigning in Comilla, he let his driver take a couple of days off. So on the night of the dinner, I had to drive Father to the ambassador's residence in Gulshan. The ambassador himself was standing at the door to receive Father and, noticing me in the driver's seat, inquired who I was. Father told him that I was his eldest son and signaled me to get out and greet the ambassador, at which point the ambassador invited me as well to join them for dinner.

Upon learning that I had been studying in the United States and that I might go back to do my PhD, the ambassador looked at me smilingly, squinted his eyes, and said that the Americans have been brainwashing me and that I should come to Moscow to study instead and that he would be happy to arrange a full scholarship for me. I replied, "Thank you, Excellency, for the kind invitation to Moscow. But I prefer to study in the United States. At least there I can choose where to get my brains washed—can't do that in the Soviet Union, can I?" Father remained a silent spectator as the ambassador and I continued with our spirited banter.

As we sat down to dinner, the ambassador turned very serious and said to me, "You seem to be a persuasive young man. You should persuade your father not to run against Prof. Muzaffar Ahmed. We want Muzaffar in the parliament. This time, your father will not be running against NAP Muzaffar—he will be running against Russian rubles!"

That the Russians were committed to spending as much money as needed to ensure that the pro-Moscow leftist NAP-M leader got elected was highly revelatory to us, because it could be a game changer for Zia and the country. Father reported this conversation to General Zia the next day. General Zia took the ambassador's threat very seriously and told Father that he himself would campaign for Father. General Zia came to Comilla to campaign for Father twice—in Dhamti and Debidwar—during the 1979 elections. Father beat Muzaffar Ahmed once again and won his parliamentary seat for the fourth time.

During this time, with Father's blessing, Mahboob and I had contracted a consulting firm, Ghosal Associates Ltd., to do a field survey and assessment of which businesses had the best potential for growth in Bangladesh. Ghosal submitted a fifty-page report, for which we paid his consultancy 25,000 taka, identifying several business possibilities. At the top of his recommended list of potential ventures was the manufacturing of PVC pellets, which could be used to develop multiple industrial products.

Based on that report, we drew up a business plan, selected a site for the factory, and applied for bank financing to import the required machinery. However, the loan officer kept missing his deadline to complete his assessment and the loan documents for the approval of bank financing, and several months went by without any progress. We were too naïve to realize that he had secretly sold our report and business plan to another client of his for a substantial amount. That client then arranged loan from another bank and was well on his way to establishing that business himself with his business partners, with a percentage ownership of the business going to the loan officer as well.

When I shared this with my friend Kamal Rahman (Ambassador Ataur Rahman's eldest son), who was trying to set up a business himself, he said he was not surprised because he had a similar experience. He and his partners had gone to a minister for his signature to launch a business venture, but the minister refused approval unless he was given an appropriate "cut." We realized that we had a lot to learn to do business in Bangladesh. Having gotten a glimpse of how things operated in Bangladesh, we decided to take the necessary precautions from then on.

We turned to Ghosal's report once again and decided to pursue the manufacturing of sheet glass, which was another top item in his recommended list of promising ventures. The report noted the expanding business and commercial endeavors in Bangladesh, among which was the spurt of high-rise buildings in the business districts of several cities. These skyscrapers would create a potentially high demand for various types of glass for interior and exterior glass panels. Ghosal's report also identified Belgium to be the top manufacturer of various types of glass, as well as Belgium's willingness to export its glass manufacturing technology to developing countries. Fortuitously for us, a Belgian business delegation was due in the city at that time.

We contacted the commercial attaché in the Belgian embassy in Dhaka for the opportunity to discuss our business plan with him and also to solicit his help to be introduced to the Belgian delegation when they were in town. He welcomed us to meet with him. During the hour-long conversation, in between our discussion with the attaché, Mahboob and I kept conferring with each other in our mother tongue, Bangla, on what and how much we should tell the attaché during that first meeting. We also said stuff not meant for the attaché's ear.

During the delegation's visit, the minister of industries threw a dinner party for them in a floating restaurant called *Mary Anderson*, a paddleboat docked on river Buriganga at Fatullah, some ten miles outside Dhaka City. The *Mary Anderson* was built in 1933 by the Calcutta Shipyard as a luxury yacht for First Viscount Waverley, the governor of Bengal from 1932 to 1937. It was later used for official purposes by the president of Bangladesh until it was donated to the Bangladesh Parjatan Corporation by President Zia. Select members of the country's business elite were invited to attend the dinner; Father received the minister's invitation as well. He then called the minister's office not only to thank the minister for the invitation but also to express his regret that he wouldn't be able to make it, but he would be happy if Mahboob and I could represent him. The minister's reply was "Of course, sir."

On the evening of the dinner, Mahboob and I drove down to Fatullah, where we boarded *Mary Anderson*. The attaché and his wife were receiving the guests. The attaché welcomed us and shook our hands, introduced his wife to us, and then turned to his wife and said in perfect Bangla, "I met these two fine gentlemen last week. They are interested in setting up a glass manufacturing enterprise."

Mahboob and I stood there in complete shock, realizing for the first time that the attaché spoke superb Bangla and desperately trying to remember Mahboob's and my conversation in the presence of the attaché. Had Mahboob and I discussed anything embarrassing or said anything negative about the attaché? Noticing our discomfort, the attaché explained that his first diplomatic posting to South Asia was to Calcutta (now called Kolkata), where he learned Bangla and where he also met and married his wife, herself a Bengali woman.

That night, we learned a valuable lesson: never assume anything about another person until you know him well; taking someone for granted could be dangerous! Aside from this embarrassment, it was a very relaxing and wonderful dinner party, and we did meet some members of the Belgian delegation with whom we talked about our desire to pursue Belgian help to establish a glass manufacturing plant in Bangladesh. Their visit concluded with the two governments signing a memorandum of understanding that called for close business collaboration, inter alia. After several months of discussion, we had to abandon the hope of establishing a glassmaking factory because the up-front money and the total financial outlay were too large for us novices to feel comfortable in the endeavor.

I was getting a little disillusioned with all the failed effort at launching a business. Around that time, I saw an advertisement by the Ministry of Foreign Affairs for two openings at the P-2 and P-5 levels at the United Nations. I was immediately interested and prepared my application within the next few days. But knowing full well that UN jobs cannot be gotten without a strong push by one's own government, I asked Dad to intercede with Foreign Minister Shamsul Haque on my behalf.

Mr. Haque received Dad in his office and said that he would be happy to put forward my name for the P-2 position; the government had already decided to push an about-to-retire secretary with many years of administrative experience for the P-5 position. Dad thanked him, and we left his office. It was obvious to both of us that the government's first priority would be to push for the P-5 position, and if by any chance Bangladesh got it, the chances of another Bangladeshi getting the second position even at the P-2 level were remote. Resigning to que será, será, Father suggested that taking a short vacation might revive my spirit. So Mom and I decided to go to the United States for a few days. Dad suggested that I should remember to call on Ambassador K. M. Kaiser, Bangladesh's permanent representative to the United Nations at the time, to convey his regards when I arrived in New York.

Just a few days before our departure, a gentleman called our home and told me that he had learned from the travel agency where we bought our ticket that I was going to the States. He asked if he could come by to discuss a matter with me. When he came to our house, he informed me that his eldest daughter and son-in-law lived in New York City and that he wanted to send his teenage daughter to them but did not want to send her by herself. He was wondering if his daughter could accompany me, but, first, he wanted to check me out what kind of a person I was and whether it would be safe for his daughter to travel with me. When he learned that Mother was also going with me, he seemed greatly relieved and inquired whether his daughter could accompany us to New York. Mom assured him that his daughter would be more than welcome and that we would safely deliver her to her sister.

During the flight, the girl sat on the window seat, Mom in the middle, and I took the aisle seat. Mom talked with her a few times during the entire flight, but she and I never talked. When we arrived at New York's JFK International Airport, she called her sister from the airport and handed the phone over to me to take down directions to go to their place. We took a cab and went to their apartment in Manhattan, where the sisters were reunited.

Mom and I stayed at a hotel in New York City for a few days, during which time I called Ambassador Kaiser and conveyed Dad's greetings. He asked me to do likewise when I returned home. He also acknowledged receiving a note from the foreign minister asking him to push for both positions at the UN and assured me that he will try his best, although it would be an uphill struggle.

Next, we flew to Portland, Oregon, and then to Eugene to my brother Selim's apartment. It was winter. After the first night's sleep, Mom woke up early in the morning to find everything outside was white and covered in snow. She was so excited that she hurried outside the apartment and grabbed some snow in her hand; it was the first time that she had experienced snow in person.

Our Eugene visit was a good getaway for a while. This was Mom's first visit to the States, and many things amazed her. For example, when Selim discarded the plastic orange juice jug, Mom picked it out of the trash can and washed it, saying that it was wasteful to throw away useful items and that she would take it with her to Bangladesh!

I gave her the campus tour, sharing with her stories of my days at the University of Oregon. We visited many places, ate in different restaurants, and even went bowling, which was a new experience for her. All told, it was a pleasant visit. Before we left Eugene, I decided to call the passenger who came with us to New York, just out of curiosity to inquire how she was adjusting to New York life. Her sister picked up the phone. I introduced myself and asked whether I could speak with her. Her sister said no and that I was never to call her again. I did not take any offense at that because I realized that she was simply being protective. After our return to Dhaka, I was not surprised to learn that Bangladesh was unable to place any of its citizens into the P-2 and P-5 openings.

Meanwhile, Bangladesh had purchased its first oceangoing vessel called *Hizbul Bahar* to carry pilgrims to Makkah, Saudi Arabia. On one occasion, it was used to take Bangladeshi tourists to Singapore. The Bangladesh Shipping Corporation sent out invitations to a few eminent people to take the inaugural voyage. Father received two tickets, one for him and one for Mom, but was unable to use them because of pressing business affairs. He called the minister of shipping and had one of the tickets transferred to me.

On our way to Singapore, we stopped at Penang, Malaysia, where we sampled its soft sandy beaches and delicious food that earned it the nickname "the Pearl of the Orient." When we docked in Singapore, we had a surprise waiting for us. About half a dozen ad hoc barber chairs were set up in the dock area, and as we disembarked, we had to stand in several queues for our turn to have our hair shortened to the officially designated acceptable length. It was Prime Minister Lee Kuan Yew's Singapore, and what LKY desired happened. So like the hundreds of other passengers, I, too, had a haircut even though my hair was short enough.

Following the haircuts, we had to sit through a stern lecture on what to do and what not to do while in Singapore; for example, spitting in public, disposing off chewing gum in a public place, jaywalking, making loud noises, wearing unseemly outfit in public, walking barefoot in public, and a million other things were strictly prohibited. Even the slightest violation would land us in jail. Other than all that, we were welcomed to enjoy Singapore! Not surprisingly, before we left Singapore, there were newspaper reports of a few Bangladeshis who were hauled into jail for breaking the law.

After we returned to Chittagong port in Bangladesh, we had to disembark and go inside the huge customs warehouse adjacent to the landing dock. The *Hizbul Bahar* passengers, who were mostly small shopkeepers and businessmen, had done a considerable amount of shopping in Singapore, and the intention of the customs officials was to go through everyone's suitcases, boxes, and package to assess customs duties.

But the intention of these passengers was quite the opposite. They had made all sorts of prearrangements to enable them to escape paying taxes and duties. Some even had the names and addresses of government ministers prominently written on their cartons and packages, hoping to keep customs officials at bay; in some instances it worked, and in some cases it didn't. But the whole warehouse was a disaster area with the customs officials losing control totally. The shouting and yelling, pushing and shoving, and in some instances small-scale violence turned the warehouse into a mayhem of the first order. Since I had hardly done any shopping, I was spared the chaos and was able to get into my waiting car and drive off to Dhaka.

A Golden Opportunity Emerges

In June 1978, the government established the Bangladesh Institute of International and Strategic Studies (BIISS). It was the brainchild of President General Ziaur Rahman, who felt the need for a national think tank that could provide him with good analyses and strategic advice on regional and international issues that affected Bangladesh's national interests. He wanted a group of analysts who could think outside the box and provide him with policy alternatives different from that provided by the Ministry of Foreign Affairs.

Toward the end of my doctoral work at Oregon, I had written a paper on Bangladesh foreign policy in which I extolled Prime Minster Mujib's guiding principle in foreign policy pursuit: "Friendship to all and malice toward none." Since India and Pakistan had already fought three wars, and since there was an urgent need for an extended period of tranquility and stability in the region for countries to attain economic prosperity, I argued in my paper that General Zia's bold and expansive foreign policy move should include Bangladesh taking the lead in establishing South Asian rapport through some sort of an economic union echoing the European Steel and Coal Community. I sent a copy of my paper to Father, who during one of his meetings with President Zia mentioned my foreign policy recommendation. President

Zia was intrigued and asked to see me when I visited home the next time. Since the president and Father frequently met in the evenings to talk politics, one evening, I accompanied Father to the president's house in the Dhaka Cantonment.

President Zia greeted me warmly, and we chatted for a while. He appeared to be genuinely interested in my ideas regarding the foreign policy for Bangladesh and asked me a lot of questions, especially about European regional integration. I was eager to talk to him about that because I was seriously inspired by Berkeley's Ernst Haas's important work, *The Uniting of Europe*, in which he described the dynamics of the processes that led to regional integration in West Europe despite the challenges that had to be weathered. I strongly felt that the only way to deter the continuous interstate conflicts in the South Asian subcontinent was by building up some sort of a mutually beneficial economic and political arrangement.

The president listened intently. That day, I gained quite a bit of respect for President Zia for his intellectual curiosity, the time he took to listen to my ideas, for treating me like an important individual with serious ideas, and for his patience. On our way back home from the president's house, I told Father that I was impressed by President Zia. Father cautioned me that I should be on my guard and reminded me that "General Zia is an intelligence officer. He was trained in the UK and West Germany. Don't forget that." I wasn't quite sure why he cautioned me. However, when I learned that the president had created a think tank to provide him with independent analysis and ideas, I thought to myself that it would definitely be worth it to work there.

The Institute advertised several vacant deputy director and assistant director's positions. I viewed this new institute as the right place to articulate, debate, and develop policies, and wanted very much to work there. The fact that it was linked to the highest echelons of government made it doubly attractive to me.

I applied for the post of assistant director. I was called to interview at Foreign Minister Shamsul Haque's office in the Ministry of Foreign Affairs; the foreign minister was the chairman of the BIISS board. The foreign minister's secretary came to the waiting room to escort me to the foreign minister's room, when he noticed that my shirt sleeves were rolled up to my elbows. He politely reminded me of appropriate dress protocol when visiting the minister and asked me to roll down my sleeves and button them up. Then he gave me a quick head-to-toe look over and, satisfied, took me to the minister's office.

Seated around the minister's desk were some members of the BIISS board that included the secretaries of the ministries of foreign affairs, defense, and finance, and senior representatives of the three armed services. The minister asked to see my original credentials, which I handed to him, and after examining them, he passed them around to the other members. Each interviewer took turn to ask me questions, which fell broadly into two categories. The military people asked me about security concerns in the subcontinent, and the civilian members were interested in my views on the potential for South Asian integration. I was also asked to give my opinion about ASEAN (Association of Southeast Asian Nations), how effective I thought it was, whether something similar would work in South Asia, etc. Foreign Minister Shamsul Haque asked me the last two questions: what would be the challenges one would have to overcome to bring about integration of South Asian states, and did I have any questions for the interviewers. Members of the interview board listened to me attentively and often asked follow-up questions. The interview lasted over an hour. When it was over, I thanked the minister and the selection board and left feeling satisfied with my answers to their questions and rather confident that I did well. Shortly thereafter, I received the letter of appointment.

Being appointed as assistant director at BIISS was a dream come true and my first career-oriented job. I joined BIISS in February 1980 as assistant director in charge of the Soviet Union and East Bloc Desk, which meant that I was going to be the institute's lead on all issues related to the Soviet Union and its satellite states.

There were two other assistant directors, Abdur Rob Khan and Mohammad Shahiduzzaman, who had joined the institute in October 1979, four months before I did. Rob was an economist and left his economic analyst's job at the Bangladesh Bank to join BIISS. He was a homegrown product, a quiet type of a guy but with sound analytical skills, and later on became the dean of Social Sciences at North South University. Shahiduzzaman was a lecturer in the Department of International Relations at Dhaka University before joining BIISS. He had graduated from the Monterey Institute of International Studies, California. He was very knowledgeable about American foreign policy, quite articulate in his discourse, and exuded the confidence of a scholar well versed in his field. He went on to become the chairman of the Department of International Relations later on and remained active in the TV talk shows even after retirement. Both of them were excellent additions to the BIISS research team.

There were two other deputy director appointments, Mohiuddin Khan and Chowdhury Mohammad Shamim. Both Shahiduzzaman and Shamim were graduates of the Faujdarhat Cadet College, Chittagong, though Shamim was senior to Shahiduzzaman. The administrative officer was a major from the army. The head of BIISS was the director general (DG), who was Brig. Gen. A. H. M. Abdul Momen. The director general was a very polite, mild-mannered, measured man. His avuncular approach and his fairness won the respect of his staff. He was not out to prove himself as somebody to take notice of but someone who discharged his duties diligently, effectively, and without creating any waves. He was supremely aware that BIISS was going to be a tool of the government and the president was going to use it liberally.

BIISS's support staff, especially the library staff under the charming and very able leadership of its librarian, Saleha Sultana, were motivated and quite committed. Despite a limited budget and minimal staff, Saleha was able to provide fast and friendly service. In those early years, every member of the institute dedicated themselves to making BIISS one of the finest think tanks in the subcontinent.

The Soviet Invasion of Afghanistan

In December 1979, a political shockwave ran through the world, particularly through the countries of South Asia, as the Soviet Union invaded Afghanistan. No one had anticipated this, least of all the

Americans. President Zia gave us our first assignment: to prepare a briefing on why the Soviet Union invaded Afghanistan, what were the consequences for the region, and what should be Bangladesh's response.

The DG assigned Shahiduzzaman and me to prepare and deliver the briefing to General Zia and a select group from the topmost leadership. The two of us divided the task according to our academic strength: Shahiduzzaman would provide the analysis from the American perspective, and I was going to provide the analysis from the Soviet Union's perspective. With the help of our colleagues, we drafted the briefing and presented it to the DG. The DG approved the presentation.

On the evening of the briefing at the BIISS conference room, a stream of the topmost leadership started coming in: President Zia; the chief of army, Gen. Hussein Mohammad Ershad; the chiefs of the navy and air force; the chief of general staff, General Nuruddin; some senior generals like General Mannaf; the director general of the Directorate General of Forces Intelligence (DGFI); Foreign Minister Shamsul Haq, Bangladesh's ambassadors to the United States, UK, France, Pakistan, and India; the permanent representative to the UN, Ambassador K. M. Kaiser; the recently returned deputy chief of mission from our embassy in Moscow, Farooq Sobhan; and a handful of others.

Since the focus was on the Soviet Union, I led the presentation followed by the U.S. perspective by Shahiduzzaman. Then there was a break for coffee/tea and refreshment. After the health break, the DG of BIISS opened the floor for discussion and to field questions. Various participants took the opportunity to share their own interpretations and viewpoints on why the Soviet Union invaded Afghanistan and what it meant for regional security. I recall Farooq Sobhan disagreeing with me on the Soviet motive for the invasion. General Mannaf, considered by some as the "whiz kid" of the army, was sitting two rows directly behind the president. He was particularly strong in advocating his line of thinking, and at one point, General Zia turned around and called out, "Mannaf." General Mannaf did not utter a word after that.

Throughout the briefing, President Zia did not speak at all, but he was a good listener; neither did General Ershad nor General Nuruddin. Overall, everyone seemed to be digesting our presentation. We had given them enough material to ponder, unlike the experts at the Ministry of Foreign Affairs who provided the president with standard official response. It was a new and exciting experience for all of us at the institute, particularly for us presenters.

We were able to express our thoughts, ideas, analyses, and recommendations freely and boldly before such august gatherings because of cues we received from the president in one of our first meetings with him. He had laid down a simple modus operandi for us: he told us that during our briefings, we were to assume that the president knew very little about the issues being discussed, that he wanted to know everything there was to know about those issues, and that he was looking for independent views, opinions, and recommendations in addition to those he got from the Ministry of Foreign Affairs.

Over the fourteen-month period, we did many presentations for President Zia in different locations, and each time, Generals Ershad and Nuruddin and, depending on the topic, different sets of selected individuals from the top level of the government would be present. In some of these briefings, held either in the Darbar Hall of Bangabhaban, or in his cantonment office or in the BIISS conference room, we would notice that the president's attention would sometimes drift off to other pressing matters, and we would be at a loss to figure out whether our presentation was meaningful to him. Consultation with the military staff from his office revealed that the president was partial to blue color and he loved graphs and charts. So from then on, in all our briefings, we made a great effort to throw in some charts and graphs with blue as the dominant color, and it worked remarkably well. The president's attention span significantly increased, and he began to ask us questions and clarifications.

Zia, the Iran-Iraq War and Us

Our greatest challenge, however, was during the first Iran-Iraq War that broke out in September 1980. The Third Islamic Summit Conference of the Organization of Islamic Cooperation (OIC) held in Makkah, Saudi Arabia, in January 1981, established the Islamic Peace Committee to resolve the conflict between Iran and Iraq. At the summit, the OIC also voted to make Guinea's president Ahmad Sekou Toure the president of the Peace Committee and Bangladesh's president Ziaur Rahman as the vice president.

When negotiations with Iran and Iraq started in earnest, Pres. Ahmad Sekou Toure could not keep up with the hectic pace, and it automatically fell upon much younger president Zia to become the principal negotiator between Ayatollah Ruhullah Khomeini of Iran and Gen. Saddam Hussein of Iraq. For the OIC to put their trust and confidence on President Zia to negotiate for peace between two important Muslim states was a matter of great honor for him. A successful resolution of the dispute between two Muslim brothers was also a matter of prestige for Bangladesh. With that in mind, the president heavily leaned on us to prepare him for negotiations with the Iranian and Iraqi leaders.

To arm our president with the knowledge and analysis he needed, we burned the midnight oil carrying out extensive research on the historical animosity between Iran and Iraq, the causes of their conflict, the claims and counterclaims of the two warring parties, the positions and strengths of their respective troops in the battle field (which we got from the western intelligence reports and from the embassies of Iran and Iraq), and the issues that needed to be resolved. Our research included accessing the archives of the British War Museum, consulting Persian Gulf maps of the British Admiralty, and international law books for case studies on riverine disputes and on the concept of thalweg.

The president took our research notes, arguments, and recommendations with him during his multiple visits to Tehran and Baghdad, as he sat down with each leader to negotiate an end to the war. After his second visit to the region, we learned from our director general that the president was having difficulty holding the ayatollah's attention and getting his arguments across. We went back to the drawing board trying to figure out how to hold the Ayatollah's attention. I went to the Iranian Embassy in Dhaka to watch taped speeches by the Ayatollah, and one thing I noted was the Ayatollah's frequent reference to the Holy

Quran. So when we prepared the brief for President Zia's next trip to Tehran and Baghdad, we bolstered the President's talking points and arguments with quotations from the Holy Quran. When the president returned from his trip, he was unusually ebullient as we learned that those Quranic quotes made the ayatollah sit up and listen to him attentively.

Until the month of the president's assassination in May 1981, it had become a routine for the president to summon us to get our analysis and recommendations whenever there was an international incident of some import and that had potential consequences for Bangladesh—for example, the Assam Crisis, the Al Quds Crisis, etc. For us, the usual routine was to go to Bangabhaban, get escorted by the president's military secretary Brigadier Sadeq to the Darbar Hall, set up our charts, graphs, tables, and flip charts, and then wait for the president to arrive. It was during one of those briefings in Bangabhaban that I met Kaiser Ahmed, an aide-de-camp to the president, whose family and my family became close friends many years later in Ottawa, Canada.

Our interactions with the president were both exhilarating and disappointing. Once, after a night briefing, the president invited us to have dinner with him at Bangabhaban. We were very excited not only to have this privilege of dining with the president but also at the prospect of being served a magnificent dinner in Bangabhaban. We could not have been more disappointed! Hardly an epicurean when it comes to food, the president actually had an unassuming lifestyle. In fact, the president's instruction to the Bangabhaban head chef, we were later told, was that we must remember how many people in Bangladesh starve every day, and therefore the food served on the president's table must never be extravagant but be minimal. We sat at the president's table awestruck but not showing it as the food was served, which was atar roti, shobji bhaji, and dahl; I don't remember if there was any meat served. The president never failed to set himself up as an example of frugal living for others to emulate.

Notwithstanding such disappointments, we were always eager to have the chance to brief the president and to visit Bangabhaban, not least because of the many fascinating anecdotes we heard from important personalities in these briefings. Once, after our presentation, the president suggested that we take a break for a few minutes so that he could make some important phone calls in his private chamber. Just before the break ended, I found myself and our permanent representative to the UN, Khwaja M. Kaiser, in the men's posh, white-marbled washroom of Bangabhaban. I finished, and after washing as I was about to leave, I saw that he had also finished peeing, but with his left hand across his forehead, he was still leaning against the wall over his urinal. I volunteered, "Shouldn't we be going? The briefing is about to start." His forehead still against the wall and with eyes shut, Mr. Kaiser remarked, "The urinal is the best place to think. At the United Nations, we generate our best ideas at the urinals." I could not have guessed it, but there it was—sage words from a seasoned diplomat! He then washed up, and we returned to the Darbar Hall. He went on to become the President of the UN Security Council in October 1979.

Many of these meetings attended by our senior diplomats provided us with insights and knowledge that we might not have gotten otherwise. During one discussion on the Israeli-Palestine crisis, the anti-Israeli rhetoric was running high. To calm down emotions, I inserted that we should remember that Israel was the first country from the Middle East to recognize Bangladesh, long before any Arab country did. But one of our generals minced no words as he continued to talk about the victimization of the Palestinians by the Israelis and of Israel's siege mentality and its militarization. Ambassador Shamsud Doha stepped in to bring some balance into the discussion by pointing out that Israel's fear of being surrounded by hostile Arab states was genuine. He told us that Israel's ambassador to the United Kingdom had told him that Israel's fear was compounded by its lack of territorial depth. A fighter jet could leave Amman and strike Tel Aviv in six minutes, giving the Israeli defense forces hardly any time to defend against such an attack. There was silence in the room for a minute as we all let that observation sink in; it added a whole new dimension to our perspective on the Mideast crisis.

Our free access to the president, the top brass, and the opinion makers in the highest echelons of power, but more importantly, our freedom and ability to debate, express disagreements, and put forth alternative thinking and new ideas were understandably resented by the senior officials in the Ministry of Foreign Affairs, who arguably rightly saw that foreign policy making was their exclusive prerogative. One day, the BIISS DG received a directive from Foreign Secretary S. A. M. S. Kibria that all our writings, papers, and briefs for the president should be forwarded to the Ministry of Foreign Affairs, and the ministry will forward them to the president's office.

The DG did as he was told. But the president's office very soon realized that the material that they were supposedly getting from the BIISS began to read differently in substance and tone from what they had been getting before. They soon found out that the ministry was doctoring the documents and putting a foreign office spin on all of them. Right away, an instruction went out from the president's office to the Ministry of Foreign Affairs and to BIISS that, henceforth, all documents from BIISS for the president's office must come directly to them without getting routed through the ministry. The ministry did not expect that and also realized that they could not dictate terms to the president's office. Frustrated, the foreign minister did the next best thing he could—he asked the DG that he would appreciate it very much if the ministry could be kept "informed" about BIISS's work and especially its policy recommendations to the president in summary form at least.

New Brigadier Gone Amock

After General Zia's assassination on May 30, 1981, Brigadier Momen was replaced by Brigadier Abdul Hafiz as the new director general of BIISS. One day, within the first week of his takeover, when we came to office, we found some of the low-level staff—the gardener, the gatekeeper, the bathroom cleaner, the sweeper, the cook—crying and very scared. We asked the administrative officer what happened. He nodded his head in disapproval and, in muted voice, informed us that the new DG's modus operandi whenever he took up a new assignment was to cause the low-level staff to be physically beaten to convey to them that there will be no slacking off at work in the new DG's watch and also to send a similarly loud signal to the superior officers and staff of the institute.

The DG's logic, we were told, was that a beating like this once every six months kept everyone on their toes, and everything ran smoothly with no headache for the DG; that was why he had ordered the beating that morning. We were quite shocked. During the previous DG's tenure, we had established the unwritten rule that we were civilians and the DG and the admin officer were military, and coming from two different cultures, we had different ways of handling matters, and therefore we will not kowtow and be ordered around the way it is done in the military.

With the advent of the new DG, whose attitude and sensibilities were at loggerheads with ours, we realized that we would have to tread carefully to maintain our dignity and self-respect even as we try to negotiate our relationship with him. Although the next few months were tense, the new DG soon learned to appreciate our worth and the value of our work. He threw himself headlong into the institute's research activities, but his knowledge about how to run an institute like the BIISS was very limited.

My colleagues and I felt that the new DG definitely needed some international exposure to temper his preconceived and rather backward notions about the institute, its work, and its staff. He needed to visit other regional institutes to learn firsthand about their operation and their work. So when we received an invitation to participate in a conference at the Institute of Strategic Studies (ISS) in Islamabad, Pakistan, we encouraged him to attend it on behalf of BIISS. He was very glad to go, because as military personnel, he had never had the opportunity to go outside the country. We prepared him adequately for the security conference.

After the conference, he took the time to visit various sections of the ISS and to confer with its officials and research staff. When he returned, he was a completely changed man. He openly commented on how backward our female staff wearing blouses with sleeves looked compared to the smart-looking female staff wearing sleeveless blouses at the ISS. He ordered that, henceforth, we must be smartly dressed and be smart in our conduct as well.

His interactions with heads of other think tanks and research outfits were like an epiphany that he could be a scholar too. He eagerly joined in organizing national and international conferences. We were all particularly impressed by his ability to memorize, for he could recite an entire ten-page conference speech from memory. In several conferences, participants were awestruck at his ability to stand before the microphone and delivery his speech without any prop, while the participants followed his words in the hard copy they held in their hands. The transition was incredible. His other peculiarity was that he always went to the Kakrail Mosque near Ramna Park after office, although to what extent he was immersed in Tablighi activities we did not know.

After General Zia's death, General Ershad came to power. One day, I was informed by the DG that the chief of general staff, General Nuruddin, had asked to see me in his office in army headquarter. When I called on him, General Nuruddin told me that he had an assignment for me—namely, that I should do a comparative survey of the existing military regimes in the world and develop a typology showing the strengths and weaknesses of each.

I stood in his office and stared at him without saying a word. Realizing that my mind was already rebelling against this assignment, he walked up to me, put his hand on my shoulder, and said, "I know you are a civilian and do not believe the military should be in power, but the chief wants this done." I left his office without saying anything. As much as I resented it, as an officer of the strategic studies institute, I was obligated to carry out the directive. For the next couple of weeks, we immersed ourselves in examining and comparing the military regimes in Pakistan, Thailand, Indonesia, the Philippines, Iraq, and Egypt to understand how they came to power, how they sustained themselves in power, their instruments of coercion and co-option, their civilian-military relationships, the nature of the power structure, etc.

Soon after we submitted our survey, General Ershad's government sent out official invitations to Pakistan and Indonesia; BIISS was assigned to serve as the host to the military delegations from these two countries. I recall the discussion with the Indonesian military delegation. Gen. Benjamin Moerdani, who headed the Indonesian delegation and later became Indonesia's minister of defense and security, explained to us the challenges they faced and how they managed those challenges to retain the reins of power. He also spoke of the control and distribution of authority among co-opted civilian leadership.

When BIISS hosted the Pakistani delegation, the exchanges with the Pakistan military were sparse on substance but loaded with nostalgia, since the senior Bangladeshi military officers including General Ershad were previously officers in the Pakistan military. During the morning tea break, a Pakistani general and I together with another BIISS colleague, Mizanur Rahman Khan (Mizan), came out to the institute's beautiful garden for some off-line chat.

What the general said in a matter-of-fact manner surprised me; he said that he was surprised that General Ershad, who was known mainly for womanizing and drinking when he was in the Pakistan Army, was now the head of government in Bangladesh! He went on to say that the Pakistan military always thought Bengalis were far more democratically minded and intolerant of the military seizing power. Now that General Ershad was in power, he wondered what happened to that democratic sentiment.

Mizan and I simply nodded our heads and wondered ourselves at our own predicament. The BIISS hosted no other military delegation that year, and one assumes that General Ershad and his cohorts found the answers they were looking for. Ershad took the same beaten track that General Zia had followed—namely, a period of military rule to control and consolidate power followed by elections to civilianize the regime.

My days at BIISS under the leadership of the first DG, Brigadier Momen, afforded me numerous opportunities to express myself. I volunteered for many aspects of BIISS life and activity. After joining the institute, one of the first things I had done was to visit the BIISS library to see what types of books, journals, periodicals, news magazines, and newspapers were kept. I concluded that the library needed a major resource upgrade.

A library committee was formed with me as the head, and I worked closely with the librarian Saleha Sultana and her staff on essential resource procurement. I drafted correspondence to liaise and join other library networks and to establish close working relationships with other research institutes and think tanks regionally and internationally. We launched the institute's journal, the *BIISS Journal,* of which I became the editor.

To enhance our visibility and importance, I delivered lectures at the Defence Services Command and Staff College in Mirpur, Dhaka, and at the School of Military Intelligence in Mainamati, Comilla. I also became an examiner and a question setter for the annual and final exams in the Department of International Relations, Dhaka University. My colleagues and I attended a number of international conferences where we presented papers or served as a discussant or as a panelist. I attended a conference in Sri Lanka and another one in former Yugoslavia, where I presented papers that were subsequently published in international journals.

Both those conferences bring back interesting memories. After the conference in Sri Lanka's capital, Colombo, ended, all the delegates were bused to Kandy, some four hours away in the Central Highlands, for a day's outing. Kandy was the home of the Temple of the Tooth Relic, one of the most sacred places of worship in Buddhism. On the way, we stopped by the roadside, and our tour guide asked us whether we would like to drink coconut water from the fresh coconuts in the roadside trees. Many said yes. So a local boy climbed one of the trees and cut down some coconuts and served the coconut water to us.

One colleague was from Yugoslavia who had never drunk coconut water before. Within minutes of drinking the water, his body reacted violently, and he had to be taken to the hospital and have his stomach flushed. His stomach did not agree with the coconut water, and he looked miserable when he boarded his flight to Belgrade two days later. I also noticed that after almost every curried meal, the conference delegates from northern India ate *dahi* (plain white yogurt) to stabilize their stomach. They could not tolerate the hot spices used in the southern cooking.

The invitation from Yugoslavia was from the International Institute for Politics and Economics (IIPE), Belgrade, to present a paper at the International Round Table on the Politics and the Nonaligned Movement in the 1980s. I decided that it was time to critique the nonaligned movement that seemed to be going moribund and presented a paper titled "Nonalignment: The Need for Self-Scrutiny," which was compiled in the roundtable proceedings and later published in *Asian Affairs, An American Review* (Berkeley) the same year.

The highlight of the visit to Yugoslavia was a somber visit to the mausoleum of Pres. Josef Broz Tito to place a wreath on behalf of the foreign delegates. We also traveled to a few select cities by bus, among which Dubrovnik was quite memorable because of the delicious red tomatoes we ate with our meal. As we traveled through the countryside, we would often stop in parks where we were served very delicious local cheese, bread, and wine. The informal discussions with my European colleagues were intellectually quite rewarding.

Early Days Leading to Regional Integration

One of the most important tasks assigned to BIISS was assigned to Chowdhury Mohammad Shamim and me. We were asked to see the Foreign Secretary S. A. M. S. Kibria in his office. He explained to us that the president was interested to explore the possibility of regional integration in South Asia. Mr. Kibria asked us to prepare a concept note not exceeding five pages. We did as asked, which the Ministry of Foreign Affairs used as the basis to elaborate the concept further and draft an expanded think piece.

This was followed up with the most memorable and important task assigned to me at the institute. The government apparently decided to adopt a low-key approach to sound out regional governments on what their views were on such a potentially important undertaking. I was summoned to Foreign Minister Shamsul Haque's office and asked to carry a message in a sealed envelope from President Zia to Pres. Junius Jayewardene of Sri Lanka. Foreign Minister Haque explained to me that I am to personally hand over the sealed letter to the Sri Lankan president and explain to him that President Zia believed that for peace and stability in the subcontinent, there was a need for regional integration of some sort, the details of which will be worked out in consultation with the regional governments, and that he would very much like to hear the Sri Lankan view on this. The minister also told me that our high commission in Colombo will be arranging with the president's office the meeting and the logistics.

I was pleasantly surprised at being chosen to deliver this message. When I thought to myself why, I came to the conclusion that maybe the president thought that I was well versed on the subject of regional integration and that I was best equipped to answer questions on the subject if asked.

I flew to Sri Lanka and met with the high commission officials. On the day of appointment, I went to President Jayewardene's office and handed him the letter. If he was surprised to see such a young nondiplomat delivering a presidential message, he didn't show it. As he opened the letter, I explained to him the context of my visit. He read the letter and then folded it and put it back into the envelope. He then told me that I should convey his thanks to my president, especially for taking him into confidence before anyone else, and that his office will send a formal reply to President Zia shortly. He asked me to tell President Zia that in principle, he subscribed to President Zia's vision, but the approach will have to be carefully thought out. He intimated that all the smaller countries will most likely strongly support Bangladesh's initiative, but the real problem will be India and Pakistan, who have hostile relationship and distrust each other. I thanked the president for receiving me and for his verbal and soon-to-follow written message to my president. I assured him that his reply will be forwarded to President Zia forthwith. I returned to Dhaka without further delay and informed President Zia what transpired in Colombo.

As we all know, Bangladesh pursued this important endeavor with vigor, urgency and credibility, which resulted in the creation of the South Asian Association for Regional Cooperation (SAARC). It was to President Zia's credit to initiate this visionary endeavor, but in equal measure, this enterprise would not have succeeded without the farsightedness and willingness of the regional leaders to join him in this uncharted path. Notwithstanding the political turmoil and the economic challenges that the regional countries had to weather over the last few decades, SAARC has proven to be resilient in its efforts to promote understanding, cooperation, and coordination among its seven members over a whole host of critical issues affecting the region. Afghanistan joined the original seven to become the eighth member of SAARC in April 2007.

I also attended many diplomatic dinner parties in Gulshan, Dhaka, and the more I became a well-known face in the diplomatic circle, the more I had to be careful because of my job in the strategic studies institute, which required that I report all contacts with foreign diplomats. Diplomats from ambassadors down to counselors began to invite me to private dinners often with a select group of people numbering no more than ten. I also loved to play tennis, sometimes at the American Club with my American neighbor across the street where I lived who was an agricultural expert from Oregon State University, and sometimes at the Australian Club, both in north Gulshan.

The counselor for political affairs of the embassy of Japan started to invite me to play tennis with him. Then one day, after we finished our game, he said that he would like to ask me a big favor. The new Japanese ambassador had been waiting for weeks to get an audience with President Zia to present his credentials. Could I ask my father to facilitate the ambassador's appointment with the president? I told him I'll see what I can do. I informed my father about the request. Three weeks later, I received an invitation to dinner at the Japanese ambassador's residence. When I arrived, the counselor was at the door to receive me and to introduce me to the ambassador. The ambassador and I bowed a couple of times, and then he asked me to convey his thanks to my father for facilitating the appointment with the president; he had presented his credentials a few days earlier.

This whole episode had both pleasant and unpleasant consequences for me. On the positive side, I got to know many of the top foreign diplomats in the country and made some very good long-term friends. It also got me invitations to diplomatic events and meetings with foreign delegations. I also had friendly access to their embassies and their recreation centers to use their tennis courts, swimming pools, and cafeterias, not to mention indirect access to their warehouses. On the negative side, some embassies saw me as a potential source of valuable information as well as a conduit to access the higher echelons of power.

Brush with the CIA

A senior official from the U.S. embassy was our neighbor on Gulshan Avenue in Gulshan 2. He often invited me to his house to chat about international, regional, and domestic politics. One of his favorite topics was the impact of the Soviet invasion on the region. During these chats, he would occasionally show me newspaper clippings from U.S. and European newspapers and ask me for my opinion. On one occasion, he showed me a picture of a Soviet T-62 armored tank in southern Afghanistan and asked me what I thought of the picture. I told him that it looked like two separate pictures were superimposed and therefore doctored. He was probably testing me to see if I could detect misinformation.

At the end of our conversation, he said that his term of assignment in Dhaka had expired and he was returning to Washington DC, and that before he left, he wanted to introduce me to the person who was replacing him. A few days later, I met his replacement, who moved into the same house. He was younger than his predecessor but appeared to be in a rush.

He did not waste any time. Within a couple of weeks of our introduction, he invited me to his house one evening, closed the door, took me to his study, and said, "Listen, I am going to level with you. I work for the CIA, and we feel you could too." He told me I was recommended to him by his predecessor and that working for the CIA could be very rewarding for me. He quickly added that I won't be asked to spy on my own government or my country. He paused to see the reaction in my face, but I did not react and maintained my poker face.

He then continued detailing the offer. They would send me to Kuwait, where they would set me up as an assistant professor at Kuwait University. I would have the wherewithal I require, and the financial reward would be great. They would, of course, fully train me for the tasks I would be required to do. He waited for my reaction with bated breath, probably thinking how I could refuse such a promising offer.

I took a deep breath and then told him, "I don't think so," and got up and walked to the door, where I stopped to say, "Don't worry, this conversation will remain confidential because it never took place." As I calmly walked home next gate, I thought to myself their audacity in thinking that I could be bought. That was my last contact with him or the U.S. embassy or their diplomatic club in Dhaka for the duration of my work at BIISS. I should have reported this conversation to the director general, but I didn't because I thought that all my freedoms would be curtailed, I would be put under surveillance, and my life would become miserable. I was mentally strong enough to withstand temptation and felt confident that I could handle things myself.

A Companion for my Journey

Toward the end of my career at BIISS, an important event took place to bring greater joy to my life; I got married. One day, my friend Shahiduzzaman, who had left BIISS a few days before Zia's assassination to become assistant professor in the Department of International Relations at Dhaka University, invited me to visit him in the department. The IR Department was on the second floor of the Arts Building. As I was going up the stairs to the second floor, a group of girls were coming down the stairs, and one particular girl caught my eye as we passed each other. I went up to Shahiduzzaman's room and sat down to chat.

Sometime later, I saw through his office window the same group of girls in the corridor milling about in front of the department office. I pointed out to Shahiduzzaman the girl I had seen on the stairs and inquired about her. He said that her name was Nipa and that she was a student in one of his classes. Then he had the department clerk summon a male student from the same class and asked him if he knew whether she was married. He replied that as far as he knew, she was not married and that she was the daughter of a surgeon in the Dhaka Medical College. My visit with Shahiduzzaman ended, and I went home.

Our house at the time was on a one-acre plot in Gulshan 2, and there was a long driveway from the gate to the building. As I walked from the gate toward the house, my mother, who was standing on the second-floor landing facing the driveway, asked me gently, "You look happy today. Did you meet someone?" I was amazed at a mother's instinct to detect even the slightest shifts in the emotional state of her child, for she could tell right away that something good had happened to me that day. I looked up and smiled, went upstairs, and confessed that, indeed, I had seen a beautiful girl that day, that she was single, her father was a surgeon from Sylhet, and that I would like Mother to find out more about her and her family.

That evening, after dinner, when she and Father were having their coffee, she told Father what I had told her. Father was pleased with the news and immediately picked up the phone and called the president's military secretary Brigadier Sadeq's father-in-law, Commander Chowdhury, who was also a Sylheti and lived in the Mohakhali DOHS (Defence Officers Housing Scheme). Commander Chowdhury suggested that Father should call Brigadier Malek, one of the country's foremost heart specialists who knew Nipa's parents very well. After a few phone calls among various parties, my parents were able to get all the information about Nipa's family that they wanted.

At some point, Nipa's parents asked Commander Chowdhury to continue to serve as the go-between and to arrange a meeting between them and me so that they can find out more about me, directly from me. The meeting was arranged one early evening at Commander Chowdhury's home, and they discreetly absented themselves, leaving my brother Mahboob and me alone with my future father- and mother-in-law in their house. Nipa's father, Kabiruddin Ahmad, who was a professor of surgery, was a smiling and extremely polite gentleman eager to listen to what I had to say. Her mother, on the other hand, was quite talkative, frequently interjecting to tell me who their relatives were and which high positions they held. Her father had to rein her in a couple of times so that he could hear me speak and learn more about me. Her father wanted to know more about my education, my current job, and my future plan.

They must have been pleased with me and decided to invite my parents to meet with Nipa. The next step was for my family to visit her family, who lived in a two-storied flat on Elephant Road. Mother, my sister Lily, and several aunts went to their house and were entertained by her family and relatives. Mother was very happy to meet her future daughter-in-law, and when it was time to leave, Mother immediately resolved to put a ring on Nipa's finger.

Father and I were waiting at home eagerly to find out how the visit went. When they returned home, they all looked happy. My sister Lily told me that I was not only getting a beautiful wife but also getting a gorgeous *shalee* (sister-in-law). Shortly thereafter, the wedding date was fixed for early December 1982, and it was agreed that I could visit her or take her out in the interregnum.

Nipa and I went out together multiple times, and I bought her flowers. Our wedding ceremony was held on December 10, 1982, at Hotel Purbani, where we exchanged our vows in the presence of a religious official and several hundred guests, and then Nipa, I, and witnesses from both sides signed the marriage register. Mizan, my friend and colleague from BIISS, was my best man.

A wedding reception was held several days later in the spacious front garden of our Gulshan house. Among the invited guests were the current president of Bangladesh, Ahsanuddin Chowdhury; a former president of Bangladesh, Abu Sayeed Chowdhury; the foreign minister; the foreign secretary; several ambassadors of foreign missions; select elites of the city; and friends and relatives from both the groom and bride's side. The president, however, called Father to express his regrets that he was unable to attend; he sent his ADC (aide-de-camp) with a state gift, which was a gilded platter embossed with the state emblem. I recall that Pres. Abu Sayeed Chowdhury and Ambassador Sinningé

Damste of the Netherlands came inside the house to greet my wife and my family.

I was happy with my in-laws. My father-in-law, Dr. Kabiruddin Ahmed, was an extremely kind and considerate man and very supportive in disposition. His smile was natural and genuine, and he was always ready to please people. It was said that he would ask his students whether it would be OK to give a test in the class, and because of the way he asked them, they could never say 'no'; he was known among his students and colleagues as *bhodro Kabir* (polite/gentle Kabir)! Even when he had a different viewpoint, he would express it in a way only he could, and nobody ever got angry or felt offended.

Once, when I had a cold and fever, he inquired what medication I was taking. I told him that I wasn't taking any medication because my belief was that I should let my body fight it and build up its immunity. He smiled and then gently said, "Baba, we invest lots of money, time, and effort on researching diseases and developing medicines to make people better. Medicines are meant to help your body fight ailments better." He did not tell me that I should start taking medicines. His argument that there was a purpose why we develop medicines stuck in my mind forever; I no longer rejected medicine.

I was also lucky to have a mother-in-law, Taslima Kabir, who prepared the most delicious dishes. She would find out what my most favorite dishes were and prepare them for me; among which were *rui, ayir,* and *pungash* fish bhuna. I was lucky indeed to have four women in my life—my mother, sister Lily, mother-in-law, and my wife Nipa—with excellent culinary skills. After my marriage, my mother-in-law's dinner parties endeared her to our mutual relatives and friends.

She is also an orchid aficionado and knows their names by heart. Her house is full of orchids, and for many years, she was the treasurer of the Bangladesh Orchid Society. She is also a writer, regularly contributing articles on her travels to magazines, and the author of children's books. She is also known for her crochet gifts to relatives, friends, and neighbors.

After my father-in-law's untimely demise, she took over the management of his cherished work, a medical clinic for poor women and children called the Begum Rokeya Nari O Shishu Shasthya Unnayan Sangstha (BERNOSSUS), which caters to the well-being of impoverished mothers and children who fell through the cracks of the country's medical system. With my sister-in-law Lopa's help, she has done excellent work in fund-raising and expanding the operation of BERNOSSUS. I should note that my father-in-law did not want the clinic to be named after him because it would trigger unwanted jealousy and obstruction, which would sabotage the endeavor. Instead, he named it after Begum Rokeya, a pioneer of women's liberation in South Asia, whose work on behalf of women was exemplary.

Off to England

A couple of months after the wedding, at an expatriate dinner party, the head of the British Council in Dhaka, who was a good friend of mine, asked me what my plans were since I had resigned from the BIISS at the end of December 1982. I told him that I hadn't thought about that yet. He then suggested that if I was interested to go to the UK for a while, he would be happy to provide me with a British Council visiting fellowship for three months. Having just gotten married, I thought it would give me the opportunity to travel in Europe with my wife. I accepted his unsolicited offer, and in March 1983, I went to the Queen Elizabeth House (QEH) in Oxford as a visiting scholar.

At Oxford, to find decent accommodation, Nipa and I walked all across town and checked out multiple locations including the bed-and-breakfast option to rent for three months but found nothing to our liking. We found one upstairs place in a house whose rent was quite modest, but when the landlady unlocked the door to the upstairs floor, we very nearly puked from the stench of *shutki* (dried fish). She had made a generous offer including the offer to cook for us, but we simply could not stomach the thought of living in that smelly place. We finally rented a modest but tidy flat that was walking distance from QEH that had two other occupants in separate rooms, an Ethiopian and a Jewish individual, and we had to share the kitchen. One of my vivid memories of the flat is how cold it was inside the flat and the ten-pence coins that we had to constantly put into the wall-side heaters to keep the bedroom warm.

Having gotten tired of eating in restaurants all the time, we decided to cook our own food in the communal kitchen. The kitchen had the utensils but no spices except the typical British salt and pepper shakers. We decided to go to the store to buy some spices but couldn't find any store in Oxford that carried Indian spices. Then it came to me that perhaps if we could find an Indian woman in the street and follow her, she might lead us to an Indian store that will definitely carry what we need. Luckily, that is exactly what happened; we followed an Indian woman to an Indian store tucked away in a corner out of the beaten path. We finally bought the spices we needed and went back to the flat where Nipa cooked some rice, dahl (lentils), and chicken.

Nipa thought that it would be nice to invite the other two occupants to have dinner with us. We knocked on the Jewish gentleman's door, but he was not in his room; the Ethiopian fellow agreed to join us. We sat down to eat, but when he started eating dahl, he nearly puked. He was obviously not used to the taste of curried dahl, and we told him that he didn't need to eat anything that was not to his liking. It was interesting for us to observe that dahl, which was a favorite and staple meal item for Bengalis, was so unsavory to someone from another culture.

My work at the QEH was primarily research oriented and conducting weekly discussions and monthly seminars on topical issues. I also capitalized on the rare opportunity to visit other Oxford colleges, primarily All Souls College and St. Anthony's College because of their specialization in international relations, politics, and social sciences. During my short sojourn at Oxford, I met many scholars from the Oxford colleges, visiting scholars from the United States and Europe and some from Oxford's archrival, the University of Cambridge.

I also met for the first time Gowher Rizvi, who was a fellow at Nuffield College and, at the time of this writing, the international affairs adviser to the prime minister of Bangladesh. Gowher bhai was a very polite, friendly, and amiable person, ready to acknowledge a person's worth and quick with his commendations as well. Whether he could or not, he was always ready to help. He was also kind enough to invite us to his house, where we met his Italian wife and their dog.

While at QEH, I participated in many seminars, and one was on South Asia, where Gen. Hussein Mohammad Ershad had recently seized power in Bangladesh. After the seminar, an elderly Oxford professor asked me whether it was true that with General Ershad seizing power, the "generals were making general decisions and majors were making major decisions?" While it sounded funny, one could argue that there was some truth to it. He was referring to the many ad hoc committees headed by majors that were established by Ershad to address the country's pressing problems.

Following my stint at QEH, I spent a month at the Royal Institute of International Affairs, also known as the Chatham House, which was established in 1920 as an independent policy institute. Located in St. James Square, it served earlier as the residence of three British prime ministers. It is known worldwide for its nonattribution rule, commonly called the Chatham House Rule, which states that participants in its meetings may discuss its contents anywhere outside the institute, but they may not identify the individuals who participated or what a specific individual said. My Chatham House visit helped me to broaden my network of scholars and intellectuals concerned with global issues.

When I was at the BIISS, I used to frequently play tennis with the Australian ambassador at the posh Australian Club in Gulshan; we had become good friends. At the end of his term as ambassador, at one of his farewell parties, he suggested to me that I might consider doing my PhD in Australia. I liked the idea and asked him which university he would recommend. He immediately replied, "Oh, I would say the Australian National University (ANU) because of its prestigious International Relations Department. Many of the professors there are former Oxonians." He then added, "I know the chairman of the department. If you want, I can send him a note of introduction." I accepted his suggestion and thanked him for offering to do the introductions. I also mentioned to him that I will be in Oxford from March to early June 1983.

I then wrote a letter to my mentor, Prof. Thomas Hovet, at Oregon mentioning the possibility of doing my PhD work at ANU and asking him what he thought about that. He wrote back saying that my American and British education had given me a western perspective on world politics. It would be great to broaden my intellectual horizon by looking at global politics from the other side of the world; therefore, doctoral study at the ANU was an excellent idea. I was happy with his response because not only did it make eminent sense, but I also had his encouragement and support. I eagerly looked forward to pursuing the ANU option.

The Australian ambassador, whose name I should remember but I regrettably forget now, kept his promise after he returned to Canberra. I received a note from the secretary of the Department of International Relations at ANU informing me that since I was going to be at Oxford during Easter time, I should get in touch with Prof. Geoffrey Jukes, who will also be there at the same time training the Oxford rowing crew.

The Oxford and Cambridge Boat Race was the most anticipated traditional event that also reflected the intense rivalry between England's two most prestigious universities. The first race between them was in June 1829 on the River Thames and had become an annual event from 1856 onward. It was held around Easter when spectators numbering in the hundreds of thousands lined up both banks of the River Thames with their cucumber sandwiches and Pimm's (a gin-based fruit drink) to witness the contest. Geoffrey Jukes, who was formerly of Oxford University, had been training the Oxford rowing team for years, and even after leaving Oxford for ANU, he came to Oxford every year to train its rowing crew.

So, while at the QEH, I contacted his office at Oxford and set up a meeting with him. When we met shortly thereafter, I found him to be a rugged, weather-beaten, no-nonsense, straight-shooting guy. He came straight to the point without any preliminary small talk. "So you want to study at ANU? Why, might I ask?" Recalling Professor Hovet's comment, I told him that "it would be helpful to me to try to balance my western perspective with the oriental perspective in understanding world politics. I would like to understand how the Aussies, the Japanese, and the Chinese view the world. Besides, ANU comes highly recommended." He remarked, "I see. So what are you doing here?" I explained to him that I was on a British Council bursary doing some research work on South Asian security. He ended the conversation saying, "OK, you will hear from ANU. I'll be back in Canberra next month."

My visit to QEH and Chatham House ended in June 1983. Since it was our first postwedding trip and we had not gone on a honeymoon yet, we wanted to visit as many places and see as many things as we could during this trip. We frequently went to the movies and loved *Sophie's Choice,* which was just released. We took the bus to Stratford-upon-Avon, which was the birthplace of William Shakespeare, and thoroughly enjoyed walking through that medieval town and visiting the picturesque five-hundred-year-old cottage where the bard and his wife, Anne Hathaway, lived their lives. We also took the opportunity to watch the Shakespearean play *Twelfth Night* at the Royal Shakespeare Theatre there.

My father-in-law had arranged for us to meet several of his relatives in the UK and Holland during this trip. We took the train to Manchester to visit with Nipa's eldest aunt and uncle, Jolly khala and Matin khalu. Mohammad Matin was a doctor in the Manchester hospital, and khala was a nurse. Both of them were soft-spoken and caring and extremely kind to us and made me feel very welcome; I really felt at home. We enjoyed spending time with their children, Dipu, Lintu, Shan, and Meena, all of whom were younger to me. Their lovely house was on a hill at Mottram Rise, Stalybridge, and Dipu took me for a walk to see their neighborhood with quaint houses bordered by white slate walls and expansive pastures that fell off at a distance to reveal the outskirts of the city below. What is also memorable was khalu's beautiful garden that he took great care tending and, in later years, his equally beautiful indoor garden and the attached sunroom. We thoroughly enjoyed our visit there.

We also took the twenty-one-mile ferry trip from Dover across the English Channel to Calais in France and then a four-hour train journey from Calais to Amsterdam. The whole trip was quite memorable because the passage across the channel was rough and windy, and the entire train journey through Holland smelled of cow dung, which the Dutch use to fertilize their tulip fields. But the excitement of traveling with my wife kept up my spirit.

When the train arrived in Amsterdam, we were met by Nipa's *fupa* (uncle) Jalal Ahmed, who was the head of the Bangladesh Biman Office in the Netherlands. During our weeklong stay with them, we walked through the streets of Amsterdam including through the red-light district with prostitutes sitting inside glass windows, and we took the boat cruise through the waterways of the city, which was quite pleasant. We also visited Madurodam, which was a miniature park in The Hague and contained miniaturized replicas of famous Dutch landmarks and historical cities. It was indeed a pleasant visit for us.

Besides my rich academic interactions, the travels, and the fascinating places we visited, something truly wonderful that accompanied us was Nipa carrying our first child. I did not want us to be elderly parents when our children were born. I wanted us to be young and energetic father and mother to our children, and so I wanted to start our family early. Nipa was on the same page. After our visit to Holland, we returned to London and stayed at the residence of my father-in-law's cousin, architect Hassinur Reza Chowdhury (elder brother of the late Jamilur Reza Chowdhury of BUET and onetime adviser to the Caretaker Government of Bangladesh), for a few days before we returned to Dhaka. I would have preferred to stay in London until our daughter's birth so that she could have become British citizen by birth, but I did not have the money to sustain ourselves.

When we returned to Dhaka, the only person who seemed surprised that Nipa was pregnant was my mother-in-law. We were married just a few months earlier, and she expected that Nipa and I would take a few years off to enjoy our marital life before we had any children. Nipa was admitted to Dr. Mehrunnessa's Clinic in Dhanmondi, Dhaka. Our daughter was born on October 31 that year. Nipa's friends came to visit her among many others, and her IR Department friend Bindu suggested that we might name the baby Sanam, which meant "beloved" or "sweetheart." So she was named Sanam Hassan in the birth certificate. We had also thought of Fareen as a possible name, and so her name was changed to Fareen Sanam Hassan years later when we immigrated to Canada. When Mumu learned that *farine* was flour in French, she was upset and wished that we had not named her Fareen. So that made two of us—father and daughter—who were not quite happy with our names! Her nickname, however, was Mumu.

In the Land of Kangaroos and Wombats

In January 1984, I received a letter of admission to the doctoral program in international relations at the Research School of Pacific Studies in the Australian National University, Canberra. I was thrilled also to receive a doctoral scholarship that would considerably allay my financial burden. I had lived alone away from home since 1970, but going to Australia with my wife and a newborn baby was a whole new experience and a new chapter of my life. I was looking forward to broadening my intellectual horizon and to the unique flora and fauna of the Down Under.

I received a note from Prof. James Piscatori from Johns Hopkins University, USA, who was then a visiting professor at ANU. He identified himself as one of my doctoral advisers and gave me directions from the Canberra airport to my assigned graduate student housing in the suburb of Hughes in Canberra. We landed in Sydney on April 19, 1984, and then boarded the domestic flight to Australia's capital, Canberra. When we reached our assigned house, there was another note from Professor Piscatori in the living room that said that he had put some firewood and matchsticks by the fireplace, some warm clothes for us in case we came unprepared for the Australian winter ahead, and some essentials that we would need immediately, such as milk for the baby, and eggs, bread, and butter in the refrigerator. My wife and I were deeply touched by his thoughtfulness and help.

The residence at 73 Carroll Street, Hughes, was as good as we could have expected. It was an independent two-storied home, with spacious interior, beautiful utilitarian floor plan, floor-to-ceiling windows opening into a nice big front yard, a car shed, trees both in the front and in the back, and properly fenced off from other student houses. It had an old-fashioned wood-burning iron stove and a washing machine, but no dryer. We soon realized that there was no need for a dryer because of the all-year-round generally hot Australian weather. The average temperature was thirty degrees centigrade, and it was common for the barometer to hit forty plus degrees in peak summer. We learned quickly to put out the wash on the clothesline in the garden to dry only at night, usually after 10:00 p.m., or else they would turn yellow from the heat outside.

The following day, I went to the department and met Professor Piscatori, whom I found to be a friendly and unpretentious person, eager to be as helpful as he could. I thanked him for his thoughtfulness and for his generosity for the sweater I was wearing that morning. He welcomed me to the department, offered his assistance whenever I needed it, and then took me to meet the department head, who, by contrast, appeared to be arrogant bordering on being a racist.

Wearing a bow tie and trying to project an image of an upper-class gentleman, but coming across as a prick, he right away warned me that I was not to misuse the scholarship money and that I should be sure to return the sweater that Professor Piscatori had loaned me! I was shocked that he would think that I might blow my scholarship on nonacademic things and that I might not return Professor Piscatori's sweater. I found him to be imperious, very condescending, and we took an immediate dislike to each other. The chairman informed me that my principal doctoral supervisor would be Geoffrey Jukes and James Piscatori would serve as an adviser.

I then went to the office of my supervisor, whom I had met in Oxford, and made an appointment with his secretary to meet him next morning. After my day's visit to the department, Professor Piscatori drove me to my house, where I introduced him to my family.

The following day, I met my supervisor, who welcomed me, and we chatted for a while. We planned to meet the next day again for some substantive discussion. His secretary took me to the graduate student lounge and introduced me to a few other graduate students of the department. There, I met other doctoral students: two were from

Pakistan, Samina Ahmed and Nazir Kamal; an American student; a Japanese student; and several African students.

Over the following weeks and months, I got to know them quite well and also got used to the African students frequently arguing loudly over nothing, like the episodes of *Seinfeld*! I got into an argument with one of them once, though. He was a chain smoker, and so I urged him to stop smoking because he was polluting the room with cigarette smoke, which was bad for everyone's health, and also because he could be saving tons of money that he wasted on buying cigarettes. He looked at me with bloodshot eyes and asked me how many times a year I had a haircut. Then he pointed his finger at his head full of curly hair and said that he had not needed to have a haircut in the last ten years, and therefore I should add up the amount of money he had saved, which he used to buy cigarettes. Our conversation on that topic came to a standstill.

I found only two doctoral students at ANU from Bangladesh at the time; one was Sultan Ahmed from the Department of Sociology, and the other was Ahmed Kamal from the Department of History both from Dhaka University. The latter was working on a thesis on the devastating Bengal famine of 1943. There was also a master's student from Bangladesh who was a government officer from the Bangladesh Forestry Department at ANU on Australian government scholarship. Another doctoral student, Iftekhar Ahmed Chowdhury, had just completed his PhD from my department and left for Dhaka immediately prior to my joining the doctoral program. He was a successful career diplomat, Bangladesh's permanent representative to the UN both in Geneva and New York, and went on to become an adviser to the Caretaker Government from 2007 to 2009. Several years later, when we were preparing to go to UK for my postdoctoral work, we visited his home in Dhaka, where his wife read tea leaves for us to predict what was waiting for us in the future.

Initially, I had much work to do at home. Winter was coming, for May to August were winter months in Australia as opposed to these being summer months in the northern hemisphere. I had to order firewood for the wood-burning stove.

There was a thick stump in the front yard with an ax beside it; the stump was used to chop wood into thin pieces for the fireplace. Each winter, I ordered half a truck of firewood imitating my neighbors. The truck would dump the firewood in the front yard, and I would then neatly stack them in the car shed that had no car during the first year, from where I would take two pieces at a time, which I would then chop into four pieces. For the first time in my life, I learned how to chop firewood and thus became a woodcutter; I actually got a kick out of that! For the next few years, if Mother called and inquired The day of departure arrived about me, instead of saying, "Ghaash katey," Nipa could say, "Fireplacer jonney lakri kobachhey!" I would carry the chopped firewood into the living room and stack them by the fireplace. Whenever I threw a piece of wood into the stove, there would be loud explosive noises as trapped gases and sometimes insects inside the firewood exploded as they burned. We would sometimes sit in front of the fireplace with our lovely baby and enjoy the warmth; it was quite romantic actually!

We also needed a car, which we purchased almost a year later from fellow PhD student and our neighbor across the street, Sultan Ahmed, whom we visited occasionally. During one of these visits, he narrated to me that his preteen daughter had threatened to call the cops on him if he punished her brother again. Sultan bhai remarked, "Thank God we are going back to Bangladesh." He needed to dispose of his old Mitsubishi hatchback before departing for home. His asking price was A$1,500. I put A$1,200 in an envelope, sealed it, and gave it to him, telling him not to ask for anymore. He opened the envelope, counted the money, smiled, and said nothing. I appreciated his generosity.

Having attended the family- and home-related chores, I turned my full attention to my departmental requirements. I had no problem choosing my doctoral dissertation topic. I had already made up my mind when I was at BIISS what my doctoral work would be on. I had firsthand experience to guide me.

The government in power at the time was the center-right Bangladesh Nationalist Party (BNP). During almost every presidential briefing, most of which were in the Bangabhaban (presidential palace), I noticed that the decision makers were clearly split into two schools of thought; they were either pro-Indian or anti-Indian in their political outlook, with hardly any gray area in between. Every problem, every challenge that Bangladesh faced was attributed either to Indian shenanigans or to the pulls and pushes of the Islamic world and the West. The reaction of the people who mattered in the top echelons of government usually tended to be emotional and, to a certain degree, driven by religious concerns. So those who were more secular minded tended to be comfortable with pro-India leaning, and those with a religious bent tended to be focused on building strong relations with the Muslim countries and the West. One was either on one side of the divide or on the other side.

I found this to be a serious impediment to informed decision-making, and when this was exhibited by top government leaders, top generals, and senior administrators, it was downright dangerous, for it left little room for any healthy discussion, reasoned conclusion, or compromise. It was also dangerous for the younger generation who had just entered government service. Brilliance, intuitive thinking, thinking outside the box—all of which were the usual traits of a new generation of promising young government servants could easily turn into obstacles in one's career progress if he/she belonged to the wrong side.

But I did draw a modicum of hope from President Zia's demeanor during the briefings. It appeared to me that he was one person who seemed to appreciate the importance of hearing out all sides, of willing to be guided by both the experience and wisdom of the older generation of leaders as well as the unfettered thinking and bold propositions of the younger "would-be" leaders. I took President Zia's silence during the briefings and his openness to listen to the participants to mean that he did not have any preconceived notions, and if he did, he did not express them to allow the assembled participants to speak their minds. Perhaps this was a reflection of the president's intelligence training, or it could also have been a reflection of his statesmanship.

So when asked whether I had given thought to my dissertation topic, I informed my supervisor that I wanted to study the formative years of Bangladesh during the first administration of Awami League— that is, the period 1972–1975, when the Indian government played a significant role in Bangladesh's government and politics. I proposed to capture the political sentiments and the politics of that period through a set of hypotheses and test the validity of those hypotheses based on the available evidence.

I also argued that the existing theory of power relationship between asymmetric nations would not be applicable or useful in my case, and what I needed to do was to examine the asymmetric relationship through a new theoretical construct, which I would call "influence relationship"; in other words, who influenced whom and to what extent on the critical issues that defined India-Bangladesh relationship. This would help Bangladeshis, especially the decision makers and opinion makers, to evaluate their existing assumptions and prejudices. The overwhelming sentiment in the country was that India had an inordinate influence over Bangladesh, which ran counter to my assessment. I proposed to test the validity of this, which would be the central thrust of my research and dissertation.

Mr. Jukes and Professor Piscatori listened to my arguments carefully and concluded that both the topic of the dissertation and the proposed methodology were novel, innovative, and sound, and had the potential to make a major contribution to the fields of political science and international relations in South Asia. I was pleased when the department approved my thesis topic, and particularly so when the department chair agreed that both my topic and the proposed approach were "original."

My next task was to draft the research agenda, the theoretical works that I should study; examine the political history of the period; identify the military personnel, civil service, and political actors on both sides of the border who were directly involved during that time; locate and contact them for interviews; identify the domestic and international experts knowledgeable about the two countries and about subcontinental politics in general; identify their availability for interview; do the costing for travel and research work; etc.

I went to the university library and secured a carrel in the far corner of the floor holding the books I would read. I also went to the library archives to dig up the journals, magazines, and newspapers of that period that I would need to research. Sometime later, I drew up a list of people I needed to interview, the reason I needed to interview them, and their present location and availability. I was a bit dismayed to see that my potential interviewees—important political and military actors of the period of my study—were scattered all over the world at the time I proposed to undertake my interviews. While some of these actors were in these far-off locations in their own volition, others had fled Bangladesh because of the threat of political persecution.

When the list was finished, it looked like I would have to crisscross the globe from west to east and north to south to interview the primary actors of that period. I submitted the list to Professor Jukes with some trepidation, not knowing how he would react to this proposed, what appeared to be globetrotting.

The next day, I got a note in my department pigeonhole from the department secretary asking me to see my supervisor at the specified day and time. So I went to see him at the appointed hour not knowing what to expect. His office was usually dark even during daytime because his curtains were always drawn and he did not like to turn on the ceiling lights. Instead, he preferred to have his solitary green classic banker's desk lamp on. He was also a chain cigar smoker, because of which the office always appeared quite smoky.

Without raising his head, he beckoned me to sit. With his face still staring at my list of travel request, he said, "This is well researched, and I especially like the justification you provided for each of the proposed interviews and their relevance to your proposed chapter topics. You have also given quite an ambitious travel plan, but you have missed one stop, the moon!" My heart sank, and I thought to myself, *There goes my doctoral research travel plan.* He then continued. "I will recommend it to the department. The estimate, $4,700, is substantial, and it will have to come from the doctoral research vote. We'll see."

With that, the conversation ended abruptly, and I left. Once outside, I took a deep breath and walked to the bus stand to return home. I was sure that I wouldn't get the full amount I asked but should get a substantial amount of the request. The reason I did not shy away from asking the full amount that I calculated I would need was that I remembered my primary school principal, Mrs. Hubbard, once telling me, "Shaukat, if you want to go to the moon, aim for the stars, or else you will land on the rooftop."

I had to wait nearly two weeks before I heard from the department about my budget request for the proposed travel because the department was waiting for a few other travel requests to be submitted for collective consideration. I was summoned to Professor Jukes's office and informed that my travel request was approved without any change whatsoever. I was really surprised and could not be more thrilled! The next three months were spent contacting the interviewees on my list to confirm the date and time of the interviews, organizing my travel itinerary, contacting friends and relatives in various cities who could put us up, and securing the required visas for my wife, baby daughter, and myself. I would fly out of Canberra to Sydney and then to Hawaii, mainland USA, UK, Denmark, Pakistan, India, Bangladesh, Thailand, Singapore, China, Hong Kong, and back to Australia. I planned to stretch every dollar I could to take my wife and baby daughter along with me. Nipa also contributed from her babysitting earnings.

The day of departure arrived; on February 15, 1985, we boarded the plane in Canberra for Sydney and then to Honolulu, where an important political actor of the period had relocated out of fear of political persecution. I was both excited and anxious about my research trip. Excited, because I was on the verge of launching a study of a very sensitive period in the life of our nation that would be informed by firsthand accounts from the primary actors of the period, and not by hearsays, misrepresentations, and politically biased reporting.

I hoped that my research will unearth a true picture of what had transpired during that initial period under the Awami League Government, particularly on the critical issues of bilateral water sharing; international border demarcation, especially maritime boundary and Talpatti sandbar island; and the twenty-five-year friendship treaty. I also hoped that my study would make a contribution, however modest, to the field of international relations in South Asia and provide a foundation for the theory of influence relationship.

I was also anxious because our daughter Mumu was only fifteen months old, and this trip, with all its stops and starts in different countries, climates, and cultures might be too trying for her. Besides, we had fifteen separate pieces of luggage, mostly Mumu's, which we had to ensure did not get lost at airports and other transit points. Keeping an eye on everything as well as maintaining my schedule were stressful for me. At every luggage transfer point, I would haul a few items of luggage to a new point, have Nipa sit there with Fareen to guard them, while I went back and forth to retrieve the rest of the luggage pieces.

As we flew from Sydney eastward to Honolulu, Mumu looked down from the airplane at the Pacific Ocean. As she marveled at the vast expanse of water below, she said, "Abbu, dekho koto goshu pani" (Father, look at all the bathwater). She loved taking baths in the bathtub at home and spending lots of time playing with her rubber duck and other floats. It was delightful to hear her say that, and it just took the stress out of flying.

We landed in Honolulu the same day and were received by my friend Shamsuddin (Shams), who was doing his PhD in Hawaii. He took us to his apartment, where we met his young wife. Since there was hardly any additional space in their tiny apartment, he had arranged our brief stay with a colleague of his and helped us to move there, which was colorfully decorated with lots of oriental knickknacks. During our stay there, we walked in the beach whenever we could. One of the unpleasant things that we discovered during that trip was the infestation of the island by large cockroaches. Even in the beach houses, one could see cockroaches crawling all over the place; it was totally contrary to the image one visualizes of Hawaii.

In Honolulu, I was pleasantly surprised to bump into Obaidullah Khan. Obaidullah Khan was the second son of Justice Abdul Jabbar Khan, who was the former Speaker of the Pakistan National Assembly and also our neighbor in Dhanmondi, Dhaka. Obaidullah Khan, a career civil servant, was the minister for agriculture and water resources in President Ershad's cabinet at the time but had played an important role in the water negotiations with India as a secretary during the Awami League administration.

Since I was planning to interview him in Dhaka, I was curious to know what the cabinet minister was doing in Honolulu. I was stunned to learn that Pres. General Ershad had dispatched him to Honolulu with a briefcase full of U.S. dollar bills to appease his mistress Mary Badruddin, who had moved to Hawaii from Dhaka and who had demanded a house and a bank account in Honolulu as the price for her silence and for maintaining her distance from the general. I could not but feel disgusted by this level of corruption at the apex of government. The remark by the Pakistani general in the BIISS garden when we had hosted the Pakistani military delegation that General Ershad was known in the Pakistan Army as a womanizer seemed to be borne out. Also, the accusation that I had begun to hear in Dhaka about moral decay in the senior leadership of the country seemed also to be true. Mr. Khan was apologetic and just shrugged his shoulders with regard to his assignment.

From Honolulu, we flew to Los Angeles, where we stayed with my friend and colleague Chowdhury Mohammad Shamim and his wife Daisy. As mentioned earlier, Shamim, formerly of the Faujdarhat Cadet College, was my colleague from BIISS. Daisy and my wife Nipa were both Sylheti and knew each other well. Though our stay in LA was short, we did manage to visit Universal Studios, and Mumu was happy to meet with some Disney characters. Shamim and Daisy were great hosts, and we spent a wonderful weekend with them, after which we flew off to Seattle.

In Seattle, we stayed with my friends from the University of Oregon days, Jamal Rahman and his elder brother Kamal Rahman. As mentioned earlier, they were sons of Ataur Rahman, who was Bangladesh's high commissioner to Canada earlier. They were also gracious hosts, and we remember having pizza for dinner; their favorite was pizza with anchovies. We then flew to Eugene, Oregon, where we stayed with a young couple whom we did not know earlier. An acquaintance in Canberra informed us that her sister lived in Eugene and whether we would mind carrying some gifts for her sister's family. We were happy to do that.

Revisiting my old alma mater was nostalgic. I contacted an old friend, Markie, who was living in Eugene at the time and agreed to meet her in the student cafeteria in the ERB Memorial Hall. My wife

Nipa, true to her scorpion attribute, was suspicious and wouldn't let me meet Markie alone. So both of us went to the ERB and chatted with Markie for a while, after which I showed Nipa the campus. It was nice to be back to my old stomping ground where I spent four eventful undergraduate years.

We then flew across the United States to New York City, where we stayed with one of Nipa's Sylheti relatives. When he saw little Mumu, he immediately got some chicken nuggets from KFC for her. As we planned to go out for a walk in the evening, he advised me that whenever I walk on the streets of New York City, I must always carry at least a five-dollar bill in my pocket because if I feel a knife on my back asking me to hand over my money, I should be able to do that, failing which I am likely to be stabbed. Although I had been to New York City before and after and never experienced any such traumatic event, I took that advice in stride.

The visit to the Bronx Zoo was, however, memorable. At the entrance of the zoo, visitors were advised that the animals in the cages started from the smallest and the docile, and by the time one reached the last cage, one would see the most dangerous animal in the world. So one was naturally curious to know which animal is the most dangerous and walked all the way to the last cage. When I arrived at the very last cage, I found myself standing in front of a big mirror with the inscription on top, "The most dangerous animal in the world." It was my reflection on the mirror reminding me how dangerous human beings are and how we are destroying the flora and fauna of this planet at an unprecedented rate. It was a real wake-up call and a moment to pause and reflect!

All my interviews in North America and in Denmark and UK over the two-and-a-half-month period since I left Canberra went well. From London, we flew to Karachi, Pakistan, where we stayed with a family friend, Mr. Hashem, who was the head of the Janata Bank in Karachi; they were gracious hosts too. After finishing my interviews there, we flew to New Delhi, India, where we stayed with another family friend, Khalilur Rahman, who worked in the Bangladesh High Commission there. He lived in the Greater Kailash area in South Delhi. He was unmarried but had rented a spacious flat with several empty bedrooms.

The temperature in mid-May in New Delhi was atrociously hot, and air-conditioning was a must. I was intrigued to see for the first time an innovative and highly economical contraption for keeping the house cool in the summer heat. It was a big fan in a metal casing positioned in a gap where a window would normally be, near the front veranda of the second floor where we stayed. The outside part of the metal case facing the room was heavily wrapped in straws, which were continuously kept wet by a rubber hose linked to a big tub of water. As the fan blew in the air, which passed through the wet straws, the room received a continuous flow of cold air, thus keeping it really cool.

All my interview-related travels in Delhi were done in a scooter taxi that I rented each day for the whole day, and since baby taxis are open on the sides, I was buffeted by hot air all day. I recall the relief I felt every time I returned to the house after conducting my interviews in Delhi's summer heat. And there was Niranjan, who doubled as a cook and a housekeeper, who kept us well fed and took care of us during our sojourn in New Delhi.

Among the principal participants in the Bangladesh War whom I interviewed in New Delhi were chief of army staff Field Marshal Sam Jamshedji Manekshaw and Durga Prasad Dhar, an Indian Foreign Service stalwart, onetime India's ambassador to the Soviet Union, and prime minister Indira Gandhi's right-hand man and the principal architect of India's military intervention in Bangladesh in 1971. I also interviewed several cabinet members, national newspaper editors, academics from Jawaharlal Nehru University, and influential opinion makers.

Next, we went to Calcutta to conduct additional interviews. The interview with Lt. Gen. Jagjit Singh Aurora, who was the commander of the joint Indo-Bangladesh force during Bangladesh's independence war, was most memorable. He had many interesting anecdotes to share, including one regarding Bangladesh's commander, Colonel Osmani. According to him, Osmani was peeved at being superseded twice during promotions in the Pakistan Army, so he named his two dogs Ayub and Khan, after General Ayub Khan, the president of Pakistan. The India visit was extremely important for my dissertation research because I was able to interview most of the military, political, and government officials including the academic and media people who were important players during that period.

The next critical visit was to Dhaka, where I had to interview officials and people from all walks of life. The interviewees in Bangladesh came from multiple ideological and political party background, each carrying particular perspectives and interpretations of what happened during the independence war and the first Awami League administration.

I had to be careful and discerning. Some saw these interviews as an opportunity to challenge and even vilify Awami League's narratives, some saw them as an opportunity to push their versions of history, some were worried about how history will judge them and were eager to paint a positive picture of themselves and their efforts, while others were hesitant to answer my questions for fear of being persecuted.

Khondakar Mustaq Ahmed, who became president of Bangladesh for less than three months from August 15, to November 6, 1975, following Sheikh Mujib's assassination and was rumored to have had a hand in that, was in jail at the time of my visit. He demanded that I send him my interview questions in advance. When I received his responses, I found that some critical questions remained unanswered. When I asked him about those missing answers, he remarked, "Bhatija, shob kichhu ki bola jaey; amito shara jibon jeley thaktey chaina" (Nephew, it's not possible to say everything. I don't want to spend my entire life in jail). Since we were both from the district of Comilla and he knew my father well, it was natural for him to address me as his nephew, although we were not related. The interviews with former foreign minister Barrister Kamal Hossain were very helpful. The information I collected from my interviews in Dhaka was abundant and important, giving me rich material to work with. Added to that was the information I was able to dig up from the vernacular newspapers, journals, and locally published books.

Next, we flew to Beijing via Bangkok. During our overnight stay in Bangkok, Mumu woke up at night and wanted her milk bottle. Since it was past midnight, I couldn't get hold of anyone in the hotel kitchen, and so I used hot water from the bathroom tap to mix with the formula. In the morning, she had a severe stomachache, and we had to call in the hotel doctor to prescribe her medication. I should have realized that even a four-star hotel's tap water was not safe for drinking, especially in Asia and Africa. Luckily, Mumu recovered quickly; since I was guilty of this stupidity, it lifted the huge stress off of me. We flew to Beijing the same day, where we stayed with Ambassador Enayetullah Khan.

When I had started to track potential interviewees for my doctoral research, former permanent representative to the UN Khwaja Mohammad Kaiser was the Bangladesh ambassador to Beijing. I had written to him about the possibility of an interview. In his reply of November 26, 1984, he wrote, "I am happy that you are thinking of visiting China in connection with your research sometime next year. By the grace of God, if I am still alive and here, you are most welcome to come and stay with me with your family and be my guest . . . Some of the Chinese dignitaries you mentioned are very good personal friends of mine, and perhaps I might be able to help you too . . ."

But by the time of my visit in August 1985, he was gone. Enayetullah Khan, who was Obaidullah Khan's younger brother and a prominent leftist politician, had written an op-ed piece in the respectable *Far Eastern Economic Review* praising General Ershad's coup d'état, which endeared him so much to the general that he was rewarded with the plum appointment of ambassador to China in General Ershad's administration. His leftist pro-China leaning was useful to General Ershad as well.

When I learned that Enayetullah had replaced Kaiser as Bangladesh's ambassador to China, I contacted him from Dhaka to inform him of my planned trip to Beijing for my doctoral research. He immediately e-mailed me to say that he was looking forward to my visit and that I must give a talk at the Institute for South Asian Studies at Beijing University to inform the Chinese about India's role in South Asia. He sent his official car to the airport to pick us up and welcomed us to stay at his residence in Beijing.

He informed me that he had already arranged the talk and that I would find a captive audience among the Chinese intellectuals. I also relished this opportunity and delivered a lecture titled "India, the 'Hub Power' in South Asia: Political and Security Implications for

Regional Countries." The topic attracted lots of faculty and students even from outside the institute. After the talk, I was invited to the faculty lounge, where, unlike at the institute, we struggled to talk with each other. I did not speak Chinese, and they did not speak English, so we communicated in broken Hindi that both sides understood; it was ridiculous as well as hilarious.

The ambassador was very helpful in arranging my interviews with the Chinese officials and also in tracking down former officials who had strongly backed Pakistan against India and Bangladesh during the latter's war of independence. In addition to these important interviews that I had with the help of interpreters, what was equally informative and really delightful were the lively evening chats the ambassador and I had about the role of the Awami League and of the leftist and rightist political parties during the war, about the relevance of competing ideologies to the future of the country, about the type of administrative structure that would suit Bangladeshis, about the personalities who etched permanent marks on the nation's psyche, and about the period 1970–75 in general.

It was also a golden opportunity for Nipa and me to see some of China's iconic sights. We visited the Great Wall of China, the Forbidden City, the Emperor's Summer Palace, the Tiananmen Square, and the Great Hall of the People, among other places. It was early August, and the Great Wall, which is said to be the only man-made structure visible from the moon, was covered by dense fog. As we walked up the Great Wall, we began to make out the outline of some animal on the outside of the wall, until we reached closer and was surprised to discover a two-humped camel. It was a delightful experience, not expecting to see a camel up on the Great Wall. But because of the fog, we were denied the spectacular view of China's expanse one purportedly gets from the Great Wall. The only disconsolate view was the billboards of western hotel chains at the entrance of the Great Wall that suggested they were coming. We also saw the entrance to a newly discovered archeological site outside Beijing, which had yielded thousands of artefacts and figurines of an ancient dynasty. Tourists were not allowed in because the site was under excavation. These archeological findings were later displayed in various cities around the world.

We went to some of Beijing's local markets curious to see what was being sold. As we walked down the street of one market, we noticed little boys often sitting down to pee without removing their shorts but without soiling their shorts either. The mystery was solved later at a clothes stall as we examined similar shorts. A little boy's shorts had slits where the zipper would normally be, and as the boy sat down, the slit opened up automatically, allowing his penis to protrude through the opening to pee without using his hands.

Another remarkable sight was the main thoroughfares of Beijing; they were packed with thousands of people on bicycles and hardly any car. I remember jumping on top of the front hood of our taxi to take a picture of the sea of bicycles on the street. All in all, it was a very memorable and fruitful trip to China.

We returned to Canberra via Bangkok and Hong Kong on August 30, 1985, after completing my research work. Before we landed in Sydney, however, an airline steward asked all the passengers to close our eyes and stop breathing for a minute as he sprayed the entire cabin with an antigerm spray. This was a new regulation that had to be observed by all incoming flights to prevent people from bringing germs into Australia. Most of the passengers hated it, and many of them joked loudly about how they suddenly felt all clean and germ-free!

I wrote a brief report on the research work I was able to complete, expressing satisfaction with my interviews and the collection of data, which pleased my supervisor and calmed the nerves of the department that had forked out several thousand dollars for it. My next task was threefold: write letters of thanks to my interviewees, transcribe my recorded interviews, and sort out the information I had collected and strategize its use per the relevant chapters of the thesis. Once that was completed, I would begin drafting my thesis. It also meant that there would be no more travel for me until I had completed my PhD.

In the Domestic Front

We were able to settle down to a normal, predictable routine at home and at work. We had a small circle of great friends whose company we enjoyed immensely. Among them were Nazrul Islam, Jainal Abedin, Zillur Rahman, Mukhlesur Rahman, Hashmat Ali, and Ali Hossain. We used to frequently visit Nazrul bhai and Yasmin bhabi's home in Wanniassa; Mumu used to call Yasmin bhabi "giji auntie." They were very affectionate toward us, and we felt right at home at their place. Nazrul bhai, who was a geologist by training, was a consultant to the BHP Group plc, an Anglo-Australian mining, metals, and petroleum giant headquartered in Melbourne. During one of his consultancies, he asked me to write an analysis of the political, economic, and environmental implications of coal extraction in northern Bangladesh, which had deposits of about 2,500 million tons of high-grade coal; I was happy to prepare the report for BHP. Nazrul bhai and I remain in touch to this day, and we talk infrequently over the phone. Although we are not in contact with the rest of our friends in Canberra, we keep them in our thoughts.

Our social commitments and engagements increased, and we regularly participated in community activities, which included picnicking in Canberra's beautiful parks throughout the year. During one picnic, our friend Mary Hossein's parents, who were visiting from Dhaka, joined us. Her father was holding a hamburger in his hand after taking a bite when suddenly an emu appeared from nowhere and reached over his shoulder and snatched away the burger from his hand; the poor gentleman was visibly shaken as was I. Locals told us that emus often became a nuisance during picnics.

Another remarkable sight was the mob of kangaroos; they were often seen hopping around and about. My teenaged brother-in-law Rana came to visit us in Australia, and I was able to coax him into sitting with a troop of kangaroos to snap a few pictures. He was brave and obliged me.

In the winter of 1985, we joined several of our friends, including Jainal bhai and bhabi, Mukhles bhai and bhabi, and Ali Hossain bhai and bhabi, and went to the ski mountain just outside Canberra to watch people ski while we had snowball fights. Once, we also went to a traveling carnival that had a humungous roller coaster that was more like a high-speed Tilt-A-Whirl. Our friend Sylvia, whose husband Shapan was a cypher clerk at the Bangladesh High Commission in Ottawa, took the roller coaster ride. When it was over, she was disoriented and wobbly. When Nipa asked her, "How was it?" she replied, "Nipa *apa*, it was so scary I think I recited Sura Yasin three times!"

We also organized or participated in cultural shows that promoted Bangladeshi food, attire, poems, dances, and songs. On one occasion, Nipa and I served as bride and groom and exchanged our marriage vows on stage to describe to the Australian public a Bangladeshi marriage. Special song and dance events were also held, usually led by Rebecca Sultana, elder sister of well-known Bangladeshi singer Abida Sultana. Rebecca's husband was a counsellor in the Bangladesh High Commission in Canberra under Ambassador General Quazi Golam Dastgir.

Once, a group of us rehearsed a chorus song led by Rebecca in one of the programs. When we started singing on stage, I started going off key, at which point Rebecca, who was at the harmonium, whispered with clenched teeth, "Shaukat bhai, apne chepe jan" (Stop singing), but I did not pick up the cue and continued in the chorus. After the song ended to everyone's relief, General Dastgir smiled at me and asked, "Since when did you consider yourself to be a singer?" It was pretty embarrassing to say the least, not only for me but also for the entire chorus group. I have never participated in solo or chorus events since then, and rightly so!

Frequently in the weekends, we had dinner at someone's house as is typical among the Bangladeshi diaspora. It is an occasion to unwind from the week's work, meet and greet friends and acquaintances, exchange gossip, relax, and partake of sumptuous dishes. Since these dinner get-togethers were all about eating, chitchatting, and gaining calories, I proposed that we stop serving polao in our *dawats* and substitute only plain rice instead. Everyone thought that it was a great idea, but when it came to implementing it, no one was willing to be the first one because of the fear that the dinner host might be deemed to be cheap. Even Nipa feared that. My great idea just went down the drain.

I then proposed that perhaps we should organize some community sports and proposed taking our families to play badminton on Wednesday nights and men playing soccer on Sunday afternoons. Everyone was enthusiastic about that as well and asked me to organize the weekly events. So I did. I arranged with a community college to use their auditorium for Wednesday night badminton, and some families brought their children to play; but, if I recall correctly, it fizzled out after a few months. I also sought and got permission from the municipality for the exclusive use of a field to play soccer every Sunday afternoon. There was a good turnout for soccer for a long time, and we thoroughly enjoyed the activity until one day, one of our friends sprained his ankle and had to go to the hospital. The reaction was contagious. Bhabi after bhabi felt that they could not afford to have their husbands break any bones and possibly get laid off work. That, too, ended after a few months, but weekend calorie build up and *adda* did not.

There were also religio-social events that we organized. At a *milad mahfil* in our good friend Jainal Abedin's house in the suburb of Gowrie, a Bangladeshi law student named Imtiaz, who had traveled to Canberra after having studied in Ottawa, saw himself as the spiritual guide to the rest of us and started to talk about our religion, which gradually became very contentious. He got angrier by the minute as the discussion progressed because no one was willing to take his word as the gospel truth. He was angry also because Prophet Mohammad's name was uttered twice without saying, "Peace be upon him."

I, too, questioned his interpretation of Islam, which infuriated him even further. Not able to contain his anger, he yelled at me, calling me a bastard. There was pin-drop silence in the room, for everyone was stunned by his remark. Then Jainal bhai said that, as the host, he will not tolerate such offensive language and demanded that Imtiaz must prove to everyone that I was in fact born of unmarried parents. If he cannot prove that, then he must apologize and beg my forgiveness, or else he will not be allowed to leave the house!

Other guests strongly supported the stand taken by the host, not only on its merit but also because they were aware that when Imtiaz's wife was in the hospital giving birth to their second child, the elder child was left in our care, and we had washed him, clothed him, and fed him like our own child. Therefore, for Imtiaz to forget what we had done for him and to call me bastard was downright despicable. It was a tense situation, but Imtiaz was too stubborn to apologize. Since it was getting late, after a little while, I got up and left. I heard later that Imtiaz had not apologized, and it was decided to let him go with the understanding that he would be excommunicated from the community. Shortly thereafter, Imtiaz and his family left Canberra.

Nipa started babysitting several kids who were generally of Mumu's age. Managing a whole bunch of kids running around the house; maintaining their eating, napping, and playing routine; and taking them out for a walk were quite a challenge but enjoyable as well. They were allowed to play in the front yard, which was spacious and enclosed. Then for several days, we started hearing this loud "izzzz" sound in the front yard. I went out to check and tracked the sound to the top of a tall tree, where I noticed a big ball of something black and spikey slowly grinding on itself. Not knowing what I was seeing, I called the university warden in charge of the maintenance of graduate student housing to check it out. They immediately came in their truck, and then after one look, they told me that these were big lumpy caterpillars that inhabited a particular species of trees, that the entire tree will have to be chopped down, and that we must remain well clear of the tree. The next day, a truck with special machinery and contraptions came to our house, very carefully netted the giant caterpillars, put them inside an incinerator, and then chopped down the tree. It was quite an adventure of sorts for all of us.

Babysitting taught us responsibility, organization, discipline, planning, patience, and perseverance. Dealing with parents in a foreign land taught us new cultural norms, courtesy, and interpersonal relationship. We also acquired new knowledge. Once, one of the boys Nipa babysat came down with a fever, and she called his parents before administering any medication. The boy's mother's advice was to take off his clothes, let him roam about in the front yard for fresh air, and give him tea without cream or sugar, just the liquor. She explained that they had lived in West Germany for a while and that's how they treated a fever over there. This was, of course, all new to us, because we were taught to keep someone with a fever resting in bed, occasionally sponging off his body and pouring cold water over his head to lower the body temperature, but, more importantly, tightly wrapping him up in clothes until he broke into a sweat and rid himself of the fever.

Nipa was also able to indulge her highly creative side by pursuing bonsai during her spare time. I loved her bonsai work and wished that she would never give that up, but she had to because of the strain it caused on her fingers and wrist. After I purchased the Mitsubishi hatchback, we started going to the malls as well. There were two main malls at the time: the largest one and at that time the second largest in the southern hemisphere was the Belconnen Mall at one end of Canberra; and the Woden Shopping Centre, which was a short distance from our home in Hughes. At the other end of Canberra was the smaller Erindale Shopping Center in Wanniassa. Whenever we went to the Belconnen Mall, we had to go past Prime Minister Robert Hawke's residence, and Mumu would inevitably point to the PM's residence and say, "Abbu, dekho, Haque nanar basha!" (Dad, see, Grandpa Haque's house!)

Canberra, which is the capital of Australia located in the ACT (Australian Capital Territory), lay between Sydney and Melbourne; it was chosen as a compromise between the two rival cities in 1913. It is a beautifully designed city, with government offices, diplomatic establishments, historical buildings, national monuments, museums, and parks. In the center of the city is Lake Burley Griffin, an artificial lake created in 1958 and named after the city's architect. Six islands lay at the lake's center, the largest being Aspen Island, which was home to the fifty-meter-high Carillon Tower with its fifty-five bronze bells, a gift from the British government on Canberra's fiftieth birthday in 1963. Along the shores of the lake were located some of the city's iconic structures including the National Gallery, the National Portrait Gallery, the National Library, and the National Museum. A short distance from the city center was the National Zoo and Aquarium. The National

177

Science and Technology Center, also known as the Questacon, which was established in 1986 but didn't open until 1988 after we left, was Japan's gift to Australia for the 1988 Bicentenary. The War Memorial, with its massive Byzantine-style monument commemorating Australia's fallen soldiers since 1888, had their names inscribed in bronze on the walls of its colonnades. We loved to visit these iconic structures whenever we had spare time.

Occasionally, we drove to Sydney during long weekends or on holidays. Once, we went to Sydney with our friends Aref and Nasreen, who were a recently married couple and frequently engaged in lovers' quarrel. Since they were of the same age as we, they were a great company and great fun. Aref's father was also quite an interesting person. Once, he told us that his skin tone and his face looked so much like the Australian aboriginals that when he went out at night, people used to be scared of him. They proudly showed us their new home, which was unlike any of the other new homes purchased by the Bangladeshis; it had a central atrium containing plants with all the rooms surrounding it.

During another trip to Sydney, we stayed with photographer Alan Khan, brother of Enayetullah Khan. When we drove up to his house in Sydney, I noticed a Mercedes car decked in flowers parked in the porch. I also saw his nameplate by the front door that read, "Alan Kahn." Once inside, I inquired about the flower-decked Mercedes and mentioned the misspelled nameplate. Alan explained that since he was a wedding photographer, he had to have a fully decorated wedding car ready at all times for his wedding pictures.

With regard to the misspelling of his last name in the nameplate, he explained that when he first came to Australia, nobody knew him, nor did he get any business. So one day, an associate advised him that he should change the spelling of his name from "Khan" to "Kahn"— Muslim to Jewish. He took the advice, and ever since then, he had been getting so much business that he didn't have time to sleep. It was a remarkable story.

Alan and his wife were gracious hosts. They gave up their bedroom for us even though we pleaded that their guest bedroom was more than adequate for us. He also took portrait pictures of us for free and took time off his busy schedule to give us a tour of Sydney's iconic sights, including the famous Opera House and the Taronga Zoo. Their hospitality was incredible, especially since we didn't know them at all. We also met his younger brother Badal, who was visiting him at the time; he showed me a specially designed commode seat for elderly people such as their mom, who was going to visit them soon.

Besides Sydney's famous tourist sights, the trips themselves were something to remember. On the way to Sydney, forty kilometers north of Canberra was twenty-five-kilometer-long and ten-kilometer-wide Lake George, whose waters often disappeared completely. As one drove by the side of the lake, the road dipped down and vanished into thick fog, and it was a scary and tense moment until the car was visible again after a few miles. I always used to be tense driving by Lake George and imagining all sorts of catastrophic scenarios. Closer to Sydney, the federal highway ran past the small town of Mittagong, which always reminded me of Bangladesh's main port city Chittagong.

But not all my trips in Australia were fun or enjoyable. My only trip to Brisbane on Australia's east coast was a sad one. A Bangladeshi friend of ours had recently married a white Australian girl, and they were visiting Brisbane. While walking in the beach, his newlywed wife decided to go for a quick swim. Within minutes, she got caught in an underwater swirl and screamed for help. The husband dived into the ocean to save his wife and was able to pull her up to safe water, but he himself got caught in the downward swirl. The more he struggled, the more he went down until he drowned. The coast guard was able to recover his body, and he was taken to the hospital, where some of his motor senses were deemed to be still active, but he went into a coma.

We learned of this tragedy at night, and several of us in Canberra decided to drive to Brisbane the same night, a journey of almost 1,200 kilometers north of Canberra and a driving distance of about thirteen hours. When we spoke with the attending physician at the hospital, he explained to us that it was a case of "dry drowning," where his desperate attempts to breathe caused a spasm of the vocal cords, which closed the air passage and suffocated him. It was "dry" because no water had entered his lungs. We stayed in Brisbane for some time to see the test results and assessments of the doctors, but the situation was judged to be hopeless. He remained in that vegetative state for several weeks without any encouraging signs; it was finally decided to end his life.

He was only in his early thirties. When they had come to visit us the first time as a just-married couple, I had asked his wife why so many Australian girls had opted to marry Bangladeshi men, and she had replied that Bangladeshi men were very reliable marriage partners and they made great husbands and dads! This was in contrast to the view held by many Australian women that many Australian men thought of themselves as being macho and treated women as chattels.

My doctoral work continued at a steady pace. I drafted the introduction and the political background chapters to lay down the appropriate context, which was quite easy. The next chapter on the proposed theoretical approach required much creative thinking, for it was the most vulnerable chapter of my thesis; but using my advisors as sounding boards helped to flesh it out. Life at home was also on a steady keel. Mumu was going to playschool. Our only concern were the magpies that sometimes pecked on her head as she walked home from school with her mom. I was also concerned that she wasn't drinking enough water. So I took her to the doctor and shared my concern with him. The doctor asked me what she drank at home, and then he said that since she did have regular intake of liquid, though not water, the problem was fussy me and not her! But it was rather difficult for us not to be fussy because she was our firstborn. During our spare time, we worked on our vegetable patch by our front window overlooking the yard. Mumu enjoyed gardening as well and would often say, "Abbu, let's go gidding!" (meaning digging).

Visiting a Seer

One evening, while visiting Aref and his parents in their home, his father told us about this Australian man who was able to predict a person's future. He didn't read tea leaves or palms but had the ability to tell one's future just by sitting close to him. Our host said that most of the predictions made about his family had come true. So in the summer of 1986, my wife and I decided to pay him a visit. Nipa was pregnant with our second child but was not showing yet. We called the seer to make an appointment.

Once at his place, we sat down in opposite sofas about two meters apart in his formal sitting room. There was courtesy talk for a few minutes, and then he became silent, hands on his knees, hunched forward, staring down at the floor. Then he said to Nipa that she was carrying a child and that it will be a boy. He then described this boy as "an ancient soul who has visited earth a few times before!" I had goose bumps hearing him say this. Looking at me, he said that I can expect largesse from an elderly man with a walking stick and that I would be leaving Australia's hot climate to live in a country with a much colder climate. All these came true. Our second child is a boy, and my father did resort to a walking stick later in his life and left me a share of the family's money when he died. And we left Australia to settle in Canada as well. As I recall that visit, I cannot help but be truly astonished at how accurate his predictions were.

Around the time our son Nayeem, nicknamed Mishu, was born, there were a half-dozen other Bengali ladies who had also given birth, but all of them were girls. So they congratulated me for being the only one to have a boy and asked me how I had managed it; I told them that it took a lot of trying on my part!

Mishu arrived on March 3, 1987, at Woden Valley Hospital, which later merged with the Royal Canberra Hospital in 1991 to become the Canberra Hospital. The hospital was only a few minutes' drive from our home, and so it was quite convenient to visit mother and son in their ward. Three-year-old Mumu was happy to hold her *bhaiya* (brother) while sitting on mom's bed. After our first visit to see mom and little brother, as we were walking to our car in the parking lot, I asked her, "So what did you think of your baby brother?" Mumu was quiet, and then she looked up and said, "Abbu, *bhaiya* has a little tail!" That was the first time she had seen a naked baby boy.

My PhD and After

I had completed the substantive part of my thesis when one day my supervisor Geoffrey Jukes and advisor James Piscatori called me to discuss the composition of the external board for my doctoral defense. The university required three reputed international scholars in the field to be the external members who would conduct the oral examination. Having read the draft of the completed thesis, both my professors were sufficiently impressed to suggest that the external readers of my thesis should be among the best in the field and decided that they should be Prof. Myron Weiner of MIT, Prof. Howard Wriggens of Columbia University, and Prof. Marcus Franda of Cornell University. I had no objection; actually, I was flattered to have such high-profile, internationally reputed scholars in my field as external examiners, though with some trepidation. The department set up telephone calls between the department chair and the three externals in the United States, and once their verbal consent was obtained, official letters were sent to them for their formal acceptance as members of the external examination committee.

The final draft of the thesis that I had submitted to the department was 405 pages long. My supervisor thought that it was a bit too long and asked me to reduce it to 350 pages or so. I learned later that financial consideration was also in play, for the fee for the external examiners was one dollar per page. I found it rather difficult to decide what to delete but finally managed to bring the thesis down to 337 pages by pushing some material into annexes.

The department sent the final draft to the three external examiners, with a specified period in which to send their comments and recommendations. The waiting period was tough. Although I was confident that I had presented a well-researched and well written thesis, I was nevertheless quite nervous and waited anxiously to hear from them.

That day finally arrived, and I was summoned to my supervisor's office. Once again, it was a smoke-filled, poorly lit room with Geoffrey Jukes holding a cigar between his fingers on his left hand and the reports from the three external examiners in his right hand. I sat on the chair facing him, and the anxiety of what might be in store was overwhelming; it was as if my life was hanging in the balance. It was deathly quiet for a few minutes as he flipped through the pages of the report, and then his face, devoid of any expression, slowly rose, and he said, "I have produced twenty-one PhDs so far, and you are my twenty-second. Only two of them had their doctoral defense waived, though in both cases some minor revisions of their theses were required. But in your case, all three readers have praised your work, asked for no revisions whatsoever, and unanimously agreed to waive the defense. Your thesis has been accepted *in toto* as submitted. Congratulations!"

I just sat there frozen, my body totally numb. I had hoped that I wouldn't have to do any substantive work on the thesis, but what I had just heard was to me unbelievable! Professor Jukes finally broke into a smile and said, "You have done good work, Shaukat. You should be proud of yourself. I am." I began to feel alive again. I thanked him, and as I got up to leave, he stood up as well and shook my hand. I walked out of the room with wobbly knees and headed toward Professor Piscatori's office to thank him, but he wasn't there.

I swung by the department secretary's office to see the chairman. He appeared gracious and, with an appreciative nod, said, "Job well done! What are your plans now?" I told him that I intended to return home and see what I can do for my young country. The secretary also congratulated me and told me to expect some letters from the registrar's office soon. I went home. I could see that my wife was standing by the window, equally anxious, and waiting for the news. I smiled as I walked in through the gate, and she knew then that I had earned my doctorate!

In the following days, I received several letters from the registrar, one containing "edited anonymous examiners' reports." Some excerpts from the reports by the external experts are highlighted below:

> I recommend that the candidate be unconditionally admitted to the degree of Doctor of Philosophy because this thesis is an original work of the highest contemporary international standards . . . The thesis

distinguishes Mr. Hassan as a thoughtful, balanced writer on strategic matters—the kind of person who is very much needed in Bangladesh these days.

Mr. Hassan's work is as thorough and as painstaking as one could expect in a PhD thesis—in fact, his work goes beyond the expectations of a thesis—and . . . because of this should become required reading for anyone seeking to understand contemporary Bangladesh politics.

This paper is a first rate study of Indo-Bangladesh relations during the critical period 1972–75 . . . The paper is carefully researched, well written and seeks to use the concept of "influence" rather than "power." In my view, the paper is of publishable quality . . . There are significant strengths to the research . . . [It is] well documented, argued and presented . . . many insights and observations are made which shed new perspectives . . . The study also goes far beyond the usual "diplomatic history" approach to explaining relationships . . . The dissertation is well written and presented in good form with exceptually [sic] few typographical errors.

Mr. Shaukat Hassan's thesis is both exceptionally well presented and researched. The central theme of the thesis is one of fundamental importance to anyone seeking to understand contemporary Bangladeshi foreign policy and is also more widely pertinent to any assessment of India's relationships with its immediate neighbors . . . Mr. Hassan's thesis has produced a good deal of new data from the extensive series of interviews he has been able to complete in the course of preparing the thesis as well as new insights into the fast changing early years of Bangladesh's history.

On October 9, 1987, the registrar sent me a letter stating, "You will be pleased to know that today the Council of the University approved that you be admitted to the degree of Doctor of Philosophy. I congratulate you very warmly on this achievement." We left Australia soon after, only to return alone to Canberra in April 1988 to attend the degree awarding ceremony. At the time, my mother was in the United States, and my father was in Dhaka but unable to accompany me to the convocation; it was a regret I lived with ever since.

On the way back, I stopped in Hong Kong and bought the latest Olympus OM2 SLR camera. When I reached home, I was excitedly showing my wife this latest gadget that I had purchased. She heard me out patiently, and then she asked me, "Can your camera take pictures of me that make me look thin?" I was totally deflated!

My wife was ready to settle in Australia, but I wanted to return to Bangladesh. On the way back, we stopped in Singapore to spend a few carefree days with my friend Dr. Ishtiaq Hossain, who was teaching at the Singapore National University (SNU) then but now teaches in the Department of Political Science at the International Islamic University of Malaysia. He had an MA in international affairs from Carleton University, Ottawa, and had started teaching at Jahangirnagar University, Bangladesh. In fact, if I recall correctly, Ishtiaq was SNU's first PhD from its Political Science Department, as well as the department's first doctorate to get a teaching position in the department.

He showed me his office in the department, from where we went to the SNU cafeteria where I met other Bangladeshi faculty and students. A few of them were surprised to see me returning to Bangladesh and asked me the same question: when so many people were trying to go to Australia and New Zealand to study and become citizens there, why was I heading in the wrong direction? I gave them the same reply: if I wanted to live in another country, I would have settled down in America a long time ago.

We also visited with Abdur Razzak bhai and bhabi, whom we had met the first time we had stayed with Ishtiaq on our way to Australia in 1984 and who lived in the same housing complex as Ishtiaq's. They were very nice and down-to-earth people. Little did we know then that many years later, we would be very good friends of his three sisters-in-law: Rakim Rahman, who now lives in Toronto; Nasrin Rizwanullah, who lives in New York; and Shirin Karim, who lives in Maryland. Rakim bhabi and Saeed bhai had lived in Ottawa for many years, and we used to visit each other frequently. Saeed bhai loved to discuss politics, especially Bangladeshi politics. We enjoy visiting each other whenever we can. They are excellent hosts. Razzak bhai had relocated to Australia to teach at the University of New South Wales; he is now retired and lives in Sydney.

We visited various touristic places, and the trip to Singapore's magnificent Wildlife Reserves was a real delight for Mumu. One day, on the road, Ishtiaq pointed out to me the special lane created for cars with more than one passenger to expedite traffic. He explained that drivers with no passengers frequently gamed the system by picking up street urchins waiting by the roadside by the entrance to those fast lanes and dropping them off when that lane ended. It was a win-win situation for the street kids, who earned some money for providing that service, and the driver, who was able to beat the traffic and fast-track to his destination without breaking any law. It was fascinating indeed how humans constantly looked for shortcuts and ways to beat the system. After a few days of unwinding, we returned to Dhaka in September 1987.

I became quite active as soon as I came to Dhaka. I became a fellow at the Bangladesh Institute of International and Strategic Studies (BIISS). Soon after my return, I received an invitation from the Graduate Institute of International Affairs in Geneva to author a monograph for them on the problems of internal stability in South Asia, which I did and which was published as PSIS Occasional Papers No. 1/1988 in June 1988. I started delivering occasional lectures at the Defence Services Command and Staff College in Mirpur, Dhaka. In August 1988, I was happy to get a letter from the University Microfilms International, Ann Arbor, Michigan, that my doctoral dissertation was published in July and that they had filed for U.S. Copyright as well as granted the Library of Congress "non-exclusive permission to reproduce and distribute copies of my dissertation solely for the use of the blind and handicapped."

I was also made a member of a special task force created by Pres. General Ershad to find a solution to the continuing low-intensity tribal insurgency in the Chittagong Hill Tracts (CHT). Our mandate was to reach out to the leadership of the Shanti Bahini who occasionally carried out sorties against Bangladesh from sanctuaries in India across the eastern border, and to draft the parameters and agenda of the talks to be held between the government and the insurgents. General Ershad approved the use of a helicopter for night visits to meet and talk with the insurgents. We completed our tasks and handed over the results of our work to the government-appointed negotiator who launched into formal negotiations with the insurgency leaders. This resulted in the passing of the District Council Act in 1989, which unfortunately was later rejected by the Parbatya Chattagram Jana Shanghati Samiti (PCJSS) representing the Shanti Bahini.

Joining Dhaka University

While that was going on, my friend Mohammad Shahiduzzaman, who was my colleague at BIISS from 1980 to 1982 and a teacher in the Department of International Relations (IR), Dhaka University, then, urged me to apply for an assistant professor's position that opened up in the department, which I did. One day, when I was visiting the department, he took me to the faculty lounge to introduce me to some senior university officials hoping to familiarize my face among the university faculties. He introduced me to Prof. Emajuddin Ahamed, who was then the pro-vice-chancellor. The very first question Mr. Ahamed asked me was, which group I belonged to: blue, white, or pink. I was stumped. Realizing that I had no clue what he was talking about, Mr. Ahamed turned to Shahiduzzaman and sarcastically remarked, "And you want him to be a teacher in your department?"

As we walked back to Shahid's office, he explained to me the political significance of those colors that divided university faculty into competing political panels: blue meant Awami League BAKSHAL supporter (Sheikh Mujib), white meant a Bangladesh Nationalist Party supporter (Gen. Ziaur Rahman), and pink meant a Jatiyo Party supporter (General Ershad). Not belonging to any of those colors, which was the case with me, was tantamount to being an untouchable because my political identity was unknown or unreliable.

The day of interview arrived, and I faced the interview board comprising Prof. Emajuddin Ahamed; Professor Saduddin, dean of social sciences; Prof. Sirajul Islam of the English Department; and Prof. Nurul Momen, chair of the IR Department. They asked to see original copies of my credentials and publications, which I had with me in my backpack, followed by a few cursory questions about my academic background and work experience. There were several other candidates waiting to be interviewed. Sometime later, I received a note from the registrar saying that my interview was successful—I had been selected as a department teacher—and that a formal letter of employment would follow.

After several weeks of waiting, I inquired at the registrar's office about the appointment letter and was told to see the vice-chancellor, Prof. Abdul Mannan. When I went to see him, he said to me, "Don't you see what's happening in the country? All hiring, firing, promotion, demotion, and transfers have been suspended. Just sit tight, you will hear from the university when you will hear." I had no choice but to wait. The country was indeed going through a difficult phase under General Ershad's military rule.

When I finally joined the department in October 1988, within one year, I ended up alienating important people both within the department and within the university's top-level administrative echelon. My first brush with reality was in a departmental meeting when I raised the issue of how primitive the IR Department's syllabus was. I pointed out courses in the undergraduate syllabus that were obsolete and had little relevance to the modern world. I argued that international relations was a dynamic subject, and what we taught today could quickly become less relevant tomorrow because of the dynamic nature of international politics, and therefore the syllabus needed to be urgently revised and kept regularly updated.

Realizing the validity of my argument, in a typical bureaucratic fashion, the department appointed a small Syllabus Revision Committee with me as the chair. The committee got to work right away, did its research and consultations, and submitted a revised syllabus for consideration by the whole department. After much acrimonious debate, it was finally adopted, but this Pyrrhic victory alienated many of the department teachers against me, because in light of the revised syllabus, they had to substantially upgrade their lectures, reading assignments, and their own knowledge, which had remained stagnant at the level of their graduate study days.

The second clash was when I awarded a score of 90 to a student in a class test. Almost everyone was in arms because I had violated the established scoring tradition. Getting 60 out of 100 placed a student in the first division, and a few points more got one "star marks" standing, but getting 90 was simply unheard of. The agitation against me grew.

The final straw was when I proposed that there should be student assessment of the course and course teacher at the end of each semester, a practice that was absent in Bangladeshi universities. Since such feedbacks were usual practice in western academic settings and helped to maintain the highest standards within a university, I felt the urgent need to implement it to restore Dhaka University's onetime image as the "Oxford of the East." However, everyone just about went berserk! Some departmental teachers complained to higher-ups in the university about my "crazy" idea. Professor Saduddin, the dean of the social sciences, summoned me to his office and asked me, "Do you seriously believe that students have the capacity to judge us teachers?" I was told to go back to the United States before I did serious damage to the university! But I fought on, and as a compromise, the IR Department agreed that such assessments may be tried out in the department as a pilot program, but the assessment can only be of the courses, not of the teachers who taught them. It was not a total victory, but at least the idea had been planted with the hope that other departments would follow suit.

Natural Disaster Hits Bangladesh

Lying entirely on the Brahmaputra-Ganges Delta with an average elevation of three meters above sea level, Bangladesh has a long history of catastrophic cyclones and floods, and when both strike at the same time, the devastation in lives, livelihoods, and of the natural environment becomes almost unbearable. In the nineteenth century, six destructive floods were recorded, while in the twentieth century, there were eighteen major ones, all with catastrophic consequences. And in this century alone, we have already had four major floods.

A couple of months before our return to Bangladesh from Australia in September 1987, a severe flood inundated 40 percent of the country and wreaked extensive damage to infrastructure, lives, and livelihoods. Within a year, Bangladesh had to contend with another terrible disaster, the floods of August and September 1988, which flooded 60 percent of the country within a space of three days, and the capital city of Dhaka remained severely affected for about twenty days.

The main road in the Dhaka suburb of Gulshan under two
feet of water during the September 1988 floods

The greater part of Dhaka was under water, including most of the Gulshan suburb, where my parents lived, although my parents' property was spared because it was at a slightly higher elevation; the flood waters had reached just below our front door. To see the extent of flooding in Gulshan, we hired a dinghy (a small wooden boat with oars) and roamed around a bit. When we got onto the main road, Gulshan Avenue, it was already a couple of feet under water, and by the time we reached the section of Gulshan 2 bordering the Banani cemetery, which was a depressed section of Gulshan, we could see most of the ground floors of buildings and cars on driveways totally submerged several feet below us. It was an incredible sight to behold.

Ten years later, the 1998 floods were even more devastating, flooding 75 percent of the country and half of Dhaka city. The raging rivers had burst their banks, rendering thirty million people homeless and causing over a thousand deaths. Many thousands of hectares of crops were destroyed, and thousands of livestock were lost. Dead animals floating down the rivers were a common sight, and the general contamination of water supplies and the environment triggered cholera and typhoid outbreaks. Hospitals were rendered dysfunctional, hundreds of factories came to a standstill, and communication within the country broke down, resulting in an estimated 20 percent decrease in economic production. The floods and cyclonic storms seemed to increase in frequency and ferocity with each passing year. This was the reality in which I grew up, but for our two kids, the floods of 1988 were, of course, a new experience.

Visits to Khomeini's Iran

Despite the difficulties I faced in the department, or depending on one's perspective, the difficulties I seemed to have inflicted on the International Relations Department, the years 1988 and 1989 were very busy years for me. Aside from my external engagements at BIISS, with army institutions in Mirpur and Mainamati and with the Shanti Bahini, I was engaged in full time teaching duties both at the graduate and undergraduate levels, including supervision of MA and MPhil thesis students. I also received multiple invitations to international conferences to present papers or participate in scholarly discussions.

Two of these conferences, both in Tehran, were most memorable. During the first trip in January 1989, the itinerary was Dhaka-Dubai-Tehran. As I stood at the Iranian Airways counter at Dhaka Airport, a female Iranian official noticed that a woman standing in the queue did not have her head covered. She immediately called out sternly, "Khanama, cover your hair." The woman, who was an Iranian visiting her in-laws in Dhaka, panicked and quickly wrapped up her head and shoulders, remembering that she was leaving secular Bangladesh to return to Khomeini land.

As I sat in the waiting area facing the Iran Airways counter, I noticed a number of Bangladeshis who were waiting for the same flight had baskets of bananas in front of them. I asked the passenger sitting next to me why he and others were carrying bananas to Iran. He smiled and explained that banana was a very favorite fruit to Iranians but in short supply, and so the best way to please Iranian in-laws, especially the mothers-in-law, was to gift them bananas from Bangladesh.

He went on to explain that he was a doctor, that the eight-year-long Iran-Iraq War (September 1980–August 1988) had decimated Iranian doctors, and Iran had asked Bangladesh and other Muslim countries to send them doctors, and that there were scores of Bangladeshi doctors working throughout Iran. Since the main casualty of war was the male population, there was also a shortage of males and an abundance of females of marriageable age. So many Iranian families, especially in towns and villages, were happy to find husbands among unmarried Bangladeshi doctors.

After we arrived in Tehran, we were put up at Hotel Intercontinental, renamed as Tehran Laleh International Hotel. The western names of all international hotels were changed after the Iranian revolution. All photos of the Shah had been removed, and all western images and advertisements on exterior walls of buildings were painted over. Some buildings were draped with black cloths from roof to ground level, and many buildings carried the huge photo of the supreme leader, Ayatollah Ruhollah Khomeini. Our hotel had multiple Khomeini photos on its walls.

Iranian female colleagues—academics, NGO heads, and media people—who came to visit us at the hotel had to be accompanied by male companions, had to meet us in the public lounge and not in our rooms and constantly looked over their shoulders as the religious police monitored everyone and everything round the clock. It was interesting to see that these female colleagues were covered head to toe in black *chador* (wraparound), but when they moved in their seats, one caught a glimpse of their fashionable outfits including short skirts inside their chador. It was hard for the educated urban women used to Parisian lifestyle during the Shah's reign to adhere to the government dictated drab dress code.

According to one Iranian colleague's anecdote, some girlfriends of hers were sunning by the pool, and two of them were playing tennis in their bikinis inside the house of a rich man in Tehran. Even though the property was surrounded by high walls, a religious police had noticed this through a crack in the wall and arrested them, flogged them, and the owner of the house was taken to jail. There was palpable tension in the air, and any kind of contact with foreign visitors was generally avoided.

The conference was on "The Future of Afghanistan." It was a conference to solicit support for the Iranian government from South Asian academics, opinion makers, retired senior government officials, media moguls, and other relevant experts during Iran's fierce rivalry with Pakistan to bring Afghanistan under its political influence. Only about forty specially selected South Asians were invited, including the most influential Afghan warlords, which included Ahmed Shah Massoud, Gulbuddin Hekmatyar, Ismael Khan, Burhanuddin Rabbani, Mohammad Fahim, Abdul Rashid Dostum, Jalaluddin Hakkani, and Karim Khalili.

During the conference, we listened to senior members of the Iranian power structure making commitments to the warlords to stand by Afghanistan in its struggles against foreign invaders and to extend all material and political help as needed. They also wished to make it clear to the assembled delegates that Iran considered Afghanistan to be within the Iranian sphere of influence, and foreign (meaning Pakistani) interference would not be tolerated. Their expectation was that the delegates would carry this message to their own countries and influence political opinions and shape foreign policies of their countries accordingly.

Owing to the small size of the gathering and the "confidential" nature of the conference, it was possible to interact closely with each other and especially with the warlords. I remember the contrast between hugging Hekmatyar, a ruthless and malevolent warlord, and hugging Rabbani, a rather docile university professor, both of whom had later become the prime ministers of Afghanistan. Dressed in his battle fatigues and towering over me, Hekmatyar felt like a giant of a man, with a shoe size double that of mine. His girth was such that I could not reach around him with my hands. Contrasting that, Rabbani in Afghan civilian clothes appeared to be a small-built man, and I could easily reach around him when we embraced.

The warlords, each of whom seemed to have a different agenda, had separate meetings with Iran's topmost political/religious leaders, which we were not privy to. Other than meeting with some key players of the region, the feeling I came away with was that the Afghan warlords seemed hardly amenable to compromise, reconciliation, and peace and that it would be extremely difficult to deal with them. They seemed to be jockeying for power and weighing Iran's offer against Pakistan's. The fact that the majority of them had their own armies who were ready to fight at a moment's notice did not auger well for Afghanistan's future.

After the conference, we were flown to Mashhad, an hour and a half away, which is a very multiethnic city in northeastern Iran with good road and rail connections with Herat, Afghanistan (4.5 hours' driving time). Mashhad, which means "city of martyrdom," is Iran's second-largest city and the holiest because of it being the burial place of Ali al-Rida, the eighth imam, who was considered to have been poisoned by his enemies; that made Ali al-Rida an important pilgrimage site. We visited other important sites, among which was the Ali al-Rida shrine complex, which is purportedly the largest mosque in the world and dominates Mashhad's municipal life. We also visited the mausoleum of Persia's famous poet

Ferdowsi, the author of *Shahnameh* (*Book of Kings*), just forty kilometers outside Mashhad. Mashhad is situated along the traditional Silk Road and continues to be an important commercial and trade center as well.

The itinerary of my return trip home was different, Tehran-Karachi-Dhaka. I had to stay overnight in Karachi. I took a cab from the airport to the hotel. As we entered the city, I heard gunfire coming from all directions. Seeing my worried face in the rearview mirror, the driver assured me that I "may be OK" if I kept my head down. He explained that low-level civil war had been going on within the city between the authorities and political groups for some time now, and that there had been occasions when he had to ply passengers while bullets were flying in all directions. Not reassured, I spent a fretful night in the hotel amid the continuous sound of gunfire and was immensely relieved when the plane took off from Karachi Airport the next morning.

The second invitation was from the Institute for Political and International Studies (IPIS), Tehran, to present a paper at the Conference on Persian Gulf Security in November 1989. It was an equally tense atmosphere after the death of Ayatollah Khomeini from a heart attack five months earlier. This conference had both overt and covert objectives: the Iranians wanted to signal to the world that they had significant interests and were the major player in the Persian Gulf waters. The unsaid objective was to remind the three hundred plus international delegates that they were the victims of American aggression. Many of the papers presented acknowledged Iran's legitimate role in the Persian Gulf security.

At the end of the conference, all the delegates were packed into an Iranian airbus and flown to the southern coastal port city of Bandar Abbas. From there, we were put on an Iranian naval vessel and taken to the spot on the Persian Gulf where the U.S. Navy's guided missile cruiser USS *Vincenne* had mistakenly fired a surface-to-air missile and downed Iran Air flight 655 on July 3, 1988, killing all 290 passengers and crew on board. The naval commander pointed to us the spot where the "great *shaitan*" had inflicted pain on innocent Iranians. We were then taken back to the port where the governor entertained us with fine food at his palatial residence on the beach. The ambience of the day and evening is still etched in my mind. We were then taken back to Tehran that night to catch our outgoing flights the next day.

Among the over three hundred delegates, most were from the western countries especially from Europe and the United States. Some among them were Jewish American professors who flinched at the naval commander's invectives against the West and Israel. A few, however, understood Iran's wrath and were willing to take a balanced perspective. One such delegate, Hans Kochler, a professor of philosophy at Innsbruck University, Austria, and the president of the International Progress Organization, took a philosophical view of the conference. He was pleased with my paper on "Soviet Role in the Persian Gulf" and offered to arrange a lecture for me at the University of Innsbruck, which I gladly accepted.

He left for Vienna immediately after the conference, but I stayed on for a couple of days to see Tehran and do some shopping. Instead of strolling through the *souk,* I hired a taxi from the hotel to take me to various shops, but the taxi driver understood very little English and spoke English even less. He uttered only fractured phrases such as "I stop benzene," and I understood what he meant only after he stopped at a gas station; benzene reminded me of my organic chemistry classes at Notre Dame College!

I wanted to shop for some baby clothes but couldn't make him understand, so I pointed to the clothes of a child walking by. He smiled and said, "Aah *kurta!*" I felt stupid because that's the word we use in our villages. I also wanted to buy a prayer mat and tried to explain to him through gestures of prayer, and he replied, "Jai namaz?" Again, I felt stupid because that's what we say in our language too! By the time I finished shopping, it dawned on me that there were indeed many Farsi and Turkish words in Bangla and that I should have just told the taxi driver the Bengali words and he would have probably understood me!

We stopped at a restaurant to eat, which was another learning experience for me. I ordered roast chicken and rice, which was served to me with a half orange on top of the rice. I watched the taxi driver squeeze the orange juice over the rice and then eat his meal. I emulated him; it tasted great. When we ordered tea, I watched him take several cubes of white sugar and place them under his tongue and then slowly sip his tea; that was new to me as well!

Meanwhile, during the two days I was in Tehran, Hans Kochler had arranged a lecture invitation and a visa for me to go to Austria. I left Tehran for Innsbruck, got the visa stamped on to my passport at the airport, and took the taxi to the hotel Hans had arranged for me. He invited me to dinner at a restaurant that evening. I met him at a rendezvous point in a beautiful park, from where we walked to the restaurant.

When we entered the restaurant, the maître d' looked at me and said politely, "Sorry, sir, our guests must wear coat and tie." I was wearing business casual, no tie. For a few seconds, the situation was awkward. Then the maître d' asked us to wait, and he left. Within a minute, he returned holding a nice flat leather box in his hands, and he held it in front of me. Hans stepped up and opened the box; there were three folded ties inside. Hans picked a light yellow tie to go with my blue striped shirt. The maître d' set the box on top of the reception counter and then proceeded to put the tie on me; after which he escorted us to our reserved table. The entire incident was handled professionally, and I was impressed.

It was a very posh restaurant. The Wiener schnitzel (veal coated in breadcrumbs and fried) I ordered was delicious. Dinner was quite expensive, but Hans picked up the tab. We had a wonderful evening, chatting away into closing hours. The next day, Hans picked me up and took me to my lecture at the university. Hans had informed me that the faculty there were more interested to learn about the latest developments in South Asia than about the Persian Gulf, so I made a last-minute switch and gave a talk on "SAARC and Its Role in South Asian Security."

Postdoctoral Fellowship at the IISS, London

The two Tehran conferences were at the beginning and end of 1989. In May 1989, I received a very pleasant surprise—a letter from the International Institute for Strategic Studies (IISS), London, considered to be one of the world's premier strategic studies think tanks. John Chipman, the director of IISS, wrote that the institute was awarded a handsome grant to explore new areas of global insecurity that would impact the international political order in the coming decades. He wrote that one urgent area identified by forward-looking thinkers was the need to address the relationship between environmental degradation and the security of states, and that it was suggested to him by people he consulted that I should be invited to research and write the Adelphi Paper on that topic. If I was interested, I should send the IISS a research proposal outlining how I would proceed to address the proposed topic.

I was speechless; getting a fellowship to IISS to author the institute's prestigious Adelphi Paper was a dream come true for any student of international relations, and I was no exception. I immediately replied that I would be honored to come to the IISS to author an Adelphi Paper. I proposed to write on "Environmental Issues and Security in South Asia" and sent them a research outline. A second letter in late June 1989 confirmed the acceptance of my research proposal and the offer of a research associateship for a year starting from January 1990, to be funded by a Ford Foundation grant. I acknowledged the offer the following week.

I applied for a study leave from Dhaka University, and the University Syndicate was kind enough to approve in October 1989 the postdoctoral fellowship leave from January to December of 1990. After requesting the chairman of the International Relations Department to arrange a substitute supervisor for my MPhil thesis student Rumana Samiruddin, my family and I left for London at the end of December 1989.

We stayed in Hotel Bonnington on Oxford Street the first few days as I searched for an appropriate place for my family. I contacted a real estate agent who turned out to be a Bangladeshi and was able to negotiate a nice upstairs flat at 3 Squirrel's Close, Woodside Park, North Finchley in northwest London for 600 pounds a month. It was quite spacious with two bedrooms, one living room, a separate kitchen and dining room, and a full bath. The kitchen was a special attraction for our two young children because the window was huge and opened out to a beautiful courtyard full of trees. One of the tree branches reached the kitchen window that allowed squirrels to regularly visit us for nuts and fruits. We would leave food for the squirrels on the windowsill and watch them come in to grab the food.

Every weekday, I took the subway train on the Northern Line from Woodside Park to Holborn underground station, from where I walked fifteen minutes to IISS at 23 Tavistock Street in Covent Garden. The Northern Line was the oldest tube (deep level) railway that went into operation in December 1890. It was perhaps the slowest of all the tube lines, but I enjoyed the daily commute after a hard day's work in Central London. I did tense up slightly, though, every time I used the Holborn station because the stairs from the ground level to the platform were steep and easily several stories down.

Nipa got busy as well. She started babysitting and regularly walked Mumu to her kindergarten and Mishu to playgroup; both of them enjoyed their new friends and their great teachers. Being Sylheti, Nipa had many relatives in London. We occasionally visited Rani *fupu,* whose husband Jalal *fupa* had transferred from Holland to the London Biman Office; and Hasnu *chacha* and Lipi *chachi,* both of whom were wonderful to us. Their only child, Hasib, was little and called me "duabhai" instead of "dulabhai" because his front teeth were missing; he has now grown up to be a fine doctor practicing in London. We were always amused when we visited Hasnu chacha because one room in his upstairs flat, located a few minutes' walk from the Chiswick Park underground station, was filled with newspapers God knows from how many years ago. He saved them, we were told, for his father, who lived in Dhaka! Another unusual thing about him was that he continued to have two eggs for breakfast every day his entire life, defying medical advice about cholesterol! He didn't talk much and projected an image of being cerebral. He now lives in a senior citizens' home, and chachi sadly has passed away.

Our other routine was to rent movies and watch them in the comfort of our home. Most of them, if I recall correctly, were kids' movies and cartoons. We also took the opportunity to go out and see London's tourist attractions such as its wax museum, Madame Tussauds, the Tower Bridge, Big Ben, the Westminster Abbey, and the London Zoo. We went browsing in the shops of Oxford Street, such as Selfridges, John Lewis, Debenhams, and Marks & Spencer. Nipa liked to visit Mothercare and Gap. Since we didn't have a car, our usual transport were the London Underground during off-peak hours and the slow red buses.

An exciting thing that happened in the November of that year was a meeting with a suitor vying for my beautiful sister-in-law Lopa Sharmin Kabir's hand. My in-laws in Bangladesh informed us that a young doctor named Rezwan Islam, nicknamed Rubel, would be coming to Dhaka from the United States to meet with them and that they had asked him to meet with us during his stopover in London. My in-laws wanted us to give them our impression of this young man before they met with him.

We were excited to hear this and eagerly waited to meet Rezwan. When he arrived in London, he called us, and we arranged a time for his visit. He came with a friend named Burhanuddin Khan, who spoke nonstop, and Rezwan had to stop him several times so that he could speak. The meeting went well. Rezwan turned out to be a very polite, soft-spoken person of measured words. We were impressed by his calm demeanor. My in-laws and my sister-in-law also liked him. Lopa and Rezwan were married within a few days after, on November 16, 1990, although their formal wedding reception was delayed until February 19, 1993, because Lopa did not have the proper papers yet to be with Rezwan in the United States. Rezwan's loquacious friend is now the owner of a pharmaceutical company in Bangladesh and I am told is doing quite well.

My work at the institute was progressing at a good pace. There were a dozen or so scholars in residence, and we regularly discussed and debated international politics and security issues over coffee. We were from multiple continents, and the perspectives were many and varied. Even though we came from different political leanings, we saw ourselves as a select group engaged in trying to make sense out of weighty issues and unfolding events. I felt that there was genuine respect for each other's work and a sense of camaraderie among us. Among our colleagues at IISS were some academic stalwarts like Prof. Samuel Huntington of Harvard, which made our intellectual exchanges quite exciting.

There were also mundane tasks that we shared. One task was for the first person arriving in the office to make the coffee that morning. One day, it was my turn. I cut a coffee packet with the scissors and poured it into the kettle of boiling water. When a German colleague poured himself a cup, he immediately spat it out, exclaiming, "Wer hat diese Scheisse gemacht?" (Who made this shit?) I was quite embarrassed and acknowledged that I was the culprit. He said, *"Mein freund,* I'll have to show you how to make good coffee." The only difference was that he put two packets of coffee instead of one, which made the coffee thicker, blacker, and bitter. I realized belatedly that unlike most North Americans, Europeans drank thick coffee.

While at the IISS, I was invited to several conferences and to write on important international issues. The first invitation was in February 1990 from the London-based Arab Research Center as a panelist at a discussion on the Euphrates water issue. My paper on the "International Rules on the Uses of the Waters of International Rivers" was subsequently published by the *Arab Researcher* in September 1990. I was also invited to the prestigious Wilton Park Conference, which is a global forum for strategic discussions under the aegis of the UK Foreign and Commonwealth Office. Located in Sussex, it was originally a prisoner of war camp and a reeducation center during WW II. In January 1946, it was inspired by Winston Churchill to play a leading role in promoting democracy in postwar Germany. Every year since then, it has invited strategic thinkers, foreign policy experts, and opinion makers to debate political, security, and strategic issues openly and calmly and find compromises for successful policy initiatives.

I was invited to Wilton Park to participate in a "Conference on South Asia: The Regional Balance in a Time of Shifting Superpower Relations and Rapid Economic Development" in March. In attendance were senior military and political figures, foreign policy experts, security experts, academics and media and business heads from, or dealing with, the South Asian region. The chair of the morning session was Gowher Rizvi, who was a fellow of Nuffield College at the time.

When it was my turn to speak, I took aim at the three Pakistani generals sitting in the front row, stating flatly that as long as Punjabi generals ran Pakistan, regional imbalance will continue because the emphasis of the generals will remain on how to bolster the military and on armaments procurement rather than on Pakistan's economic development. I argued that Pakistan had a history of Punjabi generals consistently sabotaging democratic rule, and that as long as the military dominated Pakistan, political decision-making would be conditioned by misguided threat perceptions, and instability in the region will continue to undermine the security of the region.

The generals were livid with anger for making them what they called the scapegoat. The heated exchange between them and me continued until Gowher bhai intervened to let others speak and restore some calm. Despite the many contentious issues that were discussed and many disagreements aired, the two-day conference ended on an amicable note and with some agreed recommendations to policy makers. On the afternoon of the departure, as the Pakistani generals got into their high commission's car, one smiled at me and complained, "Shaukat sahib, you have been quite unfair to Pakistan." After they left, while the Indian general looked amused, the Sri Lankan high commissioner in London teased me, "Did you guys make up?"

I was able to finish the paper I was working on, and after several critical reviews and revisions of various sections, it was published in the autumn of 1991 as Adelphi Paper No. 262 under the title "Environmental Issues and Security in South Asia." The field of environmental security was brand new, but the insidious effects of man's tampering with nature and the potentially dire consequences as a result were already palpable in many parts of the world, and concerned scholars were beginning to take note.

The IISS wanted to be at the forefront of this effort, and my paper that linked the effect of environmental degradation to the security of states was the first of its kind, but only the tip of the iceberg in this endeavor. After my paper got published, I started to get numerous phone queries from all over the world, such as The Hague, Tokyo, San Francisco, Vancouver, and Kuala Lumpur. I even got a call from a colonel from NATO Headquarters in Brussels who wanted to know if my research for the paper included looking at the impact of environmental deterioration on a country's military and its armament procurement; clearly, environmental threats and their potential for conflict were becoming a major concern among both political and military leaders.

Canada Beckons

So, in retrospect, it was not surprising that while I was working on the Adelphi Paper one morning in May 1990, I received an envelope with a handwritten note inside from the IISS secretary. It was from Bernard Wood, the CEO of the Canadian Institute for International Peace and Security (CIIPS), Ottawa. He had stopped by the institute to meet with the IISS director on his way to South Africa. He informed the director that CIIPS had launched an international scholar search to hire an environmental security expert to work within the ambit of the newly minted "New Challenges to Security" thematic research area at CIIPS. Both the IISS and CIIPS had understood that environmental degradation did indeed create a huge potential for interstate conflict and that it needed to be seriously looked at. Environmentalists, social scientists, and conflict experts were only now waking up to this threat but were still struggling against the powerful forces of globalization that saw environmental concerns as an obstacle to their objectives. My study for the IISS was the first of its kind that tried to understand this dynamic and its impact on state stability and security.

Bernard's note stated that he would be returning from South Africa in a few days, and during his stopover in London, he would be pleased to have a chat with me regarding my work at IISS and the new thematic topic his government had funded his institute to pursue. We met a few days later when he stopped in London; the meeting was short and friendly. He had already gotten background information on me from the IISS and had checked with experts who knew me. He told me that he was interested in my work, and if I were interested to continue my work on the nonmilitary aspects of security, I should send my credentials and references to CIIPS. In early June, CIIPS personnel officer Maria Catana acknowledged receipt of my documents. On June 27, Bernard sent a letter to the Canadian High Commission in London to support my application for a visa so that I can come to Ottawa for an interview.

I flew to Ottawa for the interview on July 9. The interview with the CEO and some senior members of CIIPS took place in its boardroom and lasted a couple of hours. This was followed by a separate but brief meeting with the CEO. He asked me, among other things, whether I would be willing to enroll at the institute's cost to learn French, one of the two language proficiencies required of federal employees. I confirmed that I was OK with that, since I did study French for two years at the Alliance Française de Dhaka. After the interview, I was given a tour of the institute and introduced to the research staff and the administration.

I left for the airport to return to London the same evening. The visits with the members of the institute, including its administrative personnel, immediately after the interview was a good sign indeed. A week later, Bernard called me in London over the phone with the offer of a fellowship. I was quite happy and, thinking that a job would be waiting for me in Canada after I finished the Adelphi Paper, readily accepted the offer. On August 1, 1990, I received the formal letter of employment as a research fellow for a renewable two-year term; the letter included work permit application forms.

Nipa was also happy that we were going to Canada, the first time for both of us; but little did we know at the time about the Canadian winter! After the first winter in Ottawa, we learned that Ottawa was the second-coldest capital in the world after Ulan Bator, capital of Mongolia. Nipa lamented that I did not opt to stay in warm Australia. I also wondered whether I had made the right decision to leave warm Australia and come to frigid Canada!

As before, I had to go to the Canadian High Commission in London to get visas for my family and me. A young consular official summoned me to his counter and started asking me questions in French. I told him that I didn't really know French that well. He was surprised, and then pointing to the application form where I had ticked off "bilingual," he said, "This is a false declaration then, *n'est-ce pas?*" I had to explain to him that bilingual meant having language skills in two languages, but those two languages did not necessarily have to be French and English; they could be any two languages. He paused and then realizing his mistake asked me no further questions. We got our visas.

We landed in Ottawa on January 2, 1991. CIIPS put us up at the Minto Suite Hotel, on the corner of Lyon and Slater Streets, and across from the CIIPS in downtown Ottawa. It was bitter cold, and we couldn't go out much because we did not have the appropriate winter jackets and boots. Within a few days, we met a Bangladeshi student, Imtiaz Ahmed, who was studying at Carleton University and who is now a professor in the International Relations Department of Dhaka University, who invited us to have dinner with him at his apartment. Since we didn't know our way around, he picked us from the hotel, and we took the bus to go to his place. On the way, I mentioned to him that we will need to buy winter jackets and boots, and he suggested that we should go to a Canadian Tire store for that. I asked him why I would go to a tire store to buy jackets and boots, and he explained to me that a Canadian Tire store was like a Walmart store and carried complete household needs.

Nipa also contacted her distant cousin Shams Sadeque, whom we called Khuki apa, who lived in Ottawa. She and her husband, Zulfiquer Sadeque, invited us to dinner at their place. Khuki apa was happy to see Nipa, and vice versa. Nipa reminisced with me later that when she was a young girl, at their first meeting, Khuki *apa* had bought Nipa a salwar kameez set. In subsequent years, we would come to appreciate Khuki *apa*'s excellent organizational and leadership skills; she was a very capable person, and if given the opportunity, there was hardly anything that she couldn't do. Zulfi bhai, a federal government employee, came across as a polite and refined gentleman, quite knowledgeable in varied subjects, and a self-described news and sports junkie. They picked us up from the hotel, and we had a wonderful time at their place that night. We got to meet their two kids, Yasir and Aliya. Yasir was slightly older than Mumu, and Aliya was in between Mumu and Mishu.

We were also invited to dinner by my CEO Bernard Wood at his home; he picked us up and dropped us off at the hotel. On the way back to the hotel, we were pleased to hear him compliment us by saying that our two kids were very polite and well behaved. I thanked him for his generous comment.

Other than attending office, I devoted most of my time to looking for a place to stay. I contacted some real estate agents and was able to find a brand-new three-bedroom house at 6824 Bilberry Drive in Orleans, a residential suburb at the eastern end of Ottawa dominated by French-speaking presence. We moved out of the hotel to our new rented place on January 15, 1991. Since it was unfurnished, we had to get used to sparse living for a few months. For the first few days, we took our meals sitting on the floor.

Our first Bangladeshi visitors were Fazlur Rahman and his wife Hasina Rahman, whom we referred to as 'bhai' and 'apa' as respectful salutations, in accordance with our cultural practice. They presented us with a six-piece glass set. Hasina *apa* was a family physician in England before coming to Canada, where she discontinued her medical practice. She remains a very kindhearted person and continues to look after newcomers to Ottawa. I regret that she discontinued her medical practice in Canada, for she would have been a very kind and caring family doctor. Being from the Comilla district, she addressed me as *deshi bhai,* and my wife Nipa as *deshi bou*. Her particular weakness was store sales. She was known to buy stuff even when she didn't need them simply because they were on sale. There was even a rumor that every bus driver in Orleans knew her as the lady with shopping bags.

In later years, she herself realized that she might have overdone it because there was no more space in her house to store her unopened stuff from the sales; even the stairs to the basement were packed on both sides. She told me one day that given my reputation as one who hates clutter and untidiness and keeps a very tidy house, she was seriously considering asking me to help her tidy up her place. But then she took a pause to think about the consequences and decided not to ask me for help because, in her own words, "Apne jodi amakeo bahirey feleden?" (In case you throw me out as well with the trash!)

Her engineer husband, Fazlur Rahman, also from Comilla, had completed his PhD in Canada and worked for Canada's Space Agency. He is retired now but continues to offer his services on contract to countries that purchase Canadian satellites; the certificates hanging on his walls in his home are a testament to his engineering brilliance.

Several months after we came to Canada and had rented the first house and furnished it adequately, Nipa invited the few people we were acquainted with by then to have dinner with us one Sunday. However, one Sunday earlier, we heard a knock on the front door and opened it to find Mustafa and Chhobi Chowdhury at the door. We welcomed them in, hiding our surprise. Not seeing any other guests in the house, within minutes, Chhobi bhabi realized that they had come to dinner on the wrong Sunday. They were extremely embarrassed and apologetic and started to get up to leave. But Nipa assured them that they were welcome and that we would love to have dinner together.

We had no extra money then to take them out to a nice restaurant. While I entertained them, Nipa went to the kitchen and in no time whipped up a delicious multicourse meal, which she served to our guests. Our guests and I were truly amazed at how swiftly Nipa was able to prepare and serve that delicious dinner. I was very proud of my wife indeed! We told our guests that they must come next Sunday as well and join the rest of our guests at dinner. They did but brought with them an expensive glass set as a gift.

Over the years, we became very good friends and still live very close to each other. Both of them are now retired but happily engaged in important social work in Bangladesh and in community work in Ottawa. Mustafa bhai, who likes to introduce himself as "Mostaaaafa," is a gregarious, smiling, laid-back person who delights in wearing very colorful shirts and *panjabis*. His one great attribute is that he is not easily offended. Chhobi bhabi now hosts a weekly TV program in Canada. Both of them are very charming, sociable, and energetic couple, as are their children, Saad and Seema, and their beautiful spouses.

With the cold wintry weather and the knee-high snow outside, it became extremely difficult to walk home from the grocery stores with both hands full with heavy grocery bags; the need to buy a car became urgent. A colleague at CIIPS, Robin Hay, informed me that his wife, Imogen, was looking for a buyer to sell her car. Since I had no saved money yet but had a stable job, I went to the CS-Coop Bank for a loan.

With no collateral to offer, the bank demanded an underwriter for the loan. I went to my CEO and asked him whether he would be willing to underwrite my loan. He refused, which saddened me. I then turned to Zulfi bhai, who signed the loan application. It was a huge relief to be able to purchase the sporty GM Pontiac. During our stay at Bilberry, my mother and sister-in-law came to visit us briefly.

After joining CIIPS, I wrote to Dhaka University for an extension of my study leave for another year. They reluctantly approved the extension but with the reprimand that I should not have accepted the second fellowship without consulting the university first and without getting its prior approval. The university was, of course, justified in issuing me the reprimand, for I had circumvented the university protocol for getting an extension.

At CIIPS, I was primarily responsible for exploring the social, economic, political, and security challenges that might arise from the misuse and abuse of the physical environment. As a new area of academic pursuit, it was quite promising and exciting at the same time. It not only opened up a new vista for exploration but also created opportunities for new multidisciplinary contacts across various types of institutions, which considerably expanded my reach and enriched my perspective.

In November 1991, my newly married sister-in-law joined her husband Rezwan Islam, who was an internal medicine resident at St. Barnabas Hospital in the Bronx, New York. They were staying at a rented apartment at 1819 Williamsbridge Road, Bronx. We drove to Bronx, New York, on November 24, 1991, to visit with them. I parked my car on the road in front of the apartment building. Rezwan came down to help us with our luggage. We took the luggage out of the boot, locked the car, and went upstairs to their apartment. We returned immediately to the car to take out the passports from the dashboard, but we found the front passenger-side door open and all our passports missing. I nearly freaked out because the passports contained our visas and work permits, without which we would not be able to return to Canada.

In desperation, we reported the theft to the Bronx police. As he filled out the missing report form, the police officer said that he was pretty sure he knew who might have stolen them. He said it was most likely the Italian passport mafia who were doing a roaring business in stealing people's passports, skillfully replacing the photo with a new photo and then selling them in a hungry market. He also said that the Bangladeshi passport was one of the easiest to doctor. That was of little consolation to me.

With a copy of the police report, I then went to the Bangladesh embassy in New York and explained to them what had happened. They were sympathetic, said that I wasn't the first one to have fallen victim to this kind of scam, took a photocopy of the police report, and assured me new passports the next day. On November 27, 1991, we were issued new Bangladeshi passports, which I submitted to the Canadian Consular Office explaining to them what had happened. The Canadian consular officials said that I needed to submit documents to verify my job in Ottawa.

Luckily for me, I had made two sets of photocopies of all my important documents, including my passport, visa, work permit, and my letter of appointment, and kept one set in my study at home and gave the other set to the CIIPS Personnel Office. I called CIIPS and requested them to FedEx the documents to the Canadian Consular Office in New York. Realizing the urgency of the situation, CIIPS faxed the documents on the basis of which we were issued new visas to travel. We returned to Canada on December 3, 1991, with a huge sigh of relief. The stories I had heard about the Bronx were distant to me until that trip when it suddenly became very personal to me.

Within a year and half of joining CIIPS, the think tank ran into political difficulty. CIIPS had released a study that looked at the potential impact of Quebec separating from the rest of Canada and concluded that Quebec would survive as an independent state if it did so. This was not the conclusion that the conservative government of Prime Minister Brian Mulroney was looking for. The prime minister was also under pressure from different conservative forces to reduce the size of government, especially the multitude of Crown corporations.

Crown corporations were state-owned enterprises under the sovereign of Canada—that is, the Crown, established by an act of parliament or a provincial legislature and operated at an arm's length from the government. CIIPS being a Crown corporation was one of several such institutions that went under the chopping block. Suddenly, one morning in early February 1992, we were summoned to the conference room and told that in one hour, the government would be submitting its budget to parliament and that CIIPS was left out of the budget, meaning that CIIPS would cease to exist.

It was like a thunderbolt because more than sixty of us would suddenly be without jobs. We were told that CIIPS was given until June of that year to wrap up and shut down, and that a consulting agency would be hired to give the staff psychological treatment if needed, as well as help them find alternative jobs. It was a traumatic turn of events for all of us, but particularly harsh on those who had just married and were starting a new life, as well as on those who had purchased a house or a car with a loan from the bank with their income from their job as the collateral. This announcement was followed up with a letter dated June 12, 1992, to me from the CEO that stated that "the Institute is being 'wound down' as the Bill to dissolve our organization moves quickly through Parliament," and that all employment at the institute was terminated as of today. The letter also stated that "the services of Bradford, Dunlop, Hushion Partners" were retained until March 31, 1993, to assist us during this transition.

Like my colleagues, I had a one-on-one meeting with a consultant from the partnership but found it to be of little use. Since my work permit was still valid, I contacted colleagues in my field with whom I had been working the past year to explore work opportunities with them. They were quite stunned themselves that CIIPS was dissolved and saw it as a politically convenient move to punish CIIPS for contradicting the government's assessment regarding the Quebec separatist move. They showed great sympathy toward me and promised to involve me in their academic endeavors. They also told me that I was an asset to Canada and urged me to apply for citizenship.

Although I was mentally prepared to return home, in light of this widespread show of support and encouragement, I decided to apply for citizenship. To bolster my chances, I decided to float a research outfit. I approached two colleagues from CIIPS, Robin Hay and Jean François Rioux, who were also wondering what to do. They agreed to join me in establishing the research outfit. Robin proposed that we name it Global Affairs Research Partners (GARP). We talked with a law firm that specialized in establishing private companies, who drew up a partnership agreement "to establish a business under the name of Global Affairs Research Partners (GARP), effective the 1st day of October, 1992 . . ." It further stated that "the partnership shall offer programmes and services of excellence in research and publication in the field of international peace and security and Canadian foreign policy to the federal, provincial and municipal governments and Crown corporations . . ." The work that ensued under the aegis of GARP was quite profitable for me.

Meanwhile, I consulted with Immigration Canada, located at 200 Catherine Street in downtown Ottawa, informing them of my desire to apply for immigration. They advised me that I will have to apply for immigration to Canada from outside the country. With that being the only option, we drove to New York in late April 1993 to submit our immigration application to the Canadian consulate there. Scarcely three months elapsed before we were called by the consulate for an interview.

In early July 1993, we drove back to New York for the interview. At the interview, the Canadian official, who had my file open in front of her and was sifting through my documents, told me that I did not fall into any of the official categories for immigration to Canada. However, having gone through my academic credentials, my rich work experience, and the impressive letters of reference from well-known Canadian academics and senior government officials, she had come to the conclusion that I would indeed be an asset to Canada. Therefore, she had decided to exercise her discretionary authority to create a new category for me, that of a political consultant!

I was truly flabbergasted by her decision. I did not imagine that an immigration official could have so much power, but I was mighty pleased that she had decided to use it in my favor. She handed me a list of doctors in Ottawa and asked me to get our medicals done expeditiously. Then she got up from her chair, grabbed her crutch, hopped a few steps toward us, extended her right hand, and with a smile said, "Congratulations! Welcome to Canada." We thanked her and inquired about the plaster cast on her right leg. She said that she had broken her leg at several places in a recent ski accident. She turned to Nipa and asked her what she was planning to do. Nipa replied, now that she was becoming a Canadian citizen, she would be happily exploring her options.

On July 11, 1993, we drove through Ogdensburg, New York, to enter Canada at Prescott, which is a border town about an hour's drive from Ottawa. At Prescott, we were required to fill out various forms, one of which was a declaration of all the assets we were bringing with us to Canada or planning to bring to Canada at a later date. The border officials also issued us our Record of Landing, which was equivalent to the U.S. Green Card. My Bangladeshi friends in Ottawa and I were equally surprised at the speed with which we were processed and given the immigration visas.

Once in Ottawa, we did our medicals right away. In the third year of our permanent residency, on February 20, 1996, we received a notice to appear before the citizenship judge for citizenship hearing. The meeting was more than an hour in the morning when the judge went through all the documents I had submitted in support of our citizenship application. She mentioned that our application was the most complete that she had ever seen because it contained documents from every category listed by the government. She explained that the government list was merely to suggest the types of documents that an applicant could submit and not that there has to be a document from each category.

In any case, she was pleased with the fullness of our application and confirmed that our application was in order, there was no more paperwork left to be done, and that the next step was to take the citizenship oath, which would be very soon. True to her word, a month later, on March 27, 1996, we were called to the Court of Canadian Citizenship, on Albert Street, downtown Ottawa, to take the oath. All four of us dressed up and went to the court, where we joined scores of other nationalities and swore allegiance to Canada; after which we were given our citizenship certificates. It was a happy and memorable day for all the participants, and an important chapter in all our lives had come to a satisfactory closure.

Global Consultancies

My private consulting work started in earnest and spanned three continents—Asia, Europe, and North America—and kept me very busy for the next few years; I had to travel a lot. These consultancies, which overlapped considerably, required me to be skillful in managing my commitments, effort, and time, and significantly broadened my academic contacts, intellectual reach, and work opportunities. Experts and institutions in related fields began to seek me out. Even while at CIIPS, I had been getting invitations and presenting papers in international conferences, seminars, and workshops. In April 1991, I was invited jointly by the UN Department for Disarmament Affairs, the Friedrich Ebert Foundation, and the Coolidge Center for Environmental Leadership to present a paper at the Seminar on Environmental Stress, Conflict, and National Security held at the UN Headquarters in New York. It was a wonderful experience for me to come face-to-face with international scholars in this field, and I remember getting goose bumps as we were shown the General Assembly Hall and the Security Council Hall.

From July 1991 to May 1992, I participated in the project on Environmental Change and Acute Conflict jointly pursued by the American Academy of Arts and Sciences (AAAS), Boston, and the Peace and Conflict Studies Program (PCSP), at the University of Toronto. From July 1992 to February 1994, I was with the Center for Global Change, University of Maryland, at College Park, working on their project on No Borders: Energy, Environment and Security Solutions in South Asia, where we explored the potential for cross-border energy resource sharing in an environmentally safe manner and its implication for interstate security. The idea was to use energy as the tool to build cooperation and collaboration between hitherto hostile states in the region. In August 1992, I became a member of the Experts Panel on Population Displacement, Migration, and Environmental Refugees at the International Summer Institute of the Center for Sustainable Regional Development (CSRD) at the University of Victoria in Whistler, British Columbia. It was a great opportunity to exchange views and ideas with a new generation of experts concerned with how environmental abuse was generating human refugees. I also worked with the CSRD on its second but related project on Environmental Issues, Population Displacement, and Conflict from August 1992 to June 1993.

Retired Bangladesh ambassador A. R. Shams-ud Doha had launched a weekly news magazine named *Dialogue* that was simultaneously published from Hong Kong, Dhaka, and London. He invited me to visit his Dialogue office in Kawran Bazar, Dhaka, where he asked me to write for his paper as a contributing editor. I was happy to do so and wrote op-ed pieces on the environment, water, military, and political and security issues during the years 1992 and 1993.

From June 1993 to December 1995, I was the team leader for the India study in the project on Environmental Scarcity, State Capacity, and Civil Violence jointly sponsored by the American Academy of Arts and Sciences (AAAS), Boston, and the Peace and Conflict Studies Program, U of Toronto. This was a particularly fascinating project comprising three comparative studies of China, Indonesia, and India that sought to understand how resource scarcities triggered conflict between the affected communities and the capacity of the states to manage violence. As the lead for the India study, I was responsible for two resource scarcity studies within India: the Cauvery water dispute between the states of Tamil Nadu and Karnataka, and the land dispute in the state of Bihar.

I found the water-related authorities in Karnataka much more receptive and forthcoming with their data than their counterparts in Tamil Nadu. Bangalore, the capital of Karnataka, was fast turning into a high-tech hub and India's premier IT center, and the people were bursting with optimism and excitement for the future. I also learned that most of the city's cab drivers were Muslim. My cab driver was quite helpful in advising me on good restaurants and shopping.

In contrast, the authorities in Tamil Nadu were suspicious and hesitant to share their water data. The Tamil Nadu print media was particularly hostile toward the Union government and suspicious of foreign interference. I spent the better part of one month, mostly in Tamil Nadu, coaxing and cross-checking the water data with various sources. I also found Madras (now called Chennai), the capital of Tamil Nadu, to be a rather staid city but rich in artistic and culinary traditions. I found the food to be quite spicy. One particular dish that seemed to be everyone's favorite was chili curry. Long red chilies were dried under the hot sun in the courtyard and then sliced lengthwise to get rid of the seeds inside and then stuffed with sea salt and fried in oil with onion and certain vegetables. This was one dish I passed up. I also went shopping for *sarees* for my wife. In the shopping arcades, saree shops were in multiple floors with the price ranging from the cheapest in the bottom floor to the most expensive in the topmost floor, with prices increasing in tandem with the floors in an ascending order.

While working in these two states, I took the opportunity to visit historic sites such as the Mysore Palace, which drew the largest number of tourists each year in India, except for the Taj Mahal, the exquisitely sculptured temples, museums, and the sandy beaches.

My research visit to Patna, the capital of Bihar and the second-largest city in eastern India after Kolkata, was quite enlightening. I found non-Biharis holding senior positions in the state whether in government, private sector, the NGO sector, or the media. Many of them were in fact Bengalis who had migrated from West Bengal to Bihar and grabbed senior portfolios by dint of their knowledge and administrative skills.

My first appointment in Bihar was with the chief minister of Bihar (CM), Lalu Prasad Yadav; it was at six o'clock in the morning. I was told that the chief minister likes to start his day very early and that I would be his first appointment. On the day of the appointment, I woke up at 5:00 a.m., got into the prearranged taxi, and arrived at the CM's office at 5:45 a.m., because this appointment that was made months earlier was very important and I didn't want to miss it. I sat in the guest room until 6:30 a.m. when I got the word that the CM was on his way.

When he finally arrived, he received me with a friendly embrace instead of a handshake and apologized for the delay. I went to interviewing him immediately, and he answered my questions forthrightly. He regretted that he had not been able to solve the prickly land issue facing Bihar but that his government was working hard at it. He seemed to imply that the Union government's interest in the matter created hurdles for him, for the Congress Party in New Delhi and his Janata Dal in Bihar did not see eye to eye on many of the issues and on the appropriate strategy to solve them.

After the meeting, he got up and embraced me again, saying, "You do know that you are *my* people." He went on to explain that *my* stood for Muslims and Yadavs, the only two groups that voted him to power. Traditionally in Bihar, the Muslims and the Yadavs, who were a nonelite peasant-pastoral caste, have been downtrodden groups. Yadavs, who were traditionally linked to cattle-raising, needed Muslim support to exercise political power. As the CM's secretary walked me to my taxi, he felt obliged to explain to me why the CM was late for our meeting. He explained that since the CM belonged to the Yadav caste, despite his position as the chief minister, he was obligated to milk his cows every morning with his own hands, and that's what caused the delay. Later on, I learned that the chief minister had a captive market for his milk; he made his entire cabinet buy milk from him!

My India research, however, was delayed by another month because of the bubonic and pneumonic plague that hit India from August to October 1994. After completing my research work and the first draft report, we had our final meeting at the Pink Palace in Jaipur, Rajasthan, approximately three hundred miles southwest from the capital city of New Delhi, where we discussed my findings. Built in 1799 from local red and pink sandstone, it had become a huge tourist attraction and a conference venue over the years. Its architecture is described as a fusion of Muslim Moghul and Hindu Rajput architectural styles. Its five-floor honeycombed exterior contained nearly a thousand windows with intricate latticework designed to allow the ladies of the palace to observe what was happening in the outside world in complete privacy. It was a pleasant place to unwind after my tedious research work in India.

When the three-country study (China, Indonesia, and India) was completed, the comparative analyses and the findings of the project made major contributions to the understanding of how competition for scarce resources can trigger violence and jeopardize intrastate and interstate security. The results of this endeavor were disseminated widely through publications in several scholarly journals, through presentations in conferences and workshops, and through the print as well as the electronic media. It led to policy-relevant recommendations for political leaders to work with both in the West and the East. Perhaps the best example of the study's influence and impact was U.S. vice president Al Gore's reference to this study and his making Thomas Homer-Dixon, who headed this project, as one of his advisors on environment.

It had a secondary benefit as well that had a much wider resonance, for it led to the development of multiple environment-security courses not only at the undergraduate but also at the graduate level in a number of western academic departments.

After this important work, both Thomas and I received many invitations to speak to audiences seriously concerned about the human impact on our environment. One such invitation came to me from Harvard; I gladly accepted it. My family and I drove down to Cambridge, Massachusetts, and were put up in a cute boutique hotel for the night. The next day, I left early to deliver my lecture. My family went down to have breakfast and soon felt nervous as professorial-looking fellows stared at them at the slightest noise coming from their cutlery use. When I returned, my family told me that they had to be very quiet while eating breakfast to maintain the pin-drop silence in the room. During this short trip, we also took a Boston Harbor cruise to watch whales and visited the magnificent New England Aquarium and the bar from the TV show *Cheers*.

Peace Mission to Sri Lanka: Corridors of Peace/Tranquility

For me, the most challenging yet potentially impactful project was launched by the Ottawa-based Center for Days of Peace (CDP) from

January to December 1994. In late 1991, delegates from conflict areas in fourteen countries, including five Sri Lankans, had attended an international conference in Canada on peace building for children. The conference was hosted by the CDP. The board members of CDP embraced the notion of conflict mitigation through humanitarian cease-fires.

This novel approach to conflict resolution posited the notion that humanitarian cease-fires could be an effective tool to bring about the cessation of conflict between warring parties, which could open up possibilities for dialogue and negotiation leading to peace. Humanitarian cease-fires would allow basic human needs, including medical services, for all parties to be addressed. It was a particularly attractive proposition in conflicts where children and the elderly were the casualties of war.

So several Sri Lankans contacted the Center for Days of Peace to explore the possibilities of humanitarian peace building in Sri Lanka, with the focus on children. The CDP responded to this inquiry positively, and through their working group in Sri Lanka, they identified a facilitator, Father Joseph Fernando, the bishop of Kandy, who had the moral standing and the willingness to reach out to both the Tamil Tigers and the Sinhalese government to facilitate cease-fires so that "corridors of peace" could be established for essential health deliveries including vaccination to children caught in the conflict.

After the idea of "corridors of peace" was accepted by both the warring parties, CDP hired our consulting firm (GARP) for this very difficult and potentially hazardous task. My partner Robin Hay and I took up the challenge of managing the Project on Humanitarian Cease-Fires: Peace Building for Children in Sri Lanka. Our target group was children, since thousands of Tamil and Sinhalese, but mostly Tamil children, were dying every year because of the long-running civil war in Sri Lanka.

Our initial tasks before leaving for Sri Lanka were threefold: (1) seek the clearance of the Department of Foreign Affairs of the government of Canada to implement our project in Sri Lanka; (2) consult with Health Canada for their advice and supply of syringes to carry out the vaccination efforts; and (3) consult with the World Health Organization (WHO) to procure the vaccines. CDP successfully accomplished these tasks; after which we were sent to Sri Lanka to liaise with Bishop Fernando, who had already held initial talks with the Sinhalese government, and with Thiruvenkadam Prabhakaran, the leader of the Liberation Tigers of Tamil Eelam (LTTE), who was fighting for an independent Tamil state in northern Sri Lanka.

In Colombo, our first task was to hold a small workshop to explain our mission, to explain our conceptual approach, and to learn firsthand about the realities obtaining on the ground in Sri Lanka. The workshop was organized by the working group for Days of Peace at the Watersmeet Convention Centre, Colombo, on January 22 and 23, 1994. I took the floor to explain our mission, while Robin spoke at length on the concept of humanitarian cease-fires with emphasis on the needs of children through which confidence building and peace building could be facilitated.

We explained what the "corridor of tranquility" was. It was an agreement between the warring parties to designate a piece of land—the corridor—that would serve as a neutral ground where the Sinhalese and the Tamils would enter unarmed with their children for medical checkup, treatment, and vaccinations during a specified period. The corridor could be at any place and at any time as agreed. It was similar to a medieval practice among some Christians of not warring with each other on Sundays because it was the day of rest. Our presentations were followed by detailed discussions on the security situation, the challenges we will face, the actors involved, the appropriate timing of our meetings with the various parties within a packed social, political, and religious calendar, and the modus operandi of our mission.

An ancillary activity of our mission was to convince the Muslim leadership, who represented roughly 9 percent of Sri Lanka's population but who had deliberately abstained from taking sides in the Sri Lankan conflict, to take an active role in the peaceful resolution of the decade-long conflict. The Muslims were under suspicion by both the warring factions because they had not proclaimed their allegiance to any side to the conflict, and our mission goal was to try to facilitate the participation of the Muslim community in the island's national interfaith committee to further the peace process through dialogue. We met with Muslim leaders in Colombo, Kandy, and Trincomalee to coax them into joining the dialogues, while asking the Catholic bishop to liaise with the Buddhist *sangha* to convince them to welcome the role of the Muslims; but we found the sangha resistant and the Muslim leadership hesitant.

The workshop in Colombo was followed by meetings with the relevant government officials to explain our mandate, to reiterate our commitment to offering medical relief to children in the war zones, and to solicit the support and help of the government. The most critical meeting was with officials from the Ministry of Defence to get the authorization to visit the northern and eastern provinces. On January 13, 1994, Brigadier P. K. B. Pereira, military liaison officer for the secretary of defense, issued Robin and me the authorization to travel north to the war zones, with the instruction to report to the brigade commanders of the districts we would be traveling through, and to meticulously stick to the approved itinerary. He also warned us that our journey north was perilous, telling us in no uncertain terms that we were traveling at our own risk when we go through the free-fire zone, where anything moving is fired at. Bishop Fernando also secured some traveling documents for us from the LTTE to travel through LTTE-controlled territories.

Before leaving Colombo, we consulted with the United Nations High Commissioner for Refugees (UNHCR) regarding the growing refugee problem in Sri Lanka caused by the unending conflict. We also consulted and requested help from the Geneva-based International Committee of the Red Cross (ICRC), who put us in touch with Nicholas, who headed the Red Cross office in Sri Lanka. Nicholas appeared to be quite frustrated with his work and was blunt, telling us that he has had tremendous difficulties transporting refugees through the territories of the warring parties. He spoke of the challenges his office faced transporting Tamil refugees through Sinhalese-held territories and of Sinhalese refugees through Tamil-held territories because of the suspicion that enemy combatants could be moving in disguise. Muslim refugees presented a problem of a different sort. They were harassed by both sides because they had refused to take sides in what they called an internecine Tamil-Sinhalese conflict.

Robin, I, and the interpreter piled into a Land Rover with the Canadian flag fluttering on the front bonnet and the red maple leaf painted on its roof. There was also a flashing red light on the roof to notify all combatants of our movement. Our defense ministry approved itinerary was Colombo-Anuradhapura-Kilinochchi-Vavuniya-Sigiriya-Trincomalee-Batticaloa-Colombo. Heading north from Colombo, we crossed Sinhalese military checkpoints uneventfully. At the last checkpoint in the Sinhalese-controlled territory, the officer in charge cautioned us about what lay ahead and wished us well.

We then entered the no-man's-land, and we traveled for a while until armed LTTE soldiers emerged from nowhere and stood at the center of the road armed with AK-47s, which were the weapon of choice in their guerrilla warfare. We stopped immediately and crossed our fingers as our hearts started beating faster. One of the soldiers stepped up to the driver and asked him in Tamil who we were and what we were doing there. Wishing not to agitate the AK-47-toting guerrilla in any way, our interpreter quickly handed over to him the travel authorization from the LTTE headquarters in Jaffna. He looked at it, but, apparently, he was illiterate. He passed it on to another soldier, who looked it over but thought it best to take it to their commander, while several soldiers stood all around the vehicle with guns pointing at us. Soon, a third soldier came to the vehicle, opened the document as if to read it, and then started to nod his head side to side. At that point, Robin murmured silently, "Oh, no, our goose is cooked!" But what Robin didn't know and I did was that sometimes Tamils wobbled their heads side to side to signify acknowledgement and not necessarily a no like the rest of us do. Robin was relieved to hear my explanation and desperately hoped that I was right.

The soldier asked Robin, me, and the interpreter to follow him. As we walked toward the interior, we could occasionally feel the butt of their guns on our backs pushing us to pick up the pace. As we came to their camp deep inside the woods, we could smell urine, and then we saw a vat on the far edge. The deputy brought us to the commander of his unit. As the commander examined our authorization paper, the deputy motioned to a soldier to take us to the vat. There, the soldier instructed us to pee into the vat. Robin, the interpreter, and I looked at each other, but with guns pointing at us, we realized that we had no choice but to unzip our pants and pee. The commander then motioned to his deputy to take us back to our vehicle.

As we were led back to our vehicle, I asked our interpreter to ask the soldier why they made us pee. The soldier explained that since they could not get foreign-manufactured mines, their engineers had built their own mines. But since the Sinhalese government had banned the transport of all essentials to the Tamil territories in the north, they did not have access to acid. They needed the human urine that was normally slightly acidic to fill up their batteries whose terminals were hooked up to the homemade mines by the roadside. This was their ingenious way of mining all paths leading north to Tamil-controlled territories to stop or slow down Sinhalese military advance northward. The soldier warned us that we must stay in the center of the road because they had planted mines by the road sides randomly to deter Sinhalese troop movements outside the roadways.

As we traveled further inland, sometimes the gravel road became dirt road, but everywhere one could see utter devastation. The tops of most trees were missing as if they were sheared off. Not a single building in rural towns was standing intact. Whatever little was still standing was heavily pockmarked. Sometimes it was hard to figure out whether we were going through Sinhalese-held territory or Tamil-held territory or through no-man's-land.

We went through many towns and villages that were devoid of any human presence. When we arrived in Vavuniya in the Northern Province, the town was eerily quiet, with much of its population having fled south or overseas. From there, we drove further north to Elephant Pass, which is on the isthmus connecting Jaffna Peninsula further north to the Sri Lankan mainland in the south. The Elephant Pass was of strategic importance because it controlled access to the Jaffna Peninsula. The Portuguese had noted this, and to control the passage of goods and people, they had built a military fort at Elephant Pass in 1760, which was reinforced by the Dutch in 1776. The LTTE had tried several times to seize control of the pass but failed. In the First Battle of Elephant Pass in 1991, the Tamil Tigers suffered heavy losses. The Sinhalese army was able to retain control of the Elephant Pass throughout the 1990s and had mounted several major offensives from there. Operation Yal Devi in September 1993 was the last Sinhalese offensive prior to our arrival. However, they suffered a major military defeat in April 2000 but was able to recapture the pass soon after.

The territory immediately north of the Elephant Pass was under LTTE control. Our goal was to link up with the LTTE leadership in the north, but the Sinhalese commander prevented us from crossing over to the Jaffna Peninsula because some sort of a military stabilization effort was going on north of the pass. We waited for a couple of days for the situation there to stabilize, but it did not. The Sinhalese military commander was unsure how long his ongoing operation would last. So since we were under time constraint, we drove southeast to Trincomalee, passing through many desolate towns and parched lands with sparse human habitation. There were times when we would be quite hungry, but there were no restaurants or shops to buy food. We stopped at a ramshackle home somewhere on the way to rest. The caretaker, who was an old emaciated man, felt obligated to feed us. It was simply pathetic to see him running after a scrawny chicken to catch it, cook it, and feed us. When we arrived in Trincomalee, there was a sense of relief because we were able to bathe, clean up, and eat a proper meal after many days on the road.

We got briefings from a church group and from a Muslim group that Bishop Fernando had been able to organize. We were apprised of the uncertainties and insecurities faced by the people of the Northern and Eastern Provinces, of the displacement of thousands of peoples, and of refugee camps. The Muslim group felt that their decision not to side with any of the warring factions had actually backfired, making them appear unpatriotic and unreliable in the eyes of their countrymen. Given that the Muslims were a tiny minority at the time, and the predicament they were in, they appeared to be more conducive than before to the idea of joining the interfaith peace talks that we alluded to. They expressed their willingness to participate in the peace dialogue, which is what we were hoping would come out of the "corridors of tranquility" exercise.

We also met with some Tamil members of the community, who informed us of the horrendous conditions under which the Tamils in the Jaffna Peninsula were surviving. We heard anecdotes after anecdotes of survival strategies enacted by the war-ravaged Tamils of the north. We learned that there was a long list of essential items that the Sinhalese government had banned from reaching the Jaffna Peninsula to force the Tamils to their knees. Petrol, kerosene, and other sources of energy were banned. Cooking oil and other essential food items were banned. All educational material was banned.

There was no electricity in homes, schools, and offices. Hospitals used hurricane lamps and torchlights as long as these were available. Despite many hardships, teenage Tamil students prepared for their O level and A level examinations by bunching together in footpaths under streetlights that randomly lit up only for a few hours at night when bombings usually stopped. It was a remarkable display of commitment to education even in conditions of conflict, which perhaps explains why Sri Lanka achieved the highest literacy rate among South Asian countries as far back as in 1895.

The Sinhalese air force regularly bombed and sank the boat loads of essentials that the Tamils from Tamil Nadu in India tried to send to their beleaguered compatriots in the peninsula. We were told that because of this complete encirclement of the peninsula, its residents didn't have adequate food to eat and clothing to wear. Tamil girls, for instance, used the two halves of coconut shell tied together as bras and palm fronds as skirts.

There had been so much bombing of the Jaffna Peninsula that Tamil kids were adept at figuring out the type of bombers bombing them from the sound of their engines, as well as the type of bombs from the sound of their explosions. Unlike kids who collected stamps, coins, marbles, cards, and comic books in other parts of the world, Tamil kids in the Jaffna Peninsula collected the manufacturer's metal tags from exploded shells. Every church in the Jaffna Peninsula had converted its basement into an underground bunker where people ran for shelter during bombing raids. Our informers also confirmed the high fatality rate among Tamil children in Jaffna. The stories we heard all night were endless, and they left us speechless and horrified. Our trip to Trincomalee ended with visits to some refugee camps around the city.

After we returned to Colombo, we met with our partners in the peace process to debrief them on our trip, as well as assess for ourselves how to move forward given what we had observed and learned from the trip. The working group agreed with the government and military officials that holding "corridors of tranquility," even if the LTTE agreed to them, was not feasible at the moment and would have to be postponed for a more opportune time. It was very disappointing for us and the CDP because we had taken the risks but had failed to complete the mission.

Following that decision, Robin left for Ottawa, but I stayed on to conduct several other tasks. One such task was to visit the refugees on the island of Mannar. ICRC's Nicholas was helpful. He facilitated my visit to the tiny 125-square kilometers island of Mannar, which was linked to mainland Sri Lanka by a thirty-kilometer causeway. Geological evidence had confirmed that there was ancient land connection between India and Sri Lanka. The existing chain of limestone shoals between Rameswaram Island, off the southeastern coast of the state of Tamil Nadu in India, and Mannar Island, off the northwestern coast of Sri Lanka, was locally known as the Adam's Bridge, or Rama's Setu in India. Written records in Hindu temples suggest that Adam's Bridge was above sea level until AD 1480 when a cyclone broke that link. India has been contemplating building a sea bridge and a tunnel to connect the two countries, but the cost was estimated to be around US$33 billion, although the real obstacle might continue to be the sour political relations between the two countries.

With the help of the International Committee of the Red Cross (ICRC)–Sri Lanka, I prepared a report on Sri Lanka's war refugees. They were primarily civilians and noncombatants caught in the cross fires, who had taken shelter in the outskirts of Trincomalee on the northeast coast, Batticaloa on the eastern coast, and on the island of Mannar, with some strewn throughout the mainland particularly in the south.

Meanwhile, our peace efforts in Sri Lanka soon became known to

225

others, particularly to the UNICEF. As soon as our work in Sri Lanka ended, I was invited by UNICEF–Bangkok to hold an exploratory workshop in Bangkok to promote the concept of humanitarian cease-fires for children in the conflict zones of southern Asia stretching from Afghanistan to the Philippines. The Centre for Days of Peace was excited at the prospect of the dissemination of their Sri Lanka work and approved my trip to Thailand. I flew from Colombo to Bangkok, where I conducted the one-day workshop that was attended by over fifty NGOs and CSOs who were brought together by UNICEF for this purpose.

The group known as the Friends of Burma in Canada and the Burmese leaders in exile, especially in the Scandinavian countries, also learned of our peace efforts. While I was conducting the workshop in Bangkok, I received a request from the Burmese diaspora for a meeting with the Burmese Karen National Liberation Force (KNLF) to discuss the possibility of providing inoculation to their children who were victims of the conflict between them and the Burmese government known then as the State Law and Order Restoration Committee (SLORC).

I informed them that while I had clearance from Foreign Affairs Canada for my work in Sri Lanka and Thailand, I did not have permission to cross the border into Burma. The following day, the diaspora leadership informed me that they had contacted the KNLF leaders in the Karen state, who agreed to cross the border and meet me at a designated warehouse on the Thai side of the border. The UNICEF–Bangkok, however, expressed their inability to assist me to link up with the Burmese rebels because of political reasons.

Fortunately for us, the Mennonite Mission working in western Thailand who had attended the workshop came forward with the offer of organizing the meeting with the rebel group and of providing lunch and also a jeep for me to travel to the border. The meeting with the Karen rebels was held inside a run-down warehouse in an unused aerodrome by the Thai-Burmese border, where I explained the concept of humanitarian cease-fires for children, and advised them on whom to contact and how to organize it.

In hindsight, the only success of these two meetings in Thailand was the wide dissemination among the NGOs of the notion that children suffering in war zones can be an effective conflict resolution tool if done properly. In both these cases and in Sri Lanka as well, this tool remained unimplemented because of the failure of diplomacy to make the warring parties agree to humanitarian cease-fires in the case of Burma, and the wrong timing in the case of Sri Lanka. My work on conflict inducing issues continued unabated.

From January 1994 to December 1995, I was a member of the experts panel for the project on Development and Security in Southeast Asia jointly pursued by the Institute for Strategic and Development Studies, University of the Philippines, Quezon City, and the Centre for International and Strategic Studies, York University, Toronto. I had to go to the Philippines twice during the duration of this project. We got introduced to the NGO community of the Philippines, and the postconference evening suppers on the beach were particularly memorable.

However, February 1994 was a particularly busy month for me when I presented a paper on *The Environmental Dimensions of Armed Conflict* at the International Consortium for the Study of Environmental Security in Montreal, and another paper on the *Major Issues Impacting on Sustainable Development in South Asia* at the Asia Branch of the Canadian International Development Agency (CIDA). In June 1995, I presented a paper on *Confidence Building and Conflict Reduction* at the Ninth Asia Pacific Roundtable, ASEAN-ISIS in Kuala Lumpur, Malaysia.

Friends of the United Nations

The year 1995 was also the fiftieth anniversary of the founding of the United Nations. The international citizens group based in New York called the Friends of the United Nations dedicated to promoting the objectives of the UN Charter had decided two years earlier to celebrate the fiftieth anniversary of the UN by recognizing fifty communities or individuals worldwide who had made significant contributions to promoting the ideals and goals of the United Nations. The Friends of the United Nations commissioned an international panel of advisers comprising "a Who's Who of international diplomacy, academia and media (including CNN founder Ted Turner)" to select fifty model communities and individuals who had demonstrable achievements in realizing the objectives of the UN in various fields. The cochairs of this elite international panel were Dame Nita Barrow, governor-general of Barbados; and Pierre Marc Johnson, former premier of Quebec, with Nola Kate Seymoar as the coordinator. I was invited to be a member of this august panel of advisers.

Invitations were sent out to individuals, nongovernmental organizations, voluntary associations, citizens' movements, federations, networks, coalitions, spiritual/cultural communities, cooperatives, associations, unions, and professionals throughout the world to nominate individuals or communities for their exemplary work in advancing the UN's mandate. Among the four criteria for nomination, the principal one was a clear "demonstration of a successful model that advances the goals and vision of the UN." Communities nominated were required to "demonstrate concrete positive accomplishments reflecting citizens' participation" within ten broad categories:

1. peace and security
2. environment and sustainable development
3. economic and social development
4. human rights
5. human settlements
6. education and health
7. women and children
8. cultural development
9. food, agriculture, fisheries, and forests
10. humanitarian activities

The initial nomination phases of the program were sponsored by the United Nations Environment Programme (UNEP), the United Nations Human Settlement Programme (UNHSP), and the United Nations Development Programme (UNDP). Support for later phases came from the Sasakawa Peace Foundation, the International Institute for Sustainable Development (IISD), and other private donors.

The worldwide response was quite impressive as the Friends of the United Nations considered 360 communities during a two-year search. After a grueling exercise of research, fact-checking, and vetting, fifty of the world's most extraordinary grassroots communities—many of which had overcome adversity or conflict—from thirty-two countries were short-listed and handed over to a selection committee comprising some members of the international advisory panel. The job of the selection committee, of which I was a member, was to further vet these submissions and approve the list for recognition and award. Each of these communities demonstrated "positive, practical solutions to difficult problems, such as peace building, conflict resolution, environmental protection, sustainable development, reduction of poverty and illiteracy, food security, positive multicultural relations, protection of human rights and advancement of the rights of women, children and indigenous peoples."

The original plan was to invite the selected fifty communities to come to the United Nations to present their achievements and share with each other their experiences and lessons learned, with the hope to cross-fertilize ideas and incentivize other community endeavors. But the program ran into difficulty when a political controversy was triggered by the inclusion of four communities from the People's Republic of China and especially the Tibetan community at Dharamsala, India. The Chinese government strongly objected to the inclusion of the Tibetan community. The board of the Friends of the United Nations and the selection committee reviewed the issue and overwhelmingly decided to confirm the inclusion of the Tibetans "as an exemplary community meeting the criteria for the Awards." However, because of the Chinese objection, the UN secretariat felt the need to back out from holding the ceremony on site at the UN.

Despite this setback, forty-three of the fifty communities were able to participate in the Study Conference in New York on September 22– 24, where they were divided up into several working groups to present their life's work on behalf of the UN's goals. I was invited to chair the working group on Food, Agriculture, Fisheries and Forests. The awards ceremony and luncheon were held at the Cathedral of Saint John the Divine in New York on September 24, 1995. The stories of these fifty communities and the synthesis of their lessons were compiled under three categories—common security, common development, common rights and responsibilities—and published under the title *Creating Common Unity* by Weigl Educational Publishers Ltd. in December 1997.

It was an incredibly difficult task to choose only fifty out of the 360 very deserving nominations, because the great majority of them had significantly improved the lives of millions of people in multiple spheres of human activity all over the world. Writing the letters to those who were not among the selected fifty despite their excellent work was equally difficult. The whole experience was very informative and rewarding to me.

IDRC's Foray into Development, Environment, and Security Studies in South Asia

From April 1995 to June 1997, I was also the lead consultant for the project on Sustainable Development, Environmental Security, and Disarmament Interface in South Asia by the International Development Research Center (IDRC), Ottawa. It was a huge multinational, multidisciplinary project, and my responsibilities were to select, induct, and manage scholars and experts from multiple disciplines (environment, anthropology, political science, international relations, conflict studies, and security studies) from six SAARC countries (Bangladesh, India, Maldives, Nepal, Pakistan, and Sri Lanka); to conduct four workshops in Colombo, New Delhi, Kathmandu, and Goa; to edit the proceedings of the workshops; and to write the conceptual approach chapter and the project overview chapter of the final product, which was a book under the title *Sustainable Development, Environmental Security, Disarmament and Development Interface in South Asia,* which was published by Macmillan India Ltd., New Delhi, in 1997, with the help of a Ford Foundation grant.

However, the project fell short of what was originally hoped for. The conceptual framework linking the three distinct themes—sustainable development, environmental security, and disarmament—in a manner that would be useful to the research exercise became a tough intellectual challenge. Although two consultants were asked separately to produce the conceptual framework for the project, at the methodology workshop in New Delhi, one was rejected outright for failing to establish any kind of thematic link.

The second conceptual framework that was authored by me was considered to have a western bias and not sufficiently reflective of regional political and cultural realities. I was asked to incorporate the suggestions of the workshop participants and resubmit a revised framework. Although that was done, most of the thirteen papers on the thirteen topics finalized at the methodology workshop failed to fully adhere to the revised framework.

There were other serious issues as well. The papers failed to project a regional perspective as was unanimously agreed to, to distance the project from narrow nationalistic interpretations. The participants in the workshops felt that their perspectives and interpretations were not given sufficient importance, which led to a national versus regional tug-of-war. Some of the participants, such as Nepal and the Maldives, believed that since the project was being handled by the IDRC office in New Delhi and not by the IDRC head office in Ottawa, its activities were tinged with Indo-centrism, and therefore India's smaller neighbors would get the raw end of the deal.

The fact that the project coordinator was an Indian professor based in New Delhi did not help to ameliorate their misperceptions. Even the project steering committee was seen to be heavily weighted in favor of India. The dominance of Indian "guidance" of the project was especially evident toward the end of the project when a number of decisions were made without prior consultation with the authors of the research papers. This resulted in a written complaint by the Nepali contingent (with alleged support from the Bangladeshi and Pakistani contingents) to IDRC, New Delhi, and the Ford Foundation, New Delhi.

The last workshop was in Goa, which is situated on the southwestern coast of India facing the Arabian Sea. It is the smallest Indian state but with the highest GDP per capita. The Portuguese merchants who landed there in the early sixteenth century conquered the city, and for the next 450 years, it remained a Portuguese overseas territory until it was annexed by India in 1961 in a fit of nationalistic rage. The admixture of Portuguese and Indian traditions, culture, and cuisine; the rich flora and fauna; the white sandy beaches; the river cruises; and its famous night life made Goa an enchanting place to visit.

Since the workshop occupied the better part of the day, workshop participants reveled in the Goan night that was livened up with bright lights, excellent pubs, discotheques, music, dancing on the beach, and delicious food. Those of us who were scheduled to fly out of Goa the next morning really regretted having to leave so soon.

Overall, the project was a hugely challenging task for me. I was primarily responsible to bring together experts from the subcontinent who did not usually see eye to eye on critical issues and usually towed their government's line tried to make them put the regional interest over country interest first, to convince them to leave behind their suspicions and hostilities and debate the issues calmly and in a scholarly fashion, and to reach consensus that benefited all. I tried hard to mitigate their political and cultural sensitivities to ensure that the project will be able to draw on their experiences and expertise to attain its goals without alienating anyone.

I also got to meet and make friends with multidisciplinary colleagues from the countries of South Asia. These new relationships with different scholarly communities in South Asia not only broadened my own intellectual horizon and provided me with a much larger network of thinkers and doers but also raised my stature as an up-and-coming Bangladeshi scholar in a field where the Indians dominated and usually had the final say.

After the completion of the last workshop in Goa, we summarized the findings from the four workshops and then drew up a set of recommendations for each country's political leaders to act on. We also held press conferences to disseminate our findings. It was a very exciting work indeed!

Visit to Palestine

I visited Palestine three times. My first visit to Palestine was in the beginning of March 1996. I had formally joined North South University two months earlier in January 1996, and so I had to take special unpaid leave in March to complete an IDRC project in Palestine that I had signed up for earlier. It was a very important project for the Palestinian people, which was to assist the Palestinian authorities with the preparation of negotiation documents. One of the terrible things that Israel had done after it occupied Palestinian territories of West Bank and the Gaza Strip in the Six-Day War of 1967 was to seize all historical documents including treaties and maps that would have allowed the Palestinians to negotiate with the Israelis from a position of strength and authority. But Israel deliberately destroyed or seized those documents to deny documentary evidence and to weaken Palestine's negotiating position.

IDRC received this special request from several Palestinian agencies to help them reclaim and reestablish historical evidence to strengthen their case against Israel in the courts. I was sent to Palestine by the IDRC to assess the situation as well as the type of help Canada could provide to strengthen Palestine's documentary evidence.

Another colleague from IDRC but with a different remit and I flew from Ottawa to Cairo, and a third colleague, who was a female from our Cairo Office, joined us for our flight from Cairo to Tel Aviv. Each of us was pursuing separate projects, but we had to familiarize ourselves with each other's projects to pass Israeli interrogation. We were intensively briefed by our Cairo office in terms of what to expect. We were required to carry with us hard copies of the list of people and institutions we would be visiting in Palestine with their full contact details, and hard copies of our travel itinerary and hotel bookings.

We were also briefed on Israel's sensitivities and the do's and don'ts. We had to fly Israel's El Al Airlines. The security was beyond belief. The body check was thorough, as was our luggage. I remember my camera and pen being dismantled and reassembled by Israeli security officers at

Cairo airport. We were also asked by Israeli security at the boarding gate in Cairo the purpose of our visit and a whole bunch of other questions.

Once in flight, I saw fully armed Israeli security personnel, one stationed near the entrance to the cockpit and another standing in the rear by the toilets, during the entire one-hour flight. After landing in Tel Aviv, we walked across the heavily guarded tarmac into the Immigration and Passport Control Hall. When it was my turn, I handed my passport to the Passport Control officer. The Israeli official looked at my Bangladeshi passport (I was not a Canadian citizen yet) and smiled as he pointed out that it was not valid for travel to Israel.

Printed on the top of page 6 of my passport was "Countries for which this Passport is Valid" and below that was stamped "All Countries of the World except Israel." I told him that I was not there to visit Israel but to transit through Israel to Palestine. He nodded his head to signify that he understood my point. He then told me that he would stamp the entry visa on a separate piece of paper and place it inside the passport, and that I should make sure that I did not lose it or take it out of the passport, failing which I would get into a lot of trouble.

The next thing that happened was a young Israeli soldier with a mini Uzi submachine gun across his shoulder asked me to follow him inside. We went behind the passport booths to a circular space with several rooms encircling the covered space. We waited there for a few minutes until my other two colleagues were brought there by two other young soldiers. Then the three young soldiers were replaced by three older security officials with no guns, each taking one of us into a separate room.

The rooms were sparse, with no furniture except for a small rectangular table in the center. The security officer had my passport in his hands. We stood on opposite sides of the table, and he asked me to empty my small carrying case on the table. He quickly rummaged through them with one finger and then returned to my passport and started the interrogation.

As he flipped through the passport pages, he asked me questions to verify my answers against the contents of my passport: what was my name, my parents' names, the place my passport was issued, places I had visited before coming to Israel and why, etc. He then asked me who my other two colleagues were, since we had already declared ourselves as a team from IDRC. Then he left the room, shutting the door behind him. Minutes later, he returned and asked me what each of us was supposed to do during our visit. He then left the room and returned a few minutes later. Then he asked me who I would be meeting while in Palestine and what was the purpose of my meetings. I had already given him the hard copies that explained all that. He left the room again and returned after a short while. We learned later that each time the security officers left us, they met outside our doors to cross-check our answers to see if there was any kind of discrepancy in our answers. This type of interrogation lasted about an hour; after which we were escorted out of the building and put into three separate Israeli taxis; our luggage were already inside the taxis.

Our IDRC security briefing in Cairo had cautioned us that the taxis we would be put into would be driven by Mossad agents, and therefore we should avoid conversation with them as much as possible and that we should be alert not to contradict what we had told the interrogating officers. As we drove toward the Israeli-Palestinian border, the driver was all smiles and courteous and asked me what I thought of the Israeli people, when was the last time I visited Israel, would I like to come back again, did I have any friends in Palestine, etc.

I reciprocated by delivering polite, monosyllabic answers. At the border checkpoint, the Israeli security official once again checked my passport before allowing me to cross over to the Palestinian side. The Palestinian driver was also friendly and asked me whether I was OK and where I was from. He knew from experience that the passengers he picked up at the checkpoint were always subjected to Israeli interrogation. He then asked me about my hotel in Ramallah and how long I would be visiting Palestine. He advised me to always assume that I would be under Israeli surveillance even in Ramallah because Mossad had its eyes and ears everywhere and that I should be especially careful when I went to restaurants in the evening.

My hotel booking was done by our IDRC desk officer in our embassy in Tel Aviv. The hotel was a five-storied building. It was late afternoon when I arrived in Ramallah, and after checking in, I went to my room to freshen up. Then I came downstairs to unwind and have a cup of tea. Within minutes, there was a huge commotion on the main floor as armed security forces entered and cordoned off the area from the main entrance of the hotel to its stairs. There were so many armed military personnel lining the cordoned-off route that I had to stand up on my chair to see what was going on.

I saw Palestinian president Yasser Arafat and German chancellor Helmut Kohl walking past us and up the stairs. The commotion subsided as quickly as it had started, although the security personnel remained in their positions and outside surrounding the hotel building. I learned from the people drinking tea with me that the hotel belonged to Yasser Arafat, the topmost floor was his residence, the floor below was his presidential office, the middle floor was for his security personnel, and the first two floors served as a hotel for international guests.

The German chancellor had decided to come to Ramallah to meet with President Arafat after he had concluded his meetings with the Israeli president Ezer Weizman and Prime Minister Shimon Peres. It was a brief unplanned meeting and lasted about an hour in the late afternoon; after which the chancellor flew back to Bonn the same evening.

The IDRC and its partner institute in Ramallah had jointly fixed my itinerary for the visit. The next few days were a fixed routine; a colleague from the partner institute came to the hotel to apprise me of that day's planned activities, briefed me on what I needed to know, and then accompanied me to all the meetings in various offices and research centers. I noticed that going from one place to another was a real challenge because the Israelis had set up road blocks everywhere to impede the free movement of the Palestinian people as well as to monitor them closely. There were towers in street corners manned by fully armed Israeli soldiers to maintain twenty-four-hour surveillance, and the atmosphere of intimidation was quite palpable. In short, Israel had "bantustanized" the whole city.

Every office I visited and every government or private person I spoke with betrayed similar levels of frustration and anxiety. They seemed to be living on the edge. They spoke of frequent and unannounced visits by Israeli security personnel, of confiscation of materials at will, and of threats of arrests and incarceration.

At the Palestinian National Archives, officers told me of their constant efforts to hide and protect from the Israelis whatever little were left in the archives. They told me alarming stories of unilateral Israeli decisions and actions aimed at minimizing Palestinian presence in the region. They brought out several maps to show me the historical locations of Palestinian villages and settlements and more current maps that showed how Israelis had bulldozed many of them into nonexistence to change the realities on the ground and destroy the evidentiary basis of Palestinian claims. They took me to some of these sites that had been leveled to the ground.

I was able to visit many places including government offices, institutes, college and university campuses, restaurants, and everywhere there was a huge amount of not only frustration and fear but also fierce determination to survive and not let Israel push them out of existence.

My days in Ramallah, Jerusalem, Bethlehem, and Hebron were spent with the project people and in interviews of local experts who were mainly historians, archivists, religion professors, anthropologists, and travel guides. Their vast knowledge in their respective fields and the passion of their narratives overwhelmed me.

I had the added benefit of guided tours of each city, which made me appreciate what the Palestinian people were struggling to preserve for their future generations. The professor who was my guide in Jerusalem knew intimately the history of each iconic site within the city, the city's struggles over the centuries, and its present predicament. He took me through the city's underground passageways, the secret tunnels through which citizens escaped when invaded, and the multiple concentric walls surrounding the city.

To see the holiest places of Judaism, Christianity, and Islam, we entered Jerusalem's Old City through one of the eight gates of the Old City Walls and then through another gate of an inner wall. Between these concentric walls were Jewish shops on one side and Muslim shops on the other side, each community selling their wares with gusto. Pointing to them, the professor said to me that he could never figure out how these same shopkeepers and their customers who were friendly and peacefully going about their business inside could turn so hateful and violent outside in the streets!

As we walked to a gate in the innermost wall, I saw Israeli soldiers guarding the entrance. They frisked us and let us enter. Inside were the sacred sites of three Abrahamic religions. I visited the Church of the Holy Sepulchre, built on the site where Jesus Christ was supposed to have been crucified, making it Christianity's holiest site. Among the many holy relics inside the church, I saw the large slab where Jesus's body supposedly lay, and inside the box under the slab were remnants of the last garments Jesus supposedly wore. Various sections inside the church were owned by different Christian denominations. The ornate decorations inside the church were clearly visible even in partial darkness. Outside the church, there was the Ethiopian Monastery in one corner of the Church courtyard that contained frescoes depicting the Queen of Sheba's visit to Jerusalem c. 945 BCE.

I went to the Haram Al-Sharif, or as the Jewish people call it the Temple Mount. Beneath the golden Dome of the Rock lay the sacred stone where according to Jewish and Muslim beliefs Abraham offered his son for sacrifice. The Muslims also believed that Prophet Mohammad (PBUH) stepped off the same stone to begin his night journey to heaven. The sacred stone was housed in an enclosure wrapped in black cloth when I visited the Dome and cordoned off on all four sides by metal railings. There was a small opening near one corner of the railing, and one could walk to the enclosure, where there was a small opening to stick one's hand inside to feel the rock inside.

I wasn't going to miss this opportunity, so when I stuck my hand inside the opening, I felt a solid rock with an imprint in the shape of a foot, but it seemed like a large foot much larger than mine. The rock felt very slippery probably because of the thousands of hands touching it over the years. On the opposite side of the entrance to the Dome were stairs going down. I took the stairs to explore the space below, and I saw a whole bunch of women praying. I asked the caretaker of the Dome about these women, and he explained that the women's section of the Al-Aqsa Mosque was under renovation, and so the women used the space in the basement of the Dome for their prayers. As I was coming out of the Dome of the Rock, a Japanese tourist clicked his camera for a picture, and he was immediately escorted out and his film seized. He had disobeyed the sign outside by the door that warned that photography was forbidden.

The Al-Aqsa Mosque was a tiny distance from the Temple Mount. From the front of the Al-Aqsa Mosque, I could see the Mount of Olives, which was the traditional burial site in Jerusalem for three thousand years and which boasts over 150,000 graves. I could also see the Hebrew University from the courtyard of Al-Aqsa. I wanted to go to the Wailing Wall (Western Wall) in the Jewish Quarter but was not allowed in because I wasn't a Jew. The Wailing Wall was what was left of the Second Temple of Jerusalem that was destroyed by the Romans in 70 CE.

My tour guide took me to the rooftop of the building across from the Western Wall from where I had a clear view of the wall and of the Jewish people wearing *kippah* (*yarmulke* in Yiddish) nodding their heads back and forth as they recited their verses from the Torah and inserting short prayers inside the many pigeonholes in the wall before they left. I went to the Tower of David, sometimes called the Jerusalem Citadel, also in the Old City of Jerusalem. The Tower of David Museum containing exhibits that date back four thousand years and that trace Jerusalem's history from its beginnings as a Canaanite city up to modern times gave me a better sense of how the city evolved through the ages. My tour guide also pointed out to me the Muslim Quarter, the Jewish Quarter, and the Armenian Quarter. It was also fascinating to walk down the bustling alleys and bazaars of the Old City of Jerusalem.

I visited historical sites in other cities as well. In Bethlehem, the biblical birthplace of Jesus, which was south of Jerusalem, I visited the Church of the Nativity, which was built by Emperor Constantine the Great around 325 CE. Further south some twenty miles from Jerusalem, I visited Hebron, which with its six-thousand-year history was considered to be one of the oldest cities in the world and was famous for the Cave of the Patriarchs. It was also famous for its glassblowing industry. It was fascinating to watch how liquid glass was shaped into beautiful forms. I bought quite a few glass containers, jars, and cylinders for my home. I was also surprised to learn that the West Bank brewed some of the best beers in the world. There were many private breweries producing novelty beers and exporting them all over the world.

My visit to the West Bank was also a wonderful opportunity for me to pray in the Al-Aqsa Mosque, Islam's third-holiest site after Makkah and Medina. Between the Dome of the Rock and the Al-Aqsa Mosque, both of which were at a raised level, a few steps down to a lower level rested a circular water tank with multiple water faucets for Muslims to perform their ablution before their prayers. At the time of my visit, it was undergoing maintenance work, and so we had to walk indoor into a large washroom that contained a series of water faucets to perform our ablution.

With the sound of *ajan,* I heard Muslim shopkeepers pulling down their shutters and coming to pray. As I started washing with water from one of the faucets in the washroom, I saw others standing next to me go through the motions of ablution without even turning on the faucets; they were just mimicking water use. I could understand this behavior in a dry arid place where there was no water available to perform ablution, but, here, that was not the case, which I found to be strange.

After I finished washing, as I was heading out of the washroom, I saw a man standing in the middle of the door hunched over his mop. I saw people giving him *bakshish* (tip) as they left. So on my way out, I gave him a ten-shekel coin I had in my pocket. He looked at it and threw it on the floor; presumably it was beneath his dignity to accept the coin, which was roughly equivalent to three U.S. dollars. I did not turn back or pick up the coin as I walked past him.

I walked over to the Al-Aqsa Mosque, which was probably less than one hundred steps away, and as I was entering the mosque, a man sitting on a chair by the entrance handed me a cellophane bag and asked me to put my shoes in it and place it close to me during my prayer; he explained that shoes do get misplaced and even stolen.

I was veritably shocked to hear that. I could expect that happening in some mosques in Dhaka, but certainly not at Al-Aqsa! The mosque was carpeted and quite spacious inside. The carpet had rows of green and white imprint of jai namaz (Muslim prayer mat), making it easy for worshippers to line up properly. But when I went into *sajdah* (placing forehead on the ground), I could smell the dust in the carpet. Again, I was surprised that the upkeep of Islam's third-holiest shrine was so wanting. Aside from all that, it was a most humbling and heartfelt experience that God granted me. I had the opportunity to pray at Al-Aqsa three times, and for that, I am eternally grateful to my creator.

Two nights before my departure date, the elderly professor who was my walking tour guide invited me to his home for dinner. It turned out that he was a bachelor. He also had a twenty something girl as his dinner guest. She was a very charming but shy girl who had just finished her university studies and started work at a research institute. After dinner, the professor invited us to sit on the carpet with cozy cushions all around as he served dessert. He started telling me stories of different families he knew and how they had suffered under Israeli occupation.

Then he started telling me the story of his female dinner guest. Both her father and her elder brother had lost their lives during the first intifada in 1987–1993. As the eldest child now, she had to look after her elderly mother and a teenage sister and a preteen brother. Her extended family had also suffered, and they themselves needed help. Following the intifada, life under Israel's brutal suppression had become unbearable, particularly for families whose members had participated in the intifada.

Then the professor looked at me and said that I could be a savior by sponsoring her to immigrate to Canada! He said that having spent several days with me as my tour guide, I appeared to him to have a kind heart, and this would be a great way of helping a distraught Palestinian family survive honorably.

During his storytelling, it never occurred to me that he was leading up to something. I had failed to detect his motive for inviting her to dinner to meet me and for telling me her family story. I paused briefly as they waited in anticipation of my response. I told them that as much as I would love to help her family, I myself wasn't a Canadian citizen yet, and even if I were, a sponsorship by me would be rejected outright because she and I were neither related nor from the same country. He then asked me if I could explore some alternatives for her. She remained totally silent as we discussed the issue until it was time for me to thank him for the dinner and leave. I do feel sorry that I could not be more helpful, as I also remembered my graduate school friend Abdullah, whose family had also suffered under the Israeli occupation but who had found a way out by marrying Babette and settling down in France.

The day of departure was tense for both my colleagues and me. We had to go through intense exit interviews as the Israeli security wanted to extract from us as much information about our stay and of our activities as possible. They also thoroughly checked our baggage. After we passed immigration and control, as we were sitting down in one corner of the departure lounge, I noticed our female colleague's teary eyes. I asked her if everything was OK. She replied that as soon as she returned to Cairo, she would draft her resignation letter and submit it first thing next morning. I asked her whether that wasn't a bit drastic, and she said no. After a pause, she continued. "The security officials said that I had been meeting with people connected with the intifada and who wished to harm the state of Israel. They wanted to know what we talked about. They asked me whether I was carrying any material for them, and I said no. But they did not believe me. So they took me to another room where I was subjected to body search, including cavity search. It was humiliating! I'm not working in this project anymore." The Israeli security who had been shadowing her wanted to make sure that she was not a courier or a conduit to transmit messages or anti-Israel material abroad. After I returned to Ottawa, I learned that she had indeed quit IDRC.

The Home Front

There were major developments in the home front as well during this period of our life. We had stayed in our first house on Bilberry Drive only a year, and on February 1, 1992, we relocated to a different house at 6941 Avenue du Bois, which was only a street away and closer to the Park and Ride bus terminal. Nipa converted our walk-out basement into a kids' paradise of sorts and started babysitting several kids. She would take them out every day, if the weather allowed, for a walk and other activities, which the children loved. The parents of the kids were very pleased with the care with which she looked after them.

Our daughter was now a preteen and facing the challenges that came with that age. One day, she came home from school quite upset; somebody had teased her for her brown skin. She told her mom that from now on, she was going to wear only clothes that totally covered her body head to toe. When I came home, Nipa told me that I needed to have a chat with my daughter. So I did and could understand her concern. She was approaching that age when looks mattered very much. I sat next to her on her bed and asked her, "Why do you think white girls in their bikinis spend hour after hour suntanning by the pool or on the beach? Isn't it because they want a tan so that their skin color is just like yours? You are so lucky that you were born with it, whereas they have to work hard to get it. They try so hard to look like you. You have nothing to be embarrassed about." I recall that my pep talk seemed to have made a difference; she no longer seemed to be worried about what others said of her. But when she became a teenager and was attending high school, one day, she came home from school and told her mom that she would have to be patient with her because her teacher had said that teenage girls have lots of mood swings! Indeed, we were forewarned!

Another time, she was excited to receive an invitation from an Indian family who lived on the next street in our neighborhood to celebrate Diwali with them. Diwali, or the Festival of Lights, started on the thirteenth day after *Poornima,* or the full moon, and was a five-day celebration of the triumph of good over evil, of light over darkness, of knowledge over ignorance, and of new beginnings. According to Hindu mythology, it was the celebration of the victory of god Rama, who was one of the two avatars of Vishnu, the preserver of the universe, over the demon god, Ravana. In some parts of India, Diwali also marked the beginning of the Hindu New Year. Rows of *diyas* (oil lamps) and candles were lit inside and outside Hindu houses to welcome Lakshmi, the goddess of fortune and wealth.

Mumu was hesitant at first and asked me whether she should accept the invitation, since it was a Hindu celebration and she was a Muslim. This gave me the opportunity to tell her that one must strive to be a world citizen, and for that, one needed to learn to appreciate the diversity of religions, cultures, and traditions that Allah had blessed us with; this diversity existed because the Almighty had willed it.

I encouraged her to accept the invitation so that she can learn firsthand about the Hindu religion and about the Hindu people and their cultures and traditions, which would make her a more wholesome human being. This was, of course, contrary to the beliefs of many Muslims who were locked into a rigid mind-set and intolerance. When she returned from the ceremonies that night, she was very excited and regaled us with the full account of the rituals she observed. She said that after she rang the doorbell, the door opened, and she was lifted off her feet and carried to a sofa, where they washed her feet with milk, and on and on. She spoke of the string lights and candles, the delicious sweets, the family relatives and friends, the gaiety, and the jovial atmosphere. She was happy to have not missed it. But I was surprised to hear of her feet getting washed with milk because the cow is a sacred symbol of life to the Hindu people, and in South Asian cultures, we do not touch anything sacred with our feet.

It was also the time when several Bengali parents were sending their kids to a Bangla school to learn the mother tongue, and the fathers took turn to drive them to and from school. One day, it was my turn. The kids were packed into my Dodge Caravan and we set off. Soon, the kids were talking among themselves in English. So I suggested that when they are in my van, I expect them to speak in Bangla only because that would be a good warm-up for the Bangla class. There was total silence. Realizing that I had shut them off, I started to feel guilty. So I told them that I will ask each of them to translate a Bangla word into English; they all agreed. I started off with the eldest kid, who was a boy. I asked him, "What is the English word for *haati?*" He didn't know, and so one of the girls said, "Come on, bhaiya, it is elephant!" He replied, "Oh, yes." I said, "OK, let's try another word. What is the English for *ghora?*" Again, he couldn't translate it, and again another girl said, "Bhaiya, you know it means horse, don't you?" By now, he was quite embarrassed that the girls younger than he knew but he didn't. So I said, "OK, one last try, what's the word for *goru?*" The boy immediately replied, "Oh, I know that, my dad calls me that all the time!" All the kids burst out laughing. The normal translation is cow, but *goru* is also a pejorative term in Bengali used against someone to signify that he is an idiot!

On the return journey from school, I could not remember the house number of one of the girls in my van. When I entered her neighborhood, I asked her if she knew her house number. She said she didn't, but she knew for sure that "it's the house with the garage." I smiled and told her that it seems that all the houses on her street had garages. She paused and then replied, "Oh, it's the garage with a car inside!" Armed with those definitive pinpoint coordinates, I downshifted to first gear and asked her to look out the window to see if she could identify her house. It wasn't long before she was able to find the house with the garage with a car inside. Every time I visit that house, I am reminded of that precision guidance by my cute little passenger, who is now happily married to a tall Dane and lives just outside Copenhagen.

Our son is two and a half years younger to his sister and enjoyed the company of his sister and her many girlfriends. I do not remember now what exactly it was that he had done, but one day, he had done something that he was definitely not supposed to have done. I was cross, so I told him that he deserved to be punished unless he could give me one good reason why I shouldn't punish him. He was scared. He thought for a moment and then said, "*Karon ami tomar ekmatro theley*" (Because I am your only son)—the last word, "chheley," couldn't make it through his missing front teeth! I just melted inside, grabbed him by his arms, and whispered into his ears to be extra careful next time.

My mother and my sister-in-law Lopa had visited us once when we were living in our first house on Bilberry Drive. But both Nipa's parents and my parents visited us in our second house on Avenue du Bois. My parents came during the winter, when the snow in our backyard was waist high. I remember my father sinking into the snow in the park behind our house, and I had to pull him out. Nearly every morning during the weekdays, from her bedroom window, Mother watched me walk through knee-high snow to the bus terminal. It was quite an adventure for all of us as we tried to negotiate our way around in snow-covered Ottawa.

That year, in March 1992, we had gone to the Niagara Falls for the first time. It was really exciting to watch the 167-foot-high falls. Canada was lucky, because although the falls were on the American side, the view was best from the Canadian side. We visited Niagara Falls once again a few months later in July, when we rendezvoused with Nipa's eldest aunt, Jolly khala, and Matin khalu, from Manchester, UK, who had come to visit Canada. We brought them to our home to visit with us for a few days.

My father-in-law had been under treatment for non-Hodgkin's lymphoma, which was a cancer that originated in the lymphatic system. He had gone to Manchester for treatment while staying at Matin khalu and Jolly khala's house. As soon as he felt somewhat better, he yearned to come to Ottawa to see his eldest daughter, Nipa, and his grandkids. When he and Ma finally came, we were shocked to see how emaciated he looked, but the smile on his innocent face was ever present. Unsurprisingly, he was the same doting father to Nipa and a loving grandpa to Mumu and Mishu. We were not only very happy to see him but very sad as well because we knew that his chances of pulling out of it were uncertain.

During his stay with us in Ottawa, many of his former students, who were now doctors in North America, called to inquire about his health and to wish his fast recovery. One of his medical school friends, Dr. Amir Ali, who was practicing in Calgary, drove 3,300 kilometers from Calgary to Ottawa to see him. Nipa's parents stayed with us for about a month and returned to Manchester to continue with his chemotherapy.

After staying nearly two and a half years on Avenue du Bois, we purchased a house at 2097 Gardenway Drive in a brand-new neighborhood but on the opposite side of the Queensway in Orleans. First, Father visited us; Mom remained in Dallas at my brother Shahalam's place. Father maintained his military routine of timely wake-up, timely namaz (prayers), and timely meals, but he enjoyed his brief visit. When he returned to Dallas, Mom was curious to know about our new house. Soon after when I called Mom, she said Father had told her that he liked the house, that it had black-and-white décor; and that the backyard had no trees. I informed her that we had planted a white birch in the backyard just after Father left. There was a pause as Mom tried to picture everything black and white in our house, and then she said, "Shesh porjonto gaachtao shada lagali?" (Even the tree you planted is white?)

This was the first house we had bought after living in two rented houses before, and we were very proud to have our own house. We would often go to the construction site to watch it being built, which is why we have scores of pictures of the house from the time of the excavation of the site to completion. We had extended the back exterior wall by two feet into the yard to give us some extra space in the living room and in the kitchen. We had nice neighbors on either side. One neighbor, David, worked in the Canadian Mint, and his wife Lisa and their two daughters sometimes visited us. For many years, David addressed me as "abbu" because he thought that was my name since the children that Nipa babysat always called me abbu, until one day he found out that *abbu* meant "Dad." He was surprised and embarrassed and said to me, "All these years I have been calling you *Dad?* Damn!" The neighbor on the other side ran a business from his home, printing blank official forms for various Canadian government departments. We lived at this address for the next ten years and built up lots of memories.

The following summer, Mother came to visit us, and we decided to go to Niagara Falls with her; unfortunately, it was peak tourist season. By the time we reached Niagara Falls, which was about seven to eight hours' nonstop drive from Ottawa, it was close to midnight, and we couldn't find any hotel rooms to rent. We retraced our drive on the QEW to go to nearby cities in search of a hotel but still had no luck. We finally found a room in a motel and were relieved to be able to just hit the sack. But there was one problem; I had forgotten to pack my pajamas. Seeing my dismay, Mom offered me one of her petticoats to wear for the night. Everyone started laughing, but I was too tired to worry, and so I accepted the offer, and that night, I slept wearing

Mom's petticoat! My kids got a real kick out of that and still remind me of that trip.

We visited the Niagara Falls many times, and every time it was wonderful. When the kids were young, we would take the tram ride that ran by the side of the falls and visit the flower clock, the Children's Wonderland with its rides and many other attractions, the waterpark with playful dolphins, and the children's carrousel. During one summer, my mother-in-law went with us, and she and Mishu opted to go on the Ferris wheel. As chance would have it, just when they reached the very top, the ride lost power and froze on the spot, with them hanging several hundred feet up in the air.

As I kept looking up to check on them as well as video them, I thanked my stars that I wasn't on it because if that had happened to me, I would have had a panic attack. I had become fearful of height after the accident on the Rockies when I had been blown off the mountain into a ravine by a blizzard. After that happened, I had gotten on a ride with my kids once but felt my heart pounding faster as we went up; at that moment, I had to yell out to the ride master to stop the wheel so that I can disembark. I had decided then that I will not subject myself to my acrophobia again.

During every trip to Niagara Falls, we made sure to get on the Maid of the Mist, which took its passengers very close to the pounding waters of the falls. The 85,000 cubic feet of water falling per second from a height of 167 feet generated so much mist that it inevitably drenched every plastic raincoat-wearing sightseer on the boat, not to mention its deafening sound. We also enjoyed the laser show at night and the wonderful food in the many restaurants.

Our Christmas holidays were equally memorable. My in-laws were frequently with us. My sister-in-law Lopa and brother-in-law Rubel, both of them doctors, usually drove up to Ottawa from Wausau, Wisconsin, to celebrate with us. Lopa and Rubel were great fun. Lopa was a vivacious, spirited, fun-loving chatterbox, while Rubel was quiet, composed, and desperately trying to keep up with his beautiful wife; they complemented each other beautifully! Lopa's restless demeanor and her unflinching attention to everyone's well-being always kept everyone on their toes, especially her mother, whose health was of great concern to Lopa. Sometimes it went overboard, as was the case with her mother.

One day, they went to the grocery store, and Lopa told her mom she could pick whatever she wanted. Since they usually did not buy eggs but kept only egg white in their fridge, my *shashori* (mother-in-law) was desperate to enjoy the taste and smell of real eggs and grabbed a carton of eggs and put them in the trolley. As they passed the blood pressure machine, Lopa asked her mom to check out her blood pressure. When she saw the high blood pressure reading, Lopa was shocked. She immediately grabbed the eggs to put them back on the shelf, saying, "No eggs for you," much like the Nazi chef in the soup kitchen in the *Seinfeld* episode! My shashori helplessly watched as the eggs floated away right before her eyes. Perhaps her only consolation was that she could at least secretly share this sad predicament with her eldest daughter in Ottawa!

The Christmas tree in our house always went up in early December, and decorating it with beautiful trinkets was great family fun. Christmas shopping was exciting, as was secretly wrapping presents in colorful wrapping papers and tying bows around each of them. It was exciting to see the Christmas tree lit up and wrapped presents all around it. Even more exciting was Christmas morning when we gathered in front of the tree to open our presents. Some common items that almost everyone got nearly every Christmas were sweaters, tuques, socks, gloves, and thermals out of respect for Wisconsin's and Canada's severe winter.

Once all the presents were opened and admired, we would get busy stuffing all the wrapping papers and bows into giant black garbage bags for disposal. The next phase was Nipa preparing the turkey for the oven, while we got busy preparing other food items for the Christmas dinner in the late afternoon. There were games to play and stories to share as joy and laughter kept our spirits high. Nipa always bought all sorts of Christmas stuff for us to wear on our head or playful things to pop open before saying grace. Sitting down to enjoy the Christmas dinner with family was the ultimate moment of the day. It was always a sad day when Lopa and Rubel packed their bags to return to Wisconsin after the Christmas holidays.

We also took turns to drive to Wisconsin to visit Lopa and Rubel.

They have a beautiful, spacious home atop a hill in Wausau, which is wonderful in all seasons but especially in the fall when the leaves change color. I usually took the southwestern route, driving from Ottawa via Toronto-Detroit-Chicago to Wausau, Wisconsin. On the return trip, I once took the northeastern route driving from Wausau northeast toward Lake Michigan, over the Sault Ste. Marie International Bridge to Canada, and then through Sudbury and North Bay to Ottawa, which is a shorter drive of roughly sixteen hours.

During one of these visits, Rubel's father was visiting them. Dr. Mohammad Serajul Islam was a chest physician trained in heart diseases, who had worked at the World Health Organization (WHO) as a temporary national consultant and as UN staff physician who served in Pakistan, Malaysia, Saudi Arabia, Sudan, and Tunisia. He is a kind, affectionate gentleman with an inquisitive mind. He also has a tremendous knack for writing and reciting poems. We always have great conversations when we are together.

During this particular trip, I learned that he was under a strict dietary regimen imposed on him by his son Rubel. One day, after Rubel left for work, I told him that we shall go for a drive to see Wausau's parks and lakes and then have lunch outside; he was very happy to hear that. After our tour, I asked him what he would like to eat. In sheepish voice, he told me that he really yearned for KFC, but Rubel would never allow that. I felt very sorry for him and told him that it would be OK to have it once, and I won't tell Rubel about it. However, I said to him, there was one condition! When Rubel asks us what we had for lunch, he has to keep quiet when I tell Rubel that we had nice, thick, juicy steaks just to see the expression on Rubel's face.

We then stopped at a KFC and bought enough for all of us, went to a park, and sat on a park bench and enjoyed our lunch. It was nice to see a happy man in my minivan. That evening, after Rubel returned from his hospital work, as expected, the first question he asked was what we had for lunch. I calmly told him that we had a splendid steak meal with all the usual accompaniments. Rubel froze still. He looked at me with great disappointment and said, "Hassan bhai, you have destroyed my weeks of effort at one go." He looked so devastated that I couldn't help but assure him that in fact we did not have steak and that I was just pulling his leg just to see his reaction!

Notwithstanding this episode, I have always had fun time with my brother-in-law. Although he doesn't talk much, on occasions, he could be quite entertaining. Once he was relating to me his experience with a southern cop when his sister Shuborna was visiting from Bangladesh. He was driving in one of the southern states with Shuborna in the backseat. Suddenly, he heard the siren of a highway patrol and had to stop. The police officer informed him that he was speeding and asked for his car registration and driving license. Then he was issued a ticket with a very hefty fine. After warning him to stay within the speed limit, the police officer left. The next thing he heard was "Thank you, bhaiya," from his happy sister in the backseat. Puzzled, he asked why she was thanking him. She explained that she had seen only on TV how American cops stopped drivers and issued them speeding tickets; thanks to him, this was her first real experience witnessing cops stopping drivers and issuing tickets! It was a story worth remembering.

Every time Rubel's dad and mom planned to visit them in Wisconsin, we invited them to visit us in Ottawa as well, but only his mom visited us once. Rubel's mom, the late Sufia Islam, who had worked at the CIDA Dhaka Office until her retirement, was a very kind and amiable person. She and my mother were kindred spirits.

On September 11, 2001, when the Twin Towers in New York City were under attack, Rubel's mom and dad were in the air heading toward the United States. Their flight was quickly diverted to Montreal Pierre Elliott Trudeau International Airport. Rubel was obviously very concerned and called me immediately for help. I assured him not to worry and that we would take care of his parents.

Nipa and I drove up to Montreal airport, picked them up, and then took them to a hotel. They looked totally stressed out and needed immediate rest after a very harrowing experience. They were not willing to come to Ottawa with us because they were desperate to be united with their own son and daughter-in-law at the earliest. So I constantly checked with the airline to find out about their next flight to the States and kept Rubel abreast of the developments at our end. Only after we managed to put them on their flight to Wausau did we return to Ottawa, with much relief to Rubel.

Nipa's younger brother Rana Javed Kabir and his wife Samina Chowdhury had visited us once in 1999. Their next visit was after they got their immigration visa to Canada; they stayed nine months with us from April to December 2003. They moved out and bought their own house in Aylmer, Quebec, when we put our Gardenway house up for sale.

Our trips to the United States were mostly to visit relatives, and Nipa and I have tons of family, relatives, and friends down south, which was our euphemism for the United States. Although we rarely had any problems with the U.S. border officials, when we were traveling with our Bangladeshi passports, they would flip through my visa pages and inevitably ask me why I went to Iran and what did I do there, since I had been to Iran several times. I would then have to launch into a lengthy explanation.

After 9/11, it didn't get any easier, even with my Canadian passport; we would occasionally need to answer stupid questions. On the photo page of our Canadian passports, under "Place of birth/Lieu de naissance," it read "Dhaka BGD." Immigration officials at the border checkpoint would say, "So you were born in Baghdad?" which would be the prelude to lots of follow-up questions. So the second time I was asked this, I told the border official, "I was born in Bangladesh. Dhaka is the city, so BGD has to be the country, and Baghdad is not a country, is it?" The official stared at me unappreciatively, which reminded me that it was never a good idea to challenge or argue with an immigration or customs official at any border.

Talking about 9/11, on that day, my brother Selim, who lived in Seattle at the time, was fly fishing in some remote Canadian waters north of the U.S. border. He had no idea what had happened in New York that day. As he was returning to the United States, he was stopped at the border and asked what he was doing in Canada. He told them he loved to fly-fish and that's what he was doing.

Since he was a young Muslim lad, crossing the border to the United States alone, the U.S. border officials were wary. They asked him to open his car trunk. Inside, they found his fishing gear and several types of knives. But what saved him was a huge, freshly caught fish wrapped in newspaper. The officers checked his credentials, and only after they were completely satisfied did they allow him to enter the United States. As he prepared to leave, he asked the officers why he was detained, and it was only then that he learned about the terrorist attacks on America. He had deliberately not turned on his car radio to enjoy some peace and quiet and missed the entire cataclysm!

We made frequent visits to Long Island to visit with Nipa's youngest aunt, Tanju khala, who was a talented and successful hairdresser with her own hairdressing salon in Manhattan. Visiting them was always fun, because Tanju khala's husband Pervaiz khalu, who was younger than I, was hilarious and always had stories to tell. He narrated to us about his recent pilgrimage to Makkah.

He was part of a small group of young, like-minded persons accompanied by a young hujur from their mosque in Jackson Heights in Queens, New York. In Makkah, they had completed initial parts of the hajj ritual and were chitchatting while resting in a room near the Kaaba, when the hujur urged everyone to get up and come outside to perform the next ritual, which was the symbolic throwing of stones at the *shaitan* (Satan). Noting the heat outside, Khalu said, "Hujur, shob shaitan-to ghorer bhitorei, aikhaney amra dhiladhili korlaito hoy, bahirey jawar dorkar-ta ki?" (Hujur, all the Satans are right here. Why don't we just stone each other? Why bother going out in this heat?) Shocked at this statement, hujur shouted, "Tauba, tauba!" and exclaimed that their hajj might have been irreparably compromised!

My shashori also has many relatives in Long Island from her home district of Dinajpur, Bangladesh. Most of them were well-to-do pharmacists, and they always received us with open arms.

During another trip, I looked up Hussain Shareef Ahmed, my colleague and friend who had assisted me with the NSU convocation and who was then the assistant dean of Enrollment Services at Hofstra University, Long Island. His wife was not home. He proudly showed us a wall plastered with certificates his son had earned.

Another trip to New York was to attend the Holy Cross College reunion. Since Nipa was a graduate of the college, it was a great opportunity for her to reconnect with her classmates and some long-lost friends. I accompanied her as the spouse. What was interesting to me at this reunion was the discovery that a great number of Holy Cross College girls had married boys from St. Joseph's High School, me included. It was as if these two institutions were fated to create marital pairs!

We drove to Dallas several times to visit with my brother Shahalam and his family. During our very first drive from Ottawa to Dallas to Disney World near Orlando, Florida, and back, I drove my Dodge Caravan 7,700 kilometers through seventeen states in seventeen days. It was memorable for several reasons. It was the first time that I had driven such a long distance and gone through so many cities and states.

We visited my cousin Rafiqur Rasul in Columbus, Ohio. We went through Hope, Arkansas, which was Pres. Bill Clinton's birthplace. We visited the house where he was born and the school he had attended. We were really struck by how poor his family was. But what was most memorable was the police car that trailed us as soon as we left Memphis, Tennessee, until we crossed the state border and entered Arkansas.

It was close to midnight when we neared Memphis, and our children were fast asleep in the backseats. Since it was before the days of GPS, I had to occasionally stop the van by the roadside to read the road map that I had gotten from the CAA. In this instance, I stopped to see if I could locate a hotel to spend the night.

The police car stopped behind me, and one of the police officers walked over to me with one hand on his holster and asked to see my driver's license. He inquired what I was doing there so late at night. The other police officer checked out the inside of my van through his torchlight and saw my kids fast asleep in the backseats. I told the officer that I was looking for a hotel to spend the night. He gave me direction to the nearest Holiday Inn in his southern drawl, which I barely understood.

After registering for the night, when we got to our hotel room, I looked out through the window and saw the police car parked inside the hotel compound. It was there all night and followed us the next day until we crossed the state line into Arkansas. What was striking was their seeming suspicion of out-of-staters, or perhaps of my Canadian license plate, which looked different from the license plates in the States.

I also recall the dilapidated condition of the roads in those southern states. The freeway throughout the length of the state was cracked in many places, and the road shoulders were in disrepair. There were pieces of torn tires strewn by the sides every now and then; one could occasionally see garbage spilled by the sides including old mattresses! One could tell that these states were indeed quite poor compared to the northern states.

After spending a few days with my brother, we left Irving, Texas, and drove eastward through Louisiana, Mississippi, Alabama, to Florida to go to Disney World, where our kids were delighted to meet and take pictures with Disney characters and enjoy the various rides and shows. The thrill rides, water rides, big drops were their favorite, but I didn't go with my kids to any of these because I was too much of a chicken. Nipa was and is the brave one, always ready to hop on to any ride with the kids.

At one point, I was so exhausted after the long drive that I asked my family to go ahead and have fun while I rested on a bench. When I woke up, I found myself looking like a hobo because I had wrapped around me a shawl with a hat on my head while I was napping! The pictures they took while I was dozing off were that of a veritable beggar, a tramp, or a bum—you get the drift!

On our return journey, we drove straight up north overnighting in Atlanta, Georgia, in the home of Nipa's cousin Tanweer Akram (Chandan). Our next stop was in Washington DC in the home of another cousin, Khursheed Ahmed (Nichol). Nichol and his then wife Tonu took us to one of their malls and bought little Mumu a big pink toy car; Mumu was thrilled to get that from her uncle. She was also happy to get a Barbie doll from us. The next day, we drove nonstop for twelve hours to Ottawa, except for a brief stop at the Canadian border customs.

We had driven to Disney World straight from Ottawa the second time in 1997. On the way back, we stopped in Charleston, South Carolina, to visit with my sister-in-law Lopa and her family. Her husband Rezwan

255

had recently changed hospitals and moved from Atlanta, Georgia. Her mother-in-law, who was with them at the time, had recently had an open-heart surgery, and so it was a good opportunity for us to see how she was recuperating. She was in good spirit and healing well.

From Charleston, we drove north to Washington DC and spent the night with cousin Nichol. It was on that trip that on the day of departure, we drove six hours from Washington DC to the Canadian border only to realize that we had left our passports in the bedside drawer in Nichol's house. We panicked because not only we couldn't enter Canada without our passports but also Nichol was supposed to leave for Myrtle Beach, South Carolina that morning. With no cell phones in those days, I remember desperately calling him from a public phone booth in a roadside town to tell him to delay his trip so that we can pick up our passport. We drove back to their house to pick up our passports. I think I decided then that henceforth our passports should be in Nipa's handbag because girls never forget their handbags/purses.

Our other long driving trips were to Wisconsin to visit with Lopa when they moved from Charleston to Wausau, Wisconsin. She had joined the Marshfield Clinic Health System in Wausau as an internal medicine physician, and her husband Rezwan (Rubel) was an oncologist also at Marshfield until he transferred to Saint Michael's Hospital in Stevenspoint, both in Wisconsin.

We drove there several times, both in the summer and late fall, and took full advantage of the seasons. During one of these visits in the fall, Nipa and I strolled down their street up in the hill and marveled at the rhododendrons changing color. At one point, both of us lay down on our backs on the ankle-deep leaves on the ground and looked up to catch the sunbeams trying to pierce through the beautiful canopy as the tree branches swayed in the soft breeze. It was very peaceful and quiet except for the rustling of the leaves in the breeze and a moment to ponder the beauty of creation and how insignificant we were in the greater scheme of things. During that trip, I was the only one who didn't have the guts to take the gondola ride to the snow hills because of my fear of heights.

Our visits to Boise to see my sister Tina and brother-in-law

Rawnaque, both of whom work for Micron International Inc., had to be by air because of the considerable driving distance. That is not to say that I haven't driven such a long distance. I do have a record of driving nonstop from Eugene, Oregon, in the West Coast to New York City in the East Coast one summer with a Chinese student during my undergraduate days. It was a marathon trip clear across America that took us four days of nonstop driving, aided by NoDoz pills that kept us awake; we stopped only for gas, food, and washroom.

I visited Boise several times and twice without Nipa because she couldn't get leave from work. Most of my visits were to the home they had before the current one. That house was on the foothills of one of the mountains that surrounded Boise, and perched on top at one side overlooking their cul-de-sac driveway was a huge boulder that looked like it could roll down any moment. Every time my other brothers and I visited Tina, we wondered what would happen if an earthquake struck Boise or its vicinity.

Rawnaque and Tina's two lovely daughters, Mayisa and Nusha, were growing up fast and outgrowing their home. Rawnaque had been eyeing new homes and going to open houses for a while, and they were able to finally choose a home they liked. It was very spacious with beautiful timber interior in a posh neighborhood. We all fell in love with it when we saw it through Google Maps. So my youngest brother, Tawfiq (Tito), from Dallas, and I from Ottawa flew to Boise to help them move to their new home. While no house move is fun, and it involves lots of work and patience, I have to say that the excitement of moving into this new home more than made up for the sweat that was shed. Even unpacking the dozens of boxes and putting away the contents in their appropriate places did not seem like a chore to me. My last visit was to see Mother, who had flown in from Dhaka to Dallas and then to Boise. By then, there was an addition to Tina's family, a most adorable and cute shih tzu whom they named Jazz.

My brothers and sisters also visited us several times. In May 1994, Shahalam, his wife Luann, and their two kids, Ryan and Justine, drove up to Niagara Falls to celebrate Luann's birthday. Then they drove up to Ottawa. I was about to go out to run some errand and pressed the garage door opener, and as the door rolled up, I saw them drive into our driveway. It was great to see them.

I took Shahalam and the kids out on a tour of the city and regretted that Luann hadn't joined us, but Shahalam assured me that she was having a great time at home, because her idea of a great vacation was to be able to sprawl out on a sofa reading a novel. One day, they simply vanished. I looked for them everywhere including in the basement, but they were nowhere to be found. Later on, I opened the garage door to go out and found both of them in their car parked in the driveway, sitting in the front seats with legs up on the dashboard taking in the sun. Although it was warm weather in Ottawa, the two Texans were freezing!

Tina's Wedding

December 1995 was a special month in our family history, for our youngest sister got married later that month. We had been preparing for the wedding for months, and it included constructing a palanquin to carry the bride to the groom like in olden days in Bengal. There was much festivity and fun. Tina had met Rawnaque while attending the University of Texas at San Antonio, from where she had graduated summa cum laude in biology. This brings back memories of Tina's early schooling.

She was academically the most brilliant among us brothers and sisters. She always aced her exams and always stood first in her class from kindergarten through high school. But she was also the only person who ever cried when she got her school report cards. We used to tell her that students cried because they got poor grades or failed in certain subjects or did not get promoted to the next class, "But you stood first in your class as usual, so why are you crying?" Of course, there was no reply.

Rawnaque had graduated as an engineer. He was of a quiet demeanor with a good head on his shoulders. He could also be funny. He and our youngest brother, Tawfiq, seemed to have hit it off well together. Rawnaque turned out to be quite likeable, and very soon after their wedding, we started to treat him like a brother rather than a brother-in-law. Their wedding reception took place at Shena Kunjo, which is the Bangladesh Armed Forces Convention Center located in the Dhaka Army Cantonment, and their bou-bhat (reception) was held at the RAOWA Club, which is the meeting place of the retired army officers' welfare association, also in Dhaka.

Among many memorable moments during those celebrations, one was the fact that for the first time in a quarter century, our whole family, including our spouses, had come together from different parts of the world to celebrate our little sister's wedding. One of our guests from Canada attending the wedding, Manzur Huq, offered to capture that moment by photographing our entire family together. That photograph remains in our family album as a precious memento of that day.

A year later, however, on December 8, 1996, tragedy struck our family. Our sister Lily's eldest daughter, Tanya Karim, just one month shy of nineteen years, died in San Antonio of chronic myelogenous leukemia (CML), which is an uncommon type of cancer of the bone marrow that causes an abnormal increase of white blood cells in the blood. While advances in treatment allow most patients to achieve remission these days, at the time, there was no cure for the disease. As a last resort, doctors even tried experimental drugs on Tanya but to no avail. The anguish over the demise of such an innocent, caring, and loving person dying so young hung over the family like a pall for years to come. Our youngest sister, Tina, in whose care Tanya was in her final days, suffered from guilt for many months.

The North South University Years

I was engaged in my project work in India for the IDRC in 1995–97. In the summer of 1995, I learned that my father was not well; so I decided to make a quick visit to Dhaka to see him. As I sat down by his bedside to inquire about his health, he cheered up and asked me about my work in India. I told him that I was heading up a multidisciplinary, multicountry project that was trying to understand how environmental crises affected a country's or a region's political stability and security.

He then told me that his friend Moslehuddin Ahmed, who had founded Bangladesh's first private university, the North South University (NSU), was looking for an expert who could advise him on creating the country's first Environmental Studies Department. I was impressed to hear of Mr. Ahmed's effort; first, because of his initiative to create a private university; second, because of the focus on an environment department.

While the quality of education in East Pakistan had always been superior to that in West Pakistan, the quality had significantly deteriorated after Bangladesh's independence. The 1971 war had created major dislocation in the education sector: many teachers at all levels, but especially at the tertiary level, had been deliberately targeted and killed by the Pakistan Army; the administration during the first few years was in disarray; and educational facilities throughout the country were in shambles. Even though billions of dollars had poured into the country in the form of UN aid, the nascent government did not have the capacity or the wherewithal to utilize much of it, especially in the educational sector.

The situation deteriorated further with the mandatory introduction of Bengali as the medium of instruction at all levels; this was a major shock to the existing English medium educational system. After two decades of decay and corruption in the public sector education, it became obvious that the country did not have the appropriate skills in English to compete in the world, and the need for private sector education in English was being widely felt. The Khaleda Zia government subscribed to this general sentiment and decided to open up education to the private sector. Mr. Ahmed's initiative was readily approved by the Khaleda Zia cabinet in 1992 under the Private University Act 1992, and the North South University went into operation in early 1993.

With regard to environmental studies, while the Department of Geography at Dhaka University offered a couple of courses on environment-related issues, no university in Bangladesh actually had either an undergraduate or a graduate program that offered degrees on environmental studies. For a country like Bangladesh, which was on average only a few meters above sea level, which was seriously overpopulated, which had a high degree of deforestation with only 15 percent forest cover, and which was continually ravaged by devastating floods, environmental issues should have been at the top of national concerns. And yet there was no academic department addressing these urgent issues. It was Muslehuddin Ahmed's foresight to appreciate the country's urgent needs that led him to decide to create an Environmental Studies Department at NSU. So, on Dad's suggestion, I made an appointment to see Mr. Ahmed, who was then the president of NSU.

Mr. Ahmed was happy to receive me and showed great interest in my environment-related work, which I shared with him in some detail. He then told me of his urgent desire to establish an Environmental Studies Department at NSU and thought that my international experience in dealing with environmental issues that spanned across the globe from Canada to the Philippines would serve the university well.

Realizing that I will not be able to commit myself full time to NSU because of my work in India, he suggested that I might come in as an advisor to the president and guide him to set up the department. I was happy to do so and promised to send him an outline of how I would approach this task. I sent him the task outline within a month. Meanwhile, all the required paperwork and approval from the NSU board for the establishment of the department had been completed. I continued to advise him informally for the next several months.

By the end of 1995, I had completed the research component of my project work in India and had considerable flexibility with my time. I informed Mr. Ahmed that I could make myself available full time to work for NSU. He was pleased to hear that and asked me to join the university full time and head the new department. The letter of appointment was issued on November 16, 1995, and I became the department's first chairman from January 1996. It was a renewable three-academic-year contract. I started the department with six students, all female, and with three teachers including me; the rest of the teachers were from other public universities recruited on term contract.

My family remained in Ottawa, which gave me the freedom and the necessary time to devote to the needs of the nascent department. The excitement of building the country's first such department from ground up thoroughly engaged me, on average, twelve hours a day. As one can imagine, we had to start from scratch. When the establishment of the department was publicly announced, response from potential students was disheartening.

Very few people thought of environmental studies as a serious academic pursuit. In general, women students were more interested on environmental issues than were men, who preferred to study business, economics, or computer science, with an eye to finding a well-paying job after graduation. My first job was to hold an "open house," where parents and prospective students were invited to find out about this new department. We explained what such a department would teach, how it would contribute to addressing the country's environmental challenges, the areas in which there would be high demand for environment related expertise, and the opportunity for jobs and careers in the public and private sectors and internationally.

We also distributed leaflets and brochures on environmental studies. I spoke to them about my personal international experiences dealing with environmental issues to gin up the interest of potential students. Among those who became interested to enroll, several of their parents, who did not attend the open house, came to me later worried about their daughters' desire to enroll. They asked me whether it was realistic to expect any jobs with such a degree and whether there can be any career studying this subject. I had to convince them not only of the importance of the field of environmental studies per se but also of its promising future in the context of Bangladesh as well as one's career.

There was, understandably, much skepticism among parents who would be doling out a considerable amount of money in a four-year undergraduate degree program at NSU without any guarantee of a good-paying job at the end. In any case, only six female students signed up for this field of study. It became doubly important for me to ensure that these six students got the best education on the subject and that all had good jobs upon graduation, so that we could cite their success to convince future students to enroll in the department.

Jumping ahead here, years later, after I had left NSU and was working for the International Development Research Center (IDRC) in Ottawa, I met two of my students, one in South Africa working for the World Bank and the other one in the Philippines working for the Asian Development Bank. I was filled with a great sense of satisfaction!

I had invested a lot of time and effort during the advisory months on developing not only an advance curriculum but one that was also relevant to the country's needs. I looked at the undergraduate and graduate curricula of the internationally rated top-ten environmental studies programs. At the time, these top-ranked programs were in Canada, USA, UK, Holland, Switzerland, and Australia.

Inspired by these curricula, I drafted the NSU curriculum and then held two roundtables where I invited the Bangladesh's environment related experts—environmentalists, climate experts, flood and water experts, soil science experts, forestry experts, specialists from SPARRSO (Space Research and Remote Sensing Organization), geographers, environment ministry officials—to discuss the draft curriculum to indigenize it to Bangladesh's needs. All the participants were surprised as well as happy to be a part of this exercise and felt that they were, for the first time, collectively thinking and discussing our country's environment-related problems and needs. They also conveyed their strong support for this effort by NSU and offered future assistance if and when needed.

The selection of teachers was equally meticulous. During my fifteen months as chairman, from January 1996 to March 1997, only two teachers were appointed full time in the department—a lecturer named Rumi Shammin, who had recently graduated from Cornell University; and an assistant professor named Islam Mohammad Faisal, who graduated with a PhD in hydrology from the Colorado State University, Fort Collins. The rest of the teachers were hired from outside the university on term contract, such as Prof. Ziaush Shams Haq, from the Geography Department of Dhaka University, and Prof. Robert McKim, from the Department of Philosophy of the University of Illinois at Urbana-Champaign, to teach environmental ethics.

The department also felt that there was an urgent need for an environment laboratory. We had unofficial agreements with the Geography Department of Dhaka University and with SPARRSO that allowed our students to use their labs. But we soon realized that we needed to have our own lab on campus, and I petitioned the president and got his approval to immediately start the consultations to build one within the department.

My commitment to establishing the department and to building up NSU and the concomitant investment of time and effort were so high that within a year, I became the victim of my own successes. Mr. Ahmed heaped more and more responsibilities on me because of my dedication, discipline, and hard work, and because of his belief that unlike most of the other faculty members, I can get things done within schedule and to his satisfaction.

In addition to teaching an undergraduate course, my departmental responsibilities included administering the department that had a total of six faculty members and three administrative staff, preparing advertisements for faculty appointment for new courses, recruiting visiting foreign and local faculty every semester, planning and designing the course offerings every semester, strategizing expansion of student enrolment, preparing the department budget, preparing the five-year projection of faculty need and student enrolment, designing a cutting-edge environmental studies syllabus by revising it at the end of every academic year, supervising course and faculty evaluation by students, overseeing examinations and grading, supervising the setting up of the environmental lab, and developing links with ranking environmental departments around the world, inter alia.

Within a few months of my chairmanship, the president pulled me into multiple committees, making me simultaneously a member of the University Management Board, a member of the University Curriculum Review Committee, a member of the University Admissions Committee, a member of the University Library Committee and then chairman of the Library Task Force from April 1998 to January 1999, the chairman of the University Convocation Committee for the years 1996 and 1997, as well as the University Marshall for Convocation 1996 and 1997.

Being a member of so many important university committees not only gave me high profile and raised my stature among the faculty and administration but also created challenges for me. Department heads and faculty members started to believe that I had direct, unfettered access to the president and board members and that I could get anything done. Since I was never afraid to voice my opinion, express a dissenting view, or fight for a cause I believed in, members of the faculty saw me as an effective conduit to convey their feelings and sometimes their demands as well.

While department heads forwarded their departmental requests to the president through the proper channel, they viewed me as a powerful ally and often approached me bilaterally to support their demands in committee meetings. Sometimes they sounded me out first on a potentially contentious issue before raising them in committee meetings or formally approaching the president. I too felt strong kinship with faculty members and built up strong camaraderie with the department heads, as well as with junior faculty.

I was particularly fond of our registrar, Zafrul Karim, who was a very likeable and affable gentleman and a highly capable and efficient administrator. He was respected by his office staff, who was also dedicated to offering diligent service from the registrar's office.

The president of NSU had full confidence in me and held me in high regard. There were moments when we would be alone and we would share with each other many things about the future of the university including our visions for NSU, which were basically the same: build up NSU into one of the finest universities in South Asia.

While he was usually reserved and measured in his speech, he did let his guard down with me occasionally. I recall asking him once why he named the university North South University. He said that when he was Bangladesh's ambassador to Rumania in the mid-1980s, he had the occasion to meet West German chancellor Willy Brandt and to ask him about his foreign policy initiative called *Ostpolitik*. The chancellor explained that it was his dream to normalize political relations between Eastern Europe and Western Europe, and particularly between the Federal Republic of Germany (West Germany) and the German Democratic Republic (East Germany). Mr. Ahmed was inspired by that and resolved then that, one day, he would like to found a university and name it North South University to bridge the intellectual gap between the north and the south.

I recall another moment when he was introducing the senior faculty and officials of NSU to the presidents of several American universities with whom we had Memoranda of Understanding (MOUs), and who were invited to NSU's first convocation in 1996. He introduced each one of the faculty by their name and their designation, and when it was my turn to be introduced, he paused and then said, "And this is Dr. Shaukat Hassan, who is half of NSU!" It was both flattering and embarrassing.

Being singled out for praise made me doubly sensitive to faculty dynamics. I wanted it to be clear in everyone's mind that my commitment to the university was absolute, that the interest of the university was supreme in my mind, and that there was never any personal motive involved. I wanted everyone to know that I was not territorial, and my every thought and action with regard to the university was always preceded by such questions in my mind as, how does this benefit NSU? Will this promote or undermine NSU's image? Therefore, it became necessary for me to earn the trust of the department heads by taking them into confidence and sharing with them my interactions with the president and the board members. I endeavored to make sure that they did not feel left out or ever doubt that I was one of them.

To that effect, I created the informal departmental heads group. Professor Waheeduzzaman, who headed the Graduate Business Program, proposed that we go out to lunch once every week. The heads of the departments, each excelling in their own disciplines and highly dedicated to building up the university, were a close-knit group. They were all excited about the prospects for their individual departments. Professor Musa, heading the Undergraduate Business Program, Professor Mollah, heading the Economics Department, Professor Haque heading the Computer Science Department, and every other head of the department were very supportive of each other, united in the common purpose of making NSU the finest private university in the country. They liked the idea of lunch meeting once every week very much, and we started having these weekly get-togethers where we aired our concerns, shared our departmental challenges, solicited ideas from each other, and floated new ideas that would advance the university's goals.

These weekly lunches assured the faculty heads that they were in the know with regard to developments at the highest levels of the university and that I was willing to fight for the interest of every department and not just the Department of Environmental Studies. It also gave us the chance each week to check out the fantastic restaurants that were popping up in Banani and Gulshan at the time. Sometimes we invited others as guests to our lunches to broaden our information-gathering network.

Since I had initiated this group, I assigned my secretary Suraiya Amina to coordinate with the secretaries of the other departments and make the reservations in the restaurants. Suraiya was a polite, soft-spoken, bright, young lady who discharged her responsibilities well and was of great help to me. It was a loss to me when she had to resign her job to accompany her husband, who was a BUET teacher, to the United States.

There was, however, a downside to having the departmental heads group. Among our objectives were to align our policies, present a united front against administrative intrusion into academic affairs, protect the interest of faculty and students, and keep open a robust communication channel. To that effect, we felt the need to work with the registrar on academic issues, and sometimes on university policy issues, so that both are on the same page.

The head of the Graduate Business School suggested that we might ask the representative of the registrar's office who was on secondment to his office to keep us informed of the registrar's activities. I was asked to convey that message to him, which I did. Unfortunately, that turned out to be a clumsy approach, because when he reported this to the registrar, it was natural for the registrar to assume that there was some kind of a conspiracy afoot against him and that we were using his guy on secondment to act as a spy. Our relationship with Zafrul Karim took a nosedive from then on. The way I conveyed the message and the message itself were totally wrong, because our original intent was not to alienate the registrar but to work with him. I never had the chance to rectify the situation or my relationship with Zafrul, and I regret it to this day. After Mr. Ahmed's departure from NSU, Zafrul also left and later became the registrar of Presidency University.

During my tenure, the NSU president participated in the meeting of the International Association of University Presidents (IAUP) held in the Netherlands. The IAUP was founded in 1964 in Oxford, UK, with the mission to provide a global vision of higher education, sponsor effective networking between university executives, and promote peace and international understanding through education.

Among those with whom Mr. Ahmed conferred at the meeting was the president of the University of California at Berkeley, who strongly supported the U.S. role to promote higher education in the private sector in the developing world. He invited the NSU president to visit Berkeley before returning to Dhaka. At Berkeley, the president met with the heads of its various environmental programs and discussed with them NSU's environmental studies program.

The president of UC Berkeley was impressed with NSU's effort and offered to sign an MOU between the environmental programs of the two universities. President Muslehuddin was so elated that he called me from Berkeley to discuss the MOU, which he signed before he left Berkeley. It was an unexpected gesture from Berkeley, one of the best-known universities in the world and a giant step forward for NSU. It should be pointed out that many of the MOUs NSU signed with top-ranked American universities during Muslehuddin Ahmed's presidency no longer exists, and these have been replaced by MOUs with universities below par.

One day, I received a call from a director in the Bangladesh Ministry of Environment and Forest (MEF); he asked whether he could meet me in my office. When he came over, he explained to me that the minister for environment was invited to deliver a keynote address at a global environmental conference that was being held in Honolulu and that the ministry would be grateful if I could draft the minister's speech.

I was surprised and flattered that the ministry would reach out to our department for assistance. I asked him for the talking points that should be incorporated into the speech. He meekly explained that the government regularly signs international treaties without fully understanding their import and implications and that no in-depth analyses had been done of the documents that followed from the Earth Summit of 1992 in Brazil. He said that I probably knew as much if not more about the treaties, conventions, and agreements on the environment than anyone in the ministry, and so I was the appropriate person to draft the speech.

Seeing his desperation, I agreed to draft the speech. The next day, I sent the draft speech to him with a note that I will finalize it after the ministry's and the minister's comments, suggestions, and edits. Not receiving any feedback, I assumed that the MEF had done the edits and finalized the speech. About a week later, the speech that the minister delivered at the conference in Honolulu was published in the Dhaka newspapers, and I was shocked to see that the minister had delivered exactly the same draft speech that I had forwarded to the ministry, with no changes whatsoever. When I called the director and asked him about it, he said that the minister was satisfied with the draft and so didn't want to change anything.

On another occasion a few months later, I received a call from the Ministry of Foreign Affairs inviting me to the ministry to discuss with and analyze for a select group of ministry officials the significance of the international treaty that Bangladesh had recently signed, as well as provide advice regarding its implementation. I realized then that the governmental ministries had low intellectual and analytical capacity and that they needed urgent help.

The Birth of the Department of General and Continuing Education

The above two incidents led me to draft a proposal to create a new department at NSU that would cater to subject-matter training for government officials. I marketed the idea to the president as an outreach program to serve the broader public, and I also told him of my recent experiences with the two government ministries. I reminded him that during the Pakistan time, government officials were regularly sent to Harvard or to Johns Hopkins or to the Fletcher School of Law and Diplomacy at Tufts University for three-to-six-month training or refresher courses on particular topics of international significance.

I explained to him that Bangladesh was probably at a disadvantage at the negotiating table because of the low intellectual, conceptual, and analytical capacity of its civil servants. This is not to say that our civil servants were incompetent; they were generally competent, but most of them lacked the confidence and the cutting edge. I knew that the Ministry of Foreign Affairs had very bright and highly skilled people, but I also knew that there were not enough A. K. H. Morsheds or Farooq Sobhans or Iftekhar Ahmed Chowdhurys to take on the world, and that while most of the officers were potentially bright, they were still young and inexperienced. Mr. Ahmed thought that was an excellent idea and even liked the name I proposed: Department of General and Continuing Education (GCE). The proposal was put before the board, and it was approved.

With the establishment of the Department of General and Continuing Education (GCE) in March 1997, Mr. Muslehuddin Ahmed decided that I should hand over the chairmanship of the Department of Environmental Studies to Dr. Islam Mohammad Faisal, who had joined the department nine months earlier, and assume the chairmanship of GCE to give it a strong foundation. So I was appointed as the chairman of the Department of GCE in April 1997.

My responsibilities were similar to those of any academic department. But it also opened up major possibilities. According to its name, the department was mandated to provide general education as well as continuing education. This provided me with a broad scope to offer a wide variety of subjects, which became elective courses for students as well as expanded the university's liberal education curriculum.

We were able to offer courses in multiple disciplines, such as anthropology, geography, history, law, philosophy, sociology, psychology, political science, global security, public administration, gender studies, biology, zoology, Bengali language and literature, and world religions during my nearly two-year tenure. The instructors for these courses were recruited from Bangladesh's public universities.

It was a win-win arrangement for NSU and the instructors. On the one hand, it gave these instructors the opportunity to teach at the country's most prestigious university and enhance their academic credentials. They also earned an amount equal to their annual salary from teaching a single course at NSU. On the other hand, it was a great outreach program for the university as it opened up the opportunity to build strong relationships with other institutions of higher learning. It was also a way of disseminating NSU's academic rigor and of its culture of transparency and accountability that were generally missing at public universities.

There was also the need to reach out to other important constituencies such as government service holders, teachers and administrators in rural schools, and NGO personnel to offer them refresher courses as well as the opportunity to upgrade their knowledge and skills. I started consultation with the Ministry of Foreign Affairs on what would be the best mechanism for us to offer our services that met their needs. The discussion had just started and was quite promising.

At a diplomatic dinner, some dinner guests were curious to know about the new department at NSU. I gave them a brief description of what the department's avowed purpose was, and in the course of the conversation, I mentioned that I was toying with the idea of initiating distance education that would initially target the students of districts bordering the Dhaka district, and that my first hurdle would be to set up the online course. I also mentioned my hope of broadcasting specially designed lessons, such as on the state of environmental degradation in the country and how that would impact our lives, to students and teachers in remote corners of the country, especially where the government's investment in education has been lacking.

One of the diplomats informed me that the USIS was replacing its decades-old radar with modern radar and that I should try to get the old radar, which could help the university to provide distance education. The next day in office, I made a few phone calls and tracked down the person I needed to talk to in the U.S. embassy about the discarded radar. My American colleague confirmed that the radar that had been on USIS's rooftop for decades was indeed very old and that a decision had been made to replace it with a modern one with considerably increased capacity and efficiency. He went on to say that every day, information packages and contents were sent from the USIS headquarters in Washington DC and downloaded at the local USIS library but that the data inflow had become so enormous that the existing radar's capacity was wholly inadequate to the modern requirement.

He mentioned that they were going to disassemble the old radar and pack it and ship it back to the States. I then explained to him our department's plan and that since they were going to discard it anyways, would the USIS be willing to give it to us *gratis* but for a very good cause. He assured me that he would raise the matter with their office in Washington DC and get back to me soon.

A couple of weeks later, he called me back and informed me that the USIS was pleased to support private sector education in the country and would be happy to donate the radar to NSU. They would need a formal request from NSU outlining its need for the radar and also accept the responsibility to transport it from the USIS premises to NSU campus. I discussed the matter with Muslehuddin Ahmed, who was happy that we could lay our hands on the radar for free and approved the arrangement. He sent off the letter.

While waiting for USIS's formal approval for transfer, I started scouting for an appropriate place on campus to set it up. However, the difficulty was that the campus was on rented property and there was already plan afoot to look for a suitable real estate for a permanent campus. The radar installation would require a solid concrete foundation, and no building owner would allow NSU to locate such a contraption on their rooftop. Since NSU was still a few years away from relocating to a permanent campus, we were ultimately unable to take the radar.

Since research and learning were integrally linked to the reputation of any university, fairly early NSU also established the Institute for Development, Environment and Strategic Studies (IDESS). However, within a short period of its launching, the IDESS director resigned and left for a better opportunity in the United States. The president once again turned to me and made me the director, in addition to my departmental chairmanship. As director of IDESS from January 1996 to January 1999, my responsibilities included filling up the void left behind by departing research personnel and staff; raising research funds from international donor community; directing research projects; developing research linkages and collaborative activities with other in-country and subcontinental institutions; liaising with government officials/agencies, the media; establishing cordial relationships with donor agencies in Bangladesh; preparing and securing the institute's annual and supplementary budgets; preparing advertisements for research fellowship appointments; negotiating for the Fulbright fellowship program at IDESS; supervising the preparation of research proposals; supervising presentation of research proposals to funding agencies; overseeing and monitoring research work; and running day-to-day administration.

A Quick Visit to Narikel Jinjira

Within the first few months, I was able to negotiate two grants for IDESS, one from the Ford Foundation, Dhaka, and the other from the research wing of the Grameen Bank. The foundation grant was used for two purposes: to hire researchers for short periods and to procure necessary research tools like computers for the institute; while the bank grant funded a research project in Narikel Jinjira (St. Martin's Island) off the southern coast of Bangladesh.

Since there was simmering tension in the island, the Narikel Jinjira project was undertaken to identify the factors that were likely to trigger conflict, and to suggest proactive measures to prevent conflict on the island. I decided to join the research team to visit Narikel Jinjira for two reasons; first, to make a personal assessment of on-the-ground situation and the dynamics at work there; and, second, to explore the feasibility of setting up an environmental research facility on the island.

Getting to the island was, of course, a big challenge, for there was no regular means of communication with the mainland at the time. One option was to hire a boatman who had a sturdy-enough fishing boat with a motor and would be willing to rent it for the return trip. The other option was to seek help from the Bangladesh Navy, which would require a lot of paperwork without any guarantee of success in the effort. A third option was to seek the help of foreign missions who had commercial presence in the Bay of Bengal. We learned that the German embassy in Dhaka had a motorized vessel that they might be willing to lend to the university. However, when we contacted the German embassy about renting their vessel, they regretfully informed us that their vessel was undergoing refitting and therefore not available. So we fell back on the first option.

The lead researcher of the project made all the arrangements. We hired a minivan from Dhaka to Chittagong and then to Teknaf, a town located on the southernmost tip of Bangladesh. He rented a shallow engine boat with which we went to the island, which is about nine kilometers south of Teknaf on the Bay of Bengal. The journey over water took more than two hours. As we neared the island on its eastern coast, we saw fishing boats moored along the shoreline and fishes hung on strings left out to dry by the bank.

The boat came as close to the shore as possible, and we folded our pant legs and disembarked into ankle-deep water and walked up the sandy beach to the road, which was just a narrow mud strip. Lined on one side were a number of huts where elderly women sold basic amenities and island girls sold trinkets made of fish bones and sea shells for the occasional tourist. We boarded flatbed rickshaws that took us to the island's only "resting place" that the lead researcher had reserved for us. It was just a covered open space with rattan mats on the red floor and a few decorative pillows thrown here and there.

We washed up with water drawn up by a tube well pump and sat down cross-legged on rattan mats where food was served. The choice of food was incredibly limited; there was no meat on the island, only fish, fish, and more fish. And it wasn't even fish curry; it was fish that was fried to such an extent that it was hard and brittle. Even vegetables had to be brought from the mainland by boat once every several weeks. Our meal was rice, dahl, and dried fish galore, but somehow the meal was delicious, which was perhaps a reflection of how hungry we were more than anything else. We had brought our own water bottles.

After a short rest, we spent the entire day traveling across the six-by-six-kilometer island and canvassing people about their state of affairs. It was a new experience for the islanders, for they had never been canvassed before. The womenfolk were more eager to talk to us than were the menfolk, who were cautious and reluctant.

The islanders had many complaints, and almost all of them seemed to me to be quite legitimate. They complained that the government in Dhaka, irrespective of political parties, did not give a hoot about them and totally neglected them; that even when the island was hit by tropical storms—which was quite frequently—the government's response was usually tardy and lukewarm; that communication with the mainland was only by boats, and even that was unpredictable and unreliable, and that the government had shown no interest to improve the situation; that the island's only economy was fishing, but when boats returned with low catch, survival became a problem; that the Bangladesh government's forced settlement in the island of Bengali refugees from West Pakistan after independence had exacerbated the social problem; etc.

The women had additional problems, and those had to do with their errant husbands. They complained that when the men sold their catch to the buyers from the mainland, they often wasted much of the money on booze and whoring and that they could never give a proper or honest accounting of their catch or their earnings. The interviews were honest and heartfelt and a real eye-opener for the research team.

We visited all parts of the island. Whereas the east coast had white sandy beaches, the west coast was mostly very rocky and full of pebbles. Interestingly, I saw the same thing in Sri Lanka, which I was to visit a few years later. We saw a solitary blue-colored house with windows locked from inside standing on the northwest coast. I went for a closer look and found it to be padlocked with a heavy chain across its front door. When I asked our local guide about the house, he said that it belonged to Bangladesh's famous writer and novelist, the late Humayun Ahmed; that it was chained because of a payment dispute with the locals; and that the writer had virtually abandoned the place because of the fear of the irate locals.

We traveled to the south of the island where even rickshaw or bicycle travel was not possible because there were no roads or path; one had to walk through soggy and partially submerged patches of low land to go to the island's southern tip. Our initial assessment was that it would be incredibly difficult to set up an environmental research station on the island because of the lack of fundamental needs pertaining to travel, communication, accommodation and sustenance, and work supplies. Our interviews, however, provided us with a huge bank of information to work with.

We had planned to return to the mainland on the same day, and mindful of the boatman's warning that the waters of the bay start churning up toward the evening as the wind begins to pick up then, we boarded our not-so-seaworthy vessel well before the sun started to set. But halfway to our destination, the boatman's facial expression started changing for the worse as he pointed to the dark horizon in the distance behind us. He told us that a storm was brewing, and it was unpredictable how fast it would travel or in which direction it would ultimately turn. He asked us to wrap ourselves up in the blankets and to sit close to each other balanced in the front and back of the boat. We were afraid because the boat was rather slow and wondered what would happen if we got caught in the storm. We could see the dark specter get larger, but thankfully it still remained far away by the time we docked in Teknaf.

Having visited the island and collected some valuable information, the research team concluded that building an environmental research station on the island was not feasible at the moment. It also concluded that there was an urgent need to develop proactively a conflict mitigation strategy to ward off future conflagration. There was agreement that the island's women needed to play an active role in island life, and a good starting point would be to train them on basic accounting so that they can manage the island's economy rather than leave it in the hands of fishermen whose priorities did not appear to be sound or sensible.

Accordingly, a training program for the women was designed and implemented. There was initial resentment among some menfolk, but when they realized that women were far better in understanding family needs and priorities and were good money managers, men started to accept the new reality and cooperate. The project went into the next phase, which was to design and implement a conflict mitigation strategy that sought to address three critical issues: island-mainland dynamics and political relations, issues between the settled refugees and the native islanders, and promoting additional livelihoods to complement the fishing economy.

Besides the Narikel Jinjira project, there were a number of other project proposals that I wished to pursue, which were based on knowledge gained from my various earlier project work in India and from my experience while working at the BIISS. Both had convinced me that there was so much distrust and misgiving among the leaders and peoples of the countries of South Asia that it undercut any possibility of rapport and collaboration, and that a critical first step toward restoring normal relations was to initiate a series of confidence building measures.

I thought of a number of areas that we could and must target, such as periodic dialogue between the editors of major newspapers in South Asia with inter alia the aim of setting up a code of conduct that will guide subcontinental news reporting; dialogue between the chambers of commerce and industry to promote good business practices and mutually lucrative businesses; and periodic dialogue between academics to promote better understanding of issues critical to the region and endeavor toward collective solutions.

However, I thought that I would like to start first with the parliaments of the region. Since the parliament was the people's elected body where the affairs of the state and governmental policies were discussed and vetted, a promising confidence building measure could be interparliamentary dialogue where parliamentary delegations from SAARC countries could meet periodically to discuss contentious issues and work toward amicable solutions.

I drafted a letter addressed to Sangma Tura, the Speaker of the *Lok Sabha* (the lower house of India's bicameral parliament), explaining my proposal, and mailed it to him together with a concept note on the proposed dialogue. I was delighted to receive a positive response from the office of the Speaker, who acclaimed the idea and invited me to visit New Delhi to discuss the proposal further. Excited by the prospect of getting this interparliamentary exchange started, I went to see Humayun Rasheed Chowdhury, the Speaker of the Jatiya Sangsad (Bangladesh Parliament), in his parliamentary office. He listened to my proposal, thought there was considerable merit in it, and acknowledged that getting the positive nod from the Speaker of the Lok Sabha was indeed a good beginning. He asked me to leave the concept note and proposal with him so that he can give some thought to the proposal and said that he would get in touch with me soon. I was very pleased with the Speaker's response as I left his office.

A couple of weeks passed by, but I didn't hear anything from the Speaker's office. I was getting anxious because I did not want to lose the momentum and was eagerly waiting to get his approval so that I can take the next steps. I tried to get a second appointment with the Speaker but couldn't; in fact, I never got to see him again, and worse yet, I learned shortly thereafter that one of his relatives associated with another institute was pursuing the idea! I was very surprised because I never expected my idea to be hijacked by someone of Mr. Chowdhury's stature. Mr. Chowdhury had served Bangladesh honorably as its ambassador to important diplomatic posts, as a foreign secretary, as a foreign minister, and as the president of the forty-first session of the UN General Assembly in 1985. Anyway, it was a disappointing experience for me, and it put a damper on my other project pursuits.

There were a number of other items on my IDESS to-do list, such as exchange programs with other institutes in the region that would allow students, faculty, and researchers to spend three to six months in each other's institutions; organizing some international conferences on topical issues either singly or jointly with BIISS or the Bangladesh Institute of Law and International Affairs (BILIA) or other national institutes; workshops on domestic issues; etc. But a big constraint was budget, because NSU was unwilling to invest on "nonessential" areas or activities. Added to that, a new worry emerged that demanded immediate attention.

Proctorship and Its Challenges

By the summer of 1996, the university faced a number of very serious nonacademic issues that required immediate attention. It was reported internally that an increasing number of students were turning to drugs. They were primarily kids from affluent background who somehow lost their direction and fell prey to drug pushers. This came as a shock to the senior administration. Since it had potentially serious repercussions, we debated what would be the most effective way to handle this problem. Class attendance of these otherwise bright kids who had become drug addicts had plummeted, together with their grades. There was no chance that they would graduate if the problem remained unaddressed. Given the cost of education at NSU, the financial loss to their parents was huge. Parents were also uncertain how their children went off track. They wondered whether it was the university's fault or it was the parents who had failed these kids. There was also the social stigma that both the addicts and their parents faced, and of course the image and prestige of the university were at stake. Handling the issue discreetly and urgently was indispensable.

Response to this crisis, which was still very limited within the student body and quite manageable if addressed urgently, varied among the senior faculty and administration officials. One opinion shared by the hard-nosed was that these students should be summarily expelled from the university before they infected others and before the word got out. They were quite intolerant of students who they felt were deliberately misusing or wasting their parents' money and undermining the prestige and honor of their families, and therefore they ought to be punished through expulsion. They also felt that whatever rehabilitation was required ought to be the responsibility of the parents.

I took a diametrically opposite view with minority support. I argued that a university has obligations to its students and to the society at large. The job of an excellent university is not only to impart high-quality education but also to mold the physical, moral, mental, and ethical character of its students, so that they become good citizens who

279

are ready and able to shoulder the challenges they will face in life, as well as help their country and society advance and prosper.

The second equally challenging problem was the physical security of the NSU campus. Theft of university assets, damage and defacement of university property, increasing eve-teasing and fear of assault felt by female students after evening classes were among the concerns being increasingly reported to the university authorities.

During my tenure, political disturbances and *hartals* by disgruntled students and politicians were a common occurrence throughout cities and towns, and it was expected that every educational institution should join these countrywide protests. Mindful not only of the need to finish our courses on time but also of the security of our students attending their classes, we decided to take some bold measures to stay undeterred, focused, and on course. We required our teachers to deliver their lectures on weekends as well. For some courses, we taped the lectures for distribution to the students in those classes. We held all our classes during normal weekdays as well, but locked every door on campus on the outside with chains and padlocks to give the impression that our university was locked down and had joined the protests, while, actually, classes were being held inside.

But the issues of drugs and physical security of campus required different solutions, and the upshot of the debates on those issues was the unanimous decision to recruit a proctor of the university. Once again, the president turned to me and made me the proctor with the full support of the faculty and the administration. So I became the proctor from August 1996 until my departure from the university in January 1999. My new additional responsibilities included overseeing the security of the physical assets of the university, recruiting security guards, overseeing the management of campus security guards and their duties, contracting security agencies to provide special services to the university, overseeing the maintenance of law and order on campus and general security, enforcement of the university's "no drugs" and "no smoking" policies, overseeing provisions for special security for female students, maintaining working relationships with law enforcement agencies, maintaining working relationships with drug rehabilitation centers, monitoring political activities on campus, and periodic briefings for the university president on campus issues.

Many of my relatives and friends lived in the posh suburbs of Gulshan and Baridhara and had hired security companies to protect their homes and their businesses from unwanted intrusion. I consulted with some of them to get their opinions on the quality of service provided by these companies. I talked with restaurant owners about the quality of protection they were getting for their premises. I also consulted my colleagues at NSU about their experiences with security companies.

Having gotten a profile on a number of security companies, meetings were scheduled with them in which the registrar, the administrative officer, and I interviewed them. Most of these companies were founded by and run by ex-army officers, and the personnel were also usually of army, intelligence, or police background. Since the quality of service offered by these security companies varied measurably, it was not difficult to choose a company that had the training, the resources, and the deployment capability that fit the particular needs of NSU. We signed a contract with a security company for one year.

The university also decided to create a student counselling center and to recruit a student counsellor, whose primary tasks would be to address the drug problem and provide counselling to needy students, teach an undergraduate psychology course, as well as work closely with the proctor to maintain law and order in the campus. Within a month of my assuming the post of proctor, Ms. Durriya Meer was appointed as the student counsellor from September 1, 1996. She was a young, talented, and able counsellor and quite hardworking and dedicated to special needs students; she was also very discreet. She immediately reached out to the city's existing rehabilitation centers and made arrangements for our students in dire need for therapy. It was a pleasure to work with her on this important task of reclaiming hitherto promising students from drug addiction and putting them back on the path to a bright future. Although it would take some time to completely wipe out the drug problem, it was a relief to us that the university was on the right track.

Bangladesh's First University Convocation

The year was 1996, and the first batch of students who had enrolled in North South University in 1993 was ready to graduate. The last university convocation was held at Dhaka University twenty-six years earlier in former East Pakistan. There had not been any graduation ceremony in the new country of Bangladesh.

Mr. Muslehuddin Ahmed was very eager and excited that NSU should organize a memorable graduation ceremony and thought of it as the university's signature achievement. His intention was to assign not only someone very senior but also someone he could completely trust to take over the management of the convocation from start to finish. He called me to his office and asked me if I could start the preparatory work until he found someone of higher academic stature and experience.

I was excited to get this assignment, a first for NSU and a first for Bangladesh. I returned to my office to draft an outline of how I am going to approach this task. As I began to think about it, I began to realize the gravity of this assignment, that everything will have to be done from scratch since there was no pro forma or template to follow, that there were huge expectations in all quarters from the president to the faculty down to the graduating students, and that tremendous pressure and even panic may set in as we approach the final day.

My immediate assessment was that this task was so gargantuan that it could not be done by me alone, and that I would need a fully invested, reliable team to support me. I also knew that the university had limited resources, and therefore whatever requests I will have to make have to be minimal and prioritized. I decided to start off with only one convocation assistant and my secretary, Suraiya. I wrote a memo to the president to assign to me Hussain Shareef Ahmad, a lecturer in the Department of Business, as my assistant. I chose him because he was an amiable, dedicated, highly capable young man whose sense of responsibility impressed me. I also found the chemistry between us to be excellent. The president readily approved my request, and Shareef was happy to come on board. From that day on, he and I rolled up our sleeves and plunged into convocation work, not only fulfilling our normal duties as faculty but also working extended hours to make the convocation ceremony an event to remember.

To move on all fronts simultaneously where possible and with urgency, we created mini task teams and assigned each team discrete tasks with deadlines. Our convocation work proceeded at full steam, and Shareef and I spent every minute of our time outside our departmental commitments to discuss, plan, and strategize. We reached out to whichever office was necessary to get whatever human or material resources we needed. To facilitate our joint work, I dedicated the spare space in my department on the fifth floor to our convocation work, building several workstations for convenience and efficiency.

Shortly after we started our work, Prof. Salim Rashid, of the Department of Economics at the University of Illinois at Urbana-Champaign, came to visit us. He was serving as a part-time unofficial advisor to Pres. Muslehuddin Ahmed at the time and was sent to check on the progress we were making. After I finished briefing him on what had already been accomplished, what was under way, and what needed to be done, he expressed his satisfaction and told me that he felt the convocation work was under control. He then added that the president had asked him to take charge of the convocation, but having seen personally how we had organized our work and were going about it, and our enthusiastic volunteers, he felt the entire task was in the right hands. He said that he will decline the president's request and recommend that I should continue my work and that I should be made the convocation chairman.

With the vote of confidence from his confidant, the president was somewhat relieved from the concern whether I can handle it and officially designated me as the convocation chair. He also appointed me as the university marshal and appointed Shareef as the assistant university marshal. He also approved the tentative budget.

After much senior-level discussion regarding the convocation venue, the Bangladesh Army Stadium (at that time known as the Ershad Stadium), on Mymensingh Highway in Banani, was finally selected from a list of multiple sites. It was available for use on the date we wanted it; it was very near to our campus; there was no traffic problem and therefore accessibility was easy; there was no capacity problem and therefore we would have ample space for seating and setting up snacking tables and stalls; and the necessary monitoring and security apparatus could be easily deployed.

With the venue selection confirmed, we assigned our head of administration, Mukhlesur Rahman, who was a retired army colonel himself, to contact the appropriate authorities and do the necessary paperwork to get the permission for its use. He was also asked to consult with the intelligence services and the presidential security service to make arrangements for the necessary security if the president of Bangladesh accepted our invitation to attend the convocation. The office of administration was also responsible for advertising the needed convocation services, compare the bids, and make the final selection of the suppliers—namely, decorators, caterers, printers, costume suppliers, videographer, and photographer.

The group comprising the department heads and the registrar that was responsible for making up the list of potential foreign dignitaries who could be invited came up with names of persons with international stature; they included Presidents Clinton and Carter, philanthropist Bill Gates, and Nobel laureate Amartya Sen. I was assigned the task of contacting them informally to ascertain who would be available and willing to deliver an address at the convocation. If we received positive acknowledgement from anyone, then the NSU president would send a formal invitation to participate in our convocation.

Since the telephone on Mr. Muslehuddin Ahmed's desk was the only one that had a direct international line, I had to come to his office at odd hours to make the calls to the offices or homes of the dignitaries on our list because of the time difference between Dhaka and the cities in the United States. I called the Carter Center in Atlanta and spoke with President Carter's appointment secretary about our desire to invite the president to our convocation. She thanked me but regretted that the president was in bad health at the time and would not be able to travel to such far-off distance.

I called President Clinton's foundation in New York and learned that the president was heavily booked until the end of the year and therefore not available. I called Bill Gates's office in Seattle and was informed that at the time of our convocation, Mr. Gates will be visiting several African countries on foundation business.

I then called Amartya Sen at Trinity College, Cambridge University, and was told that he was away on sabbatical at Harvard. I took his telephone number at Harvard and called him there. His wife, Emma Rothschild, answered the phone. I explained to her the reason for my call and wondered if she could convey the message to Mr. Sen. She replied, "You know he will be quite upset when he hears this. He loves to go to Dhaka whenever he gets the chance, and I am sure he would have loved to attend your convocation. But he has recently been hospitalized and he will have to convalesce for a while, doctor's orders. But I will pass on the message. Thank you for calling. Wish you a happy convocation." I was sorry to hear about Mr. Sen's failing health.

In any case, our attempts to attract international dignitaries to the convocation had ended in total failure. The earlier concerns whether we would have to issue a first-class or business-class round-trip ticket and a speaker's fee to our international invitees were no longer there. It was decided that we would invite the presidents of the U.S. universities with whom we had signed MOUs and try our best to get the president of Bangladesh, Shahabuddin Ahmed, as the chief guest. Accordingly, letters of invitation went out promptly to the presidents of our partner universities in the United States. A request was also forwarded for an appointment with the president of Bangladesh.

The day of appointment with the president of Bangladesh at Bangabhaban finally arrived, and Mr. Ahmed informed me that he had gotten permission from Bangabhaban for me to accompany him to meet with the president. I knew how eagerly he waited for this opportunity to personally invite the president of the republic. He told me that the chairman of the NSU board, who outranked him in the pecking order, would insist that the chairman should meet with the president to invite him, but Mr. Ahmed felt strongly that as the founder of the university, it was his right to meet and invite the president. So on the day of appointment, he and I drove up to Bangabhaban.

We were ushered into one of Bangabhaban's resplendent drawing rooms. The president was sitting in a comfortable sofa and signaled us to sit down on sofas across from him. We were offered tea. The president asked us how we were and how NSU was doing. After a few minutes of informative talk, he gave the floor to Muslehuddin Ahmed. The NSU president thanked the government for its help, with special thanks to President Shahabuddin, who was the chancellor of all private universities in Bangladesh, for his support. After finishing his pitch, he got up and handed over to the president the invitation card and a copy of our convocation brochure.

The president thanked him as he read the invitation card and went over the brochure page by page; he seemed to be genuinely interested. Then he buzzed his ADC and handed the invitation card to him, asking him to check the convocation date against the president's appointments calendar. We waited for a little while. The ADC returned to inform the president that there were no presidential engagements on that date. The president smiled and then turned to us and uttered the words that we were eagerly waiting to hear from his lips. He said that he would be happy to attend NSU's convocation.

We were elated. We thanked him, told him we would work with his ADC to make all the arrangements, and then bade him farewell. Once in the car, we were two happy, smiling people heading back to campus. Getting the president to attend Bangladesh's first university convocation in twenty-six years was a feather in Muslehuddin Ahmed's cap! After returning to his office, he sent out a message to the heads of the departments and the registrar about the president's acceptance of our invitation. He personally called the chairman of the NSU board and informed him of our visit to Bangabhaban and of the president's affirmation to be the chief guest. Subsequently, the young, talented, and hardworking Kashmiri Ali, who got the NSU contract to supply the convocation apparel—gown, cap, sash, sleeve, and cape—went to Bangabhaban to get the president's measurements for his convocation gown and hat size.

Our convocation work went into a new level of vigor now that we knew that the president was coming. We wanted it to be the most memorable occasion for all the participants: our foreign guests, our graduating students and their parents, the faculty, and the entire NSU. Once all the convocation tasks were completed, we conducted a dry run to ensure that on the day of convocation, everything will run like clockwork.

Convocation day, December 18, 1996, was a proud moment for NSU when I held up the national flag and led the convocation procession with the president of Bangladesh and the rest of the invitees following me from the gate of the Army Stadium to the convocation podium. After everyone was seated, the national anthem was played, and then I, as the university marshal, announced the starting of the ceremony. Then there was recitation from the Holy Quran, followed by speeches by NSU president, the chairman of the board of governors; address by Dr. Ray Hoops, who was the president of the University of Southern Indiana, USA; address by the valedictorian; address by the minister of education; and finally address by the honorable president of Bangladesh and the chancellor of North South University.

Leading NSU's first convocation procession, December 1996

In his address, President Shahabuddin told the graduands that while acquiring knowledge was important, it is not "a substitute for the nobility of character . . . [and] a rigorous honesty in their dealings with others." He praised NSU, saying that "despite many challenges, the NSU has earned reputation at home and abroad," and noted with satisfaction that while the Private University Act 1992 "envisages financial assistance to 5 percent students, the NSU is providing education to its 7 percent students free of cost." After the conclusion of his speech, the honorable president conferred the degrees, at the end of which the ninety-six graduates of the class of 1996 screamed and tossed their caps into the air, signifying the successful end of an important chapter in their lives. The entire event progressed flawlessly, and there was much joy, merriment, and videos and picture taking for posterity.

On January 20, 1997, at the first meeting of the Academic Committee after NSU's first convocation, the NSU president expressed his satisfaction at the success of the event. The president and the committee commended me for my "excellent work as Chairman of the Convocation Committee."

The year 1997 was memorable to all Bangladeshis, for in April of that year, Bangladesh had won for the first time the ICC Cricket Trophy in Kuala Lumpur, Malaysia, by defeating Kenya in the finals; a total of twenty-two cricketing nations had participated. It was the qualification tournament for the 1999 Cricket World Cup. It also catapulted Bangladesh to test status in 2000. My NSU convocation assistant was able to get for me a mini cricket bat with the autographs of all the Bangladeshi championship players including that of its coach, Gordon Greenidge, a Barbadian who had played for the West Indies for seventeen years. I presented my son Mishu with the autographed cricket bat.

Fractures within NSU

No convocation was held in 1997, and the official reason was that there were not a sufficient number of graduands to warrant a convocation ceremony that year. The precipitous deterioration of relations between the board members and the NSU president began to slowly consume the university and did not help the situation either. The atmosphere at the management level turned toxic faster than anyone had anticipated.

The primary issue was control over the finances and the future direction of the university. The board members were primarily industrialists who viewed the university as a commercial enterprise and were hell-bent on controlling its annual revenue. Some of them were founders of private banks and fought over the ownership of NSU's bank accounts. Regrettably, however, as one senior university official pointed out, the board members were also the same people whose names were on the list of bank defaulters published by the national newspapers.

The NSU president, on the other hand, saw the university as an academic enterprise and fought the board members for primacy of academic interests over commercial interests. The fight between them and within the board itself became so nasty that the board broke up into three distinct factions, each vying for supremacy over the others. But with the exception of a few, all the board members had one common cause—namely, that the president must go or be forced out if he doesn't depart willingly. They needed someone to replace him urgently so as to bring the university under their absolute control, and they found the right man in the person of Hafiz Siddiqi, who was the dean of the Business School.

Siddiqi was a man of calm demeanor, of gentle nature, soft spoken but astute at manipulation, having mastered the art when he was a teacher at Dhaka University. He camouflaged his greed for power very well. My relationship with him, as with everyone in the university, was cordial. We respected each other, and he thought of me as highly dependable.

One day, I got a telephone call from him inviting me to have lunch with him at Saffron restaurant that had opened in Banani the previous year. During lunch, he shared with me his plans. He told me that the chairman of the board had hired a powerful lawyer skilled in wrecking people's lives and will not stop until Muslehuddin was removed. The chairman had promised to make him the vice-chancellor of the university. Siddiqi then told me that he would like me to replace him as the dean of the Business School, and together we could control the university on behalf of the board.

I was horrified by his suggestion. I also pointed out that I had never taken a business course in my life and it made absolutely no sense for me to be the dean of Business School. Besides, there was Mohammad Musa, who was the head of the Business Department, and Waheeduzzaman, who was the head of the Graduate Business Program, both of whom had a legitimate claim to the deanship than I did.

Siddiqi countered saying that deanship was a political appointment and did not necessarily require me to be a business professor. He told me that no one would contest my appointment because of the many positions I held and because of my reputation and standing in the university. He assured me that he would handle any political problem that might arise. I told him that implementing his plan would cause rift within the faculty and was tantamount to surrendering the academic future of the university to commercial greed. He rebutted that the NSU board thought highly of me and suggested that he and I should call on the chairman of the board at his residence to hear him out.

I grudgingly agreed to do that because I was also curious about what the chairman had to say. I accompanied Siddiqi to the chairman's house one evening, and we waited for the chairman to return from work. When he entered his drawing room, he at once launched into a diatribe against Muslehuddin Ahmed and told me that he wouldn't rest until the president was booted out of the university. He also stated that the president had no support within the board. I was truly aghast at the chairman's hatred for the president and his commitment to go to any length to achieve his goal. And I was equally shocked at Siddiqi's cowardice and betrayal of the president and the university.

A few months earlier, Siddiqi had gotten into trouble with the authorities at Dhaka University (DU). The DU authorities had written a formal letter to Muslehuddin Ahmed informing him that Hafiz Siddiqi had gone to the United States with official leave from the university and with the understanding that when he returned to Bangladesh, he would provide equal number of years of service to DU. The letter accused Siddiqi of failing to fulfill his obligations under that leave arrangement, as well as accused NSU of "stealing" him with a higher salary.

Furthermore, the letter demanded that since he had not returned to DU, he must forthwith return the 12 lakh taka in salary that had been deposited by the university into his account during the years he was abroad. Siddiqi, however, was unwilling to return a single taka to DU and begged the president to find a solution that would allow him to stay at NSU as well as retain the salary money.

The president was in a bind. He did not wish to create bad blood between NSU and the premier public university but at the same time wanted to help his friend. He conferred with Siddiqi, and they both agreed that one way out of this mess was for Siddiqi to no longer hold a professorial/teaching position at NSU; instead, he would be rehired as a consultant to the university. The DU authorities were peeved at what seemed like a Machiavellian move. Anyway, this unpleasant saga ended with the president bending over backward to help Siddiqi at the expense of Dhaka University.

As the president narrated this to me one evening after the board had forcefully prevented him from entering NSU, I could see in his anguished face that he felt he had compromised his principles to help a friend who then betrayed him by siding with the board members who had kicked him out of the university he had founded.

The university decided that it will hold the second convocation on December 18, 1998. Siddiqi turned to me again to chair the convocation committee and to serve as the university marshal. He told me that he felt that there was no one else who could pull it off as smoothly as I could. But his real concern was that he was on the hook to demonstrate to the board his capacity to run the university and conduct the convocation as well as Muslehuddin Ahmed had done.

I acquiesced in his request for the sake of NSU and once again conducted the 1998 convocation ceremonies. But I knew full well that once I delivered the convocation, Siddiqi would find a way to get rid of me for not embracing his plans and doing his bidding. I returned to Ottawa to spend my Christmas holidays with my family. My contract with NSU was to expire on January 19, 1999, so I requested the new contract to be sent to me before I left Ottawa for NSU. There was no response from NSU.

I thought I should let the chairman know, so I wrote to him on January 30, 1999. He passed my letter to Siddiqi. A new contract dated February 22 was sent to me, which denied me the 10 percent increment that was due to me. On the contrary, it slashed my salary that was in the old contract. I faxed my response on February 24, expressing my disappointment at the salary cut and the denial of the increment and requesting reconsideration. Siddiqi's very able special assistant Omar Khasru faxed me back on March 14 stating that they had received my fax of February 24 on March 4, that NSU would be unable to meet my demands, and ending, "I hope you will find enough reasons to return to NSU. I fondly and appreciatively remember the great effort you put in before and during the 2nd NSU

Convocation. Please accept my regards." That was the last correspondence that I had with NSU. I was disgusted with Siddiqi's underhanded attempts to get rid of me; I decided not to return to NSU.

The board made Siddiqi the pro-vice-chancellor in 1998 and vice-chancellor in 2003, confident in the belief that he would be a pliable sycophant ready to carry out the board's bidding irrespective of whether it served the university's interest and the greater good or not. He did for the board members exactly as he was told to do, but was retired in 2010 presumably because he no longer served their purpose.

Before I left NSU, a tragedy struck my wife's family. My father-in-law, who had been suffering from non-Hodgkin's lymphoma and was under treatment in Manchester, had returned to Dhaka. He started to deteriorate, and it became necessary to admit him in a hospital for treatment and urgent care. But there was tension within the extended family with regard to the choice of hospital.

My father-in-law's family, primarily his sisters, wanted to admit him to Holy Family Hospital in Eskaton Garden, where he himself was a visiting physician at one time. They believed that Holy Family Hospital would be the best choice because it was well equipped, offered a wide range of medical services, and had a good relationship with the family. But my mother-in-law decided to admit him in Dr. Zaman's Clinic in Gulshan 2, which was a private clinic and had fewer patients to take care of. When I learned that he was in Dr. Zaman's Clinic, I myself wondered whether it was the right choice because of rumors that patients who went to the clinic usually did not return alive because a number of them had actually died.

Dr. Zaman was a heart specialist himself, and he prescribed quite a few medications to my father-in-law. I went to see him in the clinic, which was only a couple of blocks from our house in Gulshan 2. He was cheerful but very weak and emaciated. His deterioration, however, accelerated, and so more and more medicines were administered to him. It came to a point when we were all concerned about the medicines cancelling each other's effects. Then his organs started failing one by one; at which point Dr. Zaman agreed to set up a medical board, which he had resisted previously.

Although the list of medicines being administered changed, it was too late; he died in April 1998. His demise spelled the end of a very gentle and caring human being, and a very conscientious surgeon who had put his Hippocratic Oath before everything else, best exemplified by the many free surgeries he did on patients who couldn't afford to pay. He was so loved by my father and mother that it was a hard blow to them; my mother asked rhetorically, "Why does Allah always take away the best among us so early?"

The year 1998 was overall a difficult year for us, and it had started ominously. A massive ice storm struck eastern Canada and northeast USA, a swath of land from eastern Ontario all the way eastward across southern Quebec, New Brunswick, and Nova Scotia in Canada to northern New York and central Maine in the United States. As described by one source, "It caused massive damage to trees and electrical infrastructure all over the area, leading to widespread long-term power outages. Millions were left in the dark for periods varying from days to several weeks, and in some instances, months. It led to 34 fatalities, a shutdown of activities in large cities like Montreal and Ottawa, and an unprecedented effort in reconstruction of the power grid. The ice storm led to the largest deployment of Canadian military personnel since the Korean War, with over 16,000 Canadian Forces personnel deployed, 12,000 in Quebec and 4,000 in Ontario at the height of the crisis."

The scene in Ottawa was horrific. The entire city was white and covered with ice for many weeks. The thick ice on power lines weighed them down to the ground. Hundreds of trees were permanently damaged as the sap inside the tree trunks and branches froze solid and expanded, causing them to explode. With no electricity or gas for weeks, people were hard pressed to cook their meals. One saw pictures of people trying to use firewood in their fireplaces as makeshift kitchen to cook their meals. I had been used to ferocious cyclonic storms that regularly wreaked havoc in Bangladesh, with millions of homes destroyed, thousands dead, and corpses of animals and humans floating by in bloated rivers in its aftermath. What I experienced in Ottawa was the colder version. The ice storm reminded me once again how powerful and destructive Mother Nature could be and how fragile human communities were.

IDRC and My Africa/Palestine Work

The Ottawa-based International Development Research Centre (IDRC) is a Canadian federal Crown corporation, established by the Parliament of Canada in 1970 under the International Development Research Centre Act., which directed IDRC "to initiate, encourage, support and conduct research into the problems of the developing regions of the world and into the means for applying and adapting scientific, technical, and other knowledge to the economic and social advancement of those regions." In 1999, IDRC had multiple regional offices; although as of this writing, it has only four regional offices, located in Kenya, Jordan, India, and Uruguay. It continues to be a unique institution because of its emphasis on supporting research designed to adapt science and technology to the needs of developing countries. In the process, IDRC has contributed to strengthening the research capacities and the expertise of local counterparts to identify their own problems and formulate effective measures to resolve them.

I joined the Peace Building and Reconstruction Program Initiative (PBR) of IDRC on April 22, 1999, as a senior program officer, after leaving North South University in January. I was hired because of what I brought to IDRC, "a wealth of experience and strong academic and policy analysis expertise in the areas of international development and security, encompassing conflict resolution, peace building, disarmament, human and environmental security."

My disbursement budget was modest, under $2 million, with which I was able to fund and manage a multitude of joint projects covering a variety of critical concerns in Africa and Asia. All the projects were developed in consultation with local institutions and experts, and implemented by them as well with the technical and financial support from the IDRC.

The IDRC work was very exciting to me because it gave me the opportunity to consult with the citizens and experts of the countries of the third world, jointly design innovative projects that addressed their immediate and future concerns, and the freedom to travel across Africa, Asia, and the Middle East. The most attractive part was that most of the projects that were developed and implemented were based on research done not by western academics but by African and Asian researchers and experts. My primary job was to provide advice, technical help, funding, and monitoring. But almost every project threw up unforeseen challenges that my colleagues and I had to cope with. To illustrate what I mean, let me briefly touch on some aspects of these challenges in a few of these projects.

The *Good Governance and Security Sector Reform* project with the Center for Democracy and Development in Accra, Ghana made the officials of the target countries often unwilling to fully share information because they feared the project would expose the level of corruption in their countries. Government officials also feared retaliation from their superiors, unsavory postings, and even possible job loss. In such situations, culturally sensitive approaches and low-keyed information gathering by my local counterparts were needed.

The *Budgeting for Defense in Africa* project with the Stockholm International Peace Research Institute was another very sensitive one because it sought to understand how African leaders, most of whom were unelected dictators, managed their military expenditures in complete secrecy. In fact, as the project revealed, the military budgeting process was in many cases completely outside the normal budgeting process, and citizens of the country did not even know how much was apportioned for military procurement and expenditure. The country's national budget sometimes did not include the military budget, and if it did, it was only a single-line item without any detailed breakdown.

The project on the *Regional Security Architecture in the Horn of Africa* with the Nairobi-based Africa Peace Forum faced the challenge of bringing all the countries in the Horn of Africa on to the same page. The asymmetric power relationship, say between Djibouti or Eritrea and Ethiopia or Somalia, made it very difficult to start with the same sets of facts because the perceptions of the small and large countries diverged sharply. There was much suspicion and doubt on the part of the smaller states.

The project on *Israel in the Middle East: New Avenues for Peace* with the Ramallah based Palestinian Institute for the Study of Democracy had its own challenges shaped by the region's historical experiences. The first challenge was to convince the government of Israel that the project, its goals, and its participants were not anti-Israel from the get-go. One advantage we had was that Canada was generally seen to be a neutral and fair-minded country, and the Israelis were willing to assume that we were not out to malign Israel's image. However, access to information was severely limited, securing permission to interview Israeli officials was a bureaucratic nightmare, and the free movement of project people was seen by Israeli security officials as a security risk.

The project on the *Future of Burma* with the International Institute for Democracy and Electoral Assistance (IDEA) was unable to get input from within Burma, and the primary participants were the Burmese diaspora in Scandinavian countries and in Canada. Attempts to get input or even feedback about various scenarios of Burma's future from the various ethnic groups within Burma proved to be very difficult and were limited. The Burmese military saw the activities of the diaspora as inimical to its interest, and therefore any external project was suspect.

The project on *Globalization and Its Impact on Bangladesh* looked at the interplay between the forces of globalization, their impact on the physical environment, and how that effected social evolution. My former BIISS friend Mizanur Rahman Khan partnered with the Winnipeg-based Disaster Research Institute to complete this project. Among the outputs of the project were a video documentary and a book titled *Globalization, Environmental Crisis and Social Change,* published by UPL, Dhaka. I hoped that I could do more projects with Mizan.

The project on *National Reconciliation Policies in post-Conflict Countries* with the Center for the Study of Violence and Reconciliation (CSVR) in South Africa sought to explain why conflict mitigation efforts were failing. It sought to look at the strengths and weaknesses of the traditional versus modern approaches to conflict resolution and to find a more effective way of handling disputes before they degenerated into conflicts. The principal finding was that in South Africa's rush to modernity, traditional dispute resolution approaches that worked quite effectively in the country's villages and towns were abandoned and replaced by the modern justice system that emulated the colonizers' systems. But this transition was incomplete. So, on the one hand, the traditional informal approach to seeking justice was abandoned, and on the other hand, the modern formal structure with courts and lawyers was yet to be fully implemented, thereby creating a "vacuum" in justice delivery. For the average person, justice became inaccessible, costly, time consuming, and bureaucratic, but there was no fallback option because the traditional system of seeking resolution had broken down.

Visit by a Prince

In November 1999, I got a call from a colleague of mine in Toronto with whom I had been consulting to do a project on the massive deforestation problem and its security implications for Cambodia. He excitedly told me that our proposed Cambodia project had found political support from Prince Norodom Sirivudh, who was visiting Canada at the time to seek Prime Minister Jean Chrétien's support on a number of international issues affecting Cambodia, as well as support for his political party FUNCINPEC (*Front uni national pour un Cambodge indépendant, neutre, pacifique et coopératif*), or the National United Front for an Independent, Neutral, Peaceful, and Cooperative Cambodia, which was founded in 1981 by King Norodom Sihanouk. Prince Norodom Sirivudh was Sihanouk's half brother and a former minister of foreign affairs (1993–94) and then deputy prime minister (2004–06).

Prince Norodom Sirivudh of Cambodia at dinner at our house
during his official visit to Ottawa, November 1999

He said that the prince was going to be in Ottawa to meet with the prime minister and would like to meet with me after his official meetings. I consulted Nipa about this unexpected meeting, and we both thought it would be an honor as well as fun to formally invite the prince to dinner at our house. I sent off the formal invitation to the prince and received immediate confirmation of acceptance. Accordingly, after finishing his meetings, Prince Sirivudh accompanied by my friend came to our house, and we welcomed him warmly.

His princely bearing was obvious right from the start from his soft speech and mannerism as he thanked my wife and me for inviting him to dinner. He was very polite, and generally quiet by disposition. My wife cooked a few special Bengali delicacies, helped in part by my mother-in-law, Taslima Kabir, who was visiting with us at the time. The prince made it a point of tasting all the dishes in very modest amounts and liked all of them. After dinner, we retired to the formal sitting room for dessert and coffee, and the prince asked me about the project that we were planning in Cambodia.

He was pleased that we were planning to address, in his words, "a very critical issue facing Cambodia" and suggested that we try to incorporate into the project related issues such as problems with land tenure, population explosion, and uncontrolled commercial logging and use of fuel wood that were exacerbating deforestation in Cambodia.

He also suggested that we liaise with his office in Phnom Penh if we run into difficulty with the bureaucracy. It was an extremely useful conversation for our project, and we expressed our gratitude for his offer of help.

After our conversation ended, the prince pulled out two gifts, a beautiful tie for me and an equally beautiful scarf for Nipa. As he prepared to leave, he thanked us once again for inviting him for a home-cooked meal and for our hospitality. For us, it was a great occasion indeed to be able to entertain royalty, and for me in particular, for receiving his assurance of support for our planned project. The prince spent the night at Hotel Fairmont Château Laurier and flew out to Paris the next day.

As for the project, regrettably, it never materialized because we lost our bid for a McArthur Foundation funding. The selection committee in their letter to us explained that while the objectives and design of the project on deforestation were impressive, in their view, the existing political turmoil and uncertainties in Cambodia and the insecurities that existed for foreigners working and traveling in Cambodia did not warrant investing funds for a research project there at this time. Our elation of receiving royal support for the project was crushed by the disappointing rejection letter.

Second Visit to Jerusalem

The second time I visited Palestine on IDRC project work, I went alone. It was in April 2000, four years after my first visit in 1996. For me, there were only two official ways of visiting Palestine: one was through Israel, and the other way was through the Allenby Bridge land border crossing from Jordan. However, going through Israel was simpler and easier, and so IDRC chose that route for me. I landed in Tel Aviv's Ben Gurion Airport, and, like my previous visit, I saw the same level of security deployment all around, both outside the terminal building and inside it.

This time, I was traveling with my Canadian passport and faced no hassle at Passport Control. But once again, a young Israeli in military uniform and carrying a mini Uzi submachine gun escorted me to a small room behind the Passport Control area, where I was interrogated by an older security official. After the interrogation, he handed me my passport and escorted me to a waiting taxi. The taxi took me to the Israeli-Palestinian border checkpoint, where Israeli officials again checked my passport and then allowed me to cross over to the Palestinian side, where I got into a Palestinian taxi to go to Grand Park Hotel in Ramallah.

A colleague from the IDRC desk in the Canadian embassy came over to pick me up for dinner that evening. We went to a nice restaurant with the interior of adobe arches, beautiful carpets and colored cushions scattered across the floor, and hookahs at every sitting arrangement. The interior was rather dim, lit only with beautiful lanterns. There were only a handful of people eating their meals and a group chatting with hookah hoses in hand.

My colleague informed me that this was one of a few safe places in Ramallah where foreigners usually frequented because it was a small, family-run restaurant, and Mossad agents and informers would be too obvious here. It turned out to be a relaxing evening as we downed a couple of delightful Palestinian dishes. He ended his meal by ordering a hookah. He explained to me that the *shisha* here wasn't tobacco but compressed dried fruit combo of apple, strawberry, pomegranate, and mint, and that I should try it. I took a couple of puffs and then passed it on to him.

This time, I had come to Palestine to monitor the project on *Violence against Women* in the Gaza Strip. Since Gaza was on the western side of Israel, I had to hire separate taxis to travel through Palestinian territories and through Israeli territory. The next day, I took the taxi to the border checkpoint, where I switched over to an Israeli cab to travel across Israel.

I noticed a stark difference in the vegetation on either side of the border. On the Palestinian side, we drove through dry, arid land with sparse vegetation that was mostly prickly shrubs, dwarfed orange and olive trees, and brambles. On the Israeli side, it was lush green vegetation. This was, of course, due to Israel's confiscation and redirection of the waters of the Jordan River, which severely curtailed Palestine's share of its water. The Israelis also practiced drip irrigation that allowed water to drip slowly and directly into the roots of plants, thereby minimizing water loss through evaporation. This highly efficient system of micro-irrigation was invented by an Israeli engineer named Simcha Blass, who was an important contributor to Israel's water development.

After traveling through Israeli territory, I arrived at the Israeli checkpoint in Gaza. I had to get off the Israeli taxi and then take the Transit Tunnel to Gaza, go through the Gaza checkpoint, and then take another taxi to my hotel in the Gaza Strip. The approximate driving distance between Ramallah and the Gaza Strip was about eighty-five kilometers, and taking into account the delays at the checkpoints, it took me about ninety minutes to arrive in the Gaza Strip, which itself is only 360 square kilometers in area with its width varying from a minimum of 6 kilometers to a maximum of 14 kilometers. It had a population of about 1.7 million then, making it the third most densely populated polity in the world.

At the Transit Tunnel that connects Israel to the
Gaza Strip, Gaza Checkpoint, April 2000

But a huge chunk of its land along its border with Israel had been converted to a security buffer zone by the Israelis leaving the Gaza people very little usable land. Israel also controlled Gaza's air and maritime space and seaways and six of Gaza's seven land crossings.

Even worse, Gaza was dependent on Israel for its water, electricity, telecommunications, and other utilities. This meant that there were no factories or industries in Gaza where the inhabitants of Gaza could earn a living. Israel maintained direct external control over Gaza and indirect control over life in Gaza, and Egypt in the southwest controlled whatever freedom was left to the people of Gaza. In short, given this "indirect occupation," which left Gaza totally at the mercy of its neighbors, it was not surprising that its people would develop almost a siege mentality. It also affected their level of patience and tolerance and their family relations.

The IDRC project in Gaza was a sister project under the rubric of *Violence against Women* that we did in the Soweto Township of Johannesburg, South Africa. The Soweto project looked at violence against women perpetrated through rape. The violence against the women in Gaza was of a different kind. Women in Gaza were subjected to a great deal of domestic abuse, so much so that violence against women had become statistically significant and quite alarming.

It was an eye-opening experience for me, for I came face-to-face with the reality that the Palestinians living in the Gaza Strip faced on a daily basis. I personally witnessed able-bodied Palestinian men wake up before sunrise and rush to the check point at the Israeli-Gaza border to stand in line for the gate to be opened by the armed Israeli guards so that they could go to work in the factories on the Israeli side of the border. And then when it was time, the Israeli guards told the men that there was no work in the factories that day and that they could go home. Although the guards knew that they wouldn't be opening the gates that day, they did not tell the assembled men ahead of time to create maximum psychological effect. The men got depressed and left.

The same thing happened the next day. When the same thing happened the day after, many of these men were so frustrated and angry by then that they started yelling and screaming at the guards and kicking the border fence. Then they went home and kicked open their doors and took out their anger on the first person they saw, which was usually the wife. With no work for days on end, often there was no food on the table, and tempers flared up leading to further abuse. What was even more astonishing was that not infrequently the mother-in-law also subjected the wife to verbal and psychological abuse, blaming her for failing to ration food properly so that there was food on the table every day.

After observing this for a few days, I arranged an informal roundtable in our project office in Gaza with the wives and the mothers-in-law to discuss the situation, the lack of gainful employment, coping mechanisms, and to try to find alternative solutions to minimize violence against the Gaza women. When I asked the wives that when they became mothers-in-law themselves, how they will treat their daughters-in-law, their response was amazing. They said that they would be repeating exactly what their mothers-in-law were doing to them now! They would be heaping abuse on their daughters-in-law the same way as they were getting it from their mothers-in-law.

It was presented to me as being a *fait accompli,* a part and parcel of the unchanging Gaza life to be replicated down the road! I concluded that there should be a phase two of the project, which should be designed inter alia to explore how gainful employment could be generated in the Gaza so that the Gaza people were not at the mercy of the Israelis, and what social measures could be adopted to change their existing mind-set.

At the conclusion of my work in Gaza, my project colleagues and I had a wonderful meal at a seaside restaurant. The entire coastal drive was very bumpy but pleasant except for the intermittent security towers on the beach that reminded one of Israel's grip over Gaza. I returned to Ramallah and spent some time visiting historical places that I had missed the first time I was in Israel and Palestine. I visited Masada, which was an ancient fortress in the Judean Desert in southern Israel. The climb up to the fortifications was long and winding but worth it because I got to see the ruins of King Herod's Palace, the Roman-style bathhouse with mosaic floors, and the Dead Sea at a distance.

I also visited Jericho roughly forty kilometers east of Ramallah. According to some archaeologists, it is eleven thousand years old, making it the oldest continually inhabited city. Among the places I visited in and around Jericho were the Mount of Temptation, where Jesus supposedly fasted for forty days, and the Greek Orthodox Monastery of St. George. The monastery was carved into a cliff of the Wadi Qelt, which was a deep scenic limestone gorge, and the view from the outside of this isolated monastery was unforgettable. Back in Ramallah, I went to the Al-Aqsa Mosque once again to pray and this time entered through the Damascus Gate. I also had a delicious meal with friends at an Armenian restaurant.

Third Visit to the Holy Land

My third visit to Palestine was only two months later, in April 2000. After my second visit in February, I had taken an extended trip through the African continent to visit my projects, following which I returned to Palestine to participate in our Peace Building and Reconstruction Program Retreat where all the team members of our PBR program participated. We were in Ramallah for five days where we brainstormed about our future programming direction and project themes. It was a very useful exercise that allowed us to take stock of what we have been doing in the previous budget period; the successes we achieved, the challenges we faced, and the lessons we learned; and how to incorporate those lessons as we planned ahead. It was also the least eventful of my three visits to Palestine over the previous five years.

First Extended Tour of Africa

I flew from Tel Aviv to Cairo in late February 2000 and put up at Hotel Marriott. Cairo was the starting point for my Africa trip that took me all the way to Cape Town at the southern tip of the African continent. I took this extended trip to take stock of the projects I have been managing remotely, to meet our African project partners face-to-face, and to meet potentially new partners to discuss with them the feasibility of new projects. It was very useful for me and our partners in the field because it allowed us to put a face to our e-mails and to chat heart-to-heart regarding our projects and the personnel involved that was not always possible through correspondence or even though telephone calls. Conference calls were ineffective most of the time because of unstable Internet connections with Africa, lack of appropriate level of security, and time differences.

Before leaving Cairo, I decided to take time out to visit some of Cairo's famous sites. I went to see the pyramids at Giza, about eight kilometers southwest of Cairo, and found that their depiction in postcards belied their impressive dimensions up front. In one of the pyramids, there were steps leading to an opening through which tourists went inside to take pictures. I emulated the rest and went inside through very narrow passageways to a couple of openings that had a few items kept there for tourists to take pictures. After I came out, I couldn't find my guide who was arranged by my IDRC office.

So as I strolled around, a man with a camel approached me and asked to stand next to his camel so that he could take a picture of me. I obliged, and then the camel owner asked me for twenty Egyptian pounds since I had a picture with his camel. I was confounded that I had fallen for this cheap trick. By then, my guide found me, and I told him what had happened; he scolded the camel owner in Arabic and gave him five Egyptian pounds and shooed him away.

My guide then took me to see the Sphinx, a colossal limestone statue of a recumbent mythical creature with the face of a woman, body of a lion, and wings of a bird, and whose task was to guard the treasures of the Giza plateau. Measuring at twenty meters high and seventy-three meters long, it was believed to be around 4,500 years old. Its nose was missing because, according to one theory, a Sufi Muslim named Muhammad Sa'im al-Dahr mutilated the statue in the fourteenth century to protest idolatry. But the rest of the face was also heavily pockmarked because, according to my guide, Napoleon Bonaparte had instructed his troops to use the face for cannon fire target practice.

From there, I went to the famous Al Azhar Mosque, around which was built Al Azhar University, claimed by some as the oldest university in the world and the center of Islamic scholarship since AD 975. Others, however, claim that the oldest existing and continually operating educational institution in the world is the University of Karueein, which was founded in AD 859 in Fez, Morocco. While there is dispute among historians, it seems to be generally agreed that the oldest European university was the University of Bologna in Italy, which was founded in AD 1088, and the oldest English-speaking university was Oxford University in England, which opened in AD 1096.

I entered the Al Azhar Mosque to take a look inside. My guide then told me an interesting story about Napoleon Bonaparte's failed attempt in AD 1798 to conquer Egypt. He said that, initially, Napoleon had won a series of victories against Egypt's Mamluk rulers. After every victory, Napoleon made it a point to ride on horseback into mosques to show his revulsion for Islam. To prevent him from doing the same to the sacred mosque of Al Azhar, the locals hastily erected concrete barriers from the top of the doors halfway down so that Napoleon would be forced to disembark from his horse, bow his arrogant head, and crouch to go inside the mosque. I had thought then that I would like to read up on that, but I never did, mainly because I had forgotten about it.

I also visited the Cairo souk, which was no different from the souks in Tehran and Istanbul where I had the occasion to shop. Since my guide wasn't with me that time, I asked a passerby where I could find a taxi to return to my hotel. He pointed me in the direction of the nearest taxi stand and then extended to me his cupped hand; it took me a few seconds to realize that he had demanded bakshish (tip) for helping me. As I walked away from him, my opinion of Egyptians took a decidedly downward turn!

After finishing my project work in Cairo, I flew to Nairobi and spent a few days at the beautiful Fairview Inn. During each of my stops, I was picked up from the airport by staff from our local IDRC office and then thoroughly briefed on our project work in that region. It constituted a series of meetings that covered virtually everything that had to do with project implementation, monitoring, and evaluation, with occasional project site visits when feasible.

From Nairobi I flew to Maputo, capital of Mozambique. There, for the first time, I experienced the joy felt by local partners of successfully completing a project, as well as their sadness and disappointment when projects failed for no fault of their own. One such failure was narrated to me by a colleague who was running a demining project in Mozambique. It was a million-dollar landmine clearing project sponsored by the United Nations and funded by Canada/IDRC. The project team had carried out a very tedious, time-consuming, and dangerous job of surveying the location of the hundreds of landmines planted by the Americans, the Russians, and the Chinese in support of their factions in the Mozambique civil war over many years, and up until the 1990s. Many of these mines were planted near key infrastructures such as electricity pylons, dams, bridges, and railway lines.

After the civil war ended, the land remained inaccessible for use because of the mines, and each year, countless numbers of civilians, particularly children, were maimed or died from landmine explosions. During the survey, a red flag was planted near each landmine located so that the mine-clearing experts would know the location of each landmine. Sadly, however, just after the survey was completed, there was a massive flooding of the Zambezi River, which flowed eastward along the border between Zambia and Zimbabwe to Mozambique and then flowed through the country to empty into the Indian Ocean. The flood waters simply washed away the red markers, as well as displaced the landmines, requiring the need to do the landmine survey once again. It was a tragic waste of effort, time, and money, and it postponed Mozambique's economic recovery effort by several years.

From Maputo, I flew to Johannesburg (called Jo'burg by expats and Jozi by the locals), which was my most important stop because of the number of projects we ran from our Johannesburg office. I was amazed by how vibrant the people were as they enjoyed their postapartheid freedom with much gusto. There was a sense of optimism and joy in the air. It was particularly pleasant to see South African white folks, many of whom had fought against the apartheid and were members of the African National Congress (ANC), mingling with their black compatriots in social settings such as in restaurants and national sporting events without any hesitance, and working shoulder to shoulder on joint projects to change their country's image from being a pariah nation to one that was respected and welcomed by the world.

Conversations with my black colleagues also revealed full acceptance of their white partners and little ill feeling toward them, with a whole lot of forgiveness. I was also impressed by the energy, dedication, and commitment shown by all our project partners in South Africa, including the energetic engagement of the Institute for Security Studies (ISS) in Johannesburg, which saw itself as an African institution rather than a South African one, and whose avowed goal was to enhance human security in the entire African continent. Discussions with colleagues at ISS gave me a much broader perspective on and a better understanding of Africa's problems and choices. It also gave me lots of new ideas regarding future projects for the African continent.

I took full advantage of my trip to South Africa by visiting as many places as I could. Going to Pretoria, the administrative capital of South Africa, was in my list. Unlike other countries of the world, South Africa had three capitals because of disagreements among its four provinces as to which city should be its national capital. As a compromise, it was agreed that Pretoria would be the administrative capital, Cape Town would be its legislative capital, and Bloemfontein would be its judicial capital.

The proposal to change Pretoria's name to Tshwane ("little ape") after a Zulu leader who had founded a tribal settlement in the area in the eighteenth century had been strongly resisted by the predominantly white population of the city, who wished to retain the name Pretoria named after the Voortrekker ("pioneer" in Dutch) leader Andries Pretorius. Within South Africa, Pretoria is also called Jacaranda City because of the thousands of pale indigo-colored flowers of the jacaranda trees planted in its streets, parks, and gardens.

The dominant sight in Pretoria was the Union Buildings that constituted the official seat of the South African government and the offices of the president. Built from sandstone, the buildings were semicircular in shape and were the site of presidential inaugurations. The interior of the buildings had to be accessed through heavy doors, and inside were carved Rhodesian teak fanlights, dark ceilings, and heavy wood furniture. Almost a decade and half after my visit, a nine-meter-high statue of Nelson Mandela was erected at the Union Buildings.

Visiting Pretoria was incomplete without tasting braai (Afrikaans for barbecue or roast) meat, so I gladly accepted my South African colleague's invitation to an evening of braai. It was wonderful to witness the rituals of cooking thick steaks over coal and then consuming the meat with his friends sitting around the fire. Braai was so much a part of the cultural heritage that South Africa's National Heritage Day was renamed as the National Braai Day. This experience prepared me well for the braais I attended in the UN security compound headed by a South African in Kabul, Afghanistan, a decade and a half later.

Visit to Robben Island on the Atlantic Ocean

I also had to go to Cape Town for project-related work. I had originally planned to take the thirteen-hour southwestern drive from Johannesburg to Cape Town to see the countryside, but my South African colleagues dissuaded me, arguing that there were still pockets of highway banditry on that route. They advised me to fly instead, which would take me just over two hours, which I did.

One of the items in my "must see in South Africa" list during my visit there was to go to Robben Island, where Nelson Mandela spent eighteen years of his twenty-seven years in prison, the rest being in Pollsmoor Prison and Victor Verster Prison. Fearing international outcry if the death sentence was passed as demanded by the prosecution following the Rivonia Trial in 1962, the courts sentenced Mandela and seven other fellow activists to life imprisonment on charges of conspiring against the Apartheid state. After Mandela's release in 1990, UNESCO declared Robben Island as a World Heritage Site.

The island took its name from the Dutch word for seals (*robben*) because of its large seal and penguin population. It was roughly oval in shape, measuring 3.3 kilometers north to south and 1.9 kilometers wide, with an area of 5.08 square kilometers. It was quite flat and only a few meters above sea level. Located in Table Bay, named after the flat-topped Table Mountain that overlooked it, Robben Island was about seven kilometers in a northerly direction off the coast of Cape Town.

It had served as a whaling station and then a leper colony and finally a place for exile for almost four hundred years. For much of this period, Robben Island had been in colonial service. From the late seventeenth century, political prisoners from the Dutch East Indies and Muslim holy men who had traveled south from Egypt and Mali were incarcerated in Robben Island for their opposition to Dutch colonial rule.

I took the thirty-minute ferry ride from the Victoria and Albert Waterfront in Cape Town to Robben Island. It was very windy, and the choppy waters of the Atlantic made the trip a ride to remember. After we docked at the concrete quay, we walked several hundred feet to the prison gate, whose overhead marquee read, "We serve with pride."

Robben Island on the Atlantic Ocean where Nelson Mandela
was incarcerated for eighteen years, March 2000

After entering through the gate, we were given the tour of the island on what looked like elongated open golf carts. Many of the tour guides were themselves prisoners here and therefore familiar with the island's layout and its checkered history. The tour included the museum, the lime quarry, the bluestone quarry, the courtyard where prisoners crushed stones, the island graveyard, the eighteen-meter-tall lighthouse with its flashing electric lantern gallery at the top, the military bunkers, and the maximum security prison.

Our guide also talked of how all prisoners were exposed to asbestos from the mines on the island. For me, there were several highlights of the guided tour. One was Nelson Mandela's prison cell, an eight-by-seven-foot space containing an iron bedframe, a brick for pillow, a coarse blanket, and a tin pail that served as a toilet. Another was the garden where he was allowed to plant a flower bush whose base served as a hiding place for his secret writings while in prison. The third was the asbestos mine where he worked eighteen years.

Standing in front of any of these sites, closing one's eyes and then trying to visualize what Mandela went through all those years and then to remember how he decided to forgive his torturers and opted to build a "rainbow nation" gave one the true measure of this great man and his humanity!

Toward the end of the half day tour, as we moved around freely, I noticed a mosque at one side. I was very surprised to see a mosque on such a remote location. I went to its entrance to read what was written there. It talked of a Muslim holy man who had traveled all the way from the north of the continent to its southern tip and then founded this mosque. According to the Cape's history, Sayed Abdurahman Moturu, who was one of Cape Town's first imams, was banished to the island by the Dutch East Indies Company in AD 1743, where he died in AD 1754. The Moturu Kramat, which is a shrine that was built in 1969 to commemorate his life and work, has since become a place of pilgrimage for Muslim political prisoners in South Africa, including Muslim prisoners on Robben Island who pay homage here before leaving the Island.

On our way back to the mainland, the captain of the ferry set a southward course and informed us that he was going to show us where the waters of the Atlantic Ocean and the Indian Ocean met. After a fairly long while when we arrived at that point, it was actually scary to see the stark difference between the violent, churning waters of the Atlantic readily distinguishable from the relatively calm waters of the Indian Ocean; the boundary between the two waters was visible for as far as the eye could see. As we headed back toward the mainland, the view of the Table Mountain from the distance was indeed spectacular. It was a Portuguese explorer, Antonio de Saldanha, who supposedly climbed to the top of the Table Mountain in AD 1503 and was awed by its flatness and named it Taboa do Cabo ("Table of the Cape"). I had hoped to take the five-minute aerial cableway ride to the summit of the Table Mountain but did not have the time to do so.

My Africa trip was very useful to me and my project partners. It allowed me to monitor the progress of the projects and do some project evaluation, but, more importantly, it gave us the chance to have frank discussions on the challenges we faced, political and otherwise. On occasions, I had to revise project expectations or their trajectory to ensure their timely completion. This did not always work according to plan, and some projects inevitably got delayed because of a variety of reasons beyond the project team's control. There was also the concern that failure to disburse fully the allocated fund for a project had a stigma attached to it and sometimes led to a negative assessment of the project and the people in charge. So the project ethos was that it must be brought to a successful conclusion.

Besides the projects themselves, these travels were a tremendous learning experience for me. I met people from different cultures, traditions, and ethnicities, and of different religions and languages. I learned that logic and reasoning did not always guide a person's actions; emotion, mind-set, and personal background often played a critical role.

There were the occasional project-related hurdles as well that one was not always prepared for. For example, our IDRC office in Johannesburg had assigned me a car for my business meetings. After one such meeting, when I walked to my car, I found the two back wheels missing. There was a street urchin sitting on a waist-high concrete pillar on the pavement. Seeing me, he said, "Looks like you need two wheels! I got two over there," pointing to a couple of wheels lying on the pavement on the other side of the road with several kids guarding them. Realizing that those wheels were from my car, that this was a street gang and these streets were their territory, I went back to the meeting place and called the IDRC office and told them what had happened. They told me to stay put and help was on the way. I got picked up by another office car, while a gentleman from the office remained behind to deal with the situation.

Later that year, in December 2000, I had to go to the Philippines on project work. I had funded a project to strengthen the capacity of the indigenous people to fight for their rights. I was working with Victoria Tauli-Corpuz of the Indigenous Peoples' International Centre for Policy Research and Education, commonly known as the Tebtebba Foundation, to mitigate conflict between the indigenous peoples and the government of the Philippines. This required me to travel between Baguio City and Manila.

I had arrived immediately after the typhoon season had ended, but the pollution in the atmosphere was incredible. I landed at Manila's Ninoy Aquino International Airport during daytime, but the city was enveloped in a haze of particulates, and visibility was limited. When I got into an airport taxi to go to my hotel, I noticed a cellophane package next to me on the backseat. The driver noticed me looking at it through his rearview mirror. "Sir, that is a mask. Please put it on." "A mask?" I asked. "You see the pollution in Manila? We do not want tourists visiting our country to die. We want them to enjoy and come to Pilipinas again and again," he replied. "Do you provide one to every foreign visitor? A new one every time?" I asked. "Yes," he said. "It must get very expensive for you." "All the taxi services in Manila agreed that we must give masks to foreign guests. So we all contribute every month to buy masks," he replied.

I have to say that I was quite impressed by their concern for foreign visitors coming to their country. It was very conscientious of them to think of our well-being, as well as take responsibility in whatever small ways they could in the face of the pollution. It was a relief for me to spend most of my time in Baguio City, which was roughly 250 kilometers from Manila, or about two to four hours' driving time depending on the traffic, away from the hustle and bustle and pollution of Manila.

My years at IDRC gave me the opportunity to travel to Asia and Africa quite a bit. These travels, particularly in Africa, gave me the chance to engage in many informal chats, after-dinner discussions, and lively debates with people from different countries and communities, all of which broadened my horizon and appreciation of other cultures and their concerns. But this was just a prelude to the much more demanding work that lay ahead for me in the coming years. The contract at IDRC ended and I left IDRC for the Canadian International Development Agency (CIDA) after three years.

New Opportunities and Challenges at the Canadian International Development Agency (CIDA)

In the late summer of 2002, my friend David Brooks, who was the director of the Environment Program in the Environment and Natural Resources Division at IDRC, informed me that the Democratic Institution and Human Rights Division (YDI) of CIDA was looking for someone to manage their newly established Security Sector Reform (SSR) program. He felt that because of my fairly extensive work in the security sector field, CIDA would benefit much from my knowledge and experience. I could also put my stamp on the direction and content of this new program within the context of the government's priorities in that field. I found his arguments rather convincing and decided to apply for the position. CIDA was also a much bigger organization than IDRC and would give me a much larger playing field.

My meetings with the YDI Program people and interview with the director of the YDI Division at CIDA were quite positive, and it led to my joining CIDA as the team leader for the SSR program in September 2002. I needed to get certification in French, so a year later, I went on a three-month crash course, which I am proud to say I completed with a score of EEB. Although I was hired as the lead for CIDA's SSR work, my actual portfolio of work included quite a few other important files, and I soon found myself to be CIDA's policy lead on the Extractive Industries Transparency Initiative (EITI), the Global Organization of Parliamentarians against Corruption (GOPAC), Transparency International (TI), the Private Sector/Corporate Social Responsibility (CSR), and the Muslim Communities Working Group (MCWG).

I also had a significantly larger budget to work with. Since I was now in the policy branch, I did not have much programmatic travel. However, as the policy lead on the above files, I had to attend meetings all over the world but mostly in Europe to represent CIDA and the Canadian government's position. In the first few years, I had to attend meetings in Bergen, Oslo, Paris, Berlin, Madrid, The Hague, and Kiev frequently. In subsequent years, my meetings expanded to include Vienna, London, and Istanbul as well as non-European cities around the world.

Korea and the 38th Parallel

Many of the work-related international meetings I attended over the years are memorable for different reasons. One such meeting was in Seoul, South Korea. One of the international organizations we were funding was the Berlin-based Transparency International (TI), which published the noteworthy Corruption Perception Index (CPI) each year. The CPI ranked the perception of corruption in each country from the least corrupt to the most corrupt, and every two years, it organized a global forum on anticorruption in a different continent. The Eleventh International Anti-Corruption Conference (IACC) was held in Seoul in May 2003. The Canadian delegation was led by John Williams, a member of parliament, the chairman of the Standing Committee on Public Accounts, and also the chairman of the Global Organization of Parliamentarians against Corruption (GOPAC), and I was CIDA's voice in the delegation.

I recall several noteworthy incidents during that conference. As I was about to enter the main conference hall for the opening plenary, I came upon the ambassador from Bangladesh, whose name I cannot remember now. He looked quite stressed out. I inquired what the matter was. He told me that he had been searching the entire city of Seoul to rent a Mercedes-Benz car for Moudud Ahmed, minister of law, justice, and parliamentary affairs, and the head of the Bangladesh delegation, who had insisted on going to the conference in a Mercedes-Benz car only! Since other embassies were also renting brand name cars for their delegations, nothing was available. Luckily for the ambassador, his staff was able to borrow someone's private Mercedes car through their personal contacts at the last minute, thereby probably saving the ambassador's job. Such are the idiosyncrasies of ministers especially from third world countries!

The second interesting incident was when the chairman of the opening plenary invited the head of the Saudi Arabian delegation, who was a Saudi prince, to present his remarks. The speaker just before him was the U.S. secretary of treasury who had delivered a thirty-five-minute speech. The Saudi prince walked to the podium and said, "Bismillah hir Rahmaner Rahim. We are a Muslim country. We have no corruption in Saudi Arabia!" And then he walked off the podium and returned to his front-row seat. The entire audience of 1,500 or so delegates in that plenary hall fell silent, and many jaws dropped in consternation.

As for me, being a Muslim, I was thoroughly embarrassed. Some of my delegation colleagues looked at me hoping that I might be able to shed some light on this bizarre behavior. I simply nodded my head in disapproval. I could have perhaps defended him if there was a shred of truth in what he had said, but we all knew how corrupt the Saudi royal family was. In any case, that was arguably the shortest address that any invited dignitary had ever given in a global forum.

The final and the most memorable moments of that trip were when the Canadian delegation visited the Korean Demilitarized Zone (DMZ). The DMZ is a relic of the Cold War between capitalist United States and Communist USSR, now Russia. At the end of the Second World War, the Korean peninsula was divided up into the Chinese-supported Communist north and the United States-supported capitalist south. However, war broke out between the two Koreas in June 1950 when North Korean forces invaded South Korea.

The DMZ, which stretches east-west for 150 miles along latitude 38 degrees north (hence known as the 38th parallel) and is 2.5 miles wide, was established in July 1953 as a buffer zone between the Cold War adversaries as a part of the cease-fire negotiated by the United Nations and the Communist forces. It was an area where military installations, military personnel, or military activities were forbidden. Since we wanted to visit the DMZ, a South Korean foreign ministry official escorted us there and handed us over to the U.S. military. A U.S. Marine from Alaska was assigned to give us the guided tour.

Unlike the other members of the U.S. military detachment and their South Korean counterpart who looked very steely jawed and emotionless, our Marine escort was cheery and quite willing to enlighten us with all sorts of stories. He said that everyone in the DMZ lived from one day to the next, not knowing when the North Korean dictatorship will go crazy and attack the U.S.-South Korea joint force, and that over the years, there were numerous incursions from the north. He said that there was, however, a smidgen of hope that the North Korean military might not be as insane as their leader and might hesitate to start a war, but one could never really tell.

The Alaskan marine gave us a guided tour of the fortified structures on the South Korean side. As we stood in a balcony facing the North Korean side, the Marine pointed out to a mounted machine gun on a similar balcony on the other side with a stiff, grim-faced North Korean soldier staring at us just a few hundred feet from us. The gun was aimed directly at us as an intimidation tactic. The dividing wall had built-in sensors throughout its length and was quite high with electrified steel coil fencing at the top. The Marine pointed to a tree on this side and narrated the tragedy that befell a few months earlier. One of its branches had gone over the demarcation wall, which was a violation, and so a Marine with a saw in hand got up to trim it. Unfortunately, he slipped and fell on the other side, and he was instantly shot dead by the North Korean soldiers on guard. There was no love lost between the two sides.

Standing just inside the demarcation line on the South
Korean side at the DMZ, May 2003

We were shown a number of flat tin-roofed warehouses straddling the demarcation line whose purposes I cannot recall. But what I do remember was the big, rectangular blue warehouse with double-sided tin roof. It was used as a meeting room by the two sides during emergencies to talk things over before resorting to outright war. But what was unusual about the meeting room was that it was built across the demarcation line so that half of the room was on each side of the international border. The conference table was also placed in a way such that half the table was on the South Korean side and the other half on the North Korean side, and the two negotiating sides sat on their side of the border because neither side wanted to be accused of crossing the demarcation line, which would be tantamount to declaring war. According to our Marine escort, if my memory serves me right, this meeting room was used only twice since 1945! He also told us of several infiltration tunnels secretly dug by North Korean infiltrators. We were also shown the bridge that connected the two Koreas. One of our delegation members was brave enough to walk almost to the dividing line on the bridge, risking being shot at by the North Korean guards.

Move to Our Fourth House

We had purchased our first house in 1994, where we spent ten wonderful years. But our family was growing up fast. Our daughter had just stepped into her twenties and our son was in his late teen; it was time for us to move to a bigger house. I put up our house for sale, but a whole month went by without getting any offer. I then decided to get a realtor to conduct the sale. He was an elderly gentleman with a young female colleague as his partner. They came to the house and advised us to remove all house decorations from the walls to make it look less cluttered and to repaint the house. They also asked us to ask our house guests to move out to make the house look less used. I conveyed the realtor's advice to my brother-in-law Rana, which did not go down very well.

Sitting at the Conference Table on the South Korean side facing the North Korean side at the DMZ; the demarcation line ran right through the middle of the table, May 2003

The realtor also arranged several open houses for prospective buyers and advised us to do some baking before the open house because the aroma of baking is supposedly pleasing to the senses, putting potential buyers in an agreeable mood. Within a month, the house got sold, but we were able to negotiate actual delivery in early May 2004 to coincide with us taking delivery of our brand-new house in May. We had purchased a much bigger house on a just-developed neighborhood a short distance away. It was a very attractive neighborhood with its own artificial lake, park, and playground, and with the provision for several new junior high and high schools under the English, French, and Catholic school boards. We were lucky to have the option of choosing a plot that backed into a huge open field that was reserved for a high school to be built subsequently; luckily for us, the school did not get built to this day, thus giving us a beautiful backyard with no neighbors behind us but a huge open space.

Ours was the second house on the street. Michael and Debbie Duncan, same age as we were, were the first homeowners across the street from us. Michael was a quiet type of a guy, but Debbie was the "watchdog" in our block; she always kept her eyes and ears open and knew everything that transpired in our neighborhood. We felt safe leaving our home under Debbie's watchful eyes whenever we went away on vacation.

I recall an interesting incident when we were visiting our daughter in London. Nipa had flown from Ottawa to London, while I had flown from Kabul via Dubai to London, switching to Qantas Airlines for the Dubai-London flight segment. I had my luggage tagged to London, but Qantas lost my luggage. Now, my wife Nipa is adept at Facebook, or in my niece Naureen Karim's words, *"Boromami-toh* Facebook-*er guru"* (Aunt Nipa is the guru of Facebook). A few days later, Nipa received a message from Debbie in her inbox that an Air Canada transport van had dropped off two luggage pieces by our front door, and since we were not home, she had put them inside our garage (we had given her our garage door code). That was helpful Debbie! The other good thing that happened was that since all my clothes were in my luggage, I had nothing to wear in London. This was a wonderful opportunity for my daughter to take me attire shopping in London, and by the time she was done with me, I was transformed from an old fuddy-duddy to a chic dad! I must say I liked the new look.

Our friendship with Debbie and Michael grew stronger over the years. Often she would keep an eye over our house when we were on vacation. She and my mother-in-law had a common interest in knitting, and they spend hours chatting together whenever my mother-in-law visited us. My mother-in-law liked to give gifts and once surprised Debbie by giving her a nice piece of jewelry. Debbie was also good at selecting the most reliable service providers, and I have often followed her lead in awarding the contracts for snow blowing in the winter and lawn maintenance work in the summer.

We moved to our new home on May 10, 2004. We had frequent visitors during those early years. One of them was Nipa's aunt Rezwana Choudhury Bannya, one of Bangladesh's famous Rabindra Sangeet singers. It was her first visit to Canada, and it was in the early winter. When she woke up the morning after, she was amazed to see snow falling outside. She was so excited that she dashed off outside in her bedroom slippers to grab some snow and exclaimed that she had often wondered how it would feel to touch snow. It was quite an experience for her indeed!

Meetings in Europe

For me, the year 2004, when we moved to our current house, started with a trip to The Hague in late January, to London in May, to Berlin and Bergen in September, ending the year with a trip to Paris in December. During all my meeting-related trips over the duration of my working life, I made it a habit of taking either a half-day or a full-day tour of the city, and often these were on the double-decker, open-air hop-on-hop-off buses. I always found them to be a very efficient way of spending my time and money to see the wonderful sights a city has to offer.

In The Hague, where government representatives met to discuss governance issues as well as to agree on an international governance agenda, I met two important personalities who impressed me; one was Malaysia's onetime deputy prime minister Anwar Ibrahim, who had been thrown into jail in September 1998 on charges of sodomy and corruption. The sodomy conviction was overturned in late 2004 by the Supreme Court of Malaysia. We had a brief chat, and he explained to me that he was on a European tour to meet with European leaders to clear his name and seek their political support. I asked him about the sodomy charge, which he categorically denied claiming that it was a politically motivated trumped-up charge by the government because he was a political threat to them. He appeared to be a tragic figure.

The other person who impressed me was Mohammad "Mo" Ibrahim, a Sudanese-British billionaire businessman with years of experience in the telecommunications sector. He had founded Celtel, which boasted twenty-four million mobile phone users in fourteen African countries at the time of its sale. He was very much interested in governance issues and, in his own ebullient way, described to me his plan to create a foundation whose twin goals would be to usher in good governance and develop the next generation of leaders for the countries of Africa. He told me of his commitment to help Africa transition from its "dark past" to a vibrant future and give Africa's new leaders the tools and skills to compete with the rest of the world. I was quite impressed by his passion.

True to his commitment, two years later, in 2006, he established the Mo Ibrahim Foundation to improve governance and leadership for Africa. The foundation launched four initiatives: (1) created the Ibrahim Index for African Governance by relying on four indicators: safety and rule of law, participation and human rights, sustainable economic opportunity, and human development; (2) Governance Weekend held every year in a different African country where prominent state and nonstate actors gathered to debate issues of critical importance facing Africa; (3) the African Leadership Prize given annually to a former African executive head of state or government (awarded only five times in twelve years to leaders found worthy of receiving it); and (4) leadership fellowships that were awarded each year to mentor future African leaders. The Hague meeting was rewarding for me as I was able to network with committed governance actors from every continent.

In May that year, I met with colleagues from the Department for International Development (DfID) in London to discuss the potential for developing joint Canada-UK position on governance and anticorruption issues; this was in preparation for our Utstein meeting in Bergen later in September that year.

But in September, I first went to Berlin for the first time. Berlin used to be the capital of Germany until it became the capital of Communist-controlled East Germany during the Cold War. With the collapse of the Berlin Wall in 1989, it was once again officially designated as the capital of united Germany in 1991. After two days of intense meetings, I took the third day off to see as much of Berlin as I could before departing the next day for Bergen, Norway. And Berlin, like Paris, offered incredible sights that were steeped in history, arts, and culture.

I visited the Brandenburg Gate, which is an impressive eighteenth-century structure with a four-horse chariot on its top looking over the city. This twenty-six-meter-tall gate was built on the order of Prussian king Frederick William II on the site that marked the start of the road from Berlin to Brandenburg. Since its creation, it has often been the site for major historical events, including the occasion in 1987 when Pres. Ronald Reagan called on Russian president Mikhail Gorbachev to tear down the wall. I also visited the Reichstag Building, which was opened in 1894 and housed the Imperial Diet of the German Empire until 1933 when it became the Reichstag of the Weimar Republic. Following much-needed restoration work, it reopened in 1999 to serve as the parliament (the Bundestag) of united Germany. It was just a block away from the Brandenburg Gate. I could not go inside it because of the long queue for ticket.

The infamous Berlin Wall that forcibly split the German people into East Germans and West Germans was another must-see item on my list. Built in 1961, it was 4 meters high and 155 kilometers long, with 293 observation towers and 57 bunkers that stationed East German border guards to stop East Germans from fleeing West across the wall. Although the wall was taken down in 1989, a segment remained as a reminder to the united German people of their dark history. This 1.3-kilometer-long remnant of the former wall was now the East Side Gallery, the longest open-air gallery in the world covered with vivid paintings to remind everyone what life was like during the Cold War. Another place I stopped to see was the Checkpoint Charlie on Friedrichstrasse. It was the most famous point in the Berlin Wall where people crossed over from East Berlin to West Berlin. It was still manned by a soldier on the day I visited it, perhaps to keep alive the history of its past.

The bus also swung by the underground bunker where Jews were held during the Communist regime; the 370-meter-tall Berlin Television Tower with its observation deck and revolving restaurant hyped to be Europe's third-tallest freestanding structure; the 70-meter-tall Victory Column with an 8-meter-high gold statue of Queen Victoria on top; and Berlin's largest church, the Berlin Cathedral Church with its 75-meter-high dome and a huge collection of sarcophagi and coffins in its crypt. Berlin was so rich in history, arts, and culture that a one-day tour of Berlin was wholly inadequate; one should dedicate at least a couple of weeks if not more to imbibe its riches.

The Utstein meeting in Bergen on how to tackle corruption was most fruitful, perhaps because huddled around the table were only six like-minded participants. The Utstein Group was formed in 1999 at Utstein Abbey on the west coast of Norway when four prime ministers (from Sweden, Norway, Holland, and UK) met to discuss a common path to tackling poor governance. Later on, Germany and Canada were invited to join. The six countries then committed themselves to dedicate resources to fight corruption in developing countries. My five colleagues and I represented our respective governments, and our remit was to discuss our modus operandi on how to fight corruption, as well as develop some common understanding, approaches, and expected outcomes. Our discussions were candid with no holds barred, and the meeting concluded satisfactorily with several agreements.

On the final evening, we were invited to a dinner hosted by the Norwegian government. It was at a seafood restaurant inside a wooden building on the wharf, which was the focal point for locals and foreign visitors alike because of its fine restaurants, shops, galleries, and a museum. Bergen was situated on the west coast. It was Norway's second-largest city and was proud of its nickname, the "fjord capital." With two hundred days of rainfall every year, it also claimed to be the rainiest city in the northern hemisphere.

Bergen was unforgettable in many ways. Its piers were lined with fishing vessels constantly supplying the fish market in the wharf with fresh supplies every day. One couldn't escape the strong smell of the fresh catch, the whiff of the fish delicacies that were the centerpiece of restaurant menus, but, above all, the scent of the sea mist coming in from the fjord. I made many trips to Bergen during my CIDA years, and each time I saw a different side of the city, from its cobblestone streets, the multicolored houses on its hillsides, beautiful spray-painted street art, and unique street shopping to visiting the Bergen Aquarium, which comprised over fifty small and large aquariums of land and sea life in and around Norway; the Old Bergen Museum, which depicted old Bergen, which was Europe's largest city with wooden houses; and the Floibanen funicular, which connected the city center to the summit of Floyen 320 meters above sea level and only a six-minute ride up. Needless to say, I have a very fond memory of Bergen.

The year 2004 ended with a trip to Paris. Our delegation was led by our vice president for policy, and one of our delegation members was from the province of Quebec in Canada. He spoke French except that it really wasn't French but rather Quebecois, which was a bastardized version of Parisian French. Although our French host conducted the meeting in French, he looked uneasy whenever our delegation member from Quebec spoke. At the first health break, our French host pulled our vice president over to one side and told him that he did not mean to be impolite but could he instruct his colleague from Quebec to speak in English because he was massacring the French language! Although our Quebecois colleague found that to be quite insulting, the rest of us found that quite humorous.

The year 2005 commenced with meetings in Kiev, Ukraine, a country that I visited multiple times since then. The Ukrainian people had launched the Orange Revolution in late November 2004, and the massive countrywide protests that involved civil disobedience, sit-ins, and general strikes especially in Kiev, the capital of Ukraine, had continued until January 2005. These protests were led by opposition movements in the immediate aftermath of the runoff vote of November 21, 2004, Ukrainian presidential election, which was marred by massive corruption, voter intimidation, and electoral fraud according to several domestic and foreign election observers. In the face of these protests, the results of the original runoff were annulled, and a revote was ordered by the Ukrainian Supreme Court for December 26, 2004. This second runoff vote was conducted under the intense scrutiny of domestic and international observers, and Viktor Yushchenko was declared the winner with 52 percent of the vote; he was inaugurated on January 23, 2005, as the next president of Ukraine. Following his takeover, his government decided to take immediate steps to align Ukraine with the Western democracies. The new administration reached out to Canada requesting its assistance in this transition toward democratic norms.

Given the large Ukrainian population in Canada, the Canadian government was ready and willing to provide Ukraine with the needed development assistance. CIDA was designated as the lead agency of government in this effort, and I was one of several persons sent to

Ukraine to do an initial assessment of how to prioritize the aid. Our ambassador to Ukraine had scheduled for me a series of meetings with various ministers in the new cabinet, and after a briefing from him, I started having my meetings one by one.

The most critical meeting turned out to be with the minister of justice, who implored me to help Ukraine get rid of the arcane and backward legislation and laws of the Soviet era that he felt were holding back Ukraine from modernizing swiftly. He mentioned Ukraine's inability to draft modern legislation that would reflect its forward thinking; the widespread corruption in Ukraine's judicial system; the need to train Ukraine's judges, prosecutors, and lawyers so that delivery of justice would be fair, efficient, and timely; and, in general, to help Ukraine expedite its transition from a Soviet satellite state to a modern democratic state.

It was obvious from my meetings with various ministers that the new government wanted to capitalize on its popular support and fulfill the people's demands and expectation as much and as fast as possible. It was also clear to me that the new administration made joining the European Union (EU) its highest priority and therefore wanted to pursue reform with great haste to demonstrate to the EU its seriousness to join the comity of democratic nations.

At the conclusion of my visit, which was in late February 2005, I briefed our ambassador on my findings and returned to Ottawa with a rough draft of a series of recommendations that I would be making to my government. I submitted my report to the director general of the policy branch with recommendations on how Canada can and should proceed with the assistance. Central to my recommendations was a close collaboration between Ukraine's Ministry of Justice and our Justice Canada, especially its International Legal Assistance Programs (ILAP), which had over the years provided legal advice, technical assistance, and training to the judiciaries of many countries such as Afghanistan, Algeria, Argentina, Bangladesh, Czech Republic, Hungary, and Jamaica, among others.

Ukraine needed legal reforms both to modernize its laws as well as to strengthen its law-related institutions, which included civil code reform, legislative drafting, upgrading criminal prosecution procedures, anticorruption measures, procedure for appointing judges, regulations pertaining to the legal profession, and the like. The ILAP had been providing these and other types of assistance at the request of other governments and with financial support from CIDA and the Department of Foreign Affairs and International Trade (DFAIT).

After a lively debate with colleagues in CIDA's programming branch and some nuanced changes in the recommendations, the vice president of policy approved my direct engagement with Justice Canada. I had periodic meetings with my colleagues from the ILAP, who were happy to support Ukraine reform its justice sector and took up my recommendations in earnest, which were deemed to be necessary, urgent, and doable, and had the support of our ambassador in Ukraine.

My trip back from Ukraine, however, nearly got me into trouble. I had visited multiple touristic sites in Kiev, and one particular place sold medieval weapons. I was particularly attracted to the maces and flails on display, so I bought a twenty-inch-long mace to bring home. I had only a carry-on baggage with me, and I could fit the mace inside the carry-on diagonally only.

At the airport, the mace showed up in the security screen. I was asked to open my luggage. The airport security person was shocked to see a mace inside. He stared at me for a minute and then said, "I can look the other way and let you go. But what is your destination?" "I'm going to Canada via Paris," I replied. "You are going through Charles de Gaulle? Do you know what they will do to you when they find you are carrying a mace into the cabin?" he asked. "You are very right. Carrying the mace in my carry-on isn't very wise," I conceded. "But I am not going to leave the mace behind, so what do you suggest?" I asked. "The only choice you have is to check in your carry-on," he said. "But I don't have any lock for my carry-on, and I don't want the mace to get stolen," I protested. "Well, that's a risk you'll have to take, or you will be eating insects in an offshore French jail like in *Papillon*, so it's your choice!" he said.

The image of a starving Steve McQueen desperately trying to grab a bug running across the floor to eat flashed through my mind,

327

and without further hesitance, I took his advice and let him do the necessary luggage transfer tagging. The entire return trip was stressful, not knowing whether I would be stopped and questioned in Paris or Montreal. I nervously waited for my carry-on at the Montreal Airport luggage carousel. The first thing I did after retrieving it was to check whether the mace was still in there, and it was. I'm now the proud owner of a medieval mace, and while I bought it only for decorative purpose, it still makes a good conversation piece!

A Major Shift in My Portfolio

A major change of emphasis in my work portfolio came about after my Ukraine trip in February 2005. The focus on security sector reform for which I was originally hired was no longer high up on CIDA's agenda; instead, it was replaced by a new emphasis on governance and anticorruption. My colleague John Lobsinger, a CIDA veteran, was designated as the policy lead on governance issues, and I was designated as CIDA's policy lead on anticorruption. It also coincided with the departure of the director of our Democratic Institutions and Conflict Division (YDI), Robin McLay, leaving John and me to be acting directors of our division interchangeably.

My interest in fighting corruption had emerged during my Africa work at IDRC. At the time I joined CIDA after leaving IDRC, I was told that the issue of corruption was not a major consideration in CIDA's eighty plus countries of operation and that it was viewed within CIDA with a small *c*. But CIDA's subsequent engagements with the Utstein Group, the DAC GovNet, and the World Bank's Extractive Industries Transparency Initiative (EITI) brought about changes in its understanding of developmental challenges and in its development programming trajectory. Corruption in our partner countries was now seen as a big *C* issue. So the thrust of my work changed accordingly, and my international meetings became more and more corruption related. My engagements with the UNODC, OECD, the World Bank, and the AfDB, among others, became more frequent and intense, and I now had a dedicated budget to do my anticorruption policy work. My travel itineraries now included Vienna, Brussels, and Washington DC, and I thoroughly enjoyed this new focus on anticorruption work.

In the summer of 2005, I had to represent Canada at the meeting of the OECD DAC GovNet Task Team on Anti-Corruption (TTAC) in Vienna. Ten European countries and Canada and Australia met to discuss how to push the international anticorruption agenda forward. In the past, the TTAC had excluded the United States from their meetings because there was no meeting of minds between the European countries and the United States. This time, the United States was invited to attend the meeting as an observer, as also was the World Bank.

One critical agenda item was how to launch anticorruption programming because of its sensitive nature, and hence the issue of methodology became all important. For example, CIDA had approved a $28 million anticorruption program for Indonesia, but it did not get approval from the Indonesian government. After months of delay, CIDA learned that the Indonesian government thought that the project was indirectly labeling the government of Indonesia as corrupt. So CIDA dropped the word "anticorruption" and designated it as a good governance project, and it got approved by the government right away. Since no donor wanted to alienate its development partners, programming approaches, therefore, became of paramount importance.

Each development agency—SIDA, NORAD, DANIDA, MinBuza, SDC, GTZ, CIDA, DFID, EU, and DFAT—had developed its own methodology for its anticorruption work, and therefore it became nearly impossible to coordinate efforts and compare results. It was decided that we should make an effort to agree on a single methodology that every development agency would use so that results are verifiable and comparable. Not surprisingly, the United States disagreed and insisted that the methodology that the USAID used should be adopted by all other agencies; this was unanimously rejected by every agency. It was agreed by the ten nations that an international consultant would be hired to draft the anticorruption methodology after all ten nations provide their input to the consultant.

Another issue was where to test the new methodology to measure its effectiveness. The World Bank came up with a suggestion. They informed us that Cameroon was one of the heavily indebted poor countries (HIPC) and that the World Bank had made its aid conditional on Cameroon taking immediate and effective measures to fight corruption within its governmental system. The World Bank volunteered to ask the Cameroon government whether it would be willing to serve as the venue to test the new methodology. We all agreed and authorized the World Bank to do so.

A Conservative Government Takes Over in Canada

Meanwhile back home, a dramatic shift in Canada's politics took place in early 2006. The various conservative political factions were able to unite under Stephen Harper, who led the Conservative Party to a narrow victory against the Liberals on February 6, 2006. Little did we know that Harper would win a total of three consecutive elections—the first two would be minority governments and the last one a majority government—and remain prime minister of Canada until November 4, 2015.

What was even more drastic were the irreversible changes he brought to Canada's social and political orientations. Our domestic policy, foreign policy, and developmental policy changed beyond recognition. Within the first month of his assuming power, I remember all of us getting an advisory from the prime minister's office (PMO) in which each page had two columns. The left column had rows of words and phrases that we regularly used in our official memos to the PMO and in our MOUs, and the right column had the new corresponding words and phrases that we were required to use henceforth. It was made clear to us that it was mandatory that the words and phrases on the left column were never to be used again and were to be replaced by the corresponding words and phrases in the right column with immediate effect. This exercise signaled an unmistakeable shift toward the conservative agenda of the government.

Our development programming in the continent of Africa abruptly diminished because, according to Prime Minister Harper, it was a waste of resources to give them to the poor and corrupt countries. He ordered that we should shift our development focus to South America, whose countries were better markets for Canadian goods and therefore worth investing in so that it increased their ability to buy Canadian exports. Overnight, Canada's traditional values of empathy, human rights, and human concern that guided its foreign policy and foreign aid were replaced by pure commercial interest and insensitivity to human concern.

The Public Service of Canada was also very concerned at Harper's avowed promise to reduce it in size, ostensibly to reduce the size of the government, but in reality to punish it because of his belief that its members voted liberal. This, unfortunately, started a massive brain drain early on, and many members of the public service did not wait to be pushed out but took the first opportunity to move out to the private sector. This, of course, was great for the conservatives in the public sector who saw it as the opportunity of a lifetime to move up the career ladder at an accelerated pace. The result was a public service staffed with people with very limited knowledge and experience and one wholly inadequate to fend off the pressures and demands of other countries.

In June 2006, I went to a meeting in Paris. The agenda of our meeting was comparatively limited, and so it was a bit more relaxing trip than usual. My sister-in-law Lopa had heard of my upcoming trip from Nipa and called to tell me that her husband Rezwan's uncle and aunt lived in Paris and that they would be happy to meet me. She told me that Rezwan would text me their address in Paris and also call them to let them know that I will be contacting them when I am in Paris. Accordingly, I called them toward the end of my visit. They immediately invited me to their apartment. They were simple but gracious folks and were happy to invite me to their home. I met their children. Their son told me of his dream to become a soccer player and maybe someday play for Paris Saint-Germain FC. I wished him bonne chance! After the introductions, they took me to a Chinese restaurant. I loved the food, which I usually do at any Chinese restaurant. Following lunch, we took the subway to see some of Paris's iconic sights, including the Arc de Triomphe, the Eiffel Tower, and the Louvre Museum. All in all, it was a pleasant outing for me in Paris.

The Machete Men in Cameroon

It had been a year since the GovNet TTAC had recruited a consultant to draft the anticorruption methodology, which had gone through multiple inputs, iterations, and revisions, but now it was ready for testing. The World Bank had also consulted with the Cameroon government, who was eager to comply to signal their seriousness to fight corruption within their administrative system. The GovNet TTAC decided that a small delegation that would include Canada and a U.S. observer would be sent to Cameroon in mid-July 2006 for a week to meet with the high officials of the Cameroon and launch the anticorruption work using the new methodology. The U.S. observer was Bert Spector, the anticorruption specialist working for the Management Systems International (MSI), who would hire me half a decade later to manage USAID's anticorruption project in Afghanistan.

We arrived in Cameroon's capital, Yaoundé, on July 16, 2006. Right away, we could see what a poor country it was. Yaoundé looked like a dilapidated rural town with slums abounding everywhere one looked. Walking through the streets, one saw lots of commercial activities that were primarily small, family-run businesses; streets were crowded with people, mobile vendors, and money changers; and traffic was less vehicular and more bicycles, pushcarts, flatbeds on wheel carrying basic goods. There were a few high-rises in specific sections of the city, but the roads were generally below par.

During one of my strolls around my hotel, I was approached by a money changer who insisted to change my dollars for the local currency promising me the best exchange rate. I decided to test him and exchanged fifty U.S. dollars. When I compared the rate with the certified money changers and the bank, I found that the rate offered by the street money changer was indeed much better. I thought that this was too good to be true and succumbed to the fear that I might have gotten counterfeit currency, but when I had my currency notes examined by the bank, they turned out to be genuine. My faith in the street vendors was restored!

Our first meeting was with the president of Cameroon. We waited beyond the appointed hour when the vice president arrived to meet us. He apologized that the president was otherwise engaged and so our meeting was with him. He assured us of his government's commitment to combat corruption and welcomed our effort. He hoped that Cameroon's agreement to participate in this endeavor would convince the World Bank of their sincerity to pursue reform and that the WB would release its financial aid to Cameroon. We met other ministers and high officials of the government, all of whom were using the same talking points. It was agreed that the UNDP office in Yaoundé would spearhead the anticorruption effort, and the participating donors would bear the cost. I volunteered to provide the first tranche of the money needed for the endeavor from my anticorruption budget after securing the approval of my DG.

One evening, our delegation was invited to a dinner reception at the residence of the French ambassador to Cameroon. It was a beautiful spacious house up in the hills overlooking the capital. After a lovely evening of lively discussions, good food and wine, Bert and I were ready to leave when we learned that our car was not available for reasons I cannot recall now. The French ambassador stepped in and graciously offered his own car to take us back to the hotel. Finding no other alternative, we thankfully accepted his offer.

Within ten minutes or so as we started going downhill slowly, suddenly there were some machete-brandishing, rough-looking guys standing on our path. As our car slowed down, we were surrounded by a few of the machete-swinging hoodlums. Our local driver immediately instructed us to make sure our car doors were locked and windows were rolled up all the way. The driver turned to me and said that I will have to pretend that I am the French ambassador and that he will do the rest. As Bert and I looked at each other, he said, "Your French better be good!" Little does one realize that in moments like that, even a good French speaker could easily sound like he is speaking anything but French!

One of the guys with machete signaled the driver to roll down his window. Our driver rolled down just a little so that they could talk. He asked who the two were in the backseat, and the driver indicated with his thumb pointing backward toward me that I was the French ambassador and sitting next to me was my colleague. The machete guy replied that if the ambassador was in the car, then why wasn't the French flag flying on the car bonnet? The driver replied that the flag was not flying because it was nighttime and the ambassador's trip was personal and not official.

There was a pause for a minute as the machete-swinging guys looked at each other trying to figure out if that was the protocol. Then he took a couple of steps toward our window, lowered his head to peer through the glass, and then knocked a couple of times on the glass with his machete. Bert lowered it a tad bit. The guy looked at me sitting on the other side of Bert and said, "Bonjour, Monsieur l'Ambassadeur!" Realizing the do-or-die situation, I maintained my poise and my ambassadorial visage and replied, "Bonne journée, monsieur, et bonne nuit." I signaled Bert to roll up the window, which he did.

At that point, our driver started rolling gently forward. The machete guy stepped back, and the other gang members stepped back as well. We slowly rolled downhill and picked up speed on flat surface until we finally arrived at the hotel. I asked the driver to wait as I called the ambassador from the lobby to report to him about the incident. The ambassador replied, "Mon Dieu!" and then asked me not to send the car back that evening but to instruct the driver to bring the car to the residence in the early morning.

We were very cautious during the rest of our stay, although the protocol office had heard about the incident from the ambassador and called us to apologize for the incident and assigned an armed police vehicle as our escort for the duration of our stay. Bert and I flew back to Zurich on Swissair, and from there we flew to DC and Ottawa separately. Although the GovNet TTAC expected me to return to Yaoundé at the conclusion of the project that I had initially funded, I opted out of it without any regret.

Dar es Salaam, Arusha, and Zanzibar

Two months later, I prepared to go to Tanzania. Several years earlier in October 2002, the Parliament of Canada hosted an international gathering of 170 parliamentarians and 400 observers to discuss the role of parliamentarians to combat corruption, and one important output of that conference was the creation of the Global Organization of Parliamentarians against Corruption (GOPAC). CIDA was an early supporter of GOPAC, having provided Canadian 100K for the first global forum in Ottawa, and it continued to support GOPAC over the years in its efforts to establish various thematic global task forces. CIDA also assisted GOPAC whenever it could to create national chapters and regional groupings to serve as GOPAC hubs.

GOPAC also held a global forum every two years to promote collaboration among parliamentarians from all across the world to fight political corruption and to provide parliamentarians a platform to set the international anticorruption agenda. Since I was CIDA's policy lead for anticorruption, I became intimately involved with GOPAC and worked very closely with its founder chairman, John Williams, who had headed our delegation to the IACC in Seoul.

The Parliament of Tanzania invited GOPAC to hold its second global forum in its East African Parliament Building in Arusha from September 19-23, 2006. Since neither Dodoma nor Dar es Salaam—the two capitals where Tanzania's parliament met—had the capacity to hold an international meeting the size of GOPAC's global conference, the decision was made to hold the conference in the Arusha International Conference Centre (AICC), home of the East African Legislative Assembly. The GOPAC Constitution required that global conferences be organized in conjunction with a regional chapter, so the African Parliamentarians Network against Corruption (APNAC) became the cohost.

At the top of John William's agenda was the creation of national chapters. He asked me if I could draft a concept note for the creation of national chapters and present it to GOPAC's board of directors at its second forum in Arusha. I readily agreed, seeing that as an opportunity to inject my ideas at GOPAC's nascent stage. I flew from Ottawa to Amsterdam to Dar es Salaam, and then to Kilimanjaro International Airport on Monday, September 18, 2006, and registered at the Ngurdoto Mountain Lodge for the duration of my stay in Arusha. The next day, Tuesday, was reserved for preconference tours to Tanzania's national parks—Ngorongoro, Lake Manyara, and Kilimanjaro National Park— hosted by the Parliament of Tanzania. The participants were given the option to choose any one of the three tours.

I opted to take the tour to Ngorongoro Conservation Area. We left the hotel in late afternoon, and it took us just above three hours by a tour bus. Ngorongoro is a Maasai word that meant "black hole." Two and a half million years ago, a large volcano had erupted and collapsed on itself, creating the largest caldera in the world, 22.5 kilometers wide. The Ngorongoro Conservation Area comprised vast expanses of highland plains, savanna, woodlands, and forests where many types of wildlife such as wildebeests, zebras, gazelles, giraffes, and lions coexisted with seminomadic Maasai pastoralists who grazed their cattle in the grasslands.

After we arrived, we were introduced to the Maasai chief of that region and some of his lieutenants, who then gave us a guided tour of the forests and the plains. We saw a couple of lions not very far from us and some zebras at quite a distance, as the Maasai chief explained to our English-speaking guide the lions' sleeping, roaming, and feeding habits and timing. After nearly an hour of walkabout, the sun had gone down, and we returned to camp and found that tents were already set up and fires were burning in four corners with a huge fire burning in the center, and all around it were colorful cloth on the ground for people to sit down under the clear open sky.

Inside one of the tents on one side were rectangular tables with large containers of food. We queued up to fill our plates; I chose pilau, meat with plantain, grilled meat, and lentil porridge. As we ate, the Maasai chief regaled us with stories of Maasai bravado. It was a very enjoyable evening of feasting, storytelling, laughter, and relaxation.

When it was time for our departure, the Maasai chief's voice suddenly turned serious, and he said that it was in Maasai tradition to offer a visiting guest a Maasai maiden for the night, and pointing at me, who was sitting directly opposite him, he said that the maiden had chosen me! There was complete silence as we looked at each other not knowing what to make of it. The government officials also put up a serious look. The translator looked at me and said in an equally serious tone, "Well! We cannot offend the Maasai chief. I guess we will have to leave you behind for the night!" It was tense all around me, and I was beginning to get scared. I told him, "Please tell the chief that I am much honored, but I am also very, very, very married." After he translated my response, everyone held their breath, as the Maasai chief lowered his gaze and stared at the fire for a while, and then he burst into laughter, followed by the government officials and the translator. It took the rest of us a minute to realize that they had planned this stunt all along to see how we foreigners would react and so that they could get a good laugh at our expense. But I was relieved that it was not real. We returned to our hotel at around 10:30 p.m., and I just hit the sack.

Conference registration was next day at 8:00 a.m. at the Arusha International Conference Center (AICC). My presentation on Global Integrity Initiative was the second item on the first day's agenda. It was a forty-five-minute PowerPoint presentation to the GOPAC board of directors followed by another forty-five minutes of questions and answers in a closed-door meeting. Parliamentarians from different regions making up the board asked many questions, and some of them were quite interesting, such as the differing understanding of the concept of integrity, of ethics, and of corruption. I was asked to revise my concept paper to incorporate the suggestions made by the board of directors and then send it to the GOPAC secretariat for wider distribution.

The global conference itself ran into some difficulties. While most of the some 280 parliamentary delegates had no issue with GOPAC's leadership, many African parliamentarians felt that the APNAC should be recognized as the primary parliamentary forum because it was established before GOPAC came into being. But after some intense discussions and a straw vote, GOPAC was the unanimous choice among the parliamentarians as the lead agency to guide the work of parliamentarians across the world. This vote was important because the World Bank was planning to provide substantial support to GOPAC, and it would have withdrawn that support if APNAC was designated as the lead agency.

The conference ended successfully, and its final report contained eight resolutions, one of which was the endorsement of the United Nations Convention against Corruption (UNCAC) and similar international anticorruption conventions and the commitment to support their work by creating a global task force of parliamentarians who would work in concert in their respective countries.

To the Land of Spices

The conference ended in the afternoon of Saturday, September 23, 2006. I decided to capitalize on the weekend and on the rare opportunity to visit Zanzibar, an island only about fifty kilometers off the coast of Tanzania on the Indian Ocean, with a population of around one million, 95 percent of whom were Muslim. I had heard so much about this Spice Island over the years that I decided to visit the island before leaving the region. The ninety-minute flight, one way, was a further incentive to avail this opportunity.

I decided to take the late-afternoon flight on Precision Air from Kilimanjaro International Airport to Zanzibar. Shortly after we were airborne, the captain announced that Mount Kilimanjaro would be visible on the right side of the aircraft in minutes and whether we would be interested to see its crater. We all exclaimed, "Yes!" He then told us to get ready with our cameras. Shortly thereafter, we could see Africa's tallest mountain and highest peak at 19,341 feet. Much of Mount Kilimanjaro was dry and snowless. The captain announced that when he had started flying many years ago, the snow line was halfway down from the peak; now the snow line was only a few hundred feet from the top, and he attributed this receding snow line to global warming.

He flew the plane so close that we could see the crater as if it was only a dozen feet away. The crater looked deceptively small in diameter, as if someone could run and jump from one side to the other. The captain circled around the crater twice, each time changing the direction of his flight so that passengers on both sides of the plane had the chance to take pictures. I was able to take several pictures myself.

We then flew in the southeasterly direction to Zanzibar. I spent two nights on the island. The timing was right. I was visiting in late September, which was toward the end of Zanzibar's spring, and the weather was cool and dry. The first thing I did when I woke up the next day was to hire a taxi for the whole day, ensuring that the driver could speak some English and serve as a tour guide. I doubled his daily rate from fifteen to thirty U.S. dollars, which was considerably cheaper than what it is these days. He was quite happy and enthusiastically took me to places that I wouldn't have thought of going to.

First, he took me to Paje Beach on the southeast coast. The beautiful white sand, the tall palm trees swaying in the light breeze, the crystal-clear blue and turquoise waters, and a couple of kite surfers getting ready at a distance created a picture for me that I could never forget. We drove northward and stopped at Kendwa Beach, another white, powdery, sandy beach that extended for miles with clear turquoise waters all around. The driver told me that the northeast was the posh region of the island where all the rich people lived. It was the island's prime location with its top-end accommodation because of opportunities for excellent diving and reef exploration. Next, we stopped at Nungwi Beach in the northwest of Zanzibar; after which we ended our beach tour because, according to the driver, the beaches on the west coast were nothing to crow about.

From there, the taxi driver drove south along the west coast to Zanzibar's capital, Stone Town, with its many winding alleys and byways and old Arab-style buildings. What was remarkable about the buildings was their huge wooden doors with inlaid intricate metal decorations that reflected the Indian, Arab, and Swahili influences of the past. There were many places to see in Stone Town. There was the nineteenth-century Sultan's Palace on the waterfront overlooking the ocean where the Sultan and his family lived until the 1964 revolution deposed him and the palace was renamed the People's Palace and later became a museum. There was also the seventeenth-century Old Fort on the waterfront built to defend the island against Portuguese marauders. I saw remnants of the fortifications, as well as of the amphitheater. My driver and I took a break at the Forodhani Gardens to have some samosas and tea.

He then took me to a coastal fortification comprising an underground holding place, which was a huge room with thin slits that served as air vents at the very top of its fifteen-foot walls to allow air for captured men and women to breathe. A concrete underground passageway connected the holding place to an opening closed off with iron grills at the oceanfront where ships waited for their cargo of slaves destined for the Americas. I walked into the underground holding place and stood there imagining what it must have been like to the scores of chained slaves huddled there not knowing what their fate was; it was an eerie feeling.

The driver and I walked the full length of the underground passageway to the opening at the other end where the wrought iron gate was nearly all gone. There was a sense of relief when I felt the warm ocean breeze on my face, but I instantly remembered that for the slaves, the experience was quite different because slave handlers with whip in hand must have been waiting there to direct them toward the waiting slave ships where they were packed like sardines and carried off to a horrific future.

I took the time to read the inscriptions and the history of the place and was shocked to learn that the first slave traders were not the Europeans but the Arabs; the first slave trade from Africa was actually from the east coast of Africa to the sultanates of the Middle East. According to historians, the primary source of slaves before the slave trade began in earnest was the Bosnian coast. The Slav clans were constantly at war with each other, and the victorious clans sold off those they captured from the defeated clans, and the Bosnian coast was the most lucrative slave market. This continued for centuries until the Arabs conquered the region and the Balkan source of slaves dried up.

With the expansion of Arab power in the Middle East, the Mediterranean region, and North Africa, the Arabs expanded the slave trade to the continent of Africa, and the Savannah and the Horn of Africa became the primary source for slaves. According to the historians, the male-female ratio of slaves captured by European slave traders for the American markets was 2:1, while for the Arab slave traders in Africa's east coast was 1:3. This was because the demand in the Americas was economic and they needed sturdy men in the cotton fields and for other outdoor work, while the demand by the Arab sultans was for their harems; hence, girls numbered three times more than boys. The Omani sultan of Zanzibar bought thousands of slaves from Arab slave traders for their clove plantations as well.

The next day, Monday morning, I went to the reception to change some dollars for the local currency. First, the receptionist and then the manager regretted that the hotel wouldn't be able to change any foreign currency because it was running low on the local currency. The manager explained that since the bank was closed that day—I cannot remember why—I would have to wait till Tuesday morning to change money at the bank. This seriously undermined my plan, and I had to scale down my activities for the day. I told the taxi driver my situation and arranged with him a half-day spice tour.

Zanzibar has been an important trading center in the Indian Ocean region for centuries and attracted the attention of the Arabs and Europeans alike for its abundance of spices, earning the sobriquet "Spice Island." The island produced a plethora of spices but was probably most famous for its cloves, which were considered the king of spices, until Indonesia took over. The island's pineapples were still considered to be the sweetest in the world.

Our spice tour guide walked us past tree after tree, stopping to explain the value of each tree. He stood before a neem tree and asked us if we knew what this tree was used for in our own countries. I told him that I had seen men from our villages using the twigs to brush their teeth. He replied that in Zanzibar, it was used by midwives to abort unwanted pregnancies. He explained that the leaves and twigs were boiled in water, the white foam was discarded, and the rest of the water was cooled and drank to trigger abortion, and that it was a safe method with little side effect.

341

We walked to another tall tree with a vine wrapped around it. He explained that it was a pepper vine that cannot grow by itself but needs another tree to grow on. He then showed us several other pepper vines. Next, he pointed to bamboo mats on the forest floor containing green, red, and black peppers on separate mats. He said that Zanzibar exported the three types of peppers after they are dried under the sun. The color of the peppers depended on the time they were plucked from the vine and on the drying time under the sun. At the end of the tour was a covered shed with tables of packaged spices. All of us bought quite a few packets of different spices. Almost all spices were available except saffron, which is not grown on the island. All in all, it was a very informative and learning experience for us. I left Zanzibar the following day, happy that I had undertaken this trip.

A City of Churches

A month and a half later, in mid-November 2006, I went to Guatemala City to participate in the Twelfth International Anti-Corruption Conference (IACC); it was my first visit to Central America. The Eleventh IACC had taken place in Seoul in 2003 in which I participated. Although the IACCs took place every two years in a different continent each time, I cannot recall why this time it was being held after three years. Participation in the IACC varied from 1,000 to 1,500 delegates and observers. Since I joined CIDA in 2002, I had attended all the IACCs for multiple reasons. I was CIDA's policy lead on anticorruption, and therefore IACCs where the world's anticorruption experts and practitioners gathered were must-attend conferences for me. CIDA has occasionally funded Transparency International (TI), which organized the biennial IACC, and I was required to monitor the event. And CIDA's former president Huguette Labelle was chairman of TI's international board. An additional attraction for me has been to meet familiar faces from Bangladesh, like former foreign minister Kamal Hossain, who was a member of TI's board; my longtime friend Iftekhar uz Zaman, who is the executive director of Transparency International

Bangladesh; and Manzoor Hasan, executive director of the South Asian Institute of Advanced Legal and Human Rights Studies who attended occasionally.

What I remember most distinctly during the drive from the airport to the hotel was how "old-world" Guatemala City looked. All the structures were really old Spanish-built buildings, many of which had a recess on the roadside exterior wall with a miniature statuette of Jesus Christ to enable passersby to light a candle. I had never seen as many churches anywhere in the world as I saw in Guatemala City; there seemed to be a church in every road intersection. The whole city seemed to be deeply religious. During the spare hours, I hired taxis to drive around the city and visit its outskirts. Most of the people I met during these trips were women involved in outdoor work like sweeping, cleaning, washing clothes, hanging them out to dry, knitting, selling clothes that were spread out on mats, etc. Most of the men I saw looked like daytime laborers with dark lips as if they had been chewing tobacco—all this in the capital city.

At the conference, I met a new Bangladeshi. She was Selima Ahmad, president of the Bangladesh Women Chamber of Commerce and Industry. At lunch, I was walking to an empty table with my lunch tray and looking around hoping to see Kamal Hossain when I spotted this lady in sari. I asked her where she was from, and when she said she was with the Bangladesh delegation, I invited her to join us. It was interesting to hear of her women-focused work in Bangladesh.

On the last day of the conference, we bumped into each other again when we started talking about shopping. I told her that I might buy some souvenir to remind me of Guatemala. She said that she was interested in gemstones, but she was afraid to go out alone; she asked me if I would consider giving her company. Since I have bought gemstones from many places during my past travels, I thought I could check out the gemstones in Guatemala as well, so I agreed. After the conference ended, she and I took a taxi to the streets known for shops that sold gemstones. We checked out a few shops, and she did buy some stones, but I didn't.

Tragic Ending of a Family Member

My father came to visit us in Ottawa in January 2007. He said he was having problem with his vision. So I made an appointment with my ophthalmologist. The diagnosis was that he needed immediate cataract surgery on his left eye. The surgery was done successfully on January 15, 2007. A month or so later, he left for Dallas. In mid-April, I got a call from my brother Shahalam in Irving, Dallas, telling me that Dad was at Richardson Hospital. He had slipped on the wet kitchen floor at my brother Mahboob's home in Garland, Dallas, and was found on the floor. Mahboob picked up his limp body and put him to bed. He was incontinent several times.

When Shahalam called to inquire about Dad, he learned what happened and immediately had Mahboob call 911 to take Dad to the hospital. Once in the hospital, Dad went into coma and never regained consciousness. I immediately flew to Dallas from Ottawa to be by his side, followed by our cousin Rafiqur Rasul, who drove down from Kentucky to see him, and then came my sister Tina from Boise, Idaho. A doctor's letter from Richardson Hospital addressed to the U.S. embassy in Dhaka was attached to visa applications by other family members in Dhaka to come to Dallas to see Dad, but visas were denied. Dad passed away on April 20, 2007, after remaining in coma for seven days. After his death, his *janaja* (funeral rite) was arranged by the Muslim community in Dallas.

Then followed a round of conference calls between family members in Dallas, Boise, Ottawa, and Dhaka to decide where to bury Dad. The choice was either in a cemetery in Irving, Texas, or in Dhaka or in his village Comilla. Since I was the eldest child, the responsibility of reaching a consensus on this and conducting the burial ceremonies fell on me. My siblings were in disagreement, and some insisted on having it their way. After hearing their arguments and counterarguments, I decided to bury Dad in Bangladesh.

It was not difficult for me to reach this decision. I reasoned that Dad was unknown in the United States, but he was a highly respected retired army man, a very well-known jute businessman, a respected political figure, a philanthropist, and, most importantly, a freedom fighter who had given blood and nearly his life for his country. He deserved to be buried in Bangladesh. Arrangements were made to fly his corpse to Dhaka. My siblings and I flew to Dhaka from the States and Canada as well, and the corpse arrived in the same flight to Dhaka. In Dhaka, we had to make an arrangement with an air-conditioned morgue because of the oppressive heat at the time, while we had to decide where to bury him. Dad had left no will.

In Dhaka, I faced my greatest challenge regarding where he should be buried. First of all, every important constituency with whom he was affiliated insisted on giving him a *janaja*. The Retired Army Officers Welfare Association (RAOWA) Club held a janaja for him in its premises. The Gulshan Central Mosque (Azad Masjid) of which he was an early benefactor since we were an early settler in Dhaka's posh suburb of Gulshan held a janaja for him.

There was a real tussle between multiple communities regarding his actual burial site. My father being one of the senior most Bengali officers in the army, when the Bangladesh Army learned of his death, they insisted on giving him a guard of honor and a proper military burial in the army graveyard near the navy headquarters. The people of Debidwar, where he had built the orphanage and a college and from where he had won every election to parliament, insisted that he should be buried in the college grounds as a mark of respect and of recognition of his selfless contribution to his district. The people of his village Gourshar insisted that he should be buried with his ancestors, that he was the son of their village where he had built a primary school and therefore they had the first right to him.

I discussed with my family members the pros and cons of each of the options and finally reached the consensus that we should bury him in the Shujat Ali College grounds. It would be a mausoleum of sorts with a brief description of his life, so that not only the present generation who know him well but also the future generations will know this illustrious son of Bengal and what he did for his country. What was further appealing to me were the words of those who prayed in the mosque that Father built. They said that he should be buried in the vacant space between the main college building and the mosque because the orientation of the grave would be such that toward the end of the prayer when worshippers turned their head sideways to the left to say, "Wa As-Salaamu Alaikum Wa Rahmatullah" (May Peace and Mercy of Allah be Upon You), hundreds of worshippers would be looking at the grave while uttering those words.

We took the body to Debidwar and placed it on a cordoned-off table placed on a podium at one end of the huge field in front of the Shujat Ali College for people to see him for the last time. We also had the Debidwar police manage the queue and do the crowd controlling, for there was a sea of people from entire Debidwar and neighboring thanas who came for one last glimpse of the man who had made such a difference for the good in their lives. Despite the police vigilance, we noticed some deliberate attempts by hired thugs of Father's political opponents who had repeatedly lost in the elections and bore considerable grudge against him trying to create disorder and disarray to throw the corpse off the table. But we managed to keep control of the situation.

The wake ended with speeches from the podium delivered first by my youngest uncle, Fazlul Hossain, who was the longest-serving headmaster of Debidwar Reazuddin Model High School until his recent retirement; then by onetime member of parliament from another thana, Fakrul Islam Munshi; and finally by me. The first two speakers spoke of Father's lifetime achievements and his contribution to society. My job was different. Tradition dictated that as the inheritor of family responsibilities, I had to proffer a public apology for anything Father may have done or said that may have hurt someone's sentiment, and to ask for their forgiveness. Following the speeches, we lowered his body into the grave according to the instructions of the hujur, who then led the burial prayers, and finally we arranged a police detail to patrol the area and protect the grave from politically financed miscreants.

With that came an end to the illustrious life of a village boy who walked barefoot for miles to go to school, who had to cross water bodies holding his books on top of his head so that they didn't get wet, who dared to dream big, and who sent his kids to the finest schools and then across the ocean to America so that they could realize their own dreams.

Through it all, he served with honor and distinction, first, the British Empire and then Pakistan and, finally, his homeland, Bangladesh. His philanthropy gave his district of Comilla an orphanage, a school, a college, a mosque, and scholarships for the needy.

During every flood season, he spent his time in his district of Comilla monitoring the rise of flood waters and frequently gathering people together to sandbag the banks of the River Gumti to save the villages it flowed through. Twice in the early '70s, Father missed casting his votes in parliament. The Parliamentary Whip complained to Prime Minister Sheikh Mujibur Rahman that Shujat Ali spent more time in Comilla than he did in Dhaka and missed segments of several parliamentary sessions. When the PM raised the issue with Father, he acknowledged that that was correct because he was doing important constituency work as part of his pledges to the people who voted him to parliament. If the PM had a problem with that, then Father was ready to quit parliament. The PM never raised that issue with him again, perhaps because he knew that the only person who could win against the National Awami Party (NAP-M) chief professor Muzaffar Ahmed, who was from the same constituency, was Father.

Family Trip to Italy

We tried to bury this sad development by bringing some cheer into our lives by planning a trip to Italy. Since Fareen had graduated from the university the previous November and would be leaving us soon for her master's program later in the year, and since we had a friend who was living in Rome at the time, we thought the timing for a European vacation was right. We got in touch with Nasrin Rizwanullah in Rome to sound her out about our plan, and right away, she and her husband Mohammad Rizwanullah, who worked at the UNHCR office in Rome, invited us to stay with them. So in late July, the four of us flew to Rome. We met Rizwanullah bhai's mother, who was visiting them as well. She was an elderly lady but also an accomplished Bengali writer who had published several books.

They had rented a big and spacious house with more rooms and space than they needed, and the iconic sights were walking distance from their house. We walked to Rome's largest and most famous fountain, the Fontana di Trevi. Built in AD 1762, it was twenty-six meters high and fifty meters wide depending on how one measured it and featured statues of *Abundance* and *Health.* The centerpiece of the fountain was the Greek sea god Oceanus, whose chariot was being pulled by two sea horses, one wild and one docile, which represented the opposing moods of the sea, with two Tritons who were mermen (men from waist up and fish from waist down) leading the horses.

A common occurrence at the fountain was that each day, hundreds of tourists stood with their backs to the fountain made a wish and then tossed a coin over their heads into it. According to legend, tossing one coin meant that one would return to the Eternal City (Rome), tossing two coins meant that one would return to Rome and find love, and tossing three coins meant that one would return, find love, and get married. It was estimated that up to 3,000 euros were thrown into the fountain each day, and the annual take was over a million euros. The money was put in sacks and handed over to the police, who weighed the sacks and then deposited the money for donation to a local charity that helped the homeless and the hungry.

Not wanting to miss the opportunity, we, too, made our wishes before the wishing fountain and threw in our coins. I wish I could remember what I wished for. If I were to guess, it was probably that I wished our son and daughter would complete their education from reputed schools, find jobs that would make them happy and solvent, find good life companions, and live a healthy life.

From there, we walked to the Spanish Steps, which linked the Trinità dei Monti church, which was under the tutelage of the French king with the long Spanish Square below. The Spanish Steps continue to be best known as a meeting place, although a law was passed after our visit prohibiting sitting down on the steps because of the degradation that had taken place over the years. A short distance from the Spanish Steps was the Roman Pantheon, an ancient brick-and-concrete building built around AD 128, as the brick stamps on the side of the building revealed. As its name suggested, the Pantheon was a Roman temple dedicated to all the gods and goddesses of pagan Rome. The temple had a massive domed rotunda measuring forty-three meters in diameter, and at the top of the dome was an opening, or the oculus, which was just over eight meters wide, which had no covering and allowed light and rain to enter the Pantheon. There were no windows except for the oculus, and the geometric patterned marble floor of the rotunda was gently sloping with twenty-two well-hidden holes that drained the rainwater. The Pantheon contained the tombs of several Italian kings and of poets and artists, including the famous artist Raphael. Over the years, visitors to the Pantheon have been impressed by its rotunda and have sought to replicate it in their own countries. Perhaps the best examples are the U.S. Capitol rotunda and the rotundas in various U.S. state capitals.

From the Pantheon, we walked to the Colosseum, which was less than one kilometer away. Enough of the structure that predated the Pantheon seemed to be still standing, allowing visitors a glimpse of its past where gladiators regularly slayed each other and where the public's frenzy peaked when Christians were fed to the lions. A man in an ancient Roman army commander's outfit with leather tunic and plumed helmet and sword in hand stood in front of the entrance ready to take pictures with visitors. So we took a picture with him and Mishu standing side by side. Opposite the Colosseum was the Imperial Forum, still evoking its ancient glory and magnificence. The ruins of ancient Rome were all around us to be captured in photographs.

In early September, we also visited the Vatican City, which was the headquarters of the Roman Catholic Church and its government, the Holy See. The Vatican City became the smallest independent state in the world on February 11, 1929, when the Lateran Agreement was signed between Italy's Benito Mussolini and Pope Pius XI. We went early to be at the front of the queue when a stern-looking Vatican matron approached us and said that Mumu would not be allowed in because she was wearing a sleeveless top and her arms were showing. We hadn't done our homework, so we didn't know that entry to the Vatican Museums, Vatican Gardens, the Sistine Chapel, and St. Peter's Basilica was prohibited to visitors wearing low-cut or sleeveless tops, miniskirts, shorts, or hats. So we stepped out of the queue and went outside the Vatican compound in search of a shop to buy a shawl for Mumu.

To our pleasant surprise, just outside on the street was a man with his mobile cart who saw us coming and immediately said, "You need a shawl, right?" On top of that, he was a Bangladeshi and spoke to us in Bangla. He picked a shawl for Mumu and assured her that now there wasn't going to be any problem. We paid him, thanked him for his help, and returned to the queue. Once inside, we moved around freely except for areas cordoned off by signs hanging on metal chains. We went down to the crypt and saw the many sarcophagi of modern-day popes and kings. The most important, of course, was the cordoned-off area of St. Peter's grave, the first pontiff of Rome. The dome of St. Peter's basilica, considered to be the tallest dome in the world at 136 meters, was particularly famous because of Michelangelo's painting that took nineteen years to complete in AD 1547. Unlike the Pantheon, at the base of the dome were windows that allowed sun rays to stream in, giving one the sensation of the dome floating in the clouds.

We decided to take the stairs to the top of the dome, and each of us braved the 550 steps to the top to get the enchanting view of the city. We had to occasionally rest to catch our breath on the way up. The return journey was scary because there was no railing guard to prevent us from falling except for a dangling rope in the center. We stayed as close to the exterior wall as possible as we very slowly went down the spiral staircase until we reached the main floor. I cannot remember if we went to the Sistine Chapel, which is the papal chapel in the Vatican Palace that is the residence of the pope. The Sistine Chapel is, of course, famous for being the venue where the conclave of the College of Cardinals meets to elect the next pope. A white smoke (fumata bianca) signified that the assembled cardinals have elected a new pope.

The St. Peter's Square was the huge plaza in front of St. Peter's Basilica. It was surrounded by 140 statues on columns depicting various Roman Catholic saints, including St. Dominic, St. Francis of Assisi, St. Benedict, and St. Bernard of Clairvaux. At the center of the plaza stood a thirty-four-meter-tall, 330-ton red granite obelisk. This four-thousand-year-old

Egyptian obelisk was a part of the spoils of war after Octavius conquered Egypt in 30 BC. It was brought to Rome around AD 41 and placed in front of the Basilica to celebrate the triumph of the church over paganism and heresy. In later years, the obelisk was placed at the center of the plaza so that the shadow cast by the obelisk marked the movements of the sun at midday on the signs of the zodiac. It also helped the church get a better handle on the summer and winter solstices.

Standing on a balcony of St. Peter's Basilica overlooking
the The St. Peter's Square, September 2007

After completing our sightseeing in Rome, we took the Eurostar to Florence, which was 260 kilometers north and only ninety minutes away by high-speed train. In Florence, we walked through its posh plaza as well as strolled through its markets that looked very much like a bazaar and did some shopping. From the posh shopping area, Nipa bought some beautiful Murano glass jewelry and scarves, while from the shops in the bazaar, I bought some really nice but inexpensive silk ties; I can't remember what my children bought.

At one point, we came upon a couple of Bangladeshis selling trinkets from a cloth spread out on the street. When we introduced ourselves as Bangladeshis also, they were very pleased to see us. They were keen to find out how to immigrate to Canada and asked me questions to that effect. It was obvious that they had entered Italy illegally and was looking for ways to go to North America. Suddenly, another Bangladeshi stationed at the end of the road signaled them that the police were coming. They immediately grabbed the four corners of their cloth and dashed off to evade the police. We sat down at a street-side café for a delicious lunch. It was rather exciting to go through an authentic Italian menu (with English translation in much smaller font below each item) and then place our individual orders. We had a very casual lunch as we watched tourists of many nationalities pass us by. For dessert, Nipa had to have a cone of strawberry ice cream that matched her pink top!

Famous for its culture, Renaissance art and architecture, and monuments, we had to visit some of Florence's famous galleries and museums. We went to the Galleria dell'Accademia to see Michelangelo's famous sculpture of *David*. My wife thoroughly checked him out and was so impressed by his physique that she said, "Eesh, aijay, amar ekta David lagbe!" For some reason, I suddenly felt obsolete. This was the second time she had indicated to me that I was losing it. The first time was when I was teaching at North South University, which meant I was living in Dhaka while she was living in Ottawa. After several years of living separately, she told me one day that she had seen in the mall ample, young, handsome men with headful of hair to choose from if I continued to stay in Dhaka.

We also visited the Uffizi Gallery to see Botticelli's *The Birth of Venus* and Leonardo da Vinci's *Annunciation*. Although we could have spent days going through Florence's rich art and architectural history, our time was limited. We returned to the Eurostar to head north to Pisa, only sixty-nine kilometers and fifty minutes away.

From the Pisa Central Station, we took the bus that directly went to the Leaning Tower of Pisa, located next to the Cathedral of Pisa in the Piazza dei Miracoli (Square of Miracles). The town of Pisa got its name in 600 BC from a Greek word meaning "marshland," which is why many of its historical structures have sunk over the years. The construction of the Tower of Pisa started in AD 1173, and it took more than two hundred years to finish in AD 1399.

But because of the marshy soil, the tower was no longer its original height of sixty meters, and it had sunk unevenly, thus giving it the leaning look. Before restoration work was completed in 2001, the tower leaned 5.5 degrees, and now it leaned about 4 degrees, which meant that the top of the tower was horizontally almost four meters away from its base. Tourists were allowed to climb its 251 steps to the top, but we decided not to. Instead, our kids were content with trick photography that showed each of them bracing against the tower with their palms as if they were holding the tower from falling to the ground.

For me, it was also exciting to see on top of a column the bronze sculpture of the she-wolf *Lupa Capitolina* suckling the twin brothers Romulus and Remus, who, according to Roman legend, were born in 770 BC and founded the city of Rome in 753 BC. The original sculpture was in Rome with several replicas elsewhere. I had read the history and antiquities of ancient Europe, the Mediterranean, and the Levant and was familiar with the legend of Romulus and Remus, and to actually see the sculpture that I saw in books on antiquity was a thrilling experience. We took the train back to Florence, where we stayed the night, and then returned to Rome from where we retraced our steps to London. We spent a few days in London; during which time we took the boat cruise on the River Thames to see a different London from the waters. It was great for the family to spend a few days with Mumu before she started school at the London School of Economics and Political Science (LSE).

A Loved One Leaves the Nest

Our daughter Mumu had graduated from Sir Wilfrid Laurier Secondary School in Orleans and had gone to Carleton University, Ottawa, to study economics. She graduated from Carleton U in November 2006 with a bachelor of arts with high honors in economics, concentration in financial economics and minor in Spanish. She then applied to several top universities in North America including Queens University at Kingston, McGill University in Montreal, and the University of Toronto. She got accepted to all, but my preference was for her to go to the prestigious London School of Economics and Political

Science (LSE) in the UK even though it would cost nearly twice as much because of the UK pound to Canadian dollar exchange rate.

I wanted her to attend LSE because of its global reputation and the global access that its graduates enjoyed. She also liked the idea and immediately starting saving money for LSE. For months, she was holding down three jobs at the same time and saved a substantial amount of money to take with her to London. She started at LSE in October 2007 and rented a two-bedroom apartment that she shared with a girl from Jamaica. For her master's program, she chose to do her internship at the OECD and had to live in Paris for four months from July 2008 until October 2008. Although she graduated from LSE in October 2008, she continued working on her OECD Project at La Defence, Paris, remotely with occasional project visits from London. Her first job in London was in January 2009 but moved to IMS, London, full time in July 2009. After serving fifteen years at IMS, in September 2014, she joined Janssen, UK, which is a subsidiary of the global giant Johnson & Johnson Pharmaceuticals.

Before she left for London in 2007, one day, she came to visit me at CIDA and was struck by the cubicle that was my office. She had visited me at CIDA twice before, and each time my office happened to be in a different location but on the same twelfth floor. The first time she came was just after I had joined CIDA. My office was a spacious room with a view of the Ottawa River. I had a painting on the wall, a palm plant on the floor, and plants on my desk. The second time she came, my office was a smaller room with no windows, no artwork on the wall, and no palm plant on the floor. The third and final time she came, my office was a six-by-eight-foot cubicle among dozens of cubicles on the twelfth floor.

Stunned by the size of my office and seriously worried about my job, she asked, "Abbu, did you get demoted?" She probably thought that I must be underperforming at work and therefore my directors were not happy with me, which accounted for the continuous downsizing of my office. While her question to me was rather funny, I understood her concern. I explained to her that the new conservative government was downsizing, and with many of CIDA's worldwide operations cut, CIDA had to abandon several of its buildings and cram its staff into limited space. We no longer had the luxury of individual rooms to ourselves. Talking about the twelfth floor, I found it quite interesting that the three jobs I held in Canada until retirement—at CIIPS, IDRC, and CIDA—my office in every one of them was on the twelfth floor! I wondered if I should ask a palmist or an astrologer whether the number 12 was my lucky number; I never did.

Beneath the English Channel

It was after Mumu had relocated from Paris to London that she had to take the Channel Tunnel, or sometimes referred to as the Chunnel, to go to La Defence in Paris to complete her internship at the OECD. During that first trip, I accompanied her from London to Paris. I was actually nervous, not relishing the idea of crossing the English Channel through a tunnel under it. I imagined the waters of the English Channel coming crashing down on us and visualized all sorts of morbid ending!

The British and the French had been toying with the idea of constructing a tunnel under the English Channel for decades. Tunnel drilling on both coasts had in fact started in 1881, but Britain stopped it the following year fearing that it could turn into an invasion route from the continent. It was only in 1955 that Britain dropped its defense-related objection, and in 1957, an Anglo-French consortium called the Channel Tunnel Study Group was formed. But there was little progress. The idea was once again revived in 1986, and discussion was held over two options: either a rail tunnel under the English Channel or a very long suspension bridge across the narrowest part of the English Channel, which was about thirty-five kilometers across the Strait of Dover; the latter idea was rejected.

It was agreed that the rail tunnel project would be privately financed by a consortium of British and French corporations and banks, and the tunnel would be operated by an Anglo-French company to be called Eurotunnel. Accordingly, eleven giant electricity-driven tunnel boring machines called moles, the most complex of which weighed 1,300 tons and cost $42 million a pair, started digging on both sides of the Strait of Dover in 1987–88, and the tunnel officially opened six years later on May 6, 1994. It was estimated that the moles had removed as much as 7.8 million cubic meters of chalk marl from the English Channel bed, enough to build three Great Pyramids of Egypt!

By any measure, it was a remarkable engineering feat, especially since the digging was simultaneously from opposite directions and had to meet at the rendezvous point. The Channel Tunnel was the longest undersea tunnel in the world, with its undersea section thirty-eight kilometers long with an average depth of forty meters below the seabed. There were actually three tunnels, each fifty kilometers long, two of which were single-track tunnels for trains and one service tunnel, connecting Folkestone (Kent) in UK with Coquilles (Pas-de-Calais) in France. It cost 4.65 billion pounds, which exceeded the original budget by 80 percent.

In any case, I was relieved that my daughter and I came out alive at the other end, and, of course, it was helpful to know that it took only thirty-five minutes at a top speed of 160 kilometers an hour to cross the English Channel. While we literally zoomed through the Chunnel, the ride was very comfortable and smooth. I was less anxious on the return journey.

Our Silver Anniversary

Although the year 2007 started painfully for me with the demise of my father in April, it did end on a happy note. Nipa and I celebrated our twenty-fifth wedding anniversary. We hadn't planned anything elaborate, but we weren't prepared for the surprise either. Unknown to us, Mumu, who had just started her graduate program in London at the time, had been planning a huge surprise anniversary party with the help of our family friends' daughter Nabila, who was in Ottawa. Mumu secretly reserved the East India Company restaurant on Somerset Street in downtown Ottawa, selected the menu, and invited all the guests including her maternal grandmother, her grandmother's youngest sister,

Tanjina, and her family who lived in Long Island, and her aunt Lopa and her family from Wausau, Wisconsin.

Lopa and my mother-in-law arrived in our house under the pretense of family get-together during the Eid-ul-Fitr celebrations, while other relatives made different living arrangements away from us so that we wouldn't know that they were in town so that the surprise was complete. The secrecy was so complete that Nipa was truly surprised. Seeing all our friends there was wonderful, and seeing our relatives was even more so. The food was great. I was asked to give a speech, which turned out to be hilarious because I gave a comic rendition of how one of the elderly guests had given away the secret to me a few days earlier quite unintentionally and innocently and how I had an inkling of what was going to happen that night.

My sister-in-law Lopa, who has a big heart, insisted on covering the entire cost of the party. For us, it was a night to renew our love, our vows to each other; a night of receiving blessings from our relatives and friends; a night to remember. I am also reminded of Tanjina khala and Ferdaus khalu's twenty-fifth anniversary celebration that took place a few years later in Long Island. At one point, one of his friends congratulated him and raised his glass to wish him wedding bliss for the next twenty-five years, to which Ferdaus khalu responded, "You mean with the same woman?" I can't remember whether he had to spend the night in the garage!

Madrid Visit

In late May 2008, ten governments, the World Bank, and several observers from international financial and anticorruption organizations came together in Madrid to brainstorm on the topic of extractive industries. We met in Madrid to review how countries with extractive industries can be encouraged to join the Extractive Industries Transparency Initiative (EITI), how to enhance collaboration among multi-stakeholders, how to strengthen the collection of data, and how to streamline procedures that were already in place. The meeting itself was highly successful as all the governments were on the same page more or less.

But the problem was with Spanish hospitality. The Spanish government wanted to impress us with their hospitality and arranged a multicourse dinner for the delegates. The hors d'oeuvres, however, were unsightly and tasted slimy. No one, and I mean no one, ate them. The servers waited for a long time to remove the plates, thinking that we were taking our time to eat them, but then realized that no one wanted to eat them. Then came an aubergine dish that was equally tasteless, and most people didn't eat it. The rest of the courses were also unappealing to say the least. It came to a point where all the delegates were extremely hungry and desperate to get out of there. As soon as we were able to leave, most of us dashed out looking for a taxi to go to the nearest fast-food place to eat. It was the most embarrassing experience in an official setting that I had ever encountered. From that day onward, I have always avoided Spanish food. Even the Spanish paella that my wife and kids like does not attract me. I must confess though that when I was an undergraduate student in the United States, I used to love to cook packaged Spanish rice and have it with chicken or egg omelet.

Family Vacation in UK and France

An outcome of Fareen moving out to London was for us to visit her every year and use that opportunity to vacation in Europe. So a month later, in late June 2008, we decided to go on a family vacation to UK and France. In the UK, we wanted to visit the Stonehenge on the Salisbury Plain in Wiltshire, England. We took the air-conditioned deluxe coach from London to Salisbury and reached the Stonehenge in less than two hours. The Stonehenge, which was carbon-dated to 4000 BC, had a number of its tallest stones, known as sarsens, still standing. At thirty feet tall and weighing twenty-five tons each on average, these stones gave the visitor pause, forcing him to reflect on its antiquity.

For a while, there was a general belief that the Stonehenge served as the temple of the Druids, but that belief was discarded after carbon-dating confirmed that the stones existed at least two thousand years before the Druids did. At the Stonehenge, we were issued headphones that narrated an audio history of the Stonehenge. The stones were laid out in a circular or horse-shoe shape and cordoned off by a rope, but we were able to stretch our hand and touch the stones. Standing next to them to take pictures gave one a pretty good sense of how huge those stones were. We had finally seen the Stonehenge that we had been seeing in pictures all these years.

At the Stonehenge, Salisbury Plain, Wiltshire, June 2008

Our next trip was to the city of Bath in the county of Somerset, just 180 kilometers from London. The city got its name from the famous Roman baths that the Romans built in 43 BC and called it Aquae Sulis, which meant "the waters of Sulis." The city became known for its hot springs, Roman baths, medieval heritage, and Georgian architecture—all of which convinced Queen Elizabeth I to bestow on it the title of a city in 1585. Today, one can add to its attractions the boutique shops that attracted thousands of tourists each year. We went inside the Roman baths, but the water was algae green. We visited the outdoor market and strolled in the streets and by the riverbank. It was a pleasant day to spend outdoor.

On the way back to London, we stopped by Windsor Castle in the county of Berkshire. It has been the official residence of British royalty for a thousand years and currently the official residence of Queen Elizabeth II. On the day we were visiting, the standard was not flying from the Round Tower, which meant that the queen was not in residence. The construction of the original castle was started in AD 1070 immediately after the Norman invasion of Britain in October 1066 and Saxon England's defeat in the Battle of Hastings. We decided not to take the castle tour because very little time was left before the tour would end and the grounds would be closed; so we just posed in front of the castle entrance for pictures.

The trip to Bath and Windsor was courtesy of our cousin Neela and Shaheen Chowdhury, who live in London. It was their idea to show us both places. Shaheen drove us around and served as our guide during the entire trip. Shaheen, Neela, their lovely daughter Esaba, and handsome son Israr are a wonderful family, very friendly, and very enjoyable company. We always have a barrel of fun and laughter when we get together. And I love to joke around with them. Many moons ago when I turned fifty, my Egyptian family physician had advised me to lay off red meat especially organ meat such as beef liver and giblets. But because my doctor said no to them, they became doubly attractive to me. However, I have been resisting organ meat rather successfully.

But when I started working in Afghanistan, I would often stop in London during my Kabul-Ottawa-Kabul trips and stay at Neela's during the transit. One day, she served fried beef liver at dinner, and I ate it with gusto while mentioning my doctor's prohibition. Neela replied that if I liked it that much, then she will always make it for me during my visits, since they were only once every four to six months. So before my travel, I would inform her of my London arrival date, and she would assure me that fried beef liver would be waiting for me!

Shaheen has a great sense of humor. He is jovial in disposition, very knowledgeable, politically well informed, and loved to discuss with me trans-Atlantic politics and its implications; the U.S. president and the British prime minister were our staple topics! However, it was only fairly recently that we discovered a remarkable talent that he had successfully hidden from us all. He composed beautiful poems, a veritable bard indeed! Who knows what else lurks beneath that jovial patina!

From London, the four of us went to Paris on July 1, 2008. We took the Channel Tunnel, which was an exciting trip by itself. We visited almost all the touristic places an outsider would normally visit. We visited the Basilica of the Sacred Heart of Paris, commonly known as the Sacré Coeur Basilica. Situated on top of the Butte Montmartre, at 213 meters above sea level, it was the second-highest point in Paris after the Eiffel Tower, which stood 300 meters tall; the view of Paris from its steps was magnificent. The Sacré Coeur was also the most-visited church after the Notre Dame Cathedral in terms of annual visitors.

Behind the Sacré Coeur church was a huge space with kiosk-type setup where budding artists honed their painting skills. Some of them were commercial painters trying to entice tourists to sit down for a personal portrait for a small fee. From there, we took the subway to the Louvre Museum, which served as the royal residence for French kings in the sixteenth and seventeenth centuries. It was my second trip to the Louvre. It carried the largest collection of famous paintings in the world. There was a huge crowd queued up to see Leonardo da Vinci's famous painting, the *Mona Lisa*. We were prohibited from taking pictures with flash on. We also took pictures in front of the statue of Aphrodite, the Greek goddess of love, beauty, and passion.

From Paris, we decided to take the bus to Sun King Louis XIV's Palace of Versailles, which was only an hour away. He was referred to as the Sun King supposedly because he had chosen the sun as his personal symbol. Louis XIV had moved his court and government to Le Chateau de Versailles in 1682 to get away from the hostile Parisian public and to create sufficient distance from the nobility to make them yearn for his royal presence.

The Chateau, with seven hundred rooms, more than two thousand windows, and sixty-seven staircases, was second in size only to the Louvre, which was built in the twelfth century and was still the largest of all European palaces. The Palace of Versailles was home to the immediate royal family, some members of the French nobility who were directly in the service of the king, as well as all official government offices. It was considered to be France's most famous royal chateau and a magnificent example of French baroque architecture.

361

Right from the eighty-meter-long steel gate at the entrance that is decorated with one hundred thousand gold leaves, the entire visit was magical to us. As we walked through each room of the palace, we marveled at how incredibly preserved each room was and at the impeccable attention to the finest details. The tour guide explained to us the history of each room, what historical events took place there, and the role of each room alongside the rest of the rooms of the palace. The décor of each room reflected the functions it served in statecraft. Thus we learned about which room was used for what by King Louis XIV and his successors.

The king's personal quarters, his bed, work desk, and other historical curiosities were explained to us in detail. It was interesting, and at times disgusting, to hear how the nobility jockeyed for the privilege of attending to the king's bathroom needs every morning to secure his favors in court. Le Roi Soleil ruled France from May 1643 until his death in September 1715. His seventy-two years of reign was the longest in European history and established France as the preeminent power. He had achieved absolute power in France and declared himself as *L'etat, c'est moi* ("I am the State").

We also saw Marie Antoinette's bedroom. She was the Holy Roman emperor Francis I and Habsburg empress Maria Theresa's fifteenth and last child. Married at the age of fourteen to the future Louis XVI of France, she met a horrific death. During the French Revolution and following the storming of the Tuileries in August 1792, Emperor Louis XVI was guillotined in January 1793 at the Place de la Revolution in Paris. Nine months later, Marie Antoinette was tried by a revolutionary tribunal, found guilty, and guillotined in October 1793. History recorded her famous words to be "Let them eat cake," which was supposedly her response upon learning that her starving peasant subjects had no bread to eat.

At La Galerie des Glaces, Versailles Palace, July 2008

The most famous room in the palace was the Hall of Mirrors. The grandeur of the 73-meter-long Hall of Mirrors, or as the French call it *La Galerie des Glaces,* with its 357 mirrors, 17 glass doors, many chandeliers, and ceiling paintings was spectacular. The Hall of Mirrors was where Louis XIV held court and entertained foreign dignitaries. It also served as a venue for important historical events. At the conclusion of the Paris Peace Talks following World War I, French prime minister Georges Clemenceau chose the Hall of Mirrors in the Palace of Versailles where the Treaty of Versailles was signed on June 28, 1919, between the victorious Allied Forces and defeated Germany.

We walked out to the rear of the chateau to stroll in its magnificent gardens and see the Grand Canal and the fountains. The patio was huge with many steps. We walked all the way to the golden horses partially submerged in the artificial lake. We took tons of pictures both inside and outside the Chateau de Versailles. As we left the Chateau de Versailles, I couldn't help but wonder at its ornate interior, its architectural grandeur, its opulence and magnificence, and its place in French and European history. We took the bus back to Paris.

Next, we decided that without a visit to the French Riviera, our trip to France would be incomplete. But the Riviera was almost ten hours to the south forming the French coast. We decided that it would be great to experience France's technological wonder, its high-speed train service, the TGV (Train à Grande Vitesse). Traveling at approximately three hundred kilometers an hour, the TGV would also cut down the travel time by half, which meant that we could reach Nice on the southern coast in just over five hours. We took the taxi to Paris' Gare de Lyon, one of the six main train stations in Paris and the one from where trains departed for southeast France. The interior of the train was elegant and utilitarian, and the high-speed train journey was very pleasant, although towns and villages flashed by us and we could hardly see anything, unlike the much slower train journeys in UK, which I thoroughly enjoyed because I simply love the English countryside. I relished my train journeys to Manchester to see Matin khalu and Jolly khala or to Milton Keynes to see Nipa's cousin Rubaiyat.

After arriving at the Gare du Nice, we spent several hours strolling through Nice's open markets, seeing the sights, and shopping. Since we had several items on our to-do-list, such as visiting the Palais des Festivals where the annual Cannes Film Festival was held, driving the full length of the Riviera toward the principality of Monaco, sightseeing in Monaco, and visiting the quaint shops up in the hills that divide France and Italy, we decided to rent a chauffeured van so that we won't have to worry about directions and local laws and also get a running commentary on places we would be visiting. That turned out to be an excellent decision. The chauffer knew the geography and the laws of the region and was able to guide us every step of the way; he was also very polite, friendly, and quite helpful. First, he took us to the Palais des Festivals et des Congrès in the town of Cannes on the French Riviera, roughly thirty minutes west of Nice; he knew where to park the van, the exact entrance, and what to look for inside. We spent some time there and then set off for the drive back to Nice.

When my mother-in-law heard that Nice was in our French itinerary, she suggested that we might stop by the residence of Madanjeet Singh to say hello. So our first stop heading east from Nice was at the Singh residence in the tiny village of Beaulieu-sur-Mer, ten kilometers east of Nice. We did not know him, nor did we ever meet him before. He was a former Indian diplomat who had joined UNESCO in 1982 and had become a UNESCO Goodwill Ambassador in 2000 and was a very accomplished person. He had gone to Bangladesh on a visit and was due to fly out of Dhaka on the day of the *Bishwa Ijtema* (global congregation). But there was a serious problem with that because millions poured into the city that day and the next two days to attend the Ijtema, creating total logjam for vehicular traffic.

At the residence of Madanjeet and France Singh in the village
of Beaulieu-sur-Mer on the French Riviera, July 2008

The Ijtema was the second-largest annual Islamic gathering after the annual hajj gathering in Saudi Arabia. It attracted devotees from over 150 countries to pray, listen to scholars reciting and explaining verses from the Quran, and demonstrate Muslim unity, solidarity, mutual respect, and reiterate their commitments to Islamic values.

Since it was going to be nearly impossible to go to the airport from his downtown hotel on that day, the previous night, his acquaintance Prof. Jamilur Reza Chowdhury brought him over to my in-law's place, which was a stone's throw from the airport. Madanjeet and his wife stayed at my in-law's place that night, and next evening, my brother-in-law Rana drove them to the airport through a backstreet. Having enjoyed Rana's hospitality and having spent the night in the safety of their home, Madanjeet later on sent a letter of appreciation to my in-laws for their kind gesture and generosity.

So when we decided to swing by their place, we called them and introduced ourselves and told them that we would be happy to visit them if they were available. They were happy that we were coming. We were received warmly. Madanjeet was an elderly, soft-spoken person with a nice smile. His wife France Singh was gracious but more businesslike. It was obvious that she was in charge of everything to the minutest detail. After we were done with the introductions, in came their two dogs that were so tall and big that they were more like elephant-lets, and it scared all of us because we were not used to pets. Realizing our discomfort, France Singh ordered her housekeeper to keep them away from us.

She told us that they had arranged to take us to lunch at a seaside restaurant, which turned out to be very elegant and quite pricey. At lunch during small talk with Madanjeet, I mentioned what a lovely house he had on the Riviera coast. He lit up and said that actually he was able to live this great life because he had invested in his son's software company, and when the stocks soared in value, he sold his equity, netting him enough money to establish the South Asia Foundation in 2000 and buy the house and live very comfortably ever after. I asked him what his son was doing now, and he replied that his son was pursuing his real passion, which was having his own musical band. Lunch was wonderful as was the conversation and the company. After lunch, we extended our invitation for them to come visit us in Canada, and then we bade them good-bye and were back on the road to Monaco.

We stopped a few times by the Riviera to sit on the benches on the beach, to watch the world go by, and also to take pictures. What was very noticeable to me was that there were lots of Arab men there strolling in the beach eyeing bikini-clad girls, a few of whom were topless, while their hijab-clad women were patiently sitting on bedspreads with their babies; I could not believe this overt double standard!

We headed east toward Monaco. As the road climbed to higher elevation and meandered through the hills, we often stopped to take pictures of the magnificent private sailboats and yachts moored in the stunning azure waters of the Mediterranean. When we arrived in

Monaco, which was actually only about a half-hour drive from Nice, we were floored by the number and magnificence of the private yachts in its harbor; one could understand why Monte Carlo was considered to be a billionaire's city.

On the road to Monte Carlo overlooking the Cote d'Azur, July 2008

Our chauffeur showed us the sights in Monaco, including the historic Monte Carlo Casino, which received its charter from Prince Charles III in 1856, the various places where *James Bond* scenes were filmed, the Monaco Grand Prix race track, the Marine Museum and Aquarium, the Jardin Exotique, and the Palace of Monaco, where the prince and the Grimaldi royalty lived.

After making the rounds in Monaco, we headed east toward the Italian border. As we climbed into higher altitude, we came across many picturesque villages hidden away between hills, and in those villages were many more quaint shops carrying exotic stuff. We actually bought mementos from the hilltop medieval village of Eze. Its meandering cobblestone streets and the incredible view of the Cote d'Azur are simply unforgettable! There was one last thing left to do before leaving the Riviera. My son and I had to take a dip in the waters of the Mediterranean so that I could brag about it, and we did!

We returned to Fareen's apartment in Paris where she had started her internship with the OECD in July 2008. We spent a few more days visiting other iconic sites. We went to the Eiffel Tower and climbed some of its steps. We bumped into several Bangladeshis who probably entered France illegally, who were selling trinkets that were spread out on a cloth on the pavement. While we were talking with them, they suddenly grabbed the four corners of the cloth, picked it up, and started running; what we saw next were several gendarmes pursuing them. This was the daily fare of illegals spread all across West European countries. They entered these countries and the American continent with the hope of landing a job so that they could send money to their poor families back home either to put their younger siblings through school or as dowry for their sister's wedding or for the survival of their family. It made me think once again that fundamental structural changes had to take place within the Bangladesh society to rectify this situation.

We also visited the Arc de Triomphe. Before leaving Paris, we visited Fareen's office at the Place des Corolles at La Defense, Paris. Interestingly, La Défense was named after the statue of La Défense de Paris by Louis-Ernest Barrias, which was erected in 1883 to commemorate the soldiers who had defended Paris during the Franco-Prussian War (July 1870–May 1871), which resulted in the defeat of French hegemony in continental Europe and the creation of a unified Germany.

In the Land of My Childhood Dreams

As I mentioned earlier in the section on my childhood days, from the time I could read, I had been fascinated with epic tales, sagas, myths, and legends, and Greek heroes and legends were my particular favorites. I had always dreamed of visiting Greece one day and seeing for myself the historical places. Occasionally, however, I would have competing travel requirements, and the last week of October was one such example when I needed to be in Bucharest and in Athens at almost the same time. I decided to go to Athens.

Transparency International (TI) held its Thirteenth International Anti-Corruption Conference (IACC) in Athens, Greece, from October 30 to November 2, 2008. The conference theme was "Global

Transparency: Fighting Corruption for a Sustainable Future." The assumption of the conference was that mankind's common future will be defined by certain critical issues such as human security, climate change, energy security, and compromised livelihoods. These posed unprecedented challenges to the ecosystems mankind depended on, and to tackle these properly, combating corruption had become essential. Like in previous IACCs, participation in thematic committees by delegates was robust, and at the end of the conference, a number of resolutions and action plans were adopted.

I took the day off after the conference to tour the country as much as I could. I joined a tourist group with similar intentions, and we took off in a large air-conditioned van very early in the morning. The van was equipped with translations in several languages, and it stopped at many places mentioned in the Greek legends. When we went outside the van to have a closer look at those historical sites, the driver continued to regale us with the legends of the place. Among the places we visited were the Tomb of King Agamemnon, who had summoned a mighty Greek naval fleet and sailed against King Priam of Troy to reclaim Helen of Troy, who had been stolen by Priam's son Paris from Agamemnon's brother, King Menelaus, who was Helen's husband, thus launching the ten-year Trojan War.

We visited the Temple of Poseidon, whom legend described as being the vengeful god of the oceans and the seas. We stopped at the 1400 BC Oracle at Delphi, which was dedicated to Apollo, the Greek god of archery and music, and was situated on a plateau of Mount Parnassus. Delphi was an ancient religious sanctuary and home of Pythia, the highest priestess of the ancient world, who served as the oracle of Delphi.

We also visited the Parthenon, which took its name from Athena Parthenos, the Greek goddess of wisdom, courage, and war, among other things. In ancient times, the Parthenon's unexcelled size and opulence were an expression of Athenian wealth and symbolized Athenian political and cultural preeminence in Greece. It is located on the Acropolis, which means "high city," and overlooks the entire city. We also stopped at a couple of places with ancient amphitheaters that still exist in dilapidated conditions. The tour included a mandatory stop at a shop that carried curios, trinkets, artifacts, and touristic stuffs. I could not resist buying some souvenirs such as miniature Hellenistic jars and tumblers. It was a very memorable Greek tour for me as I got to see the places associated with the heroes right out of the pages of Greek legends. I resolved that, one day, I would like to bring my wife and children to Greece to share with them this wonderful experience.

At the GOPAC in Kuwait City

Barely two weeks later, I had to ready myself to go to Kuwait. Following the Second Global Conference of Parliamentarians against Corruption in September 2006 in Arusha, Tanzania, the Third GOPAC Conference was held in November 2008 in Kuwait City in partnership with its Arab chapter, ARPAC, and the Parliament of Kuwait. The focus of the Conference was on the role of parliamentarians in the UN Convention against Corruption (UNCAC) and its effective implementation and oversight. But the conference turned out to be a demonstration to the delegates of Kuwait's opulence and hospitality.

The conference started with a big reception at the prime minister's opulent residence. Every day, conference work was followed in the evening with a splendid dinner as if cooked by Michelin chefs, laid out on long tables magnificently garnished with accoutrements and bouquets of flowers imported from Holland. The food was very rich, tasty, and plentiful; the delegates were impressed.

Our conference ended in the midafternoon of November 19, 2008; after which we were taken to the desert to enjoy a Kuwaiti cultural show and dinner from 6:00 p.m. to 10:00 p.m. It was a late afternoon of fun of the kind we were normally not used to. We were shown how to get on a camel and ride it without falling off. There were even mini camel races organized for the novices, meaning us. Most fell off the camel's back, while I managed to hang on for my dear life; after all, *bhat kheye boro hoechhi na!* (Bengali saying: "I grew up eating rice"—meaning, "Of course, I can handle it.") The Kuwaitis had thrown over the camel's back what looked like thick soft carpets as makeshift saddles for the comfort of the delegates, but not being proper saddles, these kept on sliding off, which was a major reason why so many of the delegates could not stay on the camel's back for the entire race.

We were also introduced to falconry. A falconer gave us a quick history of falconry in the region and of its introduction to England and Europe through the crusading kings. Then he told us about the training of falcons to prey on wild animals and other birds, and how over the years it remained as a sport among the royal families of the Middle East. Finally, he told us how to handle a falcon and transferred a full-grown falcon with a safety hood over its head and eyes from his wrist to my left wrist, explaining that in some parts of Asia—namely, Mongolia—birds of prey were held on the right wrist.

Holding a falcon in the Kuwaiti desert, November 2008

I was at first hesitant to take the falcon, fearing that it could rip off my eyes with its powerful beak. The falconer assured me that as long as I didn't make any sudden moves, I would be OK. So I decided to brave it, but, first, I pushed back my glasses to ensure that they were ensconced properly to protect my eyes. He then threw a suede leather piece over my left wrist and gently moved the falcon over to my wrist. Next, he slowly pulled up the eye cover of the falcon. I was quite tense then until I was told to relax for the cameras. The falconer told the delegate taking the picture not to use his flash, and I begged him to double-check that the flash was indeed off.

The next episode in which I participated was a pretend sword fight. I was asked to pick a sword of my choice from a whole array of swords with gem-encrusted hilts that were neatly placed next to each other on a table covered with a velvet table cloth. Immediately after, I drew the sword from its scabbard, held it in front of me, and asked that a photo be taken, lest I am not around after the so-called pretend sword fight. The instructor showed us a few moves when my sword and my opponent's sword would actually meet. It turned out to be fun and not dangerous at all because of the way the "fights" were managed. There were also go-karts for us to frolic in the desert sand dunes, and most of the American delegates went for that.

But none of us—except, perhaps, the Kuwaiti delegation—was prepared for what was planned for the farewell dinner that evening. It was held in the desert near the Kuwait-Iraq border. Several huge white tents were erected to serve different purposes: one tent served as a huge dining hall, and the rest of the tents were for guests to sit. One tent in particular that stood out from the rest was adorned with regal trappings because members of the royal family would be hosting the senior government officials from third world countries who led their country delegations. All the tents had huge expensive carpets covering the sand floor, with large-size pillows on these carpets. It was very uncomfortable for the American and European delegates to eat sitting down on the carpets.

In terms of the food served, it was like a king's table from the Middle Ages, of splendidly furnished dishes including exotic dishes such as pheasant roasts, duck roasts, whole goat roasts, and venison roasts. There were multiple food stations all around the central table carrying nuts of every kind and other sauces and garnishes. There was no doubt that the Kuwaitis were out to make this GOPAC gathering a memorable event to the assembled parliamentarians for a long time to come. The extravagance, the opulence, the hospitality were indeed unforgettable. At the end of dinner, each of us male delegates got a gift of a Kuwaiti aristocratic outfit comprising the *keffiyeh* (scarf), *agal* (black double-ringed cord to hold the scarf in place), *thawb* (ankle-length tunic), and *bisht* (flowing outer cloak worn over the thawb). The women delegates got their version of it. All in all, it was an occasion to remember indeed.

From the Middle East to Chicago, USA

In May 2009, we went on a road trip to the south of the border. Nipa's cousin Khuki apa and her husband Zulfi bhai had recently moved from the Canadian Consulate General in Los Angeles to that in Chicago, and we decided to spend a few days with them. As always, their hospitality was superb. Khuki apa cooked special dishes for us and looked after our creature comfort. She and Zulfi bhai also took us to various places of interest. We spent a whole day walking through Chicago's downtown and its parks.

The downtown skyline was of special interest to our son Mishu because of the architectural uniqueness of its buildings. The oval-shaped, shiny silver Bean was quite a curiosity to all its visitors because of the distortions it reflected as one moved closer to it. We walked to the nearby Grant Park, where President-elect Barack Obama gave his victory speech on November 4, 2008, before an estimated crowd of 240,000. We paused there for a while to try to capture the spirit and emotion of that moment. I remember watching on television thousands of blacks and whites overwhelmed with emotion, including Oprah Winfrey crying, not believing that America actually elected a black man to reside in the White House—a shocking denouement for the racist segment of the American population who went out with vengeance to elect someone who was the antithesis of Obama. Our stroll through downtown took us through one intersection that had a huge statue of a traveler who had by his feet a two-tone, tan-colored suitcase with prominent labels "Dhaka, Bangladesh" and "Shanghai, China" on it. It made us feel great that of all the cities in the world, "Dhaka" would be on it.

Traveler's statue with luggage, Chicago, May 2009

We also took the open-air river cruise, which showed a different view of Chicago. The cruise guide pointed to each building we passed and gave us brief historic tidbits about it. At one point, he pointed to the 110-storied Sears Towers and credited Bangladeshi architect Fazlur Rahman Khan as its inspiration and architect. My family and I could not but feel very proud of our countryman's achievement. Known as F. R. Khan, he was born in Dhaka in 1929 and obtained his bachelor's degree in engineering from the University of Dhaka in 1950. In 1952, he received a scholarship to attend the University of Illinois at Urbana-Champagne, where he got two master's degrees in applied mechanics and structural engineering and a PhD in structural engineering. Khan's highly innovative approach to building skyscrapers soon earned him the reputation of being the "father of tubular designs" for high-rise buildings. His most cited achievements include Chicago's John Hancock Center and the Sears Tower, which are among the tallest buildings in the world, and the King Abdul Aziz University, Jeddah, Saudi Arabia. He died in March 1982 in Jeddah and was buried in his hometown of Chicago.

There were two other places to which Zulfi bhai took us. First was the Bahai Temple in Wilmette, about thirty minutes north of downtown

Chicago and on the shores of Lake Michigan. Claimed to be the oldest existing Bahai Temple in the world, its shiny, lily-white, cone-shaped structure was visible from a distance, and as one neared the temple, one got to see the exquisitely kept gardens around it. The temple had nine arched entranceways, and the pillars of the arches were adorned with symbols of the world's great religions: the Jewish Star of David, the Christian Cross, the Islamic Crescent Moon and Star, and the Swastika of Hinduism, Buddhism, and the Native American religions. The Bahai religion respected the teachings of all these religions and considered them divine, hence it was inclusive and in some sense syncretic. We parked the car, walked to the front door, took off our shoes, and silently entered the temple. There was pin-drop silence all around. The whole place was impeccably maintained. Even though we were Muslims, for me, the serenity and the religiosity of the temple were overwhelming.

The Bahai Temple, Chicago, May 2009

Our next visit was to the Abraham Lincoln Presidential Library and Museum in Springfield, Illinois. Right at the entrance of the museum stood the statues of the Lincoln family members. Inside the building, we saw dioramas of Lincoln's childhood. One tiny room that he shared with his siblings, with his normal-size bed that was, however, too small for the tall lanky lad. We saw his reading room with a small bookcase containing the books he read as a young man. We saw the replica of his yard where he cut wood, with his ax resting next to the tired boy. We saw diorama of the presidential box in the Ford's Theatre, where Lincoln was shot in the head by a .44-caliber derringer pistol on April 14, 1865, by John Wilkes Booth. The museum was rich in artifacts, memorabilia, and photographs. The collection included the original handwritten Gettysburg Address and a signed Emancipation Proclamation. Walking through presidential libraries, as I did while visiting the LBJ Presidential Library and Museum in Austin and the Jimmy Carter Presidential Library and Museum in Atlanta, gave one a sense of rendezvous with history and a wholly different measure of the man who sought to lead the world.

. . . And Then to the West Coast, USA

My niece Naureen Karim graduated from Eastern Oregon University in La Grande, Oregon, with a BA in international business in June 2009. While her mom informed all our family members of Naureen's graduation, Naureen never expected that I would fly from Canada to attend her graduation. So I decided to give her a surprise and flew to my sister Tina's place in Boise, Idaho, and then drove with Mom and my sisters Lily and Tina to La Grande. Naureen was pleasantly surprised to see me. It was regrettable that her dad could not come from Bangladesh for the ceremony.

We sat through the outdoor graduation ceremony in the remarkably pleasant summer weather of the eastern Oregon desert. After the ceremony, she introduced us to Kana, her Japanese roommate, and to her other graduating friends. We took lots of pictures; after which I took our family to the graduation lunch. Naureen had chosen the restaurant and made the reservation. We were very happy that we could attend her graduation, because her elder sister, Tanya, who aspired to be an economist, succumbed to untreatable blood cancer at the tender age just short of nineteen, leaving a huge emotional hole in our hearts.

Tanya was the eldest among our children's generation, and we had high expectations for her. Naureen was my sister Lily and Shafiq's only other child, and we were very sensitive to her well-being and her future. She now lives and works in Dallas, Texas.

Mishu's Graduation

Our son Mishu had graduated from the same high school as his sister did, but he wasn't sure what subject to study in the university. He had been toying with the idea of studying architecture. While we had nothing against architecture as a subject, we were concerned that architecture had no future in Canada. We had close friends and relatives who were architects but could not find work primarily because there was hardly any large-scale construction going on anywhere in Canada. One friend had relocated from Winnipeg to Ottawa but, still not finding any gainful employment in the architecture industry, ultimately decided to return to Bangladesh, where he was purportedly doing well. Another friend's younger brother had moved from Ottawa to Toronto to improve his luck but, after much frustration, retrained himself in another field to be gainfully employed. When we visited Chicago in the summer of 2009, we had also visited Nipa's architect cousin Zerin, who also advised Mishu that many architects were finding it hard to put food on the table.

Given these dire stories regarding architects and their futures, we steered Mishu toward engineering. But after studying engineering at the University of Ottawa for two years, he came to the conclusion that engineering was not for him. He informed us that he felt his real calling was architecture and what he really wanted to become was an architect. Since he felt so strongly about it, we decided to support him. He transferred to Carleton University from where he graduated with a bachelor of arts in history and theory of architecture on June 11, 2010.

Afghanistan beckoned

I had mentioned in my opening page the telephone conversation I had in the spring of 2011 with Bert Spector from MSI regarding the job offer in Afghanistan.

As mentioned earlier, I was in an intergovernmental meeting with European colleagues in Vienna. The Utstein Group on Anti-Corruption, based in Bergen, Norway, and comprising seven countries plus Canada, was also meeting in Vienna at the same time. I represented Canada in its steering committee. I decided to sound out my Utstein colleagues about working in Afghanistan. Their unanimous view was that nothing could possibly be achieved because of the complexity of political and security issues there. They were international experts on corruption in their own right, and their opinion mattered. I needed to think through this carefully.

I had no illusion about how challenging the job would be. I found it ironic that the USAID would allocate millions of dollars over three years to assist the newly established High Office of Oversight and Anti-Corruption (HOOAC), some of whose senior officials had highly questionable reputation. The Afghan presidential elections themselves were declared fraudulent by international election observers, and yet the American support for Pres. Hamid Karzai remained steadfast. It was in this environment that the USAID chose to launch its anticorruption program in Afghanistan.

After returning home from Vienna, e-mail exchanges followed between Bert and me. Several weeks later, Bert called to tell me that the initial review of my candidacy by the USAID/Kabul had gone through and that they asked for three references. I mulled over a few names that came to mind easily. One was Liz Hart, the director of the Utstein Group's Anti-Corruption Resource Center, an American who was a part of the USAID/Kabul team until she left for Bergen a year earlier. I sent her an e-mail asking whether I could propose her name as one of my referees. Her immediate reply was "Going to Afghanistan? Are you out of your mind? If you are really serious, of course, I would be happy to serve as a referee." I had thought of suggesting her as a referee because I thought her assessment of me would carry a lot of weight with her former USAID colleagues in Kabul.

Next, I e-mailed Robin McLay, my former director at CIDA and at the time the executive director of the Institute for the Study of International Development at McGill University, Canada. He was a very good friend and always ready to provide advice and assistance if asked. He readily agreed to be a referee. He also thought that I should enlist the help of an international heavyweight and mentioned Stephen Wallace, the former associate deputy minister at CIDA and at the time holding the prestigious position of secretary to the governor-general of Canada. While at CIDA, Stephen was our vice president for policy and had been instrumental in mainstreaming my anticorruption work in CIDA's development programming. I thought that was an excellent suggestion and e-mailed Stephen right away. Stephen replied the next day, congratulating me for getting the job that he opined would normally be reserved for American experts. He said that I had a huge challenge ahead of me but that I was the man for the job. I sent Bert two additional names of referees who were experts with international reputation in the field of governance.

MSI's official letter of appointment came in the middle of June. This was followed by a call from MSI's CEO Marina Fanning, who welcomed me to the MSI "family" and asked whether I could join right away. I demurred, explaining that I needed time to negotiate my leave from CIDA. I was also waiting for the renewal of my federal top secret clearance, among other things. I got six weeks to sort out my affairs at CIDA and in Ottawa. I informed the acting director of my division, Mark Dawn, about my decision to leave for Afghanistan. Given the difficult transition that was taking place at CIDA, he was not surprised. He congratulated me and arranged an agencywide farewell party. My division took me out to lunch and gave me a touching farewell. Each of my colleagues took turns to scribble a few lines to describe what they thought of me. Below are a few samples:

> *Your depth of knowledge and experience on your files brings credibility to our work.*

379

Canadians should be happy to have you serving as a member of any Canadian Delegation and truly living the spirit of transparency and anti-corruption that you and our country [sic] is working towards.

I'm so glad we work together & I appreciate your insight and frankness when we talk about things at work. Your opinion on things is really of interest to me & warm wishes for 2011.

I really admire your commitment to your work and your kind hearted manner. You have been very supportive of me and I have really appreciated your mentorship. Thank you.

You are surprisingly un-jaded for an experienced bureaucrat and scholar. Please keep that spirit.

Always knows the answer and smiles when he says it!

Very organized.

Kind-hearted, can tell that you are a great father and love your family so much . . . Very supportive. Love having you on our team.

They also presented me with a diary and a pen with my initials etched on it to write down all my experiences in Taliban country. I also received individual gifts from colleagues. One student intern, Jason Tan, who was working on his master's at the University of Victoria, gave me a thank-you card and a box of chocolate for being his external supervisor and examiner of his thesis. He wrote in his card:

I wanted to formally thank you for your support in the development of my thesis. The final product would not have been possible without the ongoing support you provided, the countless discussions, and your very open door-like policy. All of these are very much appreciated. The tact and formality you exercised throughout the process I will definitely use in my future endeavors. I do truly wish to thank you at this critical point in my young career. Sincerely, Jason Tan.

I called or e-mailed friends all over the world to inform them of my impending move to Kabul. The responses were uniform; first, disbelief and then congratulations!

After much soul-searching and, I must say, against my better judgment I had agreed to go to Afghanistan. Even after I signed the contract, it did not fully dawn on me that I was actually going to go to Afghanistan, until I received the Delegation of Authority from MSI's CEO Marina Fanning, and the Power of Attorney from the Department of State signed by Secretary of State Hillary Rodham Clinton. Before my departure for Kabul, I was asked to come to the MSI Office in Washington DC for two days of intensive briefing. Nipa was interested to come with me as well since she had many friends and relatives in the DC and surrounding areas, so we decided to drive from Ottawa to retain our freedom of movement.

Bert arranged all my meetings including with the CEO, the president, and other senior officials of MSI, and I got quite an extensive briefing from the project personnel who had been flown in from Kabul to meet and brief me. After the two days of briefing, I had no doubt that I could direct this project to the complete satisfaction of the USAID and MSI, but one nagging concern was security. The fact that the security setup and protocol were so detailed and extensive raised my sense of insecurity more rather than diminish it, because it gave me a clearer understanding of the horrendous insecurity that pervaded Afghanistan including Kabul. But I had opted to cross the Rubicon, and there was no turning back!

We also met Nipa's relatives and friends. One of her friends was Rumni, who took us out to a wonderful lunch. Her husband was working for the IMF at the time and had visited Kabul on business. He appeared to be taciturn in disposition, at least the first time when he met strangers, but opened up when he heard of my impending assignment in Afghanistan. With a mischievous smile, he cautioned me to beware of Afghan girls because, in his words, "Afghan *meyera choke diye hashi deye*" (Afghan girls smile with their eyes), implying that they could be dangerously alluring. I was amused and told myself this I got to see! We spent a wonderful afternoon with Rumni and her hubby.

We returned to Ottawa. The month of fasting (Ramadan) was going to start shortly on August 1. I left Ottawa for Afghanistan on July 24, 2011, with considerable trepidation and a huge amount of anxiety. As I handed over my passport and ticket to the lady at the Air Canada check-in counter, she asked where I was off to this time. I replied, "Afghanistan." She paused, looked at me, and said, "Oh! Really?" It felt unreal to me as well. Kabul, Afghanistan? I never imagined I would one day work in Afghanistan, certainly not in the post-9/11 environment.

I paid for the excess weight, two overweight suitcases packed with essentials that I thought I would need in Kabul, not knowing what would be available there. I recalled the last time I paid for excess baggage; it was when our daughter Mumu went off to London to start her master's program in international health policy at the London School of Economics. Mumu and Mishu had adjusted their summer holiday dates so that they could arrive from London and spend at least a week with Nipa and me before my departure for Afghanistan. It was a wonderful week as a family, eating out, going to the movies, and spending family time at home. After checking in, we sat down at the Tim Hortons corner to snack, as was our custom whenever we saw off a family member. As I drank my English toffee coffee, I became pensive. Mumu asked, "Abbu, penny for your thoughts?" I replied, "I'll miss Tim Hortons. They are pulling out of Afghanistan together with our troops."

It was time to go. I hugged my daughter Mumu, son Mishu, and wife Nipa. I reminded Mishu to set up Skype for Mom so that we could all remain in regular touch. I boarded my flight, took my seat, buckled up, and looked out the window all the while immersed in my thoughts. I tried to look at the bright side. I was going to be USAID's country director for its anticorruption program in Afghanistan. I was going to be working with high Afghan officials assisting them with policies, strategies, and action plans to fight corruption. I would have a direct hand in strengthening Afghan government's capacity to advance its anticorruption agenda. Given the complex environment in Afghanistan and the high level of corruption in the country, even a little amount of success would be significant; that comforted me. The plane finally took off. I looked out the window and watched Ottawa recede into the distance. Only the beautiful sunny July weather remained with me as the plane banked left and climbed up to vanish into the white clouds.

At Frankfurt Airport, I spent most of the day in the Star Alliance Lounge reading the different security analyses of what might happen in Afghanistan during the month of Ramadan. One analysis concluded that during the holy month of Ramadan, in deference to the requirements of fasting, the Taliban might cease its military offensive and we might see a much-needed lull in the war-stricken country. But there was also countering security analysis that predicted that the offensive may become even more daring and hard-hitting because the Taliban commanders were likely to tell their followers that dying in the battlefield during this holy month was the easiest passport to heaven. Reading these differing security analyses left me wondering even more what I was stepping into. It reminded me of President Truman's dilemma when he had gathered the top economists of the country for some sound economic policy advice. When asked what their advice was, they replied that, on the one hand, he could do this, and on the other hand, he could do that, to which President Truman reportedly exclaimed how he wished there was a one-handed economist!

I caught the late-afternoon flight to Dubai, where I boarded a private Afghan airline and landed in Kabul on July 25, 2011. Prior to landing, I noticed Afghan as well as foreign women passengers taking out their shawls and covering themselves up appropriately, with Afghan women putting on the hijab as well. The male passengers de-westernized their appearances as much as possible also.

When we landed, I could sense the tension in the air immediately. There were soldiers with guns at few meter intervals along the path from the plane to the terminal building. I had detailed instructions from my American and Afghan handlers what to do and not to do between the time I landed and the time when I finally arrived inside MSI compound. I stood in the queue for foreigners at the passport and immigration counter, which I thought was actually dangerous because a trigger-happy Afghan secretly working for the Taliban regime wouldn't have to search for foreigners to mow down.

I wasn't the only one who was nervous; it seemed both Afghans and other foreigners were equally nervous and fearful of what might happen next. There were ample armed Afghan soldiers constantly checking the queues to keep the tension in the air at a constant high. At the passport counter, I was asked to take off my cap, place four fingers and the thumb of each hand on a fingerprinting machine, and take off my glasses for a facial photograph and a deliberately lengthy examination of the Afghan visa in my passport to convey their suspicion that it might be doctored or even fake. It was a relief to see the entry stamp finally land on the visa page, while the visa officer stared at me all the while. Not a single word, expression, or gesture was offered during the entire process. If their government was going to allow foreigners into the country, these airport officials seemed determined to make them feel uncomfortable if not miserable.

I took my passport and swung around to the luggage area where the carousel was already filled with passengers' luggage. Every time a passenger emerged from the passport control, there was a mad rush by waiting porters to secure his business. I was told that MSI had a special luggage handler on its payroll who would be contacting me in the luggage area. We made contact without much delay, and he asked me to stay by his side to identify my luggage. He pulled both of my bags into his trolley and then by the exit door put them on a machine for security check, in case I was bringing contraband stuff from outside.

After the security check, we exited the terminal building. He pushed the luggage cart across a huge compound and then across an internal road and then across another compound, which was a high-security parking lot, at the end of which were waiting the 4A Project's director of administration and finance Jay Stanford; security risk manager Gareth Williams (Gaz to his friends), formerly of the British Second Parachute Regiment and who had just ended his assignment with the

British Forces stationed in Basra, Iraq; and security manager Anurag Gurung, formerly of the Third Battalion/4 Gurkha Rifles of the Indian Army. I watched Gareth transfer a few U.S. dollar bills during his handshake with the luggage handler as Gurung transferred the luggage on to the B6 armored land cruiser. The driver was an Afghan who had undergone special training, especially on evasive maneuvers, satellite communication, and greater awareness of roadside IEDs.

Gareth sat in the front with the driver, and I was required to sit immediately behind him. Anurag sat in a different cruiser. Next to me on the backseat lay a Kevlar vest and a helmet and half a dozen water bottles on the door pockets. After we took our seats, Gareth gave me a quick ten-minute briefing on security protocol that I was required to observe at all times. As soon as we exited the airport zone, the cruiser took a slight detour to go to a security checkpoint from where Gareth retrieved his sidearm that had to be surrendered before entering the airport security zone. The approximately thirty-minute road trip from the airport to the MSI compound was deathly quiet with occasional government security vehicles moving in different directions. Almost every building had thick, reinforced concrete walls with electrified fences on top and CCTV cameras all around. What was really eerie to me was the absence of public that one would normally see in any city.

Gareth called the security at the MSI compound gate a few minutes before our arrival to alert them that we were coming. Extra security lined up outside and inside the gate. When we arrived at the gate, the steel pillars retracted into the ground and the gate opened, while security in the rooftop scoured the neighborhood with their high-grade binoculars. The MSI compound was quite well fortified with extra-thick, reinforced concrete exterior wall with electrified steel coils on top, CCTV cameras, and fortified security posts on every corner of the compound and the roof. The only weakness that I noted later seemed to be a rear entrance, which was not as fortified as the rest of the compound. The compound had two buildings. The main building in the front contained the project offices, library, conference room, store room, the security section, etc. The building in the back had two big bedrooms, one for the COP and one reserved for senior colleagues visiting from MSI Headquarters in Washington DC.

Before I had embarked on my three-year assignment in Afghanistan, my family had given me two gifts to take with me that turned out to be very practical and precious. One was an iPod with my favorite Bengali, Hindi, and English songs in it. As days turned to weeks, weeks into months, and months into years, I took solace in those songs and listened to them every night before falling asleep. The second gift was from Mumu, a daily diary—*One Line a Day: A Five-Year Memory Book*—with my daughter's remark, "Abbu, don't forget to write a few lines on the highlights of the day before you go to bed." I followed her advice diligently, and every night before retiring, I jotted down briefly what transpired that day. I am glad that she gave me that diary to capture the highlights of the day and that I followed her advice, because as I flip through the pages now, details of events I mentioned in the diary flood my memory, which I might have forgotten otherwise. What follows below are a few excerpts from entries I made in that diary.

The Afghanistan Diaries

July 26, 2011. My second day in Kabul started with a full security briefing by Pax Mondial, the security company that MSI had hired to provide security to the project personnel. The first couple of weeks were taken up by my stocktaking of the state of the project, which included one-on-one interviews with every staff member, foreign and Afghan, including interviews with the security personnel. To the staff, this appeared to be a seismic shift from their experience with the previous two American directors who had not even bothered to know who all the project people were, nor did they listen to those they interacted with. Most of the staff had never exchanged a word with the directors. I started getting very positive feedback from the staff who felt that I was a team player and that they felt comfortable in approaching me if there was an issue that needed to be flagged. Previously, because the directors made themselves inaccessible, project staff felt compelled to e-mail MSI head office directly, and so people at headquarters were flooded with complaints about which they really could do very little. With my advent and my approach, that suddenly stopped and the buck stopped at my desk; MSI Office in DC was relieved.

I had also ordered a full security review of the compound, with the specific order to identify the most vulnerable points in our security architecture. Two upgrades were recommended. The small wrought iron gate in the rear of the compound was deemed to be rather weak and wholly insufficient to hold back a major push by Talban insurgents, and the safety room for the expatriate staff located in the basement could easily turn into a trap under a sustained attack. It was decided that both the safety room and the operations room would be moved to the rooftop; the ops room would have to operate at 100 percent capacity.

August 1, 2011. It was the first day of Ramadan. Fasting in Kabul was a tough experience for me. *Sehri* (meal eaten by Muslims before dawn to start their daylong fasting) was at 3:13 a.m., and my first sehri was a bowl of cereal with milk. Since I was used to taking milk with 1 percent fat for years, the full-fat milk in Kabul left an oily taste in my mouth, and I could not drink the Kabul milk ever again; since then, sehri was only a bottle of water. Even *iftar* (meal taken to end a day's fast at sunset) became a disappointing experience because every Afghan meal was meat, meat, and more meat and no vegetables whatsoever. My first iftar was of lamb steak, which was mostly thick fat, which Afghan's loved and I hated.

August 5, 2011. I had noticed early on that a bunch of preteen neighborhood kids occasionally gathered to play cricket in the vacant lot that was next to the MSI Compound. They did not have proper equipment. They used three uneven slim tree branches as stumps without any bails and a worn-out tennis ball as the cricket ball. For the cricket bat, they used a piece of flat wood. I decided that I would give them a cricket set as Eid gift, in the Canadian spirit of community service. I gave Khyber, our office manager, the money to purchase the cricket set and to give it to them.

Then I noticed that after the first day, they were not playing any cricket anymore. I asked Khyber to find out what happened. He sent one of our off-duty guards to go to the home of one of the kids and inquire. The guard learned that they had a fallout among themselves over who had the right to store the cricket set. I realized that my act of kindness was breaking up their friendship, so I called them to our compound and informed them that while the cricket set was their collective property, from now on, it would remain in MSI storage. Whenever they wanted to play, they could check it out but return it after their game was over. They grudgingly accepted the solution, and their cricket game as well as their previous friendship resumed forthwith. I cannot recall how Khyber and others resolved the ownership/storage issue when our project ended three years later.

August 10, 2011. I planned to see Kabul as much as I could within the first six months because I wasn't sure how soon things might take a turn for the worse. I had heard stories about ancient artifacts one could get at the Bush Market, so I asked my security team to take me to the Bush Market for a visit. It used to be known as the Brezhnev Market when the Russians were in Kabul. Now that the Americans were the occupiers, it was renamed as the Bush Market, which was essentially the local black market that carried western products among other things.

Since I was the head of the project—the chief of party, or COP—the security protocol for road travel required that I must notify my security team at least twelve hours ahead of my intended travel, a reconnaissance of my route would take place, alternative routes and nearest safe houses would be identified in case we came under attack, a backup armored vehicle would be fueled and ready to tag behind my B6, and my security monitoring room in the MSI compound would be in full gear for continuous communication and updates between the road security detail and security setup at the office compound. And there was always the Kevlar vest and helmet right next to me in the backseat in case I needed to put them on. Every road trip was a full-fledged security exercise.

The Bush Market looked like the hawkers' market in Dhaka but with much more fascinating stuff. Some of the shops in the rear carried battlefield armor—swords; gem-encrusted scabbards; short, long, serrated, straight, and curved knives; shields, scythes, and maces from earlier centuries. There was also a plethora of jewelry worn by royalty, each having the distinct style and design of the particular kingdom and the time period. There were also modern battlefield items, much of which was stolen stuff from the NATO forces, and particularly the U.S. Army. A pair of night-vision binoculars caught my eye. My Afghan interpreter suggested that he should do the bargaining. I finally bought the US$600 binoculars for only US$20! That night, I went to our rooftop and focused it on the houses at least five miles away on the sides of the mountains. The clarity of view on that pitch-black night was amazing. Unfortunately, on the way home, the rough handling by airline luggage handlers damaged it. I had also bought a khaki vest for AFN 470, or US$10.

I also went to Finest, Kabul's largest private shopping chain, where I bought some videos, some pastries, a bar of chocolate, and a can of unsalted roasted cashews. Both of these trips were officially logged as nonessential trips outside the MSI Compound.

August 11, 2011. A permanent fixture in my weekly routine was to report to the project's COTR, or the contracting officer's technical representative at the USAID, who monitored the project's progress and ensured its accountability. The COP of every USAID project was required to update his/her COTR once every week on the progress, including challenges that the project might be facing. My meeting with our COTR James Wasserstrom was on every Thursday usually in midmorning. The setup was very elaborate and tedious. I had to go to the Green Zone, which was designated as a safety zone marked by high perimeter barbed wall and military check posts. Jim had to inform twenty-four hours earlier the military check post that was designated for my entry into the Green Zone, so that when I presented my USAID-issued ID, they would check my name and picture against the list of approved visitors, subject me and my possession to a vigorous physical search, and then let me in. Jim would be on the other side hidden from direct sight waiting to escort me to our meeting place, and our meeting would usually last one to two hours.

One major problem with this setup was that I would be dropped off at the military check post at the infamous intersection called Massoud

Circle, which was a vulnerable point for foreign visitors. There had been several instances when the Taliban had attacked foreign personnel who were being processed through the checkpoint. The U.S. military did not allow any vehicle to wait there or in its vicinity for security reasons, so I could not wait in the armored vehicle while others ahead of me were being processed. I always felt unsure and insecure as I occasionally had to stand in line to be ID'd and body checked. These tense moments were the downside of the project and lasted the entire three years until the project's natural conclusion in November 2014.

August 13, 2011. Thirteen days into fasting, I got a surprise Skype call from my sister Tina in Boise, Idaho, to inquire about me. Her eldest daughter, Mayisa, sang "Anastasia," and younger daughter Nusha sang the "Ariel" song for me before going to bed; it was very sweet of them. The Skype talk left me in a happy mood. I asked my Afghan chef to make some samosas for iftar; he gave me a blank stare and asked what a samosa was. The next day, I went carpet shopping, really exquisite woolen and silk carpets from Afghanistan and Iran for my home.

August 15, 2011. Halfway into the month of Ramadan, I organized a Khatm-e-Quran (complete recitation of the Holy Quran) for the office staff during the lunch hour, both as a religious gesture and with an eye on security implications. I was supremely aware of the fact that while the project's Afghan staff were used to working with foreigners, everyone else especially the security guards carrying the guns, knives, and grenades might not be comfortable answering to foreign personnel. They were very poor Afghans who were barely educated, deeply religious and trying to eke out a living for their families but susceptible to religious militants and could be easily turned from friend to foe.

A Khatm-e-Quran especially with the foreigners also participating could send the right signal and allay their concerns. I asked the Frenchman, the Scot, the Americans, and the Gurkhas in my expat team to attend the event, and that they could leave the room from time to time to monitor the perimeter security. The Khatm-e-Quran went off quite well, and subsequent feedback through my Afghan staff revealed that the security guards were very impressed and happy that we took this initiative. The presence of non-Muslims wearing appropriate outfits at the Khatm-e-Quran was interpreted as a mark of respect for Islam and that they were friends of Afghanistan.

August 19, 2011, began as a terrible day. Immediately following sehri, a huge explosion ripped through the British Council, Kabul. A bomb-laden truck rammed into the outer security gate and exploded, destroying the outer security perimeter. A second bomb-laden truck drove through the opening into the main building and rammed into the front entrance, exploding and destroying the ground floor. The Taliban insurgents had carried out this attack to mark the defeat of the British by Afghan forces eighty years earlier and secure their independence. I had to cancel all travel outside the compound and ordered a complete security lockdown. This was going to be a recurrent phenomenon during the entire period of my stay in Afghanistan.

The security situation deteriorated further. We received intelligence that the government was worried that a significant number of insurgents purportedly trained by Pakistan's ISI (Inter-Services Intelligence) had infiltrated across the Peshawar border and their whereabouts inside Afghanistan were not known. We spent a few tense days in security lockdown, until we got the word from the U.S. military and government sources that most of them were finally apprehended while a few had escaped to Pakistan.

My senior non-Afghan staff was antsy from being cooped up in the compound for several days when they would normally be partying and drinking with their buddies in the UN compound or in their favorite restaurants, so I decided to take them out to dinner. We went to an Indian restaurant called Namaste; the food was OK, but the main objective of being able to get out of the MSI compound was fulfilled. They were able to unwind a bit.

August 16, 2011. I received an e-mail from CIDA informing me that my top secret security clearance had been renewed by the government. I had taken unpaid leave of absence from CIDA for a year, and retaining the high-level security clearance was very important to me for the type of work I did within my government and with other friendly governments. I was happy that it was renewed and not revoked.

On that day, it rained for a few minutes in the afternoon for the first time since I arrived in Afghanistan. Kabul was located in a valley between mountains, and a pall of smog hung over the city all the time.

When I had flown into Kabul for the first time in July, as the plane was descending, I had looked out through the window to catch a glimpse of the city, but all I saw was this dark cloud enveloping everything below. Minutes before the plane was about to land, we suddenly saw the outline of a city still shrouded in pollution. The Afghan passenger next to me explained that the pollution level was like that all year round and that the Kabul air was not healthy.

So that afternoon when it rained just for a few minutes, I had been walking in the garden for some exercise. I noticed that the water dripping from my hair on to my shoulders was muddy and sticky. When I touched my head with my hand, my hair felt sticky and matted. I realized that I needed a shower, and when I turned on the showerhead, I could see muddy water running down my body. Even the few minutes of rain had brought down the pollution from the sky to the ground, and wherever it was wet, it was muddy and sticky. Living with pollution suddenly became up close and personal.

August 27, 2011, was literally a shocker. At 1:10 a.m., Kabul was rocked by an earthquake that measured 5.9 on the Richter scale. The hypocenter was estimated to be two hundred kilometers below ground. I woke up as my bed shook for about ten seconds. During the three-year life of the project, I weathered through multiple earthquakes, and I learned early on to call my family members immediately after the earthquake to assure them that I was OK. After the first earthquake, I asked our security company, Pax Mondial, to bring in an earthquake disaster expert who could train us on what to do during and after an earthquake. The disaster management expert they brought in was quite good and trained us through videos and other tools the do's and don'ts during and after an earthquake. It restored some semblance of confidence and hope during such trying circumstances.

August 28, 2011. A group of Afghan staff members came to me with a request. They pointed to the fully equipped gym we had in the basement, which was primarily used by the expats, but Afghans were not into gym work. They wanted some form of entertainment to pass time during their break and during security lockdown. It could not be TVs showing Hollywood or Bollywood movies because that would alienate the Afghan guards and heighten security risks within the compound. However, a ping-pong table would be ideal. I thought it was a reasonable request and authorized the purchase of a complete table tennis set. This had a tremendously positive effect on the entire staff because they could take turns to play without offending any ideology or belief system.

August 30, 2011. On the previous day, the mullahs declared that the celebration of Eid ul-Fitr, the Festival of Breaking the Fast, would start on August 30. Like many Muslim countries, Afghanistan, too, had a moon sighting committee whose job was to confirm that the new moon had been sighted and that Eid would be the next day. However, what I found hilarious was that the Afghan moon sighting committee was headed by a chairman who was blind in one eye. One would have thought that a partially blind man would be disqualified from being a member of such an important committee.

A Brush with Death?

On Eid day, Muslims throughout the world gathered in mosques to pray collectively. To maintain the tradition, I completed my ablution in my room, put on my Muslim outfit, and went down to get into the cruiser that would take me to the Iranian-financed Blue Mosque a few blocks away. I had checked earlier whether I, a Sunni Muslim, would be allowed to pray in a Shia mosque; the imam's reply was "Yes."

I had barely put one foot inside the armored cruiser when Gareth came running and extended his arm in front of me to prevent me from getting into the cruiser. He apologized and said that he cannot let me leave the compound today to attend the prayer at the Blue Mosque. I calmly explained to him that ever since I was a teen, I had been fasting the full month and had been going to the mosque or an *idgah* to join other Muslims in prayer; I was not about to change that now. He apologized again and informed me that he had received intelligence from our usual sources in Kabul that an extremist Sunni group was planning a massive suicide bombing at the Blue Mosque that morning. I was stunned. I took a pause and thought about this latest intelligence we received. In Kabul, many western intelligence outfits including the American, NATO, and Japanese intelligence agencies regularly gathered and shared intelligence with each other that was quite reliable.

I decided to listen to my head of security and went back to my room to offer my Eid prayers alone for the first time. I had just gone into my first *ruku* (bending at the knees in preparation for sajdah), when I heard an extremely loud explosion, and the shattering of glasses of my bedroom windows. Anurag came running to my room to inquire about my safety. Within a short time, we learned that a Taliban suicide squad, mainly Sunni extremists, had carried out the attack against the Shias, and nearly a hundred either had died or were severely wounded. I sat in my room wondering that had it not been for Gareth, I could have been one of those hundred dead within one week of my arrival in Kabul! I developed a new respect for my security personnel.

My head of security in the initial months was a Frenchman named Antoine Rozes. He had a lot of Africa experience under his belt but was new to the Asian terrain and cultures. It was interesting to listen to him about his military experience in the French African armies and his experience as a security officer for projects in Africa. Whenever we met during our spare time, he would tell me interesting stories about the French, about the popes, etc. His growing friendship with me, the boss, did not go unnoticed by Welshman Gareth Williams, who was in charge of the project security operations.

When Gareth returned from his six-monthly rotation in early October, he brought me a gift, a book titled *1000 Ways of Annoying the French,* written by Englishman Stephen Clarke and published as a paperback edition in September 2011. The book was absolutely marvelous and was a must-read, for it sought to systematically debunk many French claims, including the claim that the French invented the croissant or the baguette or even the guillotine, and went so far as to suggest that champagne got a market only because the British had created the fashion for fizzy drinks. What made the book thoroughly entertaining was that it was meticulously researched and had tons of eye-opening stuff that a very few people ever knew.

I showed Antoine Gareth's gift to me. Antoine flipped through the pages, raised his eyebrows, and then grimaced and finally shrugged his shoulders and smiled, acknowledging that the thousand-year exercise of the British trying to annoy the French was still alive and kicking. His parting shot was that he, the superior Frenchman, would have gifted his boss a bottle of expensive wine, not a cheap book!

August 31, 2011. It was the second day of Eid holidays, and the office was empty of Afghan staff members except for the security guards. The head of my personal security, Anurag Gurung, his assistant Hari Thapa, and I decided to watch cricket. After cricket, we decided to have a rooftop barbecue. The security detail made a makeshift barbecue by slicing a fuel drum in half lengthwise and filling it up with wood chips and charcoal.

I discovered something unexpectedly. Normally, we would put into the skewers a cube of meat and then an onion piece, another beef cube and then pieces of red and green bell pepper, another beef cube, perhaps a zucchini cube; in other words beef cubes interspersed with vegetable pieces. Not the Afghans! What I saw were skewers with a beef cube, followed by several cubes of fat from the sheep's or goat's tail area, and then a cube of beef followed again by several cubes of fat.

After they were cooked, I watched the Afghan guards set aside the beef cubes and immediately start eating the fat cubes, which were their primary choice. I could not imagine popping chunks of pure, unadulterated fat into their mouths like grapes, and yet I did not see a single fat Afghan person in the streets. It was much later when one day I drove through the narrow lanes and by-lanes of the neighborhoods on the sides of the mountains and watched Afghans of all ages and gender hauling essentials like water and firewood from the valley floor to the higher elevations and back that I realized why Afghans loved those chunks of fat and why they were so lean, sturdy, and fit. Anyway, it was a wonderful barbecue on a hot summer day with the clear blue sky filled with colorful kites. As the Afghans downed the fat chunks, I was left with the meat pieces.

September 2, 2011. It was a Friday, my only day off every week, since I worked six days a week in Afghanistan. The Afghan staff was still away on four-day Eid holidays; they would be returning to work on Saturday. Saturday to Wednesday constituted the Afghan workweek, with Thursday and Friday the Afghan weekend. I ordered dinner from the Indian restaurant Namaste for us five expats in the compound: chicken jalfrezi, prawn masala, and butter naan. My brother from Texas, Shahalam Hassan, Skyped me, and we had a wonderful chat, which started with a discussion about the Texas governor deciding to run as a presidential candidate and ended with the agreement that Russian tennis star Maria Sharapova was very sexy indeed.

September 4, 2011. It was a day full of tension. Our security manager Antoine informed me in the morning that late in the previous night, he had gotten up from bed to do a quick perimeter security check, and as he swept the horizon from the rooftop with his binoculars, he noticed that there was a van parked across the field from our villa and that someone in the van was taking pictures of our villa. He had immediately dispatched a vehicle with two armed security guards to seize the van, but it sped away as soon as it saw our guys coming.

Our villa was put under immediate heightened vigilance. I then called our security personnel to discuss options. We had been concerned with the villa for some time because it was exposed on three sides; on the fourth side was a common boundary wall with another building, which could be rented by a terrorist group to target us. In light of this, we had been toying with the idea of relocating to a more secure area but had decided to wait until we were closer to the expiration of our rental contract.

Our landlord was also threatening to increase the rent by 15 percent, which we were unwilling to accept because the rent we were paying was already above-market rate. In light of all this, I decided to inform headquarters in Washington DC that we will be actively searching for a new location that had a reasonable rent and offered better security options. I also designated Antoine Rozes and Samad Sahil to start looking for a new location with a given set of criteria.

September 8, 2011. Our project, officially called Assistance for

Afghanistan's Anti-Corruption Authority, or the 4A project, had hired Bertrand de Speville, a South African anticorruption specialist, to conduct a series of five training workshops for the benefit of the Afghan civil servants. He successfully conducted the first of the five workshops. In the evening, I took him out to dinner at Red Hot Chili, which was initially hard to locate. Today was also the day when our son Mishu was leaving Ottawa for London to study architecture at the University of Westminster.

Mishu's Second Baccalaureate, His London Jobs and Tertiary Degree

In addition to his Carleton degree, Mishu wanted to enroll in another full-fledged architecture degree program. His preference, however, was to graduate from a British university whose architecture graduates had access to the European job market in the pre-Brexit era. As I mentioned earlier, Mishu has been very close to his sister Mumu, so it was not surprising to us that he would opt to go to London where his sister was. He got admitted to the University of Westminster, London, which offered a three-year bachelor's program, and he graduated with a bachelor of science in architecture with architectural engineering in June 2013.

Immediately after graduation, he joined Bildify Limited, an architectural firm in London. After nine months, he moved to a larger firm named Granit Chartered Architects in London, where he spent the next 2.5 years. For his master's program, he got accepted to the University of Westminster (UW), the University of Toronto (UT), and the University of Glasgow (UG). The master's program at UT was a 3.5-year program. So the choice was between UW and UG, both of which were two-year programs. Since his undergraduate degree was from UW, he opted for UG.

In September 2016, he started his master's program in architecture at the University of Glasgow, Scotland. During his second to last semester at Glasgow University, he opted to capitalize on the EU's Erasmus program (European Union's student exchange program) at the

Oslo School of Architecture and Design (AHO). He graduated from the University of Glasgow with a diploma in architecture in June 2018.

September 9 2011. This was a scary day in Kabul. This day was also called Massoud Day to honor all the martyrs. On this day, Mujahideen commander Ahmed Shah Massoud was blown up by an al-Qaida terrorist posing as a photographer. Extra security measures were put in place as a precautionary step. Also, 9/11 was only two days away when the Twin Towers were destroyed by America's enemies. Our villa had to be fully secured since we were an American project.

September 13, 2011. Peace in the city was totally shattered as citizens struggled to return to their homes and their loved ones without getting killed in the face of the Taliban's simultaneous multiple attacks in different parts of Kabul including the U.S. embassy, the parliament, and the airport. I let the staff leave office early as curfew was imposed until noon the next day. By then, the last of the insurgents were finally rounded up and killed. That night, we threw a surprise farewell party for Bertrand; he was moved.

September 15, 2011. The last of the five workshops by Bertrand was completed. The postworkshop assessment by our staff yielded mixed results. We learned that many of the staff from the HOO for whom these workshops were organized did not take them seriously because they didn't think that the lessons they learned would be allowed to be implemented by their bosses. They attended the workshops nonetheless to get away from their offices and also to collect the per diems. What was equally disappointing was that my meeting that evening with Pres. Hamid Karzai was cancelled because he was preoccupied with putting down the pockets of insurgency throughout the city.

September 16, 2011. Since Bertrand was leaving for South Africa the next day, he wanted to see some historic sites in Kabul. Since it was Friday, my off day, I decided to join him for sightseeing. The security team went for a quick reconnaissance and then gave the clearance for us to proceed. First, we went to the Kabul Museum, which was open in the morning hours and closed right before the *jummah* prayers started. It was quite rich in content. The curator told us stories of how he and his family members often hid many of the museum's most valued contents from being stolen during wartime and of all the valuable items that conquerors carried away with them that could not be saved. He was full of regret that the museum was not a high priority in the government budget and that it was scarcely able to keep its doors open.

Next, we visited the Old Palace of Afghan Kings that looked like it was about to crumble. No doors or windows were left intact, and the walls were full of holes made by cannon fire and machine guns. There was a wrought iron fencing all around the palace to keep everyone at a distance from the building lest it collapsed on them. It was a pathetic sight indeed.

From there, we went to the impressive black marble Mausoleum of King Nadir Shah on a hilltop in east Kabul called Teppe Maranjan, where his son and Afghanistan's last king, Mohammad Zahir Shah, was also buried. King Zahir Shah, who succeeded his assassinated father in November 1933 and reigned until July 1973, was best known for the forty years of peaceful rule he gave his people. While undergoing medical treatment in Italy, a surprise bloodless coup in 1973 by his cousin and former prime minister Mohammad Daoud Khan deposed him and established the Republic of Afghanistan.

Although he returned to Kabul from self-imposed exile in Italy in 2002 after the fall of Taliban rule in December 2001, he renounced the throne and was given the epithet "father of the nation" by his people. He died from illness on July 24, 2007, and with that ended the 250-year dynastic rule that had started in 1747. The royal graves were in a locked chamber beneath the mausoleum, which was a modern monument with ample space all around. We took lots of pictures to remind us of this trip.

September 20, 2011. It was an eventful day once again. Burhanuddin Rabbani, an Afghan Islamic scholar, a political leader, and Afghanistan's second president (1992–1996) after the Soviet troop withdrawal, was an influential member of Afghanistan's Tajik minority. After the defeat of the Taliban, he served as interim president until the election of Hamid Karzai as the president.

President Karzai appointed him as the head of the High Peace Council with the mandate to pursue peace talks with the Taliban. But on September 20, Rabbani was assassinated by a suicide bomber who claimed to be a Taliban emissary. According to one account, although every participant in the peace talks were body checked for security reasons, asking one to remove his *pagri* (a headdress worn by men that consisted of a cap and a sash wound around the cap and sometimes hanging down the neck) was considered to be insulting. It was believed that the bomb was hidden inside the pagri when it was detonated during the welcoming embrace. There was widespread anger and demonstrations in the streets. The next day, the government declared three days of mourning for the ex-president. But the tense atmosphere kept everyone on their toes for some weeks.

September 29, 2011. Had a wonderful meeting with our COTR Jim Wasserstrom at the USAID in the Green Zone, who lauded our performance and confirmed the renewal of the project for the second year; the project had started in October 2010. I called my daughter Mumu in London to plan our Istanbul trip to celebrate Nipa's fiftieth birthday.

September 30, 2011. This being Friday, I decided to go sightseeing. First, my security team and I went to the mountains to see for ourselves how people lived and traveled. The flatlands in the Kabul valley had been expropriated by the rich and the powerful both legally and illegally, leaving no land for the poor and the weak. The latter had no choice but to start cutting down the trees on the sides of the mountains to build shelters for their families and also to use the trees as firewood.

It was amazing to see these ramshackle structures precariously perched on the sides of mountains. Most of the brick buildings had signs of cracked walls and floors that clearly indicated that hardly any cement was used in their construction. Most of the cracks and damages in the brick buildings were due to the many earthquakes that hit Kabul every year. The lanes were so narrow and uneven that whenever vehicular traffic had to pass, even though there were very few, one had to find a building built at a lower level whose rooftop merged with the lane at the upper level to provide additional space to squeeze into and allow the vehicle to pass. Since there were no trees to hold the soil together, earthquakes had the potential to cause a major loss of human lives. In one sense, Afghans were lucky not to have frequent or major rainfall because that would surely trigger mudslides all over the place.

From the mountains, we went to its foothills where Mughal emperor Babur's tomb was located. Babur, who descended from Tamerlane, was the founder of the Mughal Empire in India. When he died in January 1531, he was buried in Agra, India. But per his wishes, his mortal remains were transferred a decade later to Kabul, which was his initial capital and the launching pad for his conquest of the Indian subcontinent. He was buried in Bagh-e Babur, or the Garden of Babur.

But I was stopped from entering the garden by the security guards at the entrance because I had my video camera with me, and photography and video were prohibited. Khyber Khan, my officer manager who accompanied me, went into action. Since he and the guards were Pashtun people, he launched into Pashtu by introducing himself to the guards and then explaining that I was his father-in-law visiting Afghanistan from Canada for the first time and that he didn't want his father-in-law to think that Afghans were impolite people and that his son-in-law was a worthless Pashtun.

The guards looked at each other and then said, "Khyber jan, but video cameras are not allowed inside." Khyber responded saying that I was only an elderly gentleman from the very friendly country of Canada; what harm could I do even if I videoed a little? After a short pause, the guards let us pass. Not only was I a little uncomfortable at the suggestion that he was my son-in-law, but I also realized that Khyber used that excuse probably because he knew what would appeal to the Pashtun guards. I started to admire his presence of mind that made it possible to enter the Bagh-e-Babur, which was a well-maintained secluded garden with a building housing Babur's tomb and those of his immediate family members, and a second building displaying artifacts from his time as well as handwoven items.

There was hardly any kind of entertainment in Kabul. When the Taliban came to power, one of the first things they did was to rid Kabul of all places of vice. This meant that cinema halls deemed to be promoting decadent western and Bollywood movies were shut down and their equipment destroyed. Public baths, considered to be venues for indecent behavior, were closed up. Nightclubs and a variety of other clubs where the people gathered to socialize were condemned as being purveyors of sinful behavior.

Even foreign diplomatic establishments were not spared. The surfaces of their tennis courts, although only a handful was in existence, were shot up so that they could not be used. With the defeat of the Taliban, the inhabitants of Kabul were desperately looking to regain their normal life. Teenage boys and their friends, and teenage girls and their friends, and couples of all ages paid the token entrance fee to loiter in the beautiful gardens of Bagh-e-Babur. There were several groups of friends and onlookers playing carom, and in the far edge of the garden, there were about twenty young boys dancing to the beat of Afghan songs on an open platform. Some of the youngsters noticed me watching them and invited me to join them, so I joined them for a few minutes, and everyone clapped when I bowed out to leave. I was able to capture the serene setting of the garden including Babur's tomb with my Sony 3D video camera.

On the way back to our office compound, I saw a comic but sad sight. We passed a beat-up van with its sliding door missing and its rear lift gate up. The driver and two men were squeezed in the front seats, the middle seats were missing, and the space was packed with goats, and at the very back were several burqa-clad women facing outward with their feet dangling outside the van. I was amazed and asked Khyber why the women were not seated in the middle seats and the goats were not in the back with the lift gate closed. He smiled as he explained that the goats were far more valuable than the women and would fetch a higher market price than the women, hence their positioning in the van!

October 2, 2011. The weather was getting colder. We arranged a farewell party for Jay Stanford, our director for administration and finance. He was planning to retire to a quiet private life in the West Coast, USA. My youngest brother, Tawfiq Hassan, Skyped me from Dhaka to inform me that his company had won a joint bid to produce the e-passport, and that he was leading a delegation to Ukraine to negotiate with the Kiev-based EDAPS Consortium known for its manufacture of information systems and identification documents.

October 6, 2011. My security team and I went to Shahzdarak in one section of Kabul City to check out some villas for the project to relocate; Shahzdarak housed other international donor projects and therefore had more security set up per square meter than any other place in Kabul. The buildings did look more secure than where we were at the moment, but every vacant building we looked at was garish, lifeless, and painfully ugly. Each one of them had the standard Greek columns in the front entrance, extra and totally unnecessary embellishments on the exterior walls, bedrooms with bright multicolored ceilings with running lights that changed colors, and bathrooms that needed complete overhaul.

While my security team was gaga over the low-security risks, I had to look at the overall picture, for I was going to stay there under house arrest if you will for the next two years! I vetoed every building I inspected. They were in dilapidated condition because they had been vacant for months and sometimes years when donors left Afghanistan because of the continuous violence and insecurity. The landlords did not invest in their upkeep hoping that the new projects that rent them will fix them to their liking. I was unwilling to invest even a dime to make them livable.

October 7, 2011. It was an auspicious day for my Gurkha bodyguards, Anurag and Hari. It was Dashain, the grandest religious festival celebrated for two weeks in Nepal. Dashain honored the goddess Durga, who was created out of the Shakti, or energy of all the gods with weapons from each one of them to defeat the evil demon Mahishasura. It celebrated the victory of good over evil and hoped for the fertility of the land and a year of good harvest. Anurag bought dinner for us to celebrate Dashain. After dinner, I played some ping-pong with him to unwind.

October 9, 2011. My sister Lily's husband, Shafiqul Karim, had a niece named Zishan who had been working at the World Bank in Kabul for several years. When I learned about it from her parents, who lived in Canada but had retired and settled in Dhaka, I contacted her in Kabul and took her out to dinner at a nice Italian place called Taverna du Liban. I didn't remember when I had last seen her, so being able to catch up on those lost years was wonderful. I learned that she lived next door to Ahmed Shah Massoud's brother's house, which was a scary thought. In any case, it was a pleasant evening, and we departed with her promising that she would invite me and the new director of BRAC in Kabul for dinner at her house the following week.

It bears mentioning that BRAC (originally Bangladesh Rural Advancement Committee) was the world's largest NGO and the largest charitable organization operating principally in Asia and Africa. It had started its first international operation in 2002 in Afghanistan and had been providing essential programs in education for girls, health care, rural livelihood, and microfinancing.

When it first came to Afghanistan, it had a large contingent of female officers, which did not sit well with the Afghans who noticed that these women were unattached—that is, there were no male mentors or companions such as a husband, brother, or son with them. I was told that Afghans lodged protests with their government, which led to the Afghan government demanding that the women members of BRAC be withdrawn from Afghanistan forthwith. BRAC had no choice but to replace the female members with male counterparts or else face complete shutdown of their operation in Afghanistan.

A second negative experience for BRAC was the kidnapping of a couple of their workers by the Taliban who refused to believe that they were BRAC personnel. It took a while for the Taliban to realize that the kidnapped workers were indeed BRAC personnel and not foreign spies, and since BRAC had an excellent reputation in Afghanistan for the kind of work they were doing, the kidnapped workers were released with full apologies. But the experience of being held in a hole in the ground waiting to be executed was traumatic for the BRAC workers, and they were recalled to Bangladesh.

October 10, 2011. Went to Qargha, an artificially created resort area with a thirty-meter-tall dam and a reservoir, some thirty-five minute drive to west of Kabul, to check it out as a possible location for our office retreat that I was contemplating to develop our action plan for the project year 2. The reservoir offered recreational activities such as boating, surfing, and swimming, while the surrounding areas offered facilities for golfing, picnicking, and horseback riding.

October 15, 2011. The weather started to suddenly change for the worse and became very windy and cold. It made me sad to watch the Afghan guards shivering in the cold and howling wind as they manned their security posts. It became obvious to me that the woolen clothes, socks, and boots that Pax Mondial had issued each of them were inadequate in this inclement weather, and that it was going to get even worse as full winter hit Kabul.

Next morning, I called in the head of Pax Mondial, our security company, and told him that instead of focusing wholly on their profit margin, they needed to show a bit more compassion and provide their guards with outfits fully appropriate to the Kabul winter. He didn't like what I said and definitely didn't want me to interfere with their profit margin. I told him that it was going to be either my way or the highway, for I wouldn't be renewing our contract with them unless the guards on whom our lives depended were properly clothed; he said he'll see what he could do.

Within a couple of days, the guard's outfit from head to toe underwent significant upgrade to the relief and delight of those poor souls. I also assigned the non-Afghan security manager who was on duty at night the responsibility of brewing some strong tea and serving it to every guard on duty at midnight and at 3:00 a.m. Since adopting those measures, the attitude and disposition of the guards toward all expats in our project and especially toward me changed significantly. We were no longer bosses lording over them with unfair demands under trying circumstances but compassionate human beings who cared about their welfare and were friends helping them and their country.

Among the beneficiaries of our compassion were four street cats that used to meow for scraps by the kitchen door; these were also fed, and kitty homes lined with hay and old discarded woolen clothes were placed under the outside staircase for them, which they started to use.

October 19, 2011. Went to dinner at niece Zishan's house in the Wazir Akbar Khan area, which was a neighborhood in northern Kabul named after the nineteenth-century Afghan emir. It was considered to be a very wealthy area as well as a highly secure area because the Presidential Palace, most of the national government institutions, and the headquarters of the Resolute Support Mission were located there. It was also the location of a large number of western embassies, including the Canadian and American embassies. So it was a consolation of sorts that Zishan was residing in a safe neighborhood.

She had ordered takeaway—chicken, shrimp, dal, and naan—which we enjoyed heartily. We got to meet her World Bank colleague, and it was particularly wonderful to meet the departing and the newly arrived heads of BRAC. The conversation was quite lively and informative.

When I asked why BRAC was so successful in Afghanistan while other international NGOs were not as much, the departing head said that it was a combination of several factors. BRAC personnel did not move about the country wearing western/business clothes and in cars; they adopted the casual street outfit of the common man and either walked or biked from place to place; in other words, they blended with the public. BRAC also strictly observed Afghan traditions such as employing women to provide services to women and the girl child; focused on areas that were not considered to be politically sensitive such as health care, training in cottage industry skills such as weaving, knitting, and making handicrafts that women could employ at home; and respected the local culture and custom. They targeted areas of rural livelihood such as agriculture and nonfarm activities that yielded benefits to the community.

All of these redounded to BRAC workers being welcomed into the rural communities and to their willingness to participate in BRAC-sponsored socioeconomic activities. I had to leave the dinner party earlier than I wanted to because as the night progressed, security checks on the roads increased, often resulting in the cruiser getting pulled to one side of the road and searched and delays in checking out the official permits for the sidearm and the shotgun that my security team carried with them when I traveled.

October 22, 2011. It was a Saturday, the first business day of the week. I took my technical team and the support staff to Qargha for our office retreat to do work planning for the next year. The weather was miserable—overcast, rainy, and cold. The support team had gone there over the weekend to set up the shamiana (a South Asian ceremonial awning used for outdoor parties or events), sofas, tables, projector and projection screen with extension wires, whiteboard, flip charts and markers, multiple plugs for laptops, etc. But with the weather changing for the worse, we had to move indoors into a rather small conference room of the guest house. In any case, our retreat triggered very lively debates and brought out great practical ideas that we were able to incorporate within the Option Year I mandate. Lunch was delicious as well. Everything went smoothly except for a flat tire on one of our soft skins (vehicles that were not armored). We completed our work and left Qargha at around 4:00 p.m.

That night, our security manager informed us at the dinner table that he had really bad news. A wedding party had booked the Qargha resort that evening, and they had come at around 8:00 p.m. At around 10:00 p.m., Taliban terrorists had attacked the place from several directions, and by the time the attack ended, the entire wedding party, including the bride, the groom, and their parents and relatives, had been slaughtered; no member of the wedding party left the place alive. We sat around the dinner table in stunned silence, unable to get our head around the fact that we were there just a few hours earlier.

Nipa's Fiftieth Birthday

October 27, 2011. An important family event in our household was coming up fast; my wife Nipa was about to turn fifty in November 2011. I was working in Afghanistan at the time, and since leave from work was restrictive, I postponed an earlier leave to add my leave days to my next leave for the big event. I discussed with Mumu, who was living and working in London at the time, various options and we decided to celebrate Mom's birthday in Istanbul. I arranged to meet Nipa in Doha on October 27; she was returning from a visit to Bangladesh. I took the 8:00 a.m. Safi Airways flight from Kabul to Dubai and then connected to Doha from where Nipa and I flew together to London. At Heathrow, Mohammad, who was Mumu's Somalian taxi driver, picked us up and drove us to Neela's house.

October 29, 2011. Since we had a few days to spare before our

Istanbul trip, Nipa, Mumu, and I took the train from London Euston train station to Milton Keynes, a journey of less than an hour to visit with Nipa's cousin Rubaiyat and her husband Shoeb. The timing was great because chachi (aunty), Rubaiyat's mom, was visiting them from Bangladesh, and we hadn't seen her for a long time.

Rubaiyat and Shoeb had a wonderful story of their own to tell, which she shared with us later when she visited us in Ottawa. They struck their friendship when they were both students at the same time in the same place in England. According to her, Shoeb told her that his mom in Bangladesh was pushing him to get married and settle down, so he asked Rubaiyat whether she could help him find the right girl to marry. Rubaiyat agreed to help him, and over a period of time, she introduced him to a number of girls. But Shoeb did not pursue any of those girls because none of them was the girl he was looking for. Finally, Rubaiyat told him that she knew no more girls and asked him, "You have rejected every girl I introduced you to. The only girl left is me. Do you like *me*?" He said "Yes." With a sigh of relief, she called her mom in Bangladesh to tell her about Shoeb, and the rest was history, but a delightfully romantic one!

Rubaiyat and Shoeb lived in a cute house. They gave us a tour of Milton Keynes, including the lake area by her office. Rubaiyat worked in the Mercedes-Benz dealership and loved the option to drive new models for an initial period. That night, some of her guests dropped by, and we had a wonderful time together. Mumu left the next day to return to work in London.

October 30, 2011. We left Milton Keynes in the morning to make a quick stopover at the house of Nipa's another cousin, Shumon, and his wife Shirin; they lived in Milton Keynes as well, and Nipa hadn't seen Shumon for many years as well. After the brief stopover, we took the train back to Euston station, London, where Mumu and Mishu met us, and from there, we spent the afternoon in Brick Lane, where we had lunch and bought some DVDs and CDs. Brick Lane at the east end of London was home to the Bangladeshi community and was famed for its authentic curry restaurants. It had also developed the reputation for its warehouse art exhibitions and trendy clubs, and Mishu used to buy his art accessories from there.

October 31, 2011. It was a day of mixed emotions for Mumu, for it was her birthday and also the day when Halloween was celebrated in North America. When Mumu was younger, her girlfriends would carve out pumpkins to read "Happy Birthday" with candles burning inside on the night of Halloween. We woke up rather late that day and then went to Nipa's Rani fupu and Jalal fupa's place for lunch, where we met Engineer Reza and his wife, who were Jamilur Reza Chowdhury's friends. (Regrettably, Jamil chacha passed away during Ramadan 2020 at the time of this writing.) Jalal fupa had retired as Bangladesh Biman's head in London, and fupu had been working in London all along; they were now settled in London. After lunch, we went to the Marylebone Station to buy flowers for Mumu, and when Mumu was done with work at 6:00 p.m., the four of us went to Zizzi's for her birthday dinner. It was wonderful.

November 1, 2011. Nipa and I left Neela's house at 4:00 a.m. for Heathrow for our flight to Zurich and on to Istanbul where we arrived at 2:00 p.m. Mumu had booked all of us at the Double Tree by Hilton Hotel. The weather was great, so we did some scouting around the Grand Bazaar and then pored over the travel brochures from the hotel lobby to chalk out a "tourist plan" for the duration of our stay in Istanbul. We spent most of the next day at the Grand Bazaar where Nipa bought lots of souvenirs, ending the day by eating donair kabob from a roadside vendor. That night, both of us fell sick as well as started coughing and sneezing.

November 3–4, 2011. It rained all day, so we remained in our hotel room. Our daughter and son arrived in Istanbul in the early afternoon, and we all rested that day, especially for Nipa and me to get better and in preparation for the schedule that we jointly planned for the next day. We booked an all-day tour with a private tour guide and a taxi for the next day. We started at the Hippodrome of Constantinople known today as the Sultanahmet Square. The central attraction there was the Obelisk of Theodosius, which was a nearly thirty-meter-tall red granite Egyptian obelisk of Pharaoh Thutmose III, placed there by Emperor

Theodosius I in the fourth century AD. It had hieroglyphics on all four sides praising the emperor's victory and depicting the ensuing celebrations. Two-minute walk from the square was the Blue Mosque, so named because its twenty-one thousand blue ceramic tiles decorated its interior with exquisite geometric and floral motifs. It was built by Sultan Ahmet I from 1609 to 1616. Though not very large, it continues to be an important mosque to the citizens of Istanbul.

Next, we visited one of Istanbul's famous cathedrals, the Hagia Sophia, which means "divine wisdom." This domed monument was constructed by order of Emperor Justinian I in less than six years, from AD 532 to 537, and over its history, it depicted the religious, artistic, and political life of the Byzantine world. It continued to be seen as a symbol of peace, harmony, and tolerance. It served as the most important Christian church for nine hundred years until its conquest in AD 1453 by Turkish sultan Mehmet II when it became a very important mosque of the Ottoman Empire for the next five hundred years. In 1935, it was turned into a museum displaying the art, artifacts, and symbols of Muslim and Christian rule.

But in late March 2019, Turkish president Recep Tayyip Erdogan stated that he would change the status of the museum to that of a mosque after the local elections to curry favor with religious parties. I found this statement to be needlessly provocative to Turkey's minority Christians and displayed Erdogan's shortsightedness.

We also visited the Topkapi Palace, the principal residence and the administrative headquarters of the Ottoman sultans since AD 1478. Huge and opulent, it also guarded the Ottoman treasures. It was called Topkapi, which in Turkish meant "Gate of Cannons" because of the huge cannons displayed outside its gates. With the establishment of the Republic of Turkey, Topkapi Palace was converted into a museum in 1924.

We had a late lunch at the Konyali Restaurant perched on a hillside by the Topkapi Palace Museum overlooking the Bosphorus. The sunny weather with its nice warm breeze added to the glorious view of the marina below and of the ships and water traffic on the Bosphorus; one could even say that it was romantic!

At the Konyali Restaurant on the terrace of TopkapiPalace
Museum overlooking the Bosporus, Nov 2011

After the casual lunch, we went to the carpet-making district and watched how carpets were weaved. Since I had purchased both Iranian and Afghan carpets before, I had a pretty good sense of different types of carpets and what they might cost. One thing I learned early on was that when the shopkeeper tells you that he will give you a special price for any number of reasons, you can take it for granted that he is about to screw you over badly. We were made special offers, and when I pointed out that I had seen similar carpets in Herat or in Tehran but priced much less, the answer, inevitably, was that his product was far superior to what I had seen. That was the end of our carpet shopping, because shopkeepers saw us tourists as foreigners to be finagled out of their dollars.

November 5, 2011. The day started with mother-and-daughter shopping in the Grand Bazaar. Next, we took a two-hour cruise of the Bosphorus, which was simply marvelous. We took lots of pictures and 3D videos of special buildings, historical sites, and architectural masterpieces. The evening was special. We made dinner reservation at Galata Tower, a medieval stone tower that was one of Istanbul's famous landmarks overlooking the Old City and the Bosphorus Strait. Standing sixty-seven meters high, it was originally built in the sixth century by Byzantine emperor Anastasius as a lighthouse. However, the tower was demolished during the Fourth Crusade in AD 1204. It was rebuilt in AD 1348 as the Tower of Jesus by Genoese merchants to maintain surveillance of the harbor as they traded with the Byzantines. It has served as a signal tower to guide ships ever since. The city itself was made the capital of the Eastern Roman Empire in AD 330 and named Constantinople after Roman emperor Constantine. It retained its name until 1923 when the Republic of Turkey changed its name to Istanbul after the collapse of the Ottoman Empire.

We took the elevator on the second floor to the restaurant on the seventh floor; two more floors up was the observation deck that provided a panoramic view of Istanbul. At the restaurant, the dining tables were set against each window of the circular tower so that guests were able to get a clear view of a particular section of the city. The center area was left empty purposely so that various types of activities—such as belly dancing, knife throwing, fire eating, singing—could entertain its guests.

I do not remember much about the Turkish dishes that were served, but I do remember the ample-bosomed belly dancers, two of whom came over to our table and targeted Mishu and me to come to the dance floor with them. We politely declined. Different guests from different countries were enticed to sing songs in their own languages. It was a great night except for the fact that there was no birthday cake for Nipa. Instead, I gave her a diamond bracelet that I had purchased in Dubai earlier in the year as her fiftieth birthday gift. Her actual birthday was on November 15.

Celebrating Nipa's 50th birthday at the Galata Tower
overlooking the Bosporus Strait, Istanbul, Nov 2011

The next day, Mumu and Mishu boarded the noon Swiss Air flight to Heathrow. My cold and cough got worse, so I went to bed early. While I slept, Nipa, who had recovered from her cold earlier, went to the souk once again and also visited one of Istanbul's historical sites, the Basilica Cistern, with its 336 columns, each nine meters tall, and with two Medusa heads. The Basilica Cistern, one of about one hundred underground cisterns, was built beneath the palace to serve as water storage and water filtration system as well as to supply the palace and other important buildings with water. These cisterns were built during ancient times to supply water during dry summers. I missed seeing them.

November 7, 2011. Nipa and I left Double Tree by Hilton, Istanbul, at 10:00 a.m. to catch our noon Swiss Air flight to Heathrow, London. From there, we took the subway to Neela's place, where we had a wonderful dinner of aloor bhorta, dherosh bhaji, lamb, and dahl. The next day was our last day together during this birthday-centric trip. Nipa and I woke up late and packed our Kabul and Ottawa suitcases. Mishu met us at Baker Street Station after work, and we had latte together. We then met Nipa's cousin, my youngest shalee, Faiza, at the Marylebone Station briefly. We then went to Westfield Mall where we had dinner at Pizza Express.

When it opened in October 2008, the Westfield Mall was the largest covered shopping area in London, and by March 2018, it had become the largest shopping center in UK and in Europe. After dinner, Mumu took us to see the *Ides of March*, which was the film adaptation of Beau Willimon's 2008 play *Farragut North*. It was claimed that George Clooney, who was the film director of this 2011 American political drama, felt that the principal character's political assassination was similar to Julius Caesar's assassination on the Ides of March in Shakespeare's play Julius Caesar, hence the name. We said farewell to the kids before returning to Neela's house.

November 9–10, 2011. I left Neela's place for Heathrow at 5:30 a.m., and Nipa left at 9:00 a.m. for Ottawa. I took Qatar Airways to Doha and then to Dubai, where I spent the night at Le Méridien, Dubai. I ordered room service and was pleasantly surprised to be served by a Sylheti server,

413

who enthusiastically opened up to a fellow Bangladeshi about his life's ambition; he hoped to own a hotel one day. I encouraged him saying that it was certainly achievable if he stayed true to his goal and persevered through the toils and tribulations that would come his way. He smiled and thanked me and hoped to see me again. I left the hotel at 10:00 a.m. and arrived at cloud-covered Kabul by Safi Airways at 4:00 p.m.

November 14–16, 2011. The Loya Jirga (grand tribal council or legal assembly to make important decisions) was scheduled to convene on November 16 but was anathema to the Taliban insurgents who were outside the country's political spectrum. To derail this important meeting, suicide bombers hit the Polytechnic Institute, where the Loya Jirga was scheduled to meet. The result was a tightened security throughout the city with road blocks and police checkpoints in every street junction, restricted vehicular movements, curfew from early evening to morning, and a general advice to foreign missions and institutions to reduce their travel and impose lockdown. I had no choice but to impose lockdown for the next two days because the staff had great difficulty coming to office because of route closures and heavy security measures throughout the city. There was considerable tension and uncertainty as the Loya Jirga met on the sixteenth. The expats were the only ones in the office monitoring the news, and they reported to me that amid all the tragic news, there was one good news, which was that Bollywood actress Aishwarya Rai had delivered a baby girl! That cheered me up as I wondered whether she would be as beautiful as Aishwarya.

November 17–18, 2011. Since I am a space buff, I was excited to learn that NASA had discovered that Jupiter's moon Europa had oceans of water, which was a thrilling discovery because it meant that the probability of life as we know it existing there was high. The city remained peaceful, but security measures were still in full force. Both our cooks had to walk for miles and hours to come to the villa to cook for us to last at least a couple of days. However, despite the serious vetting of all Afghans whom we hired for the project, in the back of my mind was always the fear that either of the cooks could be blackmailed by the Taliban insurgents to poison us; we had to keep our fingers crossed and hope for the best. The Loya Jirga continued to the next day, but thankfully without any security incident.

November 23–24, 2011. It was happy news from the States. My mom and sisters Lily and Tina and her family were off to Hawaii for their Thanksgiving vacation. It was a much-needed break for Tina and Rawnaque, both of whom worked for Boise-based Micron Technology Inc., a global leader in semiconductor industry. On November 24, I went to Hotel Serena for Thanksgiving dinner with our project operations manager Tracey Brinson and security personnel James.

Dinner was disappointing because there was no turkey. It was the first time that the kids were in London, Nipa was in Ottawa, and I was in Kabul, and there was no family Thanksgiving get-together and no turkey for anyone. Hotel Serena was the poshest hotel in Kabul belonging to the Agha Khan family. I had stayed there numerous times during my total six years of work in Afghanistan. The food was always great with lots of choices, but not to have turkey on Thanksgiving was very disappointing to me. There was, of course, lamb roast and beef roast that everyone loved, but I was tired of eating.

December 1, 2011. It was my birthday, and birthday wishes started flowing from early on. First, Mishu called me from London past midnight, followed by messages from my sister-in-law Lopa, brother Tawfiq, Nipa, and then daughter Mumu. There were also Facebook and Gmail messages from sister Tina, nephew Brandon, brother Shahalam from Texas, and cousin Neela, among others. I thought of treating myself and so bought myself an Afghan kurta set. The next day, Tina called from Hawaii, and her daughters Mayisa and Nusha sang "Happy Birthday" for me. It was great to hear my nieces sing for me from Hawaii on my birthday!

December 6, 2011. This day was Ashura—that is, the tenth of Muharram, the first month in the Islamic calendar. It marked the day when Prophet Muhammad's (PBUH) grandsons Hassan and Husayn ibn Ali were martyred in the Battle of Karbala (Iraq) in AD 680. It was a solemn day of mourning for the followers of the Shia faith, who dressed themselves in black and marched through the streets in a passionate display of grief. We had to close office out of security concerns because violent altercations between the Sunnis and Shias were inevitable. Not surprisingly, insurgents exploded three bombs near Shia mosques, killing over eighty people instantly. Many more died in the ambulances and later in the hospitals. It was senseless. It was tragic. I often asked my fellow Muslim brothers why we blamed the West and the Jews only for killing Muslims, while in the Muslim homelands across the globe, Sunnis and Shias were killing each other uninterruptedly, especially the former. The usual response has been silence, because there was no acceptable answer.

December 7–8, 2011. I had a fruitful meeting in the home of Seema Ghani, who was a former deputy minister of labor and social affairs in the Karzai government. When we first met, we hit it off well together. She appeared to be a kindred spirit and exhibited a lot of spunk in handling Afghan issues. Her father was a high-ranking military officer but had to take his family to safety to UK in 1990 during the Communist regime. She returned to Afghanistan in 2002. After her brief stint in government, she became the executive director of the international Monitoring and Evaluation Committee (MEC) for Afghanistan and, subsequently, the founding member of the People's Anti-Corruption Movement and of the Afghan Women Charter.

She invited me to her home many times in formal occasions and informally as well and has been a great friend. When my project ended, I returned to Ottawa. Meanwhile, she was forced out of her MEC executive director's job through political machination by senior Afghans within MEC. When I accepted the invitation of several international donors to replace an international member of MEC, Seema took it personally as a betrayal and never spoke to me again. I regret that she never gave me the chance to explain my reasons for accepting the offer to join MEC. To this day, I have no ill feelings toward her, and I still consider her to be my friend.

Following the afternoon meeting with Seema, Tracey and I attended the cocktail reception in the evening at the U.S. deputy ambassador's residence. The next day, Tracey and I went shopping with our office assistant and guide Samad; I bought really nice pendants, earrings, and rings for my wife and my daughter.

December 9–12, 2011. The United Nations had declared December 9 as the International Anti-Corruption Day (IACD), and I received an invitation from the High Office of Oversight (HOO) to the IACD celebrations that were to be inaugurated by Afghan president Hamid Karzai. I also remembered to order a bouquet of flowers to be delivered to my wife for our wedding anniversary on December 10. So December 10, 2011, was our twenty-ninth anniversary, and Mumu called to wish us happy anniversary.

The IACD was held on the eleventh because there was no opening in the Afghan president's appointments calendar before that. The president inaugurated the IACD and delivered a lengthy speech that contained all the right sound bites particularly for his international audience. On the eleventh, I also signed a new lease with a new landlord, with relocation to start from December 13. Since I was going to go on my Christmas leave sometime soon, I went shopping once again and bought some nice shawls, Afghan outfit, and a few Afghan woolen caps for our friends in Ottawa, but specifically for my brother-in-law Rana and his two sons Zahin and Ramin.

December 13, 2011. News from home was both good and bad. Good news was that our son had completed his first-year university studies. The bad news was that my aunt, my mom's elder sister, was in the hospital for treatment for cancer of the jaw. She was an elderly lady, very fair and beautiful, who had spent most of her life in her village under harsh social conditions and still retained her softness and grace. When I last saw her a few years back, she still had that twinkle in her eyes and her beautiful smile.

December 15, 2011. We started relocation of the project office at 6:00 a.m. and had to face numerous unforeseen obstacles throughout the day. We were also concerned that there wouldn't be any Internet connection for the next twenty-four hours, so I had let my family know about this ahead of time. I wanted to finish moving before I started my holiday leave a few days later. Back in Ottawa, Mishu was in a happy mood because he was ordering an iMac with twenty-seven-inch screen.

December 21–22, 2011. I departed Kabul early morning for Dubai and breathed a huge sigh of relief when I landed at Heathrow, London, and took the taxi to Neela's. I always looked forward to seeing Neela, Shaheen, and their lovely kids and their vivacious company; theirs was a home away from home. I could unwind, relax, and find comfort in Neela's and Shaheen's warm hospitality. They were also inquisitive about Afghanistan, its culture, its people and their struggles, and were eager to hear about my latest experiences there, and I was only too happy to regale them with my latest stories.

It was doubly exciting to see my daughter Mumu as well and to fly home together from London at noon the next day. Nipa and Mishu were at the Ottawa Macdonald-Cartier International Airport to welcome us; Mishu drove us home. Needless to say, it was a great relief to leave Taliban country behind and joyful to be finally in the safety and security of my home with my loved ones in Ottawa.

Afghanistan: Year 2012

As the year 2011 came to an end, so did my time with my family in Ottawa. My departure date was around the corner, so Nipa arranged a farewell get-together and invited some friends for a postdinner cha-nasta chitchat. She served a variety of snacks from Afghanistan that included fruits, nuts, chilgoza, and exotic sweets, among other items. Our guests were a great company, as well as a curious lot, who engaged in quite a lively discussion about Afghanistan and the region. Some of them had their own stories to tell, mostly about their escape route through Afghanistan from incarceration in Pakistan during and after the Bangladesh War. It was, indeed, a splendid evening full of reminiscences and lively conversations.

Before my departure for Kabul, however, I had to make a quick side trip to Washington DC to participate in MSI's annual retreat. Our friends Musawir and Shirin Karim, who used to live in Ottawa until they immigrated to the United States, picked me up from the Ronald Reagan Washington National Airport and took me to their home in Maryland. It was a nicely decorated three-floor lakeside home, spick and span, which Musawir attributed to his Roomba vacuum cleaner. Of course, the Roomba was no Shirin when it came to keeping the house neat, tidy, and attractive.

Musawir and Shirin have been great friends over the years, and we continue to remain in touch, although perhaps not as much as we both would like to. They were of roughly the same age as we were and a fun couple to spend time with. We have made long-distance journeys together and thoroughly enjoyed our many outings. Musawir and I used to regularly play tennis in the summer and badminton in the winter, and his wife Shirin, whom I teasingly called *maharani* because of the way she appeared to "lord" over Musawir, was a great friend of my wife Nipa. Their second daughter, Zahin, and our daughter Mumu were of the same age. When they had moved to the States, their eldest daughter, Mahareen, had gotten engaged to our mutual friend Mustafa Chowdhury's nephew Tarik, and the whole family stayed with us during the entire wedding that took place in Ottawa. It was a pleasure to host them and be a part of Mahareen and Tarik's wedding preparations.

Shirin served a splendid dinner, after which I showed them my Kabul video. When I talked about the United States' role in Afghanistan, both of them became very defensive. It was somewhat surprising to me to see their former Canadian perspective on America change so suddenly after becoming American citizens. It was, of course, only right to defend one's country against real or veiled criticism. Aside from that, we had a wonderful evening together and shared the latest with each other about our mutual friends in Ottawa. After dinner, Musawir dropped me off at Sheraton National Hotel, where I was lodged by MSI. Meanwhile in Ottawa, Mumu caught the afternoon Air Canada flight back to London Heathrow.

The next day was the all-day MSI retreat on the sixteenth floor of the Sheraton Hotel in Arlington, Virginia. It was an extensive stocktaking exercise of all of MSI's projects worldwide as well as a very intensive strategic planning for the future and many things in between. For me, it was also a great opportunity to meet some of the senior officials of MSI. More importantly, Pres. Larry Cooley, CEO Marina Fanning, and Senior Advisor Jesse Bunch praised my work in Kabul; in fact, Larry expressed his desire to retain me beyond Kabul. After the retreat, Technical Director Bert Spector, Project Operations Head Tracey Brinson, her assistant Maria Isabel Osorio, and I went out to dinner before parting company.

Unplanned Detour

I caught the AC 7663 flight back to Ottawa. Nipa picked me up at the airport, and we went to Nando's for early lunch and then did some last-minute shopping for flannel shirt, scarf, and woolen sweaters and socks in preparation for Kabul's winter. I didn't quite know how cold Kabul could get in the winter until I saw some pictures. There were many unknowns about the Afghan winter that I had to contend with.

An indicator of corruption in the cities was the huge, gaudy buildings that were built with expensive imported marble with the intention to rent them out to foreign diplomatic and expatriate presence. The marble, especially in the floors of these houses, were extremely cold; it felt like one was living in igloos. Another unknown was the poor heating system within buildings, the frequent breakdown of heaters, and the paucity of qualified electricians to service them. Yet another unknown was the unreliable supply of electricity that often caused the generators to crash, leaving buildings without any heat. My project, like most others, had to keep in its payroll a full-time building manager with good knowledge of and connection with skilled maintenance people available in the city.

That same evening, I left for London and Dubai. In Dubai, I boarded Flydubai FZ 301 for the 4:30 a.m. flight to Kabul, except that for some inexplicable reason, our flight got diverted to Peshawar, Pakistan. There was no explanation from the cockpit as to why we were heading for Pakistan except the brusque announcement that we were going to land in Peshawar. The passengers were looking at each other searching for some plausible explanation for this unusual detour to a neighboring country that Kabul regularly and rightly accused of harboring terrorists who attacked Afghanistan and with whom political relations were quite sour. Some of us even thought that perhaps we were being hijacked by terrorists who had taken over the cockpit. When we asked the stewardess what was going on, she merely said that the captain will make an announcement soon.

We landed in what seemed like a military airstrip, for we didn't see any airport building or any civilians. As we taxied to a halt on the tarmac, we could see lots of military vehicles full of soldiers going back and forth, and within minutes, armed soldiers flanked the aircraft on all sides. We watched iron guard rails being dragged toward the front of the aircraft and wheel stoppers placed by the front and rear wheels. What was going on outside the plane appeared bizarre to us and only increased our worries, with conjectures and speculations among the passengers flying wildly.

At one point, the aircraft door next to the cockpit opened, and two persons in military uniform boarded the plane. While one military person entered the cockpit, the other person started to walk down the aisle and take a head count. For the next while, several military persons boarded and disembarked the plane, some looking stern for reasons not apparent to us, while others with lots of documents and papers in hand. After over two hours of drama all around us and considerable tension among the passengers, all the Pakistani military personnel finally left the aircraft, and the aircraft door closed.

As the aircraft started its engines, the captain's voice finally came over the intercom. He explained that he could not land in Kabul because Kabul airport was under terrorist attack when we were up in the air very close to Kabul. There had been several bomb blasts inside the airport and raging firefight within the perimeter of the airport and in several Kabul streets. Since the aircraft was too low on fuel to fly to an alternative safe airport within Afghanistan, the only choice was to fly to Peshawar, which was safer and close by. However, the plane had to circle over the Kabul airport for some time as Afghan authorities desperately sought permission from Pakistan authorities to allow an emergency landing in Peshawar.

We learned later that this urgent request had created a bitter row between the civilian and military authorities in Pakistan. The civilian authorities were quite willing to allow the Flydubai flight to make the emergency landing, but the military authorities were not willing to allow that because of security reasons. We were glad, indeed, that the civilian authorities were able to hold their ground against the Pakistan military for a change. In any case, we were finally airborne for Kabul but totally unsure of what lay at the Kabul end. I had my own security protocol to follow, but communicating with my security staff became impossible because Internet and all other means of communication were down.

When we landed in Kabul early morning, it was an extremely tense atmosphere. Even the tens of Afghan soldiers who were spread out at the airport and inside the airport buildings looked very unsure and unsettled. We were directed to walk toward passport control single file where we were speedily processed, perhaps the fastest that I had gone through Kabul airport ever. There was no one at the airport except for the Afghan military and a minimum number of baggage handlers, and so many of the standard entry procedures were overlooked.

The passengers had to retrieve and haul their own luggage. My project security personnel were anxiously waiting for me farther away from the terminal building than was normally the case, and so I walked an extra distance to reach them under the watchful eyes of the Afghan military. As we drove to our project compound, we had to go through numerous security checkpoints where we were stopped and searched every time, all the while listening to sporadic gunfire coming from different directions.

Our compound was on high alert for obvious reasons; first, the city was under terrorist attack in multiple places at the same time; second, we were a foreign non-Muslim presence that made us an attractive target for the Taliban; and, finally, because we were an American project, and in the minds of the Taliban, the project's avowed purpose could be different from its real purpose. Although the city was finally brought under Afghan government control by the end of the day, every foreign presence including us took extra precautions assuming the worst. Our communication with head office in Washington DC remained down for the whole day and night, causing a great deal of concern there. Only in the following morning was satellite phone communication restored, allowing diplomatic establishments and projects such as ours to restore our protocol for exchange of intelligence pertaining to security.

Revisiting Security

Not surprisingly, the year 2012 had started with considerable uncertainty. I ordered my senior security officers to review our internal security, identify loopholes that can be exploited by a determined enemy and make recommendations on how we might be able to further strengthen our security. They came up with four recommendations: that we should always maintain our supply of ammunition at the optimum level, which was not always the case with us; that we should increase the frequency of security drill from once a month to once every fortnight; that I had to relocate my bedroom and office that faced the street to the back of the building; and that all the front windows of the three floors of our building must be replaced with specially designed glass panels.

These special window panels had steel mesh running through the double layers of tempered glass and were designed to yield inward with the thrust of the blast but then recoil outward throwing the blast debris outside the building. They were designed to allow the glass to break into small pieces that interlocked with adjacent pieces, thereby preventing the sharp shards from flying in all directions killing or maiming all those within the blast radius, to absorb and dissipate the blast energy to their specially designed frames, and then to eject the blast debris outward, thereby preventing or minimizing damage inside the building. I approved all four recommendations for immediate implementation.

But the physical security of the compound was just one element of overall security. What was really hard to get a handle on was how to ensure the loyalty of the Afghan security guards on whose hands our lives depended day in and day out, especially when Afghan radios and television channels were broadcasting daily any and all anti-Muslim activities in other countries, such as the burning of the Quran by a Florida pastor in his Gainesville Church sanctuary in March 2011.

These incidents were fantastic fodder for the recruitment of uneducated Afghans of all ages by the terrorist cells. While every Afghan hired by the project, especially the security guards, was thoroughly vetted, did that provide us with one 100 percent security? The answer was obviously no. While we wanted to believe that the Afghan security guards would protect us when push came to shove, and to a large extent, we did believe that because we had no choice, there was still that nagging uncertainty because of the cultural and religious bent of the guards as well as the real possibility of someone among them having no option but to do the Taliban's bidding under extreme duress.

We were familiar with a number of such cases. Going to a restaurant was a real challenge for all expats. Every restaurant that expats visited had strong security protocol in place to ensure their safety. For example, when I went to a restaurant, which was a rare occasion to start with, my security people would visit the restaurant ahead of time to assess whether it would be safe for me to go there, to understand its security protocol, and to check out whether it had a safe room and its exit points.

After arriving at the restaurant, I would wait in my armored vehicle while my personal security guard, who would either be Gurkha Anurag Gurung or British ex-sergeant Gareth Williams, would knock on the fortified concrete cubicle window next to the steel gate of the restaurant. A small metal window panel would slide open to exchange words, following which my guard would come and get me from the vehicle and accompany me to the gate, which would open to let me in through turnstiles. As I entered one compartment of a secure passageway, everything behind me including the turnstile would be locked until I moved to the next secure compartment where I would be thoroughly frisked. Meanwhile, the first compartment would open up to allow my personal security guard to enter, but the next compartment would remain shut until I vacated it. At one point in the secure passageway, my security guard would have to turn in his sidearms and other fighting gear such as knives followed by thorough body check. We would then be escorted to the restaurant building, to be accompanied from there to our table by someone else. We would be able to retrieve our sidearm and other fighting gear only as we exited the compound. The system worked beautifully, or so it seemed.

The chink in this security protocol, however, was the restaurant security guard himself. At least on two occasions during my stay in Afghanistan, a restaurant security guard was visited at home by terrorists and told that they were going to hold his family hostage until he delivered on their demand. He had to smuggle explosives into the restaurant and place them according to their instruction and then leave, while the terrorists used remote devices to detonate them. On another occasion, the guard was forced to put on a vest packed with explosives and armed with a detonator and blow himself up when the restaurant was filled with diners; he had no choice because the terrorists forced his entire family including his elderly parents to wear explosive-laden vests that would have been detonated if he failed to do what the terrorists demanded. In situations like these, the choice is so stark that there is no way out except carrying out the demands of the terrorists.

It was horrifying to contemplate such situations, and it weighed on me heavily throughout my tenure in Afghanistan. Following the first such incident, my senior security personnel—Anurag, Gareth, and Antoine—and I discussed various scenarios of this sort and the appropriate course of action and came up with a multipronged strategy. Given the importance of having timely access to reliable, up-to-date intelligence, Antoine was tasked to strengthen our relations with the different intelligence-gathering bodies—domestic and foreign—within the country. Gareth and Anurag were assigned the task of ensuring that the security guards were properly trained and ready for action at any moment, as well as ensuring that we were at all times fully stocked up with the arsenal approved by the Afghan authority, as well as maintaining a fully reinforced safe room.

Anurag was also tasked to focus on the human dimension. He was required to monitor that every time a guard reported for duty, he was thoroughly frisked for bombs or detonators on his body; he was also frisked when he left the compound to make sure that he was not carrying anything material or security related. This was done with great care and with deference so as not to offend the guard's sensibilities.

Anurag's assistant Hari was required to carry out overall monitoring of the movements of the security guards, vehicles, and their upkeep, including fuel purchase. Both Anurag and Hari spent considerable time and effort to win their friendship and confidence by relating to them at a horizontal level rather than barking orders at them, by sharing and taking food with them occasionally, by inquiring about their welfare and needs, and by expressing sympathy with them if the situation called for.

Hari also discreetly monitored all the goings-on within and around the compound. For example, he noticed one day the cook throwing something over the wall on to the adjacent graveyard. He quickly went out to check what it was and found a couple of whole chicken roasts wrapped in aluminum foil. Since the cook would be frisked at the gate when he left the premise, he threw the chicken over the wall so that he could go around the building to pick it up on his way home. He was confronted by security and then fired on the spot but without any show of hatred or malice lest he passed valuable information about the inside of the compound to the enemy. He was allowed to take the chicken roasts for his family.

Our strategy with the Afghan guards was to make them feel that there was no "we" versus "they" and that we were all in it together fighting for the safety and security of the Afghan people. My particular focus, besides overall monitoring, was on their religious and cultural sentiments. I had to let them see that I showed proper deference to their flag, their government, and to government officials when they visited me, and displayed appropriate manners and greetings.

For example, while it was a common practice among us "westerners" as well as educated Afghan female professionals to bid good-bye by shaking hands and sometime by touching of facial cheeks, we never did that with our female Afghan colleagues outside our meeting rooms. We maintained proper distance between each other in public. We spoke with Afghans at all levels with courtesy and respect even when we disagreed. I also went out of my way to demonstrate to my lower-level Afghan staff that I cared for their welfare not only by regularly inquiring after them or talking with them but materially as well.

At the end of my first year as project head, I was rewarded with a hefty performance bonus, which in Afghan money was a huge amount. I decided to distribute the entire bonus to all the guards and the lower level staff such as the chefs, the gardener, and the drivers of the project vehicles. They were very surprised and smiled in appreciation, some even bowing their heads and kissing my hands.

I also ensured that we were celebrating Afghan national heroes and holidays, especially religious holidays. In short, I had to run a tight ship to achieve the project objectives but without giving the lowly paid staff and particularly the security guards any cause for offense. I had to demonstrate compassion and understanding to earn their allegiance. The rest was in God's hands!

****

Middle of January 2012. It started to snow heavily, and the entire city was wet and white just like Ottawa at this time of the year. I was inspired to take out my video camera to capture what looked like a snow-covered wilderness. When I posted the pictures in Facebook, our friends in Ottawa couldn't believe how similar the Kabul and Ottawa landscapes looked in winter.

The downside, of course, was that the temperature fell precipitously, causing our water tank to freeze and water pipes to burst. Also, our room heaters collapsed during the frequent power outages. Samad, our very capable and competent building maintenance manager, was able to get a certified plumber to fix the pipes and an electrician to restore power within the building. It was a great relief to all the expats to be able to take a shower after two days of only bottled water. Samad also purchased for me a made-in-China electric blanket to keep me warm at night. In frigid Kabul, that was heaven sent! Every evening about ten minutes before going to bed, I turned on the electric blanket at a low setting so that the bed was toasty warm when I tucked myself in. I then turned on my iPod and listened to songs until I fell asleep. Samad also bought a basketful of pomegranate for the chef to squeeze the juice and bottle it for me.

But we weren't out of the woods yet. I had asked Samad to get a laboratory analysis done of the quality of the water in the new compound because of the horrifying stories I heard from diplomatic and other project colleagues. The results of the laboratory analysis came in showing the fecal content in the water was several times the permissible limit for safe human consumption. All of us freaked out reading this report. We had to find a solution quickly before everyone got sick.

Our source of water for household use was the pumped groundwater from the aquifers, but what we didn't know was that in our part of the city, the groundwater level had fallen by twenty meters, and the water was quite contaminated because of the unsanitary practices of the people. The landlord of our property had installed only one water filter at the point where the ground water entered the above-ground main pipe that took the water to the rooftop water tank; this was clearly not sufficient. So we decided to install two additional water filters; one filter at the point where the pumped water entered the water tank on the rooftop, and another one at the point where the water from the tank entered into the buildings' water pipes. We ensured that all the filters were of the highest quality. In addition, I purchased two water purifiers, one for the kitchen to wash vegetables with purified water, and the other for the dining room.

The huge water shortage in Kabul was not only because of climatic and environmental factors but also because of water mismanagement and poor planning. Since there were no water reservoirs in the city, the groundwater extraction rate was much faster than the recharge rate. The Kabul River ran through the city, but because of a diversion upstream for agricultural use, there was not a drop of water in the river. It had long since dried up, and now it was the dumping ground for the city's garbage; a truly sorry sight to behold.

Kabul River, which was only 700 kilometers long of which 560 kilometers flowed through Afghanistan, originated in the Sanglakh Range, some 72 kilometers west of Kabul. It flowed eastward passing through Kabul and Jalalabad in Afghanistan and entered Pakistan just north of the Khyber Pass. Industrialization and the growing population in the Kabul River Basin in part because of the return of Afghan refugees from Pakistan compounded the environmental degradation, further increasing the pressure on water resources. A 2015 study done by the German Development Bank KfW (Kreditanstalt fur Wiederaufbau: Credit Institute for Reconstruction) revealed that Kabul's groundwater potential was about 44 million cubic meters per year, while the city's water demand was 123.4 million cubic meters, showing a serious imbalance between water supply and demand. The people of Kabul, especially the poor and the powerless, who were the vast majority, had no choice but to turn to drawing water from the receding aquifers.

The new year had started with multiple serious citywide security breach. All my official meetings in the latter half of January 2012 were canceled. We had to go into lockdown because according to intelligence sources, *Hakkani* insurgents from Pakistan had infiltrated into the city to carry out targeted bombing. With movement and other activities severely curtailed during the whole week, the expat staff resorted to watching movies on DVD. I followed suit and watched *Bride and Prejudice* on my laptop; it was a delightful movie, and I loved it for multiple reasons: there was no violence, it was fast paced, it had a sweet ending, and, not the least, famous Indian beauty Aishwarya Rai was the principal actress in the movie.

The first item of business when we came out of the lockdown was to participate in a ribbon-cutting ceremony at the Institute of Diplomacy in the Ministry of Foreign Affairs. The institute was basically dysfunctional because it had neither sufficient classrooms nor modern amenities to facilitate meetings and conference calls. MSI had used USAID funding to build modern classrooms at the institute, and so the U.S. deputy head of mission and I, representing MSI, were invited to formally launch the new setup at the institute.

January 25, 2012. I woke up at 5:30 a.m. to watch Pres. Barack Obama's State of the Union Address. His presidential victory was viewed as a most remarkable phenomenon throughout the world by both friends and foes alike, although perhaps not by the racists and bigots in America. It also generated the expectation that perhaps America was ready to have a female president as well.

Toward the end of the month, we needed some printing to be done, and I sent our office manager Khyber Khan to the Nebraska Printing Press in downtown Kabul. When he returned, he looked all flustered. In a highly agitated manner, he complained to me that while in the premise of the printing press, he was attacked by a chicken-camel, an animal he had never seen before. We didn't know what he was talking about, and I asked him to describe this animal for us. As he proceeded to describe it, it became clear to us that he was talking about an ostrich, which looked like a giant chicken but had a back like a camel! It was hilarious to us expats, and Khyber became the butt of jokes. We learned later that the owner of the Nebraska printers had an enclosure by his shop where he kept exotic species as a hobby.

The month of February started with freezing temperatures. The roads were so icy that vehicular traffic came to a halt, and my office staff dwindled because they had no transport; even those who lived at a walking distance couldn't walk to office because of the icy road condition.

Thanks, however, to the skills of my personal driver, I was able to keep an important appointment in the first week of February with the director general of the High Office of Oversight (HOO), our principal client. The driver designated to me had sided with the Communist regimes during the Soviet takeover in Afghanistan. When the Taliban expelled the Soviets with American help, his life became precarious. He somehow managed to lie very low and bide his time. When the western-supported government came to power, he managed to get a job with a foreign company. From there, by the dint of cautious and intelligent maneuvering and low profile, he came to become my personal driver. He never talked and deliberately remained in the background as much as he could. I found him to be extremely cautious, only occasionally opening up to me after concluding that I was not a threat to him. After the project ended, he asked me to support his application for immigration to the United States. I wrote a strong letter of support for him and his family and also served as a character witness for him, and in late 2019, he finally got his immigration visa to the States. It was a happy ending for him and his family, and I was happy as well that my strong recommendation carried sufficient weight on his behalf.

The meeting with director general Dr. Lodin went off terribly. He was aggressive and blunt, telling me that the international community was to be blamed for the widespread corruption in Afghanistan and that my project and all my personal effort should be directed at the international community because they themselves were very corrupt.

So instead of focusing at the root of corruption, which was western money and payoffs, why am I wasting my time on pursuing corruption among Afghans?

I cannot in all honesty say that Dr. Lodin was wrong about the role of western aid and how these vast sums wittingly or unwittingly spread corruption within the Afghan society like a cancer. But his refusal to play ball made my job that much harder. He told me that the reason he acceded to this meeting was to inform me that my project was targeting the wrong audience and that he was going to tell Pres. Hamid Karzai to tell the Americans that HOO did not need USAID assistance and that my anticorruption project should be shut down. He also said that he will ask the president to shut down the International Monitoring and Evaluation Committee (MEC), whose mandate was to monitor corruption within the Afghan government.

Dr. Lodin's threatening words were not to be dismissed lightly. He was seen as a patriot and carried great weight, having fought the Russians and having lived in exile in Pakistan during the Communist governments in Afghanistan. He was not afraid to speak his mind and expressed his views loudly and forcibly. When I shared this conversation with my colleagues at MEC, they were very disturbed; they wanted my support to rally the donors to their cause. The next day, HOO's director of policy Mr. Khuramji, who was at the meeting between Lodin and me, came to my office to apologize to me for the director general's outburst and rantings against the West and told me that HOO definitely relied on USAID's assistance and requested that we continue with our assistance program.

I discussed my meeting with Dr. Lodin with James Wasserstrom, the USAID's COTR who monitored the project and with whom I consulted once every week. He, too, had been getting annoyed with HOO senior administration's failure to implement the revised standard operating procedures and training that our project had imparted to the HOO staff. In general, the staff at HOO was quite willing to implement all the things that we trained them to do but were unable to deal with their bosses who dragged their feet or simply were unwilling to comply. In light of this, Wasserstrom wanted me to start disinvesting our efforts at HOO and start focusing on working with the Afghan civil society, which appeared to be more promising.

My very competent senior program officer Daud Omari and I launched into developing a new strategy to engage the civil society forthwith. Shortly thereafter, HOO's program director Mr. Zalali requested a meeting with me. I invited him to lunch. He had heard what transpired between Director General Lodin and me and appeared very conciliatory. He said he wanted to smoothen the "rift" in our relationship and to request that we continue supporting them financially. I couldn't tell him that we had reached the point of no return because of the nonchalant and the occasional noncooperative attitude among HOO's senior administrators and that we had already decided to disengage from HOO and focus on nonstate actors in our fight against corruption.

A new complication emerged in the office. Mohammad Amin Khuramji, the director of policy at the HOO, had requested a special favor from the MSI. He wanted the 4A project to hire a relative of his in whatever capacity possible. Not to sour the project's relationship with HOO's policy director, his female relative was hired as an office secretary even though it was a redundant position. She was in her early teens and without any training for the secretarial position. It fell upon us to train her up as a secretary.

However, she didn't seem to be much interested to work and was always late to office. There was strict attendance protocol that all staff had to abide by, but she kept on being tardy to work. The HR manager sat her down and explained to her the importance of attending office on time. A second sitting warned her that her disregard for timely attendance was sending the wrong signal to the rest of the staff. And the third sitting warned her that she is likely to get fired if she continued to be late.

Seeing no improvement in her conduct, the HR manager came to me for advice. He felt that firing her may not go down well with Khuramji, and yet that is exactly what he needed to do, unless I wished to speak to her one-on-one. I agreed and asked him to send her to me. She came and sat down motionless with head bowed. I asked her if she understood the office attendance rule; she said yes. I asked her whether she was facing some difficulty at home that is causing her to come late to work; she said no. I then asked her if I could help her in any way.

She took a pause and said no. Then she said, "You see, sir, there are these boys in my neighborhood who wait for me to come out in the morning, and then they follow me all the way to office." Sensing a cultural conflict, I offered to change her office hours so that she could perhaps avoid those boys. Or send someone to directly confront those boys, but she immediately said no. Then she continued, "I have to stop several times for them to catch up with me because they are soooo slow, that's why I am always late to work!"

I realized then that being a teenage girl, she liked being looked at and pursued by boys in the highly restrictive Afghan society where there was very little scope for boys and girls to mix and enjoy each other's company. I told her that I was sorry she was having that problem but we wouldn't be able to retain her. I took up the matter delicately with Khuramji, and he acknowledged that he understood my concern. He thanked me for hiring her in the first place. I was relieved that the matter was settled quietly and without any repercussion.

Following Wasserstrom's instruction to start focusing on civil society, my programming staff and I had a series of discussions on the challenges faced by the nonstate actors—NGOs, CSOs, print and media journalists, parliamentarians, academics—and where we should invest our future time, effort, and resources. I then apprised MSI home office (HO) in Washington DC about the discussions we had among the project staff, the conclusions we reached, and the strategy we drafted, and sought their input and approval. Bert Spector, the technical director of the project, agreed with our new strategy. He suggested that one of our civil society engagements could be with the Afghan anticorruption fighters.

MSI had initiated such a program in Ukraine with reasonable success. Called the Citizens Legal Advocacy Office (CLAO), it comprised a group of lawyers who were willing to offer pro bono legal service to citizens caught in the web of corruption. Any citizen wanting a passport, driver's license, or business permit, or wanting to pay his utility bills or getting his child admitted to school, etc., without having to pay a bribe but couldn't do so could go to CLAO and request their assistance. The CLAO lawyer would register the complaint and take the citizen through a series of steps to remedy the situation.

Our project embraced this program wholeheartedly. We called on the Afghanistan Independent Bar Association (AIBA) and proposed the CLAO program to them. We received immediate positive response with several lawyers willing to offer pro bono service during their off hours, which worked out beautifully because it coincided with the afterwork availability of the complainants. We funded a centrally located office with the required furniture, computers and printers, telephones and Internet, and other amenities. We hired an administrative assistant to manage the office. We advertised this service through social media outlets, radio, TV, newspapers, and billboards. Pretty soon, there were long line-ups in front of the office, and managing the expectations of hundreds of frustrated citizens who were victims of corruption became a real challenge. We were very happy to learn at the end of the year that the program's success rate was 87 percent, a remarkable achievement by the standards of any anticorruption program.

In the middle of February 2012, I had a meeting with Seema Ghani, the executive director of MEC who briefed me on their meeting with President Karzai. Seema informed me that HOO Director General Lodin had his meeting with the president and strongly voiced his sentiments against the international assistance Afghanistan was receiving, against my project, and against MEC. She said that the president instructed MEC to henceforth focus their monitoring efforts on the international aid money and corruption associated with that and leave domestic corruption issues to HOO. This was not MEC's primary mandate, and the donors were against it all along.

It was a dilemma for many of us in the development field because we were unanimous in our belief that the Afghan civil service was quite corrupt, but many of us also knew that Dr. Lodin was right about abuse in the international assistance program and about donors' refusal even to acknowledge that such abuse was indeed taking place. MEC was in a delicate situation and had to tread carefully. Luckily for us, we were a USAID project and within the ambit of the U.S.-Afghan bilateral assistance agreement. Our relations with Lodin remained correct, while the two HOO directors, Khuramji and Zalali, endeavored to restore normalcy like before to access our expertise and money.

Urs

February 18, 2012. I spoke with my mother, who was visiting her parental home in Lostimanika, Bangladesh, to attend the annual Urs. She told me that she was very happy to see Nana's elderly disciples and to recognize even their grown-up children. She went to Lostimanika every February to celebrate Urs, which was a commemorative gathering of my nana's disciples to celebrate his life of piety. On February 2 every year, this semireligious gathering spent several days to remember him, sing devotional songs, dance, and share meals together. Each person or family brought some token gifts—a cow or a goat, some rice, some fruits from their trees, some fish from their pond, or some cash—as their way of showing their love and remembrance.

As a child, I had attended many such Urs gathering, and it was always a quasi-religious, solemn occasion but sprinkled with some festivities and merriment for the children. After Nana's death, my nani organized the Urs each year, and after her death, Uncle Matiur Rahman has been managing it. One would have thought that with the passing of time, Nana's disciples would have been gone by now and Urs would lose its magnetism, but, interestingly, the turnout for this celebration seemed to keep growing each year. It was unclear whether this was an indication of more and more people looking for spiritual guidance in this fast-paced world. Be that as it may, it is clear that thousands of people in Lostimanika and the neighboring as well as far-off villages looked forward to this event every February.

Back in Kabul, the following week turned out to be quite unsettling. There were huge demonstrations in the streets of Kabul, and schools were shut done. Even the Afghan parliament was raucous. The issue was the disturbing news that some U.S. troops in the Bagram Air Base, about forty miles from Kabul, had burned the Quran. The anti-U.S.

sentiment, even hostility, was obvious, and it pervaded the entire country. Again, we had to go into lockdown to protect ourselves from irate Afghans who had poured into the streets with weapons on the second day of demonstration. I instructed all my staff and particularly the security guards to maintain a very low profile and remain invisible so as not to provoke the demonstrators or our neighbors. We had to ensure that none of the armor on the rooftop trained on the streets below and on neighboring rooftops was visible from outside and that the CCTV cameras gave us a 360-degree view of our surroundings. We also posted extra guards to monitor at night. The anti-West demonstrations continued for several days, keeping us tense and guessing what next.

Just when we thought that maybe the demonstrations and violence will peter out soon, violence flared up again. On February 25, two American military advisors assigned to the Ministry of the Interior (MOI) were shot dead point-blank by Afghan police working inside the MOI. The advisors were working in civilian clothes surrounded by Afghan military colleagues, but that could not prevent their death. The loss of innocent lives was tragic, and it put a stop to assigning U.S. military personnel to work side by side with Afghan counterparts in the MOI sine die.

In addition, the UN compound in the ancient city of Kunduz, in Kunduz Province, in northern Afghanistan bordering Tajikistan, was attacked, thereby prolonging the tense situation further. As if that was not enough, two weeks later, on March 11, a U.S. soldier went berserk and gunned down a number of Afghan civilians, throwing the whole country into chaos. Although we were easing our lockdown, it forced us to go into high-security mode once again. But this time, the situation got so bad that four days later, on March 15, Assistant Operations Manager Maria Isabel Osorio (Issa) and I had an urgent Skype discussion on an evacuation plan for TCNs (third country nationals). During these very tense weeks, my meetings with the COTR at the USAID were canceled. Because of these unsettling developments, MSI sent its contract officer Bill Rich, from headquarters, to assess the situation and its impact on our contract with the USAID.

The fretful month of February finally ended, but March began with the generator breaking down. Since it would take a few days to fix it, we rented another generator to restore our business activities, but as luck would have it, it caught fire as soon as it was installed. We had to rent a second generator, which thankfully worked. The scheduled meeting with the representatives of the Afghan Coalition against Corruption (AfCAC), a coalition of Afghan NGOs and CSOs that we helped to create, went really well. I was reassured of their potential to spearhead the anticorruption plans and activities of civil society and make significant headway in combating corruption.

March 8, 2012. Gurkha security assistant Hari Thapa left for New Delhi to get his Afghan work permit renewed at the Afghan embassy in India. Apparently for people in the foreign security services operating in Afghanistan, the security work authorization had to be done outside the country. Hari asked me if I would like anything from India, and I took the opportunity to ask him to bring me several tubes of mehndi. The mehndi or henna party was a prewedding celebration in the cultures of South Asia. The red-orange paste created from the powdered dry leaves of the henna plant left decorative mehndi designs when applied to the bride's palms, back of hands, wrists, and feet, and it was an essential part of the wedding celebration that extended over several days.

In mid-March, the International Anti-Corruption Summer Academy (IACSA), which was based in Laxenburg, Austria, announced its 2012 summer session to start in July, and I decided to send Daud Omari to expose him to the lessons learned from the global anticorruption work, to provide him with a strong incentive to engage actively with civil society, and as a recognition of his dedicated work. MSI head office in DC concurred with my decision. MSI was in good spirits because they had just won the contract for USAID's MISTI project in Afghanistan. I sent a strong letter of reference to IACSA on Daud's behalf.

March 20, 2012. It was Nowruz, or the beginning of the Afghan New Year, which commenced on the first day of spring (March equinox) and signified spiritual renewal and physical rejuvenation, as well as the time to express gratitude and look to the future with hope and optimism. Although not a religious holiday, it was rooted in the Zoroastrian religion and was celebrated for the last three thousand years in Iran, Afghanistan, the Central Asian Republics, and wherever the Parsis community was settled such as in northern Pakistan and in parts of India.

The number of days of celebration varied from country to country, when people greeted each other, saying, "Nowruz Mubarak" (Blessed New Year) or "Nowruz Pirouz" (Victorious New Year). The celebrations in Afghanistan varied among its ethnic communities. The Hazara people, for example, who constituted at least 9 percent of the Afghan population and were located in central Afghanistan and in Badakhshan, treated Nowruz like the Muslim Eid and visited relatives and exchanged gifts. However, the Tajik people, who constituted about 38 percent of the population and were mostly located in the north, northeastern, and western Afghanistan, seemed to celebrate Nowruz with more passion by participating in buzkashi and in wrestling matches, in addition to going on family picnics and relishing traditional food.

Buzkashi

Buzkashi, which literally meant "goat pulling," was a traditional Central Asian sport in which players mounted on horses sought to capture a goat or calf carcass and place it in the "scoring circle." The rules did not seem to be the same for all regions. In Kabul, the playground was a square layout with ten horseback riders on each team, of whom only five riders from each team competed until halftime, which was forty-five minutes long, and was replaced by the next five riders on each side in the second half, with a referee supervising the game. According to one description, in general,

> competition is typically fierce. Traditionally, the sport is mainly conducted based upon rules such as not whipping a fellow rider intentionally or deliberately knocking him off his horse. Riders usually wear heavy clothing and head protection to protect themselves against other players' whips and boots. The boots usually have high

heels that lock into the saddle of the horse to help the rider lean on the side of the horse while trying to pick up the goat. Games can last for several days, and the winning team receives a prize; top players are often sponsored by wealthy Afghans.

A buzkashi player is called a chapandaz, who is usually in his forties because of the rigorous physical fitness required. Similarly, horses used in buzkashi also undergo severe training. A player does not necessarily own the horse. Horses are usually owned by landlords and very rich people wealthy enough to look after and provide for training facilities for such horses. However, a master chapandaz can choose to select any horse and the owner of the horse usually wants his horse to be ridden by a master chapandaz as a winning horse also brings pride to the owner.

The game consists of two main forms: Tudabarai and Qarajai. Tudabarai is considered to be the simpler form of the game. In this version, the goal is simply to grab the goat and move in any direction until clear of the other players. In Qarajai, players must carry the carcass around a flag or marker at one end of the field, then throw it into a scoring circle ("Circle of Justice") at the other end. The riders will carry a whip to fend off opposing horses and riders. When the whip is not in use such as when the rider needs both hands to steer the horse and secure the carcass, the whip is typically carried in the teeth.

The calf in a buzkashi game is normally beheaded and disemboweled and has 2 limbs cut off. It is then soaked in cold water for 24 hours before play to toughen it. Occasionally sand is packed into the carcass to give it extra weight. Though a goat is used when no calf is available, a calf is less likely to disintegrate during the game. While players may not strap the calf to their bodies or saddles, it is acceptable and a common practice to wedge the calf under one leg in order to free up the hands.

While it was a much-beloved six-hundred-year-old traditional sport originating among the nomadic Turks of Central Asia, during my entire five years of work in Afghanistan, I could not stomach the thought of watching the carcass of a goat or calf being manhandled during the buzkashi sport, and so I declined an invitation from a provincial governor to attend one, and I have no regrets.

The rest of March was hectic with lots of project-related issues such as attending to contractual issues, making financial adjustments for the next six months, and finishing up the quarterly performance report before my R & R leave from March 28. Also, I had been trying to secure an additional armored vehicle from the USAID stockpile. My project had only one B6 armored vehicle for my use.

The B6 was a high-security vehicle with its body encased in 7.5 mm thick ballistic steel capable of stopping armor piercing and penetrator rounds. It was designed to be highly resistant to explosions caused by roadside and suicide bombs. The rest of the project vehicles were soft skins. In light of the constant suicide attacks and bomb blasts in the city, it bothered me that my Afghan staff moved around the city to do project work in soft skins, thereby putting their lives in danger. MSI was unwilling to procure or even lease another B6 because the cost in either case was huge. Plus with a gross weight double that of a normal land cruiser, the bulletproof cruiser was a gas guzzler and went only five kilometers per liter in the city and about ten kilometers per liter with a diesel engine and worse with a petrol engine. I learned that another USAID project had ended, and the B6 vehicle of that project was returned to the USAID. So I talked with both MSI and the USAID to allow me to get that B6 free of cost, and they both agreed. I wanted to complete the paperwork to secure the B6 before I went on leave.

A potential security development that could have delayed my departure date precipitated on the day before my leave date. The Taliban terrorists had managed to plant their agents inside the Ministry of Defense (MOD) and were planning a mass suicide attack on army buses, but alert security personnel within the ministry were able to stop it by seizing eleven suicide vests. That was a huge relief for all of us because it would have killed hundreds of soldiers and ministry staff, as well as be a huge psychological blow to the Afghan Armed Forces. I was able to depart for Dubai, catch my 2:30 a.m. Emirate flight from Dubai to London Heathrow, where Mumu would join me for our 3:15 p.m. Air Canada flight to Ottawa the next day.

My arrival in Ottawa, however, was marred by the airline losing my luggage. Luckily, all my shopping from Kabul was in my carry-on and came home intact. One of my lost luggage contained a large quantity of Afghan biryani packed by my chef. Two days after my arrival, airport customs called me to pick up my luggage. The customs official asked me to open my luggage for checking, and I was shocked to see the biryani spread all over my clothes, soiling even my suit. Nipa was really looking forward to the Afghan biryani and in fact had insisted that I have my Afghan chef cook it for her, so it was a great disappointment to see it all go to waste. The customs officer pointed out that I had failed to declare the biryani in my declaration form and fined me $400. Not only did I have to discard all the clothes in the suitcase because they became unwearable and pay a hefty fine, but also Nipa couldn't taste the biryani at all. It was a hard lesson to learn, and I told myself that I had deserved it.

But we had to get past this disappointment and focus on enjoying our home visit. Ever since Mumu and I left Ottawa, we always tried to plan our leave from work in a way that would allow all four of us to spend our time together and perhaps go on an out-of-town trip somewhere. This time, we planned it so that we could go visit relatives in Long Island, New York.

My sixteen-day leave was soon over, and on April 14, Mumu and I flew back to London Heathrow, where we had lunch together in a bistro in terminal 5, after which Mumu took the taxi to her home in Wembley, and I boarded my flight for Dubai and Kabul. A few days later, on April 17, I learned that my eldest uncle had passed away in Bangladesh. The news from Bangkok from my youngest brother, Tawfiq, the next day was better; my mom's cardiologist, Dr. Visuit Vivekaphirat, at the Bumrungrad International Hospital, had given her a clean bill of health. Tawfiq and Mom had flown to Bangkok for her medical checkup.

Back to the Grinder

One morning, I went to the dining room to make myself some coffee but couldn't find my mug that I had brought from Ottawa. The chef informed me that during my absence, our IT manager Mirwali had accidentally knocked it off the tray onto the floor and broken it. That same afternoon, Mirwali came to my office with a new mug that he had purchased to replace the one he had broken. He apologized and handed me the new mug. I thanked him and paid him fifty Afghani, which he refused to take, but I insisted, saying that it was the thought that counted.

Fully refreshed from my vacation, I plunged into the daily routine of running a multimillion-dollar project. On May 8, the Standard Chartered Bank (SCB) in Kabul, which held the project's Afghani and dollar accounts, informed us that it had decided to shut down its retail banking operation in Afghanistan and that it had reached an agreement with the Afghan International Bank (AIB) to hand over the accounts of all its retail clients. After consulting with home office (HO) in DC, the project finance and accounts manager set out to transfer our accounts to AIB. It required once again three signatures: that of the finance director in the HO, my signature, and the signature of the finance and accounts manager, Mujibur Rahman. When I first met Mujib, I told him that his name was similar to the founding father of Bangladesh, Sheikh Mujibur Rahman. He replied that in fact his father had named him after the Bangladeshi leader. It was nice to know that Sheikh Mujib was revered in Afghanistan as well. The transition of the project's banking facilities from the SCB to AIB went smoothly without affecting our project work.

But for me, potential danger was lurking around the corner as usual. On April 23, we received a high-security alert from the foreign intelligence-gathering community in Kabul that the terrorists had offered five lakh rupees (Rs 500,000 ~ US$3,500) for the death of each foreigner in Afghanistan. It was a shoot-to-kill order, and every foreigner was a fair target. What made it worse was that there was plenty of disenchanted young people in Afghanistan who had been indoctrinated in the extremist rhetoric, and the Americans were at the top of their hit list. We immediately consulted with the Afghan security forces and were able to receive from them some AK-47s and pistols to beef up the security in the compound.

It didn't help that a week later, on May 1, President Obama paid a top-secret five-hour visit to Kabul to sign the Strategic Partnership Agreement (SPA) to set the framework for long-term U.S.-Afghan political, economic, and security cooperation. Upon learning this news, Taliban insurgents launched simultaneous attacks on the Green Village—a fortified compound that housed private security companies and contractors for foreign nongovernmental organization and foreign nationals—and on Baron Hotel, which was also a preferred residence for foreign organizations and individuals. The insurgents managed to kill seven foreigners and inflicted significant damage to both locations.

The security atmosphere in Kabul became so tense that that there was immediate lockdown by foreign agencies, projects, and businesses, and all intracity movement was suspended. Even on normal days, I had to strictly adhere to security protocol. Whenever I had a meeting outside the compound, I had to inform my security staff at least twelve hours ahead of the meeting. Gareth would then identify all possible routes to the meeting place, conduct a reconnaissance by actually traveling to the meeting place himself, identify safe houses en route if any should we come under attack, and coordinate the upcoming itinerary with the security manager of the office building where my meeting was scheduled to be held.

On the day of the meeting, Gareth would double-check intelligence reports for that day, fuel up the armored cruiser, and place my bulletproof Kevlar vest and helmet next to me on the backseat in case I had to put it on. During actual travel, he would be in constant communication with our security in the compound whose job was to monitor our movement on the TV screen and keep us informed of any security-related development. This whole ritual was so time consuming, tedious, tension-filled, and costly that I had asked MSI to allow me to travel in a soft skin. I argued that I looked South Asian, my complexion was nonwhite, and I could easily blend in with the Afghan public, which would enhance my security rather than travel in an armored vehicle, thereby becoming a moving target to the terrorists. My request was denied, and the reason for this, which I learned later, was that if something happened to me, the insurance claim against the MSI or the USAID could be huge.

Our building was two storied with finished basement. The conference room, the gym, a few office rooms, the utility room, and a small storage room were in the basement. The main floor was all offices. The second floor consisted of my bedroom, my office, and a couple of additional bedrooms where my Gurkha body guards stayed. The security operations room and the safe room were on the rooftop.

One night, I was just falling asleep when I heard someone running up and down the stairs. Alarmed, I got out of bed and cautiously opened my bedroom door to see what was going on. I saw Gareth, head of our security operations. He stopped when he saw me coming out of my room. He was in his gym shorts and T-shirt with a large army sack on his back. I asked him what he was doing and what was in the sack. He was panting a little and said that the sack contained bricks weighing ninety kilograms in total. He went on to explain, "Sir, you are eighty kilograms in weight. When we travel outside of Kabul, if we are attacked by insurgents and our vehicle is disabled by bomb blast, and you are hurt, I have to be able to put you on my back and run nonstop half a mile flat to carry you to safety." I paused for a moment to allow that to sink into me and then said, "Oh, OK, carry on."

I returned to my room, and as I pondered over him running up and down those six flights of stairs to retain his stamina and strength, I marveled at this forty-something person's commitment to my safety and commitment to his job. That day, for the first time, I understood why the project was paying him so much and why about 31 percent of my budget was consumed by security needs. I developed a whole new perspective on security and a new sense of loyalty to my security staff.

With increasingly higher threat levels in Kabul, I decided to try out an alternative. From that month onward, I requested the people with whom I had the meeting to come to our compound instead of me going over to their place of business. Everyone responded positively to this request because they appreciated that we were more threatened than they. I had to make an exception, though.

I continued to go out to meet with Afghan officials with the rank of director general and above because they were quite sensitive to their position and status, and I did not want to give them any offense. I felt maintaining this protocol was necessary to secure cooperation with high officials and for the success of our project work. This arrangement lasted until the end of the project. The only place my proposed arrangement did not apply was when I met the COTR, the USAID representative to whom I reported once every week, because, as an American, he was a greater target and more threatened than I was. The assistant COTR—first, Leslie Schaffer, and then Regina McKenzie—who were also American, did, however, come to our compound when they had to replace the COTR for the weekly briefing, and I suspect it was because they wanted to get away from the confinement of the embassy grounds.

The security measures extended as well to activities not related to the project. For example, I couldn't go to a barber's shop for a haircut. Every time I needed a haircut, Anurag called the barber to the compound. The barber was thoroughly vetted ahead of time, and during the haircut, either Anurag or another security guard stood by to protect me in case there was an attack. One could never be sure who was working for the insurgents or whether a previously vetted barber had been subsequently coopted by the insurgents.

Afghans who provided services to foreigners were the primary target for indoctrination and recruitment, and therefore we couldn't afford to let down our guard. It was always hard for us expats to relax and enjoy the moment. The rare exception was when we received some good news that distracted us from our immediate concerns, and on May 24,

I did receive a piece of good news that warmed my heart. My nephew Brandon got invited by *American Idol* to attend boot camp in Los Angeles in September. All of us brothers and sisters, nephews and nieces were totally excited at the news. His parents, Shahalam and Luann, were planning to accompany him. It was a temporary respite from the daily tension, however fleeting the moment was!

A Spot of Paradise

Since frequent security breaches in the city forced us to go on lockdown and suspend our project work, we had to work extra hard, and for me extra hours in addition to my six-day workweek, to make up for lost project time. Even during lockdown, when often the project staff could not come to work, I had to work nonstop. It was getting very strenuous, and I desperately needed a break. I also needed a breath of fresh air away from the confines of my compound where I was stuck for weeks and be away from Kabul.

I asked my security to get the intelligence report on the Panjshir Valley up north. We received the message that there was no insurgent activity in the valley at the time and that it was safe to visit. I decided to spend my first Friday in June, my day off, in the Panjshir Valley, or the Valley of Five Lions. Located about ninety miles northeast of Kabul near the Hindu Kush mountain range, the valley was famous for its scenic beauty and for its world-class natural emeralds.

My security, Gareth and Anurag, two office staff, Samad and Khyber, and I set off on our three-hour journey early morning. The road from Kabul went past the Bagram Air Base and then meandered alongside a stark mountainous terrain with the narrow Panjshir River on one side, making it a journey through what seemed like a spot of paradise. The natural beauty and serenity of the valley were overwhelming, except for the occasional carcass of a Soviet T-62 commando tank lying by the roadside, a stark reminder of the Soviet invasion of Afghanistan in December 1979 when the Soviet Fortieth Army rolled across Afghanistan's northern border to prop up the pro-Soviet Communist regime of Babrak Karmal and his People's Democratic Party of Afghanistan.

The number of destroyed tanks and artillery that we passed was a testament to the failed attempt by the Soviet Army to take the Panjshir Valley because of the stiff resistance put up by the legendary Afghan Mujahideen commander Ahmad Shah Massoud and his guerillas, which earned Massoud the nickname of "Lion of Panjshir." Subsequently, he had also prevented the Taliban from taking the valley, which earned him their wrath. Massoud was assassinated on September 9, 2001, by an Al-Qaeda hit squad that posed as journalists with a bomb concealed in a TV camera, two days before 9/11. It was considered by the Afghan public as a day of tragedy. After the Taliban was ousted from power, Pres. Hamid Karzai posthumously conferred the title of "National Hero" on Massoud, and September 9 is celebrated as a national holiday, Massoud Day. He is revered by his followers, who call him *Amer Sahib-e-Shahid* (our martyred commander), and his poster is seen on public walls, inside public buildings, in street corners, and in shops throughout Afghanistan.

We stopped at a couple of places to take pictures on top of those demolished tanks. We then drove all the way to the mausoleum complex of Massoud on top of a hill overlooking the valley; one could see his home in the distance from the hill. The approach to the seventy-five-foot-tall, ash-colored stone mausoleum with multiple arches and a dark-colored dome was lined with a long water fountain in the center and a number of captured Soviet tanks and arsenal on one side, perhaps to remind visitors of Massoud's bravery and tenacity as a guerilla fighter. Inside the mausoleum was an open space with a giant photo of Massoud on a wall facing the entrance door. Past that, in the center of the mausoleum was an enclosed space where lay a black marveled tomb covered with a raised sheet of glass that housed the remains of the commander. Viewing the tomb and reading the writings on the tomb about his exploits were a somber experience indeed. Outside the mausoleum complex was a mosque under construction and a gift shop that was closed on the day of our visit.

We spent about an hour in the mausoleum complex taking pictures

447

of the complex, the valley, and its surroundings before setting off on our return journey. Driving alongside the Panjshir River, which in places narrowed into crystal-clear rapids, was an experience to remember. I stopped at a couple of places and took pictures to remind me in the future that I had been privileged to visit this enchanting valley. It was already lunchtime, and so we stopped at a roadside restaurant, with its rear side extending over the rapid waters perched on stilts.

As we waited for our food to arrive, Samad, Khyber, and I sat on the edge of the open bamboo walkway on the backside of the restaurant and dipped our feet in the cold, fast-flowing mountain water. As I marveled at the snowcapped mountains in the distance, I remarked that this was *behesth* (heaven). Then I asked Samad, who was a Tajik, what was "heaven" in his language. He immediately replied, "*Jannat,*" and then added, "*Behesth* also." I then asked Khyber, who was a Pashtun, the same question. Khyber was quiet, and I could see that he was searching his mind for the appropriate word. I prompted him once more, and he was still quiet. Then Samad stepped in and with an impish smile answered, "Sir, Khyber is silent because there is no word for heaven in Pashtu. You see, the Pashtun people are constantly fighting and killing each other here on earth, and so they never go to heaven. That's why the word *heaven* does not exist in his language!" I smiled and said, "Is that so, Khyber?" Khyber smiled back and shrug his shoulders, taking the needling in stride. We enjoyed the freshly prepared hot food and were then back on the road, regretting that we were leaving behind the beauty and tranquility of the Panjshir Valley. It was a great outing for all of us and a much-needed break from the stress and tension of living in Kabul.

4A Project Activities

The project work continued nonstop despite the unstable security conditions. By the second year of my taking over of this anticorruption endeavor, we had launched ten activities, most of them in the province of Kabul but some also in other provinces. One of those activities was to implement asset declaration by all high-ranking government officials and civil servants above a certain administrative grade.

Article 154 of the Afghan Constitution and Article 12 of the Law on Overseeing Implementation of Anti-Administrative Corruption Strategy obliged the High Office of Oversight and Anti-Corruption (HOOAC) to register and publish the wealth of high-ranking officials. But this was never implemented. We confronted this challenge head-on. First, we had to revise the existing asset declaration form to conform to international standards; the existing form was a joke. Next, we had to train the officials on how to accurately fill out these forms. We undertook a series of workshops where we trained two target groups simultaneously, the staff of HOOAC and the Afghan officials and civil servants, to correctly fill out the forms. The USAID was quite excited about this endeavor and was looking forward to the asset declarations by the corrupt senior officials of the government.

While the workshops were successful, the subsequent results were less than satisfying. The tendency to falsify wealth declaration was widespread. Those who had unaccountable amounts of wealth lied about their actual possessions, while those who hadn't made enough over-reported their wealth to create space for wealth accumulation through corruption in the future. In 2014, at a high-level meeting, I bumped into Gen. Abdul Rashid Dostum, first vice president in Pres. Ashraf Ghani's first cabinet, and asked him who filled out his asset declaration form. He retorted, "Why?" I said, "Your declaration stated that your net worth was less than US$100K. This obviously cannot be true!" Getting serious, he asked, "Why not?" I said, "Because I was told that you have a number of Arabian stallions, which alone would be worth that much." He replied, "I did not know horses were assets!"

We were unable to complete our asset declaration task because of noncooperation by many high-ranking officials and outright lies and deception by civil servants. The HOOAC whom we had trained to pursue this task was hesitant to irritate the members of the power structure and alienate senior public officials. It was one of only two activities in the 4A Project that resulted in disappointment. The other was the failure of the senior administrative officials to properly implement the various trainings given to their staff.

Another activity was to work with the youth, to inculcate in them early on notions of integrity, ethical behavior, and civic responsibility. We adopted multiple strategies to draw their attention, to educate them, and to instill in them appropriate values. Our goal was to target all levels of the educational system, starting from grade one all the way to the university.

We contracted a private video company to produce several video clips carrying powerful anticorruption messages. One clip showed a youngster sitting on his bed, tears in his eyes, bouncing a soccer ball. He usually played soccer after school, and when his mom inquired why he was not playing that afternoon, he didn't answer. The next scene showed his mother telling his father, who just came home from office, that their son was crying in his room. The father goes to his son's room and, after repeated inquiries, hears his son say, "My friends don't want to play with me anymore." "Why?" asks his father. "They said that they won't play with someone whose father is a corrupt man who demands bribes," replies the son. The father goes silent. He walks over to his son's bed to sit beside him, but his son gets up and moves away. The clip ends showing the father sitting there alone and staring at an empty space as he ponders his son's words.

A second clip showed a beggar sitting outside the gate of a mosque with his cap in front of him. Mosque goers donate money into his cap as they enter or leave the mosque. Next, a Mercedes car stops in front of the mosque, and a rich man wearing expensive shoes and Rolex watch gets out of the car. As he reaches out to put some money into the cap, the beggar puts up his palm in front of the rich man's hand and says, "I do not accept ill-gotten money even if it is alms!" The clip ends showing the rich man taken aback and several of the mosque goers staring at the rich man with a look of disgust.

We ran these and other powerful videos in Afghanistan's private television stations, and unofficial polling showed that they strongly resonated among the youth and the old alike. The USAID was particularly happy noting their potential impact on Afghanistan's corruption-ridden society. We also converted them into audio clips, since the great majority of Afghans did not have access to television and regularly listened to their favorite radio stations; the impact was even greater.

We also planned to produce a booklet containing citations from the Holy Quran that spoke to honesty, integrity, responsibilities toward parents, elders, and the authorities, and other injunctions that helped to build character and strong community. We soon learned that the Asia Foundation in Kabul had already produced such a booklet. We then negotiated with them to use their booklet. We distributed the booklets to the junior and secondary-level students during anticorruption sessions with them.

Since the common people of Afghanistan were deeply religious and attended the mosque regularly, I was convinced that the *khudba* (sermon) by the imam during the *zuhr* (afternoon) prayer on Fridays could be a powerful tool to convey anticorruption messages to the public. I consulted a few imams and floated the idea of working with them to condition the public's thoughts and actions through religious teachings, and I was quite pleased to see them embrace this wholeheartedly. But it was vetoed by the USAID on the grounds that the U.S. government could not be seen to be promoting a particular religion. I did not see this as promoting Islam but simply as a mechanism to change the mind-set and behavior of the people and so disagreed with their interpretation, but my explanations and entreaties fell on deaf ears. Of all the activities that the 4A Project undertook in the course of its duration, this proposal was the only one that the USAID did not approve, and I still believe that we missed a wonderful opportunity to utilize a powerful tool to secure our project objective.

We targeted the high school and university-level students by adopting the strategy of holding televised anticorruption quiz competitions. A booklet comprising one hundred questions and answers on anticorruption, good governance, ethics, integrity, morality, religious teachings, civic responsibility, the Afghan Constitution, the Afghan government, etc., was distributed to the students and teachers ahead of time. During the televised anticorruption quiz competition, questions from the booklet were asked by the moderator, and whichever side answered the question correctly earned points. The team with the highest points won the competition and received the trophy and prizes.

The quiz was divided into segments, and between each segment, there was entertainment such as favorite songs, dances, and comedic acts to entertain the audience in the debate hall who were mostly parents, teachers, and students of the competing schools. This nationally televised quiz educated not only the students but also their teachers and parents, and the wider audience tuned in for the quiz; it was a huge success. The first quiz competition was between the students of the Construction and Technology Faculties of Kabul Polytechnic University and was held on national television on May 16, where MEC chairman Drago Kos and I spoke before the audience and distributed the prizes to the quiz participants. Several such quiz competitions were held during the duration of the 4A Project.

Another strategy was to organize sporting events among high school students. One hour before the sporting event, we did a PowerPoint presentation and a question-and-answer session on anticorruption followed by the sporting competition. Parents who came to witness the matches were also invited to the anticorruption sessions before the games. Volleyball and football matches were organized between schools. Female students competed in volleyball; girls playing football was considered too unfeminine and culturally unacceptable. The final match of the girls' volleyball competition was held at the Suriya Girls High School on June 19. It was an exciting match and was covered by several television stations and the BBC Pastu Program. I was asked to give away the winner's cup. The final of the boys soccer match was between Habibia and Amani Boys High Schools on June 28. After the trophy ceremony, the participants in the field and the members of the audience were treated to a tasty chicken burger meal.

We actively sought partners among foreign NGOs and projects of other donors working in Afghanistan to draw them closer to the anticorruption effort. In the month of May 2012, we reached out to the Tawanmandi Project, which was managed by the British Council housed within the British embassy in Kabul. This project also endeavored to strengthen the work of the civil society and expressed its interest to jointly fund two projects we had launched. One was the Citizens Legal Advocacy Office (CLAO), which sought to offer pro bono service to victims of corruption, as mentioned earlier. They monitored CLAO's activities for several months. The other project was to strengthen the Afghan Coalition against Corruption (AfCAC), which we had created to bring all Afghan NGOs, CSOs, and volunteer organizations under one umbrella—namely, AfCAC—which then could spearhead a national anticorruption effort.

A primary benefit of this effort was to reach out to the rural and remote areas of Afghanistan that were inaccessible to us and thereby spread our effort throughout the country. Having received my commitment to provide them with the needed technical assistance and to fund them, AfCAC made remarkable progress within a short period under Daud's guidance. Meanwhile, the UK Foreign and Commonwealth Office (FCO) had been monitoring our work in Afghanistan and committed $100,000 toward our projects.

An Unexpected Boomerang?

To launch AfCAC, the first step was to invite around one hundred NGOs, CSOs, and CBOs to a conference in our large conference room. As the head of the project, I took the floor to deliver the welcoming remarks. I noticed that there were only five women sitting in the front row, and the rest hundred or so participants were all men, many of them bearded and dressed in white *alkhalla*. I opened my remarks by saying,

"Friends, Ladies and Gentlemen, we are very pleased to see so many enthusiastic participants who have come from all across Afghanistan to join our anticorruption endeavor. This gives us great hope that we can work together to improve the lives of the Afghan people. I am pleased to see that some of our sisters have also responded to our call. Of course, I would have been happier if there were many more women participants joining us in this important work . . ."

After I finished my remarks, Daud took over with the PowerPoint presentations. When it was time for the first health break, the participants dispersed to have snacks and tea/coffee. A senior bearded alkhalla-clad gentleman approached me and asked if he could have a word with me. We walked over to the compound's beautiful rose garden. The gentleman looked me straight in the eye and said, "Dr. Hassan, I am surprised you want more women to participate. As a Bangladeshi, you should know better. Look what Hasina and Khaleda have done to your country. They have ruined it. You want the same thing to happen to us?"

I was totally unprepared for that remark. First of all, I did not foresee that the observation I made about women's participation in the country's development and governance would boomerang on me like that. Hasina Wazed and Khaleda Zia were prime ministers of Bangladesh and on the whole had done no worse than the men who ran the country. While I was impressed that he and perhaps other Afghans as well were quite abreast with Bangladeshi and, I suspect, South Asian politics, I told him that I begged to disagree, and that women leaders have been and could be as effective as men, if not more, in running an enterprise including running a country. I pointed out that there were many examples around the world of strong women leaders. I also pointed out that in most countries of the world, percentage wise, women were in the majority, and to deny them their rightful place in society and to not tap their intellect and ability were a terrible loss to the country. I could see that he was unconvinced; he nodded his head in disagreement as we walked back to the conference hall.

Breaking that mind-set became a priority for me. I was determined more than ever to make sure that we not only reached out to the NGOs headed by women but also built partnerships between men-led and women-led civil society organizations to build some mutual respect, appreciation, and working camaraderie, and instructed Daud to make that a high priority in our work. I am glad to say that the project was able to partner with many women-led enterprises, as AfCAC broadened its base and reached out all across the country. On June 23, we held an important workshop in Kabul of civil society organizations where their activities and achievements were shared with the public. It was broadcast by several TV stations. Work with AfCAC continued with enthusiasm and at full speed.

Meanwhile, I received happy news from home. My wife Nipa was awarded a certificate of "The Best Spirit" by her office. I felt that she totally deserved it. She had been working for Revenue Canada for quite a few years. It was not really surprising to me that she received that recognition because she was by nature always upbeat, positive minded, and a perennial optimist. She never thought ill of others. She refuses to dwell on sad or negative things, takes bad news in stride, and moves on.

She also counsels me not to dwell on the negative. A small example will illustrate what I mean. Once, a storm had tilted a roadside garbage bin in our neighborhood, and the garbage was strewn all over the pavement and the road. When I pointed it out, she remarked that maybe I should be appreciating how the storm and the heavy rain had washed clean the environment, making it look so green and fresh, instead of looking at the spilt trash.

Her other wonderful attribute was that she was not a tattletale, which is why her women friends share with her their secrets or comments about mutual friends knowing full well that she will never divulge them. She tries hard not to hurt other people's feelings. I have always been appreciative of her and of women in general because not only do they work outside the home but they also take care of their family much better than do us men. I often think how difficult it is to figure out what to serve for breakfast, lunch, and dinner day in and day out, and yet they manage that without fuss.

****

The International Monitoring and Evaluation Committee (MEC) was also a potentially valuable partner because of their corruption monitoring and reforming agenda. We established a regular dialogue with them. I was also introduced to their newest member, Gen. Hasan Chowdhury, who had served as the chairman of the Anti-Corruption Commission of Bangladesh from 2007 to 2009 following his retirement from the armed forces in June 2005. I was pleased to see a Bangladeshi in the MEC and invited General Chowdhury out to dinner at a favorite Italian place called Boccaccio. It was an evening well spent as we reminisced about Bangladesh and shared with each other some of our work.

We also had a useful meeting with the colonels and brigadiers in the headquarters of the International Security Assistance Force (ISAF), which was the NATO-led military mission in Afghanistan established by the UN Security Council in December 2001. They were interested in the kind of work we were doing and wanted to explore whether we could be useful to them. A few days later, I had a promising meeting with Mark Kryzer, head of the Asia Foundation in Afghanistan, regarding possibilities for joint work on combatting corruption.

Ramadan 2012 started on July 20, each day requiring sixteen hours of fasting, which meant no food or drinks from sunrise to sunset. At the first iftar (breaking of fast), my security guard Anurag, who was a Hindu by religion, remarked that he was impressed that I could fast the whole sixteen hours. I told him that I was doing it since becoming a teenager and that he should try it. He took up the challenge and fasted with me the next day. When asked how he felt, he replied that he felt very good. He was happy when he Skyped his wife to tell her that he had fasted that day, and his wife was impressed and praised him for his first such effort in the thirty-six years of his life!

On July 25, on my one-year anniversary on the job, MSI renewed my contract. It was a relief both to MSI and to me that my parent organization, CIDA, had approved my extension of leave without pay for a further year. I felt relaxed, and my expat team and I geared up to watch the opening of the London Olympics two days later even though it was going to be at 1:30 a.m., Kabul time! What made it more interesting was U.S. presidential candidate Mitt Romney's remark during an interview with U.S. network NBC that given UK's difficulties with security issues, "it's hard to know just how well it will turn out," which drew an instant rebuke from the British prime minister, who said that it was, of course, easier to organize an Olympic Games "in the middle of nowhere"—a swipe at Romney's stewardship of the 2002 Salt Lake City Winter Olympics. The London Olympics became memorable to tennis aficionados because Scottish Andy Murray won the Olympic gold in tennis, the first Brit to win in 104 years!

Our work proceeded on all fronts with vigor. Three weeks later, USAID informed us that the paperwork for the transfer of a B6 armored vehicle from their parking lot to us was completed and that we could pick up the vehicle. I sent Gareth and Hari accompanied by a car mechanic to the USAID vehicle compound, where they chose a B6 after the mechanic had given it a go-over. We didn't know that within a month, we would have to spend a few thousand dollars to fix it properly. But it was still better than dishing out $15,000 per month on a rental.

In mid-September 2012, we launched a weeklong workshop on Vulnerability to Corruption Assessment (VCA) to train Afghan officials on how to detect corruption and what steps to take to combat it. We also invited the staff of the MEC to participate in the workshop. We contracted Sandra Blagojevic from Slovenia to conduct the workshop, which ended successfully.

Nipa's Jaunt in Taliban Country

Since I had decided to work in Afghanistan another year, Nipa warmed up to the idea of visiting with me in Afghanistan. We had been working on her prospective visit since late summer, and, finally, on October 3, Nipa left Ottawa for Dhaka to visit with her mom and also to attend the fiftieth reunion of the students and faculty of the International Relations Department of Dhaka University, her alma mater.

From Dhaka, she came to Kabul on October 25. The next few days, we had a wonderful time visiting touristic sites, which included King Zahir Shah's mausoleum, King Amanullah's Darul Aman Palace (abode of peace), Emperor Babur's mausoleum and garden, the National Museum, and the new Parliament of Afghanistan that was under construction, among many other interesting places in and around the capital city. Two days into her visit, my staff and security personnel arranged a rooftop barbecue and kite flying, and we all enjoyed a great afternoon. The next day, on October 28, we went to Qargha Lake, where we relaxed most of the day, and then went to Design Café in Kabul for a nice candlelight dinner. Although she left Kabul on October 29, lots of pictures were taken to memorialize her visit, including pictures of her dressed as a Mujahideen fighter with a keffiyeh and holding an AK-47!

King Amanullah Khan's crumbling Darul Aman Palace, Kabul, Oct 2012

Rooftop makeshift barbecue in Kabul, Oct 2012

Spending the afternoon at the Qargha Lake outside Kabul, Oct 2012

After Nipa's departure, it was back to the grinder. The only memorable thing that happened outside of work was Bangladesh winning the first One Day International (ODI) cricket match against the West Indies by eight wickets; it was simply phenomenal! Regrettably, however, Bangladesh lost the regular two-match series 0–2. My mother, who was visiting my siblings in the States, was planning to visit us in Ottawa when I came on a home visit over Christmas. She Skyped me to tell me that she had changed her mind because my sister-in-law Etee's health had deteriorated precipitously, and so she was returning to Dhaka instead.

On December 9, the International Anti-Corruption Day, the Afghan civil society organizations under the aegis of AfCAC decided to celebrate the day by holding displays, publication speeches, and a high-level panel discussion at the Safi Landmark Hotel and Suites in Kabul. U.S. ambassador Stephen McFarland was invited to attend. As before, I delivered the opening remarks, followed by remarks by Ambassador McFarland, who praised the excellent work done by the NGOs and then remarks by the UNODC head Gary Collins and then the speech by a deputy ministry and, finally, remarks by a few parliamentarians. The whole event was covered from start to finish and publicized nationally by multiple TV and radio stations, such as the

National Radio Television Afghanistan (RTA), Samshad TV, Ariana TV, and the Voice of America (VOA). Our civil society partners were very pleased to have the opportunity to share with the public their work that was completed under very trying circumstances.

At the end of the workshop, two lady members of the Lower House of Parliament—Humaira Ayubi and Masuda Karokhi—approached me to express their strong desire to join our anticorruption work. A few days later, Daud and I met them in our office, and we had a very fruitful discussion on how to proceed. We were excited to work with them because we had noticed at the outset that the women parliamentarians were more honest and sincere about fighting corruption and eager to join our effort than their male colleagues, who offered only lip service to combatting corruption.

This was followed by a meeting with six women parliamentarians a few days later; they were neither shy nor reserved, but quite vocal about the state of corruption in the country and, in fact, within the Afghan parliament itself. They acknowledged that both houses of parliament desperately needed reform and that it would be an uphill struggle because there was bound to be considerable resistance from the male parliamentarians. I suggested to them that perhaps their first task in this struggle might be to recruit more women parliamentarians to their cause so that they have the numbers and the confidence to do what must be done; they agreed unanimously. The second thing I mentioned was that they should develop a strategy—and Daud could help them to do that—and distribute their tasks among themselves as well as work as a group with strong backing from each other. And the third suggestion was that we should meet biweekly to monitor progress, discuss challenges faced, and develop responses to those challenges.

Their commitment became quite evident when we met two weeks later, and this time, there were twelve of them, all quite enthusiastic and bubbling with ideas. Humaira and Masuda were very careful to choose only those women parliamentarians whom they felt were not aligned to political factions, were independent minded, and were committed to parliamentary reform. They had taken up Daud's offer of help, had several sittings with him, and jointly developed a strategy and an action plan to move forward with their anticorruption work.

They had also sounded out the Speaker of the lower house and were slightly disappointed that he was not as enthusiastic as they were. We discussed the strategy and their work plan, and I gave my views on both. First, since the lower house was dominated by men (as also was the upper house, or the Meshrano Jirga) and there were only a few women parliamentarians in either house, they needed to strategize on how to involve their male colleagues if their efforts were to succeed. They needed to carefully identify male parliamentarians who were potential supporters of parliamentary reform and gradually win them over to their cause. It would be difficult but had to be done. They should pay particular attention to a few male parliamentarians who had influence over the Speaker. The harsh reality was that no legislative bill would pass without the required votes, and for which the women were dependent on their male colleagues.

Second, I reminded them that there were provincial assemblies as well and that they should plan on contacting their colleagues in their respective provinces and let them know that our project was planning to work with them as well. I committed the required funding for their proposed activities.

The rest of December ended peacefully, and on December 20, I went home to spend Christmas with my family. We were happy to have my youngest brother, Tawfiq, and his wife Sabrina fly from Dhaka to Ottawa to spend Christmas with us, although they arrived on the day after Christmas having missed their scheduled DC-Ottawa flight. The exciting topic during the holidays was the 3D video camera that I had purchased in Dubai.

The Year 2013

Year 2013 started with Tawfiq and Sabrina's departure on January 2 from Ottawa for Dhaka via Washington DC and Istanbul, followed by Mishu's departure on January 6, and Mumu's departure on January 7, both for London. However, the sad news in our family was that Sohel's wife, my sister-in-law, Etee passed away on January 3 from an incurable disease, leaving a huge void in my brother Sohel's life.

Sohel had first seen Etee at a wedding party and was smitten. They got married on December 25, 1992, and had a blissful marriage. Etee was a very hardworking, calm, and quiet girl, and always with a smile when she spoke with me. When she died, she left behind a teenage daughter, Sasha. Sasha came over to the United States to pursue higher studies. She graduated from the Borough of Manhattan Community College with an associate degree in science and then studied at the City University of New York (CUNY) for a year before moving to Irving, Texas; she is currently enrolled at the University of Texas at Dallas to complete her bachelor's degree in biochemistry.

I left Ottawa for Kabul on January 10. Before long, the insurgents attacked various parts of the city, reminding us that more would follow during the year. The resulting lockdown was a blessing in disguise of sorts as it gave us expats the chance to watch tennis, the Australian Open. Meanwhile, it snowed two inches in London, and the city was in panic, which I found quite amusing because it was negative twenty-two degrees centigrade in Ottawa and it was business as usual.

The month ended with a wonderful evening at the Afghan National Institute of Music (ANIM) listening to the Afghan Orchestra at their gala concert. ANIM was trying to make a comeback with the support of the governments of Canada, Finland, France, and the United States after the dark days of Taliban government when cultural activities such as singing, playing or listening to music, engaging in the arts, painting, games, and socializing were considered sacrilegious. In the midst of bomb blasts and chaos in the city, the concert was almost surreal. Kabul turned colder, and the marble floor and concrete walls of my room made it feel worse. The room heater broke down once again, and Samad had to purchase another electric blanket for me.

Matri Bhasha Dibosh

Meanwhile, there was unrest in Bangladesh. Mother had gone to her parental home in Lostimanika, Comilla, to celebrate Urs. I Skyped with my siblings in Dhaka to inquire about the unrest and learned that, for the first time, none of my family members had participated in the *probhat feri* (dawn procession). February 21 was an extremely symbolic day for Bangladeshis because on that day in 1952, they had demonstrated en masse against the decision of the Pakistan government to eliminate Bangla (Bengali) as a state language.

Pakistan was born in August 1947 with two wings separated by India: West Pakistan, whose people spoke Urdu, and East Pakistan, whose people spoke Bangla. However, in 1948, the governor-general of Pakistan, Mohammad Ali Jinnah, declared that "Urdu, and only Urdu" will be the common language of Pakistan and sought to eliminate Bangla as a language. The citizens of East Pakistan, who were the largest ethnic group in Pakistan, were enraged and refused to replace Bangla with Urdu as their mother tongue. They took to the streets to protest.

Civil unrest ensued, and the government's heavy-handed attempt to suppress it only increased the public's determination to protect their language. After four years of discontent, public demonstrations, and civil unrest, uncontrollable sectarian tensions led to a series of draconian measures by the government. On February 21, 1952, police tear-gassed protesting students and the public, which inflamed the situation further, leading to police firing on protesters. A number of people were killed that day as the protests spread throughout the country. Ultimately, Bangla was preserved as the mother tongue of the Bengali people.

It was the first time in human history that a people were willing to sacrifice themselves to protect and preserve their mother tongue, which is the central identity of a nation. Since then, each year, Ekushe February (21 February) is celebrated by Bengalis walking barefoot at dawn (probhat feri) through the streets of Dhaka to the Shaheed Minar, the national monument erected as a tribute to the language martyrs, to lay wreaths and sing "Amar bhaier rokte rangano ekushe February/ami ki bhulitey pari" (February 21 is anointed with my brothers' blood/can I forget that) and other cultural programs.

In recognition of this sacrifice to preserve one's mother tongue and mindful of the fact that humanity loses one language per week and that nearly half of the six thousand languages spoken by the peoples of the world are now endangered, in 2000, the United Nations declared February 21 as the International Mother Language Day. Today, it is celebrated throughout the world, not just in Bangladesh.

More disturbing news came from Dhaka. My mother-in-law's maid servant Begum had eloped with her truck driver husband, who was suspected of being a thug. It was felt that my mother-in-law should spend a few days with relatives while all the door locks of her house were replaced.

A Gutsy Girl

One day in early March, Anurag informed me that he had met a girl in the office of our security service provider, Pax Mondial, who was a Bengali. She was their business development officer. When he told her that I was a Bengali too, she told him that she would love to meet me. Anurag asked me if he should arrange a meeting with me. I was curious and wanted to know about this unmarried twenty-something Bengali girl working for a security company in Afghanistan; I asked Anurag to invite her to a dinner with us.

On the appointed evening, she came to our compound, and Anurag introduced her to me. Her name was Priyanka. We sat down to chat. "I was excited at the chance to meet you when Anurag mentioned you to me," she said. "He told me that you are a Bengali too, although you are from Bangladesh and I'm from Calcutta," she continued. "I am happy to meet you too, especially a fellow Bengali," I offered. "As you can see, I am wearing a sari. I haven't worn one for several years now because there was no right occasion for it. So I thought I'll wear a sari tonight knowing that as a *bangali purush* (Bengali man), you'll appreciate it," she said. "Well, you do look beautiful in the sari. I'm glad you chose to wear a sari tonight," I said. "How long have you been working in Afghanistan?" I asked. "Just over two years," she replied. "Isn't it difficult for you—young and unmarried—to work here?" I asked. "Not really. I speak fluent Dari and learned my ways around," she assured me. "But why are you working with a western security company in such a dangerous environment as Afghanistan?" I pressed on. "Oh, I am a rebel at heart. I applied for this job without telling my parents. I was actually surprised to get hired. But I love my job. I get to travel a lot to develop businesses for Pax. Even inside Afghanistan." "So you must travel with a male escort inside Afghanistan, right?" I asked, hoping for some assurance. "Not actually. I travel about alone," she remarked casually. "Aren't you afraid of getting caught by the Taliban?" I asked with a hint of worry. "Yes, and I did get caught twice, once in Ghazni, another time in Balkh. The first time they stopped me in Ghazni, they asked what I was doing alone without any male family members with me. I had to think fast. I started crying and told them that I was running away from home because my father was forcing me to go to school. I told my father that Allah had sent me to be an obedient wife and a good mother," she explained. "The Taliban were very happy to hear that and exclaimed, '*Mashallah, mashallah.*' Then they escorted me to my destination. It was the safest journey inside Afghanistan I ever had."

Gareth, Anurag, and I looked at each other with astonishment. "Well, your luck may run out at some point, and I shudder to think what will happen to you then," I said rather worried. "My ploy has worked for me both times so far. Meanwhile, I am hoping that some foreign person will fall in love with me and take me with him to the West," she explained with a twinkle in her eye. Gareth and Anurag sat through this conversation stunned. We had a chatty dinner into the night, and after she left, Gareth shook his head and remarked, "I'll grant you, sir, this girl has a lot of balls, but I think she is crazy!" The rest of us couldn't agree more.

Fast forward to the middle of April. Priyanka dropped by my office to see me, again wearing a sari. It was nice to see her again. She looked radiant and happy, as she informed me that she was engaged to a Kashmiri diplomat in the Indian Foreign Service who was currently posted in Berlin, but will be posted to London toward the end of the year. "This sounds like an arranged marriage. I thought you were a rebel," I teased her. "Oh! That was when I was much younger," she brushed aside my comment. "I'll be very happy if you come to my wedding in Srinagar (capital of Kashmir) on September 17. I'll send you the wedding invitation," she added. I told her that I would love to but most likely can't because I'll be back in Canada by then. I wished her a very happy future. I do not know what happened to her since then, although I am quite curious to know how her life turned out to be as I write this.

****

On April 12, I received an invitation to a barbecue at the high-security UNDP Compound in Kabul. They served excellent-quality South African beef steaks. They also had pork, which surprised me because it was banned in Afghanistan. I asked them where they got it from. The South African head of security for the UNDP explained that they regularly brought large packages of pork steak in their suitcases through Kabul airport customs and which were regularly seized by the customs official and officially consigned to be destroyed. But the packages were kept in a separate fridge. Next day, they visited the official in his house and paid him a pre-agreed amount, who then released the package, although the official document stated that the pork was destroyed. That was the long-running agreement between certain customs officials at the Kabul International Airport and the South African security team. It was corruption of a different sort, though corruption nonetheless, but outside my project mandate.

****

I hadn't seen Mother for nearly a year. During her visit to Dallas and Boise last year, she had planned to visit us in Ottawa over Christmas but canceled her visit and returned to Dhaka because Etee's health was failing rapidly. One day, during our FaceTime, she asked me to come to Dhaka and stay with her for a few days. Since I had one regional rest and recreation break still available to me, on April 13, I flew Safi Airways to Dubai and then Flydubai Airlines to Dhaka with a suitcase full of dried fruits and nuts, walnut and pistachio *shirpera* (special Afghan fudge), and a tub of Uzbeki biryani. Mother distributed them to our relatives and to my in-laws, who were pleased to get fruits and sweets from Afghanistan.

I met a whole bunch of relatives whom I hadn't seen for many years. Sadly, my fupa Sirajuddin Khan passed away on April 21 at the United Hospital in Gulshan. I was sad to see him pass because I had fond memories of him. He was always kind and nice to me, and I remembered being impressed during my teen years by his Swiss Tissot wristwatch that had a red-colored seconds hand on it, a rare watch in the '60s East Pakistan.

I visited our village home in Gourshar, which was recently refurbished. Elderly villagers who remembered me as a child came to see me and inquired about my family and about my new home in Canada. They were very interested to know how different Canadian villagers were from Bangladeshi villagers. This reminded me of First Lady Hillary Clinton's visit to Bangladesh in 1996 at the invitation of Grameen Bank. She had chatted with some village women in the courtyard of someone's homestead. She was asked how many cows and goats she owned, and she said none; they concluded that she was a poor woman indeed. Then she was asked about her children, and she replied she had only one daughter. They pitied her for not having any son and concluded that she was an unfortunate woman as well. They left the meeting feeling sorry and quite unimpressed that the American president's wife had such meagre worldly possession!

I visited our family graveyard where my grandparents, eldest uncle, and other relatives were buried. I also visited my father's grave, which was not in our village but in the grounds of the college in Debidwar that he had established.

I returned to Kabul on April 23, and the following day at 3:35 a.m., we got hit by an earthquake with a magnitude 6.5. It lasted for more than a minute. There had been additional earthquakes in different provinces earlier. Since we frequently felt tremors in Kabul, some severe and some less severe, the earlier training on how to cope with an earthquake came in very handy.

****

A powerful antidote to this constant state of anxiety was the occasional good news from friends and family that temporarily distracted us and brightened our days. It reminded me of how U.S. GIs stationed in war zones must feel when they receive letters or packages from their loved ones back home. On March 1, while Skyping with my youngest sister, Tina, in Idaho, I learned that her daughter Mayisa was in a school play acting as a deer, which seemed appropriate given her doe-eyed look. On March 8, I learned that Mumu had been promoted as a senior consultant in her company, got a salary raise, and received a Blackberry from her company; she was very excited. That made me proud.

On March 19, Mishu forwarded to me the University of Westminster's invitation to his graduation ceremony in London on July 2, which made me very happy; I asked him to reserve a box so that Nipa, Mumu, and I can sit together during the ceremony. He replied right away saying that he will try to do so and also that he had received confirmation of an internship with a London-based architecture firm, which was great news.

However, on March 23, worrisome news came from Ottawa about departmental restructuring within the Canadian government. CIDA, which existed as an independent department with its own minister reporting to parliament, would no longer be a separate entity or have a minister of its own to protect its interests. It was to be subsumed under the Department of Foreign Affairs and International Trade (DFAIT), which raised the specter of termination of scores of public service jobs.

Since I was on leave from CIDA and away from Ottawa, I suspected that I would be among the first victims of this change, because it would be an opportunity for the new director of my division to eliminate a few thematic areas of work, such as anticorruption and indigenous people's affairs, that were on her hit list. Her justification was budget cut by the new administration and hence the need to streamline work within the division. I braced myself for more unpleasant news further down the road.

The month of May started to look brighter for me. On May 1, I received a message from MSI home office in DC that the USAID had completed its review of the 4A Project and concluded that the project's management and results were "highly satisfactory" and that my performance was "excellent under difficult circumstances." This was followed by a telephone call from MSI's executive vice president Marina Fanning praising me for my hard work. She also asked me to thank my staff on her behalf for their dedication and commitment to the 4A Project. I was quite elated by these commendations from the USAID and the home office. I decided to celebrate this by a summer trip to Lhasa, capital of Tibet, with Mishu if possible.

I called the travel agency in Kabul who looked after my travel needs to inquire about a summer trip to Lhasa. They informed me that visitors to Tibet normally flew from New Delhi to Lhasa, but that route had been suspended recently by the Chinese government. Now the only way to go to Tibet was to get the travel visa in Beijing and fly from Beijing to Lhasa. There was also considerable uncertainty whether a travel visa would be granted, and since there was no direct flight from Kabul to Beijing, one would have to travel to China either from Pakistan, India, or the Middle East, making the trip quite costly. Given my limited leave days from the project, I sadly concluded that the trip to Tibet from Kabul was not feasible.

A few days later, the U.S. embassy in Kabul was in turmoil. Afghan president Hamid Karzai publicly admitted in a nationally televised interview that the CIA was supplying him with a sack of money once every week. Embassy officials could not believe that the president would willfully out this heavily guarded secret. It was learned later that the CIA provided President Karzai this weekly handout with the understanding that he would use the money to pay off and control the rambunctious warlords especially of the sensitive bordering provinces.

This bombshell was picked up by the Tehran government. It was rumored in the diplomatic circles in Kabul that when President Karzai visited Iranian president Hassan Rouhani, who was elected in June 2013, Rouhani asked Karzai how much he was getting from the CIA each week. Karzai reportedly said $45K. Rouhani offered to up that if Karzai would stop taking American money. Karzai agreed and started receiving Iranian handout but did not stop taking U.S. money, explaining that he would accept "donation" from anyone to invest in his people! How far all this was true I do not know, but it kept the rumor mills spinning in Kabul for quite some time.

****

Our project work proceeded at a steady pace. The USAID had asked us to explore the possibility of doing some outreach projects, and we had launched a few. Daud and I agreed that it was time to personally monitor these outreach activities that we had funded in the northwest province of Balkh and the western province of Herat. We consulted our security team, who stated that they would have to do reconnaissance work in those provinces before they could give us the security clearance. Under their advice, we abandoned the idea of driving long distance to those provinces because much of the countryside and the interprovincial highways were under the control of the Taliban. In fact, cell phone communication towers outside the major cities and towns in Afghanistan were under Taliban control from dusk.

Given this state of affairs, we decided to fly to Herat and Mazar-e-Sharif, the capital of Balkh. Gareth got into high gear and started consulting the foreign security companies operating in those two provinces and was able to gather valuable information that helped us to plan our itineraries. He even managed to secure commitments from them to provide backup security to our delegation during our visit if needed.

Meanwhile, the opportunity arose for me to do some mountain climbing. Every time I traveled on the Dehma Zang, one of Kabul's arterial transits, I would look out and see historical sites that I yearned to visit. One was the historic Wall of Kabul, which, according to local lore, was built to divide Kabul Kingdom between two warring brothers. Kabul's two mountain peaks, Koh-e Asmayi (Sky Mountain), which was 2,110 meters high, and Koh-e Sher Darwaza (Lion's Gate Mountain), which was 2,220 meters high, also enticed me. One day, I pointed at them and wondered aloud whether I would be able to scale them.

When I returned from my latest R & R break, Gareth and Anurag told me that during my absence, they had climbed to the top of the Kabul Wall, which ended at the summit of Koh-e Asmayi, Kabul's second-highest mountain, in less than an hour and concluded that even at age sixty plus, I was fit enough to do it too. So with that confidence boost, on May 9, Daud, Musa, Gareth, Anurag, and I set off to scale the summit.

At around five thousand feet, we were met by a soldier from the Afghan army. We were again stopped at six thousand feet when the commander of the army unit on top of the summit came down to query us. Having judged all three of us—Bangladeshi, Indian, and Welsh—as "friends," he directed us toward a path that was free from mines. At the summit, we were met by two additional army personnel who spoke broken English and Urdu. A few bottles of water from our backpacks were enough to bring a huge smile in their faces. They remarked, "We wait for Allah to send down some water for us once in a while," referring to Kabul's infrequent rains. Kabul itself sat at an altitude of 1,800 meters (6,000 feet) above sea level, which meant that at the peak of Koh-e Asmayi, we were 3,900 meters (13,000 feet) above sea level.

At the top of Koh-e Asmayi, Kabul's second highest peak,
with Gareth, Anurag and Musa, May 2013

The view from the top, with Kabul City and the Kabul Valley sprawled out between the two mountains, was spectacular. The snowcapped Hindu Kush was visible in the distance, and one could see the Kabul River snaking its way south to east as it eventually met up with the Indus River in Pakistan. The Wall of Kabul was far removed from its former glory but still evoked powerful historical memories for the inhabitants of the Kabul-Panjshir Valley. I was glad I climbed the Sky Mountain, though I would have liked to have my daughter Mumu (Fareen), son Mishu (Nayeem), and nephew Ryan, a mountaineer himself, with me at the summit! I felt indebted to my security team for encouraging me to join them for the hike to the summit and for making my wish come true.

A couple of days later, I received an invitation from MEC to join their delegation that was planning to visit Bamiyan, a province in the central highlands of Afghanistan and a very well-known tourist destination about 240 kilometers northwest of Kabul. Located at the western end of the Hindu Kush Mountains, its terrain was semimountainous with beautiful peacock-blue lakes. But it was most known for the tall Buddha statues that were carved into the sides of cliffs across from Bamiyan City. I had planned to visit Bamiyan before I left Afghanistan, and the invitation gave me that opportunity.

Visit to Herat

But our visit to Herat came up first. This was our first provincial trip, and Daud had meticulously planned it. We were scheduled to meet with the deputy governor of the province, the Speaker of the provincial assembly, some women members of the provincial assembly who were lined up by Herat's woman representative in the national parliament in Kabul, civil society organizations, and members of the print and electronic media.

On May 18, Daud, Anurag, and I were going through Kabul airport security to board our flight to Herat. Daud's and my carry-ons went through the X-ray machine, but Anurag's got switched into the additional security check lane. He was asked to open up his knapsack. After everything was pulled out of the bag, airport security found a Swiss army knife in a bottom pocket. Anurag was surprised that it was there. When reminded that weapons were forbidden to be carried on board, Anurag turned to me and said, "Sir, I didn't even know it was there." Then he turned to the security official and apologized for this oversight on his part.

By then, the manager of the security operations was already summoned, and Anurag was on the verge of getting arrested for attempting to carry a concealed weapon on board. I turned to the security manager and showed my ID and explained to him that he worked for a USAID project and that he was my bodyguard and that we were going to Herat on project-related work. I vouched for Anurag and assured them that we shall be extra careful henceforth and that this would never happen again.

The security officials conferred with each other, and then the manager turned to me and said, "Sir, as you know, this is a serious offense. OK, we shall let him go this time, but see to it that this never happens again." They confiscated the pocket knife. I assured them and boarded our plane. Anurag, who was proud of his conscientious service to me and the project, and who was always organized and methodical in his work, felt devastated because of the slipup that nearly got him arrested. During the flight, he explained to me that his compatriot Hari had used the bag earlier on, and he just grabbed it to use it, finding it empty, and didn't think to check the inside pockets.

Our Kam Air afternoon flight landed in Herat about an hour later, and we drove to Hotel Nazary from the airport. Western security companies working for other donor projects in Herat had recommended Nazary to be the most secure hotel in Herat. We and our luggage went through the hotel X-ray machine, and before long, we settled into our three separate rooms located in two separate floors. Anurag met with the hotel security manager and got a briefing on its security setup and a tour of the hotel. Though rated as a four-star hotel, it was no more than a three-star hotel. Its only distinguishing feature were the many aquariums in the reception area.

We were scheduled to meet with the deputy governor that afternoon. We drove up to the deputy governor's official mansion in our rented armored vehicle, went through strict security procedures, and were shown into his office, where tea was served in the great Afghan tradition as we waited for the deputy governor to return from his meeting outside the compound. About half an hour later, we were under attack as a tremendously loud explosion ripped through the compound. Just as the deputy governor was entering his highly guarded official mansion, the insurgents who were lying in ambush struck his security convoy. We were dashed off to the safe room, and for the next few hours, there were additional bomb blasts and gunfire on the street and by the entrance of the official compound. The damage and carnage were significant. After the situation was finally brought under control by the security forces, we rushed back to the hotel to assess the situation. All our scheduled meetings were canceled that day. We learned that even the U.S. consulate in Herat was attacked simultaneously.

Security throughout Herat City was significantly beefed up as the provincial security forces patrolled the streets, and checkpoints and barricades went up at all vulnerable points, including at the city's entry and exit points. With this high alert throughout the city and its vicinity, and since Herat city was fully secured, we decided to continue with our meetings and site visits as previously planned. We were happy that the provincial assembly representatives, the NGOs and CSOs, the media people, and others also made the effort to meet with us despite the charged environment. The deputy governor, the Speaker, and women members of the provincial assembly expressed their interest to work on anticorruption legislation for their province. The NGOs had many reform-oriented projects they wished to pursue and were very pleased to get our assurance to fund those that fell within our mandate. Our press conference on the last day was attended by a large section of the Herat media and ended successfully.

The only downside of the visit was the mediocre food. The first restaurant we went to served us burnt roast chicken that was all bones and little meat. While Daud and Anurag managed to eat it, I couldn't and had only yogurt for lunch. Then we went to a buffet place that had better choices, but the food was mediocre. The only decent place we had time to visit was the mountaintop restaurant called Hazaar-e-yek (one in a thousand) Shab restaurant, where we sat down Afghan-style and the food was much better. I mostly depended on the breakfast in the hotel.

But an upside of the visit was the chance to buy fresh saffron— one of the costliest spices in the world—right from the farm. I had heard that saffron from Herat rivaled in quality that from Spain and was better than Iranian saffron and Kashmiri saffron, which I had purchased earlier. I asked Daud to arrange a visit to a saffron field.

So during our last afternoon in Herat, we drove to a saffron farmer's house at the edge of the city. We could smell the delicate fragrance of saffron as we neared our destination, and it grew stronger as we entered the farmer's warehouse. Inside, I saw several vats of just-plucked and dried saffron that was waiting to be packaged for shipment to suppliers. After Daud introduced me as a visitor from Canada, I told the farmer that I would like to purchase saffron for my family and friends.

"How much do you want, a kilogram?" he asked. I was shocked at his suggestion and thought that he must think this Canadian is a millionaire. I knew that saffron in the superstore in Ottawa came in packets of a few grams costing about $1.10 per gram; that would mean $1,100 for a kilogram in Ottawa. I asked him how much would half a kilogram cost. He smiled and said that since I had come all the way from Canada, he will give me a "friend's price" and then picked up his calculator and said that his special price for me was US$160 for half a kilo. I pulled out my cell phone to do the math and realized that the Ottawa price for half a kilo would be about C$550, or US$407 at the existing exchange rate; so I would be paying US$160 instead of US$407!

I extended my hand and shook his and requested him to give me half a kilo. He happily packed the quantity in an appropriately sized container and then taped it all around the edge to retain the fragrance. Next, he handed me a bagful of small oval-shaped plastic containers anticipating that I would also be distributing the saffron to family members and friends. Daud and Anurag also bought some for their families. We departed the farmer's fragrant house quite pleased with our purchases, and also smelling of saffron ourselves.

However, the visit to Herat would be incomplete for me without visiting the many historical sites. Herat was established circa 500 BC as the ancient Persian town of Artacoana or Aria. It was now the regional capital of western Afghanistan and continued to be a strategic commercial and cultural center to the wider region. In 330 BC, Alexander the Great captured it from the Achaemenids and built the Citadel of Herat. It remained a strategic asset to the Seleucids, Parthians, and Hephthalites, and became the eastern bastion of the Abbasid caliphate at the end of the eighth century AD. The Ghorids captured it in AD 1175, but the Mongols and Genghis Khan subsequently nearly destroyed it.

Herat reemerged as an affluent city in the late fourteenth century AD under the rule of Timur's son, Shah Rukh. Queen Gawharshad continued the extensive rebuilding program during the fifteenth century AD, and some of the monuments in the Timurid style still stand. The most prominent was the Qala-e Ikhtyaruddin, built on the site of the ancient citadel erected by Alexander around 330 BC. Apart from its architectural heritage, Herat has long been an important center for the arts and sciences, with a rich tradition of music, calligraphy, painting, astronomy, mathematics, and philosophy. Some of Herat's famous sons were Bezhad, Jami, and Ansari.

Among the places I visited in and around Herat were the mausoleum of the eleventh-century Muslim Sufi saint Khwaja Abdullah Ansari, also known as the "Sage of Herat"; the tenth-century Masjid-e Jami; the Qala-e Ikhtiaruddin, or the Herat Citadel, built on top of Alexander the Great's ancient citadel and which was now a museum and archive; the Military Museum containing life-size statues of the Mujahideen warriors who fought and expelled the Russians, including depiction of battle scenes; the Shahid Square, which depicted victorious Mujahideens on top of a Russian T72 tank; and, finally, the mountaintop Takht-e-Safer, which used to be the resting place for travelers between mountain passes and which now served as the Herat Provincial Government's guest house for foreign dignitaries. Its large circular interior hall had showcases depicting battlefield weapons from ancient times to the modern era, battle dresses worn by warriors, and samples of pottery and carpets from different provinces.

Modern Herat was a relatively flat, well-planned city with wide roads, less traffic but much hotter than Kabul. Being physically much closer to Tehran than Kabul, it appeared to be heavily influenced by neighboring Iran in its conservativeness, orientation, and attitude, and seemed prone to rely more on Tehran for religious and political guidance than on Kabul. Notwithstanding the scary start of our trip, it was nonetheless fruitful in many ways. We returned to Kabul on May 23 after productive project work.

Adventures in Bamiyan

Our preparatory work for a visit to the province of Bamiyan had been completed by my office by the time we returned from Herat. So a week later, on June 2, Daud, Anurag, and I accompanied the MEC delegation and took the 8:00 a.m. delayed to 11:00 a.m. flight to Bamiyan. The trip to and from Bamiyan itself was an experience never to be forgotten. Bamiyan was a small town in the central highlands and therefore did not have a proper airport. The UN Humanitarian Air Service (UNHAS) ran a helicopter service once a week to ferry NGOs back and forth between Bamiyan and Kabul. Since neither the MEC nor the 4A Project qualified as an NGO, we couldn't avail that service.

Travel by road was fraught with danger because of insurgent activity and highway robbers. Besides, nobody seemed to know the exact driving distance between Bamiyan and Kabul, and estimates varied from 125 kilometers to 180 kilometers, and driving time between 1.5 hours and 6 hours. Our only option was to take the regional East Horizon Airlines, the only commercial airline that flew to Bamiyan, which offered twice a week service. We had no idea what to expect from this little known domestic service.

We were in for a big surprise indeed. The aircraft we boarded was a sixty-year-old Russian/Ukrainian-built forty-four-seat twin-turboprop Antonov An-24, an aircraft designed in 1957 in the Soviet Union. It had a dilapidated interior. It was free seating inside. Some seats had no cushion, thus exposing the wooden frame. There were no overhead signs saying "Fasten your seat belts," and then we realized that there were no seat belts! The luggage bin overhead did not have covers to lock in the luggage either! There were a couple of lines in Russian projected on the wall of the cockpit in front of the seats; none of us knew what it said.

The locks of the door of the one toilet in the rear and of the cockpit door were broken, and throughout the flight, the doors kept on opening and closing. The aircraft was one-third full when its door closed. The captain welcomed us and then reminded us to try to keep our luggage by our feet and to keep an eye out for those that were in the bin above in case they fall during unforeseen turbulence during flight.

As if that was not enough stress, what I saw next gave me real fright. A ground staff appeared with what appeared to look like a tire rod in hand, inserted it into an opening in front of the engine on the wing, and tried to turn the propeller to get it started, reminding me of '50s and '60s taxis that were started like that. With each hand rotation, the propeller revved up for a few turns and then stopped. The man kept trying to get the propeller going until the propeller finally started to spin. We watched in dismay what was clearly out of the '50s. Then he went over to the propeller on the other wing and repeated his efforts until the propeller started to spin. But as soon as that propeller started, the one on our side stopped! He then came over to our side to once again start the engine on our side. Once both propellers started rotating, the pilot revved up both engines and kept it running for about five minutes when we finally started to move. During all this time, Anurag and I watched this drama with a sinking feeling and wondered whether we will really make it to Bamiyan. When the aircraft finally took off, I recited all the *suras* I knew and prayed to God to grant us safe passage to Bamiyan.

During the entire one-hour flight, all we saw were mountains, sometimes gray and sometimes reddish, revealing Afghanistan's rich iron ore deposits. And when we were not looking outside, our eyes were on the overhead compartment watching out for falling luggage. Daud, sitting in the other aisle seat across from me, and I tried to distract ourselves by discussing potential project work in Bamiyan.

Shortly before landing, the unthinkable happened. The propeller on our side came to an abrupt stop, and the engine shut down. The pilot immediately announced on the intercom that the left side engine had stopped, but we need not worry because this had happened before and he had landed the aircraft safely. Our hearts stopped beating, or at least I know mine did! After some time, and I don't recall how long, the pilot asked us to sit tight as he was going to land. I opened my eyes and looked out to see exactly where we were landing—on the mountain, valley, or flatland?

A short gravel strip that substituted for a runway came into view. The aircraft landed with a thud on the very bumpy gravel strip. A couple of bags from the overhead compartment fell off as their owners dived from their seats to catch them; the rest of us clapped our hands acknowledging their dexterity. We were also very fortunate that no one needed to go to the toilet because the door didn't even have an inside handle for the occupant to hold it shut. We all breathed a huge sigh of relief as we disembarked in hot, dry, and sunny Bamiyan.

Our next surprise was to see that Bamiyan did not have a proper airport terminal, only a single-door portable structure sitting on gravel that served as the terminal building and some folding chairs on the loose gravel outside. There was a single "official" who asked us to gather next to the portable. Shortly after, we watched our luggage being unloaded onto a tractor and brought to us. Each of us had to unload our own luggage from the tractor. Several cars that we had rented in advance were parked outside the chain-link fence surrounding the "airport." There was a big arch at the exit point with Mujahideen warrior Massoud's picture at the center and welcoming words for visitors.

The "check-in counter" of Bamiyan Airport on a gravel patch, June 2013

We hopped on to the cars. Even with windows rolled down, the heat inside was hardly bearable. But we had to roll up the windows because of the dust from the muddy unpaved sections of the road to our hotel a short distance away. There were only two hotels in Bamiyan: the Noorband Qala, which I would rate as a two-star, and the Silk Road, which I would rate at best three stars. The Silk Road was already fully booked several months ago, so we had to settle for the second best. Two days later, we were able to move into the Silk Road.

Bamiyan was a small town located in the central highlands of Afghanistan northwest of Kabul at an elevation of 8,495 feet (2,590 meters) above sea level. Bamiyan Province was home to magnificent ruined cities, caves with some of the oldest paintings in the world, crisscrossing mountain ranges, beautiful still turquoise lakes, and natural parks, but, most importantly, it was known for its two giant Buddha statues carved in the face of the cliff. The larger 170-foot-high statue was carved in AD 554, and the smaller 115-foot-high statue in AD 507, long before Islam had traveled to central Afghanistan. Pictures of them reveal their beauty, craftsmanship, and immense size that made them one of the wonders of the world and a significant cultural heritage of the people of the region.

Buddhism was widespread south of the Hindu Kush Mountains and a major religion of Afghanistan together with Zoroastrianism and Hinduism—all of which predated the advent of Islam in the sixth century. By the seventh century, Buddhism started to fade in importance and finally ended during the Ghaznavid takeover in the eleventh century.

After the Taliban captured Afghanistan, the statues were destroyed in March 2001 on orders from the Taliban leader Mullah Mohammad Omar, who declared them to be idols and hence unacceptable to Islam. According to the locals, the Taliban first tried to destroy them with antiaircraft and tank fire, but the statues were too formidable. They then climbed to the top of the heads of the statues, drilled big holes, and stuffed them with dynamite and then blasted them. To dissociate Islam from this infamous act, a Taliban envoy visiting the United States in the following weeks explained that the statues were destroyed to protest international aid exclusively reserved for statue maintenance when Afghanistan was experiencing famine. Whatever the true motive, the destruction of the statues was an unconscionable act.

View from the rooftop of our hotel Silk Road of the mountain where the Buddha statues once stood, Bamiyan, June 2013

The recesses where the statues once stood were visible from our hotel, and as we sipped late afternoon tea on the hotel terrace, we could not help but marvel at the two huge empty spaces where they once stood in their austere grandeur. We took time out of our work to visit the cliffs. The entire side of the mountain facing us was pockmarked with countless little caves that were once home to ascetic Buddhist monks who lived their stoic existence. We could make out the living, eating, and prayer areas inside these caves. Pointing to the fireplaces, the guide explained that this is where the monks hid their treasures when marauding armies rampaged through their region looting their possessions.

Many of the caves were linked to each other through narrow, chest-high, and often steep walkways, and sometimes they would open up to big spaces in the interior where religious functions were conducted. One such open space had a dome-shaped ceiling with footprints plastered all over the walls and the ceiling. The guide explained that this was done by the invaders to show their antipathy toward Islam. Today, these austere caves serve as dorm rooms for students from the countryside during their academic year at Bamiyan University and who are too poor to rent rooms in the town. We traversed some of these caves and walkways and took pictures.

Caves next to the missing Buddha statues where Buddhist monks once resided, and are now used by extremely poor students attending Bamiyan University, Bamiyan, June 2013

Band-e Amir

MEC and I had separate agenda, and so we worked with different timetables. But between our work, we managed to chalk out time to jointly visit the famous Lake District in the Hindu Kush mountains, which were at an elevation of approximately three thousand meters. The six deep blue lakes in the region were separated by natural dams made of travertine, a form of limestone deposited by mineral springs, especially hot springs. We were warned by the locals to complete our visit during daylight hours because tourists had been attacked by insurgents and highway robbers several times in the past. Thus cautioned, we left our hotel midmorning, drove for about an hour west of Bamiyan City to reach Band-e Amir National Park, and hoped to return by late afternoon.

As we walked through the park, we witnessed multiple waterfalls cascading down from the mountaintop creating a beautiful mist. We waded through ankle-deep warm running water from the nearby hot springs. The serene waters of the Band-e Amir, which literally means "Commander's Dam," stretched as far as the eye could see. Tourist facilities hadn't fully developed, but there were several swan-shaped paddleboats by a small landing that one could rent. Anurag and I boarded one and paddled into the center of the lake. It was very quiet and peaceful.

On one side of the lake was the shrine of Hazrat Ali, Prophet Mohammad's (PBUH) cousin and son-in-law and the fourth caliph of Islam. According to Bamiyan legend, Hazrat Ali had stopped the rushing waters from the mountains from washing away the villages below, thus creating these lakes. In recognition of that, a shrine was built on the side of the lake. After our excursion, we stopped at a nearby solitary mud-floored stall with thatched straw roof to eat chicken and naan. We thoroughly enjoyed our day out in the Lake District but hurried back to Bamiyan before sunset.

Azdagar

I also visited several other historic sites whose names seemed to come out of fairy tales. One was Azdagar, about thirty miles drive from Bamiyan City and known for the mountain range that was split right down the middle. We drove our 4x4 nearly to the top of the range with considerable difficulty, although I could see that the driver was very nervous. The view from the top in all directions was incredible. The width of the top of this mountain range varied between twenty feet and fifty feet. The crack ran a considerable distance, and along most of the crack, one could not see all the way to the bottom. Our driver-cum-guide asked us to put our ear to the ground, and when we did, we could hear the sound of rushing water deep below. It was intriguing to think that there could be a fast-moving water body/river flowing below this mountain range. Again, the local lore was that it was Hazrat Ali who had split this mountain range, and so a shrine was dedicated to him next to the crack, and a green flag of Islam was fluttering near the shrine. Another mountain range facing us was even taller and imposing; it seemed to be within touching distance, and yet it was several miles away.

The split mountain range in Azdagar, June 2013

Shahr-e Zohak

Next, we visited Shahr-e Zohak, or the "Red City," named after the red-colored cliffs. It was a thirteenth-century hilltop fort sitting on a seismically active zone some seventeen kilometers from Bamiyan City at the confluence of the Bamiyan and Kalu Rivers. It was built by the Shansabani kings in the twelfth century, although archaeological evidence pointed to a fort on this site at the time of the White Huns in the sixth century. During the Mongol invasion, Genghis Khan's favorite grandson was killed during an assault on Shahr-e Zohak, provoking a revenge attack that left all the inhabitants of the Bamiyan Valley dead in its wake.

The colloquial name "Zohak" was taken from the legendary serpent-haired king in Persian literature. We looked up at the citadel and wondered how one scaled it. The towers of the citadel made of mud brick on stone foundations were wrapped around the sides of the cliff, making the red city impregnable. There were no entrances to the citadel. It was accessed only by ladders that the defenders lowered when necessary and then pulled up behind them. The barracks within the citadel could accommodate over two thousand soldiers during a siege. One could see steps leading up to the ramparts for spectacular views of the surrounding mountains and valleys. Because of the location's strategic value, invaders throughout history have tried to capture and control it, but these impregnable heights repelled every invader except Genghis Khan.

Shahr-e Gholghola

Shahr-e Gholghola, or the "City of Screams," was the thirteenth-century remains of the Ghorid period. Rising above the Kakrak Valley, which housed the famous Buddhas, this citadel was Bamiyan's last stand against the Mongol hordes. It was reputed to be the best defended of Bamiyan's royal citadels but was captured by intrigue rather than by force of arms. Bamiyan's ruler Jalaluddin held off Genghis Khan's siege, but he could not anticipate the treachery of his daughter. She secretly left her widowed father's castle in a fit of pique over his remarrying a princess from Ghazni. She betrayed the castle's secret entrance, expecting to be rewarded by her own betrothal to the Mongol ruler.

But Genghis Khan did not trust one who had betrayed her father, family, and people; he executed her and slaughtered the rest of the defenders. History captured the noise of the Mongol horde's exacting vengeance on Gholghola's defenders by giving the citadel its modern name, the City of Screams. Fortifications around the sides of the cliff were still visible. One could also see holes all around the citadel at different levels, which were probably ruins of military posts, as well as cave-like openings that linked various sides of the citadel through internal passageways. There were stories that local inhabitants occasionally heard screams coming from the ruins around the date of that slaughter.

Aside from these side trips, our days in Bamiyan were spent meeting potential partners for the 4A Project. They were very eager to solicit our help in fighting corruption and pursuing reform-oriented work in the province. Bamiyan was an underdeveloped province and mostly populated by the Hazara ethnic group, which comprised around 9 percent of Afghanistan's population of roughly thirty-one million, of which 46 percent were Pashtuns. It was also small in terms of both population and the size of the economy, and the level of corruption was much lower than that in the Kabul or Herat Province.

The governor of Bamiyan was keen to share with us the challenges he was facing running the province and wanted across-the-board reform in his administration. He acknowledged that there was corruption in the provincial administration but wanted us to focus our efforts first on his own office. He was keen to overhaul the traditional way of doing things and replace it with modern methods of governance with greater transparency and accountability.

After our meeting, he immediately summoned the senior administrative staff of his office for a separate "heart-to-heart chat" with us, urging them to lay bare the obstacles and bottlenecks in their work and within the system and to seek our help to achieve greater efficiency and transparency. The meeting with them was quite productive and ended with their commitment to list the issues they were facing, prioritize them in terms of urgency and importance, and then sit with us to work out a strategy on how to address them systematically and expeditiously.

We also met with the acting Speaker of the provincial council because the Speaker was in Kabul at the time. He was receptive to working with us, but his six provincial council colleagues who were attending the meeting as well seemed to be less enthusiastic. We attributed their lukewarm response to their low level of education and exposure and their inability to quite understand the importance of transparency and accountability issues. They seemed to be rather suspicious of our motives, a reservation born out of years of dealing with the majority Pashtuns who consistently short shifted them. The acting Speaker subscribed to our initial reaction that the provincial council was lacking sufficient women representation and that it lacked necessary reform-oriented legislation. He promised to take up our concerns with the Speaker, as well as our offer of assistance in provincial council reform efforts, when he returned.

The meetings with the civil society organizations were also promising, although they appeared to be disorganized and isolated in their work from each other. They were also quite small in number. What was notable, however, was that women appeared to be more engaged in socioeconomic activities than were men, and the number of voluntary organizations mostly led by women outnumbered the men-led NGOs. We had several meetings with them, the final one being a group meeting where most of the civil society organizations and activists were present. We drew up a tentative must-do list and a tentative action plan to be further refined with consultation with Daud.

We also reached out to the media, the academia, and a few donors who were active in the region. The media was weak, and we decided not to spend any effort on it at this early stage of our engagement. The academia had inadequate governmental support and was underdeveloped, and research capabilities within the province were rudimentary. Our meeting with the vice-chancellor of Bamiyan University gave us a good picture of what was at stake. He listed the inadequacies that existed within the university—namely, lack of qualified teachers especially in subjects important to the central highlands in general and to the province in particular, absence of residential facilities particularly for female students, inadequate library resources for teachers and students, and inadequate funding. The picture he painted was of a stagnating future. We raised with him issues of corruption in student admission and in marking of exam papers among others, and he acknowledged that could be possible, but he was unaware of it.

All in all, our Bamiyan visit was highly informative and provided us with a reasonably clear picture of what needed to be done in the governance sector, what were the obstacles that we were likely to face, where the opportunities lay, and how to strategize our engagement in the province. We were clearheaded about what could be done and what couldn't be done, who were our most promising partners, and how to build the partnerships we needed to deliver results.

We were scheduled to catch the second weekly flight out of Bamiyan, which was four days from our arrival date, and so we checked out of the hotel and went to the airport. Upon arrival, we learned that the return flight from Bamiyan was cancelled because of a reason that one would hear only in the dictatorial third world country. A minister had come from Kabul to Bamiyan on official business, with his wife accompanying him. They were scheduled to leave on the return flight, but his wife insisted on visiting Badakhshan Province, lying further northeast bordering Tajikistan and China. So the return flight was cancelled as the minister and his wife took off for the north.

Having no choice, we returned to the hotel only to find that our rooms were already rented out to people who were in the waiting list and were staying at Noorband Qala. Both the hotel manager and we were in a quandary. The hotel manager fully understood our frustration and sympathized with us. After much soul-searching, he made a special provision to accommodate us. He put up a shamiana on the rooftop and provided makeshift beds for us there. He also arranged to serve us food on the rooftop and tried to attend to all our needs, all the time apologizing to us for the conduct of the Afghan minister and his wife.

Meanwhile, the Eastern Horizon Airways promised to dispatch another aircraft the following morning to bring back the Bamiyan passengers who were stranded. The next morning, Friday, June 7, we checked out of the hotel, but the hotel manager declined to take any payment for the overnight stay and for the food. He said that the temporary rooftop setup will remain intact until he saw the aircraft actually take off with its passengers, just in case! We profusely thanked him for his kindness and generosity and were relieved to be on board for our return flight to Kabul.

It was a relief to be back on familiar territory and to be able to unwind after a hectic five days of business and pleasure in Bamiyan. Not only did we find a promising province to launch our governance reform work, but also the places we visited provided incredible sights and would remain memorable for the rest of our lives. The following evening, it was a pleasure to invite our Ottawa friend Abdullah bhai's daughter Sameera Hussain and her coworker Atiyah Rahman to dinner and to reminisce about Ottawa. Sameera had come to Kabul on June 2 on BRAC work and was scheduled to leave on June 17.

On June 13, we received confirmation from the USAID/Kabul that our three-year project would be further extended until November 15. That evening, I took Sameera out to a farewell dinner at Le Jardin a few days before her departure from Kabul for Dhaka. There were other good news; Mumu texted on June 14 from London that Mishu's architectural show that she had attended was "incredible," that Mishu was graduating from Westminster University with an upper second-class honors, and that Mishu was scheduled to leave London on June 23 for Pisa and Florence on postgraduation holiday.

But June 2013 was also quite a terrible month in terms of insurgent activity. These insurgents were primarily trained in Pakistan and regularly came across the border to target government installations; defense, police, and intelligence ministries; NATO military presence with American military convoys as their primary target; and foreign diplomatic presence. Their threefold objectives were to cripple the Afghan government, to force foreigners to leave their country, and to reestablish Taliban rule.

On June 10, insurgents attacked the Kabul airport at dawn, killing several airport staff until all seven insurgents were killed by the Afghan military by midmorning. The insurgents attacked again the next day, June 11, and this time, their target was the Supreme Court, where dozens of workers were massacred. Then on June 18, there was a huge bomb blast near our office. Their target was the Hazara leader Mohammad Mohaqiq, who had publicly expressed serious worries about NATO plans to pull out combat troops by end 2014, and the French government proposal to pull out their troops a year earlier, by 2013. He had also expressed strong skepticism about dialogue with the Taliban who had inflicted brutalities on the Hazaras and other minorities during their rule between 1996 and 2001, saying, "I don't believe in a miracle occurring, that the Taliban will change their way of thought, accept the Afghan Constitution, believe in democracy and the vote of the people."

Although Mohaqiq survived the attack, his armored vehicle was severely damaged. The blast occurred near the AFCAC secretariat, blowing out its windows, which wounded a dozen people and killed three passersby. The next attack was on June 25 on the Presidential Palace, causing damage to the palace grounds. All these attacks were inevitably followed by office lockdown, skewed schedules, and suspended travel.

Meanwhile, our workshops in the provinces were coming up. On July 26, Daud, Anurag, and I once again left for Herat to conduct workshops with the members of the provincial council and with the CSOs group. Sayed Fazlullah Wahidi, the governor of Herat, was pleased to see us return to Herat to work on governance reform. Breaking protocol, he came to see me at Hotel Nazary the same night and discussed a variety of provincial issues, followed by a formal meeting with Daud and me the next day. In total, we met three times, and each time, he was complimentary about our work with the multiple stakeholders in his province. On the third day, he invited us to iftar at his residence; his hospitality was over the top.

The workshop with members of the provincial council on anticorruption measures went off quite well, helped considerably by the active participation of the two national MPs from Herat and Balkh provinces who accompanied us under project fund. The half-day meeting with the NGOs/CSOs on reform measures and particularly on monitoring and reporting on corruption was also a great success. The turnout was much better than expected, and almost every participant took turns to speak to their issues. It became obvious that they had major concerns and were ready to tackle them head-on, one of which was the lack of communication between the NGOs and the governor's office. At the conclusion of the meeting, there was much enthusiasm around the table because of their newfound sense of empowerment derived from the technical and financial support that we promised to provide. Having completed our tasks in Herat, on July 29, we took the evening Safi Airways flight back to Kabul.

The month of August started with a bomb blast at the Indian embassy with extensive damage to its front entrance. The same day, August 3, the U.S. State Department issued a worldwide security alert and shut down twenty-one U.S. embassies for two days. The next day, half a dozen terrorists were caught in the outskirts of Kabul who were on their way to carry out multiple suicide attacks simultaneously.

A Surprise in Flight

The stress on all of us was becoming unbearable, and so I decided to take my R & R leave in early August, timing it to catch the Rogers Cup Tennis Finals in Montreal on August 11. I left Kabul on August 6 by Safi Airways for Dubai. I was seated on the front row in the economy class, when immediately after takeoff, a flight attendant asked me if I was "Dr. Shaukat Hassan." When I answered yes, he asked me to kindly follow him. He took me to the first class and pointed to an aisle seat in the first row next to an elderly bearded gentleman sitting by the window. The attendant then introduced me to the gentleman, saying that he was Ghulam Hazrat Safi, the founder owner of Safi Airways who wanted me to sit with him.

I was pleasantly surprised and felt honored to be sought out for his company. As the attendant served me a glass of orange juice and a mélange of roasted nuts, Mr. Safi smiled at me and then said in Dari— which was translated by the attendant—that he knew me well from the kind of work I was doing and that it was important work because how Afghanistan developed depended a lot on our work. I thanked him for appreciating our work and volunteered that I was committed to my work and to the betterment of the Afghan people and of Afghanistan even though, often, the going was tough.

He nodded in affirmation, adding that he fully understood how difficult it must be not only in terms of physical security but also equally in terms of navigating political pushbacks and interference. But, nevertheless, he thanked me for my endeavor and inquired how long my project would go on. When I told him it would end in mid-November, he looked away with a heavy sigh and then stared outside into the inky black sky while gently twirling his orange juice glass between his thumb and fingers. The attendant then sat on the aisle seat next to me to continue translating Mr. Safi's comments. We softly chatted off and on until it was time to land, when he wished me good luck and then handed me his business card. I thanked Mr. Safi and wished him good health and good fortune as we parted company.

With Ghulam Hazrat Safi, the founder owner of Safi Airways, on our flight from Kabul to Dubai, August 2013

A week later, on Sunday, August 11, Nipa, Mishu and I were on the road driving to Montreal to watch the Rogers Cup Tennis Final where Rafael Nadal defeated Milos Raonic by a score of 6–2, 6–2 at the Uniprix Stadium in Montreal. I would have preferred that my countryman won, but I wasn't too upset that Nadal won because he was one of my two favorite men tennis players, the other one being Roger Federer. It was a very enjoyable day in Montreal, although it would have been even better if our daughter Mumu was also with us. I returned to Kabul on August 20.

An Upset Minister

One of the important tools that we had been using in our anticorruption work was *vulnerability to corruption assessments*

(VCAs). We had a trained team headed by Aziz Ariaey, who used VCAs to detect corruption vulnerabilities within any business system and suggest how to eliminate those vulnerabilities and simplify the procedures within the business line to make it efficient, transparent, and accountable. After completing the VCAs, we wrote up the assessments with recommendations for step-by-step implementation, all the while monitoring and reporting on the implementation results. These VCAs were done in the government ministries to identify and eliminate corruption within their systems.

In one particular instance, after reading our VCA report, the minister in charge of that ministry asked to see Aziz Ariaey in his office. The minister thanked the 4A Project and Aziz in particular for the VCA work done in his ministry. Tea was served as the minister continued to flip through the pages of the report. Finally, the minister asked, "So this is a substantive report and contains many recommendations. In fact, there are so many of them that I don't know where to begin. Can you suggest where to start?" Aziz replied, "Sir, you might want to identify what is your priority and start there." "Everything is my priority," retorted the minister. "Well . . ." Aziz was struggling to give the minister a better answer. "Let me put it this way," said the minister. "Tell me the single most important action that I can take to bring real qualitative change and improve the work of the ministry." Aziz knew exactly what that single most important action was and unhesitatingly said, "You, sir." Somewhat perplexed, the minister asked, "What do you mean?" Not known for his diplomatic tact, and frequently blunt in speech and conduct, Aziz replied,"Well, sir, you are the greatest obstacle to reform. You should resign."

The minister's eyes nearly popped out of his head as he went ballistic, turned five shades of red, stood up, and yelled, "Get out!" at the same time barking at his orderly to take away the cup of tea that was served to Aziz. Aziz immediately hightailed from the ministry fearful of getting arrested by an irate minister. He returned to the office but did not report to me immediately, worried whether the minister might have already telephoned me to tell me how he was insulted by Aziz. He finally gathered his courage and told me what had happened.

I was stunned at Aziz's artless response to the minister and told him that while being truthful was extremely important, telling it to the minister's face was not the right thing to do. Mindful of our project work with the ministry being jeopardized, I immediately called the minister to apologize for the conduct of my staff. The minister knew in his heart that the VCA had correctly identified him to be the primary obstacle to reform, so after the initial outburst, he calmed down and assured me that we could continue working with his ministry, but Aziz Ariaey was never to set his foot in the ministry. Word of this altercation between Aziz and the minister had leaked out somehow, and it is possible that it reached President Ghani's ears as well. A few years later, Aziz was appointed by corruption-fighting president Ghani to be the chairman of the Electoral Complaints Commission of Afghanistan. That was quite a promotion.

Trip to Mazar-e-Sharif

Preparation had been going on following our Herat visit for a similar trip to Mazar-e-Sharif, the capital of the province of Balkh. It was the largest city in northern Afghanistan and the fourth-largest city in Afghanistan, located short distances from the border with Uzbekistan and Tajikistan. It was called Mazar-e-Sharif, which means "Tomb of the Prince" because of the impressive blue-tiled mosque and sanctuary in the center of the city known as the "Shrine of Ali" or the Blue Mosque. The religion of Islam gained a foothold in Mazar in AD 651, and its Islamic and Hellenistic archeological sites and religious shrines made it a great tourist attraction. Unlike most other provincial capitals, it sat on a very fertile region producing cotton, grains, and fruits.

The 4A Project had conducted an initial survey of potentially promising Afghan provinces for anticorruption work using several criteria, among which were the size of the population, the province's importance to the country's economy, its political importance, and receptivity to anticorruption work. Mazar-e-Sharif was deemed to be a prospective candidate, not least because of the province's strong and vibrant nonstate stakeholders. On August 31, Daud, Shakib, Gurung, three parliamentarians, and I left for Mazar-e-Sharif by Kam Air.

We landed in what was clearly the most modern airport in Afghanistan. It was built by the German government and was understandably, neat, tidy, and very organized. There were plaques everywhere thanking the German government for their generosity. Unlike Herat, whose culture and outlook were heavily influenced by Iran, Mazar-e-Sharif reflected the values, culture, and outlook of the Turkish republic. The names of buildings and roads, the products in the shops, and the menus in restaurants were more Turkish than anything else.

The next day, we held a workshop with members of the Balkh Provincial Council. Once again, the active participation of the three parliamentarians from the national Wolesi Jirga convinced the council members of the importance of governance reform to a stable and progressive political and economic order. They agreed to create an anticorruption commission within the provincial council, which was a serious first step toward reform and therefore a great achievement.

The next day, we had a very productive meeting with the chancellor and the heads of faculties and departments of Balkh University, which gave us the opportunity to probe their faculty hiring, student admission, paper grading, and other policies and procedures. We were happy to learn that the university senior administration had anticipated corruption opportunities and already set up an anticorruption commission to regularly monitor and report on any discrepancies as well as suggest remedies.

The two workshops with the civil society organizations were a real learning experience as they shared with us lots of shady stuff going on in the province, although they were hesitant to discuss them in public. What was also noticeable was their guarded and circumspect comments about their dictatorial governor, Atta Muhammad Nur, who had been holding on to that office since 2004. They were, however, quite critical of the national government in Kabul and voiced their sentiments freely and publicly. Our press briefings went off well, although we were forewarned by members of the civil society not to make any adverse comments about the governor and his office.

We had contacted the governor's office in advance to inform them of our plan to visit the province and to seek an appointment with him as we did in the case of Herat and Bamiyan. But we had received no response from his office, which we interpreted to mean his unwillingness to meet with us to discuss governance reform. So we did not correspond with the governor's office further. After we arrived in Mazar-e-Sharif, we contacted his office once again, but we were told that he was away in Kabul on business. So once our project work was done in Mazar-e-Sharif, we returned to Kabul on September 4.

The next day, we learned that the governor was angry that we were in Mazar-e-Sharif during his absence and that he was furious at the hotel manager where we stayed for allowing us to stay there. He immediately passed a *farman* (edict) requiring henceforth all hotels in the province to seek prior approval of the governor's office before renting out to out-of-province officials or foreigners visiting the province. It became somewhat clear to us why the NGOs and CSOs were so hesitant to criticize the governor or his office.

Our work with the women members of the lower house of parliament, the Wolesi Jirga, who had formed the Parliamentary Anti-Corruption Committee (PACC), was gaining traction. They were the most committed and active partner we had in the fight against corruption. They knew that there was massive corruption within the parliament and within the government, and they knew exactly what needed to be done to bring reform to both. They also knew what their strengths and weaknesses were in trying to fulfill their objectives.

With the help of our senior project manager Daud, they undertook a gap analysis of their own abilities and realized that they needed to empower themselves with the necessary tools. They asked us to train them in three specific areas to start with: first, how to become effective parliamentarians so that they can represent their provinces properly and hold the government accountable; second, how to do budget analysis, amendments, and monitoring, which was a critical function of a parliament; and, third, on Extractive Industries Transparency Initiative (EITI). Afghanistan was a late comer to the EITI and was lagging considerably in its discharge of EITI-related commitments.

It was, indeed, surprising to hear them tell me that they didn't really know what being a good parliamentarian meant, and how to be one, and ask me to help them better themselves so that they could remain true to their parliamentary pledges. Admission of one's weaknesses is always a good start in the path to betterment, and I was happy to see that these women parliamentarians were fully open to self-evaluation. Thankfully, they did not suffer from a sense of self-importance and certainly didn't show any arrogance as many of their male colleagues often displayed. I immediately reached out to my colleague Prof. Rod Monger, at the American University of Afghanistan (AUAF), to organize the training workshops for the women parliamentarians.

Rod was a professor of business and highly entrepreneurial. He was playing an active role in expanding AUAF's capacities and had recently set up the International Center for Women Entrepreneurs (ICWE) at AUAF to create a platform for training promising women leaders for Afghanistan. He was quite eager and excited to organize the thematic workshops.

The four-day workshop for PACC started on September 7 and ended on September 10 and was held at the ICWE. The first all-day workshop was on Afghanistan's mineral wealth, which was plenty and an eye-opener to the PACC members, and on EITI, its mandate, modus operandi, role of a country member, and Afghanistan's record vis-à-vis its EITI commitments. The next-day workshop dealt with the mandate, roles, and responsibilities of a parliamentarian, debating tactics, as well as the strategies and tactics involved in caucusing and in intraparliamentary dialogue. The last two days were devoted to budgets and the budgeting process and how to hold the government accountable to parliament and to the people.

The three thematic workshops were a genuine learning experience for the PACC members, and they greatly appreciated accessing these skills. It was reassuring to see their enthusiasm and eagerness to try out their newly learned skills on the parliament floor. They also loved the certificate distribution ceremony and the dinner at the end of the workshops.

Attending an Afghan Wedding

A few days later, Daud, Gareth, Anurag, and I received invitations to attend the wedding of Samad's elder brother. There were a number of wedding halls in Kabul City whose exterior always flashed with multicolored running lights at night against the black Kabul sky and whose inside was garishly decorated. It was in one of these halls that accommodated several hundred people where the wedding reception was held, but with strictly separate, partitioned sitting of the two genders. The men sat together in the "outer" hall, while the women mingled together in the "inner" hall, and no man was allowed into the women's hall unless he was a close relative of the bride.

Not familiar with Afghan culture regarding wedding gifts, I asked Samad what was the normal custom. He said that gifts were generally brought to the bride's family after the wedding, which was quite different from my culture where wedding guests were expected to bring the gifts with them and deposit them at a designated spot by the entrance. I asked Samad whether giving money instead of a boxed gift was acceptable, and he said that it was. So I bought a wedding card and put U.S. dollars inside it, befitting my status in the eyes of my Afghan colleagues, sealed the envelope, and handed it to Samad, requesting him to give it to his sister-in-law.

At the wedding reception itself, we were among the honored guests and were assigned to a reserved round table near the dance floor. First, there was a round of a very sweet drink. This was followed by dinner comprising baked fish first and then roast chicken and then meat biryani served in big platters placed at the center of our table. There was a separate plate of naan. The biryani platter was replenished as soon as the first platter was nearly empty. Dessert comprising several types of very sweet dishes was served after dinner. We asked Samad to join us at the table, but he insisted on directing the catering service to our table to ensure that we were served properly and adequately.

Meanwhile, the dance floor was open from the start, and only young male dinner guests danced with each other as the musicians played their songs and music. During the entire reception, we did not see any female guests, and the groom and his father jointly visited us once to welcome us and thank us for coming. After dessert, the dance floor was packed with young and old Afghan men enjoying the wedding night to their hearts' content. We left before it got too late, and Samad summoned the groom and his dad to see us off. We congratulated the groom once again, thanked them for inviting us, and bid them farewell. For us, it was a good break from work and a chance to witness a typical urban Afghan wedding.

A New Opportunity Knocks

A week later, on September 17, Drago Kos, who was a senior international member of the Joint Anti-Corruption Monitoring and Evaluation Committee for Afghanistan (MEC), invited me to dinner at one of the expatriates' favorite watering hole, the Design Center Café. He informed me that General Hasan from Bangladesh, who was one of three international members in MEC, had informed them of his decision to resign from the committee for health reasons. He was an elderly gentleman who had joined MEC after retiring from his last posting as Bangladesh's ambassador to the Middle East.

Drago informed me that the committee felt that I would be an excellent replacement, and since my USAID project was ending in mid-November, they would like to recommend me to the international selection board if I agreed. Needless to say, I was pleasantly surprised and nodded my assent. Drago requested that I forward the committee an updated CV. Ten days before my departure from the project, on November 5, MEC's chairman Prof. Yasin Osmani invited me to a farewell lunch at Majid Mall Buffet and informed me that I would be a great addition to the committee and that I should submit a formal application. Also present at the lunch was Afghan committee member Yama Torabi, Canadian policy advisor Grant McLeod, and Professor Osmani's eldest son. When I informed Drago about Professor Osmani's support for my candidacy, he was very happy that the Afghan component of MEC was also keen for me to join MEC.

The Afghan National Election and the Anticorruption Pledge

The Afghan national election was on the horizon, and there were scores of political parties and political candidates who declared their candidacy. The two principal presidential candidates were former foreign minister in Hamid Karzai's government Abdullah Abdullah and Karzai's economic minister Ashraf Ghani. Daud and I saw the national election as an opportunity to leverage our anticorruption work, and we decided to draft an anticorruption pledge. We suggested to AFCAC that spearheaded NGOs/CSOs effort to combat corruption that they might consider demanding that all the presidential candidates should publicly sign the anticorruption pledge as a commitment to abstain from engaging in corrupt activities and to actively combat corruption if elected. AFCAC members thought that that was indeed an excellent idea and asked us to draft the pledge for them. We then handed to them the draft we had already prepared. AFCAC members debated over the draft, made a few changes, and then voted unanimously to adopt it. We saw this as a potential game changer, and the real challenge was to get the presidential candidates to publicly sign the pledge.

Jim Wasserstrom of USAID/Kabul to whom I reported every week was pleased with our innovative approach to leverage the elections. He asked us to provide a "success story" every two weeks for the USAID information pamphlet. We mailed him three success stories in the fourth week of September and many more until the end of the project period.

Meanwhile, back at the ranch, Nipa and I had been discussing a vacation trip after my project ended. Mumu suggested that we should consider going to Morocco where she and her girlfriends had planned their vacation in mid-October. We liked the idea, but we wanted to include Spain as well and asked Mumu to do the itinerary for us. She was happy to do all the arrangements, from doing the itinerary, buying the tickets, and booking the hotels, which was a great relief for me because I didn't have to do any thinking for the trip. Our vacation was planned for three weeks, the second last week of November in Spain, the last week in Morocco, and the first week of December in the UK, timed to coincide with my brother Shahalam and his wife Luann's vacation in London from November 24 to December 2 so that we can jointly celebrate by birthday on December 1 in London.

On October 5, we learned that our landlord Haji Rashid and his nephew, who were visiting their home province of Logar, about a two-hour drive south from Kabul, were both killed by a carefully planned suicide bomb attack when their car stopped at a red light. Haji Rashid had impressed me as being a mild-mannered, soft-spoken, deeply religious man. When we first met during the negotiation to rent his property, which was our current project office cum residence, he was deferential to me, telling me that he was honored to be in the presence of an educated man because he himself was an uneducated man who hadn't even completed his secondary school education because his parents were too poor to send him to school.

The second time when we met to sign the rental contract prepared by our lawyers, he opened up further and told me how fortune had shone on him and made him a millionaire. He said that after he dropped out of school, he had hitchhiked to Kabul in search of a job. He used to get up very early in the morning, perform his namaz, and then sit by the roadside with his bamboo basket and a shovel waiting for construction contractors to pick him up for the day's work. He spent several years of his childhood being a day laborer until one day, a schoolmate, who, unlike him, had managed to finish his higher education and become an engineer, saw him by the curbside and stopped to inquire how he was doing.

His friend had won a contract from the U.S. military to build the electrified concrete boundary wall surrounding the Bagram Air Base. His friend then hired him to dig up the dirt to lay the foundation of the boundary wall. His friend was billing the U.S. military almost five times the market price for the construction material and minting money right and left, and the U.S. military didn't care. His friend had given him a very lucrative digging contract, which after several years of work at the base amounted to millions in Afghan money. Haji Rashid spent his profit on building several houses and renting them in U.S. dollars for a hefty annual income.

After several months into the rental contract, one day, he called my office for an appointment with me. He came to see me with his college-age son. When we met for the third time, he meekly apologized for "disturbing" me and then said that he wanted his errant son to see what an educated man looked like. He explained to me that he did not want his son to be an uneducated nobody like himself and pleaded with me to explain to his son the value of a good education and how that could bring honor and dignity to the family.

As I started to gently explain to his son the value of education and how he could lift up the entire family after his father passes away, he argued back saying that his father didn't need to be educated to become a very rich man, so why should he have to go to school to be rich? We went back and forth as Haji Rashid watched us, and then, finally, his son ran out of arguments. My appeal to his pride and to his hidden talent and potential seemed to make him take a pause, and he stopped arguing with me altogether. Haji Rashid got up, thanked me for my time, made his son thank me for devoting my valuable time to give him good advice, and then departed with the expectation that my chat with his son will convince him to go to college. I do not know what happened after that, because I never got to speak with him again before he was assassinated. The news of his death was very sad indeed.

4A Project Wrap-Up

Since the project was going to be over in a month, I was very busy attending to multiple tasks simultaneously to meet the deadlines. At the top of my list was the completion of all the project reports that were expected of me both by MSI head office and by the USAID. Second, I needed to find replacement funders for ongoing projects that had shown excellent results and had a promising future. It was imperative that those projects should continue and not be disrupted or shut down because of lack of funding. I had started sounding out the heads of other projects similar to the ones we were seeking support for from as early as the summer of 2013.

Discussions with Abdul Basir, the executive director of the multiple donor-supported Tawanmandi Fund, were positive. They were interested in taking over the funding of the national NGO group,

Afghan Coalition against Corruption (AFCAC), and of the Citizens Legal Advocacy Office (CLAO), which had been showing positive results. They spent a few months observing and monitoring the work of AFCAC and CLAO and were impressed enough to agree to fund them.

I also held a series of discussions with Peter Dimitroff, the COP of the Afghan Independent Bar Association (AIBA) project, and his deputy about transferring the reins of the Parliamentary Anti-Corruption Caucus (PACC). Their project dealt with strengthening the rule of law and the role of parliament, and PACC was a good fit for them. Daud was busy with several other projects that had been completed and needed the finishing touches, including wrapping up loose ends. MSI sent project operations director Tracey Brinson and project manager Sean Williams from head office to Kabul to assist me in completing the wrap-up.

Additionally, I took upon myself the responsibility of trying to ensure the future of my staff and undertook to use my network and influence to find job placements for them in other projects run by international donors after our project ended. I also started writing recommendation letters for each one of them.

Eid-ul-Adha fell on October 15, and as the staff prepared to go on Eid holiday, the excitement of Eid was mixed with the sad realization that after they return from the holidays, there will only be a few more weeks left before each will go his/her separate way. The camaraderie and friendship, and the elation and challenges, of working together for three years through the trials and tribulation of Kabul life would be over soon, and there was already an air of nostalgia about it. But we were never allowed to forget even for a moment the tough, insecure environment in which we were forced to operate, for on Eid day, the governor of Logar Province was assassinated at the Eid prayers. It was a stark reminder that you could not put your guard down for even one moment if you valued your life.

But be that as it may, all good things had to come to an end, and the 4A Project was not an exception. In anticipation of the termination of the project on November 15, I made it a point of strengthening my liaisons and doing some robust networking. Throughout the remaining weeks, I went out to dinners with friends and colleagues in Afghanistan such as Professor Osmani, Drago Kos, and Seema Ghani of MEC,

Henrik Lindroth of UNDP, Dr. Hassan of UNAMA, Prof. Rod Monger of the AUAF, and COPs of other projects.

On October 17, Mumu left for Marrakesh, Morocco, to join her friends who were already there. This turned out to be a boon for Nipa and me because Mumu was able to use her knowledge and experience of vacationing in Morocco to develop our trip to Morocco in considerable detail; she knew what the pitfalls were and how to avoid them and was also able to hire for us a reliable tour guide. Among other developments on the family front, my brother Sohel's only child, Sasha, left for higher studies in the United States on October 29. Having lost his wife shortly before, his daughter's departure from Dhaka left him totally alone, which was quite hard on him. The same day, knowing how much of a tennis buff I was, Mumu texted me to inquire whether I would be interested to watch the tennis competition that was scheduled to be held at Albert Hall, London, during our visit there; I immediately replied affirmatively.

It was also a time for farewells. AfCAC threw a farewell dinner for me at Star Hotel. The food was delicious, the gifts were chosen to remind me of Afghanistan and its peoples, and the farewell speeches by the heads of NGOs in the coalition were heartfelt. They also gave me a plaque containing a Certificate of Appreciation and hoped that I would return to Afghanistan soon. I received letters of commendation from MEC and from the HOO. At my last International Community Transparency and Accountability Working Group (ICTAWG) meeting on November 4, I received words of commendation from multiple international members for my active participation and contribution to its work. Jim Wasserstrom and his deputy Emily Wann from USAID invited me to a farewell dinner on November 7. Henrik Lindroth of UNDP invited me to a farewell dinner at Mai Thai restaurant on November 10. He expressed his desire to see me work for the UNDP in Afghanistan. The next day, I received a citation from the Radio Television Authority of Afghanistan for our work with the national media. As mentioned earlier, Professor Osmani, chairman of MEC, also invited me to a farewell lunch and asked me to send my application to join as an international member of MEC.

On November 11, my ticket from Kabul to London and Nipa's

ticket from Ottawa to London, our meeting point to commence our vacation, were confirmed for November 15. Additional happy news for us was that Mumu and Mishu confirmed that they would be able to take off from work and join us for a few days in Barcelona, which was one of several Spanish cities in our itinerary. Although we would have liked them to join us for the entire Spain-Morocco jaunt, we were happy that we would be able to spend at least a few days with them. The day finally dawned when on November 14, 2013, Sean and I departed Kabul. We had to leave for the airport four hours ahead of time for the thirty-five-minute drive because it was Ashura when the Shias would be on the streets in remembrance of the martyrdom of Prophet Mohammad (PBUH), and violent clashes between the Shias and Sunnis were highly likely. I flew Qantas Airways from Dubai to London and landed at Heathrow at 5:00 a.m. the next day, but without my luggage!

The first phase of the Afghanistan chapter in my life had come to a close. I had lived through a violent period experiencing suicide attacks, bomb blasts, and tension-filled existence, never quite sure whether my personal security was adequate, where the next attack would come from, and whether the precautions taken by my security staff would be enough to protect us from being blown apart or maimed for life. Being surveilled and videoed at night by a suspicious van, leaving Qargha after completing our office retreat just a few hours before the full-fledged terrorist attack on the resort that killed hundreds, avoiding the mines on the mountain side as we scaled Koh-e Asmayi, living through a terrorist attack on the police station a few houses from our office compound, avoiding insurgents and highway robbers on the way to Panjshir, surviving a terrorist attack while waiting in the office of the deputy governor of Herat, being stopped by Gareth from attending the Eid namaz at the Blue Mosque where minutes later multiple bomb blasts killed and maimed hundreds, and experiencing the shattering of my bedroom windows from that blast were all brush with fate.

But the work I did in Afghanistan was important, highly challenging but quite satisfactory. Some resulted in immediate visible achievements, while other works were foundational, planting the seeds of prospective returns and of a bright future. For the sake of American taxpayers whose money was financing the U.S. effort to democratize and stabilize Afghanistan, I hoped that it was not money wasted. I hoped that the massive sacrifices that were being made by NATO and particularly American troops would not go in vain. And that the brutal killings of innocent American experts trying to help their Afghan colleagues in various ministries would somehow end. As I departed Kabul in mid-November, I said good-bye to Afghanistan. But what I didn't know at the time was that my work in Afghanistan was not yet finished and that I would be called back within a few months.

Vacation in Spain and Morocco

On November 15, 2013, we boarded EasyJet from London Gatwick for Barcelona, Spain. We had been planning to visit Nipa's youngest uncle, Waziul Islam (Khuku mama), who had married a Spanish lady, Lourdes, and settled down in Barcelona a couple of decades earlier. He had two children, Dunni and Jasmina. They had visited us in Ottawa some years back when they were really little. After arriving in Barcelona, we registered for three nights at Hilton's Alexandra Barcelona, a boutique hotel in the heart of the city.

Khuku mama came to the hotel to pick us up. It was nice to see him after so many years. He hadn't changed at all, the same smiling, straight-talking, protective Khuku mama. After he had done his aeronautical engineering in London, he had returned to Bangladesh. My mother-in-law helped him get a job with the aircraft maintenance ground crew of Bangladesh Biman. But within a few weeks, he quit. Every family member and, most of all, my mother-in-law were very surprised at his sudden decision to quit. He explained that he had been with his maintenance crew inspecting several aircrafts during the short time he was there, but that he was horrified to see how some members of the maintenance team simply ticked off the boxes without doing the actual inspection. He said that he wasn't going to take responsibility for that and therefore did not want any part of it. He had abruptly left for Europe.

That morning, Khuku mama told us that he would give us a tour of the city, so after we packed into his car, we headed for the marina, by which time it started to rain. The wind had also picked up, and we could see the ocean waves turning violent. But he was prepared with several umbrellas in his car boot. We got off at the marina and held on to our umbrellas as we took pictures of the marina and of the yachts anchored in the marina bobbing up and down in the strong waves. We also photographed some architecturally interesting buildings. One was of Hotel Arts Barcelona located on the beachfront with a huge fish-shaped structure on the roof. We got back into the car and decided not to get out anymore because of the rain as Khuku mama drove us around the city pointing out the various sights and landmarks. As we passed by the campus of the University of Barcelona, Nipa suggested that I should try to teach there so that we could spend a few years in Catalonia; I thought that was a great idea.

In front of Antoni Gaudi's famous Church of the Sagrada
Familia (Holy Family), Barcelona, November 2013

The next day, the weather cleared up, and we set out on a walking tour of the city. We picked the streets that were famous for Catalan architect Antoni Gaudi's buildings. Gaudi is credited with being the father of Catalan modernism, and I was struck by how the buildings seemed to compete with each other in their ostentatiousness. Others describe his work as highly individualized and unique. It is interesting that his last name is Gaudi, similar to gaudy, which stands for something garish and tasteless. It is an inescapable fact that he designed buildings unlike any other one would see anywhere in the world.

We particularly enjoyed walking in Park Güell, located on Carmel Hill, which provided some fabulous views of Barcelona. The park was full of trees and shrubs and offered tourists an eyeful of unusual and colorful sculptures, mosaics and tiling, and twisting walkways. There was one area with many small fountains and hundreds of pigeons. We also took the hop-on-hop-off bus and saw many of the city's landmarks, including Gaudi's famous Church of the Sagrada Familia (Holy Family). At the time of our visit, the church was still incomplete, although construction of the church had begun in 1882 and only a quarter of the basilica was completed when Gaudi died in 1926. We could not see inside the church because the queue was too long and we didn't have the time to wait.

Our visit nearing its end, we invited Khuku mama's family to visit us in our hotel room. They were excited to come. Nipa gifted Lourdes and Jasmina bottles of perfume, which they were very happy to receive. Mama invited us to his apartment also, apologizing that he couldn't invite us to stay with him because his place was too small to accommodate us. We had lunch that Mama prepared, which was quite tasty. At one point, his son's girlfriend came over, and Mama winked and said to me, "Khub shoondor na?" (Isn't she pretty?). We had lunch, after which we all went to the nearby mall, where we did some shopping. I picked up a sweater for myself, which Lourdes insisted on paying for. We wrapped our trip to Barcelona, and early morning on November 20, Nipa and I flew Vueling Airlines to Granada, while Mumu and Mishu flew EasyJet back to London Gatwick.

Granada, Seville, Cordoba

We were eager to visit the cities of Granada, Seville, and Cordoba to see the grand imprints left behind by the Moorish Islamic civilization that ruled the Iberian Peninsula for nearly eight hundred years from AD 711 to AD 1492 until Granada, Islam's last bastion in Iberia, fell under the onslaught of Catholic forces under Ferdinand II. For us, it was the beginning of an exciting journey for the next few days, and Granada, which was located in the foothills of the Sierra Nevada Mountains and was the longtime capital of Moorish Andalusia, was the first stop.

In Granada, we stayed at Villa Oniria, a splendidly renovated nineteenth-century mansion with an exterior garden with fountains surrounded by aromatic plants and an interior courtyard that also had a water fountain. We decided to take the daytime Granada City Sightseeing Tour, which was an extended tour and covered many historical, cultural, and architectural relics such as palaces, fortresses, churches, bell towers, monasteries, convents, and plazas. But the most exciting stop was the Alhambra (the Red Castle because of its red exterior walls), a sprawling hilltop fortress complex encompassing royal palaces with terraces that overlooked reflecting pools, fountains, and orchard gardens.

Alhambra was originally constructed as a small fortress in 889 CE on the remains of Roman fortifications, but it was renovated and rebuilt in the mid-thirteenth century by the emirs of the Nasrid Dynasty who made Alhambra their royal residence and court of Granada. Following the Christian Reconquista in 1492, it became the royal court of Ferdinand and Isabella, and one of the first acts of this royal court was to sanction the voyages of Christopher Columbus in search of new worlds. Many centuries later, Napoleon tried to destroy Alhambra because it symbolized Muslim rule; this was no surprise because his unexplained hatred toward Islam was widely known, even as he ordered his soldiers to use the face of the Sphinx as target for cannon balls and as he himself spared no opportunity to desecrate mosques by walking into them on horseback.

The tour of the Alhambra was fascinating because of its aesthetic beauty, with the eye marveling at almost everything it saw. The exterior of the palaces comprised column arcades with passageways opening into beautifully planned gardens with fountains. The palace buildings were quadrangular with their rooms opening into a central court, many of which were decorated with sculptures and fountains with running water. The beautiful intricate designs on the walls and ceilings and the exquisite details on doors and archways were something to behold. No wonder that Moorish poets described Alhambra as "a pearl set in emeralds." The Alhambra remains today as Spain's most magnificent Islamic architecture and one of its major tourist attractions. Visiting the Alhambra was quite fulfilling for us, and we would recommend anyone visiting Spain to go see it.

Nipa and I also visited an empty bullring to see an actual arena where matadors display their bullfighting skills. I stood there at the center and tried to imagine the audience yelling, "Bravo!" and "Olé!" while Nipa was busy taking pictures. Our walks took us through streets lined with pomegranate trees, from whence the city was supposed to have derived its name, "Granada"; in fact, the fruit is so abundant that it appears on the city's coat of arms. Our only shopping was buying some jewelry and a pashmina shawl. We left Granada on the morning of November 24 on a three-hour bus ride to Seville, which became the capital of Andalusia after the expulsion of the Moors.

In Seville, we stayed at the wonderful Hotel Casa 1800, another restored nineteenth-century mansion centrally located in the Old Town. The rooms were beautifully appointed with elegant furnishings, hand-carved furniture, and attractive chandeliers. There was a rooftop terrace and a pool with a spectacular view of the city. Its location was also great, just a few minutes' walk to the Seville Cathedral and a short walk to Plaza de España in the Parque de María Luisa.

We walked by the majestic fifteenth-century Seville Cathedral, which housed Christopher Columbus's tomb. It was also famous for the Giralda, or the bell tower that was built by the Moors as the minaret for the Great Mosque of Seville. There were several castles within short distances. The Alcazar of Seville (from Arabic al-qasr, or "the castle"), adjacent to the Seville Cathedral, was originally a residential fortress built by the Moors but destroyed when the Christians conquered Seville. On its ruin was built the ornate Royal Alcazar for King Peter of Castile and which serves as the residence of the royal family during their visit to Seville to this day. The Plaza de España was a beautiful square with a large fountain and a pavilion. Some of its buildings were supposed to have been settings for filmed scenes from Lawrence of Arabia. The Parque de Maria Luisa, which stretched along the Guadalquivir River, was a splendid place to visit because of its many monuments, pavilion, tiled fountains, ponds with ducks and swans, and many birds. It was also rich in flora with pines, palms, orange and other trees, and flower beds, making it a veritable botanical garden.

Seville was also known for flamenco dancing, and we couldn't resist going to a flamenco show at the Flamenco Dance Museum, a short distance from our hotel, one evening. On our last evening in Seville, we decided to order a dish of nachos con guacamole and paella valenciana minus the mussels and snails.

Another place of considerable historical curiosity that was in our must-see list was the Great Mosque of Cordova (Mezquita de Cordoba), now known as the Cathedral of Cordova. So we decided to make a quick one-day trip to Cordova by tourist coach on November 24. It was only a forty-five-minute ride each way, and the trip was worth it. The Great Mosque/Cathedral has an interesting history. It is said to have been built on the ruins of a Catholic basilica built by the Visigoths who had converted to Christianity in AD 586. After the Umayyad conquest of Hispania in AD 711, the basilica was divided into half for Christian and Muslim worship. In AD 784, Abd al-Rahman I purchased the Christian half and converted the basilica into a mosque. In the next 450 years, his successors further expanded it to its present stature, but in AD 1236, the Reconquista expelled the Muslims and converted it to a church.

The Grand Mosque remains to this day as a shining example of ornate Moorish architecture. Seeking to emulate the splendor of the Umayyad Mosque of Damascus, its interior comprised evenly spaced 856 columns with radiant white and red double horseshoe arches, which led one observer to describe it as "countless pillars like rows of palm trees in the oasis of Syria." The centrally located blue-tiled dome was decorated with stars, and the ornately decorated and richly gilded *mihrab* (prayer niche facing Makkah) lay at one end. As with all mosques, the prayer hall was rectangular with aisles perpendicular to the *qibla* (direction Muslims face during prayer).

A number of exquisitely decorated chapels were added after Christian conquest. The walls of the mosque were decorated with beautiful calligraphy of Quranic inscriptions. The courtyard was surrounded by arcades with stained glass windows, and inside the courtyard were citrus trees, mosaics, and fountains. The mosque had fortified walls, watchtowers, and a tall minaret, which was later converted to a bell tower. The mosque boasted nine outer gates and eleven inner doors, each door leading to an aisle inside the mosque. A bridge linked the mosque to the Caliph's palace. Over the years, the Mezquita de Cordoba has charmed many of its visitors. In 1931, South Asia's philosopher and poet was moved to offer *adhan* (call to prayer) at the cathedral and pray there; he then penned the poem "The Mosque of Cordoba" in which he wrote:

> Sacred for lovers of art, you are the glory of faith,
> You have made Andalusia pure as a holy land!

We also visited the Torre de la Calahorra, or the Calahorra Tower, and the Roman Bridge. The tower was built by the Almohad Caliphate as a fortified gate to protect the Roman Bridge on the Guadalquiver. It offered panoramic view of the surroundings. We returned to Seville the same evening.

Marrakech, Morocco

Early next morning, on November 26, we took Iberia Airways from Seville to Madrid and then the afternoon flight the same day from Madrid to Marrakech, Morocco. I was impressed by the architecture of the Marrakech Menara Airport. We took a taxi to the old town, a short five kilometers away. While Marrakech had modernized, it still kept intact the medina, which was the densely packed, mud-walled medieval city dating back to the Berber Empire. It comprised chaotic crisscrossing unpaved lanes and by-lanes and dilapidated mud houses. Mumu and her girlfriends had been to Marrakech before and thought we should get the experience of living inside the medina instead of a modern hotel in the city. She reserved a room at the four-star spa Riad Anyssates located within walking distance from the Jemaa el-Fna Square and the souks. The taxi driver let us off at the entrance to the medina since taxis were not allowed to enter the medina. We had to pull our luggage through a narrow unpaved lane with aesthetically unpleasant surroundings until we had to turn to an even narrower passage that led to the riad.

Once inside the riad, it was much more pleasant. It was a nine-roomed building with a central courtyard containing a tiny swimming pool and dining area. It also had a Jacuzzi, hammam, and massage. The room was spacious with traditional furniture and furnishings but with modern amenities like free Wi-Fi. We particularly enjoyed the free breakfast that was served on the terrace with a panoramic view of the city.

After settling in, we got a description of the medina from our riad host. He recommended that we start our visit with the Jemaa el-Fna square and gave us directions to walk there. When we reached the square, we came upon a huge open space bustling with people and activities of all sorts. It was packed with entertainers such as snake charmers, fire breathers, monkey handlers, henna tattoo artists, and musicians taking turns to perform their particular artistry. There were hawkers and merchants with their wares pursuing tourists and often becoming a nuisance. On the opposite side of the square was a whole bunch of horses and carriages lined for services of all sorts.

The square opened up to souks radiating out in different directions that were full of shops selling traditional textiles, carpets, beautiful pottery, and jewelry. Another section of the square was lined up with street food restaurants serving traditional dishes, and smoked sheep's head seemed to be a favorite dish. To the uninitiated like me, that didn't sound appealing at all. As we checked out the restaurants, restaurant boys with menu in hand touted their specialties and competed with each other for customers. We had our first Moroccan tagine dish for lunch that day. As we waited to be served, we noticed tourists in rooftop bars trying to capture the hustle-bustle with their cameras. The whole atmosphere was abuzz with excitement. When we returned to the riad, we shared our experience with our host. He smiled and said that if that was exciting, then we should visit the square at night. When we returned to the square that evening, we were not disappointed. The entire square was lit up with multicolored lights, and there were loud music, stage performances, acrobats, and other types of entertainment; it was packed with tourists and locals, and the atmosphere was truly electric.

The next day, we bought the twenty-four-hour hop-on-hop-off bus tour tickets to see the iconic sights of the city. We stopped at the Palais Bahia, a late nineteenth-century palace built during the time of Sultan Muhammad ibn Abd al-Rahman. It was magnificent. The decorated pink-and-white entrance to the palace grounds opened up to a garden path that led to the palace. There were two tree-filled courtyards; the grand courtyard was paved with blue and white tiles laid out in geometric pattern as was typical in Islamic architecture, with a central fountain with green and white tiles around it. Surrounding the courtyard was a gallery with decorated and painted stucco walls. The ornate chambers of the palace had painted and sculpted wooden ceilings, some with decorated alcoves while others with exquisitely designed fireplaces. I have to say that all the Moorish palaces reflected the best in Islamic architecture, architecture being one of the finest Islamic art form. And the presence of domes, minarets, mihrabs, alcoves, arches, courtyards, gardens, fountains, and geometric patterns was a dead giveaway that it was Islamic. Today, the Palais Bahia is occasionally used by the king of Morocco to receive foreign dignitaries and host important events.

We also visited La Mamounia Palace Hotel, which was built in 1929 on the fifteen-hectare palace garden that was gifted by Sultan Mohammed ben Abdallah to his son Mamoun. It was built facing the beautiful Atlas Mountains. We couldn't tour the interior because of repair work going on at the time. The beautiful La Mamounia Gardens were adjacent to the palace-hotel. Not far from it was our next stop, the famous rosy-pink-colored Koutoubia Mosque, the largest mosque in Marrakech. It was named after the Arabic word for bookseller because booksellers plied their trade at the foot of the mosque from the time of its reconstruction in the twelfth century. A notable feature was its 253-foot-high Moorish minaret that is visible for miles.

Another stop was at the famous Jardin Majorelle, named after painter Jacques Majorelle. In 1919, he left France and came to Marrakech to continue his passion for painting. In 1924, he purchased land to begin landscaping, which resulted in the present-day garden. The garden is said to be an expression of his individual spirit for it contains vegetal shapes and forms representing five continents, stamping him as one of the greatest plant collectors of his time. Some of these plant forms have to be seen to be believed. Particularly fantastic was his collection of cacti; their size and variety were stupendous. We finished off the tour of the garden with a lovely lunch in the courtyard.

The night bus tour offered us another view of the red city. I was surprised to see that Christmas hollies and Christmas lights festoon the roadside trees and the street lampstands already in late November, and Marrakech wasn't even Christian! Even in Canada, we don't see Christmas lights in public buildings, streets, and monuments until the first week of December. In any case, the whole city looked beautiful and sparkling during the night bus ride.

Fascinating cacti in Marrakech's Jardin Majorelle, Morocco, November 2013

Our Moroccan visit was going to remain incomplete without visiting Casablanca, so we decided to make a day trip to the city that was made famous by Humphrey Bogart and Ingrid Bergman in the movie *Casablanca*, which was wholly filmed in the Warner Brothers Studios in Burbank and Van Nuys Airport, Los Angeles, California! We rented a taxi ensuring that the driver was familiar with the city of Casablanca and understood some English. We left the medina in the early morning for the two-and-a-half-hour drive to Casablanca, located 244 kilometers up north on the coast. We drove through desert land with stunted trees here and there, but mostly sparse. We stopped at a restaurant to eat lunch.

When we arrived in Casablanca, we drove straight to the Hassan II Mosque standing on a promontory between the harbor and a lighthouse, looking out to the Atlantic Ocean. Touted to be the largest functioning mosque in Africa accommodating over one hundred thousand worshippers during prayers—twenty-five thousand worshippers inside and eighty thousand outside its front and side entrances—it has the second-tallest minaret in the world at 210 meters (sixty stories high) topped by a laser whose light is directed toward Makkah. It has a retractable roof. Its nine-hectare ground contains a madrasa, hammams, a museum of Moroccan history, conference halls, and a library described to be the "most comprehensive in the Islamic world." The mosque also has a courtyard with forty-one fountains and is surrounded by a garden. When Nipa and I tried to enter the mosque through the front entrance, she was stopped and directed to enter the mosque through a side entrance into the section reserved for women; I don't know how Nipa felt, but I felt a strong sense of discrimination.

Following the mosque visit, we took the coastal drive through Casablanca's Corniche, or the beachfront. We saw the lighthouse, the port, and some stretch of the beach. The taxi driver then gave us a tour of some of the landmarks of the city, and we saw the Royal Palace, the Cathédrale du Sacré Coeur, Notre Dame de Lourdes with its brilliant stained glass window, and the central marketplace. We returned to Marrakech the same evening. On our last night there, we revisited the Jemaa el-Fna square and purchased beautiful hand-drawn different-colored ceramic plates, serving platters, a red tagine, and other decorative pieces.

On November 30, 2013, after checking out from our riad, at the airport, I bought a pair of indoor slippers and a two-piece satin pajama. We boarded Ryan Air for our afternoon flight from Marrakech to London's Luton Airport. We took a taxi from Luton to come to Mumu's flat at Wembley, but the driver had a terrible time finding her place despite Mumu's continuous direction over the cell phone. It was indeed a great Spain-Morocco vacation for us.

2014—DfID's Assignment

My first consultancy offer in 2014 came from the UK office of the Sydney-based international development agency named Coffee International Limited. They had won the bid from the Department for International Development (DfID) of the United Kingdom, which was responsible for administering British overseas aid. The consultancy required carrying out a short-term scoping exercise in Ukraine following the Euromaidan Revolution, which was triggered by President Yanukovych's surprise refusal in late February 2014 to sign the association agreement with the EU and by the public's unwillingness to tolerate the corruption that had become the hallmark of Yanukovych's government and administration. It had ushered Viktor Yushchenko into power.

DfID wanted to take the lead among the European development agencies to support Ukraine's democratic transition and especially its anticorruption efforts and wanted to know how its resources might best be used and who the best partners would be in this effort. The emphasis was on identifying the immediate rather than longer-term opportunities.

Coffee International, which was recommended to contact me for this consultancy, did their due diligence in checking out my background and references, and then approached me with their offer, which I readily accepted. I had enjoyed my previous work in Ukraine. I had last visited Ukraine in early 2005 immediately after their Orange Revolution, which was precipitated by massive countrywide civil disobedience, political demonstrations, and strike actions from late November 2004 to January 2005, leading to the ouster of Viktor Yanukovych and the election of Viktor Yushchenko.

I flew to Kiev on March 24 for a week's work, which was later extended to April 5 on my request. I checked into the Hotel Senator Maidan in Kyiv city center and spent the rest of the day contacting individuals and organizations in my list and setting up appointments. The scoping exercise involved essentially three things. First, a preliminary desk research to understand the genesis of the recent political upheaval and the evolving political context that had implications for Ukraine's future. Second, reaching out to a maximum number of stakeholders to try to capture the extent and depth of concerns regarding corruption. They included civilians and government officials concerned with governance and anticorruption reform, and who were currently planning to or were engaged in designing anticorruption measures. As a result, the list of interviewees comprised interlocutors representing the business community, international financial institutions (IFIs), donors and implementing partners, the civil society (NGOs and INGOs), parliament, the media, and the government.

And, third, interviews and follow-up interviews of important actors.

The Euromaidan movement had affected the Ukrainian society at multiple levels. It generated public support for the demand to urgently clean up the country's governance structures. It galvanized civil society organizations (CSOs) to act with a common purpose. It strengthened the links between CSOs/NGOs and the public, uniting them against the government. It elevated CSOs as an equal partner with the government in anticorruption negotiations. It forced the government to publicly concede that corruption was undermining the economy and had to be addressed immediately. It forced parliament to work with civil society in the development of required reformist legislation. And it led to joint initiatives by the government, parliament, and CSOs to address the country's economic woes.

It also legitimized civil society's role as monitor and overseer of government's and parliament's efforts to promote transparency and accountability in their work. It made civil society a political force, forcing both the government and parliament to acknowledge that they must not be seen to be on the wrong side of history.

The scoping exercise led to consultations with national and international stakeholders, ranging from the European Union (EU), International Finance Institutions (IFIs), and international donors, to the government, parliament, and CSOs. It revealed, on the one hand, tremendous enthusiasm and urgency among Ukrainians to utilize this window of opportunity to initiate and effect as much governance and anticorruption reform as possible prior to the presidential elections in late May 2014. On the other hand, it highlighted a cautious optimism and a wait-and-see posture among the majority of the development agencies.

In light of this cautious approach by other European governments, I recommended that Her Majesty's government might wish to seize this opportunity to demonstrate leadership in a number of areas, ranging from international advisory services and technical assistance in key areas, to institutional strengthening and operational funding. I also recommended the top candidates who could receive immediate assistance. DfID was "very pleased with the report" and commended me "for a Stirling piece of work." They mentioned the relevance of my report "to the rest of the portfolio that DfID are working on" and were "pleased with the recommendations" that I provided. Within a month, DfID launched a number of projects aimed at strengthening Ukraine's reform efforts.

Call to Join MEC

Shortly after my return from Kiev in early April 2014, I received a message from Jim Wasserstrom/USAID in Kabul inquiring what I was up to these days. I replied that I had just completed a consultancy in Ukraine and that there was no further commitment in the immediate future. He wrote back saying that he thought I would be a great candidate to fill the void at MEC left by General Hasan's resignation, that I had strong support from the UN Assistance Mission in Afghanistan

(UNAMA) as well as from senior MEC members, and that I should apply for the post.

I wrote back thanking him for his confidence in me and for his support and mentioned that Professor Osmani and Drago Kos had already intimated to me before my departure from Kabul that I would be a good addition to MEC. I also informed him that I would be interested to replace my Bangladeshi compatriot as the third international member of MEC. The other two international members were Drago Kos, who was the former chairman of the Commission for the Prevention of Corruption in Slovenia and the current chairman of the Anti-Bribery Commission of the OECD; and Eva Joly, who was a Norwegian-born French judge, the chairman of the French Green Party who represented that party as a candidate for the presidency of France in the 2012 presidential elections, and a member of the European Parliament since 2009.

Following Gen. Hasan Mashud Chowdhury's resignation in November 2013, members of the MEC Nominations Committee comprising the United States, the UK, and the UNAMA had launched an international search in January 2014 to find a suitable replacement. The committee received a total of six applications, although were it not for the hazardous nature of this assignment in Afghanistan, there would have been scores of applications for the prestigious position. I learned later that after scrutiny of the six CVs and their reference checks, five candidates were selected for interviews.

Following the interviews, the Nominations Committee in their letter dated May 25, 2014, requested Prof. Yasin Osmani, chairperson of MEC, to forward my name to Pres. Ashraf Ghani for his approval so that the committee could confirm my appointment. On June 1, Dr. Rashed Behroz, executive director of MEC Secretariat, informed Mr. Hassan El Hag, the head of the Civil Affairs Unit of the United Nations Assistance Mission in Afghanistan, that "His Excellency, the President of Afghanistan, issued Presidential Order #1747 dated 10/3/1393 (May 31, 2014) that approved the nomination of Mr. Shaukat Hassan as an international member of MEC." I subsequently received my appointment letter as one of the three international members of MEC.

It bears remembering that MEC was a nonnegotiable product of the International Conference on Afghanistan that was held in London on January 28, 2010. Foreign ministers and senior representatives from more than seventy countries and international organizations came together to chart the future course for a stable and secure Afghanistan. Among them were the UN secretary-general Ban Ki-Moon, British prime minister Gordon Brown, British foreign secretary David Miliband, U.S. Secretary of State Hillary Clinton, and from the Afghan side Pres. Hamid Karzai, Foreign Minister Dadfar Spanta, Finance Minister Omar Zakhilwal, and former finance minister Ashraf Ghani.

The one-day conference hosted by the United Kingdom, the United Nations, and the Afghan government was aimed at staying the course on the democratization of Afghanistan and the elimination of insurgency from the country. In light of the huge international financial aid that Afghanistan was pledged, the conference communiqué stated that the Afghan government undertook to establish "measures to tackle corruption, including the establishment of an independent Office of High Oversight (*sic*) and an independent Monitoring and Evaluation Mission." On the point raised by Finance Minister Zakhilwal that 80 percent of development funds for Afghanistan were disbursed without any Afghan government control, the conference agreed that within the next two years, the Afghan government would get control over half the total funds provided Kabul demonstrated real progress "in improving its performance, in particular in the fight against corruption."

President Karzai, shortly thereafter, created the High Office of Oversight and Anti-Corruption (HOOAC), which was the principal client for the first two years of the USAID project that I had managed, and the International Joint Anti-Corruption Monitoring and Evaluation Committee (MEC), which I joined during its twelfth mission in June 2014. During my tenure that ended in February 2017, I served as an international member and as chairman of MEC and participated in eleven missions, each lasting two weeks. During almost every mission, we had the privilege of meeting with the Afghan president to share with him our findings and make recommendations. We produced six-monthly reports that detailed not only the state of corruption in the administration but also steps taken to remedy the situation based on recommendations made in the previous six-monthly report. We also undertook special inquiries deemed critical to the government as requested by the office of the president.

During every mission, MEC made it a point of visiting at least one Afghan province to see firsthand the state of governance there, to confer with the provincial governor, the high officials of the provincial administration, and the nonstate actors. These meetings were very useful and provided us not only with information and data that one cannot capture through desk research but also various perspectives on issues facing the province. These outreach efforts yielded considerable varied and rich information that allowed us to make reasonably accurate assessments of what was wrong and what was on track in provincial administration and to make realistic recommendations. At the end of every mission, we conducted a press conference where we presented our mission report and fielded media questions.

During my tenure, as also before and after my tenure, MEC addressed dozens of important issues among which were some critical ones that directly affected Afghanistan's good governance capacity, economic stability, and the democratization process itself. And at the very center of it all was the inability or more often the unwillingness of government/civil service officials to tackle corruption. The six-monthly reports and the special reports spell out our work, and these are available in the MEC website for anyone interested to read.

Each of the provincial visits yielded memorable moments that would be hard to forget. For example, during MEC's Herat provincial visit, we had been talking with the governor and other senior officials about the pilferage of aviation fuel at the land border by customs people themselves. The fuel was then sold to neighboring markets at an exorbitant price, netting the customs people hundreds of thousands of dollars each year. To illustrate how bad corruption among the customs officials was, the governor, in one of his lighter moments, narrated to us a very interesting if sad story. He said that the senior-most border customs official was due to retire, and so his staff wanted to give him a farewell party and a going-away present he will remember forever. They spent days discussing what to give him and couldn't reach a consensus. Then, finally, they did. They decided that his retirement will be extended by one extra day to allow him to make as much as he could that day, no holds barred, without him having to share his take that day with anyone! And that is what actually happened; the earning that day was so phenomenal that the retiring official was purportedly over the moon!

Since each mission was only two weeks in duration, it did not give the MEC members enough time to do all the things we wanted to do. So we tried to maximize our efforts during these visits as much as we could. During our Herat trip, we had discussed the possibility of making a quick day visit to the province of Farah, Herat's neighbor to the south. Since Farah had no airport then, we decided to drive to the Farah-Herat border to meet the governor of Farah and his senior officials. Our security team was quite nervous about the drive through the lawless roads, and so the governor of Herat decided to give us a police escort all the way to the border. But when we arrived at the border, we waited for the governor, but he didn't show up. The next day, we learned that he couldn't let go a highly lucrative deal that would make his pocket considerably heavier and had opted to abandon our prearranged meeting. For us, it was a wasted trip through unsecured territory and, more importantly, a waste of our very precious time.

Our July 2016 trip to the province of Badakhshan in the northeast bordering Tajikistan to its north, China to its east, and Pakistan to its south was another eye-opener. The most critical issue facing the province was the illegal exploitation of its mineral resources. Although Badakhshan was one of the richest provinces in Afghanistan in terms of mineral wealth in the form of gold, lapis lazuli, rubies, emerald, and turquoise deposits, the province was one of the poorest because of unplanned and largely illegal mining.

Luncheon with the Governor of Badakhshan at a park, July 2016

We scoured the daytime markets and the illegal black market and found ill-gotten gems. We discovered a number of vested interests involved, among them being the member of parliament from Badakhshan to the National Assembly in Kabul, some rogue military and police units of the province, and highly corrupt business people. We detected links between these rogue elements and the Chinese who were paying much below market price for the minerals that were being illegally extracted in the province with the help of Chinese expertise and equipment. The MEC team had split up into groups of two to pursue various lines of inquiries, which enabled us to get a handle on illegal mining, a thriving black market of precious gems, rogue police operations, hitherto unknown illegal transport routes from the mines to the border, and a highly corrupt provincial bureaucracy. Our subsequent report to the Afghan president covered all these findings and much more.

Among the urgent demands of the civil society organizations we conferred with were the need to reform the provincial police, appropriate punishment for the rogue military elements operating in the province, reporting on the corrupt activities of the Badakhshan MP, shutting down of the illegal mining operations, and holding the prominent businesses of the province accountable for their illegal conduct and collusion with the Chinese. All in all, the Badakhshan visit was quite informative as well as most secure perhaps because it was the only province in Afghanistan that the Taliban were unable to conquer or control during their rule from 1996 to 2001. It also helped the Afghan government to get a clearer picture of what was actually happening in the province.

Similarly, during our visit to the Bamiyan Province in east central Afghanistan, our extensive discussions with the governmental and nongovernmental stakeholders revealed that the two greatest concerns of the people of Bamiyan were the subversion of the recruitment process for government services and corruption in the courts and the police. The people of Bamiyan Province who were mostly Shi'ite and ethnically Hazara have facial features that are mongoloid and are thought to be the progeny of the soldiers of Genghis Khan.

One general complaint from the stakeholders whom we spoke with was that recruitment of Hazaras into government service by the Tajik- and Pashtun-dominated national government was not proportionate to their numbers and was even more skewed in provinces where the Hazaras were in the minority. The other general complaint was that the courts and the police were thoroughly corrupt, making a mockery of the judicial process and of the delivery of justice. Unless these concerns were addressed urgently, the province would continue to suffer. Specific stakeholders had specific complaints, such as the teachers who complained of biased hiring process and insufficient funds and students who were bitter about lack of residential facilities especially for girls, favoritism in the admission process, and biased grading. Indeed, Bamiyan seemed to be a microcosm of Afghanistan as a whole.

It was interesting to note that throughout Afghanistan, the most recurrent and immediate concern was corruption within the judiciary, especially the courts; corruption in the security sector primarily among the police; and corruption within the national and local administrations especially with customs. There were three missions to Afghanistan in 2014 in which I participated, in June, September, and November. The intensity of work and the tight timelines during these missions took a heavy toll on its members. I desperately needed to unwind.

Havana Calling

Nipa and I had talked of vacationing in Cuba a few times. Our daughter Mumu had vacationed there earlier with her girlfriends and liked it immensely, with lots of pictures to prove it. When she returned from Havana, she told us that we have to visit Cuba. So the year 2014 ended with Nipa and I flying to Cuba on Sunwing Airlines, which was Canada's youngest airlines that serviced principally tourist destinations.

We departed Ottawa on a direct flight to Juan Gualberto Gomez International Airport in Varadero, Cuba. After landing in Varadero, we walked from the tarmac to a big warehouse-like hall where we filled out the disembarkation card and queued up in front of the passport control booths. We paid the visa fee and got the visa stamped into our passports. Everything went off quite smoothly and efficiently. As we waited for our luggage, the tour guide for our flight informed us to gather at a rendezvous point after collecting our luggage.

We were then told where we could and should exchange our dollars, pounds, and euros for the CUC (Cuban convertible peso) or for the CUP (Cuban peso). After money exchange was completed, we were to head toward the color-coded tourist buses parked parallel just outside the airport terminal, get on board the bus whose color matched the color on the top of our information pamphlet that was handed to us by our tour guide, and wait for the bus to take us to our respective resorts. Our resort was the Roc Arenas Doradas, a charming four-star resort, although by western standards, it was more like a three-star hotel.

At the currency exchange that was housed in the adjacent hall, I sought a number of clarifications and learned that Canadian cash could also be converted to CUC; that currency exchanges were available only at the airport, banks, and at the reception desks of hotels and resorts;

that ATMs did not accept credit or debit cards issued by U.S.-based companies; that if we exchanged dollars for CUP, then all the Cuban pesos had to be spent in Cuba, and whatever peso was left unspent, only a tiny amount of that could be taken outside the country as souvenir, but if we got CUCs, then the entire leftover amount could be reconverted to U.S. dollars or Canadian dollars. I converted US$200 into CUCs, not exactly knowing how much local currency we would need since most of our principal expenses had already been paid up front during the booking of the excursion trip and since things were supposedly quite inexpensive in Cuba.

We handed over our luggage to the bus driver, who stored them in the luggage compartment in the belly of the bus, and then we took our seats. A different tour guide boarded the bus and verified the names of the passengers against his passenger list. When all the passengers were accounted for, the bus started to roll. The tour guide welcomed us to Cuba and started telling us about his country and people, throwing out random jokes some of which were admittedly funny.

It was an all-inclusive Christmas vacation package from December 24 to January 2; the dates were chosen deliberately so that we could spend both Christmas and New Year's Day on the island. As the name suggested, everything substantive was paid for in advance, which included airfare, transfer from airport to our resort and return, all meals, and unlimited drinks. The package was a real boon for drinkers, since they could be at the watering hole all day long, and so the bar area of the resort was the most crowded place with the likes of Russians, Germans, French, and the Scandinavians irrespective of the day or the hour.

We have always had family get-together at home during Christmas time. But that year, the kids had decided not to come home from the UK for Christmas; so we left for our ten-day vacation in Cuba. I was quite excited about the Cuba trip because ever since my undergraduate days when I took courses on the island's political history including the Spanish-American War of 1898, the Cuban Revolution of 1953–1959, the role of capitalist Batista and socialist Castro, the Bay of Pigs Invasion of 1961, and the Cuban Missile Crisis of 1962, I have wanted to see Fidel Castro's Cuba.

I did not expect Cuba to be economically developed or Havana to be a megalopolis because of the severe economic sanctions imposed on Cuba by the United States ever since the ouster of the pro-American military dictator Fulgencio Batista in 1959. Despite these crippling sanctions, Cuba survived all those years primarily because of Soviet Union's purchase of Cuba's entire annual sugar production to preserve Cuban socialism and to use Cuba as a base to promote socialism in the rest of Latin America.

Through it all, Cuba succeeded in providing its people their basic needs, as well as one of the best health-care services in the world. Cuba's world-renowned medical treatments, especially in orthopedics, eye surgery, and cosmetic surgery, and in neurological disorders such as multiple sclerosis and Parkinson disease, have drawn to its shores hundreds of thousands of patients from all over the world, and much-needed hard currencies.

Since the 1970s, Cuba has not only sent medical personnel to many developing countries under bilateral medical service contracts but also provided free medical aid and services to countries hit by natural disasters such as the littoral states hit by the Indian Ocean tsunami of 2004, the Kashmir earthquake of 2005, and many natural disasters in Africa and Central and South America. An estimated twenty thousand children from Ukraine, Belarus, and Russia had been treated in Cuban medical facilities for radiation sickness and psychological disorders resulting from the Chernobyl nuclear plant explosion in 1986.

We registered at the Roc Arenas Doradas and promptly received two simultaneous briefings, one on all its facilities for its guests and the other on all the activities scheduled during our ten days at the resort. The room assigned to us was neat, tidy, and clean. Over the years, Nipa and I have judged the quality of a hotel primarily by its bathroom, and in this case, the bathroom cleanliness, décor, and furnishings were satisfactory. There was hot water in the taps, and the air conditioner actually worked. The outside temperature was a perfect 27–29 degrees centigrade, just the right temperature for us to enjoy our activities outside and on the beach.

Nipa wanted to get on the paddleboat and paddle toward the ocean, but I hesitated because my swimming skills were minimal while she didn't know how to swim at all. But, as all men know, the wife always wins at the end! There were many activities to choose from, and young couples seemed to be participating in almost all of them; we, however, were far more cautious and choosy. Reading our novels under the straw umbrellas or watching people's activities in the water and on the beach as we sipped our drinks or walking in the beach in the evening for miles was quite satisfying.

We took several outings on land and at sea. We took a catamaran to another island about thirty minutes away. Sticking our feet into the blue waters of the Caribbean was exhilarating. It stopped midway at a preselected spot for us to do some scuba diving. Although I am a chicken when it comes to water-related activities, I did take half a dive to peer down for a few minutes, much more than I can say for Nipa. At the island whose name I cannot recall now, we were offered two meal choices: either a chicken dish or a lobster dish, and, of course, we chose to go with the lobster. After about an hour on the island and its coconut tree-lined beach, we returned to the catamaran to head back to Varadero. On the return journey, we stopped at another spot in the ocean that held a school of dolphins trained to perform tricks for onlookers; we could actually get down waist deep to touch the dolphins. It was a wonderful day trip across the blue waters of the Caribbean.

The other memorable side trip was the day trip to Havana. We had several options: take the tourist bus, rent a taxi, or rent a '30s/'40s/'50s antique taxi and drive it to Havana ourselves. I was tempted to try out the antique car but feared some sort of a breakdown during the trip, so I just sat at the wheels of one of them for a picture.

We joined a tourist group on an early morning bus to Havana that picked up tourists from several resorts in Varadero on its way. Midway, we stopped at a tourist spot that was doing roaring business in native-made touristy products. Nipa bought a few items as souvenirs. After we arrived in Havana, we were told at what time to rendezvous at the same spot and were given the option of a guided tour of the city or of going on our own; we chose the latter.

Nipa and I walked about seeing and hearing the sights and sounds of Havana and taking pictures. We have wonderful memories of beautiful sculptures in city squares and parks, especially of *La Conversacion* sculpture by a French sculptor; of stilt walkers on streets; of pantomimes; of actual painted human figures contorted into statues in street corners; of Finch Vigil, which was Ernest Hemingway's house in the small hamlet of San Francisco de Paula now incorporated within the city limits; the Book Market, which carried books that were out of print but in Spanish; of the Havana Cathedral and the Havana dock; and of enchanting lanes, alleyways, and restaurants.

La Conversacion sculpture, Havana, December 2014

We stopped to eat at a recommended restaurant whose inside walls were plastered with pictures of revolutionaries, artists, and actors and actresses of earlier decades. The must-stop place was La Bodeguita del Medio, which was a restaurant-bar and a famous tourist destination because of the historical figures who patronized it, such as singer Nat King Cole; Salvador Allende, Latin America's first Marxist to be elected as president of Chile from 1970 to 1973; and poet Pablo Neruda, another Chilean poet-diplomat who started writing poems from the age of thirteen and won the Nobel Prize for Literature in 1971.

It was also Hemingway's preferred place for his mojito, as also of his granddaughter Margaux Hemingway. We learned that she changed her name from Margot to Margaux after learning that her parents drank Chateau Margaux on the night of her conception. Situated in Old Havana, La Bodeguita del Medio offered a bohemian charm in the '50s to writers, musicians, journalists, and the avant-garde.

To keep my memory of this place alive, I decided to purchase some Cuban cigars and cigarillos for friends and relatives back home, since I could bring to Canada within personal exemption two hundred cigarillos and fifty cigars duty- and tax-free. The other recommended item to purchase was coffee beans. Cuba was noted for its warm, sunny, humid weather, which was ideal for growing rich, dark, and delicious coffee beans.

We assembled at the rendezvous point in the early evening, from where the bus took us to Havana's famous Hotel Tropicana, where we were welcomed with a free mojito, served a delicious dinner, followed by an evening of open-air extravaganza that included a cabaret show by a couple of dozen of flamenco dancers reliving the music, song, and dance of '40s and '50s Cuba. All in all, it was an enchanting evening, a bit of which I was able to video for posterity. By the time we returned to our resort, it was midnight.

The cafeteria in the resort offered a tremendous variety of food, and especially in abundance was my most favorite item, the lobsters. During those ten days, I downed lobsters like the Russians downed the vodka, no holds barred. The only downside regarding the food was that they were all quite bland. We watched other tourists pull out ketchup, tabasco, chipotle, habanero, and sriracha sauces from their bags or pockets to spice up their food. We were advised by them to bring our own hot sauces next time we visited Cuba. The other downside was that access to the Internet in Cuba was restricted and censored by the government, and so there was no Internet connectivity. We couldn't send or receive messages, nor could we make or receive telephone calls from or to Cuba. We could, however, make arrangements for a Wi-Fi access for a particular time and duration with the reception desk at a cost, but the whole process was onerous.

The Christmas and New Year's Eve dinners were grand, and the celebrations were full of fanfare and fun activities. Guests partied until morning, but we couldn't stay the course and had to retire early. On the day of our departure, Nipa emptied one bag that contained stuff she had brought as gifts for the room service maids, which included body lotions, shampoo, writing pads and pencils for schoolchildren, etc. They were extremely happy to receive the gifts. We found a thank-you note on our bed on the day of our departure. We returned home safe and sound after a memorable trip, agreeing that we have to do this again.

The Year 2015

The year 2015 started with my MEC work. I visited Afghanistan three times—February, May, and September—and worked on a series of critical issues ranging from weak laws and administrative corruption to policy issues. Afghanistan's accounting and audit law needed serious revision. New laws on lobbying, on accountancy, and on whistleblower protection had to be drafted. Administrative crimes such as collusion of government officials with powerful vested interests to grab public land illegally, pocketing pension payments of retired public servants, stealing and selling off international food aid in the black market, stealing imported fuel, and recruiting teachers based on who paid the highest bribe needed to be tackled urgently.

There was also the need to develop policies and procedures for contractor blacklisting, on customs tax exemptions, on proper use of administrative vehicles, on security sector oversight, on monitoring aid effectiveness, and on impunity in Afghanistan.

The issue of impunity was particularly critical in Afghanistan. Everybody who was somebody thought either that he was above the law or that the law did not apply to him. Anyone in a position of authority simply bent the rules to suit him or set aside the rules and pursued his criminal activities, confident in the knowledge that he was untouchable. He was sure that he would not be prosecuted because those who would prosecute him were themselves steeped in corruption or could be easily bought off.

On the off chance that he was being seriously prosecuted in court, the standard procedure was to make the evidence disappear or to intimidate the witness if any, or to use legal loopholes to tie up the case in the court permanently knowing full well that it would take years to resolve it. Even when a verdict was rendered, the trick was to file an appeal in the appeals court where it would be years before it came up for decision.

This sense of impunity affected every tier of government and the civil service, and it was so widespread that it was the first item of concern that I expressed to President Ghani when I became the chairman of MEC. The president acknowledged that impunity was indeed a cancer in the system and needed to be addressed urgently, but that was easily said than done because it required the complete overhauling of the entire judicial system that was corrupt from top to bottom. When one took into account the powerful vested interests such as the parliamentarians and the business community that supported the corrupt system's continuity, one realized what a gargantuan task that was even for a president pledged to combat corruption.

Given Afghanistan's tremendous untapped mineral wealth, we revisited AUAF professor Rod Monger's draft concept note on the need to create a sovereign wealth fund for Afghanistan. We also created vulnerabilities to corruption assessment (VCA) units in various ministries and conducted VCAs in the pharmaceutical sector. We developed new communication tools to facilitate better intragovernmental communication and government-public exchange of information, as well as monitoring and evaluation tools.

During every visit, we held meetings with various officials such as ministers, the national security advisor, the chief justice of the supreme court, the attorney general, the director general of HOO, senior officials from the sector MEC was working on, the U.S. ambassador, the first and second vice presidents, the CEO, and, of course, the president to inform them of our work, or to be informed of their endeavors as the case may be. And no mission was complete without the exchange of information, views, and opinions with the officials of the UNAMA, UNHCR, and donors (U.S. embassy, USAID, DfID, DANIDA, SIDA, CIDA, NORAD, and EU) stationed in Kabul. Every mission ended with a press briefing and the release of special reports.

Portugal Trip, June 2015

Nipa and I had planned to spend a few days of the summer in Portugal. She, however, pulled a muscle in the back of her leg and was having difficulty walking, but despite that, she decided that she was not going to miss our Portugal trip. We asked Mumu and Mishu whether they could juggle their holiday and work plans to join us; they happily did. When our kids started living in UK, Nipa and I had decided that we should visit with them at least once every year, and once in London, we would go for a family vacation somewhere in Europe. So on June 13, 2015, we boarded EasyJet at London Gatwick for Lisbon. Mumu had already reserved an Airbnb from Sao Bento Best Apartments in Lisbon.

There was a lot of rain, and we had to carry umbrellas. I guess the Airbnb people knew what type of weather we would face at this time of the year, so they kept several umbrellas handy for their guests. Our Lisbon visit, which lasted three and a half days, included lots of walking, tram, and hop-on-hop-off buses.

First, we took the bus to Lisbon's main square known as the Praça do Comércio, or the Square of Commerce, so named because of the presence of government bureaus regulating customs and port activities in light of the eighteenth-century spurt in commerce with Asia and Africa. Other buildings included galleries, shops, and restaurants. The huge U-shaped square faced River Tagus and had two arches at its two ends with statues of the famous voyager Vasco da Gama and statesman and minister of the court Marquis of Pombal perched at the top. In the center of the square, the bronze equestrian statue of King José I standing fourteen meters high above the pedestal looked magnificent.

The entire square had replaced the former Ribeira Palace, which was destroyed by an earthquake followed by a tsunami of November 1, 1755. The destruction of the palace had also led to the loss of over two hundred thousand books, which was the greatest archive of Portuguese literature. The rebuilt Praça do Comércio is now the venue where Portugal celebrated its independence day on June 10 every year. But the Praça do Comércio has a tragic history as well. On February 1, 1908, Portugal's king Carlos I was assassinated by two gunmen as he and his family were passing through the Terreiro do Paço. The assassins belonged to the Republican Party, which overthrew the monarchy two years later.

After getting our feet wet on the steps that emptied into the Tagus River, which before the earthquake formed a grand marble staircase to receive royal dignitaries directly into the Ribeira Palace, we walked under the Augusta Street Arch to go to the popular Rossio Square, also known as the King Pedro IV Square, which over the years has been the place for bullfights, celebrations, popular revolts, and execution. From there, we took the bus to the district of Belém, famous for its houses with colorful tiles, its seafood restaurants, and the residence of the royal family. Among its historic landmarks that celebrated Portugal's seafaring past, the most impressive were the sixteenth-century Tower of Belém and the sail-shaped Discoveries Monument.

Next, we visited the Ponte 25 de Abril, or the 25 April Bridge, which, at under 2,300 meters, was Europe's longest suspension bridge that spanned the River Tagus. It consisted of a six-car lane upper deck and an electrified double-track railway on the lower deck. Built to resemble the Golden Gate Bridge of San Francisco, it was named to remember the April 25, 1974, military coup in Lisbon that overthrew the authoritarian regime of Estado Novo. We also visited the 110-meter-tall *Cristo Rei*, or *Christ the King*, the Catholic monument across the

River Tejo, which was inspired by Rio de Janeiro's *Christ the Redeemer* statue.

We also wanted to see the Palacio Nacional da Pena, or the Pena Palace, which stood on a hill in the Sintra Mountains. King Ferdinand II must have been a nature lover because he ordered a huge variety of trees and ferns from all corners of the globe to build the two-hundred-hectare forest land to surround his palace. It was a real delight to see trees of the Pena Park that were as beautiful as they were exotic. The palace itself that was built on the site of a Convent of the Order of Saint Jerome was actually rebuilt after the Great Lisbon Earthquake of 1755 had severely damaged it, and the renovation incorporated both European and Islamic architecture. It was delightful to walk through the palace and its many terraces, and in particular the Queen's Terrace, which contained a sundial cannon designed to fire every day at noon. The palace also had a clock tower. The palace is often used for state occasions by the president and other high government officials.

A short distance from there lay the Castelo dos Mouros, or the Castle of the Moors, which was a hilltop medieval castle built by the Moors in the eighth and ninth centuries. It was captured by Christian forces following the fall of Lisbon in 1147. After a short walk through the forest, we entered a gate in the Curtain Wall. We passed through an archaeological site that was part of the medieval Islamic Quarter and the Christian necropolis. At one point, we walked over a glass floor with human skeletons and bones lying beneath. As we entered the castle ground, there were several towers. Mumu and I could not resist climbing the sixty steps to the top of the first tower. The view of the countryside in all directions from the castle walls was magnificent. We could even see the Palace of Pena at a distance. It was quite windy, and we did not dare to climb the hundreds of steps to the top of the Royal Tower, so named because King Ferdinand II supposedly spent his time painting there.

Back in Lisbon proper, Mumu chose La Paparrucha for dinner. It boasted a terrace that provided a lovely view of the city. We sat indoors and could still see lit-up Lisbon through the wide window. The restaurant specialized in Argentinian cuisine, and its main attraction was meat grilled on the traditional *parilla* (the actual open-fire hearth and grates where meat is cooked). It was a very delicious dinner, though quite pricey, but the ambience of the place and the presence of all my family members made up for that. The only experience in Lisbon that I didn't enjoy was when we sat down for lunch in a street that was temporarily closed off to traffic each afternoon, and families living in houses on either side of the street served their home-cooked meals to tourists and passersby. The menu was mostly fish based, so we ordered fish dishes. I was well into my lunch when I realized that the fish had been grilled with all its scales still on it. I just couldn't finish my meal. Nipa was able to peel off the skin and eat whatever she could salvage. On June 16, 2015, we caught the afternoon EasyJet flight back to London Gatwick.

Missed Opportunity at NSU

In late summer of 2015, I learned from a visitor from Dhaka to Ottawa that the North South University (NSU) in Dhaka had been going through difficult times for several years now because both the previous two vice-chancellors had performed below expectations, that NSU did not have a vice-chancellor now and that NSU's Board of Trustees (BOT) was looking for a new person to steer the university forward. Since I had been associated with NSU for a number of years and was regarded well by the BOT, I sent a message to the chairman of BOT inquiring whether there was any scope to offer my services to NSU. The secretary to BOT replied immediately in glowing terms. He acknowledged my message to the chairman; stated that the chairman "expressed his heartfelt thanks" for remembering them, for successfully conducting two convocations in 1996 and in 1999, and for a "lot of contributions to NSU in different ways and in different capacities in its early days." He said that he was happy that I had not forgotten NSU and wanted to know in which capacity I would like to serve NSU.

I wrote back stating that I was interested in the position of vice-chancellor. I also mentioned that I was in Kabul at the time and would be returning to Ottawa shortly. The secretary wrote back saying that the chairman would be happy to see me if I could swing by Dhaka after my Kabul mission ended in the second half of September. Our mission was scheduled to end on September 22, but we were able to complete our tasks ahead of schedule. Also, some of the meetings with ministers and senior officials that were scheduled for the last week of our mission fell through because they were abroad or had to cancel at the last moment for other pressing reasons. The MEC members were ready to depart early. I pondered my options, and noting that I was only a short distance from Dhaka, I informed the chairman's secretary that I would be happy to meet the chairman and that I would buy a separate Dubai-Dhaka-Dubai ticket for that.

I met the chairman in his chamber at NSU on September 19. He welcomed me warmly. I remembered his face from earlier board meetings when I was at NSU. He was pleased to see me and informed me that when he first started his career as a jute businessman, he used to look up to my father as his mentor and had received lots of guidance from him. He mentioned that he and other board members remember my contributions to the university in its formative days. We reminisced for a while, and then he informed me that he had arranged for me to meet with several board members after our meeting so that we could reconnect and exchange our views and aspirations for the university.

We then walked to the boardroom where were seated five other board members, three men and two women members. We had a good conversation; the members wanted to know, if I were selected, what I would be bringing to the university, whether I would be willing to relocate to Dhaka and commit to remain with the university for at least four years, etc. The final question was whether I would be willing to accept the post of pro-vice-chancellor instead of vice-chancellor. I told them that I was interested only in the post of vice-chancellor.

The meeting ended cordially, and we walked back to the chairman's room. After some pause, he told me that the board of trustees had been quite dissatisfied with the previous two vice-chancellors and had learned some hard lessons; as a result, they had actually decided not to recruit a vice-chancellor. Instead, BOT wanted to recruit a pro-vice-chancellor who would be actually doing the vice-chancellor's job. He would be closely monitored and assessed over a four-year period after which he will be upgraded to the position of vice-chancellor if his performance was found satisfactory.

The chairman asked me to reconsider my decision and accept the pro-vice-chancellor's position. He then asked the secretary of BOT to introduce me to the faculty and then give me a tour of the new campus, which I took to be his expression of strong interest in me. I was impressed by how far NSU had progressed over the years, converting many of the ideas we had dreamed of in those early years into reality. After the tour when I was ready to leave, the secretary told me that the chairman had approved complete refund of my Dubai-Dhaka-Dubai ticket. It was a pleasant surprise. I took a few additional days to visit with relatives and friends in Dhaka and then returned to Canada.

After a week, I received a message from the secretary asking me whether I had made a decision. I replied that I would be willing to come in as the pro-vice-chancellor provided I received assurance that I would be promoted to the position of vice-chancellor after two years, instead of four years, if my work was found to be satisfactory. He wrote back saying that "as per private university act, all 3 positions of Vice Chancellor, Pro-Vice Chancellor and Treasurer, are statutory positions and for a term of 4 (four) years. Accordingly, the BOT recommend and the honorable Chancellor (President of the country) approve these appointments for a term of 4 (four) years. Therefore, there is no scope of making it for 2 (two) years." Since this was a statutory requirement, I didn't have any choice and decided to accept the four-year assignment.

For the next few weeks, negotiations on salary and package started in earnest until we came to a final agreement. And then the unexpected happened. The secretary informed me that while reviewing my CV once again, they noticed that I did not have the "minimum teaching experience of 10 years as required by the Private University Act." Although I had the minimum teaching experience, I did not hold "full-fledged faculty positions" for ten years. I wrote back saying our interpretations were different, but if that was the position of the BOT, then I would not pursue the appointment further. I thanked him, the chairman, and the BOT for their earnest efforts, and expressed my regret that I could not meet the requirements of the act. With that ended my effort to rejoin NSU!

The Year 2016

In the year 2016, I went to Afghanistan three times, in February, April, and July. Our fourth mission that year in October was cancelled unavoidably. Also, I became the chairman of MEC following the July mission that year. The April mission, however, was most notable because of the extended meeting and the heart-to-heart chat we had with Pres. Ashraf Ghani, who was elected just eighteen months earlier in September 2014. He had won with Pres. Hamid Karzai's support and on a platform of combating corruption.

In the dying days of his presidency, Karzai had acknowledged that corruption was undermining all development efforts in the country and felt that his former finance minister, Ashraf Ghani, was the right man at the right time for the job. In one of his farewell speeches, Karzai appealed directly to his compatriots who had looted the Afghan treasury and the Kabul Bank to bring back the money from abroad and invest it for the economic development of their own home provinces, offering amnesty as the carrot; but no one had taken him up on his offer. At the time of his departure, countrywide polling of the Afghan public revealed that corruption ranked the number-one public concern, even higher than security, which ranked second.

To recall, one of the final achievements of USAID's 4A Project that I had managed was to require every presidential candidate to take a public anticorruption pledge, and Ashraf Ghani was the first one to take that oath publicly. He had raised high hopes among the electorate that, if elected, he would undertake serious reform of government, and now pressure was mounting on him exponentially. The existence of MEC was for him a positive development, and one of his first announcements after becoming president was to assure his government's support for MEC.

On April 21, President Ghani sat down with us and articulated his approach for fighting corruption in the country. He said that his top-three areas of effort to combat corruption would be to reform the institutions, reform the instruments, and reform the wider framework. In terms of institutions, he said that, first, he wanted to reform the "four critical building blocks," which were the Supreme Court, the Attorney General's Office, the Civil Service Commission, and the Auditor General's Office.

On the Supreme Court, he managed to install a reformist chief justice, although he lost the battle in parliament to nominate a woman chief justice by eight votes. He also replaced 630 judges with reformist judges, of whom 120 were senior judges of the appellate and the provincial courts. Regarding the Attorney General's Office, he replaced the incumbent with a person of high integrity and was in the process of replacing all the thirty-four advocates general of the thirty-four provinces, as well as six hundred prosecutors who had only high-school-level education. The Civil Service Commission, which was, in his view, the driver of corruption, was going to be replaced with people of integrity. And the auditor general, whose abuse of authority was widely known, was also going to be replaced.

On the issue of reforming the instruments, the president noted that his office had reviewed thousands of the contracts and found none to be compliant with existing laws. With procurements and contracts accounting for 30 percent of the GDP, this was a serious ethical breach. To rectify this, the president brought procurements and contracts under his direct authority and himself became the chairman of the procurement commission. The president also wanted asset declarations from all government employees as laid down by the Afghan constitution.

On the issue of reforming the wider framework, the president highlighted several drivers of corruption—namely, institutional capture, political capture, land, and narcotics. He mentioned to us some actions he ordered, among which were firing ninety generals who refused to go on retirement on their due date and stopping influence payments sometimes amounting to a million dollars for doing political favors. He cited political capture in appointments, in land grabs, and in contracts. It was also quite clear that sequencing was the key to getting it right. "We first need to free the government, then the economy, then the people," he said. We were elated by the president's commitment to pursue reform and for welcoming us to work closely with his government. But we also knew not to get our hopes high too soon because the implementation of presidential orders and legislative efforts was in the hands of officials and civil servants.

My Nephew's Wedding

For my family, the year 2016 had started with great anticipation when in January we received a wedding invitation, and it got more exciting as the month of March approached, for it was Ryan and Christen's wedding on March 12. Ryan is my second-eldest nephew. His father, Shahalam Hassan, who had come to the United States in September 1980, had settled in Irving, Texas, and Ryan was his and Luann's firstborn. Ryan was the first boy within my extended family to get married, and it was a joyous occasion for all of us not only because it was his wedding but also because he was marrying Christen, whom every member of my family loved dearly. She was of a kind and soft heart, very giving and caring, and had a wonderful cheery personality. She easily blended in with us and our South Asian culture. Their wedding was also an opportunity for all of us family members to get together once again. Our children, Mumu and Mishu, had to plan their leave from work in London in advance to be able to attend the wedding. So the four of us arrived in Dallas in late March to join the rest of my family at the wedding.

The preparations for the wedding picked up steam, although it was not as intense as a typical South Asian wedding with five to eight separate events. In between wedding preparations, the boys found time to unwind by playing soccer and board games, while the girls and women busied themselves with wedding-related shopping, organizing Christen's mehndi party, and other activities. Christen wanted her mehndi party and the rehearsal dinner to be in the courtyard by the swimming pool of Shahalam's house, which was huge with over a dozen rooms and a detached cabana. With the trees in the courtyard decorated with lights and the formal dining arranged under the trees, it was a magical night for the couple.

Ryan and Christen's wedding could be described as a bit of a fairy tale. They had met each other in sixth grade while attending a charter school called North Hills in the posh neighborhood of Irving, which was later renamed as Uplift North Hills Preparatory, and their romance continued unabated. After graduating from medical school, which he attended with full scholarship, Ryan moved to Salt Lake City for residency in 2014.

Although Ryan wanted her to move with him to Utah, she told him what was in her mind: "I'm not quitting my job and moving unless I'm engaged." Young love being a powerful aphrodisiac, in January 2015, Ryan came home to Irving from Utah, and, in Christen's own words, "He set up a 'fake' geocache with my ring in it. It was very creative— geocaching is something we used to do a lot." After that, everything else fell in its place rather neatly. After Ryan proposed, Christen finished the school year teaching middle school art and moved to Utah in June 2015. Ryan was in his second year of residency as a pediatrician at the Primary Children's Hospital attached to the University of Utah in Salt Lake City.

The young lovebirds got married in March 2016 at the beautiful Las Colinas Country Club, and the formal reception was held at the club's ballroom. Since they had only a few days left for honeymoon, they flew to California and did a road trip up Highway 101 from Los Angeles to San Francisco plus time at the Napa Valley wine country.

Ryan concluded his residency in the summer of 2017 and moved to Portland, Oregon, with a full-time job as a pediatrician at Oregon Pediatrics in Happy Valley, just outside Portland. Christen did not return to teaching but dived into her secret passion of making hand-sewn felt goods such as ornaments and garlands that she sells in person once a year during Christmastime. More recently, she transitioned to selling high-quality wool felt in a variety of cut sizes and yardage as the bulk of her business. She is very relieved now after having successfully persuaded Ryan not to take off and join the Médecins Sans Frontières, which is what he had in mind when he was in medical school.

Back to Ukraine

Following the April mission but before the July mission to Afghanistan, on June 8, I received a message from Svetlana Winbourne, who was a technical director at MSI and Bert's colleague, asking whether I was available to go to Ukraine to do some groundwork in preparation for MSI's bid for the USAID's SACCI project. The Anti-Corruption Support to AC Champions (SACCI) Activity was a five-year, US$22 million project to provide institutional support to recently established organizations championing anticorruption—namely, the nearly two-year-old National Anti-Corruption Bureau of Ukraine (NABU), whose mandate was to investigate corruption and prepare cases for prosecution but could not indict suspects; and the National Agency for Prevention of Corruption (NAPC), whose responsibility was to focus on ethics and conflict-of-interest issues as well as monitor government officials' lifestyles. MSI sent me a long list of topics and issue areas on which they needed additional information and clarity. Consequently, my interview list was extensive spanning the government and the nonstate domains. I accepted the ten-day assignment without any hesitance.

As before, it was exciting work for me not only because it gave me the chance to follow up on my previous work there and to hear my colleagues' assessment of how effectively NABU and NAPC were discharging their responsibilities, but also because it gave me the chance to touch base with all my colleagues. The target groups I worked with were different, however. In 2005, my client was primarily government ministries, but in 2014 and 2016, they included the nonstate actors such as the civil society organizations, the media, the academia, and the parliament. The only difference between 2014 and 2016 was that I was dealing with an amorphous situation in the aftermath of the Euromaidan Revolution in 2014, whereas in 2016, my primary focus would be on the newly established anticorruption bodies, NABU and

NAPC, and the relevant vested interests. It was a hectic two weeks, but I was able to complete my tasks and prepare a draft report that fulfilled Svetlana's and Bert's expectations.

True to my habit, I organized my work in a way that would allow me to sightsee. My consultancy assistant was an ambitious young Ukrainian man named Yaroslav Muraviov, who was courteous and efficient. He organized my meetings, identified additional contacts, served as an interpreter when necessary, and arranged local taxi transport to attend meetings. For some meetings, we just walked. He served as my tour guide as well. Unlike the hop-on-hop-off buses that I usually took when I was alone on other trips, this time, the sightseeing in Kyiv was mostly on foot, and I got to see and learn more about Kyiv's history and culture than I would have otherwise.

A short walking distance from the hotel was the Independence Square, also known simply as Maidan. It was the central square of Kyiv located on Khreshchatyk Street. Since the 1990s, it had become the place for radical protest movements, such as the 1990 student "Revolution on Granite," the 2001 "Ukraine without Kuchma," the 2004 Orange Revolution, and the 2013–14 Euromaidan. The Maidan no longer hosted cultural shows and other forms of entertainment such as Christmas fairs and New Year celebrations to show respect to the large number of civilians who were killed during the Euromaidan protests. Across from the Khreshchatyk Street was a modern but rather pricey mall where I purchased several souvenir items, including a couple of coffee mugs.

We walked some distance farther and took the Kiev funicular to go down to the riverfront where we went on a boat cruise on the Kyiv Dnipro River, which was an opportunity for Yaroslav to point out the palatial estates on the riverbanks built with corruption money and to identify their owners who were among the most corrupt.

Among the other places Yaroslav took me to was the Kiev Pechersk Lavra, also known as the Kiev Monastery of the Caves, which served as the preeminent center of Eastern Orthodox Christianity in Eastern Europe since its founding in AD 1051. Together with the Saint Sophia Cathedral, it was declared as a UNESCO World Heritage site and also named as one of the Seven Wonders of Ukraine in 2007. I also saw the Golden Gate of Kiev, named to emulate the Golden Gate of Constantinople. It was built in the eleventh century as the principal entrance to the fortifications protecting Kiev. Although it was destroyed during the Middle Ages, it was rebuilt by the Soviet Union in 1982; its brick and wood work impressed me.

The Motherland Monument was another exciting site to visit. This sixty-two-meter-high stainless steel structure towered over the city and claimed to be the highest monument of its kind in Eastern Europe. St. Michael's Cathedral, located opposite St. Sophia's Cathedral, was another historic site that I visited. Its blue exterior and glittering golden domes easily attracted tourists. Built by a prince in AD 1108, it was destroyed by the Soviet regime in the 1930s. Today, it stands as a sobering reminder of the ten million or so Ukrainians who perished in 1932–33 as a result of Stalin's orchestrated famine to wipe out the peasantry.

It was really nice to have the opportunity to spend a few days with Yaroslav, who was a very helpful and genuinely nice guy. He shared with me his immediate goal, which was to work for the U.S. embassy in Ukraine and then go to the United States for higher studies. He also introduced me to his girlfriend, who appeared to be loving and caring. I do not know if any of those goals came true, but I have my best wishes for him.

A Visit to Central America

Aside from my MEC missions in Afghanistan and my Ukraine visit that year, a new opportunity arose to travel to Central America. Transparency International's Seventeenth International Anti-Corruption Conference (IACC) was scheduled to be held in Panama City on December 1–4, 2016. MEC had attended the Sixteenth IACC in Putrajaya, Malaysia, in September 2015.

In light of the many invitations to MEC to participate in international anticorruption conferences, there was a serious and a necessary discussion among the committee members on whether MEC should participate in any of these international anticorruption conferences, and we had unanimously decided that we should attend at least the IACCs to inform ourselves of the latest developments worldwide on combating corruption and to inform the world community about MEC's work, and perhaps also to expand our bona fides.

Since there was budgetary implication as well, we needed a formula to decide how many and who would represent MEC. We agreed that every member should have the opportunity to represent MEC, and so the MEC delegation to each IACC should comprise a board member, alternating between an international member and an Afghan member who hasn't represented MEC at the IACC before, accompanied by the executive director. We also agreed that if the IACC was held in the western hemisphere, it would be far cheaper and more sensible for a member from the West to attend. Since the Sixteenth IACC was in Malaysia, we agreed that an Afghan member should attend. Since the Seventeenth IACC was in Panama, I, from Canada, was the nearest to Panama City, and it was decided that I should be the one to attend. Accordingly, I represented MEC at the IACC in Panama City.

I very much wanted Nipa to accompany me so that we could spend a few days together in Panama after the conference, sort of a mini vacation. I asked her to arrange her leave from work accordingly. In late November, MEC sent me my Ottawa-Toronto-Panama City return ticket on Air Canada, and I purchased Nipa's ticket according to my itinerary. I booked us at the IACC-recommended hotel, the Sheraton Panama Hotel and Convention Center. The hotel was quite posh and situated on the coast. We had a splendid view of the Pacific Ocean from our room. Across the street was the huge modern convention center equipped with the latest gadgets to host large conferences and meetings such as the IACC. Outside the convention center were flags from different countries fluttering in the ocean breeze. Inside the entrance of the convention center, in the dining area and in the corridors were tasteful displays of Panamanian paintings, sculptures, and other cultural artifacts; all in all, the ambiance was distinctly Panamanian.

I also registered her at the IACC so that she could attend it, as well as partake in the various events, in the welcoming and farewell dinners, and in the trips arranged by the government. I figured her international relations background would interest her with the agenda and proceedings of the conference. As it turned out, she attended the plenaries. The opening ceremony was splendid, revealing the culture and music of Panama. The cocktail in the evening, while sumptuous, served cold and hot hors d'oeuvres that were pork-based, and so Nipa and I had a very limited choice of finger foods to snack on. We enjoyed the dinners, and Nipa especially liked the incredibly appealing table after table of dessert spreads.

The conference was inaugurated by Juan Carlos Varela, president of the Republic of Panama, and after four days of intense deliberations by an estimated 1,500 participants from 135 countries, it was brought to a close by Isabel de Saint Malo, vice president and chancellor of the Republic of Panama.

The Seventeenth IACC was particularly interesting because of all the topical issues that were in its agenda. The general theme of the conference was "Time for Justice: Equity, Security, Trust," and the dozens of papers that were presented raised and debated many of the critical issues of the day. Among the topics covered were "The Panama Papers"; "Anti-Corruption and Open Government Partnership"; "Corruption and Migration: Connecting the Flows of Money and Refugees"; "How Tax Havens Foster Corruption"; "Shady Business Deals of Three Leftist Governments"; "Understanding How Human Traffickers Exploit Corruption Networks"; "How to Stop Illicit Financial Flows from Developing Countries"; "Police Crimes"; "Transnational Kleptocratic Networks"; and dozens more. There were several "Films for Transparency Screening" that portrayed test cases of corruption.

Each of the topics generated intense interest and debate and was a real eye-opener for the rest of us. For example, the presentation on "The Panama Papers" focused on the changing nature of investigative journalism, the increasing risks for journalists, the challenge of managing the incredible amount of data that were generated, which was at the terabyte level, the creation of the Global e-Hub, and the global impact so far, which was 4,700 plus stories by 376 journalists all over the world that resulted in, inter alia, the following:

- Investigations, protests, and call for elections in Iceland that led to the prime minister's resignation
- President of Transparency International-Chile had to step down.
- Cartel-linked suspects were arrested after Panama Papers revelations.
- 150 civil and criminal probes were launched in seventy-nine countries.
- Europol found connections with terrorism, Russian organized crime, etc.
- The Panama Papers investigations wiped out US$135 billion of the value of nearly four hundred publicly traded companies.
- Laws were revised in Mongolia, New Zealand, Panama, and Taiwan.
- More than 6,500 companies and people were investigated.

The discussions on the floor on the topic of the Panama Papers raised many embarrassing questions for the Panama government about the inflow and handling of the corruption money in the country. Panamanian officials explained that a combination of weak bank laws, ineffective mechanisms to track the inflow of money, and lax governmental oversight led to massive inflow of corruption money. Also, the government's rush to modernize its economy by inviting foreign investments into the country superseded important considerations such as the need to vet the sources of money inflow. This led bank officials to forego due diligence and allow questionable accounts to be opened and transactions to take place.

As the debate on the Panama Papers ensued, participants became familiar with corporate tax avoidance by tech companies and multinational corporations, with money laundering, and with names of dictators, corporate strongmen, political figures, senior government officials, and movie moguls, including Bollywood stars who had transferred money to shady accounts abroad.

Discussions on other topics of the conference were also riveting, which made the Seventeenth IACC memorable for the critical topics it covered and for the full-throated airing by disparate voices. This was not at all surprising to participants from other continents who knew well that the countries of South and Central America had been suffering from such evil for many decades. It also demonstrated how concerned and how active civil society organizations, academic researchers, and the media in Panama were on the issue of corruption and on the need to combat it.

After the conference ended, Nipa and I did some sightseeing. We were tempted to drive clear across the width of Panama, also known as the Isthmus of Panama, from the Panama City on the Pacific coast in the west to Colon on the Caribbean coast in the east, a driving distance of under seventy-five kilometers and less than an hour of driving time, but decided to focus on tourist sites within shorter distances. We visited the archeological sites in old Panama City. Panama City was founded in 1519 by a Spanish explorer Pedro Arias Davila, but the English privateer Capt. Henry Morgan sacked the Spanish settlement in 1671, turning the city into ruins and which is now called Panama la Vieja. We visited the ruins to catch a glimpse of the remains of fascinating old Spanish architecture.

We went to see the Panama Canal, which connected the Pacific Ocean with the Atlantic Ocean via the Caribbean Sea. The idea of connecting the two mighty oceans originated with the French in 1880, but diseases and financial problems prevented construction. After Panama gained independence in 1903 by revolting against Colombia, the provisional government junta negotiated with the government of Theodore Roosevelt of the United States to start the construction of the canal, which was finished on August 15, 1914.

The United States retained control of the canal the rest of the century until President Carter signed over its full operation, administration, and maintenance to Panama at noon on December 31, 1999. The canal is a man-made eighty-kilometer (fifty miles) waterway constructed in one of the narrowest points connecting North and South Americas. The bulk carrier *Fortune Plum* was the millionth ship that transited the canal on September 4, 2010, since operation began with the passage of SS *Ancon* from the Atlantic Ocean to the Pacific Ocean on August 15, 1914.

The huge increase in global maritime trade and the increasingly large-sized container ships that have emerged had overwhelmed the capacity of the Panama Canal, and the expansion of the canal became an urgent necessity. The Panama Canal expansion project, also called the Third Set of Locks Project, was launched on September 3, 2007, and completed on June 26, 2016. It added a new lane of traffic, two new sets of locks, one each on the Atlantic and Pacific sides, and excavated new channels to the new locks. It also widened and deepened the existing channels and raised the maximum operating water level of Gatun Lake that is a part of the Panama Canal. This expansion doubled the capacity of the Panama Canal allowing ships one and a half times the size of previous vessels to transit the canal.

We watched the canal's operation with great interest from the visitors' center at the Miraflores Locks. Since the two oceans were at different levels, ships had to be raised twenty-six meters above sea level using a system of locks with two lanes that operated as water elevators and then lowered to the sea level at the other end to facilitate the crossing through the isthmus. We were happy to take pictures of the locks operating and ships transiting, as well as of us with the locks in the background.

At the Miraflores Locks on the Panama Canal, Dec 2016

I might mention, for contrast, that another stupendous achievement was the Suez Canal, whose principal architect was French diplomat Ferdinand de Lesseps. Planning for the Suez Canal had officially started in 1854. It took ten years to build and was officially opened on November 17, 1869. The 193-kilometer-long (120 miles) Suez Canal stretched from Port Said on the Mediterranean Sea to the city of Suez on the northern shores of the Gulf of Suez, connecting the Mediterranean Sea to the Indian Ocean via the Red Sea. It separated Egypt from the Sinai Peninsula.

It is noteworthy that both these feats were rivaled by two other examples of human ingenuity, courage, and determination—namely, the Seikan Tunnel and the Channel Tunnel, which were not waterways but undersea tunnels. Japan's Seikan Tunnel, which passes beneath the Tsugaru Strait, which separates the Sea of Japan from the Pacific Ocean, was conceptualized in 1939, but construction started in 1971, and the tunnel went into operation in 1988. With its railway tracks located 140 meters below the seabed, it is the world's deepest railway tunnel. It is fifty-four kilometers (thirty-four miles) long.

Among the other tourist sites we visited in Panama, the BioMuseum was most fascinating. Located on the Amador Causeway at the south entrance of the Panama Canal, the BioMuseum was the creation of renowned Canadian-born American architect Frank Gehry. Opened on October 2, 2014, the museum highlighted Panama's natural and cultural history, how the Isthmus of Panama was formed and how it impacted the ecology of the western hemisphere. It comprised eight galleries for permanent exhibits, covering four thousand square meters, and each gallery narrated a different but interconnected story.

The first part of the story tells visitors of the creation of Panama and its natural and cultural evolution. The narration accompanied by sights and sounds depicted the tectonic clash of the two continents, which resulted in Panama emerging from the sea three million years ago, resulting in two very different oceans being formed and its huge impact on life in the planet. Two large semicircular aquariums showed how the Pacific Ocean and the Caribbean Sea evolved once they were separated by the isthmus. Also, a three-level projection space with ten screens provided the visitor a display of sight and sound featuring Panama's natural heritage.

We were reminded that when the isthmus was formed, it created a land bridge between the two continents, allowing for the first time in the earth's natural history for an extraordinary exchange of species between North America and South America. Life-size animal sculptures of all eras, shapes, and sizes told the story of this unique and ongoing natural event. In addition to the galleries, the museum also contained a public atrium, a space for temporary exhibits, a gift store, a coffee shop, and exterior exhibits in a botanical garden. I would strongly recommend to anyone visiting Panama to visit the BioMuseum and the Panama Canal.

The other things I noticed were that the climate, the flora, and the economic infrastructure of Panama City were similar to that of Dhaka. The weather was as warm and rainy as in Dhaka. The malls, roads, and restaurants reminded me very much of Dhaka as well. But, there, the similarity ended. What was strikingly dissimilar was that the entire population of Panama (roughly four million) was less than half that of Dhaka City (nine million).

With the U.S. dollar as its currency, a banking sector with more than one hundred banks, the second-largest free trade zone in the world, the second most competitive economy in Latin America, a simplified tax structure, direct flights to eighty-six cities in the western hemisphere, the only country in Latin America that is hurricane-free and earthquake-free, excellent medical care and business services, high-speed Internet, relatively inexpensive real estate, and a guaranteed safe access to pension funds, Panama projected itself as the dream destination for retirement.

For outdoor activity lovers, yachting, surfing, rafting, kayaking, trekking, rappelling, and fishing were further incentives to relocate to Panama. I could easily see why hundreds of Americans had chosen Panama as their retirement home. I did pick up a copy of the *Panama Planner* musingly and flipped through its pages during our return flight to Ottawa. It made a convincing case of why retired foreign citizens should choose Panama as their permanent retirement home!

The Year 2017

The next year started with the Twenty-Second MEC Mission to Afghanistan from January 18 to February 3. It also capped my six years of dangerous but worthwhile engagement in the Taliban-dominated country, and I was relieved that I did not have to go to Afghanistan anymore. I was happy to be at home with my wife, and I became happier when Mumu came to visit us in Ottawa in late May.

A week later, she returned to London, and then she was on her way to Malawi via Addis Ababa with seven other colleagues from her London office to do some charity work for SOS Children's Village. In the seven days there, she and her friends laid the foundation and built half the wall structure of a one-room school building in a remote village in Malawi, which had no place to educate their children. They were followed by a second office squad to complete the school building in Malawi.

She later narrated to us the excitement and fun associated with that charity work, and the pictures they took with the happy and smiling little kids who were going to have a school building of their own spoke volumes. Mumu has always been very committed to helping others in need, promoting diversity, and actively engaging with other cultures from her childhood. Since returning from Malawi, she has been taking her team to Mallorca, Spain, every summer to cycle and raise funds for a children's charity.

Returning to Bangladesh to Manage a New Challenge

At the beginning of the year, the Virginia-based Management Systems International (MSI) had already selected me to be their chief of party (COP) for a huge anticorruption project that the USAID was planning to launch in Bangladesh. But after Donald Trump was sworn in as the next president of the United States on January 20, 2017, American foreign policy began to shift radically. Trump right away took an anti-immigrant, anti-Muslim stance. He also believed that funding anticorruption projects in underdeveloped countries was a waste of American money, somewhat similar to Reagan's policy regarding the use of federal funding to finance international students. Instead, his administration wanted to focus on fighting terrorism. Accordingly, the State Department and the USAID shifted their fund allocations from anticorruption projects to countering violent extremism (CVE) projects, and the anticorruption project in Bangladesh was put on the back burner.

A month prior to visiting Boise in late May 2017, I was again contacted by MSI and informed that the proposed anticorruption project in Bangladesh had been halted and that the USAID had now announced a CVE project for Bangladesh that would use the money allocated earlier for the anticorruption project. They also told me that they will bid for the project and that they would like me to be their chief of party (COP) for the CVE project, *Obirodh: The Road to Tolerance.* Given my past conflict resolution and security sector work, and the fact that I would know Bangladesh inside out and certainly much more than any other non-Bangladeshi expert in this field, I was an easy choice for them.

But there was fierce competition from much bigger and influential implementing partners (IPs) like Chemonics. There was also a new catch. Unlike other USAID projects where the implementing partner interviewed and selected the COP and DCOP and requested approval from the USAID country mission, for the Bangladesh CVE project, the USAID/Bangladesh Mission decided to interview the proposed COPs and DCOPs of all IPs bidding for the project themselves. The USAID Mission wanted to ensure that the COP had the necessary experience, skill set, demeanor, and creativity to manage the project that, by its nature, would be an extremely challenging task to deliver on. MSI was fortunate to be short-listed, and the USAID Mission in Dhaka wanted to interview me at the earliest, with a CVE expert from their head office in Washington DC as part of the interview panel.

The timing of this interview in early June couldn't have been worse for me because I was in my sister Tina's new house, which did not yet have either Internet or telephone connection. I had planned to stay in

Boise for a couple of more weeks and help Tina settle in, but I had to rush to MSI Office in Arlington, Virginia, where they had relocated from DC, and sit for the interview through a conference call from Dhaka. Despite the tight turnaround and the obvious stress, I was able to convince USAID/Dhaka that I was the right person to manage their CVE project in Bangladesh.

During the interview, I stated that I believed Obirodh was a very appropriate and timely project for Bangladesh because the country's traditionally secular and progressive disposition was suddenly under a threat not faced before. This, to me, was deeply concerning. Second, I said that I was also aware that Bangladesh had the highest population density in the world with half its population under the age of twenty-five, which meant that there was a significant body of youth who could fall victim to the violent extremism narrative if their expectations were not properly managed. So the security implications for Bangladesh and the region were huge. Third, I was conscious of the fact that Bangladesh had built up lots of resiliencies over the years, and these resiliencies needed to be strengthened, not weakened.

I also pointed out that we had assembled a team with complementary experience and expertise needed to successfully implement Obirodh, and that the DCOP and I shared similar academic and programming interests, and our violence, conflict, and peace-building work had overlapped in Pakistan, Sri Lanka, and Bangladesh.

We concluded our presentation to the interview panel by briefly describing our own expertise and experiences. I spoke about my work in government that gave me an intimate understanding of how the Bangladesh government worked at all levels; about my teaching and research experience in both public and private universities and think tanks; about my knowledge and experience in conflict resolution and peace-building approaches and activities; and about my ability to design and implement systems appropriate to the challenges faced by a project, such as understanding the political/security dynamics, gathering local intelligence, developing contingency plans, and ensuring the safety of my staff, partners, and beneficiaries.

I concluded by saying that if I were asked to manage such a project a few years ago, I would have thought the time wasn't right and the country wasn't ready. I didn't feel the same way today. I felt that now was the time. This project provided a great opportunity to leverage this great window of opportunity to stem this rising threat.

The next half hour was spent answering questions from the interviewers and reacting to difficult scenarios that the project might have to contend with. They wanted to test how we would react in stressful situations, negotiate political demands, navigate around unforeseen risks, and maintain the solvency and sanctity of the project at the same time.

The entire MSI team who was monitoring the interview was happy with our performance and strongly felt that we had presented a strong case to the USAID/Dhaka Mission. A few weeks later, MSI was elated to be informed that they had won the US$19 million bid. I spent the week of June 5 in Arlington familiarizing myself with this novel project. Bangladesh had recently been included in the U.S. State Department's list of countries harboring violent extremists after the massacre in the Holey Artisan Bakery in Gulshan, Dhaka, on July 1, 2016. USAID wanted to waste no time and expected the project to start no later than the beginning of September 2017.

Earlier on, when I was in Boise and had learned that I needed to sit for an interview with the USAID/Dhaka Mission in Arlington, Virginia, I had called Florin, my nephew Fayez's wife, to see if I could visit with her while I am in Virginia. Florin lived in the States with their two daughters, but Fayez lived in Dhaka tending to his business there. I was pleasantly surprised to learn that Fayez was also in town. So after my interview, I called Florin, and she immediately insisted to pick me up from my hotel and bring me to her home. It was really great to see Fayez; he had not changed except perhaps being a bit more on the *mashallah* side. Florin was as beautiful as ever; her charm and courtesy hadn't left her. We had a wonderful home-cooked meal and reminisced about old times. It was really great to see them and their now grown-up children after such a long time.

Before leaving Virginia, I also had dinner with my friend Bert and his wife at Gadsby's Tavern, which was famous for once hosting George Washington and John Adams. The plaque on the front wall read,

GADSBY'S TAVERN

Erected 1792
Popular resort and famous hostelry
of the eighteenth century.
Here was held in 1798 the first celebration
of Washington's birthday in
which he participated. And from its
steps Washington held his last military review and gave his last military
order, November 1799.
Erected by the
Alexandria Chamber of Commerce

I returned to home to spend the rest of Ottawa's beautiful summer with Nipa before leaving for Dhaka in September. Every summer, Ottawa received thousands of tourists from all over the world, especially from the United States. The summer of 2017, however, offered a new surprise. There were two mammoth-sized mechanical monsters in the shape of a spider and a fire-breathing dragon that slowly walked the streets of downtown Ottawa at once surprising and bewitching the visitors and especially the children. Everyone tried to get as close to these mechanical monsters as possible to video them and take pictures. For all the days these monsters plied the streets, everyone was enchanted. It was a very special summer in Ottawa indeed!

Mechanical fire-breathing dragon, Ottawa, June 2017

Soon, September was round the corner, and I prepared myself mentally to go to Bangladesh after a hiatus of seventeen years. The country had changed considerably. Economically, it was doing well under the leadership of the Awami League Government, and the reports from the World Bank and the IMF on its future were optimistic. The government was aiming to convert Bangladesh into a middle-income country by its fiftieth birthday in 2021. All of the above were developments to be proud of.

But on the downside, the political and social context had deteriorated drastically. The government's intolerance to dissent and its highly questionable actions against dissenters struck fear in the hearts and minds of the people. Newspaper reports of targeted killing of bloggers and kidnapping of anyone expressing an opinion that was not in line with government thinking increased drastically. Corruption was rampant at all levels, and no sector of activity was immune from it, notwithstanding the existence of a Strategic Plan for the Anti-Corruption Commission 2016–2021 drafted by the Anti-Corruption Commission formed under the Anti-Corruption Act of 2004 and the Anti-Corruption Amendment Act of 2014.

On top of all that, the killings in the Holey Artisan Bakery in Dhaka in 2016 cast a pall of fear and uncertainty over the entire country. After 9/11, the U.S. government had resolved to nip violent extremism in its bud anywhere and everywhere before it could reach American shores. The CVE project in Dhaka was a continuation of that effort.

I boarded Lufthansa flight LH 6797 on Thursday, September 14, 2017, for Frankfurt and Dubai, and then the Emirate flight EK 0582 from Dubai to Dhaka, reaching Dhaka the next day. I was now the head of the Obirodh: Road to Tolerance project, whose objective was to foster an inclusive and tolerant Bangladesh. The word *Obirodh* meant "absence of dispute," and the idea was to proactively address issues that were alienating people and making them easy prey to indoctrination by terrorist groups and organizations in the country. The Holey Artisan Bakery had proven that, already, there were terrorist cells in the country that were actively indoctrinating and perhaps even recruiting alienated youth to create instability, mayhem, and violence.

I had taken the time to seriously think about what I was about to undertake, the challenges I would face, the officials I would have to deal with, as well as manage USAID's expectations. I strongly felt that this was my opportunity to help my country of birth in whatever small measure that I could, to do good for our people who were hardworking and fundamentally honest and decent, and to try to undo the image of Bangladesh as a country that harbored terrorists.

Philosophically, I subscribed to Jean-Jacque Rousseau's belief that all people were basically good and decent until civilization spoiled them. Cultivating these innate good qualities for the benefit of society was the mark of an honest and just political leadership. But I was also aware that under bad political leadership and in a socially deteriorating environment, man had the tendency to allow their baser instincts to overcome them. Terrorism was an extreme example of that.

My reaction to terrorism was not visceral. I believed that someone didn't suddenly become a terrorist one lousy morning.There had to be personal experiences reinforced over time that led to alienation from community and society. Only when other options failed and there was no one to turn to for help did people gravitate toward extremism. And the youth seemed to be the primary victims. It was a mystery to many why students from prestigious universities in Bangladesh had carried out the bakery attack. The challenge would be to try to understand what motivated them and how to prevent that from happening ever again.

I had faith in Obirodh's goals and methodology and intended to use that as a tool to improve the country's stability and security. It could not be done alone, nor through a single project. Countering violent terrorism would have to be a sustained effort over a long period because we lived in a globalized world where no country was impervious to outside forces, not all of which were beneficial or positive. On the other hand, I could take solace in the fact that Bangladesh had a tradition of moderation. There were respect and desire for democracy at the popular level. Bangladesh had a vibrant civil society with established networks as well as strong family cohesiveness and social support structures. The entrepreneurial spirit of the new generations was an additional boon.

I knew that I needed a good team that I could rely on. They had to subscribe to the project's goals, own it and be invested in it, be dedicated and hardworking, and coordinate and collaborate with each other effectively. I wanted to know which other individuals, institutions, and organizations in Bangladesh were also concerned by violent extremism and would be interested to work jointly with us. I did not want to necessarily duplicate other individual's or organization's efforts, but, at the same time, I did not want to miss the opportunity to build on someone else's successes or promising work.

Importantly, I wanted to be transparent and accountable to the maximum extent possible. This meant that I had to establish communication with government officials especially in sensitive positions, officials in the intelligence services, the local police, academics and researchers, NGO heads, etc. I had made a list of people in and outside of government whom I intended to contact with a variety of objectives. So my first order of business would be to meet with them and apprise them of my project's goals and methodology.

After arriving in Dhaka, I spent nearly a month at the Dhaka Sheraton Four Point on Gulshan Circle 2 as we searched for an appropriate location for the project office and conducted interviews of potential staff. We finally rented two floors of a just-completed five-storied building in Gulshan 2 for the Obirodh project. Given the terrible traffic jam in the streets of Dhaka, I wanted to be as close to the U.S. embassy in Baridhara as possible. It was also a short walking distance from the Gulshan 2 police station, which was an added security measure.

The project was up and running within a short time. I had made a list of priority meetings, and after settling down in our new office, I started scheduling my meetings. First in my list was the director of operations of the Rapid Action Battalion (RAB). The USAID supervisor of this project and I met him and his deputy in his office located a short distance from the airport. We briefed them on the project and assured them that if there was anything of a security nature, we would apprise them in advance. In return, we would like their support for the project.

The director replied that this was the first time that any head of an international project, and certainly any head of an American-funded project, had come to his office on his own and informed RAB about his project. He said he appreciated that we had come to brief them and the transparency we had demonstrated and then proceeded to ask us questions in more detail. We exchanged information, although the director was less forthcoming than his voluble deputy, who was at a greater ease to answer us. In answer to my question about whether the interrogation of a certain individual arrested after the bakery incident was useful and worthwhile, the deputy readily admitted that it was not because he had simply gotten caught in the cross fire and was actually innocent. He regretted that as a result of their interrogation, that person's life had been made miserable. Neither of them shared any operational details, nor did we want to know or ask. We left the meeting with the sense that we had established a minimum degree of understanding and rapport and that they fully understood where we were coming from.

My next meeting was with Gowher Rizvi, the international affairs advisor to the prime minister, in his office that was in the prime ministerial compound. He was also assigned the task of overseeing good governance issues. As always, he welcomed me with warmth; as

I extended my hand for a handshake, he brushed it aside and gave me a big hug and inquired what I had been doing in the immediate past.

It is worth noting that after he was tapped for the advisor's position, he had called me from Harvard, where he was a lecturer of public policy at the Kennedy School of Government as well as the director of the Ash Centre for Democratic Governance and Innovation. With an illustrious academic career and a towering intellectual in his own right, it was always a pleasure to be in his company and chat on global issues. He informed me that he had accepted the offer from the prime minister, that he was excited to get started, and that he needed knowledgeable, experienced, and like-minded persons in his team. He said that I fit the bill and he would be very happy if I went to Dhaka with him.

I was quite flattered by the offer, thanked him, and then politely declined. I told him that perhaps we could revisit this conversation six months later after he had gotten a taste of how it was like to work with the Bangladesh bureaucracy. When I called on him at his office in Dhaka, I informed him that I was heading an American CVE project and that his wisdom and guidance, if and when I needed them, would be welcomed. He smiled and said, "You are just the right person for this project because of your knowledge and experience. I'm sure that you will manage it well." I asked him about the government's governance policy and the challenges he was facing among other related matters for about an hour. When it was time for me to leave, I inquired about his wife Agnese and daughter Maya. We promised each other to remain in close touch. As he hugged me farewell once again, his parting words were "You must come visit me at my house soon."

My next meeting was with Additional Commissioner Monirul Islam and Additional Deputy Commissioner Abdul Mannan of the Counter Terrorism and Transnational Crime of the Dhaka Metropolitan Police. The additional commissioner was also surprised that we visited them to inform them about our project. He said that was the first time that that had happened and welcomed it. Our discussion was quite candid. I inquired whether we could invoke the U.S.-Bangladesh Counterterrorism Cooperation Initiative signed in October 2013 and interview the people who were in custody under the country's Anti-Terrorism Act of 2009; he flatly refused saying that was not possible. But he lauded our effort to be transparent and accountable. We ended the meeting on a positive note.

From there, we went directly to the Gulshan Police Headquarter and introduced our project to Deputy Police Commissioner Mohammed Jashim Uddin, who was in charge of diplomatic security. Shortly thereafter, the commandant arrived and apologized for not being able to receive us. He was happy to learn that we already had a fairly detailed discussion with his deputy, so all that was left to do was to fulfill his desire to take pictures with us, which we did.

Aside from these meetings with the heads of the security apparatus, I also reached out to the NGOs working in this field. First in my list was a meeting with Farooq Sobhan, a highly respected retired diplomat, a former foreign secretary, and at the time of this meeting, the president and CEO of the well-respected Bangladesh Enterprise Institute (BEI), which he established in October 2000. I had first met him during the briefing for President Zia on Afghanistan at the BIISS in 1980.

But I was received by BEI's vice president Ambassador M. Humayun Kabir, who was also a distinguished ambassador with his last posting being as Bangladesh's ambassador to the United States. Humayun and I were batch mates, and during the time I was managing Obirodh, we met several times to jointly work on CVE. During that first meeting, after we concluded our discussion, we walked over to Farooq Sobhan's office, where he greeted me warmly and we reminisced a short while. He told me about his special mission to China and about BEI's active engagement in promoting regional cooperation and security. He also showed great interest in our project and asked Humayun to explore opportunities for collaboration.

My next meeting was with Badiul Alam Majumdar, country director of the Hunger Project. I was particularly interested in his work with the Rohingya refugees and wanted to explore opportunities for further work with Rohingya refugees in the greater Cox's Bazar area. There were reports about the possibility of alienated refugees falling prey to indoctrination and getting recruited for terrorist activities within the country. This was of great concern to us and interested us immensely, particularly the U.S. government. Several subsequent meetings with

Majumdar led to contracting him and his academic/research team to conduct an in-depth survey of the situation in the southeast tip of Bangladesh bordering with Myanmar.

These were followed by scores of meetings with other NGOs, CBOs, heads of research centers, government officials, academics, and media people that kept me extremely busy the first few months after the project started. During this time, we commissioned a number of substantive research. One was a survey of all the violent extremist acts and on the status of violent extremism in the country, and another was a survey by a gender specialist of the role of women in the Bangladesh society. We also contracted an NGO to develop a real-time map of VE hot spots with an interactive dashboard. Within a short time, we designed and implemented a number of quick turnaround projects.

We also had internal discussions on the most feasible place to open our regional office. The choice was between Rajshahi, which our research showed was a significant hotspot with numerous terrorist-related incidents occurring there, and Chittagong, since the greater Cox's Bazar area was overwhelmed by Rohingya refugees precipitating considerable anxiety as well as sporadic violence in the region. Following the report submitted by Majumdar and his team, we decided to take a trip to Cox's Bazar to check out the situation ourselves. The project manager's numerous contacts from his previous field work in the area and his organizational skill made the trip very fruitful. We met and discussed with scores of relevant people from the civil society organizations, academia, and the media the Rohingya situation, the response from the international donors and organizations working there, the government's response so far, and the deployment of the army to maintain law and order.

The feedback we got was tremendous, and everyone was open and eager to discuss the situation there with us. One of the meetings with the students of the only private university in Cox's Bazar, the Cox's Bazar International University established in 2013, was in the lobby of our hotel, Ocean Paradise and Hotel and Resort. We were discussing the link between free passage of drugs such as yaba pills and cannabis from Myanmar to Bangladesh and what role it played in terrorist financing.

We learned how students were being targeted by VE cells, one student giving us a full account of how his roommate was being recruited and what he had done to save him.

Another student remained behind after the meeting and told us that the entire drug operation was being masterminded and controlled by the local representative of a high government official in Dhaka with the full knowledge and protection of a minister.

The meeting with the NGO people revealed the extent of conflict between the local populations and the refugees who had forcibly appropriated farmlands, farmsteads, and were denuding the forests of its trees.

Our conversation with the military deployed in the region revealed that foreign financed maulvis had made inroads into the refugee camps and were preaching a militant version of the religion to prepare them for full indoctrination into VE; the hard-lined refugees were the first and the easiest to recruit.

Since 65 percent of the Buddhist community in Bangladesh lived in the Chittagong Hill Tracts (CHT) and Cox's Bazar, we visited the Buddhist temple and monastery and talked with the senior monks and members of the Sangha. Their *sangharaja* (senior-most monk) informed us of the frequent attacks on them by violent groups, and particularly of one attack that destroyed their monastery. He told us that that attack was triggered by a false report in Facebook of a Buddhist disrespecting the Holy Quran by sitting on it. He said that his entire community was grateful to the army for rebuilding the monastery for them at no cost. He said that his community as well as the Hindu community hoped that the army would not decamp from the area and leave them at the mercy of violent mobs. He also informed us that since that attack, he learned how to navigate Facebook and monitored it daily for any indication of potential violence against his community.

Back in the project office, despite all the project activities, the project ran into difficulty with the implementing process. The trouble was that CVE was a new topic, and there was not much field experience to learn from. Every CVE project launched until then, and there was only a handful of them, ran into considerable difficulty right from the start because the methodology was experimental, the terrain of operation was very difficult, and political sensitivities encountered were unpredictable and often very difficult to manage.

As a result, every CVE project needed to make frequent course corrections, which did not always solve the problems that continually emerged. Our project design was influenced by the lessons learned from the MSI's CVE project in Lebanon, which had ran into considerable difficulty. To sort out the procedural difficulties we faced, our programming team underwent training three times by three different experts including the USAID supervisor of the project in Dhaka because every training pointed out that the previous training was inappropriate or incomplete. This training, unlearning the previous training, and retraining wasted a considerable amount of time and delayed the implementation of the localized grants projects, and the USAID was not getting the deliverables it was expecting. Thrown into this mix was the need for the USAID supervisor to show results that were not forthcoming. What bothered me was the refusal of the USAID to acknowledge the difficult, tedious, and still evolving nature of the CVE process and their impatience regarding getting the results they expected despite the considerable effort by the project team.

What complicated matters even more was the conflicting agenda of the USAID and the State Department that was monitoring the project. The State Department's agenda was to get information about the terrorists in jail, about terrorist cells in the country, and about the indoctrination process. The State's representative in Dhaka called me a couple of times to his office to make it clear what his expectations were. I told him that I had broached the subject with the additional commissioner of the antiterrorism unit who had told me that that wouldn't be possible. The State Department representative replied that I didn't try hard enough.

In the last meeting with him, he asked me to personally interview the NSU professor who had been picked up by unknown persons from the streets of Dhaka in broad daylight, whose whereabouts were not known for several months, and who was suddenly released at night just recently. I told him that that was not within my project mandate, and, besides, I didn't know the professor's whereabouts. He pulled out a note from one of his desk drawers that had the address and telephone number of the professor and handed it to me. I gave out a sigh and said I'll see what I can do.

Back in the office, I handed the note to the project manager and asked him to see if he could arrange the interview. He located the professor and informed him of my desire to interview him. The professor replied that he was released by the powers that be with the express directive that he was not to meet anyone, talk to anyone, or discuss in any form what transpired during his incarceration. He would be under surveillance, and any breach of these conditions would result in his immediate arrest with dire consequences. When I informed the State Department representative about this, he said that I just wasn't trying hard enough.

Given this push from the State and the USAID supervisor's desperation to show result, I consulted with MSI about the situation. They told me that USAID asked them to show results or find someone to replace me who can do that. Since the situation became untenable, and I refused to do State Department representative's bidding anymore, I opted to wash my hands off of the project. I submitted my resignation and returned to Ottawa six months after I had started the project.

After my departure, many of the senior staff that were recruited left the project as well, and MSI struggled to find a replacement to run the project; for many months, they had someone in an acting capacity to hold the project together until the work that we had launched during my time started to yield results. It was sad to see that USAID wasted a golden opportunity to combat violent extremism in Bangladesh. Luckily, the Bangladesh government was able to take stringent measures to contain it, and there has not been any violent extremist outburst since July 2016.

My six months in Dhaka from September 2017 to March 2018 created some opportunities for me on the home front. After the work in Cox's Bazar was concluded and my team left for Dhaka, I stayed behind for the weekend. My wife Nipa, sister Lily, and I hadn't been to Cox's Bazar for several decades, and so we spent the precious weekend traveling the area, going to the famous Mermaid Beach, enjoying the local delicacies, especially the fried chanda fish, and shopping. The fish shops in the beach carried a huge amount of dried fish of all types and sizes, and it was fun for us to take pictures with dried fish almost as tall as us. On the downside, the former resort town had expanded totally unplanned. It had become a drug-infested, overpopulated, chaotic urban jungle, a far cry from the romantic getaway with bungalows and pristine beaches it once was when I had visited it after my high school graduation. But the weekend in Cox's Bazar was a much-needed break for me.

In December, Mumu and Mishu came to Bangladesh to celebrate Christmas and New Year with us. This was the first time that we had gotten together in Dhaka. We had a relatively quiet Christmas and New Year's celebration. We decided to take a family vacation, and the kids opted to go to the hilly district of Sylhet in the northeast of Bangladesh to see the tea gardens instead of going to the beaches of Cox's Bazar. So we decided to visit the tea gardens in Srimangal.

Nipa was particularly interested to stay at her Holy Cross College girlfriend Cynthia's resort that had established an excellent reputation for itself. We booked rooms at the beautiful DuSai Resort and Spa in Srimangal, Sylhet. On January 1, 2018, the four of us flew Novo Air from Dhaka to Hazrat Shahjalal International Airport in Sylhet, where we were picked up by a prearranged van that drove several hours to reach the DuSai Resort. We were enchanted by the ambience of the resort.

The same day, we drove to the Goain River where we hired a motorized boat to go to the Ratargul Swamp Forest, located twenty-six kilometers from Sylhet. It was the only freshwater swamp forest in Bangladesh and one of the very few such forests in the world. It covered an area of 3,326 acres, of which 504 acres were reserved as animal sanctuary. This evergreen forest located by the river Goain remained submerged under twenty to thirty feet water in the rainy season; for the rest of the year, the water level was about ten feet deep. We hired a local boatman inside the swamp to give us the tour that was simply stunning; the boatman entertained us the entire forty minutes of the swamp tour by singing Bangla songs. There was also a local kid who offered to be our photographer, and it was delightful to watch how confidently he handled our Olympus and Canon cameras as he photographed our visit. We visited a number of other places in Srimangal, including several tea gardens, a mini waterfall, and another famous hotel, the Grand Sultan Resort, where we had lunch.

Following the Sylhet visit, we returned to Dhaka and visited several iconic sites including the Jatiyo Sriti Shoudho (National Martyrs' Memorial) in Savar, some thirty-five kilometers northwest of Dhaka. It was dedicated to the memories of whose who had died in the Bangladesh Liberation War of 1971.

The remaining days with our kids were spent frequenting Gloria Jeans, other delightful eating places in Dhaka, and attending lunch and dinner invitations. We also visited my father-in-law's clinic, Begum Rokeya Nari-O-Shishu Shasthya Unnayan Sangstha (BERNOSSUS), where each of us made donations. Our kids left Bangladesh for UK and Norway soon after, but Nipa stayed behind for a few more weeks.

In late January, I joined Nipa to attend her university department's annual picnic held at the Dhali's Amber Nivaas in Bikrampur, several hours' drive south of Dhaka. Though the drive was tedious, the setting was appealing. For Nipa, it was a great reunion, as she got to see many of her friends from university days. I also met a few of her friends I had heard about but hadn't met before. This was followed by a get-together of some of her closest friends from the International Relations Department at a brunch at a golf course. It was a pleasure for me to meet them, each of whom was accomplished in his or her respective fields; some of her male friends were CEOs of private banks in Bangladesh.

Year 2018 Brings More Excitement

Since Nipa had to return to work in Ottawa, we decided to jointly apply for our Bangladesh national identification card while she was still in Dhaka. I had procured all the required information earlier and had to get our citizenship certificates from the authorities in Gulshan. When

I personally went to get the certificates, I was stunned to see that the official was handing out citizenship certificates under the table to every Tom, Dick, and Harry for a small bribe. The documents these people were submitting were mostly fake, allowing the official to extort larger bribes from them. I shuddered to think how many people of Indian nationality were legitimizing their illegal entry to Bangladesh by buying these certificates from a traitor.

Nipa and I went to the office in Baridhara that processed the national ID applications. After completing additional forms, we were ushered into an adjacent room for fingerprints and retinal scan. I asked the lady in charge when we could expect to get our IDs issued to us. She replied, "If you are lucky, I would say in two years." Surprised, I explained to her that the reason we applied for the ID was to allow us to cast our votes in the general election that was scheduled for December that year. She replied, "Ask those in power." As we stood there shocked, she added, "You will be notified by e-mail when they are ready." That e-mail never arrived to this day! I had even requested the help of a counsellor in the Bangladesh High Commission in Ottawa but to no effect. I've been told by friends that unless the relevant office in Dhaka is appropriately bribed, I would never get our national ID, which is required for all kinds of official and unofficial transactions in Bangladesh.

Soon after Mumu had returned to London from Dhaka, she received a notification to appear before the judge for her citizenship oath. The citizenship ceremony was held on February 22, 2018, and she was handed her British citizenship certificate. It was a lovely picture of her holding the Certificate of Naturalisation with the portrait of Queen Elizabeth on a stand at one side and the judge standing on her other side. According to her Lily *fupi*, Mumu was now a BBC—a Bangladeshi British Canadian! Unfortunately, we could not join her to celebrate this happy day.

One month later, there was good news again. I received a letter from the Ministry of Education, Government of Bangladesh, Dhaka, that the Reazuddin Model High School in Debidwar, Comilla, which was established in 1918, was celebrating its one-hundred-year anniversary in March 2018. The school's board of trustees had decided to award special medals to five of its graduates for their outstanding contribution to society and especially to their district of Comilla. Topping that list was my father, Capt. (rtd) Mohammad Shujat Ali. Also among the remaining four was his youngest brother, my uncle A. K. M. Fazlul Hossain, who was the longest-serving principal of the high school. A third person on the list was Prof. Muzaffar Ahmed, the leader of the pro-Moscow National Awami Party (NAP-M) whom Father had defeated three times in the parliamentary elections. It was a matter of great honor and pride for me to see two members of my own family so honored.

On March 10, my sister Lily, her husband Shafiqul Karim Bhuiya, and I drove to Debidwar to participate in the ceremony. There were hundreds of invited guests and well-wishers who overflowed the open school ground. I was invited to sit on the dais with the dignitaries that included the education minister, the members of parliament from the region, and other political and academic honchos. After the speeches, the representatives of the five deceased graduates were asked to receive the medals on their behalf. I received my father's medal, and my cousin received his father's (my uncle's) medal. After the ceremony, we took the opportunity to visit Father's grave and pray for his soul before returning to Dhaka.

Three months later, there was yet another happy occasion for the family. Our son Mishu graduated with a diploma in architecture after completing the two-year master's program in the Mackintosh School of Architecture of the Glasgow School of Art. The graduation ceremony was held at the magnificent Bute Hall of the University of Glasgow on June 15, 2018. We had planned to attend his graduation since the previous year, so Nipa and I flew from Ottawa to Gatwick and then to Glasgow with Mumu joining us as well on June 14. Mumu, Nipa, and I stayed at an Airbnb. That afternoon, we dined at Paesano on Miller Street that was famous for its pizzas. Mumu and Mishu had eaten there during Mumu's previous visit to Glasgow to see her brother. We ordered two types of pizzas, and both were delicious.

Early next morning, we went to the graduation ceremony, which was a grand occasion steeped in Scottish custom and tradition, including the male graduands wearing tartan Scottish kilts as their graduation outfit. We videoed Mishu receiving the certificate as well as his ceremonial entry and departure from the grand hall. Afterward, the graduates gathered in the courtyard to congratulate each other and have a ton of fun taking pictures. It was fun capturing Mishu in his tartan Scottish kilt. Mishu introduced us to all his friends from different countries; there were Moa from Sweden, Anna from Iceland, William from Kenya, Hasan from Cyprus, Issey, James, and Matthew from Scotland, etc. He also introduced us to one of his professors who was American. The poor professor extended his hand toward me meekly, saying, "I must apologize for the conduct of my president," referring to Donald Trump! I simply smiled and then talked about graduation-related matters. At one point, we went inside for Mishu to pose for his formal portraits.

After Mishu's graduation ceremony at Bute Hall of
the University of Glasgow, June 2018

After all the excitement, drinking, greeting, and picture taking were over, we went outside and took pictures with Mishu in the front lawn of Bute Hall. From there, we walked to Mishu's studio in one of the art buildings to see his architectural work and listen to him explain his project to us. He also gave us a tour of the architectural projects done by his fellow students. Next, we went to the Kelvingrove Art Gallery and Museum with its very impressive displays. Finally, we headed to the Ox and Finch for his graduation dinner. It was one of Glasgow's favorite places to dine out, and it was packed with graduates and their parents. We stayed the night at an Airbnb.

The next morning, we woke up to the terrible news that, overnight, a fire had destroyed the Glasgow School of Arts beyond repair! The historic building was designed by Scottish architect Charles Rennie Mackintosh. Only four years earlier in May 2014, large sections of the interior had been gutted by a fire. Architects lamented that while one could rebuild the structure, one could not restore the 110-year history of the building that had produced so many first-rate architects. We went to see the devastation; it was heartrending.

I had always wanted to visit the Scottish Highlands and movies like *Braveheart, Rob Roy,* and *Highlander* only whet my appetite. After Mishu decided to go to school in Glasgow, I thought my dream may finally come true, and it did. That morning, on June 16, Mishu rented an SUV, and we took off for the Scottish Highlands with Mishu at the wheels. We toured the Highlands the entire day. We went past the University of Strathclyde and then drove past the Bridge of Orchy village, the Glencoe Mountain, past the beautiful waterfalls in the village of Kinlochleven on to the village of Ballachulish. There, we decided to have lunch at the Clachaig Inn. The menu was exotic. We each ordered different dishes: Haggis, Clachaig Fish and Chips, Highland Game Pie, and Smoked Haddock. They were delicious indeed.

After lunch, we drove past the village of Arrochar to the seaside town of St. Andrews, northeast of Edinburgh. We visited the St. Andrews Links, and I checked all the signposts to see if by any chance it belonged to Donald Trump; it didn't. We checked out the golf clubhouse as well as the Old Course Hotel St. Andrews Golf Resort and Spa. The Pro Shop inside the latter carried the typical golf shop items that were pretty pricey as one would expect. We then walked to the sandy beach next to the golf courses where Nipa drew a heart on the sand that read "S. N. M. & M. Ottawa 2018." After stretching our legs on the beach for a little while, we drove to the city and decided to park the car and go on a walkabout.

We walked through the campus of St. Andrews University, noting the dorms where Prince William and Kate Middleton had stayed when they were students there, including many historic artifacts on campus. We visited the Northpoint Café and photographed the sign across one of its large front windows that read, "WHERE KATE MET WILLS (*for coffee!*)," reminding visitors of the royal romance that supposedly started there. We stood there savoring the moment.

Next, we visited several historic ruins, among which were the St. Andrews Cathedral and St. Andrews Castle. The cathedral, which was once the center of the Medieval Catholic Church of Scotland, was built in AD 1158 and was now a monument in the care of the Historic Environment Scotland. The castle, which stood on a rock overlooking a small beach called Castle Sands adjoining North Sea, also had a rich history of being captured and recaptured by the English Protestants and the Scottish Catholics many times and had served as a residence of English kings and Scottish bishops interchangeably, as well as a prison.

Our next stop was Edinburgh, the royal capital of Scotland since the fifteenth century. It was interesting to learn that the residents of Edinburgh were called Edinburghers! Edinburgh became famous during the fourteenth century for its wool and leather goods. The Palace of Holyroodhouse, which was built between 1671 and 1678 for Charles II, was currently the official residence of the British queen. The other iconic sight perched on a distant hill was the Edinburgh Castle, which was built in AD 1103 on an extinct volcano, and was over nine hundred years old and served both as a royal residence and a military base now. It stood at the west end of the Royal Mile, which was the most important street in Edinburgh's Old Town, with the Palace of Holyroodhouse standing at its east end. The Royal Mile was so named because of its tradition as a processional route for kings and queens for the last five hundred years.

We wanted to visit the Queen's Gallery, but it was closed at the time. All the sightseeing had made us hungry, so we stopped at the Ting Thai Caravan on Teviot Place for a wonderful Thai meal. We drove back to Glasgow late afternoon. With views of imposing mountains, peaks enveloped in cloud cover, lush green valleys, countless streams emptying into tiny falls, and serene lochs framed by bucolic surroundings throughout our journey, the entire trip on meandering mountain roads was an experience not to be forgotten anytime soon.

We wrapped up our Scottish visit by exploring the Glasgow Necropolis the next day. Some graves were covered by imposing structures with flattering epitaphs on the tombstones, while others were nondescript, thereby giving the visitor a good idea of the social stratification in medieval Glasgow. Since the necropolis was on top of a hill, we were able to take pictures of the city below from all directions.

Mishu's stay in Glasgow was finally over. We packed his belongings into close to a dozen suitcases and bags, and on June 18, 2018, we took the train from Glasgow Central to London, which was the first leg of Mishu's travel to his ultimate destination, Oslo. Since Mumu's residence was by Wembley in London, we found a storage company located within walking distance for Mishu's luggage. The plan was to leave everything in storage except the most needed items until the time Mishu found a place of his own in Oslo, at which time he would transfer the stored luggage to his new place.

Meanwhile, Nipa and I decided to extend our vacation. The four of us went to Stockholm, the capital of Sweden, for a few days. The city, comprising fourteen islands connected by more than fifty bridges, was located on Lake Malaren, which flowed out to the Baltic Sea. I had gone to Stockholm before but never as a tourist. First, we went to the visitor center that had a huge fountain by its entrance to collect info and maps. We were ready to scour the city, many of whose streets were like Ottawa's Spark Street filled with curio as well as name brand expensive shops, restaurants, and people of different ethnic backgrounds and languages. We walked through parks that offered different excitement to different people, such as an open-air concert pavilion in one and a large-sized chessboard painted on the ground in another. We did not find a single open-air chessboard that was not occupied by what looked like ardent chess players. Mopeds, scooters, and bicycles were readily available for the public's use.

We photographed beautiful statues in public spaces and famous buildings including the Royal Palace, the Parliament House, the National Museum, and the Nobel Museum. We had to queue up to get to the latter and had a good tour of the museum. Mishu especially wanted to see the Stockholm Public Library, which was designed by Sweden's famous architect Gunnar Asplund; it was quite a sight to see thousands of books neatly arranged in circular bookshelves.

We visited the city hall to see in its courtyard the EU designated "Tree of Children" under which children and adults meet so that children can share their ideas with the adults. Such a novel concept! The beautiful statues in the Haymarket Square were quite an attraction to tourists as well. Stockholm's waterfront lined with majestic hotels was even more attractive. Two lovely obelisks on the waterfront displayed wind speed, humidity, and particles in the air to the environmentally conscious Swedish citizens.

Lounging, eating, and drinking on floating restaurants by the marina lined with boats of all shapes and sizes made it quite enticing. We couldn't resist the temptation, so we sat down to snack outdoors in a restaurant by the waterfront as we watched in a huge screen England beat Tunisia in the World Cup soccer that was going on at the time. Later on, we went to another restaurant on the rooftop of one of the highest buildings overlooking the harbor to get a panoramic view of the city and watched Switzerland beat Serbia.

Of course, no visit to Stockholm would be complete without visiting the Abba Museum. Since Mumu was planning to buy a turntable, we bought her the Abba *Gold* record. In all our vacations, we tried to enjoy the beauty of the city from the water whenever possible; so in this instance also, the boat cruise provided us with another enchanting view of Stockholm.

Before we left Sweden, Mumu wanted us to have a traditional Swedish dinner and made reservations in a restaurant in the Gamla Stan (the old town). So one evening, we took a leisurely walk through cobblestone streets lined with ancient buildings with flower pots on windowsills to rev up our appetite for the dinner at Tradition, which was located on Osterlanggatan 1 close to the Royal Palace. It served traditional home-cooked Swedish dishes; all our orders were quite delectable. All in all, it was a marvelous holiday. We boarded our SAS flight to return to London; the last time I had flown SAS was nearly two decades before.

A few days later, on June 27, we minus Mumu took the coach to Brighton to spend the day at the beach. Unlike most other beaches that were sandy and sometimes powdery, the Brighton Beach was quite pebbly; we didn't get into the water. Instead, we passed a leisurely day browsing in the waterfront shops and walking in the beach. A late lunch of standard English fish and chips, tasteless mashed peas, and downed with ginger beer and diet Coke at a restaurant located on the Brighton Palace Pier gave us the boost to do some additional sightseeing of interesting buildings and parks including the Royal Pavilion Gardens. We returned to Mumu's place in the early evening.

It was a fairly long vacation and a summer well spent for Nipa and me, and now it was time to go home. Two days later, on June 29, 2018, we boarded WOW Air for our flight to Ottawa via Reykjavik. WOW Air was an Icelandic ultralow-cost carrier headquartered in Reykjavik, which went into operation in May 2012 and offered services to Europe, Asia, and North America. While the interior of the planes were beautiful, neat, and tidy, it was a no-frills carrier with labels on inside walls that read, "Honk if you need anything." The airline ceased operation in March 2019. Those of us who used it found it to be a comfortable and very affordable airline and regretted its shutdown.

There was a one-day layover in Reykjavik, and we used the opportunity to the hilt. The Keflavik International Airport in Reykjavik was quite a ways from the city, so by the time we landed and were driven to our hotel, it was dark. We simply had our dinner and shortly thereafter went to bed. We woke up early in the morning, had breakfast as soon as the café we had eyed the previous night opened, and then walked toward the city center.

There were many lovely shops to visit on either side of the streets. We walked into one that carried Viking paraphernalia, where I donned the horned Viking helmet and leather vest with a spiked mace on hand like ancient Icelandic warriors and took pictures. There were shops that carried handmade soaps with stones inside, scented candles, beautiful ornaments, and a plethora of other handmade gifts from Iceland. Other interesting shops were the ones that specialized in traditional Icelandic lava jewelry. These were black porous beads made from lava stones or igneous rocks that were ejected from the core of the earth and were purported to have unique healing properties. They were supposed to calm the nerve by stabilizing the root chakra located at the base of the spine, making one feel safe, anchored, and upbeat. Some lava jewelry contained essential oils derived from plants, of which lemon, which supposedly has energizing healing properties, and lavender, which was known for its stress-releasing healing properties and as a sleep aid, were most common. Some of the lava diffuser jewelry also contained natural gemstones, primarily amazonite and howlite, which were supposed to work in harmony with lavender and lemon oils.

There were also souvenirs like Icelandic salt and chocolates for tourists to carry home. The most impressive building that we photographed was the concrete Hallgrimskirkja church, which reminded me of the Jatiyo Sriti Shoudho (National Martyrs' Memorial) in Savar, Bangladesh. After a wonderful overnight and a day in Reykjavik, that evening, we boarded our flight back to Ottawa.

Return to Africa

In mid-December 2018, I got an e-mail from a Lisa Petter, who identified herself as a senior associate at the Center for International Development of the State University of New York (CID-SUNY). She wrote that SUNY/CID was looking for a senior anticorruption expert to travel to Kenya to assist the USAID-funded Agile and Harmonized Assistance for Devolved Institutions (AHADI) project. She said that the USAID/Kenya Mission had asked AHADI to contract an international expert on anticorruption to launch an anticorruption programming in Kenya. Lisa said that they had been checking with their colleagues in the development field to recommend such a person, and Bert Spector from MSI had messaged them,

I would highly recommend that you contact Dr.

Shaukat Hassan. Shaukat worked for CIDA for about 10 years as their Senior Governance/Anticorruption Advisor, and then worked for MSI as our Chief of Party in Afghanistan for a USAID anticorruption project. He is a very talented anticorruption specialist and has a lot of experience in Africa and Asia.

Lisa went on to say,

We were very impressed with your expertise with USAID in the practice and design of anti-corruption programming and your work advising CIDA approaches in this area. We do use your *Guide for Anti-Corruption Programming* here at the State University of New York/ Center for International Development . . . The precise terms of reference are still being developed with the Mission and the options under discussion are quite broad. We would welcome a chance to discuss them with you, if you are interested. Might you be available to travel to Kenya in January or February?

I replied that I was indeed interested and that I would be available from January 2019. Further discussions led to signing a contract with them for the Kenya work.

I was scheduled to fly to Nairobi on January 18, but as luck would have it, on January 15, members of the Somalia-based Islamist extremist group al-Shabab stormed the five-star DusitD2 hotel situated in the affluent Westlands neighborhood. The attack and the rescue operation lasted nearly twenty hours, and by the time the situation was brought under control, twenty-one people had died and twenty-eight more were wounded.

The previous attack in Nairobi by the al-Shabab was six years earlier in September 2013 when terrorists had entered the Westgate Shopping Mall, and by the time the eighty-hour siege had ended, sixty-seven mall-goers were dead. I had been booked at a hotel near the AHADI office, but after the attack, my reservation was shifted to the high-security five-star Fairview Hotel set on five acres of leafy ground some ten minutes away from the AHADI office. Access to the hotel was from three different directions with multiple police checkpoints in every direction.

In light of the terrorist attack, my trip was postponed by a week to allow the situation to calm down. I landed at Jomo Kenyatta International Airport, Nairobi, on January 23. I had applied for a Kenyan visa online but could not get it by the time I departed Ottawa, so I prayed that there would not be any major headache with passport and immigration in Nairobi Airport. I paid the fifty-U.S.-dollar visa fee and got a one-year visa stamped onto my passport.

SUNY/CID had booked me a suite since I was going to be in Nairobi for at least a month. As the hotel taxi that picked me up from the airport drove me to the hotel, I could see khaki-clad military personnel with assault weapons on the rooftop of the hotel's adjacent building that had high wire security fencing with check posts all around that building. Later on, I learned that it was the Israeli embassy considered to be the most well-guarded embassy in Nairobi. And to further enhance their security, the Israeli government had purchased the Fairview Hotel where Israelis traveling to Kenya on government or commercial business were required to stay.

To facilitate my work, SUNY/CID had decided to contract a Kenyan expert on anticorruption, Dr. Arbogast Akidiva of Strathmore University, Nairobi, who had been involved in anticorruption work for a number of years. The first few days after my arrival, I had multiple meetings at the AHADI office with the staff and the COP who briefed me on the status of the AHADI project and the extent of governance work they were engaged in.

Akidiva and I also met the mission head and his staff in charge of the AHADI project to get a sense of USAID's expectations and urgencies. The mission head pointed to the challenges posed by the Kenya Constitution 2010, which had created forty-seven county governments, each with governors and legislatures to promote transparent, accountable, effective, and responsive governance systems throughout the country. However, there was also the realization that decentralized governance was spreading decentralized corruption. The government was also conscious of its very poor ranking in the Transparency International's 2017 Corruption Perception Index.

The USAID had come to the conclusion that the earlier these challenges were addressed, the more effective the interventions were likely to be. Since the AHADI project lacked a specific anticorruption objective, the USAID felt that it might be worthwhile to explore what other opportunities existed in anticorruption programming, if any, over the remaining eighteen months of the AHADI project. The mission director also asked me to include in my report a set of "strategic level interventions" that could guide the designing of an anticorruption programming in Kenya.

Prior to the meeting with the mission head, I had developed the concept note on technical approach to anticorruption programming in Kenya that was vetted by SUNY/CID before it was forwarded to the mission head. My terms of reference stated that the "consultancy will aim to provide a sound and well documented analysis and recommendations to the USAID/Kenya Mission as to how its current and future programming could address corruption more effectively, particularly within the context of Kenya's devolved system of governance. The Consultant's efforts will include assessing entry points for AHADI programming that could be completed before the end of the award (June 30, 2019) at the county level, as well as suggesting broader programming opportunities to USAID that could be pursued outside of AHADI."

A couple of days after my arrival, Akidiva and I attended the Multi-Sectoral Initiative against Corruption (MSIC) that was held in Nairobi and was attended by President Kenyatta and a number of his ministers. It was a big gathering of anticorruption activists from a cross section of society concerned with the governance challenges facing the country. Their overall objective was to hold public consultations with each other, understand the interlinkages, and reach consensus on sectoral action plans to jointly place their demands to the government.

There were twelve stakeholder groups representing twelve sectors at that meeting, and what was fascinating about the meeting was that each sectoral stakeholder group demanded from its minister a public commitment in the presence of the president to carry out their sectoral demands. It was a vibrant, interactive full-day exchange between the various development sectors and the government. It was a great exposure of issues for us and helped us considerably to identify and prioritize the public concerns with corruption and poor governance. Akidiva and I chose to focus on five of the twelve sectors that presented their cases to the president at the MSIC. We chose

- women and youth, because both groups were bearing the brunt of society's woes, and had expressed a keen desire to be at the forefront of the fight against corruption;
- religious leaders, who could play a significant role in promoting ethics, values, integrity;
- civil society, because they upheld and fought for the public good;
- media, because of their potentially investigate role and their role in dissemination of news and knowledge; and the
- Multi-Agency Team (MAT), because it was the government's formal cooperation, collaboration, and coordination mechanism chaired by the attorney general, and comprising the Ethics and Anti-Corruption Commission, the director of public prosecutions, the directorate of criminal investigations, the Kenya Revenue Authority, the Assets Recovery Agency, the Financial Reporting Centre, and the National Intelligence Service.

Our consulting work also included key informant interviews (KII) with nonstate actors, national governmental bodies, as well as members of the county assemblies, the county executive, and officers from relevant sectors in the two target counties.

Given the limited time allocated in the contract, it was clear to me that this would have to be a rapid assessment. I had already gathered the required background Information from desk study and analysis of important documents from multiple sources before arriving in Nairobi.

To capture information from the subnational level, we consulted with the AHADI staff and decided to visit two counties, Makueni and Vihiga. Makueni was chosen because of the corruption fighting reputation of its governor, who fought the county assembly members in the previous regime who demanded kickbacks to approve his development projects. He even requested the national government to dissolve the county government so that fresh elections could be held to elect new people. He was held in high regard because of his good governance initiatives. We felt that there might be transferable lessons to learn. Vihiga was chosen because its governor had expressed a strong willingness to fight corruption and to strengthen the governmental system.

On February 20, at 4:30 a.m., Akidiva and I took a cab to Nairobi airport for our 6:15 a.m. flight and boarded Kenya Airways Jambojet for a short trip to Kisumu, since our destination Vihiga County did not have any airport of its own. From Kisumu County, we drove for nearly an hour to Vihiga. It was a drive through a rural road with sparse population scattered here and there. The Vihiga town was a typical town in an underdeveloped country with unpaved roads, primitive transport, open sewerage, small family-run roadside shops, and businesses, with dogs, pigs, cattle and fowl freely roaming the streets. We were booked at the Sosa Cottages in a beautiful rural setting in the outskirts of the town.

Our two trips to the counties—Vihiga and subsequently Makueni— to consult with officials and nonstate actors yielded a rich body of information. We invited all stakeholders to focus group discussions arranged in the cottage and provided them the opportunity to share with us their concerns and recommendations. The participants gladly opened up with no holds barred and shared their frustrations about both the county and the national governments. They were able to paint a clear picture of deliberate governmental obstruction to reform efforts; of delaying tactics; of withholding of development funds; of misappropriation of funds and other county resources; collusion by county and national government officials to corrupt the system to benefit themselves, their kin and friends; etc.

They also spoke of overt and covert discrimination against minorities and the marginalized. Talk with county officials gave us another picture of the strained relationships between the county and national governments, and of the national government's continuous attempts to stymie development efforts and control the county government by frequently delaying and sometimes withholding the transfer of funds. There was consensus at the county level that the regulatory system needed to be rationalized by reviewing all laws and statutes to weed out contradictions and opportunities for judges to give lighter sentences, by amending or repealing old laws, and by passing new legislation as well as enabling legislation to implement the new laws. Another unanimous demand was to bring the judiciary to the county level. While executive power and parliamentary authority were devolved to the county level under the 2010 Constitution, justice was not, and the demand was to bring justice closer to the people.

Our road trip to Makueni was the day after we returned from Vihiga, timed to coincide with the cabinet meeting of the county government when the county executive committee members would be available in a single location for us to interview them. It was a replica of the Vihiga fact-finding mission with the addition of consultations with the county parliamentary members who had their own complaints against both the national parliament and the national government.

Consultations in Nairobi revealed a similar picture but where corruption was more entrenched and insidious. Even hallowed institutions such as the churches were affected by it. When a bishop was asked why the churches accepted donations knowing full well that it was corruption money, his response was that the various church leaderships were greedy and competitive, and that they had lost their moral compass. Another bishop was asked about the status of interfaith dialogue, and he replied that that was not possible because the Muslim doctrine was too dissimilar to the Christian doctrine.

Discussions with senior media personalities revealed constant efforts by the national government to control the media through various tactics, to co-opt journalists and reporters, and to undermine their credibility. Our consultations revealed that two realities loomed large, one was the resignation of the population to the "need to eat" philosophy that accounted for the prevalence of corruption in the country, and the other was the sense of entitlement and impunity among the top officials of the government and the public service.

On February 25, I made a PowerPoint presentation of our findings to the USAID/Kenya Mission, which was widely received. This was followed up with a question-answer session by the USAID officials involved in governance programming. The mission head was pleased with the report and made an additional request that was not a part of my contractual mandate. He asked me to prepare for the ambassador a list of talking points that he could use in his conversation with the president. I was pleased to do that.

While I was required to submit a 15-page report, I drafted a 65 page report that contained an executive summary, a list of thirteen recommendations identifying key entry points for intervention, a list of nine areas of inquiry, a list of anticorruption good practices and transferable lessons, political talking points for the ambassador, and an example of VCA we did in Afghanistan.

I asked Akidiva to vet the report before submitting it to SUNY/ CID. After receiving the report, Lisa Petter wrote back, saying, "The Field Office asked another local specialist, a constitutional scholar, to review [the Report] at the last minute. He found the draft very sound and well-reasoned . . . I am proud of this document and glad we had a chance to work together on it." The report was accepted by the USAID/ Kenya Mission in toto without any changes. In the following months, I heard that the AHADI project was under instruction from the USAID Mission to incorporate in its work plan anticorruption programming aligned to my strategic level recommendations. It was fun work, made doubly so because of the support and cooperation I received from my colleagues Dr. Arbogast Akidiva and SUNY/CID's Lisa Petter.

Unwinding in Europe

My family and I had planned to take a long leisurely trip through Europe after I returned from Africa. Once again, Mumu did the main planning. They planned our trip in such a way as to allow them to use their weekends to be with us.

Oslo

The three of us flew to Oslo on April 17 and spent several days with Mishu as the tour guide showing us the city by tram, by train, and by walking. During one of those walks, after we had crossed the park by Mishu's apartment, Nipa spotted a pair of swings and immediately sat on one for a bit of fun, as she recounted how as a kindergarten student at Mauryam School in Mymensingh, she and her friend Nasreen used to run to the school playground to grab a couple of swings before others got them as soon as the end-of-school bell rang. For a few minutes, I pushed the swing to see how high she could go. Mumu joined her in the other one.

We passed the Oslo School of Architecture and Design, where Mishu had spent a semester as an Erasmus exchange student during his master's program at Glasgow U. We walked past another beautiful park full of multistoried wooden birdhouses hoisted in poles. Meandering through the park was a fast-running stream whose waters cascaded downstream to meet up with the river. Hugging the stream the entire length were walkways and bike paths with lots of people and their pets enjoying the spring.

We crossed a beautiful timber bridge onto a small street with quaint buildings housing a variety of restaurants. On the outside walls of several buildings were giant-size stone replicas of the human eye, ear, and other body parts. As we walked the streets of the city proper, we thoroughly enjoyed browsing in the shops carrying beautiful wares from Norway and elsewhere. We noticed numerous streets with bicycle stands with bike-for-a-small-fee for the environmentally conscious Norwegians. Like in Stockholm, there were also chessboards painted on the pavement with players in deep thought planning their next moves.

In another of our walks, we visited the fish market by the wharf full of fishing boats, breathing in the scent of the fresh catch. We walked the entire Aker Brygge area, which was a lively hub for culture, shopping, dining, and tourism, as well as famous for its pier, eye-catching architectural buildings, and marina with a statue of man on stilts standing in the water and transparent cluster of human figures embracing each other floating on strings high above between buildings.

We stopped at one of the eateries with outdoor dining serving a variety of cuisine where we had a wonderful fish lunch. After lunch, we walked past the Nobel Peace Center and the Astrup Fearnley Museum of Modern Art. We visited the Norwegian National Opera and Ballet, and from its rooftop, we took in the panoramic view of the harbor, the cruise ships, and what looked like a glass-and-steel architectural design jutting out of the harbor waters. We also saw the multicolored houses lining the harbor entrance similar to those in Bergen and in Nova Scotia, Canada.

Mishu wanted to show us the city from the top of the mountains, so we took a pleasant train ride up to the mountains all the way to the last stop at Frognerseteren. As the city receded into the distance, we saw houses here and there on both sides, some modern and some with thatched roofs. The view of the city and its harbor from the top was indeed awesome. We also took the Oslo Ruter ferry from the City Hall Pier for a tour of the islands of the inner Oslo Fjord. The fresh air, the deep sparkling waters of the fjord, and the sight of the many islands made it a worthwhile outing.

Copenhagen

On April 20, the four of us flew from Oslo to Copenhagen to spend a few more days of wonderful time together. The sights and sounds of Copenhagen were enchanting as well. The hop-on-hop-off bus gave us a splendid view of the city. We saw streets lined with trees that was nothing unusual, but the base of the tree trunk was wrapped up in green tarpaulin, which was an ingenious way to retain water for the trees that I had never seen done elsewhere before.

Among the places the bus took us was the impeccably kept Danish royalty's entrance to their castle grounds from their royal yacht. We saw the statue of Denmark's famous son, Hans Christian Andersen, sitting on a high chair staring at the sky with a book in hand. Among the other stops was by the statue of *The Little Mermaid* on a rock by the waterside at the Langelinie promenade. It is said that the 1.25-meter-tall, 175-kilogram bronze statue depicting a mermaid becoming human was based on the 1837 fairy tale by the same name by Danish author Hans Christian Andersen and was unveiled for the public in August 1913. The statue was commissioned in 1909 by Carl Jacobsen, who, after watching a ballet about the fairy tale, asked ballerina Ellen Price to model for the statue. The ballerina refused to model in the nude, so sculptor Edvard Eriksen modeled the statue's head after Price and asked his wife Eline Eriksen to model in the nude for the statue's body.

The Little Mermaid, Copenhagen, April 2019

We got off the bus at the famous Tivoli Gardens, which was purportedly the inspiration for the creation of Disneyland. It was an amusement park that opened in August 1843 and offered dozens of rides, musicals, ballet, concerts, pantomime theater, restaurants and cafés, and flower gardens, which were illuminated by colored lamps after dark.

Occasionally, one could even watch fireworks reflected in the Tivoli Lake, which was a part of a moat that once surrounded the city's fortifications. Story has it that Tivoli's founder, Georg Carstensen, convinced King Christian VIII to grant him a five-year charter, saying that "when the people are amusing themselves, they do not think about politics."

We took one of the many colorful buses plying the streets of Copenhagen to visit the Rosenborg Castle, which is a renaissance palace sitting on one side of a large park in central Copenhagen. It was famous because its basement cellars served as the repository of the Danish crown jewels and the royal treasury. The crown jewels belonged to Queen Sophie Magdalene, who dictated in her will of 1746 that "in this Royal House, there are so few jewels and not any crown jewels at all," that her jewels should not be passed on to a specific person but should be kept at the disposal of the sitting queen. The crown jewels, which belonged to the state but were at the disposal of the queen, consisted of four large jewelry sets: a brilliant-cut diamond set, a rose-cut diamond set, an emerald set, and a pearl-ruby set, plus decorative accessories such as necklaces, earrings, brooches, and a diadem.

From the back side of the castle, one could walk to the park that had multiple crisscrossing paths lined perfectly with rows of neatly trimmed trees, some of which had no leaves but had ungainly nodes on every branch and whose tips were ugly stubs. Mumu took us to another park that was very rich in flora. She showed us a special red flower that was upside down, the petals pointing down while the sepals pointing up!

Copenhagen was full of beautiful public squares with statues, water fountains, and minstrels strumming their guitars entertaining a delighted public who showed their appreciation by showering coins into their open guitar boxes or hats. In one square, there were scooters for free, and I wanted to try out one. Lacking coordination ability at my age, as the speed increased, I braked and nearly flew over the top of the handle. After steadying myself with some difficulty, I handed back the scooter acknowledging to myself that I had indeed become a klutz when it came to handling twenty-first-century mobile contraptions meant for a much younger generation.

We did a lot of walking as well. At one place, we saw a sea of bicycles reminding us of the health-conscious Nordics. Denmark claims to have two bicycles per capita! I was impressed to see many of the streets had shiny metal slivers embedded on them to guide blind people—a remarkable display of social consciousness. Danes also love their waterways, and we watched swan-shaped floats with lovers lazying away the afternoon. Our walk led us to the graveyard where many famous personalities lay buried; among them was Hans Christian Andersen, whose gravestone read, "F. 2den APRIL 1805, D. 4de AUGUST 1875," with a few additional lines in Danish below that.

When it was lunchtime, our kids wanted to take us to a famous pizza place that they had been to before. So we walked and walked and walked until we came to the place called Baest, purportedly the eighth-best pizza place in the world according to some travel/entertainment magazine. After we entered the restaurant, I was surprised to see a big portrait of a smiling president Obama with a drink in his hand hanging on the wall. Of course, we had to take a picture with him. Mumu placed the order for the starters; among which the kale appetizer was particularly delicious. She then ordered three different types of pizzas, and I have to admit they were the best pizzas that I had ever tasted. Mumu explained to us that every ingredient for the pizza came from the farms of the owner. The dessert comprising tiramisu and coffee ice cream was equally delicious. It was a great lunch after all that walking.

The harbor cruise gave us the chance to see impressive waterfront buildings and other sights not possible to see otherwise. We passed the naval yard and saw frigates and submarines. We saw the elegant white-and-gold royal yacht moored by the royal entrance. We saw a very colorful but dilapidated houseboat with a sign on top that read, "Not Everyone Can Afford a Villa." One could see the hustle-bustle of the city and its periphery even from the harbor cruise.

Prague and Budapest

From Copenhagen, Mishu returned to Oslo, while the rest of us returned to London. Two days later, Nipa and I flew from London to

Prague. Since it was just the two of us, we planned to stay in a hotel in Prague and in Budapest instead of an Airbnb, which is where we usually stayed if there were more than two of us. Mumu had been to Prague before and knew what would be the best place for us to stay. She booked us in EA Hotel Julis located in the vibrant Wenceslas Square, one of two main shopping streets in Nové Mesto (New Town) specializing in fashion and Bohemian crystals. The hotel afforded many amenities including breakfast on a large terrace overlooking a quiet Franciscan Garden.

Wenceslas Square was ideal for tourists because of its international hotels, banks, apartments, theaters, chain stores, nightclubs, cafés, restaurants, and bars. It was known as the entertainment and nightlife center of Prague. At the southern end of the square sat two iconic structures: the majestic National Museum, which was built in 1890 and displayed Czech natural history; and the equestrian statue of Saint Wenceslas, a patron of the Czech nation, built in 1912. In earlier centuries, the square was called the Horse Market where horses were traded and agricultural products and, later, saddles, fabrics, and spices were sold. It was also a place for public executions.

However, the square was best known as a witness to many watershed events. In 1905, it witnessed a massive demonstration demanding general voting rights. In October 1918, Czechoslovakia declared its independence here, but in 1942, citizens were forced to assemble in front of the Saint Wenceslas monument to swear allegiance to the German empire following Anschluss Österreichs (annexation of Austria by Germany). In six short years, in February 1948, a large gathering of Communist supporters announced the victory of the working class and ushered in a totalitarian Communist regime. In January 1969, two students burned themselves to death to protest the invasion of Warsaw Pact troops, but seven months later, in August, the anti-Soviet movement was brutally suppressed. However, the seed of independence had been planted, and in November 1989, over a quarter million people gathered in the square to launch the Velvet Revolution, which ended Communist rule. Four years later, in January 1993, Czechoslovakia broke up into its constituent states, the independent states of Czech Republic and Slovakia.

We checked out the boutique shops on either side of the square. My favorite was the bookstore that extended inside for quite a distance; it was the largest bookstore I had ever been to. The Chinese restaurant on the opposite side of our hotel also attracted us a couple of times. A fifteen-minute walking distance eastward was the historic Charles Bridge over Vltava River connecting the New Town with the Old Town, as well as making Prague an important trade route between Eastern and Western Europe in olden times. The bridge was started in 1357 and finished in 1402, and contained thirty individual and group statues erected in the seventeenth and eighteenth centuries. Built of Bohemian sandstones, environmental pollution has turned these original light tan stones to black. On the bridge itself, we found many street artists waiting to lure tourists for a sit-down portrait, peddlers selling their wares depicting Czech culture and history, and entertainers performing all sorts of tricks.

At the other side of the bridge was the Old Town Square (Staré Mesto), which dated back to the eleventh century. Once the heart of medieval Prague, it remains a vibrant cobblestoned hub exuding architectural wonder and history with landmark attractions such as the medieval Astronomical Clock, the Estates Theatre with its Corinthian columns where the first Czech opera was staged, the gothic Karolinum behind the theater that is a part of Charles University, the first university in Central Europe established by Emperor Charles IV in 1348, and the impressive Old Town Hall with its sixty-meter tower that bears the Old Town's coat of arms built in 1338. The square was lined with restaurants, curio shops, and kiosks, and was bustling with people and activities. There was a flowery carousel, and next to it a six-foot-tall hand-painted egg-like structure. As we walked through the Old Town's labyrinthine streets, alleys, and passageways to return to our hotel, we stopped midway at a shamiana-covered outdoor Indian restaurant and sampled its dinner menu.

We also took the hop-on-hop-off bus to tour the beautiful district of Mala Strana (Lesser Town), which was created in 1257 by King Ottokar

II of Bohemia by amalgamating a number of settlements beneath the Prague Castle into a single administrative unit. The king replaced the original residents with mostly German craftsmen and merchants. We disembarked in Hradcanske Namesti (Hradcanske Square) at the other end of which was the beginning of the Prague Castle Complex. Outside the gilded front entrance of Prague Castle was a huge open space with guard houses and armed security police. In front of the gate were two smartly dressed royal guards. In full public view on the cobblestone in front of the castle gate was a king's chair on a red carpet. The royal crown replica was on the seat, and the royal tunic and coat were laid out over the two chair handles. The coat of arms, helmet, shield, sword, and body armor lay sprawled out in front of the carpet, as if to inform the public what their ancient kings wore.

The view outside the walls of the castle complex was that of red-tiled houses making up the neighborhoods below. We went down a row of steps by the side of the castle complex to the city streets below. One such street behind the Prague Castle was called Golden Lane, which was lined with rows of charming houses whose ground floors were souvenir and bookshops for tourists. According to the local lore, it was named Golden Lane because in the late sixteenth century, Emperor Rudolph II accommodated his court alchemists here, who spent their lives trying to turn metal into gold. It was also famous because in the early twentieth century, the famous Bohemian novelist and short story writer Franz Kafka lived here and was inspired by the Prague Castle to write his book *The Castle*.

The Prague Castle complex, which was built in the ninth century and served as the seat of power for the kings of Bohemia, Holy Roman emperors, and presidents of Czechoslovakia, and is currently the office of the Czech Republic, is mentioned in the *Guinness Book of World Records* as the largest ancient castle complex with an area of 750,000 square feet.

We queued up by a side entrance to enter the castle complex. Inside were a combination of numerous gothic-styled smaller castles and cathedrals with magnificent towers, spires, gargoyles, and the like. These ancient buildings were clustered to form multiple huge courtyards. The most famous and largest among them was St. Vitus Cathedral, which not only provided religious services but also coronations of Czech kings and queens also took place there. St. Vitus Cathedral also held one of the largest collections of church treasury in Europe. In addition, it stored and protected the Bohemian Crown Jewels, which included the St. Wenceslas crown, royal scepter, and coronation cloak. To provide ironclad security, both the chamber door and iron safe inside have seven locks, the keys to which are held by seven people, including the president, prime minister, and Prague archbishop. When the jewels are put on public display every five years or so, all seven key holders present themselves at the castle for the unlocking process.

One learns of other little known facts about the Prague Castle. The word *defenestration,* which means throwing something out through a window, came into use in 1618 when two Catholic regents and their secretary were thrown out a window of Prague Castle because they were found guilty of violating the right to religious freedom when they shut down a pair of new Protestant chapels. Luckily for the defenestrated churchmen and administrator, they landed on a pile of manure and survived. I wonder if the three Catholics considered that as divine intervention and renewed their anti-Protestant machinations with vigor!

Another story was that in 1941, Holocaust organizer Reinhard Heydrich, who was assigned by Adolph Hitler to rule over the Czech nation, set up office in the Prague Castle and launched a campaign of disappearances and executions. To stop this "Butcher of Prague," a group of exiled Czech government officials launched Operation Anthropoid. In May 1942, two Czech soldiers parachuted into the country to assassinate him; they threw grenades into his motor car. He died of injuries a week later. The 2016 movie *Anthropoid* was supposed to be based on that story.

Nipa and I walked through the entire castle complex, stopping inside cathedrals to marvel at their awe-inspiring ornate interior and inside buildings that house the country's cultural and historical artifacts. The souvenir shops carried items that were quite expensive, but we bought a few things to remind us of our trip. At the other end inside the complex was a marketplace with many shops and an open food court of sorts.

Nipa's favorite was the Waffle Garden; she ordered a chocolate-coated waffle pyramid on a stick. Her other must-have was a *trdelnik,* which is a rolled dough that is wrapped around a stick and then grilled and filled with sugar and walnut mix. The second time she had it from a trdelnik shop below our hotel was with ice cream.

After exiting the castle complex, we reboarded our bus and completed the tour of the city, taking in the magnificent buildings, monuments, parks, and sculptures, and stopping only at selected spots. One of them was the Petrin Hill to see sculptor Olbram Zoubek's memorial depicting seven fragmentary human figures symbolizing the political prisoners of the Communist era standing on a staircase leading up the slope of Petrin Hill. It was a moment to reflect on the dark days of Communism when freedom of the human spirit and ingenuity had ceased to exist. We completed our Prague visit by taking the river cruise to see a different face of Prague, and it was worth every cent.

On April 27, we left Prague for Budapest. I had learned as a young kid that Budapest was divided into two parts, Buda and Pest by the Danube River. As a member of the Pakistan Jute Delegation to East Europe, Hungary was in my father's official itinerary. He had gone to Hungary several times and made good friends there. Once, he invited two of his friends to visit us in Dhaka, East Pakistan, and then invited them to dinner at our home.

Having heard Father talk of Hungarian goulash, one of the dishes Mother prepared for the guests was spicy beef curry. Not remembering the English word for beef, one of the guests asked if it was *marhahús* (beef in Hungarian). After seeing our blank stares, the gentleman pretended to be a bull and put his two index fingers by the sides of his temples and made the motion of charging at us, exclaiming, "Marhahús, marhahús!" emphasizing the "hús" bit. We all understood that he was asking whether the meat was beef and laughed at his pantomime. That day, I heard lots of stories of Hungary from our guests. Before they left, they presented Mother with a scarf and me with a pocket-sized magnetic chessboard. I believe I learned to play chess in that cute little chessboard. Since then, I have always wanted to visit Hungary.

We decided right away to tour the city on hop-on-hop-off buses.

The sights and sounds of Budapest were equally enchanting if not better. Every time I visit Europe, what inevitably goes through my mind is the incredible contrast between the Old World, meaning Europe, with its extremely rich history, culture, and heritage; and the New World, which has very little to show besides skyscrapers, concrete jungles, and ever-receding natural beauty. Perhaps our most memorable visit in Budapest was to the Castle District, which was the historical part of the Buda side of Budapest, with winding cobblestone streets and leafy promenades known for their baroque houses, Habsburg monuments, and cafés.

The Buda Castle, which was first completed in 1265 and sat on the southern tip of Castle Hill, was the historical palace of the Hungarian kings. With its white stone exterior, its facades with their colonnades, multiple levels of spacious cascading terraces and expansive staircases, the Buda Castle was indeed a remarkable iconic structure. The palace ground was rich in artworks and monuments, which included the statue of Prince Eugene of Savoy. The centerpiece of the palace complex was the Lion's Court, which was a large courtyard featuring the two impressive lions. Viewed from a distance, the Buda Castle was one of the most impressive structures to behold. And the view of the Danube from its terraces was also quite a sight. It was now home to the Hungarian National Gallery and the Budapest History Museum. Nipa and I walked the multiple levels of the palace grounds and took umpteen pictures from all angles. Then we walked down a side street to the nearby 21 Magyar Vendeglo, a restaurant recommended by Michelin. We were quite hungry by then. Nipa once again ordered Hungary's iconic dish, goulash. After finishing it, her damning assessment was "I liked the goulash that we had in the streets."

After our late lunch, we took the bus to Gellert Hill, which was 235 meters high overlooking the Danube. The hill was named after Saint Gerard, who was assassinated during the pagan rebellion of 1046.The bishop was put in a barrel and rolled down from the top of the hill. As we walked to the top of the hill to see the citadel that presented a panoramic view of the city, we overheard a couple speaking Bangla.

They introduced themselves as Hasnat and Touheed from Canberra, Australia. We were excited to meet some people from Canberra, where we had spent nearly four years and had lots of friends. When we inquired about our friends in Canberra, they said they knew our friends Aref and Nasreen quite well. We took pictures of each other as well as selfies and promised to remain in touch. From there, we walked a short distance to Jubileumi Park (Jubilee Park), which was inaugurated in October 1957 to mark the fortieth anniversary of the Bolshevik Revolution of October 1917. The attraction of the park was the works of the famous sculptors of the twentieth century.

We then took the bus to Heroes' Square, noted for its iconic statue complex that depicted the Seven Chieftains of the Magyars and other Hungarian national heroes. It also contained the Memorial Stone of Heroes. The square was bounded by the Museum of Fine Arts on one side and the Hall of Arts on the other. On the day of our visit, there were busloads of schoolchildren who had come to the square to lay wreaths and sing patriotic songs.

Next in our itinerary was the boat cruise, but this was different from all the rest that we had ever taken. We took the night cruise on the Danube River as recommended by the tour operators, and it was the most unforgettable river cruise ever. We witnessed the city's stunning night glow. Among the highlights of the night cruise were the Royal Palace, the Buda Castle district, the Chain Bridge, St. Stephen's Basilica, and Margaret Island. But the most stunning sight was the lights of the House of Parliament glittering in the waters of the Danube. We had seen the front of the House of Parliament during daytime but never imagined that the view at night from the Danube could be so enchanting. It was a fitting end to our Budapest visit.

Athens and the Island of Paros

On April 29, we flew from Budapest to London, and after a day's rest, Mumu, Nipa, and I flew to Athens. Mishu flew into Athens from Oslo the next day. Mumu had booked an Airbnb for us. But we just spent the night there and left Athens for the island of Paros the next morning. We had left the choice of which island to visit to Mumu since she had already been to the islands before. Her advice was to avoid the most frequented island of Santorini, which would be overcrowded with young people at this time of the year, and suggested that we go to the island of Paros instead. So we took the forty-minute flight from Athens to Parikia, the capital of Paros.

It was the perfect choice. Located in the central Aegean Sea, Paros was the third-largest island in the Cyclades (i.e., a group of islands around the sacred island of Delos) lying southeast of mainland Greece. It boasted 120 kilometers of pristine coastline with unending blond-sand beaches, green mountains, beautiful natural landscapes, and cliff-top villages made up of blue-and-white-colored houses, narrow cobblestone paths, quaint little shops carrying exotic ware, and old churches. The island was proud to be the home of the Panagia Ekatontapiliani, a landmark Byzantine church from the fourth century AD. We stayed at a beautiful boutique hotel called Apollon, located only fifty meters from the beach. It was also within walking distance from the town and the port. The accommodations were quite elegant, with well-appointed rooms with modern bathroom, beautiful sitting and dining areas, and a delightful garden with an orange tree that was full of oranges.

We took many leisurely walks through the cobblestone lanes to browse in the shops that carried enticing goods. As memento, Mishu bought a shirt, and I bought a belt, which the shopkeeper gladly adjusted for a perfect fit. I was impressed by how clean and tidy the island looked. The lanes and byways looked swept and spotless; the storefronts were artistically decorated; the houses were white with blue shutters, doors, awnings, and railings, and looked freshly painted; and restaurants here and there with outdoor sitting usually under the shade of some tree. There were lots of steps as one walked by quaint houses in the villages, and many of these houses had small gardens with orange trees of their own and bright red rhododendrons hanging over their walls. Some had cactus and earthenware decorative pieces outside their front entrance. The houses facing the sea inevitably had terraces that provided magnificent views of palm-tree-lined beaches and the open sea. We passed many churches with crosses on beautiful blue domes in the village of Lefkes.

We had rented a car at the airport for the duration of our stay in Paros. One day, we drove to the village of Alyki to have lunch by a seaside restaurant. We saw squids hung up to dry in wires in front of the restaurants. All the restaurants there seemed to jut out into the sea. We sat at a table on the edge of the restaurant and could see the pebbles under the clear blue water with small fish swimming about just a few feet down by our side. The view from our table of the Aegean, of boats with anchors down at a distance and of the shimmering silver rays of the sun on the water, was breathtaking. We stayed on to see the sunset, which was yet another sight to behold.

Lunch by the edge of the Aegean Sea, on the island of Paros, Greece, May 2019

On another occasion, we drove to the cove of Xifara Beach in the village of Naoussa to dine at the Siparos Seaside Restaurant, where Mumu had made a reservation for us. Founded in 2009 by a brother and sister, the restaurant was famous for offering its clients the perfect sunset view, a warm ambience, and a tasty blend of traditional and international cuisine. Although we missed the sunset, we had an excellent dinner that night.

Before leaving the island, we decided to drive around the entire island, so Mishu took to the wheels as Mumu navigated him. In one village, we came across a roadside sign pointing to a pottery place. Since both Nipa and Mishu are potters in their own right and have beautiful creations of their own, we stopped there to check out the pottery. Mumu ended up buying a mug, and Nipa bought a locket. Nipa had taken pottery classes at the Gloucester Pottery School in the Shenkman Center in Orleans and produced many pottery pieces, some of which she gifted to friends and relatives. One summer when Mishu came home from London, she introduced him to pottery, and our son was hooked. Soon after, he made some pottery pieces for Christmas and offered them to the shop Blanc & Turquoise in Orleans; they were all sold. Now he does pottery in his spare time in Oslo. His work colleagues in Oslo urged him to hold a pottery show last year, which he did, and his entire collection was sold in no time. So he was inspired to keep up his pottery, which, I believe, he finds relaxing after his architectural work.

After completing our leisurely drive around the island, after visiting the villages we wanted to, and after downing many glasses of freshly squeezed orange juice, cafe latte, and cappuccinos, we were ready to depart Paros. With my family beside me, in a quiet picturesque island surrounded by the deep blue waters of the Aegean, beautiful blue skies, balmy weather and gentle breeze blowing across the island, lots of exotic shops to browse, and restaurants galore, it could not have been a more idyllic vacation for us.

After four blissful days in tranquil Paros, on May 4, we returned the rented car and flew Olympic Air back to Athens, where we spent a few days absorbing the sights and sounds of the city. At the top of our list was the Acropolis. An easily recognizable iconic Greek structure, the Acropolis (which in Greek means the highest point in the city) is an ancient citadel built on a flat rocky outcrop above the city of Athens. It houses the famous Parthenon, which was a temple dedicated to goddess Athena, the patron of Athens, although the twelve-meter-high statue of Athena Parthenos is long gone. The Parthenon with its rows of Doric columns was the largest temple of classical antiquity. Commissioned by Pericles in 477 BC, it took decades to build and was completed in 438 BC, when Athens was at the zenith of its power. It was built to celebrate Hellenic victory over the Persians and to thank their gods for the victory.

The Parthenon had played many roles throughout its history. In the early decades of the sixth century, its strong fortifications allowed it to serve as the treasury of the Delphic League. In the last decade of the sixth century, Byzantine Christians converted it into a church dedicated to Virgin Mary. In the early 1460s, it was turned into a mosque following the Ottoman conquest. And from 1800 to 1803, the earl of Elgin, Thomas Bruce, removed some of Acropolis's sculptures now known as the Elgin Marbles. After successfully fighting off the Ottoman rulers, the First Hellenic Republic was declared in 1822. Despite all its tragedies, the Parthenon continues to be the enduring symbol of Ancient Greece, of Athenian democracy, and of Western civilization.

We took the hop-on-hop-off to the base of the Acropolis and then climbed the many steps to the Acropolis. On the way, we saw the Herodes Theatre, an open-air venue built in AD 161 by Greek Herodes Atticus in memory of his Roman wife Aspasia Reqilla. It has a capacity of five thousand and in the modern era has served as a venue for many music concerts and other events, such as the Miss Universe 1973 pageant; performances by the likes of Nana Mouskouri, Luciano Pavarotti, Liza Minnelli, Diana Ross, Jethro Tull, and Sting; and benefit concerts by Elton John and Andrea Bocelli, among many other artists and entertainers.

On the Acropolis itself, we saw the remains of the Old Temple of Athena; the Erechtheion, temple dedicated to gods Athena and Poseidon; the Temple of Nike, the winged goddess of victory; and many other ancient buildings of architectural and historical significance erected during the classical period, 450–330 BC. The Acropolis also provided a panoramic view of the entire city. It was interesting to note that Athens was the only major city in Europe that had no skyscraper because of the government legislation that no construction can be higher than the Acropolis. It would have been exciting to visit the Acropolis Museum, which housed many local archeological wonders, but it was closed for renovation during our visit.

After the Acropolis visit, we boarded the bus to see the rest of Athens. We saw the still impressive columns of the Temple of Zeus, the National Gardens, and the Panathenaic Stadium, among other sites. The latter is purported to be the only stadium in the world built entirely of marble. It hosted the opening and closing ceremonies of the first modern Olympic Games in 1896 and the 2004 Olympics. It is also the venue from where the Olympic flame handover ceremony to the host nation takes place.

Besides the bus tour, we also walked the streets of Athens lined with houses with flowers hanging down from pots on their windows and visited several little squares that bustled with restaurants. In one outdoor restaurant, we met a lady who came to Athens to celebrate her one hundredth birthday by climbing the Acropolis accompanied by a caretaker. What was even more remarkable was that she had no walking stick and was going to hold her caretaker's hand to negotiate the eighty or so steep steps that took a normal person some twenty minutes. We spoke with her for a little while, congratulating her on her birthday and wishing her success with her climbing adventure.

After lunch, we strolled through the streets bustling with tourists from all over the world, stopping to browse in various shops. One shop specialized in honey from a variety of flowers from the different regions of Greece. There was also on display a live beehive dripping with honey with bees abuzz. The beekeeper was telling anyone who would stop to listen, like me, which part of Greece produced which honey and readily offered his guests tasting sticks to dip into the various honey tasters. Before we left the market area, we bought a beautiful table mat with olive leaf design for our family living room and a miniature Parthenon.

On May 4, we left Athens; Mishu flew off to Oslo, and the rest of us flew to London. Nipa and I recuperated for few days in London at our daughter's Wembley flat and then left for Ottawa. It was the longest vacation trip we had ever taken, and though somewhat exhaustive, we loved every minute of it.

Family Reunion in Dallas

That summer, the summer of 2019, Mother was due for her medical checkup in Bangkok. She had had a femur replacement surgery at the Bumrungrad International Hospital (BIH) a few years back. According to her doctor at the BIH, Mother was a model patient because of her devotion to strictly following her doctor's orders. Nurses there have told my brother Tawfiq that they never see the doctor smile at any of his patients; but when Mother visits him, he lights up like a bulb and takes extra time to chat with her. My sister Lily and Mother flew to Bangkok on July 22. The plan was for Mother to go onward to the States after her checkup. Since Lily would be returning to Dhaka from Bangkok and Mother wouldn't be able to travel alone to the States, my youngest brother, Tawfiq, flew from Dallas to Bangkok to accompany Mother to the States. They arrived in Dallas on July 26.

It had been a while since my mother, my brothers and sisters, and I had gotten together in one place. Since the Muslim celebration of Eid ul Adha (the Feast of Sacrifice that commemorated Prophet Abraham's willingness to sacrifice his eldest son to God) was scheduled to commence on August 11, my youngest sister, Tina, thought that it would be fun to celebrate Eid ul Adha together and also have a family reunion at brother Shahalam's place in Irving, Dallas. She sounded us out, and all of us agreed that it was indeed a great idea.

So I flew from Ottawa to Dallas on August 8, and Tina and her family flew from Boise to Dallas the next day. We all were truly astounded at the amount and variety of dishes that Tina cooked, packed, and brought with her to Dallas. She did not want us to waste time in the kitchen and, instead, wanted us to spend the whole time in each other's company. Tina also thought of having a color theme, so all the brothers had to wear beige shorts with salmon-colored T-shirts, while the girls wore blue jeans and white tops. At one point, all the brothers held up Tina horizontal to the floor facing the camera, while she panicked and screamed! That whole week was a splendid family reunion indeed, catching up on what's been happening with each of us, sharing stories, playing games, diving and swimming in the pool, visiting places, and just having a good time.

Our Eid celebration was memorable too. Irving, where Shahalam lived, had just built a brand-new mosque named the Valley Ranch

Islamic Center, so the August 11 Eid namaz was the first in that mosque. As always, all of us dressed up in our new Eid clothes and did all the usual things that Muslims do on Eid.

The family members had contributed to purchase a cow for slaughter to celebrate Eid ul Adha, as was the Muslim custom, and had given Tawfiq the responsibility to manage it. Tawfiq and a few other Bangladeshi families living in the greater Dallas area placed their orders with a dairy farm that was located on the Oklahoma side of the Texas-Oklahoma border. The meat was ready for pickup several days after Eid day, and Tawfiq and I drove for about an hour and twenty minutes in his van to pick up the meat.

As soon as we reached the farm, we were hit by a thunderstorm, and it started pouring cats and dogs. The other Bangladesh men were also there to pick up their share. Tawfiq suggested that I sit in the front porch, while he and others sorted out the beef in the freezer. There were two other elderly Oklahomans, a man and a woman, who had taken shelter from the heavy rains under the porch.

Since Oklahoma was a southern state and a pro-Trump state, I decided to tease some political talk out of them. I asked the elderly gentleman, "Your presidential elections are coming up next year, so what do you think Trump's chances are?" The man gave me a look as if that was the stupidest question he had ever heard. He replied, "Don't you worry, boy. He's comin' back, he's comin' back," with great finality. That made me a bit more mischievous, and I turned to the elderly lady next to him and asked, "But are you sure Trump will get the women's vote, especially after what he said about grabbing a woman's p———sy and all? He may have lost the respect of women voters, don't you think?" Without missing a beat, the woman instantly replied, "But when he said that, he was a Democrat. Now he is a Republican!" I was absolutely floored by her response; the way she rationalized Trump's behavior in her mind was beyond me. I left that conversation convinced that with that kind of mentality and ignorance, no progressive politician had any chance of winning votes in states like Oklahoma!

Tina and her family left Dallas on August 17 to return to Boise, but I stayed on for two more weeks before returning to Ottawa.

EPILOGUE

After my last assignment in Africa in early 2019, I was happy to return home knowing in the back of my mind that I probably wouldn't be undertaking any more consultancy work in future. This became more apparent after the invasion of the world by the COVID-19 virus when consulting trips to other countries became hazardous and untenable. This gave me the chance to turn my attention elsewhere.

Since I had to forego the idea of converting my doctoral thesis into a full-fledged book because of the ultra-sensitivity of the current government in Bangladesh to the topic, I decided that perhaps I might take a retrospective look at my life, the path I had traveled, and write about this journey.

I must thank my creator for granting me my wish to travel all over the world, for the opportunity to live and work in different countries and continents, and for the rich experiences I accumulated. I wish many more citizens had the opportunity to meet and mingle with people of other race, color, creed and lifestyle.

Despite the globalization of many facets of our life and work, ignorance, intolerance, discrimination and hatred are still pervasive. I believe that there is no better antidote to this than education. Broadening one's horizon and developing appreciation for diversity and tolerance can bring down barriers and truly lift one up, and give more meaning to life. Travelling and exposure to and interaction with other cultures can be important components of the learning process that all governments and societies ought to encourage and facilitate.

My development work had given me the opportunity to affect positively the lives of other peoples. I took risks and put myself in danger much like my father did. At the end of the day, I am satisfied that through my international work I was able to do some good to some people, and even perhaps inspire others to do the same.

I feel that among the millions of people who have emigrated from their country of birth to distant lands in search of better opportunities, I am among the fortunate ones, and that I have invested my time and efforts wisely. I encourage others to do the same.

Life is a journey that one can neither avoid nor delay. For some it may be blissful, for others painful. For me it was satisfying. This book has been a selective recollection of that journey and a cursory reflection on my life, which is yet to travel further, I hope.

INDEX

A

Booth, John Wilkes, 376

Boroma (great-grandmother), 15–16, 26

Bossche, Vanden, 50

Boulder, Colorado, 104, 106, 113, 115

Brandenburg Gate, 322–23

Brandon (nephew), 415, 446

Brandt, Willy, 265

Brezhnev Market. *See* Bush Market

Brighton Beach, 578

Brinson, Tracey, 415, 420, 503

Brisbane, 179

Britain, 29, 355, 360

British Council, 151, 155, 391, 452

British prime ministers, 153, 360, 456

Brooks, David, 314

Brother James, 47

Brother Lorenzo, 46

Brother Nicholas, 47

Bruce, Thomas, 602

Buda Castle, 597–98

Budapest, 591–92, 596–98

Budapest History Museum, 597

Buddhism, 142, 375, 480

Bulbul Lalitakala Academy, 43

Bumrungrad International Hospital (BIH), 442, 604

Bunch, Jesse, 419

Buriganga River, 9, 44, 46

Burma, 296

Burmese Karen National Liberation Force (KNLF), 226

Bush Market, 388

Butcher of Prague. *See* Heydrich, Reinhard

Bute Hall, 572–73

Byzantine Christians, 602

C

Cairo, 233–34, 242, 304–6

Calcutta, 125, 168, 464

Calcutta Airport, 101

California, 73, 84, 132, 268, 516, 543

Cambodia, 297–99

Cambridge University, 49, 152, 285

Cameroon, 3, 330, 332–33

Cameroon government, 330, 332

Canadian International Development Agency (CIDA), 4, 227, 251, 314–15, 324–25, 327–29, 335, 342, 354–55, 379, 391, 456, 468, 534, 580

Canberra, 5, 154–55, 157, 164, 166, 172–75, 177, 179, 185, 597–98

Cape Town, 304, 308–9, 311

Caribbean Sea, 550, 552

Carleton University, 185, 205, 353, 377

Carson, Johnny, 102–3

Carstensen, Georg, 590

Casablanca, 516

Castelo dos Mouros, 536

Castle District, 597

Castle Sands, 575

Cathedral of Cordova, 511

Center for Global Change, 213

Center for Sustainable Regional Development (CSRD), 214

Central America, 342, 546, 550

Centre for Days of Peace, 226

Channel Tunnel, 355–56, 361, 552

Charles, Prince, 112

Charles III, Prince, 367

Charles IV, Emperor, 593

Chashara, 23

Chatham House. *See* Royal Institute of International Affairs

Chennai. *See* Madras

Chernobyl, 528

Chhobi bhabi. *See* Chowdhury, Chhobi

Chicago, 46–47, 87, 373–75, 377

China, 22, 79, 170, 172, 214, 217, 373, 469, 488, 523, 564

Chinese government, 229, 469

Hippodrome of Constantinople, 409
Hitler, Adolph, 595
Holey Artisan Bakery, 557, 559–60
Holland, 49, 155–56, 199, 263, 324, 370
Hollywood, 73, 393
Holy Family Hospital, 292
Holy See, 349
Homer-Dixon, Thomas, 217
Honolulu, 164–66, 268–69
Hope, Bob, 103
Hossain, Ali, 173
Hossain, Fazlul, 9, 346, 572
Hossain, Ishtiaq, 185–86
Hossain, Kamal, 169, 342–43
Hossein, Mary, 173
Hotel Arts Barcelona, 507
Hotel Casa, 510
Hotel Intercontinental. *See* Tehran Laleh
    International Hotel
Hotel Serena, 415
Hovet, Thomas, 116–17, 153–54
Hubbard, Mrs. (headmistress), 17, 163
Humaira, Ayubi, 460
Huntington, Samuel, 200
Huq, Manzur, 259
Hussain, Sameera, 489
Hussein, Hassan, 31
Hussein, Saddam, 135

I

ibn Abd al-Rahman, Muhammad, 511,
    514
ibn Ali, Husayn, 415
ibn Ziyad, Tariq, 9
Ibrahim, Anwar, 321
Ibrahim, Mohammad "Mo," 321
Iceland, 549, 573, 578
Imogen (Robin's wife), 207
Independence Square, 545
India, 10, 26, 73, 77–78, 80, 100, 129,
    133, 144, 162, 164–65, 167–68,
170–71, 187, 214–17, 225, 229–
    32, 243, 259, 261, 277, 294, 401,
    437–38, 463, 469
Indian Ocean, 307, 311, 338, 341, 528,
    552
Indo-Bangladesh relations, 184
Indonesia, 140–41, 214, 217, 329, 341
industrialization, 428
Institute for Development, Environment
    and Strategic Studies (IDESS),
    272–73
Institute for Political and International
    Studies (IPIS), 195
International   Anti-Corruption
    Conference (IACC), 315, 335,
    342, 368, 546–47
International Anti-Corruption Day
    (IACD), 417, 459
International Anti-Corruption Summer
    Academy (IACSA), 437
International Development Research
    Center (IDRC), 230–31, 233,
    235–36, 259, 262, 294, 299,
    312–14, 328, 355
International Development Research
    Centre Act, 294
International Institute for Strategic
    Studies (IISS), 197–203
International Joint Anti-Corruption
    Monitoring   and   Evaluation
    Committee (MEC), 521
International Legal Assistance Programs
    (ILAP), 326–27
International Monitoring and Evaluation
    Committee (MEC), 431, 455
International Security Assistance Force
    (ISAF), 456
International Student Speakers Club, 87
Iran, 72, 135, 191–94, 252, 390, 438,
    495
Iraq, 135, 140, 385, 415

Norodom Sihanouk, King, 297
Norodom Sirivudh, Prince, 297–98
Norway, 322, 324, 378, 570, 587
Notre Dame, 51, 516
Notre Dame College, 50–51, 53, 57, 63, 78, 80, 196
Notre Dame University, 51, 57
Notu. *See* Chowhury, Badruzzaman
Nowruz Mubarak, 438
Nur, Atta Muhammad, 495
Nuruddin (general), 133, 140

O

Obama (president), 443
Obelisk of Theodosius, 409
Obirodh project, 555–56, 560–62, 564
Oceanus, 348
Octavius, 351
Old Palace of Afghan Kings, 399
Omari, Daud, 432, 437, 453–54, 460, 470–72, 474–75, 477–78, 487, 490, 495–96, 498, 500, 503
Operation Yal Devi, 223
Orange Revolution, 325, 517, 545
Oslo, 21, 315, 576, 587–88, 591, 598, 601, 603
Osmani, Yasin, 499, 503–4, 520
Osmani (colonel), 168, 499, 503–4, 520
Osorio, Maria Isabel, 420, 436
Ottawa, 4–5, 136, 175, 185–86, 203–7, 209, 211–12, 225, 230, 233, 242, 246–52, 254–55, 257–58, 261, 263, 291, 293, 298, 320, 326, 334–36, 344, 352–53, 356, 377, 379, 381–82, 408, 413, 415–20, 427, 441–42, 459, 461–62, 466, 468, 475, 489, 505–6, 537–38, 553–54, 558–59, 568, 570, 572, 574, 578–79, 603–5
Ottokar II, King, 593
Oxford, 151–54, 158, 268

Oxford University, 154, 306

P

Paje Beach, 339
Pakistan, 10, 29, 40, 44, 50, 53, 73–74, 76–77, 79–80, 92, 129, 133, 139–41, 144, 159, 164, 167–68, 193–94, 202, 230, 250, 347, 391, 418, 420–21, 428–29, 431, 463, 469, 489, 523, 556
Pakistan Army, 10, 81, 122, 141, 166, 168, 260
Pakistan government, 9, 44, 53, 77, 80, 94, 110, 463
Palace of Holyroodhouse, 575
Palacio Nacional da Pena, 536
Palais de Festivals, 364
Palatona Training Camp, 77, 82
Palestine, 107–8, 233–35, 300, 303–4
Palestinians, 137, 233, 236–37, 302
Panagia Ekatontapiliani, 599
Panama, 547–50, 552–53
Panama Canal, 550–53
Panama City, 547, 550, 553
Panjshir Valley, 446–48
Pantheon, 349–50
Parijataka, Princess, 20
Paris, 299, 315, 321–22, 325, 327–28, 331–32, 354–55, 361–64, 367–68
Park Güell, 508
Parliamentary Anti-Corruption Committee (PACC), 496–97, 503
Paros Island, 598–601
Parque de Maria Luisa, 511
Parthenon, 369, 601–2
Patna, 215
Pax Mondial, 386, 392, 405, 464
Peixotto, Joseph, 51
Pereira, P. K. B., 220

Sylvia (friend), 174

T

Tabbara, Izziddin, 88–89
Taboa do Cabo, 312
Tacke, Richard, 63
Taha, Wahabi, 63, 88
Tajikistan, 436, 488, 494, 523
Taliban, 4, 383, 390, 398–99, 401–2, 404, 422, 430, 447, 465, 470, 480, 489, 525
Taliban insurgents, 391, 414, 443
Tan, Jason, 380–81
Tanvir, Sulaiman, 51, 55–56
Tanzania, 335–36, 338, 370
Tarik (friend's nephew), 419
Tariq, Jabal, 10
Tauli-Corpuz, Victoria, 313
Tawanmandi Project, 452
Tebtebba Foundation, 313
Tehran, 135–36, 192–93, 195–97, 306, 411, 476–77
Tehran Laleh International Hotel, 192
Texas, 255, 258, 344, 377, 396, 415, 462, 542
Thailand, 140, 164, 226
Thanksgiving, 63, 415
Thapa, Hari, 395, 403, 425–26, 437, 457, 473
Theodosius, Emperor, 409
Tina (sister), 41, 45, 61, 256–59, 344, 376, 390, 415, 468, 555–56, 604–5
Tito, Josef Broz, 143
Tito, Marshal, 111
Topkapi Palace, 410
Toure, Ahmad Sekou, 135
Train à Grande Vitesse (TGV), 364
Transparency International (TI), 314–15, 342, 368, 582
Trojan War, 22, 369

Trump, Donald, 103, 554, 573–74, 605
Tura, Sangma, 277
Twin Towers, 251, 398

U

Uddin, Mohammed Jashim, 564
UK Foreign and Commonwealth Office (FCO), 201, 453
Ukraine, 325–27, 402, 433, 517–19, 528, 544, 546
United Kingdom, 61, 137, 517, 521
United Nations, 68, 116–17, 126, 137, 227, 229, 307, 316, 417, 464, 521
University of Illinois, 53, 263, 283, 374
University of Oregon, 51, 53, 57, 72, 91, 117, 127
University of Toronto (UT), 213, 353, 397
University of Westminster (UW), 397, 468, 489
Utstein Group, 322–24, 328, 378

V

Valley of Five Lions. *See* Panjshir Valley
Varela, Juan Carlos, 548
Vienna, 196, 315, 329, 378
Villa Oniria, 509
Viqarunessa Girls High School, 48
Vivekaphirat, Visuit, 442
Vulnerability to Corruption Assessment (VCA), 457, 493–94, 533

W

Wahidi, Sayed Fazlullah, 490
Wailing Wall, 239
Wallace, Stephen, 379
Walla Walla, 99
Wann, Emily, 504
Wasserstrom, James, 389, 400, 431, 500, 504, 519
Wasserstrom, Jim, 389, 500, 504